Religion on the American Frontier

1783-1830

Vol. I
THE BAPTISTS

RELIGION ON THE AMERICAN FRONTIER

THE BAPTISTS

1783-1830

A COLLECTION OF SOURCE MATERIAL

BY

WILLIAM WARREN SWEET

GENERAL INTRODUCTION BY

SHIRLEY JACKSON CASE

COOPER SQUARE PUBLISHERS, INC.

New York • 1964

Published 1964 by Cooper Square Publishers, Inc.
59 Fourth Avenue, New York 3, N. Y.
Library of Congress Catalog Card No. 63-21092
Printed in the United States of America

CONTENTS

RELIGION ON THE AMERICAN FRONTIER
1783–1830
VOLUME I
THE BAPTISTS

	PAGE
GENERAL INTRODUCTION BY SHIRLEY JACKSON CASE	v
PREFACE	ix

PART I
INTRODUCTION

CHAPTER

I. THE STATUS OF THE BAPTISTS IN AMERICA AT THE CLOSE OF THE REVOLUTION 3

II. BAPTIST MIGRATION AND EXPANSION WESTWARD . 18

III. THE FRONTIER BAPTIST PREACHER AND THE FRONTIER BAPTIST CHURCH 36

IV. THE RISE OF THE ANTI-MISSION BAPTISTS: A FRONTIER PHENOMENON 58

V. ANTI-SLAVERY MOVEMENTS AMONG BAPTISTS . . 77

PART II
DOCUMENTS ILLUSTRATING THE WORK OF BAPTISTS ON THE FRONTIER

VI. EXTRACTS FROM "THE HISTORY OF TEN BAPTIST CHURCHES" (By John Taylor) 105

VII. THE AUTOBIOGRAPHY OF JACOB BOWER: A FRONTIER BAPTIST PREACHER AND MISSIONARY . . . 185

VIII. THE "RELIGIOUS EXPERIENCE" OF A CANDIDATE FOR THE MINISTRY AS RELATED BEFORE THE CHURCH . 231

IX. CHURCH LETTERS 239–247
    1. Letters transferring membership . . . 239

CONTENTS

CHAPTER   PAGE

2. Letter from the Wood River Church, Illinois, to the Illinois Association 245

3. Letter from the Twelve Mile Prairie Church to the Wood River Church requesting "helps" in the ordination of a minister . . . 246

4. Letter from the Ogle Creek Church, Illinois, to the Wood River Church asking help from the Wood River Church 246

X. EXTRACTS FROM THE RECORDS OF FRONTIER BAPTIST CHURCHES 248–271

1. Records of Severn's Valley Church, Kentucky, 1788–1790 248

2. Records of Boone's Creek Church, Kentucky, 1799 253

3. Constitution and Rules of a Church formed on Beaver Creek, Kentucky, 1798 (Mount Tabor Church), with the Records for 1803 . . 258

4. Records of the Wood River Baptist Church, Illinois, 1812–1822 261

XI. RECORDS OF THE FORKS OF ELKHORN BAPTIST CHURCH, KENTUCKY, 1800–1820 272

XII. MINUTES OF THE ELKHORN BAPTIST ASSOCIATION, KENTUCKY, 1785–1805 417

XIII. MINUTES OF THE ILLINOIS ASSOCIATION OF BAPTISTS, 1807–1820 510

XIV. DOCUMENTS RELATING TO THE FRIENDS TO HUMANITY OR THE ANTI-SLAVERY BAPTISTS IN KENTUCKY AND ILLINOIS 564

XV. MATERIALS RELATING TO THE GREAT WESTERN REVIVAL AND BAPTIST INDIAN MISSIONS . . 608–628

1. Letters describing the Great Western Revival . 609

2. Minutes of the Salem Association, Kentucky, 1802 617

3. Extracts from the Journal of Major S. H. Long, describing the Isaac McCoy Mission in 1823 . 625

BIBLIOGRAPHY 629

INDEX 639

GENERAL INTRODUCTION

The history of Christianity in America is a relatively new subject of interest. This is particularly true with regard to the place of the church in the life of the expanding frontiers as civilization moved westward. No one who has even the most superficial acquaintance with pioneer conditions can be unaware of the large part played by religious movements in the frontier settlements. The assembling of groups for worship, the organization of churches, and the activities of the missionary were among the first agencies to influence the shaping of ideals and attitudes among the early settlers in the new lands. Agricultural, industrial, commercial, political and educational interests were all closely interwoven with religious agencies in determining the course of social development within the newly formed communities.

Important as the religious factor was in the early settlements, exact knowledge of the subject is often very difficult to obtain even a few decades after the events. The documents needed by the historian are not always easy of access. Many of them were ephemeral in character and readily disappeared as more settled conditions prevailed. They had no claim to the dignity of a recognized literature. The records of a small pioneer church, the letters or scribbled memoranda of a busy and none too well educated preacher, the sermon notes of a traveling evangelist, the manuscript records of local bodies, or even the printed minutes of more formal assemblies, were easily lost from view in a new generation. When preserved, they found lodgment in out of the way places and were threatened with early oblivion. Persons into whose possession they fell might be quite unaware of their value as testimony to conditions of life in a primitive age that no one now had any desire to remember. Occasionally one hears of the destruction of papers originally the property of some pioneer preacher whose descendants lack historical interest and make a bonfire out of what seems to them only rubbish in the attic.

Convinced that important documents might soon be lost beyond recovery, the Department of Church History in the Divinity School of the University of Chicago has undertaken systematically to locate and collect these original sources for the history of Christianity in America. One can easily imagine how much more complete and valuable the so-called *Ante-Nicene Fathers* and the earlier parts of Migne's *Patrologia* would have been if the materials had been comprehensively assembled a few decades after the events instead of centuries later. An enterprise of this sort cannot be too early undertaken or too comprehensively conceived. Even when it is possible to print only a selection of documents, the effort may stimulate wider interest in the discovery and preservation of such historical records. With these ends in view a series of volumes containing original sources for the history of Christianity on the American frontiers has been projected.

The first volume, now given to the public, deals with the Baptists because these groups were the first to take an active interest in the frontier situation as migrations moved westward when the territory between the Alleghenies and the Mississippi was first settled. Next came the combined activities of Presbyterians and Congregationalists; the Methodists and other bodies, the sources for whose history are also extensively available but are reserved for future publication. The history of other movements, and the expansion beyond the Mississippi, offer similar possibilities.

The materials are presented in the chronological order of the denominational developments simply for convenience of treatment. Indeed there is much in all of the documents that is not only non-sectarian in interest but also non-religious in the strictest sense of that term. While they consist of diaries kept by pioneer preachers, private and circular letters, minutes of individual churches and associations, records of discipline, and pronouncements of religious groups on public issues such as the question of slavery, they also abound in references—sometimes brief and at other times extensive—to almost every phase of social life among the population in general. And in form and content they are a constant revelation of the cultural conditions prevailing in the territories and among the peoples from whom they emanate.

Professor William Warren Sweet, whose special field of research is that of the American church, is immediately responsible for the preparation of this first volume of "Sources" and has in hand materials for further volumes to cover the entire history of the expansion of Christianity in America.

SHIRLEY JACKSON CASE, *Chairman,*

January 23, 1931   Department of Church History,
University of Chicago.

PREFACE

The materials in this volume represent a selection of manuscript and out-of-print sources, taken from a much larger body of scattered materials. The principal depositories, especially of the manuscript materials bearing on the Baptists on the early frontier, are the libraries of the Southern Baptist Theological Seminary, at Louisville, Kentucky, Shurtleff College, at Alton, Illinois, and Franklin College, Franklin, Indiana. And here I wish to acknowledge my indebtedness to Rev. Thomas A. Johnson of the former institution, Professor H. F. Waggener of Shurtleff College and Dr. John F. Cady of Franklin College, for their kind assistance and coöperation in placing the collections in their respective libraries at my disposal. I wish also to mention the valuable assistance rendered by two research students in church history at the University of Chicago, Messrs. R. H. Johnson, now professor of history in Thiel College, and R. W. Goodloe, professor of church history in the Southern Methodist University. Mr. Johnson is responsible for Chapter V of the Introduction, while Mr. Goodloe gathered much of the material for Chapter IV and also assisted in editing several of the manuscripts.

W. W. S.

University of Chicago
January 23, 1931

PART I
INTRODUCTION

CHAPTER I

THE STATUS OF THE BAPTISTS IN AMERICA AT THE CLOSE OF THE REVOLUTION

The materials brought together in this volume deal with the expansion of the people known as Baptists into the territory between the Alleghany Mountains and the Mississippi River, from the close of the Revolution to the year 1830. We have termed this territory and the years covered "the early frontier." As is now well known to all historical students, there have been several frontiers in the history of the expansion of the American people westward. The early frontier, however, is the most significant, as far as the expansion of the American churches is concerned, in that methods were developed and types of work devised which were to be used again and again on the successive frontiers.

It is proposed in this chapter to describe the status of the Baptists in the United States at the close of the War for Independence in order to understand the forces which were present, and which were soon to bring about such a rapid growth among Baptists in America.

Up until the Great Awakening the Baptists were not only one of the smaller religious bodies in the colonies, but they were considered religious radicals of the most dangerous type, and were frequently looked upon as enemies of all political and social order. In their origin the American Baptists had no connection with the English Baptists; rather they date from the expulsion of Roger Williams from Massachusetts, and from his establishment of the Providence Plantation. Here the first Baptist church in America was formed in 1639; a few years later (probably 1644) the second Baptist church was formed at Newport, and with this beginning Rhode Island became the chief Baptist center in the colonies. In Pennsylvania, New Jersey, and Delaware, the Quaker colo-

3

nies, since here was a large degree of religious liberty, scattered Baptist churches were formed during the latter seventeenth and the early eighteenth centuries, and the first association was organized in Philadelphia in 1707.[1] These early Baptists in the middle colonies came from various sources. The Pennepek church was made up of Welsh, Irish and English Baptists; the organizer of the church at Cold Spring, Bucks county, Pennsylvania, was from Newport; Irish Baptists made up the majority in several of the early churches.[2] There were also a few scattered congregations in the southern colonies and in New York previous to the Great Awakening, but they were few indeed, and from the standpoint of western expansion, of little importance. As late as 1740 there were but twenty-one Baptist churches in Massachusetts, Connecticut and Rhode Island, Rhode Island having eleven of that number.

With the opening and development of the Great Revival which swept over the colonies, beginning in New England about 1734, the whole religious situation throughout the country underwent rapid change, and none reaped greater profit from that change than did the Baptists. At first the Baptists took little part in the revival movement in New England, probably due to the fact that most of their churches were Arminian in doctrine and the revival was strongly Calvinistic in emphasis; and also to the fact that they had been so harshly treated by the Congregationalists that they felt little inclined to join them. The Baptists reaped their chief fruit, however, through the controversies and divisions which soon appeared in many of the New England Congregational churches as a result of the revival.

We will let Robert B. Semple, one of the early Baptist historians, describe what happened in many congregations in New England as a result of the revival:

[1] Some of these early churches in the Quaker colonies were Cold Spring, Bucks County, Pennsylvania, 1684; Pennepek, 1688, see Records (MSS.) of the Pennepek Church in the Pennsylvania Historical Society; Piscataqua, New Jersey, 1689; Middletown, New Jersey, 1687 or 1688; Philadelphia, 1698.

[2] See Newman, *A History of Baptist Churches in the United States*, II, American Church History Series (New York, 1894), pp. 200-15.

"By the preaching of Mr. Whitefield thro' New England, a great work of God broke out in that country, distinguished by the name of the *New-Light-stir*. All who joined it were called *Newlights*. Many preachers of the established order became active in the work. . . . Their success was so great that numbers of the parish clergy, who were opposed to the revival, were apprehensive that they should be deserted by all their hearers. They therefore not only refused them the use of their meeting houses, but actually procured the passage of a law to confine all preachers to their own parishes. . . . This opposition did not effect the intended object. The hearts of the people being touched by a heavenly flame, could no longer relish the dry parish service, conducted for the most part, as they thought, by a set of graceless mercenaries.

"The *New-Light-stir* being extensive, a great number were converted to the Lord. . . . These, conceiving that the parish congregations, a few excepted, were far from the purity of the gospel, determined to form a society to themselves. Accordingly they embodied many churches. . . . Into these none were admitted, who did not profess vital religion. Having thus separated themselves from the established churches, they were denominated *Separates*. Their church government, was entirely upon the plan of the *Independents*, the power being in the hands of the church. They permitted unlearned men to preach, provided they manifested such gifts as indicated future usefulness. They were *Pedobaptists* in principle, but did not reject any of their members, who chose to submit to believer's baptism." [3]

The formation of *Separate* congregations began about 1744 and by 1751 thirty ministers had been ordained as pastors of *Separate* churches. Among these were Isaac Backus, of Connecticut Congregational ancestry, who became the most influential Baptist leader of the period.[4]

The experience of Backus is typical. He was converted and joined a *Separate* congregation in 1741. Soon the number in this *Separate* congregation outnumbered the members of the original church, though they continued to be taxed for the

[3] Robert B. Semple, *A History of the Rise and Progress of the Baptists in Virginia.* Richmond, 1810, pp. 1-2.

[4] Much of our knowledge of New England Baptist history is due to the painstaking work of Isaac Backus, in his *History of New England with Particular Reference to the Denomination of Christians called BAPTISTS*, first published in 1777; republished by the Backus Historical Society, Newton, Mass., 1871.

support of the Congregational pastor. About 1747 Backus began to preach. At first he tried to maintain a church of mixed views on baptism. The difficulties arising from this situation finally convinced Backus that the church should be made up of "believers, baptised upon a profession of their faith." Backus himself went through a great personal struggle before he was willing to give up infant baptism.[5]

By the process described above the number of Baptist churches in New England, in the years following the Great Revival, considerably increased. Not all the *Separate* churches became Baptist, however. Some of them returned to the older congregations, others, due to internal dissensions, were soon disintegrated, while a good proportion adopted Baptist views and became out and out Baptist churches. By 1768 there were thirty Baptist churches in Massachusetts, as contrasted with six in 1740; in 1740 in Connecticut there were four Baptist churches, in 1768 the number had increased to twelve, while the number in Rhode Island had grown during the same years from eleven to thirty-six. The first Baptist church in New Hampshire was formed from a *Separate* society in 1755 at Newton,[6] and about the same time congregations of Baptists were formed in Vermont and Maine.

While the Baptists were growing rapidly in New England as a result of the revival and the dissensions in the Congregational churches, the growth of the Baptists in the middle colonies was but normal. In 1762 the Philadelphia Association comprised churches in six colonies: Pennsylvania, Maryland, Virginia, New Jersey, New York and southern New England (Connecticut), twenty-nine in all with a membership of 1,318. In 1776 the number of churches had increased to forty-two with 3,013 members.[7]

---

[5] Backus, *op. cit.*, II, chap. xviii, pp. 103–19.

[6] Backus, II, p. 167.

[7] Newman points out that ground once preoccupied by Presbyterians is relatively irresponsive to Baptist effort. He further states that though there were schisms in many Presbyterian churches due to the Whitefield and Tennent revival, yet it is doubtful whether there was a single Baptist church formed out of the membership of a *New-Light* Presbyterian church in New Jersey and Pennsylvania. A. H. Newman, pp. 273–74.

The rapid increase of Baptists in New England and especially in Rhode Island, from about 1740 on, and the appearance of a better educated leadership, naturally led to the establishment of educational institutions, first and chief of which was Rhode Island College, now Brown University. The idea of founding an institution under the control of Baptists originated with Morgan Edwards of the Philadelphia Association, though he soon obtained the hearty assistance of a brilliant young graduate of Princeton, James Manning. The idea once suggested was immediately taken up by the leading Baptists of Rhode Island and in 1764 a liberal charter was obtained. Baptists were to be in control of the college, but Quakers, Congregationalists and Episcopalians were to share in its government. No religious tests were ever to be required and places on the faculty were to be free and open to all denominations of Protestants.[8]

While the events we have been recounting are of great moment in the general history of the Baptists in America, of much greater importance for our present study was the extension of the Baptists into Virginia and North Carolina. The Baptists in Virginia came from three general sources.[9] The first group came from England and settled in the southeastern part of the colony in 1714. There they remained unnoticed and unmolested until past the middle of the eighteenth century.[10] The second group came into Virginia from Maryland in 1743 and settled in Frederick County. These first two groups were general Baptists, that is, they were Arminian in doctrine, though later, largely through the influence of Regular or Calvinistic Baptists from the Philadelphia Association, they gave up their Arminian views and accepted the Calvinism of the Regular Baptists. These first two groups are of little importance from the standpoint of the migration of Baptists westward. We will, therefore,

[8] R. A. Guild, *Life and Times and Correspondence of James Manning and the Early History of Brown University* (Boston, 1864).

[9] Semple, *op. cit.*, p. 1.

[10] W. T. Thom, *Struggle for Religious Freedom in Virginia: The Baptists* (Baltimore, 1900), pp. 10-11.

give most of our attention to the third group which came largely from New England, bringing with them the fervor and spirit of the Great Awakening.

The early leaders of this third group were Shubal Stearns and his brother-in-law, Daniel Marshall, *Separates* or *New-Lights* from Connecticut. Stearns was the product of the Great Revival and united with the *New-Lights* in 1745. Finally convinced of the futility of infant baptism, he determined to be immersed and unite himself with the Baptists, which he did in 1751.[11] The same year he was ordained as a Baptist minister and three years later (1754) left New England, coming first to Opekon creek, Virginia, where there was a Baptist church. Here he met Daniel Marshall, his brother-in-law, who had just returned from the Susquehanna where he had been preaching to the Mohawk Indians. Like Stearns, Marshall had been converted under the preaching of Whitefield. He came of Presbyterian ancestry, but coming into Virginia, he came in contact with the Baptists, and after examining their "faith and order," was immersed and was licensed as a preacher.[12]

Stearns and Marshall preached as evangelists in Virginia for a short time, particularly in Berkeley and Hampshire counties, but here they met considerable criticism and some opposition because of their animated preaching, and charges were preferred against them in the association. The decision of the association, however, was in favor of the evangelists, though the results of their labors in Virginia did not meet their expectation.[13] This fact evidently led Stearns and Marshall and their company to leave Virginia and locate in Guilford County, North Carolina, where they settled on Sandy Creek in 1755. Soon after arriving, the little group of new settlers were organized into a church which took the name Sandy Creek, and Stearns was ap-

---

[11] For a short biography of Stearns, see Semple, *op. cit.*, pp. 366–68; also Taylor, *Virginia Baptist Ministers*, I (New York, 1860), pp. 13–18.

[12] See a brief biography of Daniel Marshall in Semple, *op. cit.*, pp. 368–76. Marshall's second wife was Martha Stearns, the sister of Rev. Shubal Stearns.

[13] Semple, *op. cit.*, p. 3; J. T. Christian, *A History of the Baptists*, Nashville, Tennessee, 1926, pp. 198–99.

pointed the pastor.[14] Stearns, Marshall and Joseph Reed, another preacher in the Sandy Creek church, were soon engaged in evangelizing throughout a wide territory. The Sandy Creek church grew from sixteen members to six hundred six; and other churches were formed. New converts at Abbott's Creek, thirty miles away, were formed into a church and Marshall was ordained as its pastor.[15] As the work grew other preachers, to use Semple's expression, were "raised" in North Carolina. Among them were James Reid, Dutton Lane and most important of all, Samuel Harriss, a man of influence in his community, who had held several offices, among them burgess of the county and colonel of the militia.[16]

There had been Baptists in North Carolina since at least 1727, when a church had been "gathered" on Chowan River in the northeast section of the colony. In 1742 William Sojourner, a Baptist minister from Berkeley County, Virginia, settled on Kehukee Creek, North Carolina. Soon there were several churches in the region and ten years later (1752) the number had grown to sixteen.[17] Like the early Baptist churches in Virginia these early North Carolina churches were General Baptists holding Arminian views, and were more or less lax in their administration of discipline, not requiring an experience of religion previous to the administration of baptism. These churches were visited in 1754 by John Gano of the Philadelphia Association and the following year two other ministers of the Philadelphia Association visited the churches and superintended their reorganization.[18] Such was the general Baptist situation in North Carolina when the *Separate* Baptists under Stearns and Marshall began their work.

The older Baptists in Virginia and North Carolina, as well

[14] Semple, *op. cit.*, p. 3.
[15] *Ibid.*, p. 4.
[16] *Ibid.*, p. 6.
[17] George A. Purefoy, *A History of the Sandy Creek Association from its organization A.D. 1758 to A.D. 1858* (New York 1859), pp. 42–43.
[18] L. Burkitt and Jesse Read, *History of the Kehukee Baptist Association*, Halifax, N. C., 1803, quoted in Christian, *A History of the Baptists*, pp. 200–01.

as all other denominations in contact with them, generally disapproved of the *Separates*. This disapproval was largely based upon the pulpit mannerisms and type of preaching generally followed by the evangelists, and by the effects produced upon the congregations.[19] They were very noisy in their preaching and Semple tells us that in the beginning of the revival they "whooped" in "many odd tones." [20] An eyewitness at one of their meetings saw "multitudes, some roaring on the ground, some wringing their hands, some in exstacies, some praying, some weeping; and others so outragious cursing and swearing that it was thought they were really possessed of the devil." [21] One of the peculiar mannerisms developed by the preachers was the "holy whine," a sing song method of speaking which seems to have arisen with outdoor preaching, and which continued to be practiced by the less educated Baptist ministers on the frontier for many years.[22]

The *Separate* Baptists had the reputation for being an ignorant and illiterate set. As is generally the case, the people attracted to the kind of meetings conducted by the *Separate* Baptist evangelists represented the lower classes economically and educationally. The intensity of their religious exercises and their excesses alarmed some and angered others who were not swept along by the tide of emotionalism. Those who held to infant baptism thought the Baptists cruel in neglecting the baptism of their infants, and to some the very name Baptist was terrifying.[23]

[19] W. M. Gewehr, *The Great Awakening in Virginia* (Durham, N. C., 1930), pp. 121–26.

[20] Semple, *op. cit.*, p. 39; Thom, *Struggle for Religious Freedom in Virginia*, p. 17.

[21] Edwards, *History of the Baptists in Virginia* (MSS.), quoted in Gewehr, p. 110 note.

[22] Broadus, "The American Baptists Ministry 100 Years Ago," *Baptist Quarterly Review*, IX (1875), pp. 1–20.

[23] Thom, *op. cit.*, p. 19. Benedict states that in the early part of his ministry, "a very honest and candid old lady, who had never been far from her retired home, said to me in a very sober tone: 'Your society are much more like other folk than they were when I was young. Then there was a company of them in the back part of our town, and an outlandish set of people they certainly were. For yourself would say so if you had seen them. As it was told to me, you could hardly find one among them but what was deformed in some way or other. Some of them were hard-

However, in spite of their lack of education, and the general contempt in which they were held by those about them, the *Separate* Baptists, under the devoted leadership of Stearns, Marshall and Harriss, and numerous other preachers, were attracting hosts to their meetings and churches were springing up with amazing rapidity. The Sandy Creek church became "the mother, grandmother, and great-grandmother to forty-two churches, from which sprang one hundred twenty-five ministers." [24] From North Carolina the work spread into Virginia where in 1760 the first *Separate* Baptist church was established. Samuel Harriss was one of the early Virginia converts and he became the apostle to Virginia.[25] In 1760 the *Separate* Baptist churches in North Carolina and Virginia formed the Sandy Creek Association and for the next ten years the progress of the *Separate* Baptists is almost unparalleled in Baptist history. Whole communities were stirred and strong Baptist churches established. Semple thus describes the work of Read and Harriss in Virginia:

"In one of their visits, they baptised seventy-five at one time, and in the course of one of their journies, which generally lasted several weeks, they baptised upwards of two hundred. It was not uncommon, at their great meetings, for many hundreds to camp on the ground, in order to be present the next day. The night meetings, thro' the great work of God, continued very late; the minister would scarcely have an opportunity to sleep; sometimes the floor would be covered with persons, struck down under conviction for sin. It frequently happened that, when they would retire to rest at a late hour, they would be under the necessity of arising again, thro' the earnest cries of the penitent; there were instances of persons travelling more than one hundred miles to one of these meetings; to go forty or fifty was not uncommon." [26]

lipped; others were blear-eyed, or humped-backed, or bow-legged, or clump-footed, hardly any of them looked like other people. But they were all strong for plunging, and let their poor ignorant children run wild, and never had the seal of the covenant put on them." David Benedict, *Fifty Years Among the Baptists* (New York, 1860), p. 92 ff.; see also Gewehr, pp. 116–17.

[24] Newman, *op. cit.*, p. 294.

[25] Semple, *op. cit.*, pp. 377–85, for a brief biography of Harriss.

[26] Semple, *op. cit.*, p. 10.

The rapid increase of this extreme type of Baptist in Virginia and North Carolina had much more than a religious significance. The growing number of Baptists in Virginia soon made them a political factor of importance. During the early period of the Virginia and North Carolina revival, the *Separate* Baptists were badly treated by the lower classes, and much of the early trouble experienced by the preachers was at the hands of the rabble. By about 1770, however, the Baptist revivalists had largely overcome this type of opposition. The people came to realize "that the Baptists were fighting their battles" and from this time on there began a popular reaction in their favor.[27] But about the same time trouble for the Baptists was brewing in another direction. The Civil authorities began now to oppose them and the years from 1768 to 1774 are known as the "Period of the Great Persecution." The historian of the Ketocton Association states that,

"When persecutors found that religion could not be stopped in its progress by ridicule, defamation, and abusive language, the resolution was to take a different step and see what that would do; and the preachers in different places were apprehended by magisterial authority, some of whom were imprisoned."[28]

Leland states that thirty or more of the preachers "were honored with the dungeon," while some of them "were imprisoned as often as four times."[29] In 1768 five of the preachers were arrested in Spottsylvania County as disturbers of the peace and one of the charges made against them was that "they cannot meet a man upon the road, but that they must ram a text of scripture down his throat."[30] One of the five, Blair, was released after four weeks, and all were promised release if they would promise to preach no more in the county, for a year and a day, but this offer they refused and the four remained in jail forty-three days.[31]

[27] Thom, *op. cit.*, Baptists, p. 21.
[28] Fristoe, *History of the Ketocton Association*, Staunton, Va. 1808, p. 69.
[29] John Leland, *Writings*, edited by Miss L. F. Green (New York, 1845), p. 107.
[30] Semple, *op. cit.*, p. 15.
[31] *Ibid.*, p. 10.

This is typical of the persecution meted out to Baptists to the outbreak of the Revolution. When the preachers were arrested, it was done on a peace warrant, on the ground that they were disturbers of the peace, and not that they were dissenters. The civil officials pretended that they were not persecuting religion when they caused the arrest of the Baptist preachers, but were acting in the cause of peace and good order. Preachers

"were not brought to the bar for religion nor for their religious opinions, nor any of their rites, modes or religious ceremonies, but as disturbers of the peace, the perverters of good order, and the calling unlawful assemblies together, taking the people from their necessary employment on their different farms and plantations, bringing the people into habits of idleness and neglect of their necessary business and interesting pursuits and thereby reducing the inhabitants to want and distress." [32]

Semple thus describes how the tide of opinion in favor of the Virginia Baptists began gradually to turn:

"In the meantime, everything tended to favour their wishes: their persecution so far from impeding, really promoted their cause: their preachers had now become numerous, and some of them were men of considerable talents. Many of the leading men favoured them; some from one motive and some from another; their congregations were large, and when any of their men of talents preached, they were crowded. The patient manner in which they suffered persecution, raised their reputation for piety and goodness, in the estimation of a large majority of the people. Their numbers annually increased in a surprising degree. Every month new places were found by the preachers, whereon to plant the Redeemer's standard. In these places, although but few might become Baptists, yet the majority would be favourable. Many that had expressed great hostility to them, upon forming a more close acquaintance with them, professed to be undeceived." [33]

Such was the general situation in Virginia as far as the Baptists were concerned, when the War for Independence

[32] Fristoe, *op. cit.*, p. 71; see also Gewehr, pp. 122–26.
[33] Semple, *op. cit.*, pp. 24–25. Chap. iii of Semple's *Baptists in Virginia* is devoted to a concise account of the "Legal Persecutions" of the Baptists, pp. 14–35.

opened. The Baptists were still a comparatively small body, but they were strong enough to make it important for either side to obtain their support and influence, and the Baptists were not slow in perceiving the advantageous position in which they were placed. In electing members to the new state Legislature, the Baptists united their voices in electing men favorable to religious liberty and freedom of conscience.[34] The opening of the battle for political freedom offered the opportunity for the achievement of religious freedom.

The first breach in the special privileges of the Establishment in Virginia was won by the Baptists in 1775 when the Convention at Richmond granted each denomination of dissenters the privilege of conducting divine service for its adherents in the army, "for the ease of such scrupulous consciences as may not choose to attend divine services as celebrated by the chaplain." [35] From now on the Baptists became active in petitioning the Virginia authorities to abolish the church establishment. In 1776 the Virginia Convention placed in the first state constitution the philosophy of religious liberty when the first independent Legislature declared against all laws punishing men for religious opinions, and exempted dissenters from taxation for the support of the establishment.[36] Meanwhile the Presbyterians, Lutherans and other dissenting groups united their petitions to those of the Baptists, and of great significance and importance in the struggle for religious freedom were the able allies, Thomas Jefferson, James Madison, Patrick Henry and George Mason.

In 1774, Madison wrote in a letter to a college friend:

"That diabolical, hell-conceived principle of persecution rages among some; and to their eternal infamy, the clergy can furnish their quota of imps for such business. This vexes me the worst of anything whatever. There are at this time in the adjacent county not less than five or six well-meaning men in close jail for publishing

[34] Fristoe, *op. cit.*, p. 90; see also Humphrey, *Nationalism and Religion in America* (Boston, 1924), pp. 371–72; Gewehr, pp. 135–37.

[35] *Journal* of the Convention, August 16, 1775, quoted by Humphrey, *op. cit.*, p. 373.

[36] Humphrey, *op. cit.*, p. 375.

their religious sentiments, which, in the main, are very orthodox. I have neither patience to hear, talk, or think of anything relative to this matter; for I have squabbled and scolded, abused and ridiculed, so long about it, to little purpose, that I am without common patience." [37]

Throughout the years of the Revolution the Baptists were carrying on their agitation for religious liberty. They had learned the expediency "of petitions, publicity, agitation, commissions and lobbying," [38] and little by little concessions were granted to the dissenters. They petitioned for a law legalizing marriages performed by a dissenting minister; [39] they assaulted the vestries and asked that overseers of the poor be elected by the community at large. But none of these partial measures satisfied them; they demanded complete religious freedom and they continued their agitation until it was achieved.

On June 18, 1779 Jefferson's bill for the establishment of religious freedom was presented to the General Assembly of Virginia, and from that time until its passage in 1785 the contest continued. Other bills were introduced and considered and rejected. The substitute bill which came nearest passage was one providing for a general assessment for religious purposes, with the provision that persons giving in taxes should declare the denomination to which they wished their assessment to go. If they made no declaration, the money should go to encourage seminaries in their respective counties. [40] The Episcopal people, of course favored the measure and the Presbyterians were wavering. Washington could see no harm in it, but the Baptists stood firm and true to their fundamental principles, and continued to demand complete religious liberty and separation of Church and State. [41] So strong, however, was the sentiment in favor of the

[37] *Writings of James Madison* (Ed. 1865), I, pp. 1-12; W. C. Rives, *Life and Times of James Madison* (Boston, 1859), I, p. 43.

[38] Humphrey, *op. cit.*, p. 382.

[39] Semple, *op. cit.*, pp. 55-66.

[40] *Journal of the House*, November 17, December 2, 3, 4, 1784, quoted in Humphrey, p. 394.

[41] Semple, *op. cit.*, p. 71.

assessment measure that it was defeated finally only by a majority of three votes.[42]

Finally, the ground was completely cleared for a final consideration of Jefferson's bill for *Establishing Religious Freedom*. On December 17, 1785 it passed and on January 19, 1786 it received the signature of the Speaker of the House and became law. Thus Virginia became the first government in the world to establish the absolute divorce of Church and State, "the greatest distinctive contribution of America to the sum of Western Christian civilization." [43]

Says Hawks, the historian of the Protestant Episcopalians in Virginia, "The Baptists were the principal promoters of this work, and in truth aided more than any other denomination in its accomplishment." [44]

While the struggle for religious freedom was at its height in Virginia, a similar struggle was in progress in New England, led by Isaac Backus, while the Warren Baptist Association [45] furnished the machinery for the assault. To the first Continental Congress (1774) Backus presented the grievances of New England Baptists, but the Congress took no official notice of his demands. Backus now turned to Massachusetts, the chief stronghold of Congregationalism, and through the years of the Revolution the Baptists continued their agitation, and although they were not immediately successful in winning complete religious freedom, yet gradually public sentiment grew against discrimination and the Baptist churches continued to increase throughout New England. In 1796 in New England, not counting Rhode Island, there were three hundred thirteen Baptist churches, an indication that the time was soon to come when the New England form of establishment must give way before

---

[42] Humphrey, *op. cit.*, p. 402.

[43] Thom, *op. cit.*, p. 73.

[44] F. L. Hawks, *Contributions to the Ecclesiastical History of the United States of America* (New York, 1839), I, p. 152.

[45] The Warren Association was formed in 1767 of churches in Rhode Island and Massachusetts. The chief purpose of its founders was to secure denominational coöperation in education, evangelization, and the struggle for religious liberty. Newman, *op. cit.*, p. 266.

the assaults of the New England Baptists and their allies. When Backus learned of the passage of the Virginia Act establishing Religious Freedom in that state, he wrote: "Equal Liberty of Conscience is established as fully as words can express it. Oh when shall it be so in New England! However, God is working wonders here." [46]

The close of the Revolution found the Baptists in the United States in a vastly different position than they had occupied at the beginning. At the beginning of the War for Independence they were but small persecuted groups, here and there, made up largely of the underprivileged classes, economically and educationally. By 1790 a social revolution had taken place. Influential and wealthy members were now counted among them, and their general reputation was equal to that of any other denomination of Christians. They had supported with almost unanimity the patriot cause in the War for Independence; they had led in the struggle for complete religious liberty which had been so gloriously won in Virginia, and was now written into the fundamental law of the nation. They were numerous and aggressive, but still making the largest appeal to the common people, to that type which was now moving in ever increasing streams over the mountains into the new empire of the west. The second chapter will trace Baptist migration over the Alleghenies and its establishment and growth there during the latter years of the eighteenth and the early years of the nineteenth centuries. [47]

[46] *Ripon Register*, p. 94, quoted in Humphrey, *op. cit.*, p. 365.

[47] In 1790 there were thirty-five Baptist Associations in the United States and 688 churches; 710 ordained and 422 licensed ministers and 64,975 members. John Asplund, *Annual Register of the Baptist Denomination in North America*, 1790, p. 64.

CHAPTER II

BAPTIST MIGRATION AND EXPANSION WESTWARD

It has been well and truthfully stated that the greatest accomplishment of the United States has been the conquest of the continent. And the greatest and most important task which the American churches faced following the winning of independence was that of following the great streams of westward moving peoples as they found their way over the mountains into Kentucky and Tennessee, or through western New York and Pennsylvania, or down the Ohio into the great new regions opening up for settlement along the streams flowing toward the Mississippi. The future of the great west and the future of the churches in America was to be determined largely by the way in which the churches met this new problem of the west. And the churches which met this new western problem the most adequately were the ones destined to be the great American churches. We are considering in this volume the way in which the Baptists met the problem of the frontier.

The pre-revolutionary settlements across the Alleghenies were made up largely of the hunters and the Indian fighters, —men of the Daniel Boone type. They were trail blazers and had little permanent influence, in that they established no cultural institutions. Many of these first settlers never took permanent root in the region, but moved on westward farther into the wilderness, and as has been pointed out, their descendants "are as likely to be found in the Rockies as in the Alleghenies." It is not important, therefore, in our attempt to trace the migration of Baptist people over the Alleghenies, that we give much attention to these first-comers. It is true there were to be found Baptists among them, such as Squire Boone, the brother of Daniel Boone, who was a Baptist preacher, and it is known that the Boones and numbers of others among these first settlers were of

Baptist stock,[1] just as there were people of Presbyterian, Anglican, and Lutheran stock among them.

The first Baptist preacher who held anything like regular preaching services in Kentucky was Thomas Tinsley who was conducting regular preaching in Harrodsburg in 1776. In 1779 John Taylor, a Virginia Baptist preacher, came to Kentucky and spent the winter among the settlers, but returned to Virginia the following spring, discouraged at the low state of religion he found in the west. Joseph Redding, another Virginia preacher, came to Kentucky in the spring of 1780, but like Taylor, also returned to Virginia, where both resumed their preaching for about two years longer.[2] During this interval Taylor was married, and also fell heir to an estate of an uncle consisting of land, negroes, stock, furniture, and several hundred dollars in money.[3]   Among the first Baptist preachers to permanently settle in the west was William Marshall. Marshall was a product of the great Baptist revival in Virginia, having been converted in 1768, and soon afterward began to preach.   Other preachers followed Marshall into Kentucky, including Joseph Barnett, John Whitaker, James Skaggs, Benjamin Lynn, all of whom were ordained, and John Gerrard, a licensed preacher. All of these ministers were from Virginia and three of them, Barnett, Whitaker and Gerrard, were responsible for forming the first Baptist church west of the mountains, the Severns Valley which was constituted June 18, 1781.

At the close of the Revolution people everywhere on the eastern seaboard were complaining of hard times. The ports of the British West Indies were closed to American commodities, while both France and Spain had adopted an illiberal trade policy with the new nation. The small farmer and the big planter alike found themselves in much the same plight. Their surplus products found no market, while both were overwhelmed with debt, which they had incurred in the

---

[1] J. H. Spencer, *History of Kentucky Baptists* (Cincinnati, 1885), Vol. I, pp. 12–13.

[2] John Taylor, *A History of Ten Baptist Churches* (Frankfort, Kentucky, 1823), p. 39.

[3] Taylor, *op. cit.*, p. 40.

expectation of greater prosperity when the war closed, and their independence was recognized. Out of this general economic depression in the east, population began to move westward in ever increasing streams. Roosevelt thus describes this first post-revolutionary immigration:

"With the close of the War came an enormous increase of the tide of immigration; and many of the new-comers were of a different stamp from their predecessors. The main current flowed toward Kentucky, and gave an entirely different character to its population. The two typical figures in Kentucky so far had been Clark and Boone, but after the close of the Revolution both of them sank into unimportance, whereas the careers of Sevier and Robertson had only begun."

The earlier population of wood-choppers, game hunters and Indian fighters was soon completely swamped by this great new stream of immigrants. It was this population which transformed Kentucky and Tennessee from backwoods communities into states. This immigration was made up not only of small farmers and people of the lower middle class, which included many Baptists, but also there were young planters, lawyers and some men of means, impoverished by the long civil war which had accompanied the Revolution in Virginia, among them.[4] This was the class of people which laid the foundations for the cultural life of the new communities, and in whose path schools and churches soon appeared.

Among these new immigrants were numerous Baptists from Virginia and North Carolina. Generally speaking, they belonged to that class economically, which would be the first to respond to the lure of cheap land. Having won their long struggle for religious liberty in Virginia, they were now glad to find an "ampler ether, a diviner air," among the canebrakes and woods of Kentucky, where they would not only be free to worship God as they pleased, without inter-

---

[4] Theodore Roosevelt, *The Winning of the West* (New York, 1890, 4 vols.), III, pp. 67–69; also Frederic L. Paxson, *History of the American Frontier* (Boston, 1924), pp. 89–94.

ference from parsons and church wardens, but also from the supercilious airs and opprobrium, with which the "first families" of the tide water were accustomed to treat them.[5] The pure democracy of Baptist church government would also tend to attract them to the freer life and the greater democracy of a new country. Their preachers came from among the people themselves and were largely self-supporting, and were liable to be as much attracted to the better land and the freer air of the west as were the people to whom they preached, and they were to be found numerously among the immigrants. "The Baptist preachers lived and worked exactly as did their flocks; their dwellings were little cabins with dirt floors and, instead of bedsteads, skin-covered pole-bunks: they cleared the ground, split rails, planted corn, and raised hogs on equal terms with their parishioners" (*Roosevelt*, III, p. 101). Thus the Baptist was particularly well suited in his ideas of government, in his economic status, and in his form of church government to become the ideal western immigrant.

An interesting type of Baptist migration is illustrated in the Gilbert's Creek church of Kentucky, which came to be known as the "travelling church." This church had been formed in Virginia, and was there called the Upper Spottsylvania church. It had as its pastor Lewis Craig, one of the most successful of the Virginia Baptist preachers. In 1781 Craig decided to remove to Kentucky, and so great was the attachment of his members to their minister, that a majority of them decided to migrate with him. Their organization was kept up on the march over the mountains, and their pastor preached again and again as they camped along the way, and there were several baptisms. On the route they came upon other Baptist emigrants from their own section and these Craig helped to form into a church. At Abingdon, Virginia, they heard the news of the surrender of Cornwallis at Yorktown, and they made the hills ring with the firing of their rifles in their glad rejoicing. In the midst of

[5] W. H. Milburn, *The Lance, Cross and Canoe; Flatboat, Rifle, and Plow in the Valley of the Mississippi* (New York, 1892).

winter, after great hardship and danger, they arrived at their chosen destination, quickly made a "clearing" and established Craig's Station on Gilbert's Creek. Here on the second Sunday of December, 1781, they gathered for worship "around the same old Bible they had used in Spottsylvania."[6]

Another such church was the Head of Sulphur Fork church in Tennessee. This church had been formed in North Carolina in 1795 and very soon afterward emigrated to Tennessee as a church, with their pastor, Joseph Dorris. From this circumstance the church was often called Dorris' church.[7]

There were both Regular and Separate Baptists among the early Kentucky settlers. A large majority of the early preachers in Kentucky had been Separate Baptists in Virginia, but for some reason on coming to the west, most of them identified themselves with the Regular Baptists.[8] By the close of the year 1785 there were eighteen Baptist churches in Kentucky, eleven Regular and seven Separate, and there were at least nineteen preachers. An attempt to unite these two Baptists groups in Kentucky was made in June, 1785, when a meeting was called at South Elkhorn, in Fayette County, to form a union association. The attempt, however, failed, due to the fact that the Separate Baptists objected to a Confession of Faith, while the majority favored accepting the Philadelphia Confession.

On September 30, 1785 six churches, which had adopted the Philadelphia Confession, met at the house of John Craig on Clear Creek in Woodford County, and there formed the Elkhorn Association, the first Baptist Association formed west of the Allegheny Mountains.[9] The Elkhorn Association

---

[6] A very attractive account of this interesting episode will be found in George W. Ranck, *The Travelling Church* (Louisville, 1891); see also Robert Semple, *Baptists in Virginia*, p. 153; John Taylor, *op. cit.*, pp. 41–42; Spencer, *op. cit.*, I, pp. 52–53.

[7] David Benedict, *A General History of the Baptist Denomination in America* (Boston, 1813, 2 vols.), II, p. 220.

[8] Spencer, *op. cit.*, I, p. 107. Of the first twenty-five Baptist ministers in Kentucky, twenty were known to have been Separate Baptists in Virginia or North Carolina, but on coming to Kentucky eighteen became Regular Baptists.

[9] Spencer, *op. cit.*, I, 108–09; Benedict, *op. cit.*, II, p. 228; see *Minutes of the Elkhorn Association* for September 30, 1785.

was formed of churches located in central Kentucky, while in the western settlements there were four little backwoods churches, cut off entirely from the newly formed association by a wide stretch of unsettled country. Accordingly, these four isolated churches in the western section sent "messengers" to Cox's Creek on October 29, 1785, and there formed the second Baptist Association west of the mountains, which received the name, the Salem Association.[10] Two years later (1787) the Separate Baptists formed their seven churches into the South Kentucky Association.   Three attempts were made to unite the Regular and Separate Baptists of Kentucky before it was successfully accomplished, and then it was brought about through the influence of the great western revival, which "prevailed powerfully" among both groups. "All were visited and refreshed by the copious and abundant rain of righteousness which was poured over the land;" and regardless of names "they unitedly engaged in enjoying and forwarding the precious and powerful work."   Under such influence a meeting of representatives from the Elkhorn and South Kentucky Associations met in 1800 and agreed on terms of union which were confirmed in October, 1801.[11]   The terms of union agreed upon were a compromise between Calvinistic and Arminian views. They are:

"We, the committees of the Elkhorn and South Kentucky Associations, do agree to unite on the following plan. 1st. That the Scriptures of the Old and New-Testaments are the infallible word of God, and the only rule of faith and practice. 2nd. That there is only one true Godhead or divine essence, there are Father, Son, and Holy Ghost. 3d. That by nature we are fallen and depraved creatures. 4th. That salvation, regeneration, sanctification, and justification, are by the life, death, resurrection, and ascension of Jesus Christ. 5th. That the saints will finally persevere through grace to glory. 6th. That believers' baptism by immersion is necessary to receiving the Lord's supper. 7th. That

[10] Spencer, *op. cit.*, II, pp. 109–10; the churches constituting this association were the Severens Valley, Cedar Creek, Bear Grass and Cox's Creek.

[11] For the terms of union between the two bodies see Benedict, *op. cit.*, **II,** pp. 237–40.

the salvation of the righteous, and punishment of the wicked will be eternal. 8th. That it is our duty to be tender and affectionate to each other, and study the happiness of the children of God in general; to be engaged singly to promote the honour of God. 9th. And that the preaching Christ tasted death for every man shall be no bar to communion. 10th. And that each may keep up their associational and church government as to them may seem best. 11th. That a free correspondence and communion be kept up between the churches thus united."

In 1790 the total population of Kentucky was 73,677, while the total number of Baptists was but 3,105, or one Baptist for about every twenty-four of the population. There were forty-two churches and forty ministers, nineteen ordained and twenty-one licensed. In 1800 there were six associations in Kentucky, one hundred six churches and 5,110 members.[12]

While the methods of work used by the Presbyterians, Methodists and Baptists on the frontier differed somewhat, yet they were all revivalistic in their emphasis, and all had a part in the great western revival which swept over the frontier settlements in the latter years of the eighteenth and early years of the nineteenth century. The Presbyterian preachers were largely responsible for starting the movement, but immediately they were joined by Methodists and Baptists and soon they were all working together in the great meetings, in the woods, which brought together thousands of people.[13] Thus one eyewitness of the famous Cain Ridge meeting states: "I attended with eighteen Presbyterian ministers; and Baptist and Methodist preachers, I know not how many; all being either preaching or exhorting the distressed with more harmony than could be expected." [14] To this famous Cain Ridge meeting "the religious of all denominations assembled, some from as many as a hundred miles distant, particularly the Presbyterians and Methodists who were in

[12] Spencer, op. cit., II, pp. 211, 541.
[13] C. C. Cleveland, The Great Revival in the West (Chicago, 1916), pp. 62–86, 130–31.
[14] New York Missionary Magazine (1802), a letter from a Presbyterian minister in Kentucky, September 20, 1801; also in Increase of Piety, March, 1801, pp. 85–87.

full communion with one another, and also the Baptists, who preach with the others, but do not commune." [15]

The revival movement was particularly strong in Kentucky. In the year 1801, 1,148 were received into the churches of the Elkhorn Association. At the Great Crossing church 353 were baptized; at the Bryant's Station church 358, and smaller numbers at numerous other churches.[16] During the same period the Salem Association added more than two thousand members. During these years the chief business of the church meetings was the reception of members, most of whom were received by experience, though many came by letter or recommendation. A typical church meeting for these years was that held at the Forks of Elkhorn Baptist church in March, 1801:

"2nd Saturday in March the Church met and after Divine Worship proceeded to business
At Sister Simmonus's request by bro Hickman the Church has agreed to give a letter of Dismission
Recd by letter Sister Price Recd by recommendation Sister Elizabeth Lutherford Recd by letter Bro Benjamin Edrington & wife Recd by experience Betsy Hickman Recd by recommendation Bro Joseph Baker & Wife Recd by experience Pompey belonging to Bro Jno Majors Recd by Experience Peter belonging to Bro Jno Price
The Church has agreed that Bro Woodride and Bro Scott is at liberty to Exercise their Gift when and where they may think proper
The following persons recd the Lord's Day morning by letter Sister Elizabeth Ship also Jno Alfred Head by Repentence Bro Majors James by Experience Susanna Majors Nancy Gibson also Bro Henry Martin by letter." [16]

From 1800 to 1803 the Baptists in Kentucky alone added 111 churches and about 10,380 members. In the latter year there were ten associations, 219 churches, and 15,495 members in Kentucky.[17]

---

[15] Extracts of a letter from Lexington, Kentucky, to his sister in Philadelphia dated August 10, 1801, *The Baptist Register*, IV, pp. 806-07.

[16] *Minutes of the Forks of Elkhorn Baptist Church* for March, 1801. (MS.)

[17] Spencer, *op. cit.*, I, p. 541. The ten associations were Elkhorn with 40 churches and 4,404 members; Salem, with 18 churches and 890 members; Tates Creek, 23

By 1820 the Baptists in Kentucky had increased to twenty-five associations, 491 churches, and 31,689 members. The period from 1820 to 1830 was one of particular importance for the Baptists in the west. These were years of controversy and finally schism. Alexander Campbell exercised more influence over the Baptists of Kentucky than those of any other state, and through the influence of his paper, *The Christian Baptist,* and his personal activity he soon had a large following among the Kentucky Baptists. Finally, between 1829 and 1832, something like 10,000 Kentucky Baptists withdrew to form the Disciples Church.[18] Besides the Campbell followers, who were known as *Reformers,* there were several thousand anti-mission Baptists in Kentucky who were finally gathered into separate churches and associations.

Let us turn to a consideration of the beginnings of the Baptists in Tennessee. As in Kentucky, the first settlements in Tennessee were made in those years between the end of the French and Indian War (1763) and the opening of the War for Independence (1775). They were located in the valleys of the beautiful rivers, in eastern Tennessee, which flow together to form the Tennessee River,—the Holston, the Wautauga, the Clinch and the French Broad. Among these first settlers were Baptists from Virginia and North Carolina, and there is some evidence that there were two Baptist churches formed in these settlements during this early period. They, however, were broken up in the troublesome times which began with the opening of the Revolution,[19] though one of these early churches was reconstituted under the name of Glade-Hollows following the war.

By 1780 a group of Baptist ministers from Virginia and North Carolina, eight in number, had moved into the Holston country and had there taken up land. They were accompanied by a considerable number of their members who had belonged to their churches east of the mountains. About this

---

churches and 1,905 members; Bracken, 16 churches, 776 members; Green River, 30 churches, 1,763 members; North District, 24 churches, 1,745 members; South District, 24 churches, 1,468 members; North Bend, 9 churches, 429 members; Long Run, 25 churches, 1,715 members; Cumberland, 10 churches, 400 members.

[18] Spencer, *op. cit.,* I, p. 642.   [19] Benedict, *op. cit.,* II, p. 214.

time also, a small body of Baptists, belonging to the famous
Sandy Creek church in North Carolina, came out "in something like a church capacity" and formed themselves into a
church as soon as they were settled on Boon's Creek. By
1781 there were five or six churches formed in what is now
eastern Tennessee.[20]

Unlike their Kentucky brethren the Tennessee Baptists
did not at once form their own independent association, but
remained under the supervision of the Sandy Creek Association of North Carolina. This relationship was continued
until 1786 when the Holston Association was formed consisting of seven churches.[21] These early Tennessee churches were
made up of both Regular and Separate Baptists, the Separates being in the majority, but their differences were soon
forgotten, and the Philadelphia Confession had been adopted
at the time of their associational organization. By 1802 there
were thirty-six churches and between 2,000 and 3,000 members in the association, and that year a new association
was formed, made up of churches in the southern part of the
settled territory, the new association taking the name,
Tennessee. In 1809 the Holston Association contained
eighteen churches, 1,213 members, and thirteen preachers,
eight of whom were ordained; in the same year the Tennessee
Association had thirty churches, sixteen preachers, fourteen
of whom were ordained, and 1,466 members.[22]

Baptist families from Virginia and North Carolina were also
to be found among the first settlers of the Cumberland country
in southwestern Tennessee. It was not, however, until 1790
that Baptist church organizations began to appear, and from
that date to 1796 five churches were organized, and in the
latter years formed themselves into the Mero Association.[23]

---

[20] Benedict, *op. cit.*, II, p. 215.
[21] The seven churches constituting the Holston Association were Kendrick's
Creek, Bent Creek, Beaver Creek, Greasy Grove, Cherokee, North Fork of Holston,
and Lower French Broad. Benedict, *op. cit.*, II, p. 215.
[22] Benedict, *op. cit.*, II, pp. 217–18.
[23] The five churches were Mouth of Sulphur Fork, White's Creek, Head of Sulphur Fork (called Dorris' church), Middle church on Sulphur Fork, and the West
Fork of Station Camp. Benedict, *op. cit.*, II, p. 219.

One of these churches, Mouth of Sulphur Fork, was constituted in 1791 with the assistance of John Taylor and Ambrose Dudley of Kentucky, who traveled through two hundred miles of wilderness, infested with Indians, to perform this service.

By 1801 the Mero Association had eighteen churches with sixteen ministers and about 1,200 members.[24] It was at about this time that the minister, who had founded the church at the Head of Sulphur Creek, Joseph Dorris, began to cause trouble in the association, due to his reported immoral conduct. On two occasions the association made examinations of the complaints against him, and, although the charges were many, yet nothing could be sufficiently proven to justify excluding him or his church from the association. Dorris had numerous friends, which made the situation all the more difficult. Finally to solve the embarrassment, it was determined to dissolve the Mero Association and to form a new one, into which Dorris or his church would not be received. This was successfully accomplished in 1803, and the new association took the name Cumberland. By 1806 this association had thirty-nine churches and about 1,900 members.[25] In the latter year the Red River Association was organized; in 1809 still another division took place and the Concord Association was the result, while the year previous, 1808, an association was formed made up of several churches in a newly settled region on the south side of the state of Tennessee, called the Elk River.[26]

We turn now to a consideration of Baptist beginnings in the region north of the Ohio. In 1788–1789 a number of Baptist people from Connecticut, New York and New Jersey formed a settlement on the Little Miami, within the present limits of Cincinnati. Some of the company, twenty-eight all told, floated down the Ohio from Pittsburgh the autumn of 1788. This group was from Essex County, New Jersey, and

---

[24] Benedict, *op. cit.*, II, p. 221.
[25] Benedict, *op. cit.*, II, pp. 220–23.
[26] Benedict, *op. cit.*, II, pp. 223–26.

several of them had been members of the Baptist church at Scotch Plains.[27] Among these settlers were several outstanding leaders, chief of whom were Judge Goforth and General John Gano of New York, and, although they had no minister at this early period, they began at once to hold divine worship, the leaders taking turns in conducting the service. The next year, 1790, the Reverend Stephen Gano, pastor of the First Baptist church of Providence, Rhode Island, visited the settlement and organized a church, at the same time baptizing three converts. This was the first Baptist church in the Northwest Territory. One of the two first ministers of this church, which took the name, Columbia, was John Smith, who later became United States Senator from Ohio, but soon repudiated his religious profession, and lost his property and reputation through his becoming involved in the Burr conspiracy.[28]

By 1797 there were four Baptist churches in the general vicinity of Cincinnati, in the valley of the Miami, and that year they were constituted into the Miami Association. In 1805 a second association was formed in the Scioto Valley. Of the two original churches of this association one was made up of Baptists of German extraction from the Shenandoah Valley in Virginia, and the other of New England Baptists. In 1811 and 1812 two other associations were organized in Ohio, the Muskingum and the Mad River. In the latter year there were sixty Baptist churches in Ohio with a membership of about 2,400. Besides these churches and associations in the state of Ohio, there was formed in 1808 the Redstone Association made up of churches partly in Ohio and partly in Pennsylvania, while the year following the Beaver Association near Pittsburgh was organized largely through the labors of a Welsh Baptist, Thomas G. Jones.[29]

The settlement of what is now Indiana did not in any real sense begin until after the close of the Indian wars which

---

[27] Benedict, *op. cit.*, II, pp. 258–59; Justin A. Smith, *History of the Baptists in the Western States East of the Mississippi* (Philadelphia, 1896), pp. 26–31.

[28] Benedict, *op. cit.*, II, p. 259.

[29] Benedict, *op. cit.*, II, pp. 261–62.

were brought to a successful conclusion by Wayne's victory at Fallen Timbers in 1794. Immediately settlers began to move across the Ohio from Kentucky, and settlements were formed along the north shore of the Ohio River and in the Whitewater Valley.[30] Included among the first Indiana settlers were, of course, some Baptists, and soon (1798) the first Indiana church was formed on Silver Creek about fifteen miles from the present city of Louisville.[31] Within a year, two other small churches were formed on the north bank of the Ohio, Owen's Creek and Fourteen Mile Creek. The McCoy family is of particular importance in the early history of the Baptists in Indiana. William McCoy, a Kentucky minister, had previously worked in the territory, while his son, Isaac McCoy, was particularly active throughout this early period, not only as a minister, but as the first Baptist missionary to the Indians.[32]

In southwestern Indiana along the lower Wabash, Baptist churches were formed between 1806 and 1808, and in the latter year a Wabash Association of five churches was constituted. In southeastern Indiana in the Whitewater Valley, the early Baptist churches were at first connected with the Miami Association of Ohio, but in 1809 the Whitewater Association was formed with nine churches.[33] The first Indiana Baptist churches along the Ohio were members of Long Run Association of Kentucky until 1811 when they were formed into the Silver Creek Association.[34] By 1812 there were twenty-nine Baptist churches in the whole of Indiana and 1,726 members.[35]

The history of the Illinois Baptists begins with the coming of James Lemen to Piggot's Fort in 1786. Piggot's Fort was located about twenty miles north of Kaskaskia. Although Lemen was not a formal member of the Baptist church, he

[30] Logan Esarey, *History of Indiana* (Indianapolis, 1915), I, pp. 123–25.
[31] W. T. Scott, *Indiana Baptist History, 1798–1908* (Franklin, Ind., 1908), pp. 37–43; Smith, *op. cit.*, pp. 54–55.
[32] Isaac McCoy, *History of the Baptist Indian Missions, 1840* (Washington, 1840).
[33] Benedict, *op. cit.*, II, p. 263.
[34] Benedict, *op. cit.*, II, p. 264.
[35] A. H. Newman, *History of the Baptist Churches in the United States*, p. 341.

had embraced the Baptist faith before leaving Virginia.[36] The first religious service held at the Fort was the year before Lemen's arrival, and was conducted by some of the residents who had been church members before coming to Illinois, for there was no minister among them.[37] In 1787 and again in 1790 Elder James Smith, a Baptist minister from Kentucky, visited the Fort and conducted services, and as a result of his labors Captain Joseph Ogle, brother-in-law of Lemen and some of his children, and James Lemen and wife and several others were converted and soon after James Lemen began to preach.[38]

Shortly after his conversion Lemen and his family moved from the Fort and started the New Design settlement, and in his large log-house, which he there constructed, services were conducted. In 1794 a visiting Baptist minister, Reverend Josiah Dodge, came to the Lemen home and baptized Lemen and his wife and several others. Two years later Baptist preachers from Kentucky conducted evangelistic services for about a month in the settlement, and as a result the first Baptist church in Illinois was organized, the organization taking place in the Lemen home, while the church took the name of the New Design church. Early in 1796 David Badgley removed with his family from Virginia to Illinois, and it was he who formed the New Design church, May 28, 1796.[39]

By 1807 there were several Baptist churches in the region besides the New Design, and in that year, a meeting was called to form an association. The Illinois Association thus formed held its first meeting at Anthony Badgley's, January 9, 1807.[40] Two years later Lemen and his friends withdrew from the association because a majority had voted to

---

[36] W. C. McNaul, *The Jefferson-Lemen Compact* (Chicago, 1915), pp. 17, 30; also H. F. Waggener, *Baptist Beginnings in Illinois*, Master's Thesis, University of Chicago, 1928, MSS., p. 7. Lemen's relation with Thomas Jefferson and his political and anti-slavery influence will be discussed under another heading.

[37] J. M. Peck, *Annals of the West*, p. 706.

[38] Waggener, *op. cit.*, pp. 12, 13.

[39] J. M. Peck, "Historical Sketches," *Baptist Memorial and Monthly Chronicle*, July 15, 1842.

[40] See the *Minutes of the Illinois Association* (MSS.) for 1807, Part II.

hold communication with an association in Kentucky that contained slave holders among its members. Immediately the association declared nonfellowship with the withdrawn members, taking the stand that the question of slavery was an individual matter and should not be made a test of church fellowship.[41] The story of the Anti-slavery Baptists on the early frontier will be told in a separate chapter.

Both anti-slavery and anti-mission agitation were responsible for causing division among the Illinois Baptists. In the year 1831 there were four anti-slavery or Friends to Humanity associations, and eleven anti-mission associations within the state.[42]

Before Missouri became a part of the United States, Baptist settlers from North and South Carolina and Kentucky were to be found in the region living under Spanish rule.[43] When these early Baptists arrived in what was then upper Louisiana, the Catholic religion was the only one recognized by law, but the commandants were inclined to favor the American settlers. During these early years itinerant preachers sometimes visited the American settlers and held services, and, though threatened with imprisonment, they always succeeded in escaping. Abraham Musick, one of the early Missouri Baptists, once went to the commandant at St. Louis to ask leave to hold preaching at his house. The Spanish official promptly denied his request, but explained his denial by saying,

"I mean that you must not put a bell on your house, and call it a church, nor suffer any person to christen your children but the parish priest. But if any of your friends choose to meet at your house, sing and pray and talk about religion, you will not be molested."

[41] Waggener, *op. cit.*, pp. 24–25.

[42] Waggener, *op. cit.*, pp. 34, 43.

[43] Daniel Boone was among those who were living in what is now Missouri while under Spanish dominion. Peck says that Boone, though never a member of any church, was religiously inclined and sustained "an amiable and moral character, and was a Baptist in sentiment." Peck further states that he preached repeatedly in his presence and conversed freely with the "venerable old gentleman, with his silvered locks and smiling, benevolent countenance, at the age of more than four score."

Doubtless the commandant knew not how easily Baptists could dispense with infant baptism, and that backwoods people could easily find their way to meeting without a bell.[44]

No sooner was Missouri ceded to the United States through the purchase of Louisiana than Baptists, from Kentucky especially, began to come numerously into the territory. At the time Missouri became a part of the United States it contained a population of about 10,000, half of whom were Americans. Moral conditions were generally bad, and so indifferent were the people to religion that many lost track of the days in the week and paid no heed to the Sabbath. Gambling and lawlessness were rampant, while morals were generally depraved and duels common.[45] The French settlers lived largely in villages, but the newcomers passed by the villages and took up large tracts of land along the river valleys.

With the Spanish restrictions removed, the people of Missouri were now permitted to enjoy religious freedom and Protestant churches were soon formed. The first Baptist church, and very probably the first Protestant church as well, was one called Tywappity, formed in 1804,[46] while the year following the Bethel church was formed, both located in Cape Girardeau County. Other churches were formed near St. Louis which at first were connected with the Illinois Association. In 1816 the Baptist churches in Cape Girardeau County organized the Bethel Baptist Association, while the year following the six small churches formerly belonging to the Illinois Association were united with the Missouri Baptist Association. The Bethel Association at its organization had seven churches, four preachers and two hundred thirty members; the Missouri Association at its formation contained six churches, three preachers and one hundred forty-two members.[47]

[44] J. M. Peck, "Historical Sketches of the Baptist Denomination in Indiana, Illinois, and Missouri," in *The Baptist Memorial and Monthly Chronicle*, July 15, 1842.

[45] Louis Houck, *A History of Missouri* (Chicago, 1908, 3 vols.), III, p. 204.

[46] Peck, *op. cit.*, p. 208; Houck states that the Tywappity church was formed in 1805.

[47] Peck, *op. cit.*, p. 208.

Settlers were now moving rapidly into Missouri, coming largely from Virginia, North Carolina, Kentucky and Tennessee. In 1817 John M. Peck and James E. Welch were sent to the west as Baptist missionaries, and began their work in St. Louis the same year. By 1818 the first Baptist church of St. Louis was formed and a school begun in a rented building, and Peck preached the first missionary sermon west of the Mississippi in the legislative hall of St. Louis and took the first missionary collection. Although Peck moved to Illinois in 1821, yet his missionary work was largely confined to Missouri for a number of years following. An interesting phase of the work of the Baptist missionaries was the formation of a Sabbath School for negroes, principally slaves, which was opened in St. Louis in 1818 and which developed into the African Baptist church. In this year also, the Mt. Pleasant Association was formed in the "Boon Lick" country, in what is now Howard County, made up of five churches and five preachers.

By 1830 Missouri contained seven associations, whose boundaries covered pretty thoroughly the settled areas of the state. Four years later the "Baptist Central Convention of Missouri" [48] was organized primarily for the purpose of providing some organized system of carrying on home mission operations. The anti-mission agitation found some supporters among Missouri Baptists and in 1839 the "Two River Old School Baptist Association" was organized. In 1840 there were in Missouri two hundred seventy-six churches, one-hundred fifty ministers and 10,775 members. [49]

The territories of Mississippi and Louisiana received their first Baptist population from South Carolina and Georgia. There was a Baptist church formed southeast of Natchez as early as 1780, while that territory was still under Spanish rule. In 1793–1795 the Spanish authorities arrested Richard Curtis, a licensed preacher, and threatened deportation, but

---

[48] The Missouri associations were: Bethel, 1816; Missouri, 1818; Mt. Pleasant, 1818; Cuivre, 1822; Salt River, 1823; Concord and Fishing River, 1824; Salem, 1827. Peck, *op. cit.*, pp. 208–09.

[49] Peck, *op. cit.*, p. 210.

he was soon released. In 1795 the authorities ordered "if nine persons were found worshipping together, except according to the forms of the Roman Catholic Church, they should suffer imprisonment." [50] Some of the Baptist settlers were arrested and imprisoned under this order. As soon as the territory was ceded to the United States, churches were soon formed and in 1806 the Mississippi Baptist Association, consisting of six churches, was organized. By 1812 there were seventeen churches and seven hundred sixty-four members.

The first Louisiana Baptists were closely related to the early beginnings in Mississippi, and the first Baptists in the region came from Mississippi. The first church in Louisiana called Bayou Chicot was formed in 1812, and in 1813 there were three churches in the state.

[50] Newman, *op. cit.*, pp. 344-45.

CHAPTER III

THE FRONTIER BAPTIST PREACHER AND THE FRONTIER BAPTIST CHURCH

The typical Baptist preacher of the early frontier came from the ranks of the people, among whom he lived and to whom he preached. He was a farmer and worked on his land five or six days each week, except when he was called upon to hold week-day meetings or funerals. He preached on Sunday and not infrequently during the week. He generally was without much education, for not only was there little opportunity for him to obtain an education, but there was a deep-seated prejudice against educated and salaried preachers.

"The experience of early Virginia Baptists in being taxed for the support of irreligious and vicious clergymen, whose only recommendation was that they had received a university education, led them to look with suspicion upon the highly educated and to prefer a ministry from the ranks of the people earning a support by following secular pursuits." [1]

The prejudice against an educated and salaried ministry was not peculiar, however, to the early frontier, but prevailed generally throughout the denomination in the early years of the nineteenth century.

Some of the early frontier Baptist preachers did, however, receive some support. At the meeting of the Elkhorn Association of Kentucky in 1787 this question was asked:

"In regard to the duty of supporting a minister, whether it be considered as a debt or a liberal contribution? Debated and cast out. Query. Whether it is agreable to scripture for churches to suffer men to preach and have the care of them as their minister that are trading and entangling themselves with the affairs of this

---

[1] A. H. Newman, *A History of the Baptist Churches in the United States*, p. 336.

life? Answer that it is not agreable to scripture but that it is the duty of the churches to give their minister a reasonable support and restrict them in these respects." [2]

In 1798 the South Elkhorn congregation raised a subscription for their minister, John Shackleford, consisting of salt, corn, wheat, pork, flour, sugar, tallow and whiskey and four cash subscriptions.[3] Raising subscriptions for ministers, however, was not always as successful as that for Shackleford. Jacob Bower tells of such a subscription which was started by one of his Deacons in Illinois. The Deacon got one or two names besides his own on the paper, but found so much opposition that he told Bower that he was sorry he had started it, when the preacher advised him to burn it. It seems that it was the custom among the Kentucky churches "to get up, and pay annually a subscription for their pastors," but for some reason this custom was not followed in Illinois in the early years (*Autobiography of Jacob Bower*, MSS.). With the beginning of the anti-mission movement, opposition to the payment of ministers evidently increased.

The attitude of early Baptists toward paying their pastors

[2] *Minutes of the Elkhorn Baptist Association, Kentucky* (MSS.), I, 1785–1835.

[3] The subscription paper reads: "We the subscribers do each agree to give unto John Shackleford the different Subscriptions against our names in the property mentioned in such Subscriptions as a compensation for his Servises in the Minister in bounds for South Elkhorn Congregation as witness our hand . . . For 1798."

	Salt lb	Corn ls Barr	Wheat ls Bu	pork lb	flower lb	beaf lb	Sugar lb	Tal-low lb	Whisky Galln
Geo. E. Smith	12½	12½	1	×	100	100	×		
John Lucas ×				100					
Shadrach Moor			1	100					
Josiah Elam				63					
Wm Dawson × 6s ca sh									
John mosle × 9s ca sh									
John Young ×									5
John Proctor			1						
Abraham hedo									27
georg Neale ×				100					
Ahijah Wood 20s sch illgs									4
Morgan Morgans 6 ca sh									
Jas Lockett									
James Smith 12s ca sh									

is thus described by the son of one of the early Kentucky preachers:

"Aware of the damaging effects of the love of money, they contributed but little to the support of the preacher; and, other things being equal, esteemed him more highly if he managed to support himself. They would have gazed with astonishment at a man, "hat in hand," passing through their congregations, begging money for their preachers; yet they often showed by their kindness and liberality to their brethren, friends, and neighbors, that this was more from principle than from the love of money, of which, indeed, they had but little to give in those days. Without the assistance they rendered your grandfather and his family in various ways, it would have been impossible for him to have given his time and thoughts, as he did, to ministerial work. In planting his crops and gathering them in, his brethren and friends often came and assisted him with their own hands, or sent their servants when they had them. The kind sisters would often come themselves or send their daughters to help your grandmother in times of sickness, and they sometimes remained for weeks together, not to be waited on, but to render more needful assistance. Many of these gentle nurses I remember well.

"As time rolled on and their circumstances improved some of the churches for whom he preached gave him small sums of money. This was first done by the Spring Creek Church in 1824. The amount made up for him there was, I think, sixty dollars. He likewise married a great many young people. Sometimes as many as three couples a day, often living at some distance from each other. For this he sometimes received small sums. Frequently at the request of friends at a distance he spent two or three weeks preaching funeral discourses, and some of these were considerate enough to make him some compensation. If they were not, nothing was ever said. His little income from these different sources, together with the excellent management and economy of your grandmother, enabled him to live in a plain, inexpensive way, and to give his time and thoughts to the work in which he felt so deep an interest. Much, though, as his heart was set on this work, he always considered his duty to his family paramount, remembering that the sacred volume placed those who did not provide for their families lower than the infidel himself.

"As they became more prosperous the Baptists of this country exhibited a commendable spirit of liberality in supporting the ministry, contributing to aid in spreading religious knowledge, building up churches, schools, and colleges, and promoting the general interests of society." [4]

The process by which a frontier preacher was "raised up" in a church was about as follows. When a "brother" was impressed that God had called him to preach, he made it known to the church and if, after the church had heard the trial sermon, it approved of his "gifts" a license was then given him to preach in a small territory, as for instance within the bounds of a single church. After further trial, if his "gifts" proved real, and he gave further evidence of usefulness as a preacher he was then permitted to preach within the bounds of the association. If, on the other hand, his "gifts" as a preacher did not seem to improve, he was advised to make no further attempts to preach.[5] Taylor gives the following account of the action of the Bullittsburg Church in refusing to ordain a minister: Each member was asked his or her mind and they all agreed that he ought not be ordained because they could "not see that he had improved any from the beginning . . . but the whole church encouraged him to continue preaching." [6]

We have in John M. Peck an excellent example of the process by which a young man was inducted into the ministry of the Baptist church. Having moved into a new settlement in New York state in 1811, even before he was well acquainted with the members of the church, he was frequently asked, "Don't you think you ought to preach the gospel?" Finally at a meeting of the church he was asked to disclose his feelings on the matter and after he had done so he left the church. In a few moments he was recalled and informed that the church had voted to have him "improve his gifts"

[4] James Ross, *Life and Times of Elder Reuben Ross* (Philadelphia, 1882), pp. 293–95.

[5] W. T. Stott, *Indiana Baptist History* (1908), p. 38; I find this entry in the Forks of Elkhorn (Ky.) Baptist church 2nd Saturday in March, 1801, "The church has agreed that Bro Wooldride & Bro Scott is at liberty to Exercise their Gift, when and where they may think proper." (MSS. *Minutes of the Forks of Elkhorn Baptist Church.*)

[6] John Taylor, *Ten Churches*, pp. 83, 84.

within its limits, until it had gained a better knowledge of his qualifications. It also voted that he conduct the meeting and speak the next day.[7]

There were two types of Baptist preachers on the frontier, the "licensed" and the "ordained." Licensing a preacher was the first step in the making of a Baptist preacher after he had been permitted to "exercise his gifts" by vote of the church. These licensed ministers frequently served in much the same way that the "local" or "lay" preachers among the Methodists served. That is they preached more or less at large. Frequently a congregation had several of these licensed preachers in its membership and many a Baptist church on the frontier was first gathered and finally organized by these licensed preachers. Frequently "licensed" preachers were called to take regular charge of congregations, when they were generally ordained.[8] Jacob Bower thus describes the process

[7] Rufus Babcock, *Memoir of John M. Peck* (Philadelphia, 1864), p. 27. Jacob Bower tells in his *Autobiography* how he began to preach. For some time he had struggled with the "call" and finally without any invitation from the church, at the conclusion of the service, he "stepped on a bench and gave out, 'There will be preaching next sunday at Brother Wellborns.' And jumped off the bench and made for the door. As I passed on several persons asked me, 'Who is to preach.' I said, come and see." (MSS. *Autobiography of Jacob Bower*.)

[8] A licensed preacher could only preach, while an ordained preacher might also administer the sacraments.

Form of ministerial license

This is to certify, that brother   is a member of the Baptist Church, in good standing and full fellowship. Trusting that God has called him to preach the gospel, we hereby license him to engage in the great work; and we offer to God our earnest prayers that he may become "a workman that needeth not to be ashamed, rightly dividing the word of truth."

By order of the church, this   day of   , 18

                                                    Pastor
                                                    Clerk

J. M. Pendleton, *Church Manual*, American Baptist Publication Society (Philadelphia, 1867), p. 171.

Certificate of Ordination

This is to certify, that brother   was, ordained to the work of the gospel ministry, by prayer and the laying on of the hands of the eldership, on the   day of   , 18 . He was called to ordination by the   church of which he was a member which had ample opportunity to become acquainted with his piety and ministerial gifts.

The ordination council was composed of   brethren from   churches, who

by which he became first a "licensed" and then an "ordained" minister:

After he had "exercised his gift" before the congregation and was encouraged "by the brethren to make more appointments." . . . he says: "I made slow progress. Laboured incessantly on the farm all the week and tryed to preach on sundays. I had no books besides my English Bible & a German Testament, and a small hymn book. After a hard days work, I would gather dry sticks, and read at night by fire light. Sometimes I would borrow books, and make the best use of them I could, while I had them" . . . "In this way I went on as well as I could, from the 2nd Lords day in May 1814 Till the first saturday in October 1816. The brethren of Hazle creek Church thought my gift was proffitable. Therefore the Church unanimously voted to give me written licence to preach the gospel, wheresoever God in his providence mite direct,. in October 1818, I moved to Logan county, (about 15 miles) and the church with which I united. Immediately called me to submit to ordination and take the oversight of them. . . . and was ordained to the Gospel Ministry on the 27th day of February in the year of our Lord, 1819." [9]

John Taylor in his *Ten Churches* has left us a vivid picture of the hardships experienced by the pioneer preacher in a new country. In 1784 he had settled with his family on his own land in Woodford County and that winter the settlers began to hold meetings in their little cabins in the woods. They had to go forty miles to get corn and then a mile to grind it before they could get bread. For meat Taylor and his family were entirely dependent upon game and he was a poor hunter, though, he says, "I would at times go out with

after a deliberate and thorough examination of the candidate cordially recommended him for ordination.

Our beloved brother, the bearer of this paper, has, therefore, the entire approbation of the ordaining council in being publicly set apart to preach the gospel and administer the ordinances of Christ.

May he, like Barnabas, be "full of the Holy Spirit and of faith," and through him may "much people be added to the Lord."

, Moderator,
, Clerk.

[9] *Autobiography of Jacob Bower* (MSS.). John Taylor preached as a licensed preacher four years before he was ordained. John Taylor, *Ten Churches* (Frankfort, Ky., 1823), p. 27: as a rule a church which licensed a preacher kept rigid control over his activities. Stott, *op. cit.*, p. 38.

the hunters and they with the common generosity of hunters would admit me to share in the profits so far as meat went." That year he lived in a cabin sixteen feet square, with no floor and without table, bedstead or stool. They used buffalo wool and the lint from nettles to make cloth for their negroes. Taylor says that altogether he cleared nearly four hundred acres of land in the heavy forests of Kentucky besides making other improvements. In one day's work, which he describes, he put up a hundred panels of rail fence six rails high,—the rails were eleven feet long—and they had to be carried from where they had been split. It was while working and supporting his family under these difficult circumstances that the first Baptist revival in Kentucky began under Taylor's preaching in the winter of 1784-1785.[10]

A good example of the farmer-preacher on the frontier is James Lemen, the founder of the first Baptist church in Illinois. Besides his preaching and anti-slavery activities, Lemen was a farmer, and like most of the farmers of those early days, made his own harness. The collars for his horses he made of straw or corn husks, which he plaited or sewed together. Once "being engaged in breaking a piece of stubble ground, and having turned out for dinner, he left his harness on the beam of his plough. His son—who was employed with a pitchfork to clear the plough of the accumulating stubble, staid behind, and hid one of the horse collars." This he did in order that there would be no work for him while his father made a new collar. But Lemen returning in the afternoon and missing the collar, mused a few minutes, and then very much to the disappointment of his son pulled off his leather breeches, stuffed the legs with straw, threw the legs across the horse's neck for a collar and proceeded with his plowing for the rest of the day.[11]

The career of Luke Williams, a Missouri Baptist preacher, is an example of the willing self-sacrifice of many of the early frontier preachers. He was licensed in 1820 and settled on a

---

[10] Taylor, *Ten Churches*, pp. 46–47.
[11] S. J. Buck, *Illinois in 1818* (Springfield, 1917), pp. 131–32, taken from the *Illinois State Historical Society Transactions*, 1904, pp. 509–10.

quarter section of land, which he could hold by pre-emption for a limited period; for he had no money to buy land. He put up a cabin, made a "truck patch" and a "cornfield" and stayed at home only long enough to cultivate, with the aid of his wife and little children, a crop of corn. Leaving home then, he would ride through all the settlements of the extreme frontiers preaching to the destitute churches. He was aided, says Peck,[12] by no missionary society, nor did the churches which he organized assist him. Williams died four years later (1824) leaving a wife and children without a title to the land on which they were living and without a shelter they could call their own.

There were five essential Baptist principles. These were (1) Separation of Church and State; (2) Conversion as a condition of church membership; (3) Individual responsibility to God; (4) Congregational church government; and (5) Immersion as the only Scriptural form of Baptism. Those Baptists who held to the rite of the "Imposition of Hands" as a symbol of the receiving of the Holy Spirit as an essential, were known as "Six Principle Baptists," and in the early colonial period there was a division among the Baptists in Rhode Island over this question.[13] On the frontier, however, this was not considered an essential.[14] All churches which held to the five principles were Baptist churches, but there was a considerable difference existing between Baptists on other matters, and there early appeared several different Baptists groups on the frontier. There were Regular, Separate, United, General, Particular, Primitive and Free Will Baptists. In England there were two principal schools of Baptists, General and Particular; the General Baptists were Arminian in their views, that is, they held to a general atonement and free grace, while the Particular Baptists were Calvinistic and held to a limited atonement and limited grace.[15]

---

[12] Babcock, *op. cit.*, pp. 139, 140.   [13] Newman, *op. cit.*, pp. 86–91.

[14] *Minutes of the Elkhorn Association* (MSS.), for 1785, reads as follows: "concerning laying on of hands on persons baptised as essential in their reception into the Church it is agreed on by us that the using or not using of that practice shall not effect our fellowship."

[15] Stott, *op. cit.*, pp. 31, 32, 33.

The origin of the terms Separate and Regular came from the Great Awakening in New England. The Separates were those who were particularly revivalistic and separated from the churches which did not support the revival, thus they became known as *Separates*. Those who did not thus separate were known as *Regulars*. These differences were carried down into Virginia and North Carolina, and finally came over the mountains into Kentucky and the west. When finally the Separates and the Regulars came together in 1801 they took the name United Baptists. The Primitive or "Hardshell" Baptists came out of opposition to missions which will be discussed in another chapter. The terms Particular and General were seldom used on the frontier.[16] In the early frontier there was little doctrinal discord among Baptists. A mild form of Calvinism was generally the accepted belief. When the Regular and Separate Baptists united in 1801, the short confession that formed the basis of union asserted the final perseverance of the saints and allowed the preaching of a general atonement, thus combining Calvinistic and Arminian views, while most of the articles were so general as to permit their acceptance by both doctrinal parties.[17] Baptists were generally strongly opposed, however, to out and out Arminianism.[18] If one of their preachers was "suspected of being unsound in the faith or Arminian in his tendencies, they turned away from him and his usefulness among them was at an end."[19] Individual

---

[16] "The first we hear of particular baptists in Kentucky, was by a respectable preacher from New England, a brother Trott—his question in Licking association was, 'That we hold to particular redemption, particular election, and particular calling,' he thought it proper to be known in future, by the appellation of 'Particular Baptists.' It was soon agreed to by the association, but with the generous reserve, that it should not affect the correspondence they had gone into, with the brethren of the general union." Taylor, *op. cit.*, p. 185.

[17] Newman, *op. cit.*, p. 335; L. Collins, *Historical Sketches of Kentucky* (Cumberland, 1847), p. 111. Collins says that in 1809 the Licking Association was known as Particular Baptists.

[18] "2nd Saturday in April the Church met Bror. Wm. Haydon cited to the church by Bror. Wm. Hickman & charged with holding Arminian principles but did not attend agreed to cite him to our meeting in May." *Minutes of the Forks of Elkhorn Church*, 1789, (MSS.).

[19] James Ross, *op. cit.*, p. 279.

churches differed considerably in their doctrinal positions. Thus the Buck Run church in its constitution contains the statement of belief in the fore-knowledge of God, in predestination, and perseverance of the saints.[20] The Mount Tabor church constitution, formulated in 1798, however, does not specifically mention predestination or election, but does hold to the doctrine of perseverance.[21]

The doctrinal independence of the frontier Baptist churches is illustrated by the constitution of the Elkhorn Association, the first formed in the west. At the first meeting of the association they adopted the London confession of faith "but something in the third & fifth chapters" and they also take exception to "Chapter 31st," which has to do with the laying on of hands as essential.[22]

Practically all the early frontier Baptist churches were not only located on streams, but were also named after creeks, valleys, runs or rivers. A glance through the minutes of the early frontier associations will reveal this fact. Thus every one of the six churches constituting the Elkhorn Association in 1785 took its name from a stream: Gilbert's Creek, Tates Creek, South Elkhorn, Clear Creek, Big Crossing and Limestone.[23] Every church in the Salem Association in 1802 was likewise named after streams. The churches with which John Taylor was connected were the South River, Lunies Creek, Gilbert's Creek, Clear Creek, and Buck Run. Of the seven churches making up the Illinois Association in 1807, the year of its organization, five were named after streams or valleys: Mississippi Bottom, Silver Creek, Wood River, Kain Spring and Richland Creek. This, of course, simply means that the early frontier settlements were located along the streams, and that the first geographic names which became familiar to the settlers were those given to rivers and creeks. The same thing is true of the early Methodist circuits. An early circuit was made up of a group

[20] Taylor, *op. cit.*, pp. 137–42.
[21] "Constitution and Rules of a Church Formed on Beaver Creek, Kentucky," 1798 (Mount Tabor church), from the *Minutes of the Mount Tabor Church* (MSS.).
[22] *Minutes of the Elkhorn Baptist Association* (MSS.), for 1785.
[23] *Ibid.*

of settlements on both banks of a river or creek. The circuit preacher frequently formed his circuit by riding up one side of the stream and down the other. He traveled as far upstream as settlement went, then crossing over he came downstream to the place where he had begun. Thus was a circuit constituted and naturally named after the stream along whose banks it lay.[24]

The initiative in the formation of a typical frontier Baptist church came generally from some "licensed" or "ordained" farmer-preacher settled in a new community. Sometimes there were several such preachers and all of them took some part in the formation of the church. Thus John Taylor describes the establishment of Clear Creek church, Kentucky:

"From the Heavenly buddings already named at Clear Creek, we began to think of having a Church there—through the winter and spring several preachers had moved into the neighborhood, as John Dipea, James Rucker and Richard Cave—we held a council on the subject of a constitution. . . . I think in April 1785 about thirty members, to the best of my recollection was in a new Church under the style of Baptist Church of Christ at Clear Creek—we soon began to Baptize our young converts, for some of them were waiting for an opportunity—we went on in great harmony through that year, we had four ordained preachers as named above; I think we Baptized between thirteen and twenty that year." [25]

Sometimes a new church was established as an "arm" of a stronger church. Thus the Forks of Elkhorn Church was formed as an "arm" of the South Elkhorn Church in June, 1788, and the *Minutes* term the South Elkhorn "our Mother church." In the constitution of this church there were "helps" from South Elkhorn Church, and from the Clear Creek Church, while there were also representatives present from the Marble Creek Church who were called in to assist in the formation of the new church. The number of the original members of this church was twenty-six, including "a negro boy named Sandy & a girl named Gilly belonging

---

[24] W. W. Sweet, *Rise of Methodism in the West* (Cincinnati, 1920), pp. 40–41.
[25] Taylor, *op. cit.*, pp. 49–50.

to bro Majors, and a Negro Woman belonging to bror Sanders by the name of Sarah." [26]

Frequently, when it happened that there were several preachers in the congregation, there was no minister chosen immediately, but they all took turns in the preaching, and sometimes there was considerable embarrassment as to which one should finally be selected.[27] Taylor thus describes how the first minister was chosen at the Clear Creek Church:

"the day was fixed on to choose a pastor, help's sent for to Elkhorn and the Great Crossing to install, (as they called it,) a pastor of the church. I think it was at our March monthly meeting, the help's came, perhaps six or eight—Lewis Craig acted as the moderator. His mode was to ask every member of the church, male or famale, bound or free, who do you choose for your pastor—I think the church was now about sixty in number. Much to Taylor's astonishment, every member but one named him as their choice, but finally Craig, the Moderator 'worked him out of his objection.'" [28]

On his selection Taylor was called upon to reply to "the voice of the church." He responded by stating that he did not feel adequate "to the great responsibility of the pastor of a church," and especially since there were three other ministers all older than himself, two of whom had been pastors in Virginia, and he therefore asked to be excused. Finally, after several of the "helps" had talked with Taylor, having gone home with him for the night, for that purpose, Taylor consented, provided the church was of the same mind the next day. This was found to be the case and immediately they proceeded with the installation.[29]

At the installation service three of the ministerial "helps"

[26] *Minutes of the Forks of Elkhorn Baptist Church*, 1788 (MSS.).

[27] This was the situation in the Clear Creek church where there were four ordained ministers. John Taylor was finally selected as the minister. Taylor, *op. cit.*, p. 51.

[28] The objection to Taylor was that his coat was too fine.

[29] "The Forks of Elkhorn Church was constituted in June 1788 and William Hickman was chosen minister of the church in november of that year." *Minutes Forks of Elkhorn Church*.

knelt down with Taylor "while they all laid their right hand on my head, two of them prayed, after which the moderator took my right hand into his, and gave me the solemn charge to fulfill the duty of a pastor to the Church," after which he called the members of the church forward to give their new pastor the hand of fellowship. This last exercise greatly moved Taylor and the others, producing "more heart melting effect than we had ever before in Clear Creek." The fact that "almost every sinner in the crowded house, pushed forward, either looking as solemn as death or in a flood of tears to give me their trembling hand" moved Taylor greatly, and this marked the beginning of a revival in the Clear Creek community.[30]

Practically all of the churches held business meetings once each month, the minister generally acting as moderator of the meeting. Each church at its formation adopted, besides a constitution or covenant, certain rules and regulations for carrying on its business and for the administering of discipline.[31] These rules emphasized the necessity of keeping order. During business no member was to leave his seat without leave; all matters of church membership were to be decided by a two thirds or unanimous vote, while temporal matters might be decided by a majority vote. The rules specified how motions should be made; how many times a person might speak on a question; while laughing, talking, or whispering in the time of public speech were prohibited.

Discipline of members occupied much of the attention of the business meetings of these frontier Baptist churches. A random turning of the pages of any of these old *Record*

[30] Taylor, *op. cit.*, pp. 53–54. Some of the frontier churches had Ruling Elders and Deacons; thus the Wood River church in 1820 ordained an Elder and a deacon: "first the prisbatry being formed to wit brethren daved badgly and william Jones Enered into the ordennation of the ead-Elder and ordaind brother Jeames tunnel Elder in this Church 2 Entered into the ordennation of a deaCon and ordaind brother abble more deaCon for this Church sind by order of the Church." (MSS. *Record of Wood River Baptist Church* (Illinois), 1920.

[31] See *Rules and Regulations of the Mount Tabor Church* (Kentucky), published in this volume. See also *Rules of Decorum of the Buck Run Church*, Taylor, *op. cit.*, pp. 140–42.

Books [32] of the early churches is sufficient to convince one that the church on the frontier was of tremendous importance in the preservation of order and the maintenance of decency. Discipline is meted out to members for drinking, fighting, harmful gossip, lying, stealing, immoral relation of the sexes such as adultery, gambling, and horse racing. Business dealings between members, where there had arisen misunderstandings and disputes, are brought before the church and even family affairs, such as the relation of children to their parents, are matters for church discipline. Particularly interesting and significant is the fact that in the churches where there were slave members,—and there were many of them especially in Kentucky,—the Church watched over the slaves with as much care as over the white members.

In matters of discipline the churches generally followed the Scriptural rule (Matt. 18:15–17) and the offended and the offending brethren were first to meet each other; if that failed to effect a reconciliation two or three witnesses were taken along; if that failed, then the matter was to be taken before the church; if that failed, then "helps" were asked to come from neighboring churches. Sisters were, in many cases, appointed on committees to visit other "sisters" who had offended against church regulations. An example of such procedure is found in the Mount Tabor church (Kentucky) in 1803, as follows: "Third Saturday in July 1803, The Church met and after worship, proceeded to business; 1st A report was bro^t against Sister Arnett, for drinking too much, and it appears she is guilty, we therefore, appoint Sisters Baugh,

[32] Some of the *Record Books* examined are: From Kentucky, *Severn's Valley Church Minute Book* (MSS.), 1787–1820; *Minute Book Mountain Island Church* (MSS.), 1801–1836; *Minutes Brashears Creek Church* (MSS.), 1807–1818; *Minutes Boone's Creek Church*, Vol. I (MSS.), 1785–1830; *Minutes Long Run Church* (MSS.), 1803–1817; *Minutes Glen's Creek Church* (MSS.), 1801–1824; *Minutes Book Plum Creek Baptist Church*, (MSS.), 1812–1820; *Minutes of the Forks of Elkhorn Baptist Church*, 1788–1820 (MSS.); *Mount Tabor Church Minute Book*, 1798–1805 (MSS.). From Indiana, *Little Pigeon Creek Baptist Church Minute Book* (MSS.); *Silver Creek Baptist and the Maria Creek Churches, Extracts of Their Minutes* published in Stott, *op. cit.* From Illinois, *Records of Wood River Baptist Church*, 1812–1822 (MSS.); *Minutes the Baptized Church of Christ—Friends to Humanity—at Turkey Hill Illinois*, 1822–1832 (MSS.).

Philips and Clack, to cite her to our next meeting." Again on the third Friday in August there is this entry: "1st the Committee appointed to labour with and cite sister Arnett to this meeting, Report they acted agreable to the order of the Church, and say she appear'd to be humble, and very sorry for what she had done, therefore, The Church restore her to fellowship." [33]

The following records of church meetings of the South Elkhorn Church (Kentucky), taken at random from the years 1804, 1805 and 1806 will illustrate the important place given to discipline: [34]

The 2nd Saturday in November 1804
    excluded Charles, a Negroe man belonging to Bro Majors, for abusing Winney a black member belonging to Sister Boulware
    Also excluded Molly a black member formerly belonging to Mr. Fitzgerald for telling lies
    Excluded Hannah Davy's wife for swearing & keeping another Man besides her Husband
    Condorus a black member belonging to Jas Sanders was also Excluded for lying, & taking another Wife contrary to the Gospel"
The 2nd Saturday in December 1804 the Church met and after Divine Worship proceeded to business.
    James Major was Excluded from the Church for Intoxication and for Shooting for Liquor
    Bro Red Major Came before the Church and was dealt with for Shooting for Liquor, and the Church directed the Moderator to give him a word of Admonition and was acquitted . . .
    Roberts Hicklin was excluded from the Church for Horse Raceing
                                    WILLIAM HICKMAN Modtr

2nd Saturday in March 1805 the Church met and after Divine Worship proceeded to business
    A Charge was brought against Sister Polly Edrington for frequently giving her Mother the lie, & calling her a fool and for Indeavouring by tattleing to set several of the Neighbours at strife with each other She was excluded for the same"

[33] *Minutes Mount Tabor Church,* 1803 (MSS.).
[34] *Minutes South Elkhorn Church* (Kentucky), (MSS.).

The 2nd Saturday in December 1805 the Church met and after
Divine Worship proceeded to business

Bro Haydon Complains against Bro James Major for threatening a Man's life and saying that his conduct had been so bad that
he never would tell it. The Church after full Examination into
the Charges agreed to bear with him.

At the request of Bro James Haydon & Bro Samuel Price the
Church appointed the following Brethren William Hubbel
Daniel Peak William Samuel Abraham Gregory and Carter
Blanton to settle some difficulties between them

Bro John Price's Annaca is Excluded from this Church for
Stealing.

William Hickman Mod.

At the meeting the second Saturday in January, 1806,
these interesting cases came before the church:

Brother Palmer complains against Bro Stephens and his
wife for not dealing with Nancy their Negroe Woman & bringing
her before the Church and for putting her in Irons Bro Stephens
was acquitted . . . A second Charge against Sister Stephens
for giving their negroe Woman the lye—She was Acquitted from
both Charges

Charges brought against Bro Jas Major for saying that John
Dupey slapt him in the face & he draw'd himself up in the Chair
and bore it, and that Mr. Pulliam said he was the patientest
Man he ever see in his life . . .

Charge the 2nd for saying he gave Dupey no cause to treat
him in the manner he did and for going repeatedly to where
Dupey was and Quarreling with him

The above Charges was Substanchiated—but when taking a
vote who can bear with Bro Major, the Church agreed to bear
with him

Bro Ramsey Boulware said he cou'd not fellowship Bro Major
and withdrew from the Church.

Cases of discipline for drunkenness or "drinking too
much" were frequent.[35] The Baptists, like most of the other

[35] *Mount Tabor Church Minutes:* "third Saturday in September, 1803 1st, Rec'd
Reprts against bror John Claspill, for drinking too much"; *Minutes Boone's Creek
Church,* April 4, 1801, "agreed to suspend Bro Leonard Bradley by the Church for
drinking to excess and is with held From the privilidges of the Church until satisfaction is given"; *Forks of Elkhorn Church Minutes,* 2nd Saturday in May, 1789,

frontiersmen, seemed to have no objection to the use of liquor when used in moderation. Practically everyone on the frontier drank liquor.

"Ardent spirits," says Finley, "were used as a preventive of disease. It was also regarded as a necessary beverage. A house could not be raised, a field of wheat could not be cut down, nor could there be a log-rolling, a husking, a quilting, a wedding, or a funeral without the aid of alcohol." [36]

Cartwright gives like testimony as to the prevalence of liquor drinking on the frontier:

"From my earliest recollection drinking drams, in family and social circles, was considered harmless and allowable socialities. It was almost universally the custom for preachers, in common with all others, to take drams; and if a man would not have it in his family, his harvest, his house-raisings, log-rollings, wedding, and so on, he was considered parsimonious and unsociable, and many, even professors of Christianity would not help a man if he did not have spirits and treat the company." [37]

Not only was the drinking of liquor allowable, even among Christian people on the frontier, but making it and selling it were also considered respectable. In 1810 in the territory of Indiana, with a population of a little more than 24,000, there were twenty-eight distilleries turning out 35,950 gallons of whiskey a year, to say nothing of the domestic manufacturing of liquor for home consumption. [38] But for a Baptist to sell liquor on the Sabbath was a different matter, and for such an infraction a Baptist brother was disciplined by the Silver Creek Church (Indiana) in 1819. [39] With liquor flowing as freely as it did on the frontier the restraining influence of the church was undoubtedly a large factor in restricting excessive drinking and drunkenness.

Persons were received into Baptist churches "by experi-

"Bror Jer Gullion cited to our next Meeting for Getting Drunk & keeping Game for Gamesters."

[36] J. B. Finley, *Autobiography* (Cincinnati, 1857), p. 248.
[37] Peter Cartwright, *Autobiography* (Cincinnati, 1856), p. 212.
[38] Logan Esarey, *History of Indiana*, Vol. I (Indianapolis, 1915), p. 179.
[39] Stott, *op. cit.*, p. 44.

ence, letter, or information, or recantation," but the member who was received upon information was to produce his or her letter "within twelve months." [40] A person making application for membership for the first time must relate his Christian experience before the church and if the church declared it a satisfactory experience the applicant was then privileged to receive baptism.[41] Judged from the great number excluded from church membership for disciplinary reasons and from the care that was taken in receiving members into the churches, there is every reason to believe that these early frontier churches were not primarily concerned about numbers. Again and again persons applying for membership are asked to wait for further examination, nor were members once excluded restored without assurance that they were sincere in their repentance; *Minutes of the Silver Creek Church*, Indiana, record the fact (June 26, 1819): "Sister Coombs is restored after having requested it four times." [42]

The first Baptist churches on the frontier were the rude cabins of the settlers, and as a rule these served for the first several years after a church was formed, for the membership of these early churches was often very small.[43] About a year after the organization of the Forks of Elkhorn Church occurs this entry in the church *Minutes:* "members appointed to seek out the most Convenient place for a Meeting hous also to fix what Size would be most suitable and make report as

[40] *Rules and Regulations of the Beaver Creek* (Mount Tabor) *Church, Kentucky.*
[41] *Records of the Severn's Valley Church*, June 25, 1790 (MSS.): "Honah Dinemah and Sarah Barton Give in thire Experience and was satisfactory to the Church and are Privileged to receive the ordinance of Baptism." *Records of Boone's Creek Church* (Kentucky), June 6, 1801, "a greed to Receive by Experience and Baptism James Vallandindham Joseph Pearce Negro Servant to Sam Talbutt Negro James Servant to Mr Speers Negro Cate Servant to Mr Watson Negro Rose Servant to L Burbridhe Negro Hannah Sert. to D Gillaspy (Negro Jane Servant to L Burbridge by Recommendation"; *Wood River Church Record* (Illinois), August, 1815 (MSS.), "received B Beck By recantation & acknowledgement."
[42] Stott, *op. cit.*, p. 45.
[43] The Bullittsburg Church at its formation contained thirteen members, Taylor, *op. cit.*, p. 81; the Forks of Elkhorn Church at its organization had twenty-six members, *Minutes* (MSS.); the Buck Run Church was constituted in 1818 with twenty-one members, Taylor, *op. cit.*, p. 138. Numerous early Baptist churches were formed with no more than six to ten members.

aforsd." [44] The father of Abraham Lincoln helped to build the Baptist meeting house on Pigeon Creek in Indiana in 1819. This church was twenty-six by thirty feet, was built of hewn logs, with a fire-place and a chimney made of brick. For this building Thomas Lincoln made the window frames, door casings, and pulpit.[45] The period of the better meeting house came fifteen or twenty years after the formation of the average church. Thus in 1822 the members of the Silver Creek Church in Indiana were ready to build a brick meeting house, and a committee of three was selected to superintend the building which was to be twenty-eight by forty-six feet, and was to have two chimneys. Two years later the trustees were ordered to procure cherry lumber for the doors.[46]

As soon as four or five little frontier churches had been organized in a given region the next step in the development of Baptist organization was the formation of an association. Strictly speaking an association of churches is unbaptist, for according to Baptist principle each church must be absolutely independent of other churches. It is true that the associations were supposed to be merely advisory bodies, but frequently it happened that although the action of an association was termed advisory, yet its power to expel churches from the association for not taking the association's advice was certainly in the direction of compulsion.[47] And

[44] (MSS.) *Minutes* for 2nd Saturday in May, 1789.

[45] The Pigeon Creek Baptist Church is still in existence. It is a Primitive Baptist Church and the minutes for the years during which the Lincolns attended are in the possession of the Clerk, Samuel Alley, at Boonville, Indiana. See also A. J. Beveridge, *Abraham Lincoln* (Boston, 1928), I, p. 71.

[46] Stott, *op. cit.*, p. 45.

[47] See "Power and Duty of an Association" by Benjamin Griffith, found in A. D. Gillette, *Minutes of the Philadelphia Baptist Association from A.D. 1707 to A.D. 1807* (Philadelphia, 1851), pp. 60 ff. Griffith declares that complete power belongs to the churches and that the association is the servant of the churches, but churches entering an association must agree in doctrine and practice and the association reserves the right to withdraw from churches or factions within churches which disagree with them in doctrine. He defends the right of the association to exclude "delegates of a defective or disorderly church" from the association, since the churches entered associations voluntarily. Associations excluding individuals or churches for doctrine or morals were simply doing what it was the duty of each church to do, and in so doing the association was not usurping any power. Griffith further advises that for the sake of the purity of life and doctrine of the church at

it is difficult to see how the Baptist church on the frontier could have met the problems presented by a new country without some kind of interchurch organization, for necessarily the individual church was very small and outstanding leaders few. It was only through the combining of the strength of these little churches, and through the leadership of such men as Lewis Craig, William Hickman and John Taylor, and the assistance which they were able to render whole groups of churches, through associational organization, that the Baptists became an effective instrument in meeting frontier needs.

The individual churches were represented at the association meetings by "messengers" who were never thought of as delegates. A "messenger" was a person sent on an errand by a church, for a Baptist church cannot, in theory, be represented by an individual member.[48]

We have already noted the formation of the early associations in the west; the Elkhorn and the Salem Associations in 1785 in Kentucky; the Holston Association in Tennessee in 1786; the Mero Association in the Cumberland region in 1796; the Miami Association in Ohio in 1797; the Illinois Association in 1807; and the first association in Indiana, the Wabash, formed in 1808.[49] Year by year new associations were formed until the whole frontier was covered with a network of Baptist Associations.

Most of the frontier associations adopted constitutions [50] as well as professions of faith. Frequently the associations held quarterly meetings; thus the Elkhorn at its first session "Agreed that quarterly meetings be appointed at Big Crossing, Tates Creek, Limestone and South Elkhorn, to be held in February, April, July and August.[51] It came to be the

large, it is necessary for the churches not to be too assertive regarding their independency. See George M. Starbird, *The Adaptation of the Baptist Associational Movement in America to its Environment*, Masters Thesis in MSS., University of Chicago, pp. 14–19.

[48] J. M. Peck, *op. cit.*, p. 29.

[49] Starbird, *op. cit.*, see chapter on "The Association on the Western Frontier."

[50] See the constitution of the Elkhorn Association, *Minutes*, 1785 (MSS.); of the Green River (Kentucky) for 1825, *Minutes*, p. 3.

[51] *Minutes of the Elkhorn Baptist Association*, 1785 (MSS.).

custom, especially after the great western revival, to hold meetings of the Associations in the woods and the general public was invited. During the years of the revival it was not uncommon for many thousands of people to attend these meetings. At the Elkhorn Association in 1800 "not less than 2000 persons" were in attendance and the meeting "was lively and refreshing" and "great seriousness appeared in the very numerous audience which attended." [52] At such meetings Sunday was the big day and frequently three and four sermons were preached from the "stand" in the woods. When the meetings were held in churches, frequently the Sunday morning congregation would pack the church an hour before the preaching while as many more would be in the churchyard. On such occasions the preacher would take his stand in a window.[53]

The two officials of the Association were the Moderator and the Clerk who were chosen by the "messengers" from the churches. Each church in the association sent a letter to be read before the Association, while churches making application for membership had to give full satisfaction as to their faith and order. Numerous queries were sent to the Association from the several churches as to doctrine, discipline, and administration. To the first meeting of the Elkhorn Association came this query:

"Whether or not persons in a state of slavery may be said to be proper gospel members? Answer A slave may be considered a proper gospel member." [54]

At the second meeting of the Elkhorn Association this "Query" was considered:

"How are we to understand that part of the 13th. chapter of Johns Gospel which relates to washing the saints feet? Referred to the next association and in the mean time it is requested that each

[52] *The Baptist Annual Register*, 1801 and 1802, edited by John Rippon from a letter written from Bourbon County, Kentucky, 1802, p. 1008.
[53] *Elkhorn Association*, 1824, p. 3; 1825, p. 3; 1826, p. 3.
[54] *Minutes Elkhorn Association*, 1785 (MSS.).

church make up an opinion and make report to the next association." [55]

Year by year the Associations issued circular letters
addressed to the churches within the Association. These
letters generally discussed some current problem, frequently
warning the churches against heresy of one kind or another,
or warning them against imposters. Associations also corresponded with other associations, but great care was taken as
to the doctrinal standing of the associations before correspondence was begun. [56] Correspondence between Associations
was sometimes discontinued because of doctrinal differences,
or because of the slavery issue, while the anti-mission movement, and Campbellism particularly, were the rocks on
which many associations as well as churches split.

[55] *Ibid.*, 1786.
[56] Starbird, *op. cit.*, pp. 73–75.

CHAPTER IV

THE RISE OF THE ANTI-MISSION BAPTISTS:
A FRONTIER PHENOMENON

The first quarter of the nineteenth century was a period of feverish missionary activity among the Protestant churches of America. From 1800 to 1805 five missionary periodicals were started in the United States, among them the *Massachusetts Baptist Missionary Magazine*. In 1796 a society was formed, supported by Presbyterian, Baptist and Dutch Reformed churches, to carry out a missionary program,[1] while interest in missions was beginning to manifest itself in several of the eastern Baptist associations. The work of the English Baptist pioneer missionary, William Carey, stimulated considerable interest among American Baptists and extensive collections were taken for his work in 1812. The American Board of Commissioners for Foreign Missions was organized in 1810, and, although purely Congregational in its origin, it soon became interdenominational by admitting representatives from the Presbyterian and Dutch Reformed churches. The first missionaries sent out by this society were Messrs. Judson, Rice, Newell and Hall, with their wives, who set sail for India in February, 1812. On the long voyage over both Judson and Rice, although coming on separate vessels, had been converted to Baptist principles through diligent study of the Scriptures, and soon after landing, they and their wives were baptized in the Baptist church in Calcutta. The announcement of these dramatic conversions to Baptist views, and the fact that the converts offered themselves as ready to serve as Baptist missionaries, seemed a providential happening to many of the leading American Baptists. Rice returned to the United States at once to urge

---

[1] D. L. Leonard, *One Hundred Years of Missions* (1913), p. 102.

the appeal on their immediate attention, while Judson remained in Burma to establish the first Baptist mission.

Luther Rice now entered upon his task of awakening American Baptists to their missionary responsibility. To his appeal there was an immediate response and in May, 1814, the General Missionary Convention of the Baptists was organized in Philadelphia, eleven states being represented by thirty-three delegates.[2] At the second meeting in 1817—the convention was to meet triennially—large plans were laid for the beginning of home missions in the west, under the conviction that "western as well as eastern regions are given to the Son of God as an inheritance."

Rice now became the field marshal of Baptist missions. He first visited the towns about Boston, and in September, 1813, started on a tour of the country, visiting Philadelphia, Baltimore, Washington and Richmond, thence through the south. The year 1814 was devoted to a tour of the northern and eastern states, turning aside in May to help form the General Convention for Foreign Missions in Philadelphia. The year 1815 found him in the west, and that same year he made his first report, showing that he had traveled 7,800 miles, raised $3,700 and organized seventy auxiliary societies.[3]

The first Baptist missionary appointed for the west was John M. Peck. Peck was a native of Connecticut, and as a youth had become a member of the Congregational church. In 1811 he moved to Greene County, New York, where he became a Baptist and soon afterward began to preach. In 1815 Peck met Luther Rice, the secretary of the newly formed Baptist missionary society, and not long after this meeting Peck began active participation in the missionary enterprise, visiting Baptist associations in the interest of missions. After a period spent in further educational prepara-

---

[2] James B. Taylor, *Memoir of Luther Rice* (Baltimore, 1840), pp. 109–13, 115–16. *Proceedings of the Baptist Convention for Missionary Purposes Held in Philadelphia in May, 1814* (Philadelphia, 1814).

[3] For the remainder of his life Rice continued his labors for education and missions among American Baptists, dying in 1836. See Taylor, *Memoirs of Luther Rice*, for an account of his various activities.

tion, Peck with James E. Welch began Baptist mission work in the Missouri Territory. The next year (1818) was spent by Peck, traveling extensively in Missouri and Illinois, planting churches and schools. The next year the Missionary Society withdrew its support from the western missions, on the ground of insufficient funds, and Peck was asked to join Isaac McCoy in his Indian work at Fort Wayne, but Peck preferred to remain with the settlers of the Mississippi Valley and soon afterward a society was formed among the Baptists in Massachusetts, and Peck became their missionary.[4]

Peck now removed to Illinois. He took up land in St. Clair County, where he lived the remainder of his life. He was a leader in many enterprises besides the establishment of churches and schools. From 1822–1824 he took an active part in the slavery controversy then at its height in Illinois, and was a recognized leader. But Peck's main interest throughout his life was that of missions. He founded an Illinois missionary society called the "United Society for the Spread of the Gospel," and was active in finding preachers to send into the various Baptist circuits, while through his influence missionaries were sent out from the east.[5]

Peck was also a voluminous writer. He prepared editorials for newspapers, was an indefatigable writer of letters and was the author and compiler of valuable books, among them Peck's *Guide for Emigrants* (1831) and his *Gazetteer of Illinois* (1834). It is stated that Peck did more to induce settlers to come to Illinois than any other person or any other single influence.[6]

The same year that Peck and Welch began their work in Missouri, Isaac McCoy received an appointment for one year as a missionary to the Indians of Indiana and Illinois. After working for some time in Western Indiana, McCoy decided to establish a mission at Fort Wayne where he opened a school (1820), whose first pupils consisted of eight English

---

[4] Rufus Babcock (editor), *Memoirs of John Mason Peck* (Philadelphia, 1864), p. 116. The facts relating to Peck have been drawn largely from this source.

[5] Babcock, *op. cit.*, p. 220.

[6] *The Baptist Standard*, December 28, 1907, quoted in Waggener, *op. cit.*

scholars, six French, eight Indians and one negro.[7] Two years later (1822) McCoy established a mission near the present city of Niles, Michigan, which he called Carey, and here he and his wife with other assistants labored four years, amidst privations and sickness, though with great success. From 1826 to his death in 1846 McCoy worked for the better protection of the Indians against the white man's depredations, advocating the removal of the Indians to territory where they might be more adequately protected.[8]

When Rice began his propaganda for missions among the American Baptists he does not seem to have met any very serious opposition, even on the frontier. Indeed, when he first visited Kentucky and Tennessee and presented the cause to them, he received larger contributions than in any of the other states.[9] When Peck came to the west he was well received into the Illinois Association and the work that he represented heartily supported, as the following entry from the *Minutes of the Illinois Association* indicates (October 10, 1818): "Brother Peck presented the plan of a society to employ missionaries, and promote common schools amongst the whites and Indians, which we desire to see carried into effect, and which we recommend to the churches." [10] The next day Peck preached a missionary sermon before the association and a collection was taken for the Indian fund of the Western Baptist Mission Society, and a society called the "United Society for the Spread of the Gospel" was formed, and "Mite Societies" were soon organized as auxiliaries throughout the association.[11]

---

[7] Isaac McCoy, *History of Baptist Indian Missions*, etc. (Washington, 1840,) p. 75. This is largely an autobiographical account and is of great value as a picture of Indian conditions of the period. See description of the McCoy Indian Mission in 1823, by Major S. H. Long, published in this volume.

[8] *Baptist Encyclopaedia* (Philadelphia, 1883), pp. 766–67.

[9] J. H. Spencer, *A History of Kentucky Baptists* (Cincinnati, 1885), I, pp. 570–71.

[10] *Minutes of the Illinois Baptist Association* (MSS.), 1818.

[11] Babcock, *op. cit.*, pp. 158–59. On January 26, 1817 the Silver Creek Church in Indiana ordered a copy of the *Report of the Baptist Board of Foreign Missions;* and to the question, "Is it proper to assist the Mission Board?" the answer is given, "It is proper." W. T. Stott, *Indiana Baptist History, 1798–1908* (Franklin, Indiana, 1908), p. 44.

Just two years, almost to a day, after the association had taken the favorable action above, this item of business appears in the *Minutes* of the Wood River Church, one of the churches in the Illinois Association:

"The Church is not willing for any of her members to have anything to do with the bord of Western Missions
3d whereas Br Jones was appointed by the Board as a Missionary for one month the Church is willing he may receive the wages appointed him for the same and then to be cautious to receive no more from the Board for like service." [12]

From about this time on for many years, there was hardly a Baptist church in the west, nor an association, that did not experience internal troubles over the question of missions. Many churches were split over the issue, as was the Silver Creek Church in Indiana in 1829,[13] while every Baptist association in the west took sides one way or the other on the burning question. Opposition to missions began generally in a mild interrogative way. Thus this query was sent to the Wabash Association in 1818: "Are the principles and practices of the Baptist Board of Foreign Missions, in its present operations, justifiable and agreeable to gospel order?" The next year the Association answered: "It is not agreeable to gospel order." [14] The following year (1820) the Maria Creek Church (Indiana) sent in a request asking that the association "point out to us the wickedness of the Baptist Board of Foreign Missions, and it will be our happiness to avoid everything that we conceive contrary to the mind and will of Christ." To this request the association replies: "We hope no use will be made of the decision of the last Association relative to the subject of missions, to the distress of Zion, contrary to the commands of Christ." Five years later the Wabash Association expelled the Maria Creek Church, "for holding and justifying the principles and practice of the

---

[12] *Minutes*, Wood River Church (MSS.), October, 1820.
[13] Stott, *op. cit.*, pp. 47–49.
[14] *Ibid.*, pp. 56–57.

Baptist Board of Foreign Missions and failing to give satisfaction to their aggrieved brethren." [15]

The anti-mission cause made almost a complete sweep of the Baptist churches of Tennessee. Previous to 1820 Luther Rice had made several tours of the Tennessee churches, had been well received and had organized a State Foreign Missionary Society. But by 1821 anti-mission sentiment had become so overwhelming that no one dared to resist it. To quote a contemporary:

"Not a man ventured to open his mouth in favor of any benevolent enterprise or action. The missionary societies were dissolved, and the associations rescinded all their resolutions by which they were in anyway connected with these measures, and in this respect, the spirit of death rested upon the whole people." [16]

[15] Stott, *op. cit.*, pp. 57, 59. Peck gives the following account of the extreme anti-mission action taken by a Missouri congregation about 1818: "I had conversed with the Elder, with Deacon James, and several other brethren, and found, if he (Elder Farrar) could have one hundred and fifty dollars during the year he could devote his whole time to the ministry. There was great destitution for fifty miles in each direction. Elder Farrar was a moderate preacher, but was a godly praying man, poor in this world's goods, but his heart was in his work, he had truly a missionary spirit. . . . Before I left this field I had in subscriptions over sixty dollars, and a fair prospect that the whole would be made up. But there was ignorance of the most inexcusable kind, apathy, covetousness, and bigotry in the church. There was minority of brethren of excellent spirit and desirous of seeing the plan carried into effect. Some weeks after my visit, the subject was taken up in the church, which in fact had no business with it. The subscriptions were voluntary. No one was pressed to give anything. The church, or at least the majority of the men who acted, were certainly under the influence of the Evil One. Like the persecutors of Christ, they were blinded and knew not what they did. The majority actually voted that the subscription-papers be brought forward and burnt! The deed was done, and I record this as the first act by the anti-nomian and anti-mission faction of Missouri. Nor have I ever heard in that state of as flagrant a violation of Baptist rights and privileges as this. The elder and the dissenting brethren bore all this treatment with Christian meekness and patience, but the church has never prospered." Babcock, *op. cit.*, pp. 120–21.

[16] Quoted in Newman, *op. cit.*, pp. 437–38: "The original churches of Tennessee were all missionary in their feelings and tendencies, and particularly so in their action, and they continued this attitude until about a quarter of a century ago. Their sympathies appear to have been peculiarly elicited by the condition of the Indians, by whom, on all sides, they were surrounded. They were as will be seen by the minutes of their associations, in the habit of sending ministers to preach to them, and to sustain the service they contributed freely." *Baptist Memorial and Monthly Chronicle* (1845), IV, pp. 305–06.

Jacob Bower, who served as a Baptist missionary for many years in Illinois and Missouri (see Chapter VII) has left us an excellent picture of the difficulties which a missionary was compelled to meet in carrying on his work during these years of bitter opposition. Once he was preaching in a schoolhouse in an anti-mission neighborhood, "and during the religious exercises they (and some of them were members of a Baptist church) were cutting down trees within eight or ten rods of the house," thus deliberately annoying the missionary and disturbing religious worship.[17] Stories were circulated that "if the people went to hear a missionary they would be taxed and would be compelled to pay twenty five cents for every sermon they heard, and every one baptized, there would be a tax of fifty cents to pay, and every year a tax of one dollar." The bogy of taxation seemed to have been particularly strong among the Illinois and Missouri Baptists. On a number of occasions meetings begun by Bower were stopped when the people learned that he was a missionary. A certain man in Greene County (Illinois) had invited Bower to preach in his house in 1832, and a good congregation had gathered, but hearing that the preacher was a missionary while the people were gathering, he forbade Bower the use of his house.

The Apple Creek Anti-mission Association (Illinois) was formed in 1830 and grew largely out of the fear of taxation for religious purposes. The following extracts from the constitution of this association are a clear statement of its anti-mission position:

19. We as an association do not hesitate to say, that we declare an unfellowship with foreign and domestic missionary and bible societies, Sunday Schools and tract societies, and all other missionary institutions.

21. No missionary preacher is to have the privilege of preaching at our association.

23. We advise the churches to protest against masonic and missionary institutions, and not to contribute to any such beggarly institutions.[18]

[17] *The Autobiography of Jacob Bower* (MSS.).
[18] *Constitution of the Apple Creek Association* (MSS.), 1830.

Two years later the Sugar Creek Association in Indiana was formed and were anti-mission from the beginning as article 14 of their constitution reveals:

"Any church suffering their members to unite with any of the Mission Conventions, Colleges, Tracts, Bible, Temperance, &tc. Societies, and failing to deal with their members, shall be considered guilty of such violation of the principles of the union, that the Association when put in possession of a knowledge of such facts shall punish such Churches as being not of us." [19]

By 1824 the oldest association in Illinois had become anti-mission, as this statement from the circular letter of that year proves. They deplore:

"the multiplicity of societies that have arisen, each striving to be greatest. Their zeal breaking over all bounds hath established the Missionary plan, and calls this a day of wonders, striving for power and money to send the gospel to heathen nations. Thus our land suffers a vast loss of money, we fear only to support a false zeal. Thus Zion is astonished at their unbounded cravings. . . . Money and Theological learning seem to be the pride, we fear of too many preachers of our day." [20]

Such was the position taken by numerous Baptist churches and associations, especially those located on the frontier, during the years from 1820 to 1840. Throughout the west

[19] *The Regular Baptist*, I, No. 8, 1839, p. 1.

[20] *Minutes of the Illinois Baptist Association* (MSS.), 1824. The following quotations taken from the circular letters of Baptist associations are typical: Circular letter Panther Creek Association: "We further say to the churches, have nothing to do with the Bible Society, for we think it dangerous to authorize a few designing men to translate the holy Bible. Stand fast in the liberty wherewith Christ has set you free, and be not entangled with the yoke of bondage." Circular letter Green River Association (Kentucky), 1842: "We confess we did correspond with our brethren when we knew they had something to do with these missionary un-scriptural societies, with a prayerful hope, that our brethren would see the evil of these things and forsake them; but to our sad disappointment, we have found it grow worse for they now have given liberty for the members to join any of the benevolent societies as they now exist; for this cause we are compelled to forsake our brethren, or the word of God. We, therefore, decidedly wish to inform our friends and brethren at large, that we believe that the Bible knows of no society but the Church of Christ, in a religious point of view; so that we cannot receive into fellowship either churches or members who join one of those unscriptural societies." *Baptist Memorial and Monthly Record*, IV, p. 302.

the Baptist church was divided against itself and peace could not come until the contending groups were separated. To add to the confusion the "Reformers," headed by Alexander Campbell, were causing dissension and many congregations and associations were divided as to "constitutions" and "creeds" which Campbell declared to be unscriptural. In many instances the scenes attending the separation were most exciting. Frequently the "movement" involved the separation of parents and children, brothers and sisters in their church relations. In every part of the state (Alabama) in which these colliding elements in the Baptist ranks existed, there came the final division. It is known throughout the state as the "big split." [21] And what was true of Alabama was true of all the other states where the anti-mission element had become strong and aggressive.

According to the best Baptist authority there were 68,068 anti-mission Baptists in the United States in 1846.[22] Of this number about 45,000 were to be found in the frontier states of Kentucky, Tennessee, Alabama, Mississippi, Ohio, Indiana, Illinois and Missouri. There were also large numbers in western Virginia, North Carolina and Georgia. Thus it is clear that anti-missionism was largely a frontier movement. It was strongest where educational facilities were lacking

[21] B. F. Riley, *History of Alabama Baptists*, pp. 108, 110, quoted in B. H. Carroll, *Genesis of American Anti-Missionism* (Louisville, 1902), pp. 166–68. For the splits in the other western states, see Yeaman's *History of the Missouri Baptist General Association*, pp. 49, 63, 64, 98. In 1836 there were 8,723 Baptists in Missouri of whom 3,336 were anti-missionary, with eighty churches and forty-nine ministers; in 1831 there were eleven anti-mission associations in Illinois, with one hundred seven churches, seventy-eight ministers and 3,292 members.

[22] Statistics of Baptists, Regular and Anti-mission, in 1846:

Regular Baptists	655,536
Anti-mission Baptists	68,068

Location of Anti-mission Baptists:

New England	245	Mississippi	1,619
New York	964	Louisiana	80
New Jersey	246	Texas	132
Pennsylvania	868	Arkansas	517
Delaware	334	Tennessee	10,186
Maryland	404	Kentucky	7,085
Virginia	4,461	Ohio	3,456
North Carolina	5,815	Indiana	3,870
South Carolina	289	Illinois	4,382
Georgia	11,603	Missouri	4,336
Florida	509	Iowa	189
Alabama	6,417		

Baptist Reporter, 1847, pp. 341, 344.

and where the people were out of touch with the usual cultural influences. Generally the anti-mission Baptists were ultra-Calvinistic in doctrine, were opposed to academic or theological education for the ministry, and were hostile to all societies for the promotion of the spiritual and social welfare of mankind. They taught that God in his own time and way would bring his elect to repentance and redemption, and that therefore any effort on the part of man to assist God in his redemptive work was not only presumptuous, but wicked. There came to be two groups of this peculiar family of Baptists, one known as the Primitive and the other the Two-Seed-in-the-Spirit Baptist.

Let us now turn to a consideration of the causes back of this peculiar frontier Baptist phenomenon—anti-missionism. It is an interesting fact that anti-missionism did not appear in the other frontier churches. The Methodists organized their Missionary Society in 1819, and the first mission established was an Indian mission at Upper Sandusky, Ohio, among the Wyandotte Indians. The first missionary was a prominent frontier preacher, James B. Finley, and the western conferences gave as consistent support to the cause as did the eastern conferences.[23] Nor is there trace of opposition to missions among frontier Presbyterians.[24] This movement, then, was undoubtedly peculiar to the Baptists, and its causes must be found by an examination of those factors which are distinctly and peculiarly Baptist.

A good share of the responsibility for the rise of anti-missionism must be placed at the door of three men, John Taylor, Daniel Parker, and Alexander Campbell. It will be necessary to state the position of each of these men somewhat at length in order to gain an understanding of the type of influence they exerted.

One of the earliest opponents of missions to appear was

[23] W. W. Sweet, *Circuit-Rider-Days along the Ohio* (New York, 1923). Chapter IV contains an account of the establishment of the Wyandotte mission.

[24] The two books dealing most adequately with frontier Presbyterianism are Joseph Smith, *Old Redstone, or Historical Sketches of Western Presbyterianism* (Philadelphia, 1854), and Robert Davidson, *History of the Presbyterian Church in the State of Kentucky* (New York, 1847), in neither of which do I find a trace of anti-missionism.

the highly respected and earnest pioneer preacher of Kentucky, John Taylor. Missions in the west had hardly started before they came under the lash of the old veteran's ire in a pamphlet in 1819 called *Thoughts on Missions*. The thing which seemed to arouse his anger, more perhaps than anything else, was the assumption on the part of the missionaries that there had been no real religious work done in the west prior to their coming. "To hear or read their reports," says Taylor, "it would seem as if the whole country was almost a blank as to religion." Their reports would indicate that there was not a preacher in the country which deserved the name, but says he, "it is probable these men think that but few deserve the name of preachers, but missionaries." [25]

Taylor makes two general charges against missions: first that the primary object of the missionaries and the societies was to get money; and second, the missionary system was contrary to the scheme of Baptist government.[26] The very method of these "great men to get money," is "disgustful to common modesty." He compares the missionaries to Judas "Who was a lover of money"; and to the horse leech which with its forked tongue "sucks blood with great vigor." [27] He supports his charge that the missionary enterprise is contrary to Baptist principles of government by pointing out that the missionary society was really an aristocracy, absolutely contrary to Baptist government, by a worshipping congregation.[28] It is supposed that Taylor later changed his mind on the subject of missions, and repented of his attack upon them, but his pamphlet had already done its work to check the cause of missions in the west. [29]

The arch enemy of missions on the frontier, however, was Daniel Parker. When the subject of missions was first introduced into the west, Parker was living in Tennessee, not far from the Kentucky line, where he was preaching in both states, and where he was engaged in perpetual conflict with

---

[25] John Taylor, *Thoughts on Missions* (1819), p. 12.
[26] *Ibid.*, pp. 5–7.   [27] *Ibid.*, p. 20.   [28] *Ibid.*, p. 10.
[29] Spencer, *op. cit.*, I, p. 575.

the Methodists and the New Lights. At first he claims to have been favorably disposed toward missions, but very soon, evidently, he changed his mind and became active in sowing the seed of discord, and soon had a number of preachers of considerable local influence accepting his views.[30] In 1817 Parker removed to southeastern Illinois where he spent the remainder of his life and where his most active work against missions was accomplished.

In 1820 Parker published a thirty-eight page pamphlet called *A Public Address to the Baptist Society* in which he vigorously opposed the "Baptist Board of Foreign Missions." In 1824 the first pamphlet was reprinted, and another, on the same subject, appeared addressed to the Maria Creek Church in Indiana. Two years later a pamphlet setting forth his "Two-Seed-in-the-Spirit" doctrine made its appearance. In 1829 he began the publication of a monthly paper called the *Church Advocate* which was devoted to opposition to missions and to the expounding of his peculiar doctrine. The paper, however, was discontinued at the end of two years because of the lack of patronage. After this Parker seems to have discontinued his writing, but to the end of his life he lost no opportunity of opposing the cause of missions. Parkerism, including his Two-Seed doctrine, was the fruitful cause of much dissension among the churches and associations on the frontier.[31]

Parker, like John Taylor, was much concerned lest the Baptist Board of Foreign Missions should destroy the democracy of Baptist church government. He claims that the very exalted title by which the Mission Board is called proves that they intend to take over the government of the ministry and to usurp the authority Christ gave his church. The Society calls men to preach and assigns them their fields, and holds education necessary for the gospel ministry, all of which Parker holds is simply usurping the work of God, who has "reserved" all this "to himself . . . and will fulfill in his own time and way." Parker also attacks missions on the ground that it is unscriptural, that: "It has neither precept

---

[30] *Ibid.*, I, pp. 376–78.   [31] B. H. Carroll, *op. cit.*, pp. 87–92.

nor example to justify it within the two lids of the Bible."
Therefore the "Board . . . have rebelled against the king
of Zion, violated the government of the gospel church and
forfeited their right to the union and brought distress on the
church of Christ." [32]

From 1813 to 1830 Alexander Campbell was a Baptist.
This had come about when the Campbell's church at Brush
Run, Pennsylvania, accepted immersion as the only proper
scriptural mode of baptism. On hearing of this decision on
the part of the Brush Run Church, the Baptists in the
vicinity urged that they join their association, and although
the Campbells differed from the Baptists in several important respects,[33] yet they were accepted and their church
became a regular member of the Redstone Baptist Association. From 1813 to 1820 Alexander Campbell was engaged
largely in educational work in western Virginia, but from
1820, for the next ten years, he was extremely active, preaching and debating, and in 1823 he started a periodical called
the *Christian Baptist* which circulated widely throughout the
west. In 1829 this periodical gave way to the *Millennial
Harbinger*, which was devoted to the advocacy of the same
principles.

Campbell attacked, through the medium of his periodical,
as well as in his preaching and debating, every denominational practice for which he found no scriptural authority.
Missionary societies, Bible societies, associations, synods,
presbyteries, creeds, confessions, church constitutions, bishops, reverends, doctors of divinity and a multitude of
other innovations fell under his displeasure and were mer-
cilessly dealt with in the columns of the *Christian Baptist*.
Soon Campbell had a considerable following both among the

---

[32] H. B. Carroll, *op. cit.*, pp. 108–23.

[33] The Campbells had developed a doctrine of the design of baptism which was
contrary to that held by the Baptists; they differed also in the practice of holding
the Lord's Supper every Sunday while the Baptists generally held it once every
quarter; the Campbell view of the Bible differed from the Baptists as did also his
view of ordination. The most serious difference was that Campbell had become an
Arminian while the Baptists were Calvinistic. For a summary of these differences
see Errett Gates, *The Disciples of Christ* (New York, 1905), pp. 95–99.

Baptist ministers and people, who became known as the *Reformers*, and it was not long until *Reformer* groups began to appear in many Baptist churches and associations.[34]

Campbell professed to be favorable to missions and to the spread of the gospel, but it is the plan or method and the medium used in carrying on mission work which he attacks. The missionary, Bible, tract and other societies he looks upon as great engines which ultimately tend to a national creed and a religious establishment. Ministerial education also comes in for a share of his scorn and he asks: "Did God ever call a man to any work for which he was not fully qualified, and in the performance of which he was not successful?" And to this question he answers, "No, if we except the modern preachers at home, and those called missionaries abroad." [35] One of Campbell's favorite methods of attack was to cite the vast expense of missionary operations, and he delights in reprinting in his paper the expense reports of the missionary societies, while he makes disparaging comments on missionary dress and their other extravagances.[36] He accuses the societies [37] not only of greed, but of dishonesty, embezzlement and actual stealing.[38] Among his chief weapons were ridicule and burlesque, at both of which he was adept.[39]

After the separation of Campbell and his followers from the Baptists and the organization of the Disciples into a church, Campbell changed his views entirely on the question of

[34] Errett Gates, *The Early Relation and Separation of Baptists and Disciples* (Chicago, 1904) is the most satisfactory account of Campbell and his whole relationship to the Baptists.

[35] *The Christian Baptist* (2nd ed.), I, p. 154.   [36] *Ibid.*, p. 79.

[37] *Ibid.*, pp. 60, 61. Here he refers to Mrs. Judson's clothes: " The visiting dress of this self-denying female missionary could not be valued at less than Twelve Hundred Dollars!!"

[38] *Christian Baptist*, I, p. 149.

[39] *Ibid.*, pp. 57–58. Campbell takes an account of a service at Utica, New York, in which two missionaries are "set apart" for work in Burma and writes a parody on Paul and Barnabas who are sent as missionaries to the Gentiles. "On Wednesday, the 11th of June, A.D. 44, the Rev. Saulus Paulus and the Rev. Joses Barnabas were set apart as missionaries, to the Gentiles dispersed throughout the world. . . ." "Mr. Paulus is a young man and a native of the city of Tarsus; he received his classical and theological education in the theological seminary at Jerusalem. He appeared before the committee a man of good sense, of ardent piety, and understandingly led by the Spirit of God to the work in which he is now engaged."

missionary societies, and after 1844 urged his brethren to unite in a more effective form of coöperation. The enemies of the movement went back to the columns of the *Christian Baptist* for their most effective arguments against the movement, and "Alexander Campbell of 1823 was arrayed against Alexander Campbell of 1849." This change of front in 1844–1849, however, could not undo the vast harm to missionary and other benevolent enterprise on the frontier, for which Campbell and his associates must bear a large share of the responsibility.[40]

Undoubtedly one of the causes of Baptist anti-missionism was due to their objection to centralization of authority. One of the fundamental principles of the Baptists is the complete independence of the worshipping congregation, and the formation of missionary societies with their officers and especially their field secretaries, with authority to send men here and there, seemed to some a contradiction of fundamental Baptist principles. This, as we have already stated, was one of the grounds upon which John Taylor and Daniel Parker attacked the missions cause. The operations of the Missionary Society [41] brought to Taylor's mind the operations of Tetzel at the time when "the Pope of Rome and the Mother of Harlots were at their zenith."

"The same principle is plainly seen in the great Board of missions in America, and Rice their chief cook, is also in their mighty convention. . . . Money and power are the two principle members of the old beast. That both of these limbs are found in this young beast is obvious and exemplified in the great solicitude of correspondence with all Baptist Associations." He says further: "I consider these great men as verging close on an aristocracy, with an object to sap the foundation of Baptist republican government." [42]

A second cause for Baptist anti-missionism was their opposition to an educated and paid ministry. The missionaries who came from the east were far better educated men

---

[40] E. Gates, *The Disciples of Christ*, pp. 240–42.
[41] The formation of State and Triennial Conventions aroused anti-mission sentiment. Newman, *op. cit.*, pp. 433–44.
[42] Taylor, *op. cit.*, pp. 21–22.

than were the farmer-preachers of the frontier and they were paid for their services. Naturally they were accused by the unpaid preachers of working primarily for the money that was in it for them. Taylor considered Rice a "modern Tetzel, and that the Pope's old orator of that name was equally innocent with Luther Rice and his motive about the same." "Tetzel's great eloquence, and success in getting money, alarmed first Martin Luther, and afterwards the chief of the States of Germany. Our Luther by his measures of cunning in the same art of Tetzel may alarm all the American Baptists." [43] Parker compares the missionaries to the money changers whom Christ drove from the temple, and he expects Christ will do the same thing for the modern traders in sheep and oxen. [44]

Undoubtedly jealousy of the better educated missionary on the part of the frontier preachers played a large part in their opposition. This was one of the very evident causes back of Parker's strenuous fight against the missionaries. He reviled ministerial education as consisting of the manufacture of graceless and lazy young men into preachers, and therefore it was abominable. [45] Peck states that sheer selfishness was one of the causes for the anti-mission spirit among a certain class of preachers. This class "knew their own deficiencies when contrasted with others, but instead of rejoicing that the Lord had provided better gifts to promote the cause, they felt the irritability of wounded pride, common to narrow and weak minds. They got no compensation for their preaching; but the smallest degree of power and influence over others is more precious than gold to such men." [46] One preacher was asked to give his objections against missionaries and he replied: "We don't care any thing about them missionaries that's gone amongst them heathens 'way off yonder. But what do they come among us for? We don't want them in Illinois." The moderator replied that this was a free country and that

---

[43] Taylor, *op. cit.*, p. 9. [44] Carroll, *op. cit.*, pp. 122–23.
[45] *Baptist Memorial and Monthly Record*, IV (1845), pp. 306–07.
[46] Babcock, *op. cit.*, pp. 110–11.

no one was compelled to hear the missionaries preach or to give them money unless they chose. To this the objector replied: "Well, if you must know, Brother Moderator, you know the big trees in the woods overshadow the little ones; and these missionaries will be all great men, and the people will all go to hear them preach, and we shall be all put down. That's the objection." [47]

The objection to missions which perhaps found the largest acceptance on the frontier was based on the argument that missionary societies and all other man-made organizations were contrary to the Scriptures. As we have seen this was the chief argument employed by Alexander Campbell. The columns of the *Christian Baptist* were filled with the bitterest attacks upon all these man-made societies. The church, he says, is the only organization authorized by Scripture and no justification for any other societies can there be found. His objection is not to the conversion of the heathen, but the only legitimate method to accomplish that desired work is to do it through the church. He advocates that a church emigrate to a heathen land "where they would support themselves like the natives, wear the same garb, adopt the country as their own and profess nothing like a missionary project"; this he claims is the only kind of missionary work that has any basis in Scripture.[48] Parker points out in his anti-mission pamphlet that God did not send Jonah to Nineveh through a missionary society, nor was he "sent to a seminary of learning to prepare him to preach to these Gentiles; but was under the tuition of a special order of God, and was in no case under the direction of any body of men whatever, neither did he look back to a society formed to raise money for his support."[49]

The doctrinal phase of anti-missionism is important for its understanding. One is almost forced to the opinion that opposition to missions and education developed first largely on the grounds mentioned above, and then a doctrine was

[47] *Ibid.*, p. 111.
[48] *The Christian Baptist*, I, pp. 55–56.
[49] Parker, *A Public Address to the Baptist Society*, quoted in Carroll, *op. cit.*, pp. 115–16; see also Stott, *op. cit.*, p. 70.

evolved to uphold that position. The activities of the
Methodists, Cumberland Presbyterians and the New Lights,
all of whom were Arminian or were leaning strongly in that
direction, tended to arouse the hyper-Calvinists and to drive
them to an even more extreme position. Missionary societies
and educational institutions were denounced as schemes of
Arminianism, prompted by a desire for money and a hope
for fame.[50] To the anti-effort or anti-means Baptist, God pre-
pares his ministers to preach, and after their call it is blas-
phemy to seek further education, though they have no objection if the education is received before their call to the
ministry. This position they based on Paul's words, "Let
every man abide in the same calling wherein he is called." [51]

The theology of the anti-mission Baptists was clear and
simple. God in his sovereign power did not need any human
means to bring his elect to repentance. In fact there was no
need to preach to the lost at all, for the non-elect could not
be saved, and all the preaching in the world would do them
no good. If, on the other hand, they were of the elect nothing
could prevent their being saved. Daniel Parker's Two-Seed-
in-the-Spirit doctrine [52] was the most extreme expression of
the anti-mission theology. This doctrine he expounded in a
pamphlet published in 1826. It is nothing more nor less than
a modification of ancient Manichaeism. Briefly it is this.
God created Adam and Eve and endowed them with an ema-
nation from himself, which is the good seed. After the fall
of man there was also planted in Eve and all the daughters of
Eve the "seed of the serpent." All children born of the divine
seed are the children of God, while all children born of the
evil seed are the children of the devil. Those children begotten of the devil are his bona fide children and to their
father they would and ought to go. Therefore sending them
the gospel and giving them the Bible were acts of such gross
and supreme folly that no Christian should engage in them.

[50] *Baptist Memorial and Monthly Record*, IV, p. 308.

[51] Newman, *op. cit.*, p. 436.

[52] Spencer, *op. cit.*, I, pp. 576–78 gives a fuller exposition of Parker's "Two-Seed"
doctrine.

The other portion of mankind, since they are the children of God from eternity, and being allied to Jesus Christ by the nearest and dearest ties, "being no less than 'particles' of his body . . . the Redeemer *nolens volens* take them to mansions prepared for them in bliss": hence Parker very wisely concluded that if such were the case the Lord had very little use for the Bible or Missionary societies.[53]

The total effect of the anti-mission movement in the west was undoubtedly harmful to religion generally and to the progress of the Baptists in particular.   The unevangelical type of Calvinism which it fostered led to bigotry and intolerance, and its absurdities brought the churches and ministers into disrepute among those who most needed their ministrations and their restraints.   Its opposition to education and to an educated ministry was particularly unfortunate for the west at the very time when educational foundations needed to be laid.   And much of the energy which might have been utilized to spread religion among the scattered and rapidly increasing population of a new country was expended in quarrels and resulted in bad feeling and estrangement among those who called themselves Christians.

[53] *Minutes of the General Association of Baptists in Kentucky*, October 20, 1837.

CHAPTER V

ANTI-SLAVERY MOVEMENTS AMONG BAPTISTS

What was perhaps the first pronouncement against the slave trade in the colonies was made by Roger Williams. In 1637 he protested against the enslavement of the Pequot Indians [1] and, although he did not mention the Africans, a statute of 1652 granted ultimate freedom to the negroes of Providence Plantation. [2] However, the Narraganset planters soon "developed an industrial system which may be compared with that of the southern colonies," [3] and there was no definite movement for emancipation among Baptist leaders until after the Revolution. There were reasons for this period of silence: Baptists were strongest in regions where there was little slave holding; they were committed to noninterference in civil affairs; while their all-important objective at this period was the attainment of ecclesiastical freedom.

The regulation of slavery was one of the chief problems confronting the country at the beginning of the national period. The Revolution, with its doctrine of the natural and inalienable rights of man, was the basis of a philosophical movement for emancipation, led by such men as Thomas Jefferson and James Otis, but the end of the war made possible the renewal of the slave trade on a large scale, and regulation became imperative. Slavery had to be considered in the drafting of a form of government for the Northwest Territory, and in the apportionment of representatives to Congress. The several states met the issue individually as they framed new constitutions. Moreover, at the time, there was a world wide humanitarian and reform movement.

[1] Letter to John Winthrop in the *Massachusetts Historical Society Collection*, VI, p. 214.
[2] *Rhode Island Colonial Records*, I, p. 243.
[3] M. S. Locke, *Anti-Slavery in America* (Boston, 1901), p. 14.

The emancipation advocates gained important concessions. The sixth article of the Ordinance for the Government of the Northwest Territory, which was passed in 1787, contained the clause, "neither slavery nor involuntary servitude shall be permitted except for the punishment of crime whereof the party shall have been duly convicted."[4] That same year it was decreed that the slave trade must end by 1807, and the opponents of slavery in the state legislatures and in Congress were successful in gaining further concessions before the turn of the century.[5]

Religious organizations were not slow to respond to the thrust of these new forces. The Methodist Conference at Baltimore in 1780 declared that slavery was "contrary to the laws of God and nature" and in 1784 voted to suspend both local and traveling preachers who refused to manumit slaves.[6] New England Congregational leaders were active against slavery, and the Quakers had accomplished abolition among their own members by 1787.[7]

Baptists were stimulated to action in three different areas, Virginia, Pennsylvania, and Kentucky. The revivalistic methods of the Separate Baptists in Virginia resulted in large accessions of negro members. Asplund states that there were 17,644 negro Baptists south and east of Maryland in 1795.[8] The negroes were welcomed as members, and the churches undertook to regulate their lives and make them amenable to the Baptist system of discipline. Evidently Baptist work among slaves caused some alarm, for, in a petition to the Virginia Legislature from Cumberland County favoring the Established Church, the charge is made that "there have been nightly meetings of slaves to receive the instructions of these teachers, without the consent of their masters, which have produced very bad consequences."[9]

[4] A. B. Hart, *Slavery and Abolition* (New York, 1906), p. 154.

[5] Locke, *op. cit.*, chap. vi.

[6] D. Hitt, and T. Ware, *Minutes of Methodist Conferences, 1773–1813*, pp. 25, and 48.

[7] Locke, *op. cit.*, p. 39.   [8] Asplund, *Universal Annual Register*, 1796, p. 82.

[9] C. F. James, *Documentary History of the Struggle for Religious Liberty in Virginia* (Lynchburg, Va., 1900), p. 85.

Several prominent Virginia Baptists manumitted their slaves soon after the statute of 1782 made such action legal. Among them were Dr. Thomas Chisman of Grafton, Robert Carter of Nomini, and David Barrow of Mill Swamp. Carter was a wealthy member of the Virginia Executive Council and was reputed to have owned from six hundred to eight hundred slaves.[10] Barrow, a minister, wrote a circular letter in which he declared "holding, tyrannizing over and driving slaves . . . is contrary to the laws of God and nature."[11] He later moved to Kentucky and became a leader of the emancipation movement there.

The General Committee of Virginia Baptists, representing the four associations in that state, after tabling a similar motion the previous year, adopted the following resolution offered by Elder John Leland in 1789: [12]

"Resolved, that slavery is a violent deprivation of the rights of nature and inconsistent with a republican government and therefor recommend it to our brethren to make use of every legal means to extirpate this horrid evil from the land; and pray almighty God that our honorable Legislature may have it in their power to proclaim the great Jubilee, consistent with the principles of good policy."

That same year the Philadelphia Association gave its endorsement to societies for "the gradual abolition of the slavery of the Africans and for the protection of the freedmen" and recommended that the churches represented form similar societies.[13] In contrast was the action of the Salem Kentucky Association, October third, 1789. In response to the query of Rolling Fork Church: "Is it lawful in the sight of God for a member of Christ's church to keep his fellow creature in perpetual slavery," the answer was given, "The Association judge it improper to enter in to so important and critical matter at present." [14]

[10] R. B. Semple, *Rise and Progress of Baptists in Virginia*, pp. 150, 178, 466.
[11] M. M. Fisher, *History of Negro Baptists* (MSS.).
[12] Semple, *op. cit.*, p. 105.
[13] *Minutes of the Philadelphia Baptist Association*, 1789.
[14] J. H. Spencer, *History of Kentucky Baptists*, I, p. 184.

The center of anti-slavery controversy among Baptists after 1790 shifted to the western frontier. No further mention of slavery appeared in the records of the Philadelphia Association prior to 1820. An abolition society formed in 1790 in Virginia had Quakers and Methodists on its rolls, but no Baptists.[15]

Several factors combined to make Kentucky an early center of anti-slavery agitation. Slaves had been admitted into the territory south of the Ohio, but there was opportunity to make provisions for emancipation when Kentucky was admitted to the Union in 1792 and again in 1799 when a new state constitution was devised. Even before the adoption of the first state constitution the Political Club, which met at Danville for parliamentary debate, had decided by a unanimous vote that the first clause of section nine, article one of the proposed constitution which prevented legislation against the slave trade prior to 1808 should be expunged.[16] According to Brown, "It is almost certainly true that only a minority of the talent, wealth, or influence within the bonds of the District desired or expected a long duration of slavery within its borders."[17]

Many Kentucky clergy joined forces with the emancipators. Their leader was David Rice, a Presbyterian. He delivered an address before the Kentucky Constitutional Convention on the subject, "Slavery Inconsistent with Justice and Good Policy" in the course of which he employed moral, economic, and biblical arguments.[18] His proposed remedy was gradual emancipation and the prohibition of the importation of slaves into Kentucky. However, a motion to expunge the slavery clause from the constitution failed by a sixteen to twenty-five vote. Of the six ministers who voted against slavery, three, Bailey, Smith and Garrard were Baptists.[19]

The political battle on behalf of those in bondage was

---

[15] S. B. Weeks, *Southern Quakers and Slavery* (Baltimore, 1896), p. 213.
[16] J. M. Brown, *Political Beginnings in Kentucky* (Louisville, 1889), p. 109.
[17] *Ibid.*, p. 223.
[18] R. H. Bishop, *The Church in Kentucky* (Lexington, 1824), Appendix III, p. 415 ff.
[19] Brown, *op. cit.*, p. 220.

continued. An act of the Legislature in 1798 put negro slaves and white bondsmen on a legal parity, placed jurisdiction of the law in the hands of the county courts and authorized them to discharge the abused slave if a master persisted in ill treatment.[20] Emancipation forces rallied to defeat legalized slavery when the state constitution was revised in 1799, but the bitter resentment against the Alien and Sedition laws which Congress had passed the previous year made all other issues before the Legislature of secondary importance.

Before 1805 emancipation work among Baptists was carried on by individual ministers and churches. The various associations either refused to take official cognizance of the movement or were actively hostile. The Elkhorn Association, it is true, did adopt in 1792 a committee report pronouncing slavery inconsistent with the principles of the Christian religion, but strong protests on the part of individual churches caused the association to recall the resolution a few months later.[21] Rolling Fork Church withdrew in 1789 from the Salem Association because the slavery issue was evaded and Mill Creek Church withdrew in 1794 for a similar reason. According to Spencer, the first "emancipation church" was organized by two clerical leaders, Joshua Carmen and Josiah Dodge. The constituents were former members of Cox's Creek, Cedar Creek and Lick Creek Churches.[22] John Taylor asserts that the New Hope Church, founded in 1791 by John Sutton and Carter Tarrant, was first in the field.[23]

A frontier characteristic was the ready response to strong individual leaders. It is not strange, therefore, that the emancipation movements among Baptists in Kentucky and Illinois were due to the courage and ability of a few outstanding leaders. The cause did not long survive after the death or defection of these men. Reverend David Barrow, called by many the ablest preacher among Kentucky Baptists, was a leading champion of emancipation. As was the case

[20] Z. F. Smith, *History of Kentucky* (Louisville, 1901), p. 367.
[21] A. E. Martin, *Anti-Slavery Movement in Kentucky Prior to 1850* (Louisville, 1918), p. 19.
[22] Spencer, *op. cit.*, I, p. 184.
[23] J. Taylor, *Ten Churches*, pp. 79–81.

with others, he began his anti-slavery activities in Virginia. He had literary ability and his fifty page pamphlet published in 1808 entitled, *Involuntary, Absolute, Hereditary Slavery Examined on the Principles of Nature, Reason, Justice, and Scripture* had a wide circulation.[24] A close colleague of Barrow's was Elder Carter Tarrant. A principal contribution of his to the cause was a set of rules defining exactly conditions of fellowship among emancipationists. Joshua Carmen and Josiah Dodge traveled widely in the interests of emancipation. They were present at the organization of the Miami Ohio Association in 1797 in order to "prevent the newly organized body from holding any correspondence with slave holders." [25]

As emancipation societies were formed in churches and pastors began to preach against slavery as an evil, a rising tide of opposition was encountered and the agitators were charged with perverting the minds of the negroes. At its regular meeting in 1805 the Elkhorn Association administered a direct rebuke to the friends of emancipation in the following resolution: [26]

"This Association judges it improper for ministers, churches, or associations to meddle with emancipation from slavery or any other political subject, and as such, we advise ministers and churches to have nothing to do therewith in their religious capacities."

Stung by this rebuke, some of the emancipation advocates withdrew voluntarily from the Elkhorn Association; others were expelled by individual churches. In 1805 David Barrow had to answer five charges pertaining to his attitude toward slavery which were brought before the North District Association by the Bracken Association.[27] The North District Association accepted his explanation with apologies,

---

[24] A. E. Martin, *op. cit.*, p. 38: "A copy of this exceedingly rare and valuable pamphlet is in the Cornell University Library."

[25] Dunlevy, *History of Miami Association*, p. 133, quoted by W. Birney, "James Birney and His Times" p. 18.

[26] Spencer, *op. cit.*, I, p. 185.

[27] D. Barrow, *Involuntary, Absolute, Hereditary Slavery*, etc., as quoted by Martin, *op. cit.*, p. 38.

but a number of the churches were not satisfied, and in 1806 he was charged with "preaching the doctrines of emancipation to the hurt and injury of the brotherhood." [28] As Elder Barrow refused to give up his anti-slavery activities he was publicly expelled from the North District Association.

Occasionally a pastor resigned because his congregation refused to endorse his views regarding slavery. Such was the case with William Hickman, one of the great patriarchs among Kentucky Baptists, who declared for non-fellowship with slave holders and preached against slavery at the Forks of Elkhorn Church. The church record has the following entry: [29]

"The second Sunday in September, 1807. After divine services proceeded to business. Bro. William Hickman came forward and informed the church that he was distressed on account of the practice of slavery, as being tolerated by the members of the Baptist Society, therefore, he declared himself no more in union with us and with Elkhorn Association. Therefore the church considers him no more a member in fellowship. This was nineteen years after he became a pastor. Alas for human frailty and inconsistency."

In 1807 the Friends of Humanity Association [30] was formed by churches and ministers that had formerly belonged to the Elkhorn, the North District, and the Bracken Associations. At a preliminary meeting August 29, 30, 31 in Woolford County a series of principles in catechetical form were adopted. These were later known as "Tarrant's Rules" as their author was Elder Carter Tarrant. The substance of the Rules was as follows: [31]

Q. Can any person be admitted a member of this meeting whose practice appears friendly to perpetual slavery?

A. We think not.

Q. Is there any case in which persons holding slaves may be admitted to membership in a church of Christ?

[28] Spencer, *op. cit.*, I, p. 186; II, p. 120.
[29] *Kentucky Baptist Historical Society Publications*, No. 1, p. 21.
[30] Also known as Friends to Humanity.
[31] Benedict, David, *A General History of the Baptist Denomination in America* (Boston 1813) II, pp. 231 ff.

A. No, except in the following, viz—

1st. In the case of a person holding young slaves, and recording a deed of their emancipation at such an age as the church to which they offer may agree to.

2nd. In the case of persons who have purchased in their ignorance, and are willing that the church shall say when the slaves or slave shall be free.

3rd. In the case of women whose husbands are opposed to emancipation.

4th. In the case of a widow who has it not in her power to liberate them.

5th. In the case of idiots, old age, or any debility of body that prevents such slave from procuring a sufficient support; and in some other cases, which we would wish the churches to be at liberty to judge agreeably to the principles of humanity.

Q. Shall members in union with us be at liberty in any case to purchase slaves?

A. No, except it be with a view to ransom them from perpetual slavery, in such a way as the churches may approve.

Q. Have our ideas of slavery occasioned any alteration in our views of the doctrine of the gospel?

A. No.

The following September the Friends of Humanity Association was formally organized.[32]

The next year, 1808, the Friends of Humanity, at a meeting at the New Hope Church of which Carter Tarrant was the pastor, approved a motion "that the present mode of association or confederation of churches in their relation to slavery is unscriptural and ought to be laid aside."[33] Henceforth, although the Kentucky Friends of Humanity Association continues to exist, anti-slavery activities of the Baptists are conducted through the Kentucky Abolition Society. The objectives of this organization, as set forth in its first constitution, were very moderate. Free negroes and mulattoes were to be given practical training and moral instruction. The condition of slaves was to be ameliorated, and justice sought for all negroes and mulattoes who were held in bondage

---

[32] Spencer, *op. cit.*, I, p. 186: see also *Minutes of the Baptized Licking-Locust Association, Friends of Humanity*, Sept. 26, 27, 28, 1807.

[33] D. Benedict, *History of Baptists*, II, p. 248.

"contrary to the existing laws of this commonwealth." [34]
In 1816 the Society petitioned the House of Representatives
in the interest of the colonizing of free people of color on the
public lands.[35] An effort was made to effect a permanent type
of organization with local chapters in different parts of the
state, and memorials and petitions were to state and national
legislative bodies.[36] For a time David Barrow acted as
president of the society and editor of its paper the "Abolition
Intelligencer." [37] Long before 1803 the Kentucky Abolition
Society had ceased to exist.

The Friends of Humanity were never numerically strong
in Kentucky. David Benedict in 1812 estimated their number at twelve churches, twelve ministers and three hundred
members.[38] By 1816 only six churches were affiliated and a
tendency to open communion and other signs of disintegration are noted.[39] Four years later the movement had ceased
to exist.

There are several causes to which the failure of the emancipation schism among Kentucky Baptists may be attributed:

1. The Friends of Humanity Association was organized at
an inopportune time. The constitutional battles over slavery
were fought in 1792 and 1799, and it was hard to stimulate
popular interest thereafter. The excitement over the Em-
bargo Act in 1807 and the War of 1812 precluded a great
interest in purely domestic affairs. Carter Tarrant, a leader
of the emancipators, became an army chaplain in 1812 and
died shortly afterward.[40] The years 1807–1820 were a relatively quiescent period in anti-slavery propaganda throughout
the nation. The day of great abolition societies had not yet
dawned.

2. Baptist associations were interested in practical union,
and they looked with suspicion on any course of action that
might lead to schism. This apparently was the reason for the
refusal of the Salem Association to consider the matter in

[34] A. D. Adams, *The Neglected Period of Anti-Slavery* (Boston, 1908), p. 129.
[35] *Ibid.*, p. 129.   [36] Martin, *op. cit.*, p. 43.   [37] Adams, p. 130.
[38] Benedict, *op. cit.*, II, p. 248.   [39] Martin, *op. cit.*, p. 41.
[40] Spencer, *op. cit.*, I, pp. 189–90.

1789. A commitment on a controversial subject such as slavery would have been fatal to the association unions in 1793 and 1801. Individual ministers hesitated to make a permanent renunciation of fellowship with the regular associations. Thus William Hickman preached against slavery and was excluded from the Forks of Elkhorn Church in 1807, but he refused to join the Friends of Humanity and was readmitted to his pastorate in 1809.[41]

3. Then too, a fundamental Baptist tenet is the noninterference of the church in political concerns. For this reason the churches and associations outside the Friends of Humanity were unwilling even to discuss the subject of slavery. The following extract from the Circular Letter of the 1810 South District Association is typical:[42] "Let it not be supposed that we are now discussing the subject of slavery. To do so in our religious assemblies would be an interference with the concerns of civil government for which we have neither precept nor example."

4. In order to grow as a movement of protest the Friends of Humanity needed support from the neighboring free states. Such aid was not forthcoming. The Illinois and Indiana Baptist associations decided to maintain correspondence with slave holding churches and associations in Kentucky even though they refused to admit slave holding members.[43] The Illinois Friends of Humanity were too few in number prior to 1820 to be of much help to the sister movement in Kentucky.

5. The economic factor was the greatest single element contributing to the premature death of the Friends of Humanity Association in Kentucky. From the beginning some Kentucky Baptists were slave owners. Slaves were listed

---

[41] *Kentucky Baptist Historical Publications*, No. 1, p. 22.

[42] Printed Minutes, *Kentucky South District Association* for 1810.

[43] W. T. Stott, *op. cit.*, p. 54. In February, 1810, Peter Hamsburg presented a letter, but it was not accepted for he held slaves. The Association, however, continued to correspond with Kentucky associations that permitted slave holding. Martin, *op. cit.*, p. 40, states that the Miami Baptist Association of Ohio rejected the overtures of the Friends of Humanity on the "ground that the Kentucky emancipators had compromised their position by admitting slaveholders to the communion table under certain conditions."

as part of the personal property of the members of the traveling church who settled at Gilbert's Creek under the leadership of Lewis Craig in 1781.[44] Hard work on the frontier
brought increased wealth and larger holdings in slaves. John
Taylor owned but four slaves when he lived in Virginia, but
he prospered greatly in Kentucky where he became the
possessor of twenty slaves and three thousand acres of land.[45]

Feeling that their continued success was largely dependent
on slave labor Kentucky Baptists began to justify their
possession of slaves by economic, moral, and scriptural
arguments. David Benedict traveled extensively throughout
Kentucky and Tennessee in 1810 gathering materials for his
History of the Baptists. He found that "The Baptists are
by no means uniform in their opinion of slavery. Many let
it alone altogether; some remonstrate against it in gentle
terms; others oppose it vehemently; while by far the greater
part of them hold slaves and justify themselves the best
way they can."[46]

The 1807 Circular Letter of the Friends of Humanity
Association clearly shows that the pro-slavery Baptists were
in the majority and were well fortified with arguments. The
emancipators feel that they have been unjustly persecuted
and that they must justify a righteous if somewhat hopeless
cause.[47] Benedict has given an excellent summary of the manner in which slave holding Baptists justified the practice: [48]

1. They had no hand in bringing them in to the country; but
since they are brought, somebody must take care of them.

2. They cost them much money, generally from three to five
hundred dollars apiece, and sometimes more; if they set them free,
all this must be sacrificed.

3. Others observed that they had inherited their slaves as a
patrimonial estate; they came to them without their seeking and
now they know no better way than to find them employment, and
make them as comfortable as their circumstances would permit.

[44] G. W. Ranck, *op. cit.*, p. 22.
[45] Taylor, *op. cit.*, p. 125.
[46] Benedict, *op. cit.*, II, p. 207.
[47] See *Minutes* for 1807, pp. 2-4.
[48] Benedict, *op. cit.*, II, p. 201.

4. Some mentioned that the Romans and other nations had slaves; that they were numerous at the introduction of Christianity; that neither Christ nor the Apostles, nor any of the New Testament writers said anything against it; that if it were contrary to the spirit of the gospel, it is strange that it is no where prohibited.

While the Friends of Humanity movement in Kentucky was struggling through its short and rather ineffectual existence, a stronger and more enduring organization was being perfected along similar lines in Illinois. The guiding genius of the Illinois movement was Elder James Lemen, who claimed to be a protégé of Thomas Jefferson. The Jefferson-Lemen papers have been published, and they consitute a valuable though disputed source of information for Baptist beginnings in Illinois.[49] The present copies are merely transcripts of the original papers, but there is reason to believe they are faithful reproductions of the originals.[50] The following item appears in James Lemen's diary:[51]

"Harper's Ferry Va. Dec. 11, 1782
Thomas Jefferson had me to visit him again a short time ago, as he wanted me to go to the Illinois country in the northwest, after a year or two, in order to try to lead and direct the new settlers in the best way and also to oppose the introduction of slavery in that country at a later day, as I am known as an opponent of that evil, and he says he will give me some help.

In 1785, according to his diary, Lemen received a hundred dollars from Jefferson's confidential agent, and the next year he arrived at Kaskaskia, Illinois.[52]

A brief résumé of social conditions in Illinois and the part

[49] W. C. McNaul, *The Jefferson-Lemen Compact* (Chicago, 1915).

[50] Buck, S. J., *Illinois in 1818*, p. 219, questions the authenticity of the Lemen family notes. He states there is no other record of the Illinois Anti-Slavery League which John M. Peck mentions in a letter dated 1851 and included in the collection. However, as A. D. Adams—*The Neglected Period of Anti-Slavery in America*, p. 116, points out "many anti-slavery organizations of which nothing definite is known undoubtedly existed." Moreover, it is certain that James Lemen was the leader of a Baptist anti-slavery movement as the printed and manuscript records of the Friends of Humanity and his work in the State Legislature are available.

[51] McNaul, *op. cit.*, pp. 27–28.

[52] *Ibid.*, p. 28.

played by the slavery issue in politics is necessary, as the Baptist emancipation movement was constantly being adjusted to the changing political and social environment. Slavery was introduced into Illinois during the period of French control. Philip Francis Renault of the Company of St. Philips bought five hundred slaves in St. Domingo in 1720 and brought a part of them to Illinois to work the mines a few miles above Kaskaskia and along Silver Creek, St. Clair County. He sold his holding to the French inhabitants in Illinois when the venture proved unsuccessful.[53] When the Illinois country passed into the hands of the British in 1763, the population numbered three thousand, of whom nine hundred were slaves.[54] The English government laid no restrictions on slave holding, and when Virginia ceded her claims on the Territory of the Northwest it was understood that the French inhabitants were to retain their ancient rights and privileges.[55]

The Ordinance of 1787 prohibited slavery in the Northwest Territory, but Governor St. Clair so interpreted the ordinance as to give the French slave masters the right to retain their previously acquired slave property. The pro-slavery party gained strength as fresh emigrants came from the south, and in 1796 General Johnson Edgar headed a movement to suspend the sixth article of the Northwest Ordinance. That same year the first Baptist Church in Illinois, the New Design Baptist Church, was organized in the home of James Lemen. Its anti-slavery bias is shown by the fact that Elder Carter Tarrant's Rules were adopted.[56]

During the time that Illinois was a part of Indiana Territory the pro-slavery men were quite active. With the approval of Governor Harrison five attempts were made from 1800 to 1809 to introduce slavery in Indiana Territory. Congress was memorialized, and a clever scheme of indentured service was proposed to circumvent the sixth article

---

[53] Perkins and Peck, *Annals of the West*, p. 788.
[54] M. D. Harris, *History of Negro Servitude in Illinois* (Chicago, 1904), p. 4.
[55] *Ibid.*, p. 5.
[56] H. F. Waggener, *Baptist Beginnings in Illinois* (MSS.) p. 14.

of the Northwest Ordinance. The slavery advocates were partially successful. The Territorial Law of 1807, which was in force until 1810 in Indiana, provided that owners of slaves desiring to move into the territory might bring their slaves with them and bind them to service by an indenture for whatever time the master and slave might agree upon. Slaves under fifteen might be held to the age of thirty-five if males, and thirty-two if females. Children of indentured servants might be held to the age of thirty for the men and twenty-eight for the women.[57] However, this respite for slavery was short lived in Indiana. During the congressional campaign of 1808 the emancipationists held "log conventions" throughout the state, at which the southern aristocracy and the slave holding system were denounced. Jonathan Jenkins, an anti-slavery man, was returned to Congress three times, and the Indenture Act was repealed in 1810.[58]

James Lemen was keenly interested in the struggle in Indiana. His diary contains this item dated Jan. 20, 1806, "I sent a messenger to Indiana to ask the churches and people there to get up and sign a counter petition to Congress to uphold freedom in the territory, and I have circulated one here and will send it on to that body at the next session."[59] In 1809 Illinois was separated from Indiana Territory, and immediately a bitter political struggle ensued over slavery. The indentured service law of Indiana Territory remained in force in the new Illinois Territory. Governor Ninian Edwards, a slave holding Baptist, and one of the ablest lawyers in the west, rendered a decision favoring it in 1817.[60]

As the slavery adherents grew more powerful James Lemen began to see the need for an active counter movement. Very early a sharp difference of opinion developed over the slavery issue. Lemen's bold advocacy of non-fellowship with individual slave holding Baptists, in a sermon preached at Richland Creek Church, caused a division in that church which was carried to the annual meeting of the Illinois Bap-

[57] Adams, op. cit., p. 208.
[59] McNaul, op. cit., p. 30.
[58] Adams, op. cit., pp. 208–09.
[60] Harris, op. cit., pp. 12, 13.

tist Association in 1809, and he was forced to choose between a compromise and a schism.[61] Conceiving his action to be in accordance with the wishes of Thomas Jefferson, he selected the latter course. The following is taken from his diary:[62]

"New Design, Jan 10, 1809
I received Jefferson's confidential message on Oct. 10, 1808, suggesting a division of the churches on the question of slavery and the organization of a church on a strictly anti-slavery basis for the purpose of heading a movement to finally make Illinois a free state, and, after first trying in vain for some months to bring all the churches over to such a basis, I acted on Jefferson's plan, and Dec. 10, 1809, the anti-slavery element formed a Baptist church at Cantine Creek, on an anti-slavery basis.

The constitutional basis of "The Baptized Church of Christ, Friends to Humanity" was "the Bible as the pillar of faith" and "the denying union and communion with all persons holding the doctrine of perpetual, involuntary, hereditary slavery."[63] From the first, the Illinois Friends to Humanity Association was regarded by other Baptists as a schismatic movement. The 1809 minutes of the Illinois Baptist Association contain this statement: "We believe it not right to commune with those who have left the general union at large." The following year a committee appointed by the Illinois Baptist Association to investigate the emancipation movement reported "they went out from us, and therefore they are no more of us." The 1809 minutes of the Richland Creek Church likewise show an active opposition to Lemen's proposals:[64]

[61] According to a committee report to the 1830 Friends of Humanity Association meeting, the churches forming the Illinois Union Association in 1807 agreed that it was "inconsistent to open an indiscriminate correspondence with Baptist Associations in slave holding states." A committee appointed by the Illinois Baptist Association found the following record in the *1807 Association minutes:* "Does this communion extend throughout the Union?" Answered, "This communion shall extend throughout the Union"—see the *Minutes of the Illinois Baptist Association for 1831.*

[62] McNaul, *op. cit.*, p. 30.   [63] *Minutes of the South District Association,* 1870.

[64] *Minutes of the Illinois Baptist Association,* 1831.

"The Baptist Church of Christ, at Richland Creek, met according to appointment on Saturday, 9th September 1809, Br. Best
moderator

1st. The business of this day to choose delegates to the Association

2nd. to exclude Br. James Lemen, Sr. for renting himself
from the church, and drawing a party with him, and other accusations too numerous to mention, and to lay under censure,
all those that justified his conduct. Signed by order of the church

John Philips, Clerk"

For a time it seemed that the Friends to Humanity movement was to be little more than a dramatic gesture. The only
constituents of the Cantine Creek Church (later known as
Bethel Church) were the seven members of the Lemen family,
James Lemen, Sr., and his wife Catherine Lemen, Robert
Lemen and his wife Hetty Lemen, Joseph Lemen and his
wife Polly K. Lemen, and Benjamin Ogle. In 1811 Silver
Creek Church with a membership of seven joined the emancipation cause. The pioneer New Design Church was dissolved in 1821, and the Fountain Creek Church Friends to
Humanity with thirty-five members was formed of the
remnant.[65] The movement was soon carried across the
Mississippi into Missouri Territory. In July, 1812, the mother
church on Cantine Creek established an "arm" at Cold
Water, St. Louis County, Missouri, and eighteen persons
were received into it. This "arm" continued to exist until
November 1839 when it was organized into an independent
church, called "The Baptized Church of Christ, Friends to
Humanity, on Cold Water." [66]   Providence Church was
formed in Boon Lick County, Missouri, in 1820.

At first the work of the Friends to Humanity was very
informal in character. The mother church on Cantine Creek
had neither a church building, before 1824, nor a regularly
appointed pastor. Meetings were held monthly.[67]   The
licensed and ordained minister among the emancipationists
found the rôle of itinerant preacher to be the most effective

---

[65] *Minutes of the South District Association*, 1852.
[66] R. S. Duncan, *A History of the Baptists in Missouri* (St. Louis, 1882).
[67] *Minutes of the South District Association*, 1870.

method of advancing the anti-slavery cause. The official history of Bethel (Cantine Creek) Church relates how this was done:[68]

"In the intervals of monthly meetings, the preachers of this church were engaged on the Sabbath and frequently on week days in preaching to the destitute in the scattered settlements on both sides of the Mississippi River. There was no failure of monthly church meetings during the first ten years of its history, and for nearly eleven years the church had never elected a deacon. In 1824 the church erected its first house of worship. It was a frame building thirty by forty feet which for several years they occupied in an unfinished state with rough benches for seats. The house cost about $550."

As has been indicated, the progress of the Friends to Humanity movement in Illinois was at first quite slow. At the end of the first six years there were probably fewer than a score of members. Then came a sudden acceleration in growth. An association was formed in 1820, and the following year eight ministers, three active churches and 149 members were represented. A remarkable expansion followed, the association doubling in membership every few years. In 1823 there were eight churches and 237 members, in 1825 eleven churches and 411 members, in 1828 nineteen churches (five of which were in Missouri) and 550 members. The next year the body divided into three districts which eventually became distinct associations, the North and the South Districts in Illinois and the Missouri District. Progress continued, though somewhat unevenly. In 1830 there were 454 members in twenty-four churches (including an African church with eight members). A year later thirty-one churches having a total of 921 members were reported. In 1833 when the count showed thirty-nine churches and 1,347 members, a fourth district, the Saline, was formed east of the third principal meridian.[69] Benedict, writing in 1848, said that the Friends to Humanity included the South District, North District, Saline, Vandalia, and colored

[68] *Ibid.*
[69] *Minutes, Illinois Friends to Humanity,* 1833.

associations in Illinois and the Missouri District in Missouri.[70]

In 1835 the formal union and joint annual meetings of the four associations of Friends to Humanity were discontinued. A study of the printed minutes of the North and the South District Associations Friends to Humanity shows a waning interest in the slavery issue after that date. The North District Association dropped the title, Friends to Humanity, in 1842. The South District Association discarded the Friends to Humanity slogan in 1844, but it was renewed in parenthesis during the years 1847–1850. After 1850 the title was permanently abandoned.

As has been intimated, the progress of the Friends to Humanity was in direct response to political and social forces both local and national. A real battle over slavery in Illinois began at the last session of the Territorial Legislature in 1817 with the attempt to repeal the Indiana Indenture Act which was still in effect in Illinois Territory. Illinois expected to become a state the next year, and Missouri was already circulating petitions for statehood. If Illinois came in as a free state the anti-slavery men would gain a great tactical victory.[71] The bill repealing the indenture system passed the legislature but was vetoed by Governor Ninian Edwards. Slavery thus became the central issue in the campaign for delegates to the constitutional convention.

The tense feeling over the slavery issue in the campaign of 1818 found release in many ways. Votes were solicited from house to house. Letters on slavery, pro and con, were printed in the *Illinois Intelligencer*. Various arguments were employed. Some urged the encouragement of the emigration of southern planters and slave holders to Illinois to meet the 40,000 population quota. Others advocated dependence on a northern constituency. A letter embodying the latter view was sent to the *Illinois Intelligencer* from Silver Creek, St. Clair County, where a Friends to Humanity Church had been formed. The writer, who signed himself "Caution," in answering his own question: "Whether would members chosen now or members chosen in 1823 be most in favor of the toleration of slavery" stated "our [72] future population will be principally from the northern states and avowed enemies to slavery. The wealthy southern planter will not part with the plantation gods which he worships, starves and whips, for the blessings of the western woods, while we are a territory, and doubtful as to the future toleration of slavery."

The only detailed account of the activities of the Friends to Humanity in the critical years prior to 1818 is given in a *History of the Jefferson-Lemen Compact* written in 1851 at Rock Spring, Illinois, by John M. Peck. The account may be exaggerated, but it is hardly likely that Peck, who traveled widely in Illinois in 1818, invented the "Illinois Anti-Slavery League" to embellish his narrative as Buck seems to imply.[73] Following is the passage in question:[74]

"The church, properly speaking, never entered politics, but presently, when it became strong, the members all formed what they called "The Illinois Anti-Slavery League" and it was this body that conducted the anti-slavery contest. It always kept one of its members and several of its friends in the Territorial Legislature, and five years before the constitutional election in 1818 it had fifty resident agents—men of like sympathies—in the several settlements throughout the territory quietly at work, and the masterly manner in which they did their duty was shown by a poll which they made of the voters some few weeks before the election, which, on their side only varied a few votes from the official count after the election. With people familiar with all the circumstances there is no divergence of views but that the organization of the Bethel Church and its masterly anti-slavery contest saved Illinois to freedom; but much of the credit of the freedom of Illinois, as well as for the ballance of the territory, was due to Thomas Jefferson's faithful and efficient aid."

Edward Coles, a Baptist who had moved from Virginia to Edwardsville, rendered yeoman service for the anti-

[72] *Illinois Intelligencer*, April 1, 1818. See Buck, *op. cit.*, p. 256.
[73] Buck, *op. cit.*, p. 319.
[74] McNaul, *op. cit.*, p. 36.

slavery cause in 1818 and later in 1824 when he was governor.
James Lemen was a delegate to the Constitutional Convention from St. Clair County, and he voted consistently with
the minority who were for immediate and complete emancipation.[75] The representatives of Union, Johnson, and
Edwards counties, territory in which the Friends of Humanity later became strong voted against slavery. The article on
slavery as finally adopted by the Constitutional Convention
of 1818 was a victory for those who took the middle ground.
Illinois was ultimately to become a free state, but there was
to be no interference with existing property rights in slaves
or indentured servants.[76]

The excitement over slavery did not subside when Illinois
entered the Union. Missouri was seeking admission as a
slave state and attracting large numbers of emigrants, many
of whom came through Illinois. The Missouri Compromise
was regarded as a defeat by many of the more radical emancipationists, and Illinois resentment showed itself in the
election of D. P. Cook, an anti-slavery man, to Congress,
August, 1819. The following clause in the Missouri Constitution defining the legislative power of the Missouri General
Assembly was offensive to emancipation leaders:[77]

It shall be their duty, as soon as may be, to pass such laws as
may be necessary
To prevent free negroes and mulattoes from coming to, and
settling in this state, under any pretest whatsoever.

However, Congress repudiated this action, and the clause was
dropped prior to Missouri's entry into the Union in August,
1821.

The organized and determined efforts of the pro-slavery
forces undoubtedly stimulated the growth of the Friends to
Humanity in Illinois and Missouri and led, as has already
been noted, to the organization of a formal association in
1820. The early circular letters of this association refer to

[75] Buck, p. 380.
[76] Harris, *op. cit.*, pp. 22–24.
[77] Perkins and Peck, *Annals of the West*, p. 773.

the general progress of the emancipation cause. James Lemen, in 1821, pointed out that the Constitution of the United States and the Illinois Constitution were against slavery. "Thus the scene is changed, and now, instead of being charged with flying in the face of authority, we can exhort our congregations to be subject to the higher powers." [78]

Slave holders were dissatisfied with the Illinois Constitution of 1818, and, during the period 1820–1824, they launched a determined effort to call a constitutional convention to make the indenture privileges more flexible. Forces were evenly matched, and a bitter campaign of house to house canvasses, pamphlets, posters, and speeches occupied the Spring of 1823. Among the leaders of the anti-conventionists were Governor Coles, a Baptist, and J. M. Peck, a Baptist preacher and agent of the American Bible Society. The latter stated that there were thirty ministers present at the formation of the St. Clair Anti-Convention Society.[79] The *1823 Circular Letter of the Friends to Humanity* shows how a feeling of alarm and indignation had struck that organization: [80]

> But to our utter astonishment, we have such men (not to say reptiles, in our bosom or in the bowels of our state) who have exerted every nerve to introduce the barbarous God-provoking practice of unmerited slavery into our happy, peaceable, and highly favored state, under the borrowed (not to say stolen) cloak of humanity.

Two years later Thomas Hamilton began the *Circular Letter* with the glad announcement that "the [81] hopes of the Conventionists have been recently blasted, and the Demon of Oppression seems to be receding from our happy land."

The failure of the attempt to call a convention in 1820–1824 broke the morale of the forces contending for slavery in Illinois, and the Friends of Humanity were free to consider

[78] *Illinois Friends to Humanity Circular Letter*, 1821.
[79] Harris, *op. cit.*, p. 93.
[80] *Illinois Friends of Humanity Circular Letter*, 1823.
[81] *Minutes Illinois Friends to Humanity*, 1825.

the problem of slavery in its national aspects. The American Colonization Society was founded in Washington in 1816 by Robert Finley, and, after 1821, negroes were settled in Liberia.[82] The 1824 report of the "Andover Society of Inquiry Concerning Missions" which contained a strong plea for the American Colonization Society was widely circulated throughout the middle west. It is not strange to find, therefore, that Rev. John Clark, the composer of the *1825 Circular Letter of the Friends of Humanity* was enthusiastic over the colonization project:[83]

> But the mercy of God appears to be interposing in the behalf of these outcasts of men. Colonization and manumission societies are forming, and auxiliaries increasing and extending from Boston even to St. Louis, for the qualifying, if needful, and transplanting them to their ancestors' native land; wherein they may enjoy their unalienable rights, and prove an everlasting advantage to the natives of that benighted quarter of the globe.

John M. Peck noted in his diary the preparation of a sermon in favor of the colonization society which he preached in 1825.[84]

Before 1830 emancipation sentiment had reached its peak among Illinois Baptists. The circular letters of the Friends of Humanity Association show a lessening interest in slavery and a concern for other problems, such as temperance, the coming of the millenium, education and missions. A circular letter prepared by Elijah Dodson, John Clark, and James Lemen in 1830 repudiated the idea that the Friends of Humanity had declared non-fellowship with the whole body of Baptists and pointed out that slave holders were not barred as members when there were legal restrictions to emancipation. In 1839 the South District Association, Friends of Humanity, appointed a committee to prepare a letter of correspondence to the Edwardsville Association looking forward to a *rapprochment*.[85] As previously stated,

[82] Adams, *op. cit.*, p. 104.
[83] Circular Letter, Friends to Humanity, 1825.
[84] Babcock, *Memoir of Peck*.
[85] *Minutes South District Association*, 1839.

the title, Friends to Humanity, was finally dropped in 1842 by the North District Association and in 1850 by the South District Association.

The interest in emancipation weakened slowly but steadily after 1830. The extent to which the North District Association had departed from its original anti-slavery stand is revealed by the 1844 minutes. After the Jerseyville Church had submitted two queries "1. Is [86] not slavery in any and all of its connections a sin and a bar to fellowship? 2. What does scripture say to this subject?", a committee gave the following reply: "1. That in our opinion there are many conditions in and connections with slavery in which there is no sin, and brethren thus situated should not be denounced as heretics, thieves, etc. 2. What does the scripture say to this subject? Your committee are of the opinion that the relations of master and servant are regarded in the word of God."

As the Friends to Humanity Association in Illinois was longer lived and more vigorous than the sister movement in Kentucky so the forces governing its growth and decadence were somewhat different. The following appear to be the important factors in the disintegration of the Friends to Humanity movement in Illinois:

1. The Baptist emancipation movement was organized to prevent the introduction of slavery into Illinois. After 1825 the radical pro-slavery party in the state acknowledged complete defeat, and there was no longer need for propaganda on the part of the Friends to Humanity.

2. Other and more immediate needs claimed the attention of the churches. A considerable portion of the *Circular Letter of 1828* is devoted to the "Heaven provoking crime of intemperance." [87] The following year the impending millennial age occupied the attention of the association to the exclusion of all else,[88] "It is more than probable that the present age in which it is our lot to be placed will exhibit the

[86] *Minutes of the North District Association*, 1844.
[87] *Circular Letter, Friends to Humanity*, 1828.
[88] *Circular Letter, Friends to Humanity*, 1829.

most stupendous, momentous, and interesting displays of Divine Providence that ever will transpire, till the second coming of the Judge of the Quick and the Dead." It is not strange, therefore, to learn that in 1830 the association gathering took the form of a camp meeting and was in session from Monday to Friday. There were many conversions accompanied by singing, exhorting, and communion services, and [89] "at each meeting it was manifest that the Lord was there." The 1831 letter asserts that the millennial age is just ahead, but the kingdoms of darkness are now very active. "Infidelity has assumed a thousand forms such as deism, atheism, Campbellism, Mormonism, Parkerism, and drunkenness." [90] After 1835, the Alton Seminary and the American Baptist Home Mission Society are major interests. The question of open communion which was to be so productive of controversy in later years was beginning to be raised.

3. There was a real desire for unity among Baptists. Efforts were made to revive the old General Union. When the Illinois Baptist Convention was formed the North District Friends of Humanity Association sent delegates. The slavery issue was no longer emphasized as it might prove a divisive factor.

4. The Friends to Humanity Association in Illinois was largely the result of the personal efforts of James Lemen, and for the first few years it was confined to his immediate family. When Lemen died in 1822 his sons and son-in-law Benjamin Ogle carried on. There was not, however, that wide distribution of leadership necessary if the movement was to include all Baptists. Baptist organization is inimical to oligarchical control.

5. There was a strong feeling among Baptists generally that Baptist associations should not bind themselves to organized programs for the achievement of moral or political ends. Theoretically, the association had no right to direct the course of action of individual churches. Thus the Ed-

[89] *Minutes Friends to Humanity Association*, 1830.
[90] *Circular Letter, Friends to Humanity*, 1831.

wardsville Association in 1838 strongly condemned slavery and urged individuals and churches to work for its removal, but at the same time adopted this qualification:[91]

"Resolved, that by the foregoing resolution we are not to be understood as commiting ourselves to any society or organization for moral and political action whatever, otherwise than the faithful discharge of our religious duties in subjection to the churches to which we respectively belong."

6. Finally, the trend taken by the anti-slavery movement after 1830 served to alienate the Friends to Humanity. Earlier, the interest had been in gradual emancipation and in schemes of colonization. William Lloyd Garrison first published the *Liberator*, January 1, 1831 in Boston, and soon afterward started founding anti-slavery societies. In December, 1833 the American Anti-slavery Society was organized in Philadelphia to stimulate the agitation.[92] The new movement called for immediate abolition and violently and indiscriminately denounced southern slave holders. The leaders were northerners such as Phillips, Lowell, Palfrey, Follen, Burleigh, Parker, and Lovejoy. The Illinois Friends to Humanity were mostly of southern ancestry, and were out of sympathy with the radical abolitionists.

[91] *Minutes of the Edwardsville Association*, 1838.
[92] A. B. Hart, *op. cit.*, pp. 183–84.

PART II
DOCUMENTS

ILLUSTRATING THE WORK OF THE BAPTISTS ON THE FRONTIER

CHAPTER VI

EXTRACTS FROM THE HISTORY OF TEN BAPTIST CHURCHES

BY JOHN TAYLOR

[John Taylor was born in Fauquier County, Virginia, in the year 1752. He was the great-grandson of John Taylor, who, with two brothers emigrated from England to Virginia in 1650. He was the son of Lazarus and Anna (Bradford) Taylor. His maternal grandfather was a native of Scotland, his maternal grandmother, of France. During his youth he was compelled to work for the support of the family and so was deprived of opportunities for an education. When about twenty years of age he was baptized and became a member of the South River Baptist Church in Virginia, and soon afterward began to preach. For about ten years he did not become a settled pastor, but traveled from place to place, preaching in frontier communities where no regular services were held. It was his plan not to found a church unless there were enough families in the neighborhood to maintain regular preaching. When he married in 1782, like many other preachers of the time, he ceased his itinerant work, though he continued to preach throughout his long life.

Taylor moved to Kentucky in 1782 and for a half century continued to preach, though he was pastor of but one church after his removal to Kentucky. He owned and worked his own farm, in the different communities where he lived, but in addition he preached on Sundays, either in the church to which he belonged or in churches in other communities. The territory covered by Taylor was from the Kentucky to the Ohio rivers. It was his custom to visit eight or ten associations every year and his council and presence was always valued by his fellow ministers.

Taylor was strong of body and bold as a lion. He was very effective as a preacher, though very plain in his style. "No man knew better than he how to reprove, rebuke, and exhort" and "when he used the rod of correction all were made to tremble." He was always willing to preach, was always cheerful, was judicious and zealous. And on the whole perhaps he exercised a larger influence among the Baptist people in Kentucky than any other single preacher during a period of a quarter of a century.] [1]

THE AUTHOR'S CONVERSION AND CALL TO THE MINISTRY

I know of no trait in the human character, more desirable than gratitude. Therefore, no favour received from God or man, should be forgotten. A favor received by one man from another, however inimical he may become afterwards, should have credit so far as the favor goes. True gratitude will rarely think that its debts are all paid even to men; and surely to God, from whom we receive so many daily unmerited blessings, how can our gratitude lay dormant? One of the greatest blessings we receive from the Lord, is the pardon of our sins. Hence, says David, Psalm 32d, 1st and 2d verses, blessed is he whose iniquities are forgiven, and whose sins are covered—so covered by the righteousness of another, that sin is no longer imputed. Paul in citing the same scripture, Rom. 4th chap. says, blessed is the man to whom the Lord imputeth righteousness without works. Therefore those mercies are unmerited. He who has received such favor, in his gratitude, should break silence with David in 66th Psalm. Come all ye that fear God, and I will tell you what he hath done for my soul, as also speak of the glory of his kingdom, and talk of his power. Paul's conversion was related three times—first by the historian, 9th chapter of Acts, and then by himself, when Lucius, the chief captain bound him with two chains, Acts 21st chapter. He also relates his conversation before king Agrippa and Festus, the Roman governor, Acts 26th chapter. Moses tells the Hebrews to remember their coming out of Egypt and all the way the Lord had led them; and as with the heart men believe to righteousness, so with the tongue confession is made unto salvation. And as I am now well stricken in

[1] Sprague, W. B., *Annals of the American Pulpit*, VI, pp. 152 ff. John Taylor wrote his *History of Ten Baptist Churches* when he was seventy years of age, and it was published in Louisville, Kentucky, in 1823, and in many respects is the best picture of pioneer Baptists.

years, and have professed hope in Christ, and been endeavoring to follow him for near half a century, I think it not amiss, to relate some of my trials through this long travel, if it is only for the benefit of my posterity that shall come after me, as also perhaps some poor lamb of Christ may be encouraged thereby.

The place of my nativity was Farquier county, Virginia; and in the year of our Lord 1752, I was born. Through the intemperate use of spirits, and what is generally connected with that kind of vice, my poor father had so far consumed his living, that hard labour was my inevitable lot in my raising. My father had moved to Frederic county, back of the Blue Ridge on the Shenandoah river, where Mr. William Marshall came preaching the Gospel of the Kingdom. At one of his meetings I became alarmed, as noted in his biography. I was then about seventeen years old, and went to that meeting with the same view, that I would have gone to a frolic; for I had heard of the great effect that was among the people under preaching, (for he was a son of thunder indeed) I went to the meeting with no more concern about my soul, than the horse I rode on. About midway of his preaching, (for I had not noticed a word he said before,) the word pierced my soul as quick and with as much sensibility as an electric shock. In a moment my mind was opened to see and feel the truth of all he said. I felt as if then at the bar of God, and as if condemnation was pronounced against me. It may look strange; but I instantly loved the very truth that condemned me, and instrument that brought it, Mr. Marshall. I had never felt such an attachment to any human being before, and the whole of a quite new quality. What knowledge I had of sin for a considerable time, was only what belonged to its practical part. From that time I felt a particularly tender affection for all I could think were religious, though it might be an old African negro, and had the world been mine, I would have given all to have been like one of them, though with it a slave for my life. Some things spoken of by Paul are as incredible as this. He often calls God to witness the truth of them. There is another thing as to

myself which is strange. With all this desire, perhaps for
twelve months, I lived in all the practical vice and folly that
I had ever followed before; but with far other feelings, as to
the guilt of my actions than formerly. There were several
reasons for this train of vicious living: As first, the attaining
of true religion seemed so perfectly out of my reach, and so
great a thing, that it never could be mine; and this heavy
doubt sunk me into dark despondency. Perhaps I never
attempted to put up a prayer to God of any kind, for six
months together, and as I was to be lost at last I had better
try to enjoy myself, or at least please my companions the best
way I could; and though perhaps I much pleased them, yet,
God help me, sin was a bitter cup to me, though I practised
it for fear they would laugh at me, for being sanctimonious,
So I continued for many days. I seldom heard preaching,
and as seldom was in company with religious people; for all
the connections I had in the world, held the New Lights, as
they were called, in the utmost contempt; but this early
conviction gradually took deeper root, and sin grew more
hateful, so that often when I would be practising it, my
guilt would become so heavy on my soul, I would be ready
to roar out aloud, and to prevent my comrades from seeing
the effect that was upon me, would abruptly leave the company and get by myself to bemoan my miserable case. By
this kind of compulsion, I forsook my companions, betook
myself much to reading the scriptures; but when I would
think of prayer to God, it looked to me both awful and
dangerous—awful for a sinner to approach an infinitely holy
God, and great danger of offending God, more than to omit
the duty. Thus I worried on, I think a whole summer season.
I began to reflect that I had forsaken all my old comrades,
and with them all my external vices and read the scriptures
a great deal; I foolishly began to conclude that I was much
better than I was before, and that I might now begin to
pray; for I was now good enough for the Lord to be pleased
with my good prayers, and became abundantly pleased that
I should get to heaven as well as the noisy Baptists, and make
no fuss about it. I now seldom went to hear preaching, even

when I had an opportunity; for the truth was, I thought myself as good as any of them. So I had cured all my former sores and was safe without a Jesus Christ. I had been my own physician, and was safe and sound. Thanks and gratitude to the good Lord, he did not suffer me to continue there. Joseph and Isaac Reding, as noted in their biography, lived neighbors to my father. Immediately after their conversion, they began to preach with great zeal through the neighborhood; the purport of which was, ye must be born again, or be damned, or never enter into the kingdom of God. I have perhaps more than once said, that under the preaching of the Redings, the poor rags of my own righteousness took fire and soon burnt me to death; for till now, in reading the law of Moses, I only understood its external demands; but by the removal of the veil of my heart, I discovered the sin of my nature; and that law which required truth and holiness in the inward parts, condemned me for the sin of my heart. The light and goodness I had thought of before, was blown out as with a puff, and I was left as a perfect blank of darkness, from which dreadful darkness, all manner of evil was constantly flowing, and with a torrent which it was impossible for me to stop. Amendment was now out of the question; for every thing I could do was like the filthy fountain from whence it came. Every spring of my soul was now an unclean thing and my best efforts as filthy rags; and my prayers, on which I had much relied, appeared abhorrent both to God and myself. My practical sins that had been numerous, and many of them of a magnitude that to this day I can never forgive myself, were in a manner removed out of sight, by the late arrival of this mighty swarm through my whole soul. Should you ask, reader, what these corruptions lay in, I could only state their outlines, as spiritual ignorance—unlawful desires—hardness of heart, and above all, unbelief; and each of these generating their thousands—and my inability such, that I could not master any one of those thousands. My first thoughts under this new discovery were, that my day of grace was past; for this doctrine was much talked of in those days; that time had been that I might have been saved, but having past my days of grace, it was now too late, and that I was given up of God, to a hard heart and reprobate mind, all of which marks, I evidently found in myself. Under these embarrassments I laboured for many months; I ate no pleasant food nor enjoyed one night's rest. My father's family took the alarm that I had gone beside myself, and to tell the truth I was driven to my wit's end, believing that I was as sure to be lost, as if I was then in hell. I was often on my knees, day and night, crying for mercy, if it could possibly be obtained. At length a new thought struck me, that was more distressing than all before, which was that I never had a day of grace; that as Esau, God hated me before I was born; and though some quarrel with God about election, it had a very different effect on me. I shall never forget where I was when this thought struck me. I was chopping fire-wood in the lap of a tree, and a deep snow on the ground, more than fifty years ago. Under this thought, I was stricken with a tremor something like Belshazer when the hand writing was on the wall, while the axe dropped from my hands. I fell on my knees with trembling awe, not to ask for mercy but to acknowledge God's justice in my condemnation. For about one month after this, I cannot describe the great variety of agonising and vexatious thoughts that attended me. I do not recollect for that space of time, that I wittingly asked once for mercy, though I was often on my knees both day and night. The purport of my addresses to God, were an acknowledgment of the justness of my doom. O, said I often to myself, that I was ever born, or that I was not some other creature than a man. I really felt as if I had no friend in heaven or earth; but as wretched Cain, driven from God's present with a mark fixed on him, so felt I. Often did I think I had better be in hell than alive here; for life was only prolonged to aggravate hell to myself hereafter. The scriptures say, that it is impossible for God to lie or change; I therefore thought my salvation impossible; for that it would counteract God's arrangement concerning me, was then my belief. No spasm could more affect the body than these awful thoughts, alternately affected my soul about this time; till at length my conclusion was brought up to a point, that no man ever saw and felt what I did, till just before God cut them off and sent them to hell, and that destruction was at the very door, and that I should die soon; and my impressions were, this night thy soul shall be required of thee. It was then near sunset. A lonesome mountain, where nobody lived, was in full view of my father's, and about two miles distant. There I intended to roam the balance of my wretched life, expecting never again to see the face of man. In what mode vengeance was to overtake me, whether by the violence of my own hands, or by other means, was best known to him who thus decreed. Such were my impressions, that perhaps no criminal ever went to execution with more agony of mind, that I left my father's house to go to this fatal mountain. Before I got to the place, and as it began to grow dark, in passing under a high, overhanging rock, it occurred to me to fall on my knees and acknowledge what I had often done, the justice of God in this awful sentence. To my knees I went under this high rock, and as I began to whisper something like this: Thy throne, O Most High, shall remain unsullied and unimpeached, when thy wrath is inflicted on me. While thus speaking my thoughts took a new and pleasing turn, on the subject of salvation, which was that the great grace of Jesus Christ, had extended to cases, desperate as mine, as Christ-despisers and Christ-killers who had been saved by this glorious Saviour. The truth was, I saw the fulness of the grace of Christ, and in a way entirely new: but could not call it mine. The effect of that view was, a sweet calm and peace of mind, such as I had never felt before. The mere possibility of salvation was to me like life from the dead; for I had long thought, for reasons given above, that salvation for me was not possible. What I met with at the hanging rock, small as it might appear, was so great to me that I changed my resolution as to dying in the mountain, or continuing there all night. I returned home, as a new man this far—the style of my prayer was changed; I now began to cry again for mercy, as the great grace in Christ had brought possible salvation to such a wretched sinner as myself. I believe I shall never forget the hanging rock while I live, nor even in heaven.

Unbelief soon overtook me again. This unwelcome intruder would force itself on me wherever I went, tempting me to discredit all the realities of religion. I did not hesitate to esteem myself the greatest sinner of human kind; but in unbelief I thought myself far worse than the Devil; for James says, the Devils believe and tremble. But neither mercies nor judgments could move me. Yet I continued a beggar for mercy from the encouragement I had received. The scriptures I read night and day, and among other parts I opened on the 9th chap. of John, where the account is given of the man that was born blind. There appeared such a similarity in this man's case and my own, that I read it with great attention. He was born blind literally; I was born so as to spiritual eye-sight. He was literally a beggar; I desired to be so at God's door. He was cast out of the synagogue; I was despised by all my friends on earth on account of religion. His parents, through fear or ill nature, would not stand by him in his extremity; my parents showed a great deal of sorrow and ill will, on account of my late great delusion. As I read, my conclusion was, if that man were now on earth, I could have a companion, whereas all the comrades I had on earth and myself had separated, our practices not agreeing together, I also much doubted whether I had any friend in heaven. This man's eyes had been opened by Jesus, and he knew very little more of him; at the hanging rock I had some glimpse of Jesus Christ, but did not know that he was mine. But the Lord found him again and asked him a new question; dost thou believe in the son of God? While I read that question I began to feel as if I was at the bar of God, and as if Jesus was near, and asked me the question. I paused and tried to believe, but my heart failed; but the next verse expressed the language of my soul. Who is he, Lord, that I might believe on him? and when I read the answer; it is he that talketh with thee; though I neither saw nor heard anything, I began to feel as if the Saviour was talking to me in company with the blind man; and when he answered, Lord,

I believe, and he worshipped him—the very language of my soul was expressed, and if I did not speak out, my heart repeated it over and over; Lord, I believe; Lord, I believe. It is added, and he worshipped him; my soul so ran in the same way, that I understood more of Jesus Christ in one moment than I had learned in all my life before. I considered him as both Lord and Christ, that he was the proper object of worship, and that it was no robbery to think of him as on an equality with the Father. The heavenly peace and joy that I felt for a season, exceeds my expression. But Satan was not far off, and desired to sift me; for I do not know that I ever had a more pleasant and rational religious exercise in my life, than at this time, and yet within ten minutes, I began to call the reality of it in question, indeed strove myself to cast it away; for I soon rose up, laid down the book, and walked hastily away, concluding if it was the Devil deceiving me (which I strongly suspected) I had better be some where else. But wherever I went my heart would keep talking as it had before; Lord, I believe; &c. My lips would say so too, so that with all my strivings by pressing my bosom with my hands, rolling on the ground, biting lips, pulling hair, frowning or groaning, all of which perhaps were used alternately. Yet the same language of my heart would be, Lord, I believe. This continued perhaps an hour. Had any person been looking at me, by my actions, they would have thought me in the utmost distress, whereas I had never enjoyed such a peace of soul before.

You will think, reader, that I am more capable than any other person, to account for this paradoxical religious phrenzy, that has been narrated. In the first place, I was dreadfully afraid of being cheated by an unsound conversion, also as a very poor judge about it. Yet I had the whole affair carved out before me; it lay in something like being caught up to the third heaven, a joy immense, so that a man must walk tiptoe that had it. What I now felt was only peace and rest of mind, and though I learned more of Christ than I had done before I was not enabled to call him mine. Therefore, it could not be conversion, and to take rest or indulge peace any where short of the new birth, was losing conversion and settling on the sand. From all this lack of knowledge in spiritual religion, we are able to account for the extravagance as stated above.

The conflict between hope and despair soon began again; for what I had yet received was only encouragement to seek the Lord. Meeting with Isaac Reding about this time, he, by extorting some answers from me, pronounced me a child of grace, according to his own experience, which gave me a very poor opinion of his religion. About the first of May 1772, I went to a Baptist church meeting for the first time in my life. James Ireland was the pastor of said church—the house being crowded, I took my stand outside, though near where the preacher sat to examine candidates for baptism. By the help of open logs, I could hear distinctly all that was related.—Eight were received for baptism, and my belief was, that only one out of the eight was converted. The others only related what I had felt myself. This grieved me much; I doubted even the preacher himself being a christian, for encouraging them poor, deluded souls, to join the church, who were in no better state than myself; and to augment my vexation, Isaac Reding whispering through the logs, invited me to come in and tell my experience. I very abruptly answered, no. My private thought was, you are sending people enough to hell already, meaning the seven they had received, that in my belief were not born again. This was a sore day and night to me, being much distressed for others as well as myself. The next day was also a grievous day to me, to see these deluded seven go into the water, and from thence as I thought, seal their own damnation at the Lord's table. I left the meeting with awful horror of mind on my own account and that of others. I slept but little that night. When I got to my father's though a fair sunshine morning, everything looked horrible; all nature seemed to mourn; the very sunshine looked to me sorrowful; every breath I drew, articulated to this amount—*Woe is me.* I could neither sit down nor stand still five minutes together with pure distress of mind, on the account of myself and the poor deluded seven I had seen baptized the day before. My belief now is, that my reason was giving way fast; for the earth appeared to be trembling under me, or as running round with me, as unwilling to bear such a ponderous load of filth as I was, prayer to God was my main alternative; for he alone could help me. Designing to go to a certain place for that purpose, and casting my eyes on a hymn book, a verse of a hymn occurred to me as follows:

"Jesus, my God, I know his name,
"His name is all my trust;
"Nor will he put my soul to shame,
"Or let my hope be lost."

This verse kept repeating in my mind till I got out at the door, when it kindled into a heavenly flame. It seemed as if the name Jesus, never sounded so sweet before. Its fulness seemed as if it would fill earth and heaven; and when this was added to it, MY GOD, my hope began to revive, while this scripture rose up in my mind, "Reach higher thy finger and behold my hands, and reach hither thy hand and thrust it into my side, and be not faithless but believing." I saw no man, nor heard any voice; but according to my sincere belief, the Lord Jesus spake the words, and to me, and was very near. A tide of heavenly joy flowed into my soul, and of the rapturous kind far exceeding any thing I had ever felt before, with a claim to him far surpassing any evidence I ever had before, which constrained me to answer as Thomas did in John 20th chap. 28th verse, My Lord and my God. This answer was repeating through my mind with such heavenly rapture, that I scarcely knew whether I was in the body or out of the body. I now believed I was born of God; that Christ was my Saviour, and that I should never sorrow, sin, or doubt again; but in part of this I was mistaken. I now could retrace my exercise, and see that what I had received at the hanging rock was of the same quality, and as saving in its nature as what I now received, and had full fellowship for my seven deluded christians, that had been baptized the day before. Two weeks after, I was baptized by James Ireland, in the same church where the Redings had their membership.

I was now in my twentieth year. I found the church no place of ease to me, for among other distresses that attended me, a new one occurred. I soon began to feel great anxieties to communicate what I felt and knew of Christ to my fellow-men. This was to me a great source of perplexity, on account of my unpreparedness for so great a work, and how awful it would be to run without sending. And though I endeavored to look to the Lord by prayer for direction on that head, I could never get a satisfactory answer. Joseph Reding soon moved to South Carolina. Isaac Reding keeping meetings in the neighborhood, it came on as a thing of course, to give him some aid in his meetings, so that in a few months I became a public speaker in the neighborhood where I lived. My conclusions were that I could live nowhere, but where Joseph Reding lived. The next winter I travelled to South Carolina, either to live there, or get him to return with me. We returned in the spring, and the church called me forward to preach, at which I have continued for more than fifty years. About four years after I began to preach, I was ordained as an itinerant preacher. The Presbytery that officiated in the ordination, was Lewis Craig, John Picket, John Cunes, Joseph Reding, and Theodorick Noel, (the father of our Silas M. Noel,) a faithful servant of Jesus Christ, who lived and died in Virginia. He began to preach when young, continued in the ministry perhaps forty years, and was one of the most successful preachers of his day. He died a few years past. I was a travelling preacher about ten years, (of which I have said something elsewhere) before I was married, soon after I moved to Kentucky, in the fall 1783. There was no baptist association in this state when I moved to it, and only five churches of that order. I have gained an extensive acquaintance with the Kentucky Baptists, perhaps by being over officious among them. I have said above I could get no satisfactory answer, as to my call to the ministry. My present impressions are, that the call lies in a good man's motives to the work, and the call of the church. If a christian has preaching talents, and the church says preach, he may go on safely. This is my call, and for no other, do I look at present, though in my youth I laboured long for evidences of my call, of which a visionary something would then have satisfied me.

I have said, a good motive to the work, and the call of the church, is all sufficient as to a man's authority to preach the gospel. By a good motive to the work, I understand, the man's own soul must be converted, for except he is born again, he cannot have a spiritually good motive, and is what Paul designs, by "the husbandman that laboureth must first be partaker of the fruit.

It is this produces a desire in him, after what Paul calls a good work—this is a feeling sensibility in him, that "one man's soul is worth more than all the world," and while the love of Christ constrains him, he will very gladly, or readily, spend and be spent, for the salvation of his fellow men. All this I felt for many months, to the amount of robbing me both of sleep and food; and adding to that the voice of the church—but all did not satisfy me, for I was not called as the ancient prophets and apostles were, but to glorify God, and benefit men, in the sole ground of the ministerial motive, and there is no self serving, in all this sacred business—in all this I have felt conscious for more than half a century.

My own belief is, that none properly understand the gospel or voice of the shepherd, but his sheep or the true christian. Therefore the voice of the church is very essential; in the call to the ministry, the bridegroom is out of the way; what the bride does in his absence, should be valid. The church ought to act under great responsibility, being accountable to the chief shepherd at his return; so help us Lord, that we may all have boldness in the day of judgement. The instruments of my encouragement, in my early days. I had three gospel fathers, to-wit: William Marshall, the instrument of my first awakening and convertion; James Ireland, the man who baptized me, and under whose pastoral care I lived for some time; and Joseph Reding, under whose care, and with whom I travelled near ten years, before I was a married man; all these men seemed tender towards me, as if I was their natural son.

But the greatest instrument of my encouragement after all, was the Bible itself—there I saw the whole will of God at once; in point of both practice and opinion, what I saw in this heaven born book, I received as the voice of God to me, and was the invaluable guide of my whole man, both in motive and actions; to this I appeal in all controversy, and by this I expect to be judged at the last day.

Of all the religious duties in which I have ever been employed, as to conscious satisfaction, baptism takes the lead; and in that blessed work, three different days exceeds. The first was the evening after myself was baptized—the second was, the same day fifty years after my own baptism, I baptized a number of people—lastly, on my birthday, when I was seventy years old, I baptized eighteen people. I suppose I have gone into the water more than a hundred times to baptize others, and in every case a sweet peace of conscience attended me. [John Taylor, *A History of Ten Baptist Churches*, etc., pp. 237-300.]

SOUTH RIVER CHURCH

Being in the seventieth year of my age, and according to David's standard, of three score years and ten, as the number of our days on earth—it is probable, this will be the last year of my pilgrimage here below—though in as much health now, as I ever was in my life, age excepted—and though I yet travel a great deal, as well as attend to my own business at home—having a few leisure hours while there, which hours I mean to appropriate to a historical statement of ten Baptist Churches, of which I have been in succession a legal member. The first Church of which I was a member, and where I was baptised, was called South River Church, being the southern branch of Shenandoah, and near the forks of said River, famous for the fertility of its soil, and discharging itself into the Potomac River at Harper's Ferry, on the north border of Virginia—said River spreads through and makes a part of the great rich valley, between the south Mountain or Blue Ridge, and north Mountain—said valley is about twenty miles broad and several hundred miles long.

The materials or converts of which this South River Church was first composed, was chiefly under the Ministry of William Marshall, whose short biography I have given elsewhere —others also laboured in said bounds, as John Picket whose sister Marshall had married, Reuben Picket, brother of John, and the famous James Ireland, after being released from Culpepper prison, laboured much and with great success on the waters of Shenandoah River—none of those ministers were ordained for several years, so that the first Baptising in South River, the noted Samuel Harris travelled two hundred miles to administer this solemn ordinance—and an awfully solemn thing it was indeed to thousands, who had never witnessed such a scene before. I think fifty-three were baptised on that day, several young ministers came with Harris, as Elijah Craig, John Waller, with a number of others. The rite of laying on of hands, on the newly baptised, was practised by the baptists in those days—this practice was performed as follows: Those upwards of fifty stood up in one solemn line, on the bank of the river, taking up about as many yards as there were individuals—the males first in the line— about four ministers went together, each one laid his right hand on the head of the dedicated person, and one prayed for him, and after praying for three or four of them, another proceeded till they went through. It would appear as if that solemn dedication might be some barrier to future apostacy; for the prayers were with great solemnity and fervour, and for that particular person according to their age and circumstances. On the same day the church at South River, was constituted under the style of a separate Baptist Church, (this was in 1770) it may be remembered, that the word separate here, did not design a separation from what was called the regular Baptists, for it may be they were not called regulars till afterwards—The word separate came from New England— The Presbyterians there is called the standing order; all who desent from them of whatever denominations are called, and call themselves separates, because they do not adhere to the standing order—Hence Subelstern (Shubal Stearns) and Daniel Marshall who went from New England to the south, when they began society there, called themselves as they had been called before (separates) thus originated separate Baptists; what was called the regular Baptists, had adopted, for their creed, what is now called the Philadelphia Confession of Faith, with the discipline annexed thereto. The separates had no public Confession of Faith, but were generally constituted on a Church Covenant, which to the best of my recollection, was truly Calvinistic—their order of discipline, was sumed up in the eighteenth chapter of Mathew. At the time of this first great baptising at South River, I was there the last two days, (perhaps the whole meeting was near a week) an ill grown boy about seventeen years old, and though I would not then have been a Baptist for all the world, I was a close and serious observer of all that past—first to the baptising, which continued perhaps an hour, for they went some distance to a proper depth of water, and took only one at a time—I think the prayers for the newly baptised continued one hour more—I happened to be near when their Church Covenant was read—I remember concluding no man on earth could comply with it. This Church progressed on with rapid growth for several years. For my own part though I was solemnly affected at the time of the baptising spoken of above, (for some of my companions were in the number) I had such fellowship for sin, that I seldom went to the meetings for a year or two, till Joseph and Isaac Reding obtained hope of conversion, was baptised and began to preach close in the neighborhood of my Fathers, by which I became stired up afresh and was baptised, about two years after I had seen the first baptising, and near the same spot, in the twentieth year of my age, and by James Friend, then Pastor of the Church. The first serious distress that took place in South River Church, as I was told afterwards, arose about who should be the Pastor of the Church—Marshall and Ireland, it seems were the men about which the contest arose—each man's children in the gospel chose their own Father as the Pastor of the Church, but whether from Ireland's uncommon preaching talents, or some other source I am not informed, but so it was, he became the Pastor of the Church.   Though

these men were complaisant to each other, it is to be doubted
whether the same tender affection existed after this Pastorial
struggle as before—I think the Church consisted of about
two hundred members when I became one among them—It
seemed my lot was to come into the Church near the close
of the harvest, for though several young gists rose up, ingethering declined, many were expelled for loose conduct,
for to that they had been very much habituated before their
religious profession. Mr. Ireland, perhaps through prudence,
took leave of the Church as their Pastor, and took the care
of one or more Churches; soon after, Mr. Marshall was
ordained to the Pastorial care of the Church, Joseph Reding
who had been preaching near a twelvemonth, in the year
1772 moved his little family to South Carolina; while there
he became a little dipt into armenianism (see his biography)
he returned the next spring, and soon became ordained an
elder of the Church with others also, for in those days some
were ordained elders, who were not preachers—Marshall
had gotten as much above the common style in divine decrees, as Reding was below it, and a heavy dispute arose
between them about doctrines, their grievances at length
got into the Church, and produced great excitement there,
this contest terminated as in case of Paul and Barnabas;
Reading took a letter of dismission and moved to Hampshire county, adjoining the Aleghany Mountains, where he
had a great opening for preaching—the struggle in the
Church did not subside with Reding's removal, the contest
continued till some of the parties got excluded. In a few
years Mr. Marshall moved into Culpepper county, and I
think from thence to Kentucky in 1779 or 80. To where
Reding moved there was so great an opening for preaching,
that my time was spent chiefly there, and when a young
flourishing Church was raised on Luney's Creek I gave my
membership there for several years, and then returned and
took my membership in my old mother Church till I moved
to Kentucky—After my return to South River Church,
Mr. Marshall having moved away, there was no Minister in
the church but myself—The Revolutionary war having not

yet closed, a number of the English prisoners being stationed through our country; those who had trades were permitted to disperse in the settlements, to work for themselves, two of whom, apparently respectable men and of good understanding Duncan M'Lain and Garsham Robertson applied to our Church for admission, having been baptised at Albermarle Barracks, while there stationed; they having no letters of dismission, came into the Church by experience. M'Lain being of Scotch or Irish extract, or a mixture of both, with fine use of his tongue, was soon invited to preach, which he readily accepted, and soon surprised the most who heard him, for he spoke with great warmth, and a mighty flow of eloquence.—Roberson was a man of very deep understanding and of much modesty and sobriety. Among others whom I baptised, was one Donald Hombs a Scotchman, who was also a British prisoner, he was a most excellent schoolmaster, a fine scribe, and much of an English schollar; having been raised a strict Presbyterian, he seemed to have studied every subject of religion.—With this European acquisition, the Church seemed much encouraged, for among these three fine brothers, one of them was a nonsuch of a young preacher, for though there were some odd things in him from the beginning, it was construed from charity, only to be a little outlandish, or overheated zeal. Things moved on pretty well, till I moved to Kentucky in the fall of 1783— the Church at this time I think was about one hundred in number. In the fall 1782 I married my present wife, about ten years after I had been a preacher. I lived one year with my little family in South River Church, who took up the subject of supply for me, the proposition was introduced with reasoning, that I had been preaching for them off and on for ten years, and as a Church they had never given me any thing. The sum being proposed, they voted to give me a hundred dollars for my past services, in such things as my family needed—this thing seemed to be done with such readiness and pleasure by the Church, it was received with equal pleasure and gratitude. During this last years stay in Virginia, there were many propositions from my old friends and mother Church, not to leave them; that I was going to a country of strangers, and Savage rage—In a word, the importunities was such, that I was almost prevailed on to stay; for it was a gloomy thing at that time of day, to move to Kentucky—but I had seen the place, and when I found a growing family to provide for, this overweighed all, and without a single friend or acquaintance to accompany me, with my helpless young family, to feel all the horrors that then lay in the way to Kentucky—we took water at Redstone, and from want of a better opening, I paid for a passage, in a lonely ill-fixed boat of strangers—the River being low, this lonesome boat, was about seven weeks before she landed at Beargrass; not a soul was then settled on the Ohio between Wheeling and Louisville, a space of five or six hundred miles, and not one hour, day or night, in safety. Though it was now winter, not a soul in all Beargrass settlement was in safety but by being in a fort—I then meditated travelling about eighty miles, to Craig's Station on Gilbert's Creek, in Lincoln county; we set out in a few days—nearly all I owned was then at stake. I had three horses, two of them was packed, the other my wife rode, with as much lumber besides as the beast could bear; I had four black people, one man, and three smaller ones. The pack horses were led, one by myself, the other by my man—the trace, what there was, being so narrow and bad, we had no chance but to wade through all the mud, rivers and creeks we came to, Salt River, with a number of its large branches we had to deal with often, those waters being flush, we often must wade to our middle, and though the weather was very cold, the ice was not very troublesome, those struggles often made us forget the danger we were in from Indians—we only encamped in the woods one night, where we could only look for protection from the Lord, one Indian might have defeated us, for though I had a Rifle, I had very little skill to use it; after six days painful travel of this kind, we arrived at Craig's Station, a little before Christmas and about three months after our start from Virginia, through all this rugged travel my wife was in a very helpless state, for about one month after our arrival, my son Ben was born.

We will return to South River Church. When I left them the only preacher they had was Duncan M'Lain, he soon became disgusted with the Church, for, after applying to them to ordain him, and they refusing to comply with his request, he went about his business and preached but little for them. But he pretty soon embraced the restoration from hell—publickly preached it—Homes followed his example— Robertson went a little farther than either of them, for he openly professed Deism, and disclaimed all the revealed religion; failing to be reclaimed by the Church, she lost her three famous European brethren at one slam, by expulsion —Homes however, in process of time, returned to the Church, was restored, moved to Kentucky, joined the Church at Clear Creek in Woodford county—by them was invited, and came out pretty much of a preacher; he united with the emancipators, seemed zealous in that cause, and is now no more—I hear that he died a few years past in the Ohio state—M'Lain regardless of Church censure, went on with great zeal through a number of the states, Philadelphia and other great cities, and was considered a great champion, to vindicate his hell redemption—but after a while he gave up that point and openly embraced Deism if not Atheism. I need say no more than that it was the same Duncan M'Lain that came to Kentucky, settled near Bardstown in Nelson county, and as I hear, died a few years ago. I know not whether any of these men became immoral in their practice— they all seemed to have esteemed me as a particular friend when I met with them—Roberton appeared like a man that feared God, and talked as if he was conscious in his belief. The Bible he said was a mere history of the Jewish nation, and no more validity in it than the history of Greece or Rome; many parts of the Bible he would say, was unworthy to have a Holy God for its author, and that other mediums more fully illustrated the eternal power and God-head; he happened at my house in Kentucky one day when I killed a beef, he replyed in a most serious way—your bible says he, indulges you in this—but what justice can there be in one animal's sheding the blood and taking the life of another— he seemed to be a man of great sympathy of feelings, and his conduct perhaps as clear of reproach as when he was in a Baptist Church, he considered prayer to God a duty—hence one night when I was from home he went to prayer in the family. Lord what is poor man—I understand this poor fellow got killed in Harmer's defeat, many years ago. The Church at South River became very much weakened, by many of my Baptist friends moving to Kentucky a few years after I did, alternately; I think brethren John Price and Lewis Corbin attended them—after they came to Kentucky their old house needed repairing, or a new one built. They sold their old house to some Presbyterians, who repaired and worshiped in it till they wore off another set of shingles. The Baptists built a new house, about two miles from the old one, at a cross roads on a water course, called Happy Creek, which changed the style of the Church, and it is since called Happy Creek Church, after which their first Pastor resumed the care of the Church—This renowned man of God, James Ireland, continued this charge till he died, which took place about fifteen years ago, after which a brother Benjamin Dauson, has taken care of Happy Creek Church, and perhaps continues it to this day.

Thomas Buck, is one of the members of Happy Creek Church, he was one of the fifty three that was first Baptised in South River—perhaps not one of the others are now alive, for it is more than fifty years ago; he was then a lad, about fourteen years old—I believe he has never been a member of any other Church—he is wealthy as to this world, and very liberal in the support of religion, his circumstance was such, that when thirty pounds was made up by the Church for my support, before I came to Kentucky, by apportionment among themselves, ten pounds was levied on him, which he paid with the greatest cheerfulness. I was at his house eight or nine years ago, and riding in sight of the old meeting house, now all enclosed, I proposed to ride in and take a look at the old skeleton, which he agreed to; one object with me was to see whether the great White Oak stump, three or four feet over, and its mighty trunk that had always laid there when I resorted the meeting house—what made this great stump so sacred to me was, the preacher (Mr. Marshall) stood on it when, I hope, spiritual life was preached into my soul, though it seemed like a blow of death to me—The case was this, report said that at these new light meetings, the people hallowed, cried out, trembled, fell down, and went into strange exercises, my object was to see and amuse myself at all this, as I would at other sport; the people were so numerous, that the preacher went to this stump, about six feet from the end of the meeting house, that all might hear; the vast concourse of people took their stand in the snow, there being no seats to sit on—and while I was amusing and diverting myself, ranging through the company to see the exercise of the people, I had got in near the stump, when this Thomas Buck broke out into a flood of tears and a loud cry for mercy; he being my old playmate, I stared at him for a while with awful wonder, and just at that time my eye and ear were caught by the preaching, the Minister was treating on the awful scene of judgment, and while he dropt these words —"Oh rocks fall on me, Oh mountains cover me from the face of him that seteth on the throne, and from the wrath of the Lamb, for the great day of his wrath is come, and who shall be able to stand." I felt the whole sentence dart through my whole soul, with as much sensibility as an electric shock could be felt. With my mind instantly opened to understand and love all that the preacher said afterwards, and though every word condemned me, I loved the messenger that brought the awful tidings, I felt as if at the bar of God, and no mercy for me. How willingly would I have cried for mercy, if I could have hoped for any. From that moment every thing belonging to religion bore an entire new aspect for me. When we got to the old house, it was an entire old waste, the trunk of the old oak was quite gone, and the old stump on which the man had preached more than forty years before, but little of it was there; we stood there some time; I placed him where I thought he stood, when he with tears cried for mercy, myself at his elbow, where I received the Heaven born stroke I have been speaking of. With grateful hearts we thanked the Lord that we stood there, more than forty years ago—Superstition would have said, take some of this old stump home with you, to look at till you die. The same kind of motive led me soon after, to pay a visit to a lonesome hanging rock, in a rugged mountain; not being able to get to it, with convenience on horseback, I took it a foot; this rock was the place where I first received relief from my guilt, forty years before; with great-full remembrance of the Lord's past kindness to me at that spot, I bowed my knees with thanksgiving to my God, for past favors, and prayer to him for preservation for days to come, and took final leave of that beloved though homely spot of nature—all this may look like a piece of superstitious want—but perhaps those contemplations, are worthy of Heaven itself—For if Abraham would say to the rich man in Hell? Remember son in thy lifetime, there will surely be a calling up into recollection, both in Heaven and in Hell, what transpired in life. While the poor damned man, with horrid recollection, will remember every five ally, every ball room, every gay festive season, with all the excuses he plead when called on to repent of his sins, with his uniform neglect of the great salvation of God, promulgated in the gospel, with all its precious invitations to him, while the queen of the south, and the men of Nineveh rises up in judgment against him, while the torments of the cursed cities of Sodom and Gomorrow, will be more tolerable, in hell fire, than gospel despisers or gospel neglectors; all these will be sad reflections in the world to come, while it will be eternally vibrating through the soul— remember in thy lifetime thou hadst thy good things, while the righteous will recollect their evil things, with an everlasting reward of grace—even so do righteous Lord. I have said that the Church at South River was first nominated as a separate Baptist Church, but in August 1783, this with a Church higher up Shenandoah River, joined the Katocten Association that was called regular Baptists, from the Church above, James Ireland and others, were messengers; from

South River, myself and others were messengers to go into this union—both Churches were accordingly received and took seats in the Association. This was done for convenience and not from contrast of doctrine. Thus I have surveyed a Church of more than fifty years standing, and though not blest with many remarkable revivals, yet lives as a Church of Christ,—here I had my first standing as to Church priviliges. [Taylor, *op. cit.*, pp. 5–15].

LUNIES CREEK

The second Church of which I was a member, was Lunies Creek, in Hampshire county Virginia, this Lunies Creek is a branch of the main south branch of Potomac River; the Church was constituted near the River called the South Branch. On this River Lord Fairfax in early times, had laid off a large boundary of land called Fairfax's Manor, this Church was on or near this great manor, which nothing on our earth ever exceeded in point of soil. The bottoms were often a mile wide, and continued so for many miles together, and the black soil generally as deep as the banks of the river was high, but as yet they were barely free from Indian range. This was not long before the beginning of the old revolutionary war—to this place Reading and myself paid a visit, from eighty to an hundred miles from where we lived, soon after the contest between Marshall and Reading. Through the country we found a few scattering Baptists, but in manners they differed but very little from other people—by encouragement Reading soon moved to the place; my great attachment to him, led me to be much with him, for he was my secondary father in the Gospel, so that Readings company at that time was more to me than all other men in the world. It was not long before the people became much affected, and some apparent conversions, but none to Baptize them, for neither Reding or myself were ordained. I prevailed on Mr. Marshall the now ordained minister of South River, to take a travel with me to see Reading and make examination of the work we had been about; him and Reading soon made up their difficulties there were two men Baptised, a David

Badgly, who some time after began to preach, and is now, though old, a living preacher in Illinois, near St. Louis. The other man was Abram Clark, a warm Presbyterian, who when we first got acquainted with him, became much affected, and at times would say to me, I love your preaching, but you shall never dip me—but when he obtained hope in Christ, he innocently broke that rash promise. Perhaps John Cunes a Dutchman attended there and Baptized a number. At Marshall's second visit a Church was constituted, and Reading ordained to the pastoral care of the Church. I believe the Church at Lunies Creek never amounted to quite a hundred members—we ranged through almost every corner of the large county of Hampshire, on Patison's Creek, a branch of the North Branch of Potomac River, we found a few Baptists, where a Church after a while was constituted, Lewis Castleman now of Woodford county, and his wife were Baptized there. The Lost River, the head branch of Capeapin River, where preaching had a great effect, and a number were Baptized, a Church since erected there that continues to this day; there one Josiah Osbourn was Baptized, and a respectable preacher now in Greenbrier, who some years past published a large pamphlet on Baptism, and much to the purpose, under the style of the Giant of Gath and David. The North River and other parts of Capeapin River, a number were Baptized, one Levi Ashbrook, a magistrate in the county, a man of great zeal in religion, and afterwards became a respectable preacher, but is now gone to his long home. A fine looking young man, the name of Smith, of good family, was Baptized by myself here. It was thought when Baptized, that he would soon make a preacher, but by getting into bad company, and following on, was since hanged at Richmond in Virginia, for the sin of horse stealing; though gave strong evidence, that he was a man of grace. Poor man what is he! Even good Hezekiah when left to himself. A place called George's Hills, on the Maryland side; there we often went: something uncommon generally attended the people here, which lay in profuse weeping, male and female; their cries at times would overwhelm our preaching, however loud, we did hope that a number of them found mercy of the Lord, and followed him in a watery grave. If I mistake not there is a Church there to this day. After ranging through the large county of Hampshire a year or two, we contemplated passing the Alleghany mountain, to the back settlements, in Monongahaly River; the settlers there were much exposed to savage fury, for the English war had now gotten into full blast. The first tour I went without Reading, but a respectable brother the name of Whitman, who had acquaintance over the Mountain, went with me—the place of our destination was Tigers Valley on the main branch of Monongahaly, and near its source, this valley was estimated at fifty miles long, and newly settled by about one hundred families. I found only one Baptist there, and that one a woman, but I thought her a precious christian. This tour was in the midst of winter, and in the mountain the snow about knee deep. The distance from one settlement to the other was estimated at near fifty miles, the trace was so bad (perhaps a carriage has never past there yet) that we were too days getting there, of course we camped but one night in the deep snow. When we got to this valley I became much discouraged; for the first time I now saw people living in a fort; I had but very few meetings in the place, and those with a confused appearance. We set out for Greenbrier, from the upper end of the valley settlement to the nearest part of the Greenbrier settlement, we travelled in one day. Everything looked equally gloomy there; a few meetings pacifyed me there, and we returned back on a different rout—the whole of this tour, disagreeable as it was, I considered an entire water hall. All that I could say, was, I had seen Tigers Valley, and had seen Greenbrier, with but little desire ever to see them again—but it was not long before I felt deeply concerned about those poor destitute people. The next June I concluded to take a more extensive tour, and lower down than before. Monongahaly River has five large branches, the first is Yohogany commonly called Yoh; the second is Cheat River; the third and main one is the Valley Fork; the fourth is a River called Buckhannon; the fifth is the West Fork, these were all peopled. I set out with a young brother, who had been lately Baptized, by the name of Wood. Our first settlement was Cheat River, where a little settlement of Baptists, who had moved from Shenandoah, were now living, on a large bottom on the River, called Tunchards bottom. All the settlement in the great glades on Yohogany River, between the south branch and Cheat River, a space of sixty miles, had been broken up by the Indians. At Cheat River we stopt and worshipped awhile. Our next stop was about thirty miles, bearing down towards Redstone, to the forks of Cheat, and Monongahaly Rivers, where was a considerable settlement of people, and a small Baptist Church, which had been constituted by Mr. John Corbly; here the people seemed to be in safety from the Indians, though after this Mr. Corbly's family was killed by the Indians not far from this place—we got to a Baptist house on Saturday evening, and on the next day his house was filled with people, to hear preaching. While the people were gathering, I found they generally took brother Wood that was with me to be the preacher; he was well dressed, had been lately Baptized, and looked very serious—at length a respectable looking man, came to me, casting a respectful eye towards Wood, asked me where the preacher lived, what was his name, and the like; I replied, his name was Taylor, where he lived, etc. Though I found he was deceived, I suffered the innocent deception to go on; he asked me to walk with him to the spring, where farther enquiries were made about the preacher. I found he was no Baptist but showed respect for me, because I was travelling with a respectable looking preacher. This was not all the times by many, in which the people were deceived, where I was a stranger.

Travelling once in Virginia, with my brother Joseph Taylor, and having a meeting appointed at Beson Town, near Redstone, a large assembly had gathered and a man preaching when we got there, when we got into the crowded house, a seat was soon made for his reception, I worked off to some back seat. By the wishful look of the people on him, with his fine black cloth, and clean neck band, he soon discovered their mistake, and though a wild ratling man, he perhaps put on more solemn looks than he would have done—and when the preacher was done, an opening was immediately made between him and the pulpit, while I had to scramble as I could through and over the people, to get to the place. However, with the man at the spring, he asked me if it was not time for the preacher to begin—we walked to the house, and I immediately went to the table and opened meeting, the people seemed to look on with wonder, and especially the inquisitive man; but they were all excusable, for though I was now twenty two or three years old, I looked to be at least four years younger than I was. I was about twenty years old when I began to speak but by those who did not know me, I was taken to be sixteen, at twenty five I was barely grown to my common stature. When I opened meeting, I addressed the people as follows: "I am now nearly two hundred miles from home, and an entire stranger to you all. It is probable you wish to know from whence I came and who and what I am." I then informed them where my home was when at it—I then told them my name, and as to profession I was a Baptist, and of the separate order—when I named separate Baptists, it produced some oblique looks, for the Baptists there were regulars, and they considered the separates a kind of heterodox people—I took this for a text: "a man that hath friends must show himself friendly, and there is a friend that sticketh closer than a brother—prov. 18 chap. 24th verse." I ventured to transpose the words a little, and read them, "a man that would have friends must show himself friendly." I then spoke of Jesus Christ the eternal son of God, whose kind thoughts were turned to our race, before the world began, as expressed in the eighth chapter of proverbs and that our native enmity, which I dwelt on at large, did not prevent those early kind designs, from being put into practice; by his kind visit to our world, in his incarnation, his active obedience to the law, his passive obedience in death, in which by help from Heaven, I was so expressive that there was a great gush of tears among the people, then added how the mighty enmity of our hearts were slain, by a supernatural power from Heaven, with the cordial submission of the soul to Jesus Christ in friendship; the certainty of the salvation of that soul because the friendship of the Saviour was more to be depended upon than any brother whatever, for that he was God and changed not—my regular brethren perhaps forgot that I was a separate for we parted that afternoon, with tears of cordial friendship—and as an evidence on their side, they made up among themselves, and gave me three or four dollars which I received as a token of their friendship.

From thence we crossed over the main River and ranged up its west fork, where we had some happy meetings, some of the people here were at home, others in forts. I fell in at a meeting of Mr. Corbly's where we enjoyed a happy meeting together, it being the first time we ever saw each other. From this settlement, it was about one days ride to Buckhannon River, where was about thirty families, where I think preaching had never been—the people here were generally either forted or a number of families huddled together in kind of block houses, for their own safety—these poor things would risk all they had and their own lives to get together to hear preaching—to them it was a strong evidence of good will for a man to risk his life to come and preach to them. There we had several meetings and the people much affected. From Buckhannon, one days ride more through a gloomy forest, brought us to Tigers Valley, which the winter before looked so dreadfully gloomy to me. But dangerous as the times were, the summer season put a more pleasant aspect on the face of things. I had several meetings there, beginning with Sunday in the thickest part of the Valley settlement, the preaching was in the woods near the fort, where a great number of people gathered, and seemed as perfectly composed as if they had no enemy in the world, for the first time I preached twice in the day before the people broke; the first text was: "the axe is laid at the root of the trees, and every tree that bringeth not good fruit, is hewn down and cast into the fire." The second text I think was this: "Come, for all things are now ready." The people seemed to listen with interested attention, and some much affected, there are some alive now in Kentucky, who professes hope in Christ from that days preaching. On this visit I became acquainted in the Valley, with some warm hearted Presbyterians, who had embraced religion in the time of Whitfield's preaching, who seemed as kind to me as to a near relation. This with other things made an opening for another visit to Tigers Valley. I returned to Luney's Creek where Reading was now the Pastor—and from thence to Shenandoah, where Marshall was now the pastor—my designs were to spend the next winter in these back settlements, which I accordingly fulfilled. This I think was in the winter of '75 and '76, the war was now increasing with mighty rapidity, and a number of regular troops was stationed in Tiger's Valley to guard the frontiers. Some of the poor soldiers became much affected under preaching, and were despised by their officers, declaring that my preaching disqualified them for fighting, their fellow-soldiers also derided their tears and sorrows. But I hope the Lord blessed some of them: The troops being stationed at Tiger's Valley, made travelling less dangerous, through the winter, and the people more at their homes. The great readiness in many of the people, to hear the word, was an ample reward for all my troubles. Through this dreary winter, I visited all the settlements where I had been before, but Tiger's Valley was my temporary home. I here made up an acquaintance with a number of tender hearted friends, some of whom were young converts. I took two tours from Tigers Valley to Greenbrier, one of which I will relate.

It was called thirty-miles from the upper house in the Valley, to the first house in the Greenbrier Settlement, and over a tremendous mountain, that divided the Monongahela waters from Greenbrier River; the trace was very dull, and a stranger to the way, and without company. I was on a borrowed horse, and unshod; but the owner thought that would be no impediment, as a snow had lately fallen about ancle deep. I went to the last house in the Valley, that by an early start, I might prevent camping in the woods at night.

The River was from twenty to thirty yards wide when I sat out, to the source of which I had to travel before I took the mountain. The freeze had been, and was then so severe, that scarce a ripple of the River but was so blocked up with ice, that it appeared impossible for my barefooted horse to cross it. I once thought of going back, but after reflecting, the obstructions seemed too trivial, to make a good excuse from, and not knowing what was ahead, I concluded to push on. I took my wrappers from my legs, and placed my horses fore feet in the middle of the wrappers and then with my garters, tied them round his legs, by which he might walk on the smooth ice, but after I could not get him a step forward; my only remedy was to lead him in to some little steep bank on the River, two or three feet high and by a sudden push, sprall him on the ice, and then lead him on across the River, this was often repeated, and the cold so sensible that I was doubtful my ears would freeze, and my hands so numbed that I could scarcely tie my wrappers, either on my horses legs or my own, and so much time was spent in those several operations, though I had set out about sun rise, I was pretty sure I should not arrive at any house that night; but my horse learned that it was better to take the ice at once after my wrappers were tied on his legs than to be dashed on it, for I suppose we crossed the River from ten to twenty times. The after part of the day became warmer and I got to a house about sun down. I had a number of meetings in what was called the little levels of Greenbrier, but the distracted state of the people, by the war, or the barrenness of my preaching, or both, I became fully convinced that if the Lord ever intended to bless that people, the time was not come, or myself was not to be the instrument.

I returned to Tigers Valley and from thence paid another visit to the several different settlements, where was very hopeful appearances, and returned home in the spring.

The hopeful prospects in the back woods, induced me to take a letter of dismission from Shenandoah, and join the church on Luney's creek—after which Reading and myself took several tours; a part of one of them I think proper to state. Our first meeting was at Cheat river, Tunkard's bottom, sixty miles from Reading's; for this was the first settlement we came to. To this meeting there came a number about fifteen miles, from a place called Monongahela Glades, where was a settlement of about twenty families—they importuned us to stop at their settlement, and preach to them— Our other arrangements did not admit, except they could be together the next day about ten o'clock, on which we would spend about two hours with them. They set off on Sunday evening from meeting, to give notice to their neighbours: one James Brane, a Baptist, conducted us to the place next day. We met about thirty or forty people, and began about the time designed. I went forward—there was nothing very visible while I was speaking—Reding dwelt on the awful subject, of a Judgment to come—the first appearance, was a young lady who began to weep and tremble, sitting by her grandmother;—the old lady for some time strove to stop her—at length she began to tremble herself, as if the Judge was at the door—From thence the effect spread through the whole house, with solemn groans and lamentations: till at length a woman, the name of Clark, dropt on her knees, in the middle of the house, with the greatest appearance of agonizing guilt, and perhaps she did not leave that position for the space of three hours—when Reding stopt speaking, the only remedy I had to prevent hallowing with all my might, was to vent the tender feelings of my heart, by exortations and feeling invitations to those apparantly broken-hearted creatures—whether Mrs. Clark had ever been concerning about her soul before I disremember, but she obtained deliverance from her guilt before she left her knees—we had quite forgotten all the meetings that were ahead of us, and our worship continued perhaps six hours, in prayers, praise, and exortations among the people—I do not recollect that we took any sustenance before we left the place, for the family where the meeting was, seemed two much affected, to think of any thing but the salvation of their souls—I solemnly surveyed the house a little before we started, and it is a fact, that the floor of it was as wet with the tears of the people, as if water had been sprinkled all over it, or with a shower of rain. Mr. Brain, our guide, the only Baptist that I know of at the place, besides ourselves went on to put us in the way, while we made the lonesom forest ring with the praises of God, as if there was not an Indian in the world, our guide parted with us late in the evening, and not long after was killed by the Indians. This wonderful meeting at this little glade settlement, the first that was ever there—if I judge from my own feelings and the effect afterwards, according to the number of people, exceeded any I was ever at in my life—I suppose one third at least, of the people present, obtained hope in Christ afterwards and resorted to some Churches thirty or forty miles off for Baptism—The husband of Mrs. Clark, at the time of her conversion, at this meeting, was on a visit to the Jersies, where he had moved from; while there, as he told me afterwards, he had a dream of a meeting in his neighborhood and about such an one as realy was there, and at said meeting, he dreamed his wife was converted—He was struck with a sense of his own guilt, from his dream, and when he found the reality of all his dreams when he returned, had no rest till he found it in the Saviour, and in a few months was Baptized with his wife. At this place, I frequently called to worship with the people afterwards, and usually while there, felt as I think Jacob did when at Bethel, where he had his dream of the ladder. Reding and myself went on our way after leaving Mr. Brain, to visit chief of the settlements where I had been before, where we found the people more affected than I had ever before seen them, and we soon became as much united to many of those poor back-woods strangers as if they had been near relations. In those back settlements, we constituted no Church, for that to us appeared needless, except there was some person to stately preach to them, neither did we Baptize any except where we found Baptists enough to make out at least a semblance of a Church, for we had not yet grown up to apostolic style. By this time Reding, with the Church at Lunies Creek counceled about my ordination, to which they agreed, and hearing of a council of ministers to meet at old Shenandoah Church on some business, Reding took the certificate of Lunies Creek Church, and we attended this meeting of ministers at Shenandoah. This step to Reding appeared the more seasonable because, in this old Church where both him and myself had been Baptized, my ordination could undergo another scrutiny. If I mistake not, the Baptists are much less careful now, in ordaining ministers, than they were in those past days.[2]—This was about four years after I had been a licenced Preacher, and had travelled for that purpose, about twice as many thousand miles as I had been preaching years, with tolerable approbation among the Baptists. The design of my ordination, was in the Itenerant way, and to administer ordainances where

[2] (Dover Association, Virginia, 1786): How is ordination legally performed? "A presbytery of ministers are fully empowered to ordain any faithful man properly recommended, whom they shall judge to be able to teach others; and that ministers shall be subject to ministers with regard to their call to the ministry and the doctrines they preach. The church where the minister is a member shall take cognizance of his moral character."

This decision, though founded in reason and Scripture, gave umbrage to some, who indulged strong jealousies respecting ministerial influence, and who held that a call from a church was sufficient ordination. (See Semple, *History of Rise and Progress of the Baptists in Virginia*, pp. 120–121.)

In 1792 the Dover Association again raised the question of ordination, concerning which Semple makes the following remarks:

On the part of the advocates of ordination without the imposition of hands, it was argued that churches were acknowledged to be independent, but if they could not obtain the full services of a minister, unless he had been previously examined and ordained by a presbytery, their independence was so far destroyed; that churches were better judges what gifts would suit them than presbyteries could be; that the imposition of hands mentioned in the Scriptures was with a view to miraculous and not common gifts; and lastly, that it had the appearance of being governed too much by forms.

To these arguments it was answered that the New Testament did surely sanction the practice of laying on of hands in some cases where no miraculous consequences did ensue; that although the imposition of hands was a form, yet it was a significant form used in all ages of the Christian Church for the purpose of consecrating or setting apart persons for holy offices; . . . that it was true that churches were, and ought to be independent, to a proper extent, but this independence did not authorize them to ordain officers contrary to revelation, unless they were independent of God also; that although a church might judge better than a presbytery what suited her, it was not reasonable that those who had not exercised a public gift should be so competent to judge public gifts as those who had.

After this subject had been investigated for years at different times and in different ways, it was finally decided in this Association in favor of the imposition of hands. After this very little was ever said about it (pp. 124–125).

the Churches were destitute of a Pastor, and called for my service. The Church at Shenandoah, with the Ministers present agreed to my ordaination, in this way, which was not uncommon for unmarried men in those days.

The presbytery who officiated in the ordination, was Lewis Craig, John Picket, John Cunes, Joseph Reding and Theodoric Noel, then a young man; being well acquainted with me, made examination in their esteem less needful. They proceeded in the common form, all of us kneeling down, with their right hand laid on my head, two or three of them prayed, Lewis Craig, I think, gave me a pertinent charge, while holding me by the right hand, with the right hand of fellowship, from them and all the brethren that were present; with me it was an awfully solemn time. I remember young Mr. Noel though an older man than myself, wrote the credentials they were pleased to give me.

Reding and myself continued travelling in the back parts, and became acquainted with a number of Ministers, in the Redstone country, to-wit: Isaac Sutton and James his brother, at that time they had two more brothers that were preachers, John and David; for family preaching they were pretty much like the Craigs in those days, we also became acquainted with John Corbly and William Wood, very active servants of the Lord, in building up Churches in these back woods, and from which Redstone association was created; all these were regular Baptists, but after becoming acquainted, though we were Separates, we found no difference as to doctrinal opinions. I remember we went to one new place called Sandy Creek Glades, where we found some of these regular Baptists; they looked a little shy at us, because of the name. For a new place there was a great gathering of people, while I was speaking, I took notice of a small, pert looking old man, who shed tears profusely, while I was dwelling on the feelings of the heart, under the influence of the grace of God. When preaching ended, he called me apart from the people to converse, his eyes being yet moist, I think he informed me he had not heard preaching for several years—He had been Baptized long ago by Benjamin Miller in the Jersies, he thought proper to tell me his hope in Christ; he stated his long agony of guilt under which he laboured, with the sensibility of his helpless case before he obtained relief, and while stating the glorious plan of salvation being opened to him, by the Lord Jesus, he burst forth in a fresh flood of joyful tears, with perhaps smiting his hands together, in heavenly agitation cried, out; "O brother Taylor, it was forty years ago, and it is now as plain to me as if it had taken place yesterday." My own sensibility could no longer be suppressed; while I partook of the same joyful torrent, could not forbear reaching out the hand of christian fellowship, (which he was as ready to do) to a man I never saw before, and old enough to be my grandfather; This man's name was Frasy, he had a numerous offspring, of children and grand-children, and many of them living near him. I one day after I became more acquainted with him, asked him how many children he had, he replied nineteen, and after my remarking it was a good number, but he considered it only moderate, for that his father had raised twenty nine children, nineteen by his first Wife and ten by a second wife; but what gave him most pleasure of all, was the prospect of our preaching becoming useful among his children and neighbours, for some of them I hope found the Lord. To this place I often went afterwards, and was respected by the people, as much as my character could possibly deserve. The place I have been just speaking of was called Sandy Creek Glades, where a considerable settlement was now living, on the waters of Yoh River, higher up the same River was called the Great Glades, where, for many miles together, no timber grew, the whole extent of the Aleghany mountains about this place was esteemed sixty miles across it. Those glades were a part of the distance and of course in the Aleghaney mountain; in the Great Glades there had been settlements but is now forsaken; from Indian danger, through these glades by different pass ways I had to go to pass from the eastern waters to the west, and the distance from one settlement to another that a hard days travel would not accomplish it, so that camping out often attended the traveller; if these were inconveniences I often met with them; I will name a few of them; travelling once with a companion, our lot was to take up quarters in a deserted Cabin, that had two apartments, in one of them we put our horses for safe keeping, in the other we built a fire and slept; in the morning we found our horses had broken out, and in the dry glade grass it was impracticable to track them, however we searched the chief of next day, but found them not, in which time we ate up our provisions; it was about thirty miles to the first inhabitants ahead, and nearly the same behind, we left our Cabin in the evening to go on ahead, with our saddles and all we had on our backs; after a few miles dark compelled us to take up camp in the great open glade, he having a gun we obtained fire, but little or no fuel to supply it; but, though in the middle of winter, the weather was not very cold, so that we suffered as much from hunger as cold, for we had walked very hard to find our horses. The next morning, without a mouthful to eat, we set out with all the cheerfulness we were master of, to make this near thirty miles, with all our luggage before we got breakfast—the trace was very slashy in these great lonesome glades, besides Yoh River and many of its branches to wade through—after we left the glades the way was monstrous mountaneous, before we got to Cheat River or Tunkard's bottom those mountains appeared pretty hard on our hunger bitten knees. We passed along by a hunters camp late in the day but they were gone, we rumaged about after bones they had cast away, and perhaps been pillaged by their dogs, but could not get one mouthful; however, we got breakfast and supper together at night. My partner who travelled with me in this little rugged tour, was a pleasant little man the name of Powel. It was at his house our great meeting had been, with but few people where Clark's wife obtained convertion while on her knees. At the time of our travel Powell was a Baptist and now lives in Woodford county, Kentucky, it is said he now loves Whiskey a little too much. Powells horse went home, mine I never got which was a considerable loss to me. Another similar tour I had about two winters after and partly on the same road. In the first instance I had no horse, in the last I had one to maney, for I had one to lead; there had been snow on the ground, but a great rain had taken it chiefly off. I started from a place called the Crab Orchard, not far from Tunkard's Bottom, it was upwards of forty miles to the first house, I set out early to gain that object before night; I soon took a tremendous mountain called Laurel Hill, but in that place called Cheat mountain; my road was so small for eight miles, that it could scarcely be followed by daylight, when I came to the great glades where the settlement had been, the road was plainer. I soon after came to a creek, over which a bridge had been made by the settlers, when there, I saw the water was up to the planks of the bridge; I pushed on but soon found the planks were afloat, but hurrying forward, the led horse first fell through and as the one I rode was going down, I sprang from him on the floating planks, with my saddle bags in my hand, and escaped clear to the opposite shore; when I turned round, here was both my horses between the cills of the bridge, and barracaded with floating planks on each side, and the water about as deep as they were high. The next thing was to counsel how to get them out, and none to counsel but myself, for the poor horses could say nothing on that head, while they stood trembling in the cold water. Those glade creeks are generally deep, with steep banks, lined with small willows on each margin, and the water running very dead. This stream was about eight steps across it, and timber laid on those planks and locked in the willows at each end had prevented their floating off—my plan was to stand on the cill of the bridge, up to my knees in water, and float the planks off till I got to my horses, and with mighty struggling with the poor animals, get them up the bank. My saddle was wet, the bridle caked with ice, and my hands so benumbed, that I could not draw on my gloves. I suppose I lost a full hour of the day, at this place, with my feet wet to my knees, my bare hands to hold the frozen bridles, one to ride with, the other to lead, my saddle-bags being dry kept me a little from the wet saddle. I hurried on lest Yoh River should rise beyond fording; I soon met with another creek, which ran over my horses, where I got a fresh ducking, when I came to the River I found it was impossible to cross it except by swimming, which I had often done in similar cases; I paused awhile, but when I found that I must go up the current to get to the opposite shore, and just below was an ivy bluff for a long distance, that was impassible but that I must inevitably be dashed against it, viewing the muddy waves foaming over the great Rocks which lay in the River, and dashing against the icy rock on the other shore, I concluded that it was not proper to tempt the Lord my God to work a miracle in my preservation. What food I had for myself and horses we consumed, and about one o'clock, turned tail to get if possible to where I came from in the morning; riding on I became so very cold in my wet freezing clothes, I concluded a little walking would comfort me. It was usual to drive my horse before me in such cases, but the beast I led being untutored that way, broke ground to run back, and both together ran off in full speed, I ran with all my might to keep in sight of them, in these great glades; I thus ran a mile or two in hopes that water ahead where they had so hard a struggle would stop them, which it did, there I caught them, I was now very wet with heat and sweat, what shall I do was the next question, swim the creek immediately which had risen higher or wait and cool first; I had ten miles to go, the sun about two hours high, the road amasing bad when I got to Cheat mountain, and so dim that I could scarce follow it by day light, the moon also dark, that there was no alternative but dash on, or camp in the woods without fire; I mounted my horse and swam the creek with all my sweat, the water ran up round my middle, and soon after my clothes froze except what lay next to my skin.—About dark I got to where I started from at morning light, getting from my horse I could scarce keep my feet; I staggered on to the house, and soon went to bed, my hands were so swolen with cold that I could scarce use them, after some warm supper I slept sound; for several days I felt in a kind of listless stuper; about one month after this I was stricken with a prodigious surfeit, a breaking out, from head to foot, in likeness of ring-worm covered with white scales, so that scarce a part under my clothes was free from it, and continues more or less to this day, which has been a good deal upwards of forty years. I had many tours similar but none quite equal to the two last named, in point of difficulty.—It never set well on my feelings to receive pay from the people for preaching, I there-fore preferred my own exertions, to supply my own wants— my father had given me a lot of broken land, on which I had cleared a field, and generally raised some corn for my horse to eat when at home, with other little mechanical arts, I nearly made a supply—a few years after I had been called a preacher, and while under great misgivings of heart, on that subject, fearing that I was running and the Lord had not sent me, I had an uncommon dream [3] though I am not dis-posed to put confidence in a mere vision of the night. It was in the spring of the year, and when I was very busy in getting my little field in order to plant corn my mind being a little more on the world than common.

I dreamed of being at a place of gathering of people, where was a dead man, a blustering man present said he could raise the dead man to life, a dispute arose between him and others, who insisted he could not do it. But at length the dead man did voluntarily rise up, when risen he looked very angry and turned his whole attention to me; with rage in his looks he informed me he was sent from the dead to warn me never to preach any more—all this though a sleep, struck me with dreadful horror of mind, he farther reminded me, that I might treat his warning with neglect, for said he there are some who will not be persuaded though one rose from the dead. All this I realised while asleep, with dreadful anguish of mind—he farther added, I am not only sent from the dead to warn you never to preach any more but when you die you will go to hell—dam you. By this time it seemed as if the pains of hell had got hold on me while a sleep, in this

[3] This belief that dreams were used as a means of revealing the will of God was very commonly held during this period. Similar accounts may be found in the memoirs of preachers in the different denominations at that time.

dum agony I lay for some time not able to make any reply,
nor dare I do it, for he stood near me and looked as if he
would tear me to pieces. At length I began to reason while
asleep—he told me he was sent from the dead, this said I in
my sleep does not assure me that he is a messenger of God, I
farther reasoned, if he was a messenger of God, he would not
be in such a rage of anger, I farther thought, if he came as his
messenger, he would not use the language he did, either to
curse or dam me. I then thought he looked more like a messenger from hell than from Heaven, and of course nothing
he has said is true, from which I came to the conclusion, that
satin saw that my preaching would be against his interest
among man, and therefore strove to frighten me from it.
And as to going to hell when I died, this was all from the
father of lies too; and while my heart used an effort to go
into a vow to God, that I would preach more than I ever had
done, the struggle waked me with uncommon agitation,
reaching out my hand to lay hold of the man, for I yet con-
ceited he stood by me to resist me, but found it was a dream.
It is worth while to take notice how full the scriptures are of
dreams that are full of meaning—witness Jacob's ladder;
Joseph had many dreams. God often spoke to the ancient
prophets by dreams, the whole old testament is very full of
the doctrine of visions from God this way. Job says God
speaks to men this way, by which he opens their ears, and
seals their instructions. Pilates wife had a striking dream.
Peter on the day of pentecost cites up Joel on the subject of
dreams, that their young men should see visions, and their
old men dream dreams: while on dreaming another occurs, as
I am now on dreams I will relate one of a backwoods woman;
soon after my first visit to Lunies Creek in Hampshire
county, a respectable looking man, asked me to come to his
house, that his wife had a particular desire to converse with
me, at a convenient time. I visited the family, and tarried all
night; among other conversation, the poor distressed woman
related to me a dream, a little before she first saw me, she
dreamed that the awful day of judgment was come, that Jesus
Christ the great judge was present, preparing to decide the

fate of the unnumbered world that was present, to each individual he gave a book to read—with the judge were two men to direct the people how to use the books each person had. When I rode up to the meeting where was a great assembly gathered, she knew at first sight that I was one of the men she had seen with the Saviour in her dream; after alighting from my horse, I had withdrawn a little to contemplate, which gave her the opportunity, with deep concern, to reflect on what she had just seen. There was all the features, complection, age and dress she had seen before in her dream, but one thing was lacking in the dress, the man she had seen in her dream had a pair of striped roppers round his legs, this she had not noticed, when I returned from my contemplations, and she saw also the striped roppers round my legs, she said she was stricken with such a trembling that she could scarce keep her feet, and when I rose up, with the Bible in my hand to speak to the people, and direct them how to use the book of God, and looking over the great and much affected assembly that was present, it occurred to her that the great day of God was at hand and she unprepared; from this stroke this dear woman never recovered till she obtained peace through a saviour. To be sure all this statement was an unaccountable to me as it was to this much affected woman, and especially when I recollected that a few days before, I had called at a store and bought a pair of striped ticking wrappers to tie round my legs. Sosomon says dreams comes through a multitude of business, but some of them seem evidently to come from God. There being no established priest [4] in Hampshire county, we met with no

[4] Apparently Mr. Taylor's reference to the "priest" here is to the minister of the Established Church in Virginia, or what is now known as the Protestant Episcopal Church. In that day the State of Virginia was laid out into districts, or parishes, and the preacher of that parish was in a sense the State preacher, supported by a tax upon all the people who lived there. Carrying over from Europe the idea of an established church, and that all other churches are false, there was at times considerable annoyance given to such new groups as the Baptists. Upon this general situation Semple makes the following comment:

"It seems by no means certain that any law in force in Virginia authorized the imprisonment of any person for preaching. The law for the preservation of peace,

legal persecution while preaching there; but this did not prevent the rage of mobs, such as open contradiction while preaching, for Satin is not fond of loosing his prey; we were only once driven from a place of preaching, having a meeting appointed, perhaps on Christmas day, in a rich and wealthy settlement, one of Satan's strongest holds in the county, the invitation for preaching was given by a man, living in a large house, and on his father-in-laws land, a large assembly met, but the old gentleman, the owner of the land, roused perhaps twenty rugged young fellows, a number of whom came armed with instruments of death, to drive all before them; a mighty uproar soon took place in the house, with some blows from the old man on his son-in-law; Reding and myself, standing by the side of the house, concluding to retire, for a deep snow had lately fallen that we could not go into the woods and but a few of the people present was of a religious cast; after our departure, they turned the meeting into a great Christmas frolic, so that Satan, the strong man kept his palace and goods in peace in this place as yet, but became much frustrated afterwards. [Taylor, *op. cit.*, pp. 16–26.]

GILBERT'S CREEK

The first winter in Kentucky, I took shelter in Lewis Craig's station, on Gilbert's Creek, south of Kentucky River, where my wife had some relations—soon after my son Ben was born—whether from the many frights, my wife took on

however, was so interpreted as to answer this purpose, and, accordingly whenever the preachers were apprehended, it was done by a peace warrant."

The first instance of actual imprisonment, we believe, that ever took place in Virginia, was in the county of Spotsylvania. On the 4th of June, 1767, John Waller, Lewis Craig, James Child . . . were seized by the sheriff and hauled before three magistrates. . . . At court they were arraigned as disturbers of the peace. They offered to release them if they would promise to preach no more in the county for a year and a day. This they refused; and, thereafter were sent into close jail. . . . Waller and the others continued in jail for forty-three days, and were discharged without any conditions. (*History of the Rise and Progress of the Baptists in Virginia*, pp. 29–32.) The Baptists supported vigorously the Revolutionary cause; one measure after another was adopted by the legislature in Virginia, until, in 1798, every restriction upon religious liberty was removed, and all religious groups placed upon exactly the same basis.

the journey, or some cause, is unknown—but when there was a call for a midwife, the alarm was such to her, that she went perfectly out of her reason, with violent convulsive fits which continued about twenty four hours, in which time she was delivered, but to this day does not know that Ben is her son, but from circumstances and information. This with other things much embittered Kentucky to me; through this alarming crisis, the life of my wife was so despaired of, that all hope was gone, though I sent for a physician, everything appeared so hopeless, that he soon left the place despairing of any relief, but when all human aid failed, God himself afforded help, and she was restored, and nothing of the kind has ever attended her since in similar cases. The first opportunity I had I gave my membership to the Church at Gilbert's Creek—this had been one of the travelling Churches from Virginia to Kentucky—Lewis Craig, with a great number of the members of his Church in Spotsylvania had moved to Kentucky, as I have been told, they were constituted, when they started, and was an organized Church on the road—wherever they stoped they were a housekeeping at once; just before I got to Kentucky, Craig with a number of others had left Gilbert's Creek, and moved to South Elkhorn and set up a Church there—the remnant left of Gilbert's Creek, kept up Church order—it was this remnant I united with, among them was George Smith commonly called Stokes Smith, a valuable preacher—Richard Cave, then an ordained minister—William Cave, who afterwards became a very good preacher and many other valuable members. I found with the clerk of Gilbert's Creek Church, the old Church book from Spotsylvania, that was of about twenty years standing. It is probable the clerk of that old Church in Virginia, had brought that book with him to Kentucky; I was much amused at time in looking over the records of this old book—the curiosity of their decisions, a mere cap border or garments, cut in any but a plain style, was matter of complaint and expulsion—one I remember was entered by a preacher against sister such a one, for delusion, without any other explanation. This delusion whatever it might be, cost

this sister her membership—all this manifested the great
zeal the Baptists had in early times against the appearance
of sin—it has also taught me ever since, the great care
Churches should take in their records, that nothing foolish
should be committed to record, or at least the whole made so
explicit that after ages may understand it, and not be compelled to use them as the books of curious arts by putting
them into the fire. This George S. Smith was a man of great
respectability as a man, and much of a doctrinal preacher,
simplicity and plainness attended his whole course—his
preaching operated but sparingly on the passions of his
hearers, for though his voice was strong and sonorous, yet
lacking that soft melody, as a Gibbionite in the house of God,
he was better calculated to hew wood than to draw water—
He continued preaching on with zeal and usefulness, for about
twenty years in Kentucky, and died in the Pastoral care of
a large Church in Jessamine county, called Mount Pleasant.

A temporary stay of about seven months, at Gilbert's
Creek, I moved to the north side of the Kentucky River,
about two miles from John Craig's station, on Clear Creek,
now Woodford county; soon after George Stokes Smith and
chief of the members at Gilbert's Creek also moved to the
north side of Kentucky; and a separate Baptist Church
being set up at Gilbert's Creek by Joseph Bledsoe, the old
Church became dissolved and the separate Baptists chiefly
took possession of the south side of the Kentucky River—
I now moved to Woodford county, in the summer of 1784 and
rather than go into the fort settled on my own land, with
no family between me and the Indian towns, and in the
height of war, but we were not long in much danger, for the
next winter the people settled out so that we soon began to
hold night meetings, at our little cabins in the woods, our
Sunday preaching was uniformly at the station. I now began
to reflect seriously on my situation; for some time we had to
pack corn forty miles, and then send a mile to grind at a
hand mill, before we could get bread; as to meat, it must
come from the woods, and myself no hunter; I would at
times go out with hunters and they with the common

generosity of hunters would admit me to share in the profits
so far as meat went, soon after I settled in my little cabin
(sixteen feet square, with no floor but the natural earth,
without table, bedstead or stool) I found that an old buck
had his lodge a few hundred steps from my cabin among the
nettles, high as a man's shoulders, and interlocked with
peavines; those nettles, the next winter we found very useful,
in getting the lint and with the help of Buffaloe wool, made
good clothing for our black people—however, I went many
mornings to visit this old buck lodge, hoping to get a shot
at him, I could some times see him but had not the skill to
get hold of him—but I at length got a fire at him and ac-
cidentally shot him through the heart, this was a greater
treat to my family than the largest bullock I have ever killed
since, for he was large and very fat. Embarrassed as my
worldly circumstances were, the face of things as to religion
gave me more pain of mind; there were a number of Baptists
scattered about, but we all seemed cold as death—every
body had so much to do that religion was scarcely talked of,
even on Sundays, all our meetings seemed only the name of
the thing, with but little of the spirit of devotion—In short,
we were such strangers to each other, that confidence was
lacking for want of more acquaintance, and our common calls
were such that we had not time to become acquainted—
Kentucky felt to me now, as the Quails did to the Hebrews,
who ate of them till they were loathsome and returned back
through their noses. There was but one church now on the
north side of Kentucky and this was south Elkhorn, where
Lewis Craig had the pastoral care; Perhaps in the month of
August 1784 I became a member of south Elkhorn Church
where I was brought under the pastoral care of Lewis Craig,
who was now in the prime of life, as to the gospel ministry,
of the age of between forty and fifty: Mr. Craig is yet living
and about eighty three years old, he is one of the old gospel
veterans in Virginia, who often suffered imprisonment there
for the crime of preaching repentance to sinners. [Taylor,
op. cit., pp. 41–47.]

CLEAR CREEK

From the Heavenly budings already named at Clear Creek, we began to think of having a Church there—through the winter and spring of 1785 several preachers had moved into the neighborhood, as John Dupea, James Rucker and Richard Cave—we held a council on the subject of a constitution, but we found a difficulty, and in this way—a number of the members had been in the Church with Lewis Craig,[5] in Virginia, and in the traveling Church through the wilderness and its establishment in Kentucky, and above all, if we had a new Church, we might loose Lewis Craig as our pastor, and though we had four ordained preachers, all of us did not make one Lewis Craig—But after several councils, we concluded rather than not have a Church convenient to us, we would go into a constitution, under this hope that brother Craig would visit us and set us right when we got wrong—to this height of respectability was Lewis Craig in those days in Kentucky—We could only apply to South Elkhorn for assistance—and the helps from that establishment, agreed

[5] Rev. Lewis Craig, a distinguished pioneer Baptist preacher of Virginia and Kentucky, was born in Orange County, Virginia, about the year 1737. He was first awakened by the preaching of Samuel Harris, about the year 1765. A great pressure of guilt induced him to follow the preacher from one meeting to another, and after the sermon he would rise in tears and assert that he was a justly condemned sinner, and unless he was born again he could not be saved. His ministry thus began before he had hope of conversion, and after conversion he continued preaching a considerable time before being baptized; many were led to Christ under his labors.

Mr. Craig was ordained and became pastor of Upper Spottsylvania church in November, 1770. But this did not prevent his preaching in the surrounding counties. In 1771 he was again arrested and imprisoned for three weeks in Caroline County. He continued preaching with great zeal and success until 1781, when he and a majority of his church moved to Kentucky. He located on Gilbert Creek, in what is now Garrard County, early in December. The next year he gathered Forks of Dix River church in the same county. In 1783 he and most of Gilbert's Creek church moved to the north side of Kentucky River and organized South Elkhorn church, in Fayette County. Here he remained about nine years, laboring zealously in all the surrounding country. . . . About 1792 he moved to Bracken County, Kentucky. Here he formed several churches, and "became in a manner the father of Bracken Association." About the year 1828 "he died suddenly, of which he was forewarned, saying 'I am going to such a house to die;' and with solemn joy went on to the place, and with little pain left the world." (Cathcart, *Baptist Encyclopaedia*, I, p. 285.)

to acknowledge us a sister Church. I think in April 1785 about thirty members, to the best of my recollection was in the new Church, under the style of Baptist Church of Christ at Clear Creek—we soon began to Baptize our young converts, for some of them were waiting for an opportunity—we went on in great harmony through that year, we had four ordained preachers as named above; I think we Baptized between thirteen and twenty that year. Clear Creek was the the second Church on the north side of Kentucky, the same year others were constituted, as the Great-Crossings, Bryants and a Church near Limestone, under the care of W. Wood. We soon began to contemplate an association; for that purpose and partly to bring about a union, with the south Kentucky Baptists, we held a conference at South Elkhorn, in June 1785, but failing in the union with the South Kentucky Baptists, we agreed to meet as an association at Clear Creek, 1st of October 1785, six Churches it seems met, one of them was from Tates Creek, south side of Kentucky—there and then Elkhorn association was formed.

We went on so prosperously at Clear Creek that everybody in a manner lost sight of Lewis Craig's particular watch-care over us—and some time in the next winter, the question began to be stired among us, about a pastor from among our own preachers; when this talk came to my ears, it gave me alarm, thinking the peace of the church might be broken on this question—for I had seen much trouble at times in Virginia. In choosing a pastor where there was a number of preachers, and my own opinion was that a church could do full as well without as with a particular pastor. Two of the preachers that were with us, Dupey and Rucker, had been pastors in Virginia, and a number of their old flocks, then members of Clear Creek church, my own fears were that between these men and their old friends, we should have a heavy church contest, which of them should be the pastor— but the question was brought into the church and the day fixed on to choose a pastor, help's sent for to Elkhorn and the Great Crossings to install, (as they called it,) a pastor in the church. I think it was at our March monthly meeting, the help's came, perhaps six or eight—Lewis Craig acted as the moderator. His mode was to ask every member of the church, male or female, bound or free, who do you choose for your pastor—I think the church was now about sixty in number. I must confess it filled me with surprise, when the first man that was asked answered that he chose me; and my astonishment continued to increase until the question went all round, only one man objected, but Lewis Craig soon worked him out of his objection, for it lay in thinking my coat was too fine. For my own part, I did think that no man in the church had the mind of Christ but this objector. Though the objection about my coat, I considered trivial, yet to me seemed as if the Lord directed it. I could scarcely believe my own ears, when I heard that the two old Pastors, with the remnant of their former flocks with them, give their voice that they chose me for their pastor—the objector soon acquiesced in the voice of the church. After which I was called on to reply—to the voice of the church, I had just heard, to which I felt constrained to answer about as follows: —"That I had never thought myself adequate to the great responsibility of the pastor of a church, and especially in the present case—that there were three ministering brethren in the church older than myself, that two of them had heretofore been pastors, and all of them better calculated to fill that office than myself; and that it must have been the want of a better acquaintance with me, which led the church to the present choice. And though I was ready by day or night to do anything in my power in a ministerial way for my brethren, yet I could not suffer my lips to consent in the present case, to what my heart, conscience, and best matured judgement contradicted. I therefore hoped that they would excuse me in the present negative"—after some other little business the church adjourned. After meeting broke, I took notice, that a kind of silent sorrowful gloom, overspread the faces of the brethren in general, for they could scarce suppress tears when they spoke to each other, and especially when they spoke to me, though this operated somewhat on my feelings, my made up resolution continued the same. A number of the elder brethren went home with me that night, their object was to labour further with me—their mode of reasoning with me was, that though Clear Creek was a young church, it was made up mostly of old members, who knew what they were about, that their judgements were not directed, by blood connection, or former local attachments— that I had Baptized but few of the present Church at Clear Creek—and in a word they had never seen a Church so unanimous in the choice of a pastor, at any place or time— at length one of them declared that he trembled for and at my obstinacy and that he looked for some heavy judgment from heaven to overtake me. These helps from a distance thus reasoning with me—prevailed on me to agree that if the Church was of the same opinion the next day, I would sub- mit—a number of preachers from a distance, together with the design of the Church's meeting, brought out abundance of people, even from distant settlements—after preaching had ended, the moderator L. Craig called the Church together, informing them, if they were of the same mind, they were the day before, I had agreed to serve them. The voice of the Church being unanimous, those helps proceeded to instal me as they called it, into the pastoral care of Clear Creek Church—their mode was three of them to kneel down with myself, while they all laid their right hand on my head, two of them prayed, after which the moderator took my right hand into his, and gave me the solemn charge to fulfil the duty of a pastor to the Church, after which he called forward the Church, each to give me the right hand of fellowship as their pastor. This soon produced more heart melting effect than we had ever before seen at Clear Creek—what wrought most on my own feelings was, almost every sinner in the crowded house, pushed forward, either looking solemn as death or in a flood of tears to give me their trembling hand— From that days meeting, an instantaneous revival took place in the settlement of Clear Creek. That summer I Baptized about sixty of my neighbours, and a number of them among the most respectable—I took notice that four experiences were received dating their first awakening from the day that I took the care of the church—we progressed on for that year, with much peace and harmony. This year Clear Creek old meeting house was built, a framed house forty feet by twenty but we soon found the house would not hold half the people that attended in good weather—I find the old house is yet standing, to me even at a distance the place look's rather sacred, because the Lord's presence has often been there, and there also I have alternately experienced great pleasure and pain—how chequered is human, and especially the christian life—This year the Church went into an agreement to make compensation to their pastor, as they now had one—seventy dollars [6] was fixed on, some said the pastor will be pacified with this small sum, as we have our meeting house to build this year. The next year a hundred dollars was voted for the pastor, by the Church, not knowing but the first seventy had been all paid. The plan fallen on was to make out an apportionment on each member, and give the several sums drawn off into the hands of the pastor, and he give the individual credit when the sum was paid—these several sums were in such produce as would answer for family use, out of this hundred and seventy dollars, I only received about forty—those who did pay never knew but that all the rest paid also. The third year it was thought best to hire a man to attend to my business, this was done by commissioners appointed by the Church, who hired a man for a hundred dollars. The trustees took care to get their money from each individual, this produced a little flouncing—thus ended my Peterspence at Clear Creek. There were a number of conversions at Clear Creek soon after I became their pastor, that was a little out of the common track, one was my own sister in the flesh, who has since married Mr. Jeconias

[6] Preachers among all the smaller denominations, particularly those which were working primarily among the people of the frontier, received very poor salaries. At its first General Conference, the Methodist Episcopal Church set as the maximum salary for any of its preachers, including even Bishop Francis Asbury, the sum of $64.00. That remained the maximum salary until 1800, and it was not until well toward the middle of the nineteenth century before any Methodist preacher was allowed to receive more than $100.00. It should be noted, however, that this was the salary for unmarried preachers, and that there was a similar allowance for the wife; and, at times, set sums for the children, according to age.

Singleton in Woodford county, near Versailles. I went to Virginia soon after I had moved to Kentucky, my sister about sixteen or eighteen years old, applied to our parents to let her come with me to Kentucky; I the more favoured it hoping that it was a religious object—but in Kentucky she soon formed an acquaintance with a number of gay sportful young ladies, and in their alternate visits, every thing sacred was so far set aside, that it was with difficulty, that family worship could be kept up—I did now heartily wish her back with her parents. A very devotional man the name of M'Donald, and a stranger to my sister had come to pay me a visit, he had great confidence in preachers, and when with them, would ask five times more questions than they were able to answer, and it would in a manner pain him to death if his questions was not answered, his object in those questions was to know to a certainty whether himself was a christian—some time before we went to bed he asked me how I thought the foolish Virgins felt, being obliged to give some answer, I entered on what I thought were the feelings of the foolish Virgins—when I was done, he broke out with doleful lementations, and that I had described his feelings so precisely, that he was only a foolish Virgin, and that the door of Heaven would be shut against him at last. Nothing that I could say afterwards would pacify him, for I had a very good opinion of his religion—my sister who sat by and heard all that passed, and ready to burst with laughter at what she thought this foolish man's talk, left the house to vent her levity to her satisfaction—The next day, we all started to meeting, my sister riding on, took a look at this foolish man as her heart had called him the night before—It first occurred to her that he was the most holy looking man she ever saw, the next thought was, this holy looking man is afraid he will not be saved at last—the next thought was, if he is afraid what will become of me—with that thought this text occurred, "Wo is me for I am undone, for I am a man of unclean lips"—the follies of her life so bore on her mind, that her conclusion was that there was no mercy for her—though there was a number in company, she left us all and fell behind weeping along alone, others who overtook her she forbore to converse with, and they forbore to ask her what was the matter—Lewis Craig that day paid us a visit, when he took his text it was the same that had occurred to her on the way, "Wo is me, for I am undone"—Craig's sermon perfectly clinched the nail, for her conclusion was that God had sent Mr. Craig to show her that there was no mercy for her. For about one month her agony and distress was such, that at times it seemed as if she would go deranged; for that length of time she lived in a manner, without food or sleep, one day from the loom house, she came rushing in with an apparent fright, and a flood of tears, and not being able to speak for a while, the first thing that occured to me was Indians, (for we were not then safe from Indians) but droping on her knees, with heart rending cries intreating me to pray for her, for that God disdained her prayers, and she feared there was no mercy for her; but the Lord soon gave her a happy deliverance, and with that clearness, that no doubt was left with any who heard the relation of her hope in Christ. I do not recollect that a question was asked her by the Church—she was among the first that was Baptized in this happy revival, and has given good evidence since, that the work is genuine, and that she belongs to the Lord. Another singularity in conversion about the same time, was in George Dale. There being another man of the same name, this was called little George Dale—I had been several years acquainted with Mr. Dale, in short he had lived a good deal at my house, my own opinion was, that as to morality, religion itself could make no amendment in him—and yet, destitute of spiritual religion, many were obtaining hope in the Lord, at length a report came to me that little George Dale was converted—I met with his brother Abram, and asked him about the conversion of his brother George—he had heard nothing of it, but he was sure he was now in the state he was born, and he did not presume he was born a christian—but he had not seen him lately—soon after George himself paid us a visit, seeing my wife at the door he called to her, how do you do sister Taylor—I am born again—I can now call you all brothers and sisters—soon after I came to the house, and found George in the greatest rapture and confidence in religion, that I had ever seen any man—as to any thing he could see to the contrary he had at once arrived to a state of sinless perfection—though naturally a very silent man, he was now all talk—first of his deliverance from a great load of guilt and of the great grace in Christ Jesus, who had done all for him—I had often seen him at meetings, apparently as unmoved as if he had no feelings while others were weeping around him—in this he soon satisfied me that in all these cases he was inwardly mourning over his hardness of heart, and that there was no mercy for him, and that God in justice had passed him by, and left him to perish in his sin—the countenance of this man did not look as if he belonged to this world, while he would exclaim—O the happiness that I shall enjoy both in this world and the world to come—this man about two weeks after, came forward with a solemn boldness to join the Church—though he told a very good experience many questions were asked him, on the subject of his great confidence; he was asked if he had felt no trouble since his deliverance, when he answered, O no, nor never shall—why, I am converted—he was further asked, have you had no temptations, evil thoughts, or rambling of mind in the worship of God since that time—his answer was again in the negative and rather expressing wonder at those questions, as he was born again—there was some doubt expressed about receiving him as he was so much better than other people, to which he replied with pleasant modesty, it made no odds, God had received him, and he should go to Heaven, for he was born again. However the Church received him, and his course since has been very even and orderly though with not so much high sail as at the beginning—I have heard of but one complaint entered in the Church against him, and that was brought forward by himself—It seems with some Baptist friends he rode to Lexington—after which he came to the Church and requested them to exclude him, for that he had gotten drunk, when he went to Lexington, and though the company with him plead an excuse for him, and that they

could barely discover intoxication in him—he insisted there
ought to be no plea for drunkenness, and for the honor of
religion requested to be turned out of the Church. But the
Church did not choose to grant his request—how very far
from this is the hypocritical sly Baptist, who will cover his
crime by falsehood till he dies a hidden drunkard. There was
a circumstance uncommon, I think it was on the day that
George Dale joined the Church, about twelve came forward
to the Church, with but one invitation; when the door was
opened to receive members, there was no delay, for all of
them, as one man seemed eager to follow the Lord; frequently
two of them would step forward at once—to the best of my
recollection there was neither female nor black person among
them, but generally young men; among them I think was
George Churchill, an orphan lad, who in stating the consciousness of his lost and helpless condition, happened to say
he was willing to go to hell; this expression was soon caught
at by a number of the Church as very improper, and used
endeavours by other questions to set the poor youth right,
by reasoning, that it was not possible for any person and
especially a pious man, (who knew what hell was, a place of
sin as well as sorrow) to be willing to go to hell—some perhaps insinuated he need not speak any further, but set him
aside at once. The lad stood silent as if undismayed, while
these things were going on, but at length replied, that he
saw at the time that it was just in God to send him to hell
and he saw no way he could be just but in his destruction—
he had no desire for God to change, to do him any good; he
saw no reason why he should be more partial to himself than
to another person—he had no doubt that God would condemn
the greater part of the world at last, and if he was willing
for God to do right in that case, he saw no reason why he
should be unwilling to be damned himself, and especially as he
deserved it more than any other person—he had since seen that
God could be just in saving a sinner through his son, but
without that consideration, he was yet willing to be damned.

Another thing which often awakened great excitement in
Clear Creek Church, was expelling their members by a ma-

jority of voices, when a complaint was brought in, and especially when the case was somewhat doubtful; one side would conclude, if we do not exert ourselves a guilty man will be continued in the Church, the opposite side would think if we do not strive hard, an innocent man will be condemned, so that we seldom had a trial of that kind, but it was with great warmth of temper—and after all, but a cross and pile chance as to the equity of the decision—nothing is more rational, than the way a man comes into the Church, he should go out, yet privileges may be curtailed by suspension, through a majority of voices, while the member is yet retained under the admonition of the Church—2nd Thes. 3 Chap. 14 and 15 verses.

I knew one of the most respectable members in Clear Creek Church, improperly expelled by this majority plan—I suppose the free male members at this time in the Church, was about one hundred—perhaps sixty or seventy acted in this case, the case being a very doubtful subject, only twenty voted, ten on each side—one ten voted for his guilt and expulsion, the other ten voted him innocent, the moderator gave the casting vote against him, and the worthy Deacon was thus slamed off by this majority plan; the excluded man attended meetings as usual, and with great calmness took his distance for a year or two, when the Church reinvested the subject, and unanimously voted the former decision wrong, and the Deacon again took his seat, by the invitation of the Church, without asking any questions—another instance of five or six complaints being brought into the church against one of the leading members, about land claims—only three members voted in this case, two against the member and one for him; one of the two rose up and insisted, that according to the rules of the church he was expelled, and demanded the record to be made, but the church would not admit this vote to stand, and by a great majority, in a second vote cleared the accused man. This with several other cases, convinced me of the majority plan of exclusion, that it was improper, though myself had been a principal instrument to get it established in Clear Creek church, then thinking that on any other plan we could never get clear of the bad people

—but after my conviction on that head, I could never get a change of the rule in the church, and perhaps Clear Creek uses this destructive rule to this day. Shall a religious man, whose privileges in a church are dearer to him than all other rights on earth, be all lost at once as by the toss of a penny— for twenty seven years I have lived in the enjoyment of a more excellent way—That of final expulsion by an unanimity of voices, and by which we fairly get rid of all who ought to go out of the church—See Buck Run rules of decorum.

A number of conspiring circumstances, induced me now to think of moving from Clear Creek—as first the increase of my family, though I had become possessed of about fifteen hundred acres of land in that neighborhood in early times—I had whittled it all off to one friend and another, to about four hundred, the farm on which I lived—I now had four children, and a prospect of more; an opening offered on the Ohio River, near the mouth of the Great Miami, now Boon county, I purchased in different tracts near three thousand acres of land—here was plenty of soil for all the children I was like to have; this was an almost entire unsettled country, and much exposed to Indian danger, this was of but small moment to me, from the great propensity I had to live in a new country—where I lived in Woodford county was now thick settled, and but little Cow range; a number of my religious neighbours were also desirous to move to the Ohio; all this well suited my then appetite, having this view, that we could have a church there at once—But another very prevailing reason with myself in leaving Clear Creek was, a very respectable individual had withdrawn his membership from the church on my account, delicacy itself will forbid going into a minute detail of all this business—I had brought money to purchase land for him in Kentucky—when he saw the land, he became displeased with the mode of the appropriation of his money, we left it to men as arbitrators—with their decision he was displeased; a very influential character from another church prevailed on him to bring a complaint into Clear Creek to which the church agreed, by sending for helps from other churches—the first decision of the church was unfavorable to the justness of my course with the offended man—on this result I stopped preaching a month or two—This gave great consternation to chief of the members of the church, not considering that their decision extended thus far—the fact was, they scarcely knew what they had decided on, for they were hurried into it by foreign agents— I was ready to confess that in some things I had failed with the complaining man, in point of generosity, but in point of justice I had never thought I had failed; the church however hasted to the same churches for helps to reconsider what they had done—the second decision gave the offended man such dissatisfaction, that he immediately withdrew from the church—all this was while I had the pastorial care, and of course before the last revival of religion I have been speaking of, and it may look strange that though several of his family were baptized in the time of the revival, his wife a member, and I often had meetings at his house, he yet kept his distance from the church all of which in process of time, proved a painful spur to me to leave the place; I sold my land and made arrangements to move, many of the brethren seemed much afflicted at my removal—but none of them all manifested such rational concern at my removal as the man who was partly the instrument of my leaving Clear Creek—and though all this may look strange it is the truth of the case, some time before I moved he sent for me to come to his house, when he reasoned with me thus—"Many of your friends seem unwilling that you should move away, but as your land is sold they ought to remember that you cannot stay without a home," and then proposed land that he had received from myself, which had risen in value at least double, on the same terms he had gotten it from me; and if it did not suit me to pay him the money, as I had laid out a good deal for land on the Ohio, he would take it on terms I had purchased at, though the land lay about a hundred miles from him; this kindness I am bound to remember with gratitude till I die. Things had been carried too far as to my removal to accept of his kind offer; and in the spring 1795 I moved to the Ohio River; and near eleven years after I had settled

on Clear Creek.—When I left the church they were well
furnished with preachers; as James Rucker, Richard Cave,
John Sutton, Donald Homes and a number of exhorters and
prayerful men in public, so that it seemed I could be very
well spared from that place; John Tanner had also lately
moved into the neighborhood much of a preacher, but not
a man of the most peaceable cast; Tanner had married
Rucker's daughter and soon stired him up to think, that the
baptists in Kentucky, were too corrupt in doctrine, and
discipline to continue any longer in union with them; they
therefore contemplated a new, pure and separate church;
John Penny a respectable minister had lately moved from
Virginia, and settled on Salt River south of Kentucky,
these men prevailed on Penny, to go into this new church
state with them; they constituted a church on Salt River,
under the appellation of "Baptists Reformed," there were
about ten members in this new church and three of them
ordained ministers—their plan was to receive no member in
this new, pure church, but by experience and good character, a letter of dismission from any other Church was with
them, only so much for nothing, but they had not progressed
long before Penny began to think he had a hard bargain,
though they had made him pastor of the new church; for
pure as they were, they soon fell out among themselves, and
this new fabric fell like Jonah's goard—Penny called for
helps from neighboring churches, and constituted what is
now Salt River church and has continued a member thereof
ever since; Tanner moved to Shelby county, Rucker returned
his membership to Clear Creek, but whether the confidence of
his brethren became impaired or he lost confidence in himself
after this Salt River enterprise, I cannot say, but his usefulness in Clear Creek was not so sensibly known afterwards; he moved to the lower end of this state, and is yet
living a very old and respectable man; John Sutton, who was
now old, became what they called a mighty scolder in the
church, perhaps he was a Welchman, and high temper the
more congenial to him thereby; but so it was, great as his
preaching talents were; for in rich expositions from the scrip-

tures he had few equals; yet he scolded himself out of credit
in the church; he was a principal leader in the emancipating
question, and became so turbulent that some of the members treating with him in the church, Carter Tarente who
was of the same opinion with Sutton in emancipation,
espoused his cause in the church, and by which a rent took
place, both in Clear Creek and Hillsborough churches; a
number of members uniting with Tarente formed New
Hope church, where Sutton and Tarente set up the first
emancipating church in this part of the world. Thus Clear
Creek lost John Sutton, he became blind but continued to
travel and preach, and died about eighty years of age;
Mr. Tarrente traveled and preached in Kentucky with great
acceptance, had alternately served the church at Clear Creek
and Hillsborough. After his connection with the emancipators, he became reduced in his worldly circumstances; took
a Chaplin's place in the army, went to New-Orleans to fulfil his commission and there he died. Holmes had also gone
off with the emancipators, so that Richard Cave only was
left at Clear Creek; but other visitors often attended—In the
great revival in Kentucky- about the close of the last century,
Clear Creek greatly partook of this blessing, so that the
church grew up to about five hundred members, a principal
instrument in this great revival was Richard Cave. For
several years Clear Creek had kept up two places of worship, at different meeting houses, they now contemplated
a division; Hillsborough church was constituted with perhaps a hundred and fifty members at the beginning. Hillsborough church has been attended by different preachers,
but by none of equal advantage, as that laborious servant
of the Lord Edmond Waller—under his ministrations they
have had several happy revivals, and is now a growing
prosperous church. But old Clear Creek has for many years
seemed to be on the decline. Though perhaps no place in
Kentucky has been better supplied as to preaching talents;
Mr. Jacob Creath served them statedly for many years, in
which time they were rich enough to build them a large
Brick Meeting House, but they have found that the best

of riches does not consist of a fine house. Mr. Henry Toler for several years past has served them as a pastor; but things have not worked quite so well as was hoped for in the beginning; he has lately left them, and in a manner destitute; they have only one young preacher among them, and though he is a member there, he has not been ordained. May this old mother church pray the Lord of the harvest to send forth labourers; they have yet a number of valuable members, and I was pleased not long since among them to discover such a cry as this; "Lord revive us." Taylor, *op. cit.*, pp. 49–81.

CORN CREEK CHURCH

I had gotten a flat bottom boat, to move my household furniture, and year's provision down the river, sixty or seventy miles, to Mount Byrd—this provision seemed needful, as I was going into the woods, my boat sunk into the river, with chief of my effects in it, and though the clear loss was only about a hundred dollars, yet many of my things were much injured by getting wet. We had some rough cabins prepared to go into, but surrounded by one of the heaviest forest's I ever saw—it was now late in March, and our bread to get the next year, only about four acres cleared and no fence around it, was our beginning at Mount Byrd. I had acquired some acquaintance with the people from my visits there; but my wife was a perfect stranger to all, a young church of perhaps twenty members, had been constituted not long before I moved, and was called Corn Creek Church, the place of worship was about four miles from Mount Byrd. The opposite shore of the Ohio, was Indian title, and the Indians hunting on their own land about a mile from my house, but they were at peace. At the first monthly meeting of the little church (Corn Creek) after our arrival at Mount Byrd, myself and family, gave our membership to the church. After I was received by the church, I informed them, that I had joined them as a member, and with no office authority among them, that though I had been long a preacher, it was not by their sanction as a church, that I was now at their disposal as one of their members, that if they required any ministerial service from me, I expected them to signify it, otherwise I should not make free among them in that way. Perhaps what myself said, brought on the same day a request to take the Pastoral care of the church. Perhaps I had Baptized more than half the members that were in the church, at the times of my visits there before I moved. The older brethren did not hesitate at that request, as they had no other preacher in the church but myself. I then opened up my own views of particular pastorship, that myself was never calculated for it, that I was ready to do any service I was capable, without that particular charge. With which the church was perfectly content— and has had no particular pastor since.

As to our earthly concerns, we had never seen such heavy labour before us, to obtain support, as now.—We had no time to pause and think, but go right on to work, the timber quite green, and standing very thick—consisting of various sorts, as Poplar, Beach, Walnut, Ash, and other kinds, with the largest kind of Buck-eye, three or four feet through, with their trunks an hundred feet long. It was usual to get from three and four, to seven and eight cuts of rails from a tree—many of the poplars were six or seven feet through, and their length an hundred feet without a limb. The looks of the soil encouraged us to rush on, in hopes of future reward—I had at that time three strong black men, and a boy and as many black women, who could help us burn brush, and roll logs. My two sons, one eighteen and the other sixteen years old, and myself, now in a manner in the prime of life, though upwards fifty years old. The sound of our axes made entertaining musick in this mighty forest. My wife and daughters, with a black woman or two in the house, made the wheels roar in our large cabins, with also the use of a loom there, made it probable that we should get food and raimant. Another thing in our favour, though for several years, we had been afflicted with sickness, the sweet air and water of the lofty bluff of Mount Byrd, restored us all to good health again. We first enclosed twenty-five acres of land in two apartments, thirteen of which we planted in corn, and two in flax and vegetables. We had ten barrels of corn per acre that year, that, with the help of a good beach mast, made us bread enough, and to spare. After laying by our corn, we cleared our ten acres we had enclosed, and put it in wheat—we then enclosed twenty five acres, with a design to clear it next winter—and twenty acres more we enclosed for the use of a pasture. After we had cleared our intended ground the next winter, we had taken down so much timber, that we found the log rolling prodigious heavy. I took notice that we spent thirty days in log rolling—and after which it was more trouble to burn up this green timber than to roll it. However, after we had planted our corn, we concluded to go to building. We did but little at brick making till after harvest, when we moved on with rapidity—we made about an hundred thousand bricks, put up a house seventy feet by twenty-two, a stone cellar under the whole of it, and forty feet of it two stories above the cellar—before Christmas had it all covered in, and moved into one end of it in February. We then cleared the ground we had enclosed, and enclosed twenty acres more for pasture—so that when we had been at Mount Byrd two years we had seventy acres of cleared land, twenty more enclosed, living in the house I have described, and a very great orchard, of apple, peach, and other kinds of fruit, so that in Gallatin county, I was a little like Job when he lived in the east, in the early days of his prosperity. It is probable, I was the richest man in the county, where I lived—but wise providence has found a way, to put me in different circumstances, since that time. I do not recollect paying one dollar for labour in making all this improvement, except to mechanics. Should it be asked if our labour was not too severe, I should no doubt answer in the affirmative—but it was all done with great pleasantness, for I have found both by experience and observation, that when master goes, all the rest goes cheerfully to business.

Through the course of this two years, I preached but little, except on Saturday's and Sunday's, or of nights. I was commonly at Church meetings on those days somewhere— and in the time of the year for associations, I commonly went to a number of them, the settlement in which I lived did not admit of much preaching, fifty families perhaps, were the amount of all the people, and they had much to do to get their living in this heavy timbered country.—The settlement however, increased, and the church at Corn-creek grew, though but slowly—there had been a revival in the place, as I have named, before I moved there. And perhaps in two or three years after I joined the church, at different times, I Baptized about twenty people, the church being then about sixty in number. And I think she never grew higher from about eighty till I moved from the place. Amen Vawter moved from Bullitsburg and joined Corn Creek Church. He was a respectable preacher, and one of the best of men; his example preached loud to the world. Soon after his arrival at Corn Creek, the Church thought proper to ordain him—this gave me great pleasure, to have a fellow-labourer in the Lord; and in the church he was of great usefulness, till he moved to Indiana—something of his biography I have given elsewhere.

Corn-creek church, though they treated with all their members according to the eighteenth of Matthew, so far as was practicable, and though their final exclusions were by unanimity of voices, yet there was not that harmony of sentiment as might be wished for; they often differed as to the mode of doing church business, this at times brought about bickerings between the members, in harsh speeches and sulky looks; and though it did not come to tumults, yet their forerunners were sometimes seen, which Paul calls swellings, which is only another word for poutings; which is a very unbecoming thing among the followers of the meek and lowly Saviour. Methodist influence began in Corn-creek settlement soon after Baptist worship was set up there; this divided the people at large, and the contest between the parties was the warmer as the strength of members was about equal on each side; with all my attachment to my fine Mount Byrd, some things began to turn up to embitter the place to me; in the first place Vawter moved away, which was a great draw back on my peace and happiness. I had built a great barn, first of brick and added to it with timber, so that it was very spacious; I had filled it with the greatest crop of small grain I had ever raised; soon after I had housed it, the same kind of fire that killed Jobs sheep and servants, destroyed my barn, a flash of lightning as in a moment burnt it down; perhaps a thousand bushels of grain were burnt with the barn, the whole loss at least a thousand dollars; this was done when I was on a tour of preaching, from one association to another, this bespoke to me that the author of this fire, would have me leave the place,[7] so that if I was a little like Job in one case, I was also a little like him in another, and though my children were not all dead, yet two of them had died at Mount Byrd. Another strong reason for leaving the place, the town of Madison sprung up opposite to where I lived, and its inhabitants trafficking with the negroes for all that they brought to market, and my absence from home, and always on Sundays placed everything I had in jeopardy; but the greatest reason of all was, a partial loss of my repute among the people; this thing worked like spreading of leaven, and a number of the people seemed to have the strongest malice against me; I was presented to the grand jury as having committed a trespass on the public good; a school house had been built at the meeting house for which I had paid my quota of money, and where we often preached in the winter, the door was locked and I had reasons to think it was to keep me from preaching in it. I often thought of what the Lord said to Ezekiel 2d. Chap. 6th Verse about dwelling among Scorpions; some of the church I found was prejudiced against me; it was some time before I could conjecture what root of bitterness all this had sprung from, but be it what it would, my mind was made up to leave the place, and that from the Saviour's direction, where if

[7] Like Mr. Taylor's attitude toward dreams, this conception that misfortune is a means used by the Lord to convey his will, was not peculiar to the Baptists. When a second attempt of the Methodists to establish a school had been defeated by fire, Bishops Coke and Asbury, just a few years before this misfortune in the life of Mr. Taylor, had declared that by such loss of the college they perceived that God purposed that the Methodists should not build schools but should give their energy to preaching.

they persecute you in one city flee to another; I knew that some of the best friends I had in the world, were in Corn-creek church who from the storm of vengeance they saw among some of the people, gave it as their opinion, that it would be best for me to move away; the origin of all this mighty spleen came from one single circumstance.

A member of the church, and a man of considerable influence had joined the Free Masons [8]; about forty miles from home, and was in that connection some time before the church had any knowledge of it—a complaint being brought into the church against him for that act, the business for a decision was laid over till their next meeting; knowing that I as one should have to give my voice in the church on this affair—I procured the constitution of the Lodge at Shelby-ville and gave it a reading, for my own information. A large gathering of people came to the next meeting, to hear a trial in the church about Free Masonry; I took the liberty to make a pretty long speech on the mysteries of that subject, in the hearing of a number of the Masonic brethren, for they were increasing fast at this time in our settlement; I confessed as they claimed its great antiquity, that it probably existed before any of the scriptures were written, that it was an

[8] This antipathy to the Masonic Order was a part of the general feeling against secret organizations of any kind, which reached its height in the National Anti-Masonic Party, operative even in national affairs at the close of the first quarter of the nineteenth century. Baptists were not alone in holding such an attitude as that expressed here by Mr. Taylor. According to Mr. McCarthy, author of "The Anti-Masonic Party," the Presbyterian Synod of Pittsburgh declared in 1821 that the "Masonic institution is unfit for professing Christians." A little later that Church "took a decided stand against the society throughout the country, bade its members renounce it, and its laymen to sever all connection with it and to hold no fellowship with Masons. . . ."

"What the Presbyterians were to the West the Congregationalists were to New England and eastern New York. They attacked at one and the same time the Unitarians, Universalists, and the Masons. . . ."

"As early as 1823 the General Methodist Conference prohibited its clergy from joining the Masons in Pennsylvania, and during the Masonic excitement it was said by the Antimasons that 'no religious sect throughout the United States has done more for the Anti-masonic cause than the Methodists.' It forbade its members to join lodges or to be present at any of their processions or festivals, and passed strict rules against ordaining any ministers who belonged to the order." (See McCarthy, "The Anti-Masonic Party," published in the *Annual Reports of the American Historical Association*, 1902, I, pp. 542–543.)

excellent institution, when first introduced among men, to
bring them from barbarism to some degree of civilization,
and unite one man to another, and a number of men into a
kind of civilized community, and by their compact they were
bound to do each other good, and moralize their own behaviour, all of which was very good, and had been of great
use to ancient beings of our race, but that it was of as little
use now, as the moon and stars are when the sun is shining;
and that their modes of tuition, even in their Lodges, were
so dark and figurative, that weak minds could not easily
get into it. If the pupil looked at an Operative Mason, with
his apron on, his hammer in his hand, his compass, his trowel,
his square, or all this figure on paper for his contemplation,
he studies the hammer, by which the uneven parts of the
stone is taken off, and with the square shaped off at right
angles to fit it for the building—so the schollar must moralise
himself by smoothing in his conduct, as the Operative Mason
did the rock—Again, the square, with exactly as many
inches as hours in a whole day, and then going off with an
exact square, so all his conduct must be regular to fit him
for society—when he studied the compass with its exact
circles, or the trowel in using the morter or cement to unite
one rock to another, teaching the consolidating of affection,
and interest between man and man, and smoothed off as with
the trowel in brotherly friendship—As morality was the
highest object of the whole establishment, the author of our
being has given us a more excellent way in the Bible, and
especially in the new testament, in which the brightest
morality and spirituality of heart is made known in the
most explicit style—and moreover, Free Masons in general,
with all their fine system of morality, were not the most
moralized men as to their actions.

I considder it a very weak thing, for a christian to give up
his privileges in the church of Christ, for the half handed
morality that was found in a Masonic Lodge. Though I
professed no knowledge of any of their bye-laws, yet the
doctrine I had propagated was a natural deduction from
their constitution; I know not whether I ever had a more

attentive assembly of hearers in my life. I then made a proposition which was agreed to by a majority of the church; to give the man in question, two months to give an answer, whether he would finally leave the Masonic Lodge, or loose his place in the church; to this a number of the church objected, saying he ought to repent for the sin he had committed—to this proposition at the given time he affected to comply; but was not as good as his word afterwards. I knew of no Masonic man present that was offended at my remarks in the church, but their progress was rather with friendly overtures—to these I made but little reply, till at length a judge of a court, from the opposite side of the river, waited on me with overtures so explicit, that I was compelled to be plain; this friendly judge was very zealous in the cause, and no doubt had friendship for me, such as it was. After illustrating the utility, advantages and excellency of Masonry, plainly importuned me to cast my lot among them; the only short reply I made was about as follows: "that it would by no means suit me to be a Mason, that if it was a good thing, I would not keep the secret, and if it was a bad thing I would not keep the secret, but would warn the people against it; and if there was neither good nor harm in it, of course it was not worth having." Finding a number of the church dissatisfied about the man who had joined the Masons, and he being a deacon of the church, they could not receive the ministration from his hands.

I made a proposition in the church, to dismiss him from his office under existing circumstances; this the church immediately accorded in—this I soon found stung him to the quick—esteeming me the instrument of his degradation in the church, seemed determined to be revenged, if we judge from his actions afterwards—and the generality of his Masonic brethren co-operated with him, which brought forward the whole sweep of vengeance spoken of above, for though he had given his word to the church to forsake the Lodge, he did not do it. The influence of the man may be known, by his being twice elected after this by the county, to the Legislature of Kentucky—others who united with him for my destruction, were men of much influence. With deep concerted and secret council, the presentment was laid before the grand jury, while to my face they were fair and mild; I was at the court, and in friendly conversation with the men the day that this transaction took place—but I had left the court house before the presentment was made; I understood it was brought forward by a harmless old Dutchman—these cunning men made him think though they were on the grand jury themselves, that he would be forsworn if he did not bring on this kind of indictment. The great crime committed against the commonwealth—a man who lived with me, in taking in a bit of new ground had run a corner of his fence over an old forsaken road, which they called a public one; I was of course legally called on to answer for the crime—it soon spread through my neighborhood and perhaps through the county; some said I was indited, others that I was presented; the magnitude of the crime was hardly known, but it would come forward next term in all its glowing colours. The attorney for the commonwealth and the judge himself, neither of whom had ever been at my house before, came about six miles out of their way on Saturday night before the court; their object I presume was to see the spot themselves where the trespass was committed —they passed by the place in the morning myself with them, going to a meeting I had; when the business came on, a respectable man of the bar of my acquaintance who knew the whole affair of this trespass, volunteered his services to make a short statement to the court, to which the commonwealth's attorney scarcely replied, and the charge dismissed by the judge, in perhaps ten minutes after it was taken up, to the great mortification of those vengeful men. This as might be looked for, was very far from curing their malicious fever, which I might give in many more instances, but time would fail. I have no doubt that thousands among the most honorable men in our nation, are what is called Free Masons, but it did not happen to be of that kind into whose hands I fell, neither have I ever known a Baptist, who joined that order of people, that was ever of much use in a church afterwards—the man spoken of is a striking instance. In this mighty blast some of the church became prejudiced against me, for those active men, were very influential, and some of their kindred belonged to the church—one of the members said to another, who was prejudiced, that it was the same spirit, that was working against me in the neighborhood, that had put Jesus Christ to death long ago. I had now been a preacher upwards of forty years, and had never been in the same situation I now was; being in less credit as a preacher at home than abroad—being now in the habit of travelling the greater part of my time, on long tours, and by visiting many associations, acquired an extensive acquaintance with the Baptists, had a stranger attended our meetings at Corncreek, he would not have known but that I was popular in the place, for even those who disliked me frequently came to meetings, though perhaps from no better motive than the Pharisees followed the Saviour. Not long before I left the place, at one of our Sunday meetings, I took this text, "The harvest is great but the labourers are few, pray ye the Lord of the harvest &c." My own soul was enlarged with prayerful desire, that the Lord would send preaching there, that would be more useful to the people than mine had been, and also urged the people to thus pray—it was soon reported, that I got so mad with the people that I even wept when I was preaching. The reader has seen already that the origin of all this storm seemed to be from Free Masonry, but it may be remembered that only a few men of that order was at the bottom of the whole of it, for others of the same connection treated me with the affection of a brother, holding those others in contempt for their conduct—one instance was the gentleman of the bar already spoken of, who volunteered my case in court, and would afterwards receive no compensation.

When I reflect soberly, my own opinion is, that the root of all these difficulties was with God himself, as a just visitation for my sins. I esteem the deceiptfulness of sin, in its subteraneous and serpentine windings, an overmatch for any man on earth, where the fear of God is but little removed from his heart, a jealous God will not admit a rival. When we moved

from Bullittsburg to Mount Byrd, we soon emerged from
great family affliction, into a state of Great health, and
though we did a great deal of hard labour, yet prosperity
attended our efforts for a number of years, till with my fine
Mount Byrd, and two thousand acres of valuable land on the
River connected with it, besides other valuable lands at a
distance, I owned about twenty slaves, clear of debt and had
a considerable amount of stock in different banks; my children growing up, and bid fair to recommend themselves to the
world. Putting all together no doubt became a thief on my
heart, though unperceived by myself or others—for I do not
know that any person considered me in any other light than a
zealous man in religion, for I do not recollect that worldly
business ever prevented my attending one of my thousands
of meetings that I have appointed, for near fifty years past—
but a holy God does not see as man sees, three times he was
displeased with holy Moses. First, for not circumcising his
son, and sought to slay him at the inn—secondly, for pleading
an excuse, desiring Aaron to be sent to Pharoah instead of
himself, and for which it is probable God deprived him of an
eloquent tongue as long as he lived—and thirdly, his intemperate spirit, and unadvised lips at the waters of Meribah, for
which he was forbid going into the promised land—all of
which might seem innocent in the eyes of men; with many
other instances in the scriptures confirming this saying—
"I the Lord your God, am a jealous God."

For David's sin of pride (unperceived by himself) in num-
bering the people, which was a very common thing in Israel,
seventy thousand men lost their lives; and for another sin of
his, the son of his own loins stole the hearts of the people, and
God bid Shimai to curse him. For the idolatry of Solomon
and the folly of his son Rehoboam, God raised up a Jero-
boam, by whom ten tribes were rent from the house of David.
So true is that saying of Solomon, that "when a man's ways
please the Lord, he maketh his enemies to be at peace with
him"—David, in the 17th psalm 13th verse, speaks of the
wicked as God's sword, and hand or rod of correction, and
though I felt as if I dwelt among Scorpions; and though as

to my course among men, I could with all my examination
see nothing of which I could accuse myself, yet from the
appostacy of my affections from the Lord, I concluded that
God's own way of chastising was the best, and was almost
ready to excuse these men, and pray the Lord to pardon
their folly and sin.

I left Corn-creek in March 1815 after living at Mount
Byrd thirteen years—the church at Corn-creek while I
lived there had grown but slowly; I had Baptized while there,
perhaps about thirty people; I think they were about eighty
in number when I left them, after which they invited supplies
from abroad for a year or two; a young speaker moving into
the bounds of the church was licensed to preach among them,
his name was Wallace; a George Kendall who was Baptized
at Corn-creek, began also to speak in public and was licensed
by the church, but by what I could learn, the people at large,
as also some of the church paid but little attention to those
young preachers for some time, till at length a William Buckley was invited to attend them, and from appearances of
success, he moved and lived among them two or three years.

Under his labours, and the zealous efforts of the younger
preachers, a considerable revival took place, so that in one
year Mr. Buckley Baptized upwards of a hundred people.
Mr. Buckley attended several other churches about this
time, and was successful at them all, but at length moved his
family to the lower end of the state, and like my poor self, left
the church in less credit as a preacher than when he came to it.

The church was again left with their two young preachers,
but they had grown, so that public worship was kept up with
respectability—however, they soon contemplated a new
church for the sake of convenience; they constituted a church
called Hunters Bottom, on the River, this new establishment
included Mr. Wallace, whom the new church has ordained
since their constitution.

Corn-creek, has only George Kendall as a preacher among
them—his correctness of opinion in Gospel doctrines, his
orderly deportment in general, his zeal for the cause of
gospel religion, and his aptitude to explain the Bible, (which

is almost the only book he reads)—has led the church to take up the subject of his ordaination, but it was found that the church was much more willing to ordain than he was to receive it. Corn-creek has existed as a church upwards of twenty years, perhaps their number at present is an hundred and thirty or forty. When I left Corn-creek the sensation with myself was entirely of a new stamp; when I left any other place before, the solicitous voice of the people was for me to stay, and this gave me pain of mind. The thing was quite reversed, and this gave me greater pain, for I knew not whether I had a friend under existing circumstances, that wished me to stay longer. [Taylor, *op. cit.*, pp. 115–127.]

BUCK RUN CHURCH

The Constitution of Buck Run Church.

As there has been a good deal of likeness in the faith and practice of the ten churches, of which I have alternately been a member for fifty years past—I think proper to give the Constitution, and rules of decorum, of Buck Run Church, at length.

Church covenant [9]—unanimously agreed to by the church —as we hope a number of us, have long since given ourselves to the Lord, we do this day in the divine presence, give ourselves in a church compact, to one another, and do solemnly covenant and agree to fulfil the duty of brethren to each other—not to expose each others faults, but in the true

[9] There are certain necessary steps which must be taken, else there can be no proper organization at all. These necessary things are two: viz., covenant and creed. Now it is not necessary that these names should always be applied, but the things which are under-stood by these names are absolutely essential to the organization of a church. A covenant is necessary, that is to say, a voluntary act by which Christians enter into relation one with another as members of a church. There must be some action of this sort. It is not necessary to adopt a form of words called a covenant, nor is it necessary to use the term covenant at all. This is simply a convenient designation, but there must be an act of union and a voluntary entering into union, or there can be no organized church life. . . .

The other constitutive element may be called a creed, that is, the doctrinal basis on which the voluntary union just described takes place. Here, again, it is not necessary to adopt any printed or written declaration of faith. This creed is not always, nor even necessarily, expressed by any formal symbol, but some kind of doctrinal agreement must lie at the root of the organization, or it cannot be a church. (Edwin C. Dargan, *Ecclesiology*, pp. 128–129.)

letter and spirit of the Gospel. That we will not forsake the assembling ourselves together, but fill our seats, both in meetings of business, and public worship, except providentially hindered. That we will watch over each other in brotherly tenderness, each endeavoring to edify his brother; striving for the benefit of the weak of the flock; to raise up the hands that hang down, and strengthen the feeble knees; making strait paths for our feet, least that which is lame be turned out of the way.

That we will bear each other's burdens, and so fulfil the law of Christ; and as the Lord has prospered us, bear a proportionable part of the expense, to keep up the worship of God in decency—and in token of our above agreement, give each other our hands, and hearts. And as it is needful to have some epithet to distinguish our church from another, our appellation, and the future style of our records, shall be "The Baptist Church of Christ on Buck Run"—and our monthly meetings to be held the last Saturday in each month, with the Lords day following—January 31, 1818.

Met at Brother Wilsons, day and date above, according to appointment, for the purpose of constituting a Baptist Church, elder William Hickman moderator, elder Silas M. Noel clerk; with the above ministers, James Sugget, John H. Ficklin, Mordeica Boulware, Theodorick Boulware; all those ministers agreed to give agency, in the constituting of the above named church.

Names of the Members in the Constitution

John Taylor	John Graves
Elizabeth Taylor	Catharine Graves
Benjamin Taylor,	Elizabeth Gatewood,
Presly Neal,	John Price,
Fanny Neal,	Susannah Price,
Julius Blackburn,	Lewis Nall,
Elizabeth Blackburn,—	Jane Nall,
Francis Castleman,	Love B. Fuller,
Isaac Wilson,	Lucy Wilson,
Nancy Triplett	Sally Head,
Lucy Nall.	

In all twenty-one, agreed to go into a constitution; the following articles after examination, were unanimously adopted:

1st. There is but one true and living God—the maker and preserver of all created beings, visible and invisible; and that in this adorable God-head, there are three personal relations, as Father, Son, and Holy Ghost; and these three are one—equal in glory, dignity, eternity, and power. Though as to the true humanity of Jesus Christ, he is often spoken of in the New Testament as inferior to the Father.

2nd. That the scriptures of the Old and New Testament, as stated in their canonical books, is the uniform doctrine of faith; and that this sacred volume is the only infallible rule of all our faith, and practice.

3d. That by the disobedience of the first Adam, all his posterity became guilty, and sinful in every part, and helpless as to any aid they can give, in the great work of converting their own souls.

4th. That according to God's fore-knowledge, previous to time, he did predestinate his people to life—and being chosen in Christ, before the world began, he did as our second Adam, the Lord from heaven, assume human nature, yet without sin—and by his obedience, in his incarnation, making an atoning sacrifice for sin, brought in an everlasting righteousness for the rebellious— and when said blessed merit, is imputed, or applied to them through faith in his blood, they are thereby justified before God, and being effectually called by his grace and holy spirit, shall finally persevere therein, to happiness and eternal glory.

5th. Since the day of the Apostles, there is no higher ecclesiastical authority on earth, than the congregated worshiping church of Christ; being God's heritage here below; Their right is to govern themselves by their own voices, select their own officers, as Bishops and Deacon's, the only officers now known in the church of Christ; these are their servants, for Christ's sake, So that no conclave of bishops, or any council appointed by themselves, or even their own officers, have a right to Lord it over the church.

6th. As it is appointed, for men once to die, there shall also, be a resurrection, both of the just and unjust; on which awful day, Jesus Christ will judge all men in righteousness; when the wicked shall go into everlasting punishment, and the righteous into life eternal.

7th. We consider baptism valid, only by profession of faith, and immersing the whole body under water.

8th. We do most seriously consider, the preaching of repentance, and the invitation of the gospel to all characters of men, to be one of the most interesting subjects of the gospel ministry, and that they who persecute, neglect or disobey the gospel, more highly aggravate their own guilt.

To manifest our good will and charitableness towards our brethren, who may somewhat differ from us, in some of the above doctrines—we do most cheeffully accord in the terms of the general union of Baptists in Kentucky, which are as follows:

1st. That the scriptures of the old and new Testament, are the infallible words of God, and the only rule of faith and practice.

2nd. That there is but one only true God, and in the Godhead or divine essence, there are Father, Son, and Holy Ghost.

3rd. That by nature, we are depraved fallen creatures.

4th. That salvation, regeneration, sanctification and justification, are by the life, death, resurrection and ascension of Jesus Christ.

5th. That the saints will finally persevere through grace to glory.

6th. That believers Baptism, by immersion, is necessary to receiving of the Lord's supper.

7th. That the salvation of the righteous, and the punishment of the wicked will be eternal.

8th. That it is our duty to be tender and affectionate to each other, and study the happiness of the children of God in general and to be engaged singly to promote the honor of God.

9th. And that preaching "Christ tasted death for every man, shall be no bar to communion."

Whereupon, Buck Run church was pronounced constituted.

Rules of decorum for said church

1st. The business of the church to be done the last Saturday of every month, beginning at twelve o'clock, any free male member failing to attend, shall be accountable to the church for such neglect.

2nd. A moderator to be chosen by a majority of voices, and until another is chosen; he is to preside in the church while at business, he is to keep order, but always under the control of a majority of the church—he is to withhold his own opinion, until all other members who wish to speak have spoken, except by the request of the church; he shall take the voice of the church when called on for that purpose.

3rd. When the church is met, after prayer, members of sister churches to be invited to seats, who may give their light on any subject, but not vote in the decision of the case—the moderator to then enquire are all in fellowship, or has any a matter of complaint to bring forward, that has been treated in gospel order.

4th. The unfinished business of the church, if any, to be now attended to, after which a door may be opened for the reception of members.

5th. Any brother having a motion, or speech to make in the church, shall rise from his seat and address the moderator with brotherly respect—a motion thus made not to be attended to without a second.

6th. No brother to be interrupted while speaking, except he depart from the subject, on which the moderator or any other brother may call to order—of which point of order the church may judge, when applied to for that purpose.

7th. No brother shall speak more than twice on any subject without leave from the church.

8th. There shall be no laughing, talking, or whispering in the time of a public speech, nor shall there be any ungenerous reflections on a brother who has spoken before.

9th. Any business in which particular fellowship is not affected may be done by a majority of voices.

10th. Any member being accused and found guilty of a crime and unanimity cannot be had for exclusion, a majority may suspend from privilege till satisfaction can be given.

11th. In the great affair of receiving into membership or of final exclusion, unanimity is required.

12th. That brother love may continue, the direction given by the Saviour in the 18th of Matthews is to be attended to, in all cases so far as practicable in treating with our brethren, and in all uncommon cases the church to be the judge, and in all public transgressions, acknowledgments are to be made to the church.

13th. We consider it the duty of members, in removing their residence to distant bounds, to apply to the church for a letter of dismission, and join some other church, with speed or as soon as duty and prudence may dictate.

Having given the Constitution of Buck Run Church, with its mode of government at length, by which the creed of my own heart on those subjects is very fully expressed; and these are not the mere ideas of a day, but my unwavering opinion from my youth—that whoever may look on the items above may see the complexion of my whole soul in thealogy. I had thought of making some enlargement on those constitutional articles, but they stand explicit for themselves—by them I have lived long, by them I expect to die, which I hope is not far distant—but always with this reserve in that article "the will of the Lord be done"—as to the terms of the general union of Baptists in Kentucky, as named in the constitution of Buck Run Church, I as fully accord in them as I did in the beginning—a few imprudent individuals shall not drive me from that salutary measure.

At the time of the constitution of Buck Run Church there was a small revival in the neighborhood, and spreading more largely through many parts of Scott county. At the Great-Crossings they Baptized many about this time; at the North Fork, and the Forks of Elkhorn, two neighboring churches, and very near on each side of Buck Run, a number were baptized.

After we became a little composed as a church at Buck Run, I named to them what I have generally done when I became a member of a church—that I had united as a mere member in a church capacity with them and with no office hanging round me, as to them, in their now church state— that though no other preacher belonged to them as a member but myself, I could not make free in any office work among them as a church, except they some way signified it by their own voice—I was a little amused, when some of them proposed for me to walk out, while they counseled on that subject—to which I replied, if they could not look me in the face and speak what they thought on that occasion, they did not

deserve a name in the house of God—and if I could not bear
with patience whatever they might say, I did not deserve
the name of gospel minister—however, it was taken up in
my presence and myself acting as their moderator, in which
I was equally officious as if they were talking of another
man, while they seemed to act and converse in that independent godly simplicity, which gave evidence that they neither
designed to cringe or flatter—but so it was, there was no dissenting voice at my serving them as a preacher; but they had
forgotten to ask my consent, but it is probable they concluded I would not deny— when the business of the day was
read at the close, the clerk had recorded that I was called to
the pastoral care of the church; after hearing my explanation,
and my aversion to that kind of charge as to myself, the record was changed, that I had agreed to preach for them once
a month, and administer ordainances till they could be
otherways or better supplied—we have been on the same
footing, on that head, for upwards of five years. I have
named a little revival when Buck Run became a church;
we soon began to Baptize some, but this has but sparingly
continued; I suppose first and last, we have Baptized between twenty and thirty since Buck Run became a church,
and these were mostly soon after our constitution; we have
grown up to the number of about sixty members; we have
very few black members among us—and another thing in our
favour, we have very few rich men among us—for very often
by rich men and negroes the cause of religion suffers much—
for while one is above, the other is below its native Godlike
dignity. Buck Run has built a snug little brick meeting
house, forty feet by thirty, it is comfortable to worship in.
From the local situation of Buck Run, it is not likely to
become a numerous church—it is adjoining and surrounded
by a very thick Catholic settlement, with their Priest and
great Cathedral not far from Buck Run; neighboring Baptist
churches also very near and in all directions; but taking this
little young church by and large, they are rather a happy
people than otherwise—and though that warm glow of brotherly love is not often seen among them, they are peaceable

among themselves—there has been but one legal complaint, ever yet brought into the church, and that was against a poor negro, who was excluded. When Buck Run had gotten their meeting house prepared to worship in, they concluded to have more preaching than once a month, therefore they invited the well known father Hickman, who filled up another Sunday in a month—after which they invited Mr. Theodoric Boulware to fill up another Sunday in the month—they were now pretty full of Sunday preaching; Mr. Boulware soon after this gave himself a member of Buck Run, when Mr. Hickman concluded that his labours would be more useful in more destitute places, and withdrew his services after preaching at Buck Run something more than one year. Mr. Boulware continues his preaching one Sunday in the month; he is much of a preacher, and considered very orthodox by all the high toned predestinarians—his preaching bears the semblance of a man snuffing a candle, as if he would take away from true religion, all the superfluities that could possibly mingle themselves with it—some are of opinion that at times he snuff's a little too deep; he has a greater aptitude to trim hypocrites, than to invite poor sinners to come to Christ. In Mr. Boulware's own way perhaps no man exceeds him—he has a fine voice both to speak and sing —speaks with uncommon elocution and is very popular with a certain case of christian man—whether Lambs fare as well under his ministrations as older sheep, is doubted by some. [Taylor, *op. cit.*, pp. 137–145.]

CHAPTER VII

THE AUTOBIOGRAPHY OF JACOB BOWER:
A FRONTIER BAPTIST PREACHER AND MISSIONARY

[The following autobiography was found in manuscript in the Library of Shurtleff College, Alton, Illinois. It was prepared at the request of the *Illinois Baptist Pastoral Union,* and was completed in 1857. Jacob Bower is representative of the average frontier Baptist preacher, and his autobiography is a revealing human document. He was born in Lancaster County, Pennsylvania, in 1786 of Dunker (German Baptist) parentage; came to Kentucky with his father when a youth of about nineteen years; was converted under Baptist influence in 1812 and about two years later began to preach. Some twelve years later he removed to Scott County, Illinois, because he disliked the idea of raising his family in a slave state. Here he continued in the ministry. In 1832 he accepted an appointment as a missionary under the Home Mission Society and for many years did valiant work, organizing new churches and forming circuits. From 1832, the year of his appointment as a home missionary to 1848 he traveled 40,925 miles; preached 2,931 sermons; aided in organizing 14 churches and ordained 12 ministers. His missionary work was performed in both Illinois and Missouri.]

To the Illinois Baptist Pastoral Union

Dear Brethren:

At a meeting of the pastoral Union held in Jacksonville October 1847. I, together with several other brethren was appointed to present a biographical sketch of my life to the next pastoral union to be held at Winchester in october 1848. And as we all failed to do so, we all, with an addition of six or seven others, were reappointed to present a sketch at the next meeting of the union to be held in Griggsville on thursday preceeding the 3rd saturday in oct. 1849.

I was born in Manheim Township, Lancaster county in

the State of Pensylvania, on the 26. day of September in the
year of our Lord 1786. When I was about three years old
my Father emigrated to what was then called the back woods
in Westmorland county. Early in the month of May before
I was six years old. I was sent to a German school, and by
the time I was six years old, I could read the New Testament.

Thank God for pious parents

I had a sister too young to go to school with me. My
parents belonged to the denomination of christians called
Tunkers, as early as I can recollect, my Father kept up
regular morning and eavning worship in the family. Commonly he would read a chapter in the German Testament,
then sing a hymn in German, then say a prayer in the same
language, and were taught to sing with them. We were
instructed in such lessons as we were able to understand,
such as this. Be good children, all good children when they
die will go to a good place, wher Jesus is, and many pretty
Angels, and they would be happy forever. Bad children
when they die will go to a bad place, where there is a great
fire, and the Devil and his Angels tormenting the wicked
forever. These instructions were ingraven on my mind, I
have never forgotten them, and were a means of continual
restraint from being wicked. In January after I was six
years old, the Lord took my good Mother home to Heaven,
and I wished very much to go withe her to the good place
she had gon to. I was yet unconcious of sin in myself, and
my anxiety to die and go to the good place wher Mother
was, greatly increased.

Sometime in July following, my Father brought home a
step Mother, and it was not long before my anxiety to die
increased more & more. Often I would steal out and sit
down by myself and weep with anxiety to die and go to the
place where Mother was. Thus it continued with me till
one morning in the month of May after I was seven years old.
About the breake of day, my Father, as his custom had been,
was offering up his mornin thanksgiving to God. And while
he was praying, I desired that I mite die and be wher Mother

was. But suddenly a thought came into my mind, that if I died I could not go to the good place, and I would never see Mother again, for she was good and had gon the good place. But I was bad, and if I died I must go to the bad place, and be tormented forever as Father had been telling me! This thought made me weep aloud as though I had been shiped; when Father ended his prayer, he asked, "What ailes you?" I said, I dont know. From that time I date my first awakening. I mention this because of some who are sceptical in relation to a child so young becoming concious of sin & punishment. Oh the great responsibility which rests upon parents with respect to the early education & training of their children. This kind of teaching, and the restraining grace of God, made a lasting impression, and had a powerful influence on my conduct in future life, so that it was often said of me, that I was quite a moral youth. I was kept from immorral· practises. I lived a farasee, trusting in my good name, and innocence, till I was in my nineteenth year.

My father hired me for twelve months to a man who was a respectable citizen, and an assistant Judge, he lived within one mile of a Baptist Meeting House. He was a warm friend to the Baptist cause, and his wife was a member of the church, and every first saturday in each month, he would send me to the meetinghouse to clean out the spring, which gave me an oppurtunity of being at meeting and hearing preaching once a month. I distinctly recollect a scene which transpired one afternoon at a baptizing, after the preacher came out of the water he gave a most thrilling exortation—I was situated on the oposite bank of the stream with some other youths, but even I was aware I found myself overwhelmed in a flood of tears, and I could not help it. I found myself on the other side among the multitude but could not recollect how I got there. When the congregation was dismissed, I wrung the tears out of my handkerchif. It was expected by some that I would soon unite with the church, I was a long time much concerned about my poor soul.

But alas for me, after this I fel into a snare of the fowler. One day a company was collected to repave the highway;

and a certain individual who professed himself to be a Universalist, he and the old Judge had a long argument on the subject, each of them made two or three speaches in turn. I began to think that if Universalism was true, there is no need of being so much concerned about my situation, I hoped that all would be well enough at last, and began to grow more careless about religion. About this time, I went in company with some eight or ten others about thirty miles to a Universalist love feast, as it was called, I stayed among them (I think) three days & nights, the result was that I imbraced their sentiments more fully.   I was taught to believe that "God so loved the world that he gave his only begotten Son, who taisted death for every man, he came not to condemn the world, but to save the world, and that he would do it, and he would not louse one of Adams race, but he would save all. I came to the conclusion that, if all the world are to be saved, I certainly would be included, therefore I was sure of Salvation. This kind of wind blew off all my convictions and trouble about my unhappy state. I was rocked to sleep in the cradle of Universalism for a little more than five years. Another sircumstance occured which drew me still deeper into the pit: two men of my aquaintance emigrated to the state of Indiana soon after my years service expiered with the old Judge, who persuaded me to go along with them. I concented & went, and stayed with them about five months. During this period I learned more wickedness, than I had learned in all my life. I became an inebriate, and fell into many immoralities. But by the restraining grace of God, I was kept from irreverently using his name. After my return from I—a in March 1807, I lived with my Father and made a crop. In December following I was maried and went to house keeping. And not withstanding I had wrapped myself up so secure in the doctrine of Universal salvation. Yet at times it would cloud up, and lighten & thunder so severe from Sinais mountain, and cause me much uneasiness for days together. However, the suposition of being saved at last would quiet me again.

My Father had previous to this emigrated to Shelby county K—y about 160 miles from where I resided in Muhlenberg county. About the first of October. 1811. I and my wife paid them a visit—stayed with them about ten days. A universalist Minister resided in the vicinity, and I made him several visits, who strengthened me some in the faith, I was verry fond of his company.

But when the time arived that we must lieve for hom, I felt unusually solemn. My Father accompanied us about four miles to a large creek, and now the time came that we must take the parting hand. I put on as chearful a countinance as posible, and said, Well Father, come let us take a parting *dram*, perhaps it may be the last we shall ever drink together. I dont want to drink a drop, said he, I have somthing to say to you, Jacob, Well Father, said I, what is it? "I want you to promise me,' said he, 'that you will serve God & keep out of bad company." Well Father I will, said I, Farewell, Farewell. I started to go accross the creek, which was about thirty yards accross, and as my horse steped out of the water to rise the bank, instantly my promise staired me in the face. Although he had given me the same council, and in the same words, perhaps an hundred times before, Yet it never produced such an impression on my mind as now. To serve God and keep out of bad company wrung in my ears all day long, I had promised my Father, and God heard it, that I would do it, but alas how can I, and he expects that I will do it. I began to feal in a way quite different from what I had ever done before. (begin here)

By the direction of my Father we stoped with a verry pious, good old Baptist, who was aquainted with my Father —put up with him for the night, I was restless—walking about—eat no super, often the deep sigh—my face in my hands &tc. My good old host made some enquieries about my Father, his family &c. and said that he thought verry highly of him, as being a pious good man. Not thinking to what kind of conversation my reply would lead us, I told him what the old Father had said to me at parting, and that I had promised to do so and the state of my mind in consequence of it. The good old man soon discovered what the matter was with me. Began most earnestly to exhort, and direct me to trust in the saviour. At the same time quoting many passages of scripture for my encouragement. But it was all dark to my understanding. I slept but little all night.

Early the next morning before it was quite light, we were on the road. But not without the good mans benediction. Soon we met large companies of Negro-s, we passed several companies, at length we met an old man walking by himself, I stoped him, and enquired of him, where they were all going so early this morning. The old negro said, "we are all going to Beards Town to see a fellow servent hung to day for killing his fellow servent." I started on with this thought, how does that man feal, knowing that he must die to day. Suddenly, as if some one had asked me. And how do you feal? You dont know but that you may die before he does. All of a sudden, (ah I shall never forget it) as if a book had been opened to me, the inside of which I had never seen: I got a sight of the wretchedness of my heart—a cage of every unclean and hateful thing. (ah thought I. here lies the root of bitterness, the fountain from whence all my sinful actions have flowed. My mind & heart have always been enmity against God, who is so holy that he cannot allow of no sin, however small it may appear in the sight of men. How can I ever be admited into Heaven with such a heart? it is utterly imposible. Lost, lost forever lost. Right here, and at this time my crumbly foundation of Universalism gave way. I discovered a just God, who, I thought, could not save me and remain just. I could see no way of escaping eternal punishment.

This day passed away as did the day before, almost in entier silence—four days brought us to my own house, at the sight of which I felt a momentary gladness. My sister who had kept house for us during our absence, met us at the gate and said, "why, Jacob, you look verry pale, have you been sick since you left home? I tryed to pass it by, and made some evasive reply, as though there was not much the matter with me.

It was the morning of the 14th day of October 1811. when the arrow of the Allmighty was made fast in my heart, somtimes I was almost in dispair, at other times I became careless and not so deeply concerned. But the ever memerable morning of the 17th day of December 1811. About 2 oclock A. M. when most people were in their beds sound asleep. There was an Earthquake, verry violent indeed. I and my wife both awoke about the same time, she spoke first, and said, Lord have mercy upon us, what is it shaking the house so? From a discription given of an Earthquake in Germany by a Tunkard preacher in a sermon when I was about ten years old, I immediately recognized it, and replied, it is an Earthquake. The Lord have mercy upon us, we shall all be sunk & lost, and I am not prepared. O God have mercy upon us all. I expected immediate distruction, had no hope of seeing the dawn of another day. Eternity, oh Eternity was just at hand, and all of us unprepared; just about the time the sun arose, as I supposed, for it was a thick, dark and foggy morning, there was another verry hard shock—lasted several minutes terible indeed. To see everything touching the earth, shakeing— quivering, trembling; and mens hearts quaking for fear of the approaching judgment. Many families ran together and grasped each other in their arms. One instance near to where I lived, the woman & five children, all gathered around her husband, crying O my husband pray for me, The children crying, Father, pray for me, O. pray for me, for the day of Judgment is come, and we are unprepared! The people relinquished all kinds of labour for a time, except feeding stock, and eat only enough to support nature a fiew days. Visiting from house to house, going to meeting Singing— praying, exoting, and once in a while ketch a sermon from a travelling Minister. Men, Women and children, everywhere were heard enquiering what they must do to be saved. This shaking continued more or less for near two years, sometimes just percievable. Deiists & Universalist in those days were scarce. But in relation to my own views and feelings. I thought that the time had been when I viewed many others much worse. and greater sinners than I was, and if they were saved, my chance for salvation was as good as theirs, and I was pretty sure of being saved. But now it appeared to me, that surely no one was as great a sinner as I, none had such a wicked heart, and such vile thoughts. God sees and knows them all, and they are an abomination in his sight. The time has been when God would have saved me, but I have passed by the day of his mercy, and I mite as well give over all hopes of being saved, and return to my former pleasures again. But my heart would respond, no, for it is sin I know that has undone me, and I cannot consent to go back into the practice of it again. I became resolved to press forward, I would pray & serve God though he send me to hell, yet I will lye at his feet and beg for mercy as long as I am out of hell. Sin now appeared exceeding sinful to me, I strove to shun it all. Holiness appeared of all things the most desierable but I could not attain to it. I often tryed to pray in the woods, but I felt no better, I could find no relief for my troubled conscience.

For several days past, I had been thinking about giving up to God, and resign myself into his hands, for I can do nothing to save myself, and all I do is so sinful in his sight that he disregards my cries & prayers. But a follish thought suggested itself to my mind, that I must not give up to God to do with me as he pleased, for I thought that the moment I did that, he would kill me and send me instantly to hell, and although I had long ago confessed that he would be just in so doing, Yet I was not willing that Justice should be executed, and I thought that as long as I was not willing, he would not do it. My toung never can till, nor my pen discribe, the struglings & anxities I passed through about this time.

All nature appeared to be dressed in mourning, and the god of nature frowning, oh what a time of melencholy.

Well, on the afternoon of the 8th day of February 1812. I saw one of my neighbors & his wife, passing by my house—going to his wifes fathers. I said to my wife, Robert & Anna are gon to her Fathers this eavning, suppose we go to your Fathers and spend the night with them, (it was about three miles) she readily consented and we went; when we arrived there, almost the first news we heard was. "Your cousin

Billy has professed to get religion and is as happy a man as I have ever seen." Joy filled my heart for only a moment, and dispair seized upon my mind. Ah, thought I; God has mercy in story for everybody, and everybody can be saved but me, for me there is no mercy, Gods mercy toards me is clean gon forever—I thought that I had seen the sun set, but alas for me I shall never see it rise again. Before the sun rises again I shall be dead and in hell. I ran away behind the barn and tryed to pray to God for mercy—returned but felt no better reconciled. The more I tryed to pray, the less hope I had of being saved. Just about midnight, I was sittin a chair, absorbed in deep thought about my condition—I well recollect thinking, Oh how much I do suffer in this world, it appeared to me as though the flames of hell kindled on me, where my greatest burdin was, right on my heart, I thought that my sufferings in this world were nothing to what they will be if I fall into the pit of ruin. Suddenly my thoughts turned to the sufferings of Christ, and what he endured on the cross. That he suffered in soul & body, his soul was exceeding sorrowful even unto death, sweting as it had been great drops of blood falling to the ground; and all his painful sufferings for the space of three hours on the cross, and that not for himself; it was for sinners that he thus suffered that they mite be saved. The next thought that passed through my mind was. If it was done for sinners, it was done for me. I believed it. The storm calmed off, my troubled My troubled soul was easy. I felt as light as a fether, and all was quiet—pieceful—tranquil and serene. This transpired about midnight, and I had not slept for several nights previous, for fear that if I went to sleep, I would awake in hell. I thought of lying down. I first walked out of doors, and everything I could see, appeared intierly new. The trees (I thought) lifted their hands up toards Heaven as if they were praising God. I cast my eyes upward, and beheld the bright twinkling stars shining to their makers praise. They appeared as so many holes through which I could look & see the glory of Heaven. Glory to God. Thank God. Bless the Lord O my soul, was busily runing throug my mind—What is the matter with me. I never felt so strange before, strange wonderful—wonderful indeed. A little while ago I felt as if I were hanging by a slender thread over the pit of ruin. God would not have mercy on me— Hell was my portion. God was just in sending me there— This was the last call—the last time, and the last moment with me on Earth. Before morning I shall lift up my eyes in hell. My burdin—my distress of soul was too heavy to be bourn any longer. And now all of a sudden I feal so light—so easy—so happy, so full of glory, and so full of love to everything I see. And so full of love to God. What is it, what can all this mean? It did not then enter my mind that this was religion; or that this was salvation. But in this calm and piecful state of fealing, I laid myself down to sleep, when I awoke, the sun was just then rising, and a bright streak of light shone against the wall, which was the first thing I saw, and the first thought I had was, O the glory of heaven. I arose—walked out, and I never saw the gees—ducks—hogs and every living creature praising God so before. The birds were singing God's praise, and invited me to unite with them in singing the praise of God, for he is good and his mercy endureth forever.

This was the Lords day morning, and the 8th day of February, 1812 I recollected an appointment for a prayermeeting about six miles off, and I had to pass my house to get there. I made arrangments for my wife to come on after the day got some warmer.

I started verry early and got to the meeting just as the people were singing. I thought that I had never heard such heavenly music; all their singing—praying—exhortation, shakeing of hands accompanied with singing, was certainly the sweetest exercise I had ever witnessed. I wept all the time, the people seamed more like Angels than human beings, O how I loved them and their religious exercises. I had a faint hope that perhaps I would soon get religion. But a great desire to be a christian.

Late in the eavning one of my neighbours and his wife, who had both of them been at the same meeting, came to spend the night with us, she had been a member of the baptist church about four years, and a precious christian. After supper was over, she said to me. "I have come over this eavning on purpose to here you tell your experiance." O. Mrs. Dudley, said I. If that is the errend you have come on, you will be disappointed, for I have no experiance to tell. I think you have, said she, for I noticed you to day all the time of meeting, and I think that you have somthing to tell. Just tell me how your mind has been exercised of late. I began and related to her the exercise of my mind & fealings from the time my Father spake his last words to me at the edge of the water under the bank of Beech creek in Shelby county the 14th day of october last, till last night about midnight, and how I felt to day at the prayer meeting, but this, said I, is no experiance. I have no religion, but I hope that the Lord will have mercy on me, for I am a poor sinner. She replied, "You speak the language of a Christian, and I think if ever you will be a christan you are one now." Hearing this from one in whose christianity I had the utmost confidence, I began to think & say, why can it be posible that this is religion. O. Mrs. D. the news is too good to be true. Here my eyes poured forth a flood of tears. I exclaimed, Can it be posible, that God is so holy, so just, so righteous, can have mercy on, and save so great a sinner as I am? I have deserved the deepest hell, and I wonder that I am out of it to night. But, said she, "God is love else we all would have been in hell long ago."

I believed what she said, and believing I rejoiced with joy unspeakable and full of glory. In those halceon days, the following hymn expressed the sentiment of my heart & fealings.

Saved by Grace, I live to tell
What the love of Christ hath done,
He redeem'd my soul from hell,
Of a rebel made a son.
Oh! I tremble still to think
How secure I liv'd in sin,
Sporting on distruction's brink,
Yet preserved from falling in.

In a kind propitious hour,
To my heart the saviour spoke,
Touch'd me by his spirit's power,

And my dangerous slumber
broke
Then I saw and own'd my guilt;
Soon my gracious Lord replied,
Fear not, I my blood have spilt,
Twas for such as thee I died.

Shame and Wonder, joy and
love,
All at once possess'd my heart;
Can I hope thy grace to prove,
After acting such a part?
'Thou hast greatly sinn'd, he
said,

'But I freely all forgive;
I myself the debt have paid,
Now I bid thee rise and live.

Come my fellow sinners, try:
Jesus' heart is full of love;
O, that you, as well as I,
May his wondrous mercy prove
He has sent me to declare,
All is ready, all is free:
Why should any soul despair,
When he saved a wretch like
me?

I was feasting on the love of God, and contemplating on
what he had done for me, oh, I had heaven on Earth, not a
cloud, not a temptation, not a single cross met me. Till the
thirsday following. I was about forty rods from my hous, I
was engaged in grubing, was thinking deeply on the great
love of God as menifested in the gift of his son, and the
mercy he had bestowed on me last saturday night, and how
good and pleasant I had felt ever since. And that my troubles
were all behind me, and shall live happy all the days of my
life, for this is the way all christians enjoy themselves. But
oh me. There was a roaring Lyon walking about which I
had not discovered, seaking to distry my peace, and tranquil
state of mind, and in part he succeeded. The first assault he
made on me was this. "You are a poor miserable decieved
wretch. You have just now been thinking that you got
religion last saturday night, and you have been rejoicing
about it ever since. But let me tell you, at that verry time
that you think God pardoned your sins, was the very time
that you was decieved. You let your trouble roll off your
mind, and it is gon, and you will never get those convictions
back again as long as you live. You have no religion and you
will never have any." I found myself standing perfecly still
with my matock clinched in my hands, surprized, and astonished at those kind of suggestions. I instantly recognized
from whence they came, and as if some one had asked me the

question. Do you not believe that if you pray to God sincearly that he will shew you whether you are decieved or not? Immediatly my heart responded, Lord I do believe it. Instantly I fell on my knees—the purport of my prayer was. O Lord God, thou knowest whether I am decieved or not, if I am, be pleased to show me wherin if thou hast not pardoned my sins, as I thought, O do send back my convictions again more powerful than ever, and help me to repent truly and set me right. But if thou didst indeed forgive me, and has bestowed thy favour upon me in the pardon of my sins, please give me some token wherby I may know it, so that I may never doubt again. While I was in the act of rising to my feet, these lines occured to my mind. "I will be with thee thy troubles to bless, and sanctify to thee thy deepest distress." Glory to God, said I, this is enough I will never doubt it again, for these lines are sufficient to put all doubt to flight as long as I live. But the tempter was not gon, he stood close by watching every turn of my mind. "This, said he, is no answer from the Lord. It is only a fiew words of an old song that you have often heard, and you have just now thought on them." Thus I found myself in doubting castle e-ene I was aware of it. And for many years after I had serious doubts, and hard strugling of mind on that subject.

Sometimes my evidence would be so bright, and strong, that not all the Devils in hell could cause me to doubt or question the reality of my hope and interest in Christ. At other times not all the promises in the Bible could remove my fears, till the Holy Spirit bore witness with my spirit that I was a child of God, an heir of Heaven.

About this time I had a great desire to be united with some society of christians. And in those days there were no societies in that part of Kentucky but Baptistst, Tunkars, and some Methodistst, and for a time I could not decide which of them to offer myself to for membership. I felt quite unworthy to be united with any, for I verily thought with myself, that if I was a child of grace at all, I was less than the least of all saints, and unworthy the name of a christian. I first thought of Uniting with the Tunkars. And if Mr. Hendrix (their preacher) had come into the vicinity, I would have been baptized by him. (by trine immersion) I thought that it must be the right way, or Father would not have been baptized that way. But I could not arrive at any decission on the subject. I therfore resolved to read the new Testament, and go the way it pointed out to me, and unite with that church which practised, and walked nearest to the divine rule. I commenced at the first chapter of Mathew, determined to read the Testament through and through again & again till I could be able to decide. I had a German Testament, and when I could not well understand the English, the German would explain it to me. It was just three weeks from the time I obtained a hope in the saviour, till Hazle Creek Baptist Church Meeting; of an eavning I would gather dry brush (sticks) to make a fire, light enough to see to read by. I read on and soon came to the conclusion that according to the book. Baptism must be recieved by immersion I could not tell what Baptism must be received by immersion I could not tell what Baptism ment. But the German Testament said *Taufen*, and this I knew was to dip, Diping &c. But here arose another difficulty, to know whether this Taufen ment once, or thrice. When I read to Rom. 6–4. Being buried with Christ in Baptism &c. I supposed that baptism must in some way resemble a burial. When I read Colos. 2–12 the words repeeted, I paused, and began to reason on this point—Lord teach me that I may understand thy word aright. lead me in the path thou wilt have me to walk. I thought that Baptism was a sign of a death—a burial and a resorection. And as the dead are buried only once, so baptism is to be performed only once, one immersion only to represent a deth to sin, a planting, or buri-ing with Christ, and rise to walk in newness of life.

I became perfectly satisfied in relation to Baptism. But I could not be satisfied as to myself being a proper subject. I resolved, however, that I would go to meeting, and I would tell the Church exactly, or as near as I could recollect, all how I had been exercised in my mind, and ask them to give me council, but I did not believe that they would receive me, for if they thought of me, as I did of mysel, they would be sure not to receive me. Council was what I wanted. I went to meeting, and after a sermon by their pastor, Eld. Benjamin Talbert. the fellowship of the church was enquired for: a door was opened for to hear expeariences. I had not heard an experience related at that place for four years. But I ventured forward—told my tale, then asked for council. The moderator said, "Can any person forbid water?" In a moment I was threwn into the strongest kind of temptation. He extended to me the hand of fellowship for the water, I first thought of refusing my hand. Thinking that he was jesting—making sport of me. But old Brother David Rhoads gathered me into his arms, and all the members rushed forward to give me their hands, som wept aloud for joy, my jealously was removed—singing and shaking of hands all through the crowd. That afternoon 16 persons were recieved for Baptism, and two came who wer rejected. The next day, being the first Lords day in March, 1812, I, with fifteen others were Baptized. And like one of old, for a time, I went on my way rejoicing. During that revival, 76 persons were aded to Hazle Creek Church, by baptism.

The thursday following about twenty of us (members of Hazle Creek church) went over Green River about 25 miles to Beaver-dam church meeting; on saturday 17 persons were recieved by experience for baptism, who were all baptized the next day. Among them was an old negro, they called him Squire, who related a most interesting experience of grace, when he was through, the Moderator said to him. "Well Squier, you told us that you saw that God would be just in cuting you off in your sins, and send you to hell did you ever see how he can remain just and save you?" he replied. "Wy it reason wid me dis way, I save de sinne for my sons sake." When the question was put to him, I thought that I could not answer it. But when he answered it so clearly, it caused me to think of this pasage of scripture. "And all they children shall be taught of the Lord, and great shall be the peace of thy children. Why, thought I, has the Lord kept this thing from me, and has revealed it to this poor unlearned negro?

But even so Father, for thus it seamed right in thy sight. Aprile meeting at Hazle creek my wife was Baptized, just one month after I was.

It was frequently said by the enimies of religion, the Baptist are all *shakers*, that when the Earth is don shaking, they will all turn back, and be as they were before. But here I will take the liberty to state, that I have witnessed about nineteen revivals of religion 11 in Kentucky, 6 in Illinois, and 2 in Missouri. And I have the pleasure of being aquainted with many, who were brought in, the time of the Earthquake, and these were as fiew, and perhaps fiewer apostates among them, as any revival I have ever seen, many of them, no doubt are now in heaven, praising God for grace recieved during that ever memorable revival. There are a host of Ministers now preaching the Gospel in various parts of the land, who were converted in that glorious revival. *O, for such another revival!* It was but a fiew days, nay but a fiew hours after I obtained a hope in the Saviour, before my mind, yes my whole soul began to be drawn out with ardant anxiety for the salvation of my companion & neighbours, and for the Salvation of Sinners in general. I delighted in going to meeting, but when I went and saw poor Sinners in the open field, exposed to ruin & wrath, and as ignorant of the way of Salvation and their awful danger, as I had lately been. Somthing would prompt me to warn them of their danger, speake to them exhort them to flee the wrath to come, preach the gospel unto them. My mind was holy absorbed on this subject. After some days had rolled away in this way of thinking, suddenly, as if some one had spoken to me. The Lord is calling you to preach the Gospel to sinners. At this I became most wonderfully alarmed. I immediatly called in question the fact, surely it cannot be, that the Lord would chouse so mean—so unworthy a being as I to enter upon such an important work.

I thought that I was the least christian in the church, and the most ignorant & unlearned—the most unlikely instrument to do good in the Lords Vinyard, of any person I could think of. If the Lord wanted a preacher in this neighborhood, he would call Brother Dudley, or Brother Stump, or Brother Vaught, any, or all of them are much more likely to make preachers than poor me. And what can I do? here are Elders, Talbert, Tatum, Faulkner, Barham, Warden, Jackson, a host of great preachers, who have been long preaching, and warning the people, and they have not succeded in converting them. Surely I need not attempt to open my mouth to them. But hundreds of times it would dart through every power of my soul, and cause me to tremble like one having an ague. Wo, Wo, Wo is me if I preach not the gospel I would crye aloud, and say, Lord, how can I? I have no learning, I cannot speake in public to acceptance, I am not qualified for the great work. I live on poor land a grewing family to provide for, poor cloths to stand up in a pulpit; people will laught at me. I shall disgrace the cause—disgrace my wife, myself and all the church if I attempt it. Still all the time these words. Ah these words would be continually coming to my mind, like an unwelcome guest. Wo, Wo, yes there is wo to me already, and what will that wo be if I preach not the Gospel? For some months, like crazy man, in the woods, on my farm, standing, siting, walking—eating or talking the subject would be upermost in my mind; often when asleep, dream of preaching to multudes, and wake myself & wife. Often on my knees, praying to God to know what he would have me to do. But still it would roll accross my mind. preach the Gospel, And that pasage in Ezekel. 33. "Son of man, speake to the children of thy people &c. But all the time fearing that I could not perform the task." Somtime in the last week in Aprile 1814 I was out early one morning looking for my horses, walking along an old dim forsaken path, I came to a log which lay accross it. Here (thought I) I will kneel down and ask the Lord once more, what his will is concerning me. I prayed most fervently as if my life was pending. I arose from the place, expecting that the Lord would make it manifest to me in some way, perhaps at meeting. But oh how I was surprized, when suddenly before I had gon a rod from the place, these words like lightnings darted through my mind, and thousands of times they have been a source of comfort to

my disponding mind. And would inspier me with fresh
confidence in God. "Fear not, I will be with thee, go on I
will never lieve nor forsake thee." At this moment my confidence in God was so strong, that if it could have been posible
that the whole world had been assembled at that place, I
could have boldly declared to them what great things the
Lord had done for me, and how he had coppassion on me,
and have exhorted them to repent and believe the gospel.
The next saturday and sunday, which was the first Lords day
in May 1814. Was Hazle creek Church meeting in course.
And on Sunday all the time Eld. Talbert was preaching. I
was trembling like a lief. I recollected the promise God gave
me in the woods; as soon therfore as the congregation was
dismissed. I steped up on a bench and gave out. "There will
be preaching next sunday at Brother Wellborns." And
jumped off the bench and made for the door, as I passed on,
several persons asked me, "Who is to preach." I said, come
and see. That week passed off verry slowly, and with much
fear & trembling, and much anxiety on the part of some of
the brethren, who were apprized of what was pending. But
I felt confident that I had a large share in their sympathies &
prayers. When I went to fill my appointment, I soon discovered that the Lord heard prayer. The lane was litterly
filled with horses, and the house with people. I trembled at
the sight—but I retiered behind a high bank—prostrated
myself on my face, and prayed to God to help me. Glory to
God, he made good his promise to me in the woods. Yes, he
did help, for if ever I was favored with the presence of the
Holy one, surely he was with me at this time. And I was
much encouraged, for this was my first effort in speaking
from a text. Several of the brethren encouraged me to make
more appointments and I continued to do so. I will here
remark, that no person need thank me for being a preacher
of the Gospel. For if ever a disobedient servent was well
whiped by his Master to make him perfor his task Task,
surely I was well shiped, and compelled to go to my work.
often have I thought on a part of the Apostle Pauls experience; where he said, "To me who am less than the least

of all saints is this grace given that I should preach among the Gentiles the unsearchable riches of Christ &c.

Well I went on through many difficulties—discouragements & encouragements. Both of a temporal, and Spiritual nature. I made slow advances. Laboured incessantly on the farm all the week and tryed to preach on sundays. I had no books beside my English Bible & a German Testament, and a small hymn book. After a hard days work, I would gether dry sticks, and read at night by fire light. Somtimes I would borrow books, and make the best use of them I could, while I had them. Among those borrowed was, Bonnets Enquieries on the Christian Religion. Booths Reign of Grace. Bunyans Pilgrim, and his Holy war. All old books. I had no means to buy new ons. But of all the books I had, I loved my German Testament the best; for several reasons, I could understand it the best—my Mothers name—birth—age & Death were all recorded in it. But I was compelled to lay it by, and take to reading, and studying the english scriptures, and this was tedious for the want of a living teacher. The first book I bought after I began the study of the english, was Jones, Speling & prnouncing Dictionary. This book was a great help to me. But often, and I may say uniformly, when I went to fill an appointment, I would lieve my path and retier to some secret spot. Get on my knees—open my Bible— read and pray to God to help me to understand his word, and that I might behold wonderous things out of his law. It was a habit I early got into. And I have not yet laid it aside, In this way I have got in possion of what little knowledge I have in Bible doctrine. In this way I went on as well as I could, from the 2nd Lords day in May 1814. Till the first saturday in October 1816. The brethren of Hazle creek Church thought that my gift was proffitable. Therefore the Church unanimously voted to give me written licence to preach the gospel, whersoever God in his providence mite direct. in October 1818, I moved to Logan county, (about 15 miles) and the church with which I united. Immediatly called on me to submit to ordination and take the oversight of them, this was one of the most solemn tryels I ever met with. I felt unworthy of so high and holy a calling. My incompetency to fill an office of so great responsibility. But was necessary that I should submit to the decission of the church, and was ordained to the Gospel Ministry on the 27th day of February in the Year of our Lord, 1819.

And on the 16th day of August following I received license from the county court of Logan to solemnize the rite of Matrimony.

My progress in the Ministry was verry slow. It was almost five years from the time I preached my first sermon before I recieved credentials of ordination. I always was of opinion that my brethren done right in keeping me back, and so thoroly examine me on points of Bible doctrine. For I have since then seen some men ordained quite prematurely, as I thought, such as afterwards proved to be unsound in their views of Gospel truth, and who were a disgrace to the Baptist cause and our holy religion.

Soon after I recieved credentials of ordination, I recieved a call from three churches, to serve them as pastor, and break to them the bred of life once a month. Which call I accepted, and labored for them ten years, till I left Kentucky. And came to Illinois; during which time I enjoyed eleven revivals, and Baptized many precious christians. Some of them I have the pleasure of continuing an aquantence with till now, who are citizens of this state & some in Missouri who continue steadfast in the faith, and still adorn the doctrine of Christ our Saviour. "I have no greater joy than to hear that my children walk in truth."

Havin a rising family to provide for—poor land to do it on, and limited means to do it with. And hearing a good report from Illinois, by brethren who had long sat under my ministry in Kentucky, who had emigrated hither, and had made a tryel of this goodly land; warmly solicited me to come hither also. In 1827, I came on a visit, preached several times, and the sound of the old bell—so delighted them, that they renewed their solicitations, and promised to assist me with all the necessaries of living for the first year. I explored the country pretty extensively—was pleased with it, and the people. And in November 1828. I landed on the spot where I now live, Scott county Illinois.

I had many objects to prompt me to come to his county. I did not like the idea of raising a family in a slave state, therfore I preferred bringing them to, and raising them in a free state. The soil was verry rich & productive, and I thought that I could give myself more to the Ministery of the word, and support my family with less labour. I arrived here on the 17th day of November, and the first saturday in December the Sandy Creek church meeting came on, I united with the church by letter, together with all who came with me, I think six of us in number. The church on the same day called me to serve them as their pastor. The spring following, we had quite an accession to our number, both by baptism & by letter, and the good cause went on most delightfully. Sometime in the year 1830, if I mistake not, A church was constituted in Sweets prairie. (Now, Manchester church) of members from Sandy creek church (now Winchester) and was called pleasent Grove, this church also enjoyed an ingethering, some 37. perhaps were Baptized, in which that good brother P. N. Haycraft became a subject of converting grace—and became a useful Minister of the Gospel. I shal refer to his name frequently in the course of my narative. There was as pleasent a state of religious dealing in this little church as our hearts could desire, for a considerable time all was prosperity.

But a certain individual in the neighborhood, who at that time was not the warmest kind of a friend to the Baptist cause, invited a Campbelite preacher to come and preach at his house, and the third time, (I think) he came, he organized a society, and drew off eight of our members, and this was a sad drawback upon us, and especially on my feelings, for some of them I had the pleasure of baptizing, and now we were compelled, according to the divine rule, to withdraw the hand of fellowship from them. But some of them, no doubt, were Christ's sheep, and it was not long before the came back bleating, and we recieved them into the fold again. In the summer of 1831 there was a call for volunteers to go to Rock Island against Black Hawk. I went with one of my sons to Winchester to fit him out for the service—gave to him the parting hand, and started for home —just as I was approaching my horse, a rifle was discarged by axident in a blacksmith shop. The ball passed through my left foot, desperatly lascerating it. Which laid me aside for a long time. Sixteen months after it happened, there were fractored peaces of bones discharged from it. The first saturday in October I was carried to Winchester church meeting. I sat and preached every time till the second Lords day in May. 1832. when I ventured for the first time to stand on my feet—preached about half the sermon, then sat down and finished.

I recollect visiting Dr. B. F. Edwards, to obtain some council in relation to my wound. He said, "You will never fully recover so as to be able to follow the plow. But God has a work for you to do, and you will be able to ride and preach, and you had better go at it as soon as you can, least a worse thing come upon you." Well I resolved to lieve my family in the hands of the Lord; for if I were in my grave, he would provide for them, and they will get along without me. So in March, I took a cruch—got on my horse—went and preached as much as I could. During the summer of 32. The pleasent Grove church, Organized and kept up a regular Sabath school, which resulted in the hopeful conversion of sixteen of the schollars, and they were adid to the church. The news of which reached the ears of some of the churche. in the Morgan Association. In September (if I recollect ritly) The Association met at plum creek church, when a resolution was passed, somthing like this. "We recommend to the churches composing this Association to have no fellowship either directly or indirectly with missionaries. The Bible society, Sabath Schools, and Temperance measures, so called, believing them to be the invensions of men in their present operation."

The resolution passed. None voted against it except the deligates from pleasent Grove church. Immediatly I drew up a resolution, Cautioning the churches of the Morgan As-

sociation, to be ware of Daniel parker and his two seed doctrine. Brother Haycraft seconded the motion, it was put to
the house, and lost—recieved no votes but the deligates from
pleasent Grove church. On the Lords Day, Elden Crow.
Davidson, and Henson filled the stand in the woods Eld.
Crow preached first, his sermon was a continual abuse of
Missionaries. Bible societies—Sabath Schools, and the cause
of temperance. I was seated on the ground, leaning against a
tree. I felt as though I could beare such abuse no longer. I
spoke loud enough for the whole assembly to hear me.
Brother Crow. We had rather here you preach Jesus to the
people. He looked at me as if he was angry, and said, brother
Moderator, I call for order, who replied, Or-der. The next
speaker was no less sparing of his abuse. But the Moderator
(Bro. Henson) was pretty clear of it.

On our way home, one of my sons who obtained a hope
during our Sabath School, said to me, "I had rather have
been at home in our sabath school than at such an Association. I would have enjoyed myself much better there."
Brother Haycroft said, "If the church represents herself
again in the Morgan Association, I shall stay away." One
or two churches in pike county, sent petetionary letters and
messengers to this Association, but they were rejected. I
supposed that some of them were fearful of geting Missionaries enterwoven among them. Brother Haycroft & myself
began to consult on the propriety of organizing a new Association, consisting of pleasent Grove. Mt. Zion (new perry)
and Blue River. These three small churches. At first I felt
fearful to go into the measure, becaus of the fiew Ministers.
Myself, and perhaps Brother Lewis, Allen. Brother Haycraft, and Brother Elledge were then Licetiate. But we
corresponded with Eld. J. M. Peck, and other Brethren in
the Ministry, who advised and encouraged us to trust in the
Lord, and go ahead. After some preliminary meetings, and
avengments. A convention met accordingly at Blue River
Meeting House in pike county on saturday June 8 1832.
After a sermon by Brother Allen, the deligates from pleasant
Grove. Mt. Zion & Blue River churches, went into a regular

form of organization. Unanimously agreed to be know by the name of, The *Blue River Association of United Baptist.*

Lords day was spent in preaching, exhortation, singing and shaking of hands, and prayer to God that this little one mite become a great one, and that peace, harmony & prosperity mite reign among the church, and that God would gran an increase. The 6th Article of her constitution reads as follows. "Each church and member of this Association shall be left free to act according to their views of duty on the subject of Missions. Bible societies, sunday schools, Temperance measures &c. And the supporting or not supporting either of them, shall be no bar to fellowship."

Sometime in the summer of 1832. Two brethren of the committy of corrispondance at Alton. Eld. J. M. Peck, & Dr. B. F. Edwards, heard of my affliction—paid me a visit—sympathised with and prayed for me. The Doctor was still of opinion that I would recover, so as to ride and preach. They enquiered into my pecuniary matters, found that my family were on the eave of suffering, and that somthing must be done for their relief, and that soon. The Doctor himself advanced eighty dollars toards our relief, which favour will never be forgotten by us, nor by *him* in whose sight a sparrow shall not fall to the ground without his notice, May he be rewarded at the resorection of the just. They also examined into my doctrinal view of the Bible. And wished to know if I would accept of an appointment from the Home Mission society. and recieve one hundred dollars sallery a year, and give myself wholy to preaching the Gospel. I told them that it would be a great favour indeed, to assist us in our present needy condition. But I was resolved to do as I had always done—preach all I could pay, or no pay. As for any help from our Antimission folks, I expected non. And my views on the subject of Missions have not changed, they are the same as they always have been, when you (Dr. Edwards) was aquainted with me in Kentucky. They, then gave me to understand, that I mite expect an appointment from the A. B. H. M. society, and to hold myself in readiness to go to work. I have been doing all I could (said I) ever

since the first of last March. On the 21st day of December
following, an appointment came to hand, dated N. Y. Nov.
19th. 1832. I let the brethren of the pleasent Grove church
know that I had recieved such an appointment, and that I
felt myself under many obligations to the Board for their
kindness, not only to me as an individual, But also for their
kindness to the church, & the people generally in the west;
for that they certainly felt great solicitude for the prosperity
of the Baptist cause. But the church had a different view of
the subject. They looked upon it as being rather an insult,
than as an act of kindness—called me to an account for
accepting such an appointment. Why, (said som) it will be
reported all over the country that our pastor is a Missionary!
After a long and tedious debate on the subject, it was resolved that I must send back my commission to the Board
without an explanation, or expression of thanks. I told them
that it will be necessary to write back a letter of explanation,
shewin reasons why I refused to accept an appointment.
The church agreed that I should do so, and when I done it, I
had to state the act of the church in this case. The rejected
my letter—said that it must not go in that shape, for all
the blame would rest on the church. I wrote a second and
that was also rejected. I framed a third, which they thought
would answer. The church then appointed one of the Deacons to take the letter and my commission to the post office,
and see that they were safely deposited, and that offensive
paper should go back from whence it came.

Now came on a trying time in the hystory of my family.
I had already borrowed mony at twenty percent, to buy
bred & meat, and other articles of living, and the question
was now. how am I to raise that money? The church knew
that I had become enthraled, by being laid aside so long in
conciquence of my wound. And of course would have to
sacrifice property to make payement. One of the Deacons
started a subscription among the members of the church,
to obtain relief for me—got perhaps one or two names beside
his own. He told me that he was sorry that he had undertaken it, for, said he, there is so much oposition against it.

I think that I shall make no further attempt. Burn, said I. burn the subscription paper and let it never be seen again, for I see plainly that the church and neighborhood are determine to starve out me and my family, and I fear that they will succede. For the church would not be satisfied till I sent back my commission, which promised one hundred dollars to relieve us, and now they are not willing that a subscription shall be circulated, only because it looks a little like Missionary, if the church goes on in this way, God will surely curse us in some way or other. In about six weeks after my commission had been sent back, it came to hand again. In confidence, I told one of the brethren that it had been returned to me again, and I thanked God, and the corresponding secretary for so doing. I trust that God will yet provide for us. Remember, said I, that Mordcai said to Esther, when the decree went forth that the Jews shall all be slain in Shushan the palace. "If thou at this time altogether hold thy peace, then shall there deliverance arise from some other quarter." The church has hitherto held her peace, and they know that deliverance must come from some quarter, and now it has come from another quarter, even affar off. God has sent it. And I dont intend that the church shall know from whence it has come, lest they will send it back again. But, said he, the church *must* know it, this thing must not remain in the dark. The next meeting the church prefered charges against me, for recieving back my commission, knowing that the church was opposed to it. I plead for the cause of Missions, and for mercy, and that the church would not exclude me, for I could not see that I was worthy of death or of bonds. And I was not prepared at this time to recant, or make any acknowledments. A motion was made—seconded and passed, to lay the matter over till the next meeting, and that the two Deacons be appointed to labour with me, and make report to the next church meeting. The let me know what night I mite expect a visit from them. I recollected the promise which God gave me in the woods in Kentucky many years ago, before I attempted to preach. "I will never lieve nor forsake thee." I read—restled with God in prayer, that he would remember his promise—Grant me his Holy Spirit to direct me in the right way. Well, the time came, & the Deacons came. I gave them a cordial reception —they were seated. One of them opened the conversation. I said, brethren, let us pray first. Prayer was offered. And they commenced their labour—I heard them patiently through. Then I began to make my defence and said, "Brethren, both of you have been aquanted with me in K-y. a long time, even before I began to preach the gospel, and you have heard me all the time I preached there, and you know that I have undergon no change in my views on the subject of Missions. You have often heard me speak of the Burman Mission—of the brethren Judson & wife, Rice & Price, being the first Missionaries from America to that benighted people. You have heard me speake in favour of sabath Schools too, for you can certainly recollect the time when I went twice to a School House in your amediate vicinity in Butler county, and lectured the Sabath School. You know also that I highly approved of the Bible society auxiliary to the A. B. society, in Russellville. That although I was not a member of that society. Yet Elders. Warden, and Tatum, both were members of the Russellville Bible society, and distributed Bibles and Testaments. Look here, said I, has not Elizabeth, your wife, got a Testament, with P. Wardens name in it and A. B. Society stamped outside on the cover? Yes. Well that book was donated to her when she was a girl. Again, you know too that Sandy creek church in Butler county in which your brother C. had you membership, every year had a subscription paper for the benifit of Eld. Talbert, your pastor, and so at every church he attended, and you know that it was the custom in the churches in Kentucky, to get up, and pay anually a subscription for their pastor. And what is the reason that the same baptist who used to do it there, dare not do it in Illinois. I sincerely wish I was back there again, you would not see my face here again soon.

But you seem to be wonderfully alarmed at the word Missionary. and I doubt whether either of you know what it means. Her, (handing down Jones's Dictionary) look for the

word, and see the deffination of it. Read. Missionary: one
sent to propagate religion. Verry well, one sent to propegate
religion. do you suppose that to be a true rendering? I
supose it is, said one of them. Jesus Christ then was the
first Gospel Missionary. Hear him, I am not come to do my
own will, but the will of *him* who sent me, as the Father hath
sent me, even so have I sent you. Go ye therefore into all
the world, and propegate religion among all nations &c.
Christ was emphatically a Missionary and the Apostles were
Missionaries. And brethren, you have often heard me say,
that if I did not believe that God has sent me to preach the
gospel, I would never attempt to preach another sermon
while I lived. But if I call in question my call to the Ministry, I must also doubt my call to be a Christian. And now
brethren you have heard what I have to say for my self & my
Masters cause. You see that I am a whole soul Missionary.
And if you consider me a preacher of the gospel, and you
have no other charge against me, than that of being a
Missionary—You must make your report to the church that
your labours with me were unsuccessful, and if the church
exclude me, and I shall have to stand alone. The presbyterians, and the Methodists understand themselves on this
point, and they are all in favor of Missions. But the practice
sprinkling in stid of Baptism, and I cannot unite with them
on that account. And the Campbelites teach, that, no
baptism, no remission of sins—denie the special agency of the
Holy Spirit in conversion, and a special call to the Ministry.
Therefore I cannot unite, nor travail with any church but
the Baptist, and if they exclude me I must stand alone as
long as I live, there is no other alterative for me.

By the time I was through making my defence, both my
good brethren were in tears, they rose to their feet and said,
No, you wont stand (atond) alone we will stand by you, and
if the church exclud you, they must exclude us also. Then
was a weepin-melting time, both took by the hand, asuring
me that they would stand by me. The God of Missions was
in our midst, and granted us great grace in answer to our
prayer.

Well, the next church meeting this refferance was called up and and the Deacons made report. "We found Eld. Bower steadfast, we could do nothing with him. We found that he was of the same opinion that he was in Kentucky, when he was our pastor there. And he explained maters and things so plain to us that we found that his was right and we are wrong, and if the church exclude Eld. Bower, She will have to exclude us likewise." After much consultation, and many remarks by the brethren & some of the sisters too. A motion was made—secconded and put to the church to know, whether the church was sattisfied with Eld. Bower. All hands up (as it was thought) the question was reversed. Two voted against him. These two suffered exclusion sooner than to live in a church which had a Missionary for their pastor—one of them soon united with the Campbelites. The other, I believe has not united with any church. The next question was to know what Eld. Bower is to do with his commission he recieved from the Board. Decided, that he keep ˙it and act under it. Thus a whole church was converted in one day (except two) to be in favour the sistem of Missions. Amediatly the church rose up and went to work; and the Lord granted us additions of such as shall be saved. The church approving of my measures—sent me forth into this wide field to labour as requiered in my instructions from the Board. And had their hearty co-operation and prayers.

About this time our good brother Haycraft (that I mensioned before) began to exercise his gift in the Ministry, and was a great help to me. Pleasent Grove church (now Manchester) was the only Missionary church in the state of Illinois that I had any knowege of except Rock Spring— Edwardvell, & Uper Alton. These churches were constituted in an Association some time in 1832. The first Missionary Association in the state. Composed of three small churches. The Blue River Association (of which mention has been made) was composed of three small church, and was the seccond Missionary Association in the state—was constituted in June 1833.[1]

[1] The South District was a Missionary body. J. M. B.

As I have already stated, I continued in pastoral relation with the Sandy creek church (now Winchester) for four years and two months—And the Lord abundantly blessed us with peace—prosperity—good fealing & brotherly love. But when the Morgan Association denounced Missionaries, and kindred institutions, at their session on plum creek in 32. This being understood by some of the members of the church, the began to be fearful that the Association would exclude them if they continued, a Missionary as their pastor. At their Feb. meeting 1833. Old Brother Reeder brought up a query into the church to know whether the church would continue me as their pastor, and fearing exclusion. The Resolved, 19 to 13 to dismiss me as their pastor. And that neither I nor any of the members of pleasent Grove church be allowed to commune with them. Yet they invited me to preach for them once a month as usual. I remarked, that I could not understand their proceedings. You have turned me off from being your pastor, and yet you invite me to preach for you at your stated meetings. Old Bro. G. replied. "We push you off with one hand, but will hold to you with the other." But the church then called Eld. J. C. Rogers to serve them as their pastor. He served them perhaps two years, during which time the church had no communion. Some ten or a dozen of the members were excluded, and the church was reported to the Morgan Association as being Missionary & in disorder, wherupon the Association excluded her—wrongfully, for they had never acted on Missionary principles. But the Association said in her minutes. "We hope there are a fiew names in sardis which have not defiled their garments with Missionary operations, we advise them to come out of her, and constitute themselves into a church and we will recieve them." Thirteen or fourteen members took the council of the Association and constituted what is called Friendship; half mile wes of Winchester.

Being under appointment from the H. M. society, and was requiered to labour all the time. I formed circuits and preached at the same place once a month. I had one circuit of two weeks, in the Military Tract & one of two weeks in

Green—Magoupin & Morgan. The Lord was wonderful good, in causing my labours to be a blessing to many. In some plases I found most rigid prejudices existing against Missionaries, and I could not obtain a hearing. And in some plases where I had been invited to preach, as soon as it was known that I was a Missionary, the hearers would drop off, till I was compeled to chang my rout. I preached in a new open Schoolhouse in Brown county, in an Antimission neighbourhood, and during religious exercises they (and some of them were members of a Baptist church) wer cuting down trees within eight or ten rods of the house. But not withstanding the prejudises of so many, who closed their eyes & ears against all information on the subject of Missions. And although the opposers would circulate abominable lies, and tell the people that if they went to hear a Missionary they would be taxed, and be compelled to pay twentyfive cents for every sermon they heard, and every one that was baptized, they would have a tax of fifty cents to pay, and every year a tax of one dollar. Yet many there were who would not believe such slang. But where ever I went I would explain the Mission cause, and as fast as it was understood & believed, there the good cause gained the ascendancy. And by the time my first year expired, I had more invitations to preach, than I could posibly fill. I would hunt out and preach for churches who wer destitute of preaching, until they could be supplied with a pastor. In october 1832. I assisted in the organization of Mt. Zion (now perry) church. For this church I preached monthly, until Eld. Jesse Elledge was ordained July 14, 1833 and for some time after.
The Lord wonderfully blessed this church, almost every meeting, he granted her a refreshing season. Every communion season (May & September) the church would attend to the ordinence of washing feet. The members often got happy—clap their glad hands and shout Glory to God. and so it was with Blue River. Pleasent Grove & Sandy creek churches, as long as I Ministered unto them. On the fifth day of october I constituted, what was called Salem in pike county, and preached for them about two years. But some

years after I ceased to labour for them She lost her visibility. And on the 15th day of october. I assisted in the ordination of Wm. Browning, of Mt. Zion church.

This year ending Nov. 19th. 1833. I rode 2037 miles and preached 264 sermons, & Baptized 52. Ordained 2 Ministers and constituted 1 church. On the 8th day of March 1834. Eld. John Logan & myself, constituted what was called Bethany (now Payson) church. I think, on seven members, he & I agreed to supply them in turn every other month, until the obtained the servises of Eld. Fisher from Quincy. On Saturday the 29th day of March seven Ministers met in Winchester, in order to hold a protracted meeting, we had eleven Such was the opposition against the Mission cause at that time in this place, that a good old Sister remarked to me. "The people say that all you preachers are Missionaries, and they are affeared of being taxed, is the reason why they will not turn out to hear them." Eld. R. was pastor of this church at that time, and this was the kind of influence he exerted over them.

A certain man in Green county, had invited me to preach at his house, and I had done so several times. But on monday June 23, a good congregation had convened, when I got there—told me before I entered his house that he forbid me to preach in his house any more, for he heard that I was a Missionary, and all the people that heard a Missionary would be taxed twentyfive cents. I told him that I had often heard so too, but it was false, nevertheless I will not intrude upon the people in your house, I preached there no more. This was in the neighborhood of a church which I constituted the second Lords day in May 1832, called Mt. Giliad in Green co. and continued to preach for them two years, and they had united with the Blue River Association. Some of the members took an alarm at such taxing reports and thirteen of the members, and a licenced preacher among them; drew off—organized a new church, and united with the Apple creek Association. And the church was left in peace and prosperity for a time.

On saturday June 29th I constituted a church in Magoupin

county called Hony creek, on seven members, it was after-wards visited by some Antimission preacher, who scaired them on the subject of Missionary taxation till they con-sented, and were reorganized, and joined the Apple creek Association, this church was lost for the want of the right kind of instruction, but it was too far for me to attend to them.

Having preached two tours at Rhoads-s point, and the Baptist in that church appeared to manifest so much kind-ness, and respect for my manner of preaching, I left a number of appointments. But when I got there, (August 20) I was informed by their pastor, that the church had the matter under consideration, and had resolved, for the sake of peace among themselves, and the Applecreek Association. Not to suffer me to make any more appointments in that vicinity, and he was requested by the church to inform me on the subject. I visited them no more but left them in peace. But the great author of Missions, (who is always mindful of the persecuted fiew) was pleased to hear our prayers, in raising up, and sending forth more labourers in this destitute field. Raised up our good Brother P. N. Haycraft, to be a flaiming tortch, and a bold champeon in the cause of Mis-sions. And on the Lorday, a August 24th, he was set appart by solemn ordination, to the Gospel Ministry, by a presby-try, consisting of Elders. Jonathan, & Joel Sweet, and my-self. But it seemed that we were not allowed to enjoy his labours long, for God had appointed him another field to labour in, and he had to go to M-o to do it. At the Salem (united) Association held in McDonough county in Septem-ber 8th. Brother West was examined, and ordained by a presbytry of Eld. Logan, Bartlett. Clark, Hale. & myself. In october the 9th 1834 the Baptist Convension of Illinois was organized in Brother A. Hix-s Barn near White Hall, in Green c. o. Such was the oposition manifested by the Anti-mission Baptist, that they would not allow us the privilege of holding our meetings in their Meeting House. A good brother remarked, as though he had been inspired by the spirit of prophesy. "Well let them keep their old shanty, it wont stand there long." Just so it has turned out. But it pleased the God of Missions to remove every obstacle out of the way. Applecreek church was removed from that place—their pastor became a fallen prophet—left this country not with the best kind of a name! But God was pleased to smile on our effotts, he enlarged our borders—lengthened our stakes & strengthened our cords, until the little one has become a great nation, and now fills the whole land.

On the saturday following, oct. 18th I went to Mt. Giliad church meeting, to the house where the had all along been in the habit of holding her meetings—and to my astonishment, and surprize of the whole congregation too. The good man of the house, publicly forbid me from preaching in that day. But, said I, it is our church meeting day in course, and you voluntarily gave us your house for that purpose, and our rules of decorum requiers the conference to be opened & closed by prayer & praise. You may pray and exhort, said he, but you shall not preach in my house any more. So we opened our meeting as usual—Noticed those offending members who had abruptly broken off in disorder, and formed a new church, and excluded them. (he one of the number) Then exhorted the church to steadfastness in the cause in which she had embarked. And to carry it tenderly toards our ering brethren, that they with loving kindness mite be won, and be restored again to the bosom of the church. "Hush and sit down, said he, or go out of my house, for you mite as well preach as to be talking in that way." And this was the last time the church met in his house. But the new church he bid welcome. But the church in a short time gained more than she had lost, and there was not a Dog left in the church to bark against the cause of Missions.

In the Year ending Nov. 19th, 1834. Rode 3133 miles. preached 299 sermons. Baptized 14. ordained 2 Ministers. constituted 2 churches. And in the year ending Nov. 19th. 1835. Rode 2900 miles, preached 152 sermons, & Baptized 2. Saturday, March the 5th The church at Sandycreek, called me again to take the pastoral care of them. Soon these excluded members were all restored again.

And the church began again to travail, and put on a different aspect, they thanked God & took courage. At their August meeting I Baptized three. And broke bred to them. This was the first communion the had for three years. And the church had a season of prosperity—for more than two years. But, about this time I witnessed a most deplorable circumstance in pleasent Grove church. A great falling off of members—at September—October—November & December meetings, so many of the members took letters, and moved away, some to Louis Co. M-o, and some to pike county Illinois. Among them was our good brother Haycroft, who we trusted would be a great help to our little Zion. And both of our Deacons, so that the church sustained a gred loss. This was a heavy drawback upon my fealings, and I have not survived it yet. But the Lord will have his own way with the children of men, and we must submit. November 19th. No reappointment from the Board. But this year 1836. I Rode 2710 miles. Preached 142 sermons and Baptized 3.

In February 1837. While on a tour of preaching. I was confined in Quincy eleven days, with congestive feavor. But the Lord was gracious—raised me up—sent me to work again. March meeting, a reformation commenced in Winchester and Sandycreek woods, which resulded in the happiet convension of many souls. Many obtained a bright hope in the Saviour, and shouted praise to his name for what he had done for them, and many of them are yet living witness for the Lord Jesus Christ, and have thus far adorned the doctrine of Christ their Saviour by a well ordered walk & a godly conversation in the world. This year the church licenced Brother A. T. Hite to exercise his gift, in the church, who has also gone to M-o.

This year 1837. Rode 1565 miles, preached 183 sermons. Baptized 63. 1838. I continued my labours as though I had been under appointment by the Board. And on the 29th of October, I attended the ordination of Eld. T. H. Ford, in payson, Adams county. The presbytery was composed of Elders Fisher, Bailey, Trabue, Elledge, and myself.

On the 3d day of November, Elders Hobbs & Davis were ordained at Centerville church Adams county. presbytry. Elders. Logan. Elledge & myself. This year 1838. Rode 29.17 miles. Preached 176 sermons. Baptized 3 and aided in the ordination of 3 Ministers.

Note. Where churches were supplied with a Minister, I always prefered that they should do the Baptizing.

1839. The church in Winchester having now increased to a goodly number of members, and during the late revival, all the male members being active and both old and young members, would bear a part in prayer meetings and the were sufficiently able to sustain a pastor all the time did at my suggestion, give Eld. Bailey of Carrollton a call, who accepted, and took the pastoral charge of them, half the time for four years. This loosed me so that I was at liberty to Itinerate more extensively. August 14th Elder Thomas Taylor was ordained to the Gospel Ministry in Manchester, Scott county, presbytry. Elders Bailey, Meriam, and myself. During this year 1839. Rode 2623. miles. preached 210. sermons. and aided in the ordination of 1 Minister.

1840. Saturday January 25. I assisted in the organization of Mt. Sterling Church. presbytry Elders. Logan. Botts. Parks. and myself.

Saturday May the 9th I assisted in constituting a church in Adams co. called Richfield (now extinct) presbytry. Elders. G. B. Davis. J. Elledge. N. Parks. and myself. May 10th. The same presbytry examined, and ordined to the Gospel Ministry Brother M. W. Coffee. who was amediatly called to the pastoral care of the church. Both pastor & the church are no more! Sat June 13th The church in Pittsfield was organized, by Elders D. Hubbard J. Elledge & myself. On Lords day I Babtized four, and supplied them occasionally for a time. September, October & November, was the most sickly time I have seen during my Missiony labours. This year (1840) Rode 3133 miles, and preached 200 sermons. Baptized 9. constituted 3 churches. ordained 1 Minister.

1841. Thursday Aprile 1st. The church at Big Spring scott

county; was organized presbytry. Elders. Bailey, Sweet, Tailor & myself.

This year 1841. Rode 2361 miles. preached 189 times. constituted 1 church 1842. Fryday January 28th Elder Moses Lemon & myself commenced a protrated meeting at Mt. Gilead church. Green co. In eight days 76 persons professed a hope in Christ and we baptized them. At this meeting I relinquished my pastoral labours with them, haveing served them as pastor for near ten years. And Eld. Moses Lemon accepted a call, and supplied them. I know not how long.

February 21st. I went to St. Louis and preached seven sermons for the African Baptist church. The church was much stired up—setled all their difficulties and disputes, and invited me to return and preach for them again. I went home—made arrangements—and returned again in March 24.

And preached about 30 sermons for them, and about 80 professed a hope in the Saviour, and Eld. J. B. Mechum Baptized them. This was a most interestin meeting. I enjoyed as much of the divine presence at this meeting as I have done at any time since I left Kentucky. On one occasion while I was preaching, with a most powerful feeling in my whole soul, and a state of deep fealing in the congregation. The old collerd pastor was siting in the pulpit behind me; frequently saying, hai-hai-hai. At length he sprung to his feet and exclaimed with a thundering voice. "I will not hold my peace when truth comes with such *power*. hai." And soon nearly all the professing part of the congregation were on their feet too, hollowing, Glory to God. Hallalujah. Hallalujah. Glory Hallalujah. Bless the Lord. praise the Lord. Hallalujah. AMEN. AMEN. &c. I think I may safely say, that I never saw a congregation of professing people enjoy themselves so well no where. They appeared to be a happy people indeed indeed. At the close of this meeting, when I was about to lieve them (and to their praise I would say it) the collected more for me, than I have ever received from any congregation for the same time of service. The sewed bountifully—they also rept bountifully. After this large accession to their numbers, they pulled down their old house, and built a splendid Meeting House on the same lot of ground; and soon had it paid for.

The month of June I spent with the churches in S. Louis c. o. preaching almost every day. Then I took a tour in Ballard & McCracken counties in Kentucky, and returned home, July 21st, in this tour I travelled about 700 miles, and preached 63 sermons, and delivered one or two Temperance lestures.

The last of July & first of August, I attended a protracted meet at Ramneys creek M. H. pike county M-o. and preached 24 sermons, with their pastor Eld. A. D. Landrum; there were between 30 & 40 professed a good hope in the saviour and were Baptized.

The 4th Lords day in August, I attended the Blue River Association, and was appointed by that body to corrispond with the Missouri Association held at Salem M. H. on Cold water in St. Louis county 2nd saturday in september. The Board of that Association employed me to preach for the churches in that Association for three months. I spent a part of September and october November and a part of December, I preached almost every day—was wonderfully favoured with the divine presence—had sweet liberty in preaching all the time, and Baptized 21 happy converts—heard of the hopeful conversion of 210 persons. This was a year in which I enjoyed much help from the Lord. and I trust that much good was done. To God be all the Glory.

This year 1842. I travelled. 2793 miles, and preached 241 sermons and witnessed the hopeful conversion & baptism of 112 persons.

1843. A fiew days after I arived home from this tour in M-o, I was attacked with a violent cold—cough—pains in my back & breast. which laid me aside from labour for a long time. And when at any time I made an attempt to speake, it was attended with much pain. I often went to meeting, when I had doubts. whether it was duty to go.

But on saturday January 21st The Church in Manchester

gave me a call to serve them one fourth of the time for one year. and (as reported by their Deacon) that the church would remunerate me for my services, I consented & done so. But at the end of the year, the church voted to give me *nothing* for my services. The *Negro (slaves) on St. Louis were possed of more honesty & liberality!!!*

I have good reason for thinking that I left my field of labour in M-o contrairy to the mind of the Lord. My labous there, were abundantly blessed, and it was good to my own soul to be there. But after I returned home, it was an up-hill business all the time. I had promised the Lord, and the people, that I would return and preach for them after I had paid my family a visit. But I was well chastened for this *lie.* And I am not done grieving about yet.

On Saturday Feb. 18th. Eld. Bailey & I. constituted a church in Martins prairie, Green c. o. called Bethel; and on saturday March 25th I was called to serve them as pastor, which I accepted, and preached for them three years. But in consequence of debility, I could not travel and preach much. This year 1843. I only travelled about 1660 miles, & preached 86 sermon, & baptized 17. witnessed the hopeful conversion of 54 persons—aided in constituting 1 church.

1844. January the 6th during a protracted meeting in Winchester I was taken violently with Bilious cholic & spasmodic affection of the diephaim; was confined one month, and continued feable a long time. In March I started on a tour to Ohio. on a visit to some friends there and returned on the 3d day of May in some better health. On my return, I received another box of Bibles & Testaments from the city Bible society N-y. to distribute among the destitute in the west.

But on Wednesday October 30th At the request of the Board of the Salt River Association, M-o. I commenced, and laboured three months for that Association. Visited all the churches (excep two) and preached to many destitute settlements—many prejudices against Missions were removed. and I left the churches generally in a prosperous condition.

This year 1844. I travelled 1822 miles. and preached, 132 sermons.

1845. This year was mostly spent in the same business and many interesting incidence transpired, some of them I will notice, as I find them in my journal. I met with frequent opposition. Not only from the Devils chuildren, But also from people professing to be the people of God. On a verry cold day, I stoped at a house to warm, in S. p. Grove, while warming, I asked the folks if the stood in needs of Bibles, or Testaments. One of them said "Are you one of those Hell fire preachers, that goes pouring down hell fire & brimstone upon the people, and preach up Eteranl Damnation to a part of the humain family. We are all Universalist in this timber and you cannot sell us any of your Bibles."

Not wishing to enter upon a controvercy with a man in his own house, I replied; "I always tryed to confine myself to the truth, as I found it in the Bible, that tells me that God will separate the righteous from the wicked at the last great day. The wicked shall go away into everlasting punishment, but the righteous into life Eternal, and again, all that are in their graves shall come forth—they that have done good, to the section of life, and they that have done evil to the resorection of damnation. And I am bound to preach the truth, and if offend the wicked I cannot help it." Well, said he, You cant sell us any of your Bibles. Have you a Bible (I asked) Yes sir, said, Because if you had told me that you had none, I am authorized to *give* you one, but as you have one I have only one word to say to you. Read it prayerfully, and do as it tells you. Love God & keep his commandments.

Not many days after this, I happened at W. a little vilage where was a protracted meeting in progress by the presbyterians. I sought a private interview with their preacher Mr. S.—told him that I had been informed that he stated in a sermon a fiew days ago in that place. That the A. & F. B. society was an entier Baptist concern, and that the had altered the common version to read immerse instid of Baptize, he said that he had made such a statement. And that he had it from good authority, and he believed it to be a fact. I shewed him a coppy, he saw the letters. A & F. B. S. he examined, and found that the version was not altered. Now, Sir, said I, you see that you have made a false impression on the minds of the public, and you are made sensible of it, will you do me, and the public the favour to correct it? he refused to do it. I am an agent for that society (said I) And it will devolve on me to correct all such eronious reports, which are prejudicial to the progress of the cause. so I took the liberty and don it.

In many plases I found myself called on to correct the same kind of mischievious reports, put in circulation by the pedobaptist. I carried the Bible question with me. By which means I succeded in heading all such reports, and set the truth before the public mind. In the year 1845 I travelled 3040 miles and preached 125 times, beside many lectures on the Bible cause.

1846. I spent in the same way, and traveled 1917 miles and preached 121 sermons. 1847. I laboured the whole year in the state of Missouri, after preaching three months for the Wyaconda Association, I preached regularly once a month for six churches who were intierly destite of preaching, and to other destitute neighborhoods. Rode, 2973 miles and preached 134 sermons.

1848. I preached for three churches, all in Monroe county, M-o. Rode, 2386 miles. and preached 133 sermons, and returned home in September. And have been Idle a long time. Since the General Association of M-o was organized, I have attended six out of nine of their meetings, and also many disstrict associations. The General Association of Illinois, and many district Associations. Of which I have not made mention in my narative—I have notised in my Journal, all the General Associations, district Associations, protracted meetings, Communions, the number of hopeful conversions, the number of Temperance lectures and exhortations, I have delivered. But I think it unnecessary to mention them here.

At all the church meetings, and protracted meetings I attended where there were a number of persons to be Baptized, I never would Baptize any, except where I was specially caled on by the church or their pastor to do so. When I recieved an appointment from The Board of the H. M. society, I thought that I was authorized to Baptise individuals on a profession of their faith in Christ. wheresoever I found them in my field of labour, who requested it, or demanded it at my hands. Having done so in five instances, and in some instances eight or ten miles from any church, and gave them a certificate of Baptism to unite with any Baptist church in General Union, who when they offered their certificate to the church most convenient to them, the preacher who supplied the church (and who was under the same kind of an appointment that I was) thought that such a cours of proceeding was out of order. And with some difficulty those persons obtained membership. He therefore prefered charged against me, for baptizing persons in the bounds of his labours, which had to be setled by a committy of Brethren. Therefore to avoide giving an offence to any of my preaching brethren. When any requested baptism at my hads, I would alwas tell them to go to the nearest church, to them, and be baptized by a regular pastor. Some have expressed their surprize at this, and asked it I were not fully authorized to administer the ordinences of the church, and if so why refuse to baptize them. which made it nessary to give an explanation. I have witnessed the hopeful conversion of some hundred under my labours, and should have been delighted to have baptized them, but for this verry cause. I have long been convinced that there is too great an anxiety existing with some of our Ministers to increase numbers irrespective of vital and sound piety, and to swell the number of Baptisms in their reports to the corrisponding secretary of the Board, and this no doubt is one cause why we have so many unworthy persons in our churches, who know nothing of a change of heart affected by the Holy Spirit. And now, even now while I am writing, I tremble for the safety of the ark in which we are sailing, *The Baptist cause;* and the greatest curse that can exist among us is, false religion. False religion in an individual or in a church, is a sandy foundation, and that structur which is built upon it will surely fall, and great will be the fall of it. O God, deliver us. Deliver our Ministers, our churches, our brethren & Sisters, and the unverse from a system of false religion and let pure and undefiled religion predominate throughout the universal world, and that all which the Father hath given to the Son, may be raised up at the last day.

Since the date of my first appointment by the Board of the H. M. society, Nov. 19th 1832 (ie) in sixteen years I have travelled about 40925 miles. and preached 2931 sermons. Aided in organizing 14 churches, and ordained 12 Ministers.

It is my desire, and prayer to God, that this imperfect biorgraphical sketch of my life, may bi a blessing to my posterity. The Church. and the World. AMEN.

JACOB BOWER.

Oct. 18th 1849 Rejected by the General Association in Griggsville because of lenght.

The above transcribed this 15th day of July. in the year of our Lord 1859.

Biographical sketch continued from Oct. 18th 1849 to July 23, 1857.

After I retured from Mo. in 1849. A church in Jersey county requested me to serve them with the gospel once a month for one year. This year they built a good Church House. The next year 1850. They invited me to preach for them twice a month. Their house was dedicated—a protracted meeting held, the church was blessed with some valuable additions, and their hous paid for. I collected money and paid off the debt & interest of $195,00. And $8,00 to aid in paying for lamps—gave them $18,17 of my own salery of $100, as They have since enjoyed several gracious revivals. May the chief Shephard preside over— and bless them abundantly. On Sunday the 22nd day of June 1851. I preach my last sermon for them. The Lord was very good to me—blessed me with good health, so that I was able to fill all my engagements with them for two years, and failed only one Sunday—it rained so that non met.

In 1852 & 3 I preach twice a month for 18 months for

Winchester church. *This is my home.* In 1853 they united
with the Carrollton Association and numbered jut 200
members. They also have been blessed with many gracious
revivals.

On the 28th day of Feb. 1850. I went to St. Louis—spent
11 days with the collerd brethren—I preached 14 sermons
for both the collered churches. Meachum—Pastoŕ of the
first, & Anderson of the seccond collered Baptist church.
10 wer baptized, & 10 more were recieved for Baptism the
sunday after I left. Both churches wer much revived, they
desired that I would visit them again soon, I am anxious to
see them again, for I have not been with them since.

On the 4th day of Sept. 1851. My wife & I took a trip to
Ohio. She was sick most of the time we wer there. During
our stay there, I preach once in Lafayette; and in Covington
twice. In Urbana 3 times—Jacksonville twice, we were
absent two months.

In the year 1852, I rode 1086 miles—preached 67 sermons
deliverd 50 exhortations—attended 42 prayer meetings—
made 111 religious visits—spent 99 days—gave one Temperance lecture—attended one protracted meeting, &
baptized 3. Recieved $5,50. 1853. was spent in much the
same way.

1854. January 10 I attended a protracted meeting at Kings-
ton Church Adams Co. Eld. Wm. Hobbs Pastor. Eld. Os-
burn was in attendance and don all the preaching. 7 Or 8
were aded to the church by baptism I spent 14 days at this
meeting—preach only twice—gave several exhortations.

Feb. 12. I went to Belmont church and preached 14 times,
in 8 days—Rainy—Sleet & snow—unfavourable wether for
meetings. I preach in many different plases this year wheresoever I had an invitation.

Here closes eighteen fifty four. And I do grieve I've don no
more, But when I take a retrospect. Of duty which I did
neglect. Yet find but fiew that I pass-d by. When called
to preach I did comply. Affliction too I suffered more. than
I have done for years before Full eighteen weeks, was I
confind. Yet the good Lord was very kind. Jan. 16, 1855. I

started on another tour to Ohio, was gon from home, three months & five days. While in Ohio, I preached ten sermons—delivered three exhortations. While at Paris Ill on my way home, I stoped with Eld. Ryley, and preach 12 sermons—gave 2 exhortations. After my return from Ohio, I accepted a call from the Belmont baptist church. On the 20th of May I began and preach 11 months, 50 sermons. Recieved $41,00.

May the 6th 1856. My wife & I made a trip to Decatur Macon Co—spent the summer with some of our children—staid 4 months—During our stay in that part of the Lords morral vinyeard, I preach 27 sermons—assisted Eld. Talmen in 2 communions. and gave 2 S-S lectures. Attended the Carrollton association at Verden on thursday the 11th of September. A delightful Association.

July 31st I sold my farm in Scott Co. and on the 6th day of Nov. we moved to Winchester. Eld. P. Bennet Pastor of the church have the pleasure of attending four or five meetings in a week. But I am deprived of the happy priviledge of preaching the blessed gospel of the son of God. I feal as a fish out of the water.

June 25, 1857. I had the happy priviledge of attending Shurtliff Colledge commencement in Uper Alton where I had the pleasure of grasping the friendly hand of many of my old aquaintance and good brethren, and shared withem their kind hospitalities and renew our former aquaintence. It was altogether the best commencment I have ever been at. The gradates certainly did great honor to themselves—to faculty & the institution.

Among the many happy greetings of beloved ones, was my good old friend & warm hearted brother J. M. Peck. which to me was the cowing part of all, from the fact that I had the pleasure of having his company in my Buggy to his mansion at Rock Spring, there I spent one week with him most agreably, and recieved many good lessons of instruction —I preach twice in his church house (oakhill) Then accompanied him to Bethel church meeting on saturday, where he filled the Moderators chare with dignity and honor to himself and the cause of God. On the Lords day he preached an excellent Sermon siting in a chair, on account of phiscial debility. But he is slowly, and I hope permanently recovering his heath—May the Good Master spare his useful life yet many years is the desire & prayer of   JACOB BOWER

Winchester Scott Co. Ill. July 23d, 1857.

CHAPTER VIII

THE "RELIGIOUS EXPERIENCE"
OF A CANDIDATE FOR THE MINISTRY AS
RELATED BEFORE THE CHURCH

[Before receiving a license or ordination all Baptist candidates for the ministry were required to relate their religious experience before the church. The following is the religious experience of a young man, of about twenty years of age, written by himself, evidently in preparation for this ordeal. This was found in manuscript, in the Library at Shurtleff College, Alton, Illinois.]

EXPERIENCE

I was the subject of religious impressions when quite young. I recollect that while attending a Sabbath School the Summer after I was 8 years old, my mind was considerably exercised on the subject, particularly while reading the Darymans Daughter, a tract which I received at S. S. I thought that I too was a sinner, & could not expect to die the happy death which this little girl did, except I become a Christian. From these impressions I made some resolutions, that I would try to become a Christian, at least, before I was very old. I would frequently try to pray before I went to sleep at night; but rarely tried to pray in the morning. Thus it is evident that it was not from any love to prayer that I prayed; but from a consciousness of guilt & a fear of being punished. But these serious impressions lasted but a short time: I soon left off trying to pray entirely. Thus early did my Heavenly Father begin to call after, & admonish his disobedient, & refractory child; and thus early did the native enmity of my heart to God, begin to be manifest. But thro' abounding mercy other means were employed to remind me of my duty to God. My dear Mother would frequently talk

to me on the subject of religion & sometimes pray with me—
at those seasons my conscience was tender—and not unfre-
quently after hearing a sermon or being at a prayer-meeting,
was my mind considerably impressed. If I recollect the
spring after I was 13 years old there was an extensive revival
of Religion in (the) (Town) Lowville the Town where I then
resided. I recollect on one Sabbath, my Parents having both
gone to Meeting, being alone I employed myself in reading
the Bp. Magazine, which my Father then took, I read in that,
a Sermon or Newyears address written by the editor, from
these words 'This year thou shalt die;' My mind was arrested.—I gave it a second reading. I saw that I was exposed
to Death every moment—that I was unprepared to die. I
believed that except I became a Christian I must be lost forever. My mind was now more deeply impressed than at any
time previous. I made new resoultions—resumed the habit
of trying to pray, hoping that I should yet become a Christian. I was the subject of similar exercises for several months
'till at length I lost nearly all of them, & became almost
thoughtless on the subject of my soul's Salvation; except
when some alarming Providence awoke in me a little sense
of my danger for a few moments.

But O the loveing kindness & forbearance of God towards
this chief of sinners! The rejected, grieved, Spirit did not
take its everlasting flight! In the Spring after I was 18, in
the year 1831 I became again the subject of its strivings.
My mind was not at rest—My Mother & others exorted me
to repent & prayed for me. This seemed to probe the wound
which I felt, deeper. There was about to be a protracted
Meeting in the Bp. Ch. near where I lived. I secretely hoped
that I might become a Christian before the Meeting terminated, and at the same time resolve to keep it to myself—
that no one should know any thing of my exercises. Such
were my selfish, incorrect, views of the Religion of Christ
at that time.

When mingling with my associates I affected an entire
indifference on the subject; but when alone the faithful
admonitions of conscience gave me no rest. It seemed to me

that every day my heart was growing harder wickeder instead of better. I began to be alarmed for fear that God would justly give me up to hardness of heart & reprobate mind. The anticipated Meeting commenced—An aged Minister conversed with me, on the subject of my soul's Salvation, very affectionately but pointedly. I felt the truth of what he said. And faithfully exorted me to repenance; and says he, 'if you live to get home, on your knees before God read the 1st Chap. of Prov and the 3ᵈ of John. I did. I was now more deeply convicted of my self as a sinner against God. My feelings were pungent, yet I strove to conceal them from my friends. For some days my feelings were various—I saw that I was indeed a great sinner, but I was too proud to become a disciple of Christ. Sometimes I sought relief in trying to banish the whole from my mind; and then trembled for fear of being left to perish and would pray for conviction in my sins. At other times my mind was filled with Infidel principles—one evening at Meeting, I requested the prayers of Christians by saying, *if* there is a reality in religion, I wish Christians to pray for me. No sooner had I sat down, than a sense of this awful sin of unbelief seemed to roll in upon my soul with a mountains weight. I began to think that I was too great a sinner to receive pardon—it seemed that *my* sins were the most agrivating— I had sinned against light—had long been resisting the strivings of God's Holy Spirit—and was now questioning the reality of the holy religion of Jesus Christ. The next eve' (Sabbath eve) I arose in public & *begged* prayers of Christians expressing, as well as I could, my feelings. Several christians united in fervent prayer in my behalf & I tried to pray for myself. Nothing but the Blood of Christ seemed to be between me & (Death) hell.—This evening the meeting closed—I arose early in the morning with this fixed resolution—to make the Salvation of my Soul, the chief business of my life—that if I perished I would perish at the feet of Jesus,—praying for mercy, & Salvation for His sake. It seemed to me perfectly reasonable that I should love & serve God with all my heart; and If I did love and serve Him, all

my life I should do no more than was my duty to do.—
Arrangements had been made that I should spend a few
months with Mr. A. Waters a member of the Bp. Ch. (and
now a successful Minister of Christ's Gospel). My younger
Brother went with me. On my way I told him what my resolutions were; and exhorted him not to put off the Salvation
of his Soul, till he become so great a sinner as I was. During
the day Mr. Waters conversed with me on the subject of
religion. I told him what my feelings were and begged his
prayers in my behalf. My mind remained about the same
till Wednesday, when I was on the borders of despair—every
sin that I had committed, seemed agravating enough to sink
me to hell—O how I had treated the Lord Jesus!—I was
ploughing—I stoped my team,—and resolved to try again
to cast my soul, my wicked heart, my all, just as I was, upon
the Mercy of Christ whom I had so much abused—I tried
to pray—and it was Lord save or I perish!—with strong
cryings and tears. But to my astonishment I soon forgot the
urgency of *my* case, and was praying for the Spread of the
Redeemers kingdom, and for the Salvation of others. In
my urgency in prayer I had unconciously lost those feelings
which were near dispare. This alarmed me. I feared that
God had left me—I tried to pray for conviction, but could
not realise those painful feelings which I had felt. My sins
looked very sinful; but I could not be distressed about them
as I had been The life of the Christian looked reasonable, and
delightful. And I felt determined to love & serve God to the
extent of my ability. I dare not indulge the least hope that I
was a christian, lest I should be deceived. The State of my
mind remained much the same during the rest of the week. On
the following Sabbath, when a convenient opportunity was
offered, I publicly related the state of my mind, and solicited
the prayers of the Saints for me. And I trust they did pray
for me: for soon my soul was happy in God; and I rejoiced in
God my Saviour. I then began to cherish a little hope that
I had passed from death unto life;—This was in April 1831.
Suffice it to say that in June I related my experience to the
Bp. Ch. in Lowville & Venmark, and was rec'd by Baptism.

Some of my exercises with regard to *preachig the Gospel of my Redeemer*. I have often thought that the very pious and devoted family of Bro Waters, was rendered a great blessing to me. As Br. W. was gone from home much of the time, the duty, of leading in family worship, morning & evening, devolved upon me. This perhaps served to make me more watchful & prayerful, than I otherwise should have been: I also enjoyed their christian instruction. It was good for me to bear the yoke in my youth. Soon after I became a member of the Ch. of Christ, my soul was particularly drawn out in prayer for those who have not the Blessed gospel preached unto them—and that they might speedily hear its joyful sound. I had an opportunity of reading the N. Y. Bp. Regr. which contained much Missionary intelligence. With this, I was, in particular, highly interested, I would look out the Missionary intelligence, first, when I took the paper to read. Often when alone reading the precious Bible, I would exclaim—O what a *Treasure!*— O that those poor heathen enjoyed what I now do!

During the autumn & winter of 1831 I read the life Rev. Samuel Pierce. Memoirs Mrs. Judson with what other Missionary intelligence I could get. Perhaps this served to awake in me this important inquiry:—Lord what wilt thou have me to do? I had become convinced, that every christian, however limited his ability or opportunity, may be useful in his appropriate sphere; and that (the) our Divine Master has an appropriate work in His vineyard, for every one of his disciples to do. I thought that it was realy the desire of my soul to be useful to the utmost extent of my ability. And I began seriously to enquire in what way I could most glorify God; and be most useful in building up the Redeemers kingdom. This was my special prayer— Lord what wilt thou have me to do?—Sometimes I wished that I was competent to instruct the poor heathen Idolitors in the way of Life and Salvation, from the Word of God. I had not long thus enquired what the Lord would have me do; when my mind was arrested with this impression;—prepare to preach the Gospel—The more I thought and prayed about it the stronger the impression was that I must some time try to preach the Blessed Gospel; and that it was my duty to prepare to preach it. Tho' I had for some time considered the work of Preaching Christ's holy gospel, as a blessed and desireable work, to the man who is called of God to preach it yet, it seemed to me that I could raise a 1000 objections against myself trying to preach it. Tried evade it by excuses—I was, it seemed to me, every way unqualified for it—had no gift for public speaking,—my education was extremely limited—was wholly destitute of means to defray the expense of an education—and above all I lacked a natural ability.—I thought that I could select hundreds of young men that were far better qualified every way than I was. Why is it not their duty to preach the Gospel? At such seasons I was often much distressed and could find peace of mind only by yeilding the point—casting myself wholly upon the Grace of Christ, with the determination, to do what seemed to be present duty to the extent my ability leaving the result with God. In the meantime I commenced going to a district School for the winter. But my mind was not at rest (with regard) in refference to the duty of preaching the Gospel. The work seemed the most delightful one, that I could possibly engage in; were I qualified;—and were I sure that I was called of God to the Work.

I had been careful to keep all my trials, on this subject, to myself. For was fearful that they were the temptations of the Adversary.—On the 12th of Feb. I think, Eld. T. A. Warner, who was pastor of the Ch. asked me, if I had not some exercises of mind, relative to the duty of Preaching the Gospel. I acknowledged to him that I had, and related to him, the trials of my mind on the subject, as well as I could. I recollect, that, in the eve', I was much ashamed to think that I had told him so many of my exercises.

Missionary intelligence was increasingly interesting—my mind dwelt much on the situation of those without the Gospel and the great call for labourers among them. One night in my sleep I thought I was with two Bros. in a cottage with a company of swarthy heathen teaching them how to read, & preaching the gospel of Christ unto them.—It was a heaven to my soul—I awoke—I thought they were the happiest moments of my life. This made some impression on my mind; and I tried to search my heart to see if I was willing to devote my life to such a work. I thought I would joyfully if I could most glorify God in so doing. Soon after this I think I enjoyed more of the sensible presence of God in my soul than ever before; and my mind was more deeply exercised relative to the duty of Preaching Christ. Sometimes when thinking of the destitute portions of the Earth— of the millions who are perishing for the lack of knowledge— I would exclaim weeping, "Lord here am I send me." And at other times a sense of my inability seemed to forbid it entirely.

In April, Br. Calvin Horr related his exercises relative to preaching the Gospel to the Ch. and rec'd. a license.

At this time I was much affected but was not willing to have my exercises known to the Ch.—Soon after I had further conversation with Eld. Warner—asked council of him—he advised me to cherish the impression, & make it a special subject of prayer. I also had an interview with Eld. J. Blodget—an aged Minister in whom I had the most implicit confidence, & to whom I had been to School when quite young; I told him my trials & solicited his advice & prayers. This man of God gave them as freely & affectionately as a Father. He advised me make known my feelings to the Ch.—he thought perhaps it would be a relief to my mind. Eld. Warner concured with him—soon an opportunity was given me to relate to the Ch. my exercises. I did; that I might have their advice & prayers.

I did not feel it my duty to engage immediately in trying to Preach; but that this duty was before me, & that I ought to use every means in my power to qualify me for it. My Brethren advised me to cherish this impression of duty prayerfully, and to be free in exercising my gift in exortation whenever I felt it my duty. Eld. W. advised me to try go to School as soon as I could. My mind was now greatly revived. I resolved to try to do what seemed to be present duty, to the extent of my ability; and to leave the result with God.

I had a great desire to go to school, but my Father needing my labour it was not practicable for me to go.

In the following Spring 1833. My impression of duty was about the same, and my resolutions the same.

My Father told me, that, as I had a desire to acquire an education; he would try to do without my labour, but that he could not give me any encouragement of assistance from him; for he was not able.

(I was 20. Decr 16, 1832) By labouring for one of my neighbours, about 2 months, with the kindness of some brethren & friends; I was enabled to attend a select School 13 weeks.

CHAPTER IX

CHURCH LETTERS

1. Letters transferring membership

2. Letter from the Wood River Church, Illinois to the Illinois Association

3. Letter from the Twelve Mile Prairie Church to the Wood River Church requesting "helps" in the ordination of a minister.

4. Letter from the Ogle Creek Church, Illinois to the Wood River Church asking help from the Wood River Church.

CHURCH LETTERS

South Carolina Benutton (?) Districk
Wee the Unighted Baptist Church of Jesus
Christ Known by the Name of the Shole Church
Met in Conferince and our beloved Brothor——
Josiph White Requisted a Lettor from us therefore
Wee Dismis him as an Ordorly Member in full
fellowship With us When Joined to, a Nothor
Baptis Church in ordor Signed by ordor of the
Church this 17 day of Augoust——1805

ROBᵀ RELL CC

February 15th A.D. 1806 the Church of Jesus Christ
Linville holding the Doctrine of particular and Eternal
Election by Grace Effectual Calling final preseviarance
in Grace Believers Baptism by Immercion &.
being met together in Church meeting on petition of
Sister Temperance Bradshaw have granted her this letter
Sertyfying that She is in our Christian fellowship
and when join,d to Any other Church of Same
faith Dismis,ᵈ from us Signed by order of the
Church   AMBROSE CARLTON Paster

239

Oct 1808 Wea baptis Church of Jesus Christ on
Blackburns fork Do grant unto our beloved brother
John Russel a letter of Dismission and he is hereby
dismist from the Cares of this Church when jay (nd)
to another orderly baptis Church sign in bahalf of the whole
JOB MORGAN CC

Oct 1808 Wia baptis Church of Jesus Christ on
Blackburns fork Do grant unto our beloved Sister
Dorrethe Russel a letter of dismission and she is here
by dismist from the Cares of this Church when
Join d to another order by baptis Church. Signed in beha-
lf of the whole   JOB MORGAN CC

September 16th–1809 We Baptist
Church of Christ on the Linquin fork
of Little river do dismiss our beloved
Sister Margaret means She being
in full fellowship with us being
dismist from us when Joined to any
orderily Baptist Church Sind
in behalf of the hole   ABRAHAM ENLOW

The Baptist Church of Christ in Wayn County Kentucky
    on otter
Creek Holding Believers Baptism by amersion the final
    preservance
of the Saints & haveing received a letter from William Ogle
    Requesting
a letter of his Standing with us we do sertify that he was a
    member with us
in Good Standing and Receivd a letter of Recommendation
    from us
and this Sertify that when joined to aney other Babtist
    Church of the
Same faith and order Dismisd as Such from us Done at our
Meeting the third Saterday in October 1820
                              RICHARD WADE Clk

South Carrolinia Pendelton District
Baptist church of Christ by the name of
new hope to whom these Lines may come
Greeting we commend unto you our beloved
Sister Elizabeth Bates as an orderly member
in full fellowship——and when joind to any
orderly church in our union is Legally
dismisd Sind in behalf of the Church
April 1st 1810   ADIN WIMPY Clk

Louisiana District of St Louis March 16th 1811
the Baptist Church of Jesus Christ at Cold Water to any
Church of the same faith and order—Whereas our Brother
Thomas Ellis is about to Remove his place of Residence
from amongst us this is to certify that he is a member
Amongst us in good standing and full fellowship and When
Received By you Dismist from us Done at our Church meeting
and signed by order of the Church this 16th March 1811
                                    WILLIAM PATTERSON Clk

Sant Clare County Febuary 25 1812
Illinois Territory We the baptis Church
of Christ at wood river meting Hous do
dismiss our beloved brother and sister Allin Ingrom
and Rebeckah Ingrom as a ordily member and
in full fellowship with us and fully
dismist when joind to any other Church
of the same faith and order signd by
order of the Church
                                    C C
                                    GEORGE MOORE

Baptist Church of Christ on Bays Fork W. County
Kentucky to the Church of Christ on Wood River St Clair
County Illinois Territory greeting, very dear brethren we
     recd your
letter requesting us to send you our charges against Charles
     Reavis

and Jesse Ennes which are as follows (to wit) November
26th 1808
Charles Reavis excluded for disobeying the Church and defrauding his
creditors——September 28*th* 1809 Jesse Ennes was excluded
for drunkenness and rioting these are the charges we have
against them as stands on record. We leave them with you
to act
at your discretion as the Lord may direct
your satisfaction will be ours in that case. We
are your sister in gospel bonds Farewell (by order of the
Church at our meeting November 28th—1812

STEPHEN CLAYPOOL senior **C.C.**

We the United Baptist Church of
Jesus Christ at Shoal Creek
Do hereby certify that our well
Beloved Sister Lucy Hill is in
Full fellowship with us & is hereby
Dismissed from us when Joined to
any other Church of the same faith
and order ————————
April 2[d] 1813   signed by order

SIMON LINDLY **C.C.**

Indiana Territory—we the Baptistt
  Posey County—Church of Christ
at Bethel & holding the doctrines
of election the final preserverance
  do dismiss our sister
in the Lord Polly Fulk and she
is hereby dismissed when joined
to any other Church of the same
faith and order.
               Sined by order
of the Church this 24th Feb 1826

Whereas Brother Richard Conley and Patsey Conley
his wife are mambers in good standing with

us and prays letters of Dismission from usto
join some other Church it is granted them
and they are Dismissed from us when they
join any other Church of our faith and order
Don By order of the Babtist Church at——
mount moriah at thare august meeting—1819

ELISHA HEDDEN Clk

State of South carolina Pendleton District
We the Baptist Church of Christ at
Conneross Setting in conference the Saturday
Before the fourth Sunday in September 1816
Brother John Moar Applying for a letter
of dismission we dismiss him in full
Fellowship when join,d to any other Church
of the Same faith and order Assign,d in the
Behalf of the Church

EDWARD COFFE Clk

State of South carolina Pendleton District
We the Babtist Church of Christ at Conneross
Setting in conference the Saturday before the
fourth Sunday in September 1816
Sister Mary Moar applying for a letter of
Dismission we dismiss her in full Fellowship
When joind to any other Church of the same
faith and order Assign,d in the behalf of the
Church

EDWARD COFFE Clk

The Baptis Church of Christ at Pleasant Point Pulaski
County Kentucky of the general union this is to Certify
that our Beloved sister Polly Parke is in good
Standing with us and such we recommend our sister
to any Church of the same order and when
joined will be dismised from us

Signed by order of the Church April the 15th 1817

AARON BARROW Clk

We Commend unto you Nancy Young our
Sister which is a servent of the Church which
is at Republican Meeting house in White County
Tennesse State that you Receive her in the
Lord as becometh saints   Signed by order of
The Church   September the 21th 1818

ELIJAH WARD C

We Commend unto you James Reding our
Brother which is a servent of the Church
Which is in White County Tennessee State
That ye Receive him in the Lord as becometh
Saints of the Lord   Signed by order of the
         Church   ELIJAH WARD C
      Republican meeting
      house

   Harrison County State of Indiana
fourth Saturday in October 1821
The Church of Christ at Little Flock holding
Believers Baptism by immersion eternal election effectual calling and the final perserverance
of the saints through grace and the judgement
to come Send greeting to any other church of
the same faith and order,
         Beloved Brethern
              Whereas our very dear Sister
Elizabeth Smith have applied to us for a letter
of dismission in consequence of her being about
to remove from our State and County we
recommend her as a worthy member in full
fellowship with us and when received by you
will be dismissed from our immediate care
we hope dear Brethern that you will prove
a blessing to one another and may God
in his goodness bless you all.
      Farewell
         By Order of the Church
                        PAUL FRENCH clk

State of Tennessee   October first
Mc Minn County   Satturday 1829

We the baptist church of christ at
Big Spring holding believers babtism
by immersion and final perse
verance of the Saints through grace
& do hereby dismiss our brother
John Hammel a lisend minnister
of the gospel in full fellowship
for the purpose of joining some
other church of the same faith
and order done by order of the church
in church confernce

RUSSELL LANE
assistant C" Clk

A Letter from the Wood River Church (Illinois) to
The Illinois Association.

State of Illinois

Madison County

We the United Baptist Church of Jesus Christ at woodriver
To the Ministers and Messengers Composing the Illinois
Association to Convene att Richland Creek meeting house
St Clear County on the
Very Dearly beloved brethern in the Lord we have a renewed obligation thank God for the approaching anual
meeting we therefore gladly Correspond with you by letter
and dellegate to this end we have chosen and sent our beloved brethern & c to set with you who can declare our
situation more particularly pray receive them into Counsil
we have nothing new or strange to write our principles are
the same the Bible is our Rule and Standard of life we have
still to lament the languishing state of Zion Particularly our
own leanness nothing but Coldness apear in the professors
of Christianity while sin abounds in the world dear brethern

pray for us that the good shepherd would visit this flock
& lead us into fresh pastures & smile upon zion that his word
may be glorified to the ends of the earth

Dear brethern we conclude with this prayr that the lord
would watch over you and guide you into ways of
Righteousness   we are your little sister in the gospel farewell

A Letter requesting "Helps."
in ordination.

The twelve mile Prairie Church to the Woodriver Batist
Church sendeth Christian Love.

Beloveds, we wish you to send us your Elder in order to
examin & ordain, if proper. Br Sam⌐ Smith to the work of the
Ministry, the appointment on the Second Saturday of December next at Brother Timothy Higgans' at ten oclock
A. M.

By order of the Church ———

Clerk

DAVID BADGLEY

pro tem

October *4th* 1823.

Letter requesting help from
one Church to another

Illinois,   St Clair County Jan.y 20ᵗʰ 1822
The United Baptist Church of Jesus Christ,—called Ogle
Creek Church; Sendeth greeting—Grace to you and peace
from God our father, and from the Lord Jesus Christ.———
Dear brethern,
        Troubles having got in our Church and matter of
great weight, we humbly pray you to send us help from your
Church, say two members or more to meet at Job Badgley's
on the third saturday in April next,—as likewise we have
sent to several other Churches, and may the Lord God of

heaven and Earth bless you and us, and be with us,—and direct us in all our undertakings, for which we humbly pray for Jesus Christs sake, this to the United Baptist Church of Jesus Christ, called Wood river Church.————————

Signed by order of the Church,

JOB BADGLEY Clerk

Pro tem

CHAPTER X

EXTRACTS FROM THE RECORDS OF FRONTIER BAPTIST CHURCHES

1. Records of Severn's Valley Church, Kentucky, 1788–1790

2. Records of Boone's Creek Church, Kentucky, 1799

3. Constitution and Rules of a Church formed on Beaver Creek, Kentucky, 1798, (Mount Tabor Church) with the Records for 1803.

4. Records of the Wood River Baptist Church, Illinois, 1812–1822.

[The Severn's Valley Baptist Church is the oldest Baptist Church west of the Alleghany mountains. The Manuscript Records are in the Library of the Southern Baptist Theological Seminary, Louisville, Kentucky. They have been partly destroyed by fire, and the minutes for several of the early years are not legible. The Records printed here are for the years 1788 to 1790.]

SEVERNS VALLEY CHURCH RECORD.

March 20 (1788) The church Meeting as trial and proceeding to business agreeable to request Thomas Gilleland and Wife Came and Was Duly Sworn Concerning Brother Johnston The Church hearing the Evidence have thought Expedient to Lay him under Censure Untill farther Acknoledgment
Sept 27th The Church meeting and proceeding to Business as follows Brother Vertrees and Brother Larue is appointed Messengers for the association (Three lines marked out)
October 25th The Church Meeting and Proceeding to Prayr Brother Johnston by making ample confession of his fault Which Was Satisfactory to the Church is agane Restored to his former priviledges
Dec^r   Brother John Larue Appointed Ruling Elder and
5th.   Brother Robbert Hodgings Appointed Deacon

Janu^r 2 1789	The Church Meeting and proceding to business agreed that Brother John Larue Cite Rebeckah Logston to the next Meeting of business to answer the Complaint laid in against her
Feb^r 4th	Philip Philips offered as a member Gave a Relation of his Experience and Was Satisfactory to the Church
	Susanah Phillips R. as a memb^r
Feb 21	The Church of Christ Meeting and Proceding to Business as follows Brother Phillips Choses Clerk for the Church (The next entry not legible)
March 22^d	Sister Rebeckah Logston By Making ample Satisfaction to the Church is restored to her seat again.
April 25	The Church meeting and Proceding to Business (The next four lines marked out)
May 28	The Church Meeting at Nolin and Proceding to business as follows as the absent Members that Were not at our Last Meeting are not Satisfied With the Conduct of John Allin Tharp he is not Rc̄d——
Jn 26th	Met together in the Vally no Business in Particular Brought before the Church
Sept 25th	The Church of Christ met at Nolin and after prayer proceeded to buseness

The Church Consists of forty-five Members
<table>
<tr><td></td><td>Brothers Josiah Dodge John Larue and Robt Hodgen Ware apointed Members to attend the Sociation at Cox is Creek on the 3d of october</td></tr>
</table>

Maragret Byres was Rec^d by letter

Lidia Winchester Was Rec^d by Experience

Octob^r 24	The Church of Christ Met at Severns Vally and as there was no business of consequence came before the Mimbers the Met and dismiss^d with prayer————————————
Novr 21	The Church Met at Nolin and after prayer proceeded to business...............

Brother Dodge Was appointed Moderator A Motion Was Made and agreed unto that it is the

Duty of all Heads of families in this Church to keep those of there families that are under there care under the same order and Disiplin as they themselves are bound to observe both in their Walk & Conversation also to use their endeavor (The next several lines illegible)

Dec[r]   The Church Met at Savrens Vally and after
26th 1789 prayer proceded to business

Gimimea Johnston Was Received as a member by Experience————A motion was made Respecting the Soply of those who Labour in the Gospel and it was agreed that those who Contributed any nesessaryes for that purpose Should give an account of the Same to the Deacons Who are Request to Set down thire names and also the Contributions made by them and have a true list of the Same to Give into the Church from time to time when Required

Jan[r],   The Church met at Nolin and After Prayer
22[d]   proceeded to business
1790

Brother Josiah was appointed Moderator
No perticular Business was brought Before the Church they Dismys[d] with prayer

Feb 26   the Church Mett No Business being Brough Before the Members the Mett and Dismiss[d] with prayer————————————————

March   the Church Mett and Dismiss[d] aftr pr.
27th

Apr   the Church Met and after prayer proceeded to
24th   Business Several of the Members haveing not filled thire Seats according to the order of this Church a list of thire names are given
(The next several lines not legible)
Brothers Dodge and Brother Larue are appointed to Wait on Brother Bozier in order to Reconsile a Matar in Controversy betwee him and John Davis and Report at the next Church Meeting; Should

they find by his conduct that he Refuses Deeling justly towards S^d Davis or Contrery to a Christian Conduct the above appointment——

May 22^d   The Church met at Saverns Vally No Business being laid Before the Church they Met and Dismissd with prayer

June 25th   The Church Met at Nolin and after prayer proceded to Business Honah Dinemah and Sarah Barton Give in thire Experience and was satisfactory to the Church and are Privileged to receive the ordinance of Baptism.

August 22   the Church met at Nolin No perticelor Business Was Laid before the Church the Met and dismiss^d with prayir

August 23   The Church having assembled and and taken to Consideration that Some Business ought to be seen Imediatly into Concluded to call a Church Meeting on Satarnday the 28 Same Inst

August 28th   The Church Met according to appointment Recbekkah Logsdon being listed to appear to answer and give in her Reasons for Reporting that Joseph Kirkpatrick had attempted to Violate her Chastity——

(Several lines here not legible)
and after consedering.....................the circumstances on Both Sides the Church Ware of opinion that nothing apeared against him worthy of Censure and therefore he was continued in his former standing

And that She Should be Admitted to her former privilages on Conditions of hir giving Satisfaction to the Church by Expressing her Sorow for her Conduct promising amendmendment through Divine Aid and also make Some Acknowledgment to him by Asking his forgivness

John Lerue Reported that at the Request of the Church he had cited Benjamin Johnston and Philip Philips to appear on this Day and Shew there Reason Why that Brotherly Love did not abound between them as ought to Remain between Member of one Church The Church being first Acquanted by Each of the parties that this was the case he also Reported that Johnston Refused to attend and on hearing the other Party the Church agreed to appoint Bennam Shaw John Lerue & Sam'l Watkins to attend————at his house and know this Eavning to know his Reasons for not attending and Endeavour to Reconcile thire Differences and Make Report to the Next Meeting of Business

Septr
5th

A Consultation held by the members it Appeared Expidient that the members appear in their places on Monday the 13th Inst at the house of Br Philips to attend to Business which Requires Instant attention ——————

Septr
13

Met according to Consultation and the Brethern Shaw Larue and Watkins and Report that Br Johnston Still Refused to attend and persisted in Refusing to attempt to Settle the Difference

Resolvd that the Grove Opposite to the Mouth of Middle Creek Being a Survey of five hundred acres

(Several lines not legible)

to Br Johnson .... payment of L57.00 which was to be Discharged in good land) in the following Terms the five hundred acres to be at the price of fifty pounds the note for twenty five pounds to Discount its nominal Sum the beef for which the Receipt or Note for L32–10 to be Rated at Sixteen Shillings & Eight pence hundred without allowing for the fifth Quarter and that am't added to the twenty five pounds and the Ballance to fifty pounds to be paid in Current trade to Br Philips by Br Johnson in the term of————
——————————and that Brn Josiah Dodge and

Jsan Dye be appointed to make the offer and in
case Brother Johnson Refuses the Grove on the
terms it is ordered that Br Philips pay br Johnson
the Sum of fifty Seven pounds ten Shillings in
Good farming land Out of one of his surveys on the
waters of Rough Creek or Indian Camp at the
Rate of twenty pounds per an hundred acres to
take Quantity to the am't at any Corner of the
Survey of which it is a part the length to be not
more than three times the Width and that Br
Philips or his Atty Make the Deed in the Space
of one year

RECORDS OF BOONE'S CREEK CHURCH FOR 1799

[The Boon's Creek Baptist Church was organized in 1785, and
is therefore one of the oldest of the Kentucky Baptist churches.
The complete records of this church, in two manuscript volumes,
are deposited in the Library of the Southern Baptist Theological
Seminary,˙ Louisville, Kentucky. Volume I contains the records
for the years 1785–1830. The Records here printed are for the
years 1799 to 1801.]

Jan^r 26th   The Church Conveyned in order after prayer
1799   proceeded to Business and receivd by Letter
Hannah Holmes & then Adjourned
Fef^r 7th   The Church Conveyned in Order and after Prayer
1799   proceeded to Business—
Whereon Complaint was made to the Church
that Bro George Winn had been guilty of Disorderly Conduct by Publickly saying he would
not attend the next Church meeting & also De-
clareing that he would not give another farthing
in Support of the Ministry, On which the Church
Agreed to suspend him untill he give satisfaction
and Cite him to Attend our Next Church Meeting,
Brother Samuel Moor & G Valandingham to Visit
him and converse with him on this Occasion——
Whereas it is now Represented to this Church
that the Seperate Brethern Constituting the

Church Called Bosmans Fork Church,—Are desirous of Affecting a Union with us we therefore. to shew our willingness thereunto, do Agree to appoint (Brethern) John Hazelrigg. Owin Winn— Randol Noe. Leonard K Bradley, Samuel Talbot & George Valandingham to confir with s^d Church on the Subject, previous to our next Church Meeting & then & there make report

March 23rd 1799   The Church Conveyned According to Appointment and after prayer proceeded to Business.

Agreed to postpone the Matter relative to Br G Winn untill our Next Meeting & Br George Valanding-ham is hereby Requested to Cite him to Attend

Also Agreed to postpone the matter respecting the Union Untill Our next Meeting and Appoint Brs Jno Hazelrigg. Owin Winn & George Valandingham as a Committee to reconsider the preposials made at the other Conference & prepare Amendments if Necessary & make Report at our Next Meeting

Also Agreed that the Church Meet again on the first saturday in April in Order to receive the Report———

Also Agreed that Br William Thomas be Dismisted According to his Request & that the Clark prepare a Letter for him before he starts to the Miammies the Church then Adjournd———

April 6^{the} 1799   the Church met according to her Last Appointmt and after prayer proceeded to Business——

Whereon the matter respecting Br George Winn Came forward & finding No Satisfaction given, the Church once more Agreed to postpone the matter untill Next meeting———

Also the Amendments to the union bill was brought forward by the Committee and being received by the Church, Agreed that a Coppy thereof be transmitted to the Church at Bosmans Fork by the hands of Brother Samuel Boon

April
27th
1799

The Church Met & After Prayer, Br George Winn Came forward and made such Acknowledgments, that the Church agreed to restore him again, Also Agreed to postpone giving an ansr to the Church at Bosmans fork, untill Next Meeting Also Agreed that Sister Margett Stuttiville have a Letter of Dismission when Ever sha may Apply for it then Adjournd————

May
25th
1799

The Church Conveynd in Order & After Prayer Proceeded to Business————————·

Whereon the Church Again Agreed to Postpone giving an Ansr to the Church at Bosmans Fork Respecting the union, untill our Next meeting—

the Business respecting a Call to Br Bambridge was convers'd on, and Unanimously Agreed that our Brethern Samuel Boon Leonard K Bradley and Randol Noe, prepare a Letter in Behalf Of this Church to Br Marshal, Respecting the Call to Br Bambridge as minister if this Church————————

Then Adjourned————————

June
22nd
1799

The Church Met in Order And After Prayer proceeded to Business Whereon the Church Requested that Brs Samuel Moor & Randol Noe Visit Br John Hazelrigg & Request him to bring forward the Reply respecting the union with Bosmans fork Church (at our Next Meeting)——

Also that Br George Valandingham prepare a Letter (in Behalf of this Church) to Our Next Asson and present at our Next Meeting for Inspection

Also Agreed that the following Brethern (towit) Owen Winn Randol Noe, Leonard K. Bradley Saml Talbert & Dennis Bradley be Appointed to Converse with Br Marshel Respecting his Dissatisfaction with Br Bambridge

July
27th
1799

The Church then Adjourned in Order

The Church Conveynd in Order & After Prayer proceeded to Business

Brother John Hazilrigg Agreeable to request, ————brought forward the reply Respecting Bosmans fork Church & it was rejected,

Also the Letter for Next Ass^{on} was Read & Received & Brothers George Winn Owin Winn & D. Bradley are Appointed as Deligates to represent s^d Church & carry her Letter into Ass^{on}

Also the Brehern Appointed at last meeting to converse with Br Marshal Reports that he says he intends to converse with Br Bainbridge the first Oppertunity with an Expectation of a Mutual Satisfaction, Betwixt them

The Church then Agreed & Chose Br John Hazelrigg Leonard K Bradley & Samuel Tablirt to revise the Letter brough forward by Br Hazelrigg Respecting Bosmans Fork Church, (Which was done Immediately and Brought forward by the Committee & Recein'd————

Brother Bambridge attending to the Call of the Church. Agrees to Attend this Church Statidly the first Sunday in Every Month The Church then Adjournd

Augst
24th
1799

The Church Conveynd in Order and After prayer proceed to Business

When the Money collected to Defray the Expences of Recording Our Minits was put into the hands of Br Owin Winn, 12/7—

a Complaint Lodged Against Br Leonard K Bradley for fighting the Church Agreed that as Br Bradley was Absent they would pospone the Matter untill Church Meeting

Br Owen Winn Appointed to Cite Br Bradley to Attend Our Next Meeting

Sep^{or}
31st
1799

the Church Conveynd in Order and after Prayer Brother Leonard Bradley gave the Church Satisfaction Respecting the Charge that was Against him for Fighting

But as there Appears to be a Difference between Br Bradley & Br George Winn, it is Agreed that it Lay Over untill Our Next Meeting

and Brother Dennis Bradley Cites Br G. Winn to Attend

Oct
25th
1799

The Church Met in order & After Prayer proceeded to business, Whereon it was concluded that as Br George Winn is unable to attend the Present meeting the Business respecting him & Br L K Bradley is Referd & Br Owen win is appointed to cite him to attend Our next meeting —then Adjournd

Nov^{r}
2nd

Brother G Winn still being unable to Attend the Church agreed to refer the matter to our Next Meeting, and appoint G. Valandingham Randol Noe Own Winn Dennis Bradley & Saml Talbot as a Committee to Attend with Leonard Bradley & Labour with Br G Winn and make Report in writing or Otherwise to our Next meeting Adjornd

Nov^{r}
30th
1799

the Church sitting in Order, agreed to hear the Report of the Committee Respecting the Matter of Grief subsidering between George Winn & Leonard Bradley (which report says they are reconciled, from which the Church is satisfied

April 4th
1801

The Church met according to appointment and after Prayer procee'd to Business

a greed to suspend Bro Leonard K Bradley by the Church for drinking to excess and is with held From the privelidges of the Church until satisfaction Is given members Recd into the Church the date above Thos Clarke Joseph Baty Henly Moore James Gest George Johnson Anna Gest Linny Mc Daniel Abraham Servant to Owin Winn

One servant to Leonard Burbage and then adjourned

   allso agreed to let George Johnson have a Letter
   April 4th 1801

May 2^d   The Church met according to appointment and
1801   after Preaching procee'd to Rec'd members into
the Church By giving the right hand of fellowship
Namely Sarah Baty Polly Cotton Wm Talbutt
Presley Talbutt Jane Servant to Bro Baty Racel
Servant to Bro Nicols George Servant Samuel
Moor Sarah servant Br G. Winn and then procee'd to Heare Expearances and then adjourned

May 3^d   Paptise Anna Wilson Polly Moore Nancy Moore
Patsy Gillaspy Salley Cotton Charles Grimes Cabel
Plunkit Grace Servant to Mr Cade Jane Servant
to Mr Jno Parish Margret Servant Ditto Rec^d
by Recommendation and Rec^d them in?

June 6th   The Church met according to appointment and
1801   after Prayer proceed to Business?

   also a greed to let John Hazelrigg and wife have
a letter of Dismission

   allos a greed to Restore George Mure and wife
to fellowship? allso a greed to Receive by Experances and Baptism James Vallandindham Joseph Pearce Negro Neroe Servant to Saml Talbutt
Negro James Servant to Mr Speers Negro Cate
Servant to Mr Watson Negro Rose Servant to
L. Burbridhe Negro Hannah Ser^t to D. Gillaspy
(Negro Jane Servant to L. Burbridge by Recommendation

   And then adjournd

Constitution and Rules of

A Church Formed on Beaver Creek Kentucky 1798.

A Covenant of a baptist Church on Beaver Creek entered
into the 5th of November 1798 (with seven members)

And Constituted by Elders, William Hickman, Carter
Tarrant, and Alexander Davidson.

Agreed to be constituted on the essential doctrines of the Gospel viz.

first, We believe in one only true and living God and that their are three persons in the God-head. the Father Son and Holy Spirit.

2nd. We believe that the Scriptures of the old and new Testaments, are the word of God, and the only rule of faith and practice.

3rd We believe that we are saved by grace thro faith and that not of ourselves it is the gift of God.

4th We believe in the doctrine of original sin.

5th We believe in mans impotency to recover himself from the fallen state he is in by nature.

6th We believe that sinners are justiyd in the sight of God, only by the imputed righteousness of Christ.

7th, We believe that the saints shall persevere and never finally fall away.

8th We believe that baptism and the Lord's Supper are ordinances of Jesus Christ, and that true believers and them only are the fit subjects of these ordinances, and we believe that the true mode of baptism is by immersion.

9*th* We believe in the resurrection of the Lord and universal Judgement,

10*th* We believe the punishment of the wicked will be everlasting and the Joys of the righteous will be eternal.

RULES AND REGULATIONS TO BE OBSERVED IN CHURCH DECIPLIN

First, In all Church meetings, it is the duty and place of the Minister or Elder to keep good order, and be forward in carrying on business, and that no member leave their seat without leave,

Second, In all cases touching fellowship the Church shall act by a majority of two thirds, and in case a majority cannot be had the member shall be debar,d from Church privileges untill a majority of 2 thirds can be had, and should any individual shew obstinacy the Church may deal with him or her, as appears right on the case,

Third, In Temporal matters, or such as do not immediately touch fellowship they may decide by a majority.

Fourth, Any motion made and seconded shall be put to the Church and no motion, or question shall be put without a second,

Fifth, Any member making a motion, or speaking in the Church shall rise from his seat, and stand and address the Elder and direct his discourse to him,

Sixth, In all debates the members shall direct their discourse to the elder and not to the contending party,

Seventh, No member shall speak more than three times upon the same subject without leave from the Church,

Eighth. If two shall rise at once to speak the Elder shall determine which rose first, and give him leave to speak first, and afterwards the other may speak,

Ninth, All members shall be receiv,d by experience, letter, or information of a member of our union, or Recantation, the member who may be receiv,d upon information shall be bound to produce his or her letter within twelve months.

Tenth, All offences must be dealt with in gospel order, but publick offences or such as does not come under the denomination of trespass against an individual ought to be dealt with in a publick manner in Church,

Eleventh, From Scripture authority we count it a duty for all members to attend each Church meeting unless providentially hinder,d and especially the Male members, therefore if any member neglect this duty, we count it a breach of good order and agree that all such must be dealt with as the Church direct,

MOUNT TABOR CHURCH

(Taken from MSS. Volume of Mount Tabor Church, 1798–1870)

Third Saturday in July 1803,

The Church met and after worship, proceeded to business; 1st A report was bro^t against Sister Arnett, for drinking too much, and it appears she is guilty, we therefore, appoint Sisters Baugh, Philips and Clack, to cite her to our next meeting.

2nd. Recd a peitition from Concord requesting helps, to set with them the first Saturday in August next, therefore we appoint and sent Bren R. Hunt, G. Right, J. Baugh, and Wm Baugh.

3rd The Church agree that bren Ferguson, and G. Right, hire the finishing of the meeting house, and that each free male member pay an equal part thereof; dismist in order;—

Third Friday in August 1803

The Church met and after worship proceeded to business,

1st The committee appointed to labour with and cite sister Arnett to this meeting, Report they acted agreable to the order of the Church, and say she appear,d to be humble, and very sorry for what she had done, therefore the Church restore her to fellowship

Saturday, The Church set after preaching, &ct.

1st Opened a door for the reception of members, and rec,d James Bradsberry, be recantation, 2nd Sister Dinah Allin apply,d fro a letter of dismission, which was granted; dismist

Third Saturday in Septr 1803

The Church met, and after worship, proceeded to business,

1st, Rec,d Reports against bror John Claspill, for drinking too much and appoint bre,r Phil. Baugh, Jas Bradsberry, and G. White to labour with and cite to next meeting,

2nd Rec,d an accusation against bro,s Wm Bradsberry, for fighting and using rough language, Agreed to refer it to next meeting

RECORDS OF THE WOOD RIVER CHURCH

[The Wood River Church was organized in 1806 and had as its pastor Rev. William Jones who served the Church from its organization to his death many years later. Jones was largely responsible for the organization of the first Baptist Association in Illinois, in 1807—The Illinois Association. The Church—now extinct—was located one mile east of the present town of Upper Alton, Illinois.]

1812

the first Satterday in July 1812 the Church met according to appointment after Devine worship B James Rantfrow, moderator. Ready for Business & the Church found in peace
                                                    GEORGE MORE Clk

August 1st The Church met & after worship ready for business brother William Jones Moderator chose the following brethern to attend the association J Beman George Moore & Able more & that the clerk prepare all them against next meeting
                                Signd by order
                                                    G MOORE Clk

first Sattarday in Jeneary 1813 Church met and after sarvis proceed to besness and then com forard Charls Jackenes and give in expearance and was Received
                                Signd by order
                                                    G MOORE Clk

the first Sattarday in febuary the Church met and nohing don
                                                    GEORGE MOORE Clk

the first sattarday in March Church met and nothing don
                                                    GEORGE MOORE Clk

First Saterday in July Church met & after worship ready for business & the church considers that Henry Williams has acted disordely & neglected to hear the Church he is therefore excluded
Second Brethen Russel, White & Beaman apointd deligates to the next association & bro Rentfro to Prepare a letter against next meeting

first Saterday in August Church met and after worship redey for business, the letter to the asociation was red and received.

first Sattarday Fubuary 1814 the Church met in pace and nothing don

the first Sattarday in March the church met and nothing don

first Sattarday In June the Church met and af sarvis proceeded to besness first there being a report in circulation that bro' Beck has Defrauded a certain M' Beman in Selling s'd Beman an unsound mare the members of this Church being Destressd with the report apoints Brother Joseph White to request brother Paul Beck to atend our next meeting & clear himself if he can, of s'd report. Signd by order

GEORGE MOORE Clk

First Saterday in July the Church met & after Worship ready for business. bro' White informed us he had told B Paul Beck the Church requestd his atendance at this meet as he is not here the Church agrees to wate with him til august meeting   Signd by order

GEORGE MOORE Clk

August first Saterday the church met & after worship ready for busness Some of our mebers having talked with brother Beck & he not being Present nor no incouragement that he would come to meeting he is therefore excluded for neglecting to hear the Church. Signed by order

GE° MOORE Clk

Sep'—the 3' 1814 The Church met & ater worship ready for business bro Jones Moderator 1st the letter to the ass" read

amended & receivd. 2nd brethers G. Moore C Kitchins & Jas Beman apointed deligates to the association 3rd brother John Russel & Sister Dorathy his wife Dismissd by letter
Signd by order   GEORGE MOORE Clerk

the first Sattarday In october the chirch met and after prer the chirch Redey for Bisness the first chose Brother Beeman modorrattor 2 Brther William Jones and Eliezabeth his wife give in thare ltters and was Received 3 he was chosan Standing modorrattor ————————————————————
4 Brother Chechens Chodd Clark to seet the (   )
Sind by order of the hole
                                   GEORGE MOORE C C

Novimber the first satterday the chirch met and nothing don
                Sinded by order
                                   GEORGE MOORE

December the first satterday th chirch met and after prar a door was opened for to receive members into feloship and John finley and Mary finley com forad with a letter and was Received into feliship
                Sined by order
                                   GEORGE MOORE

Jegneuary 7th 1815 the church met and after prar redey for bessness and was found all peace   sined by ordo
                                   GEORGE MOORE Clk

Febuary the church met and after prar redey for Beesness and nothing don
                Sined by or.
                                   GEORGE MOORE

March the chirch met and after prar proseeded to beesness and pitcht on the last saterday in April for fasting and praying and nothing mor

sind by order of the ho
GEORGE MOORE

the first sattarday in april the chirch met and after prar wredey for bisness and agreed to have preching on sattarday as well as Sonday   sined by ord.

GEORGE MOORE Clk.

The first Sattarday in may the chirch met and after prar redey for bisness and foun all in pece and ceumuning on the day folling

Sined by ord of the hole
GEORGE MOORE Cl.

the first Sattarday in June the chirch met and after prar proseeded to bisness and chused brother bagley modatear and proseeded to talk a bout fixing the meeting hous and also a peoint brother beeman to speake for the plank for the floors if so be that he cold geet some shoerty for a bout twoo acers of land whare about the house and grave yard is of Joseph Vane

On the first Saturday in July the Church met and after divine service proceeded to business 1st. the reference concernin plank brought forward 2d Br Beaman to engage the plank and the Church to furnish him with the Money for that purpose 3d

the first Satterdy in August the Church met & after Devine worship ready for Business 1st received B Beck By recantation & acknowledgment 2 rec^d B reavis By letter 3^d the Chose william Jones Beman & findlely as members to the assasiation and B Clark to write the letter

first sattarday September the Cherch met and prar Redy for Bisness and nothing don
Sineed order of the hole

GEORGE MOORE

first Sattarday in October the Chirch met and after prar the then redey for bisness and all found in peace sined by order

GEORGE MOORE Cl

First Sattarday in Novmber the Chirch met and after sarvis redey for besness and all found in peace sined by order of the hole

GEORGE MOORE Cl

first Sattarday in December the Chirch met and after sarvis redey for bisness and al found in peace   sined by order of the hole

GEORGE MOORE Cl

first Sattarday in ginuary the chirch met and af sarvis redey for bisness and found in peace   sined by order of the hole

GEORGE MOORE 1816

first Sattarday in febuary the chirch met and after sarvis redey for bisness and all found in peace sined by order of chirch

GEORGE MOORE Cl

the first Sattarday in march the chirch met and after sarvis redey for bisness Sister hill aplied for a letter of dismisan

and it was granted and the chirch found in peace sined by ord
of the hole   GEORGE MOORE

the firs Satterday In April the Chirch met and after Sarvis
the chirch redey for bisness and all foundin peace

the first Sattarday in May the chirch met and after sarvis
redey for bisness and all found in peace
                                    sined by ord
                                    GEORGE MOORE

the first Sattarday in June the chirch met and after worship
redey for bisness and all found in peace
sined by order of the hole
                                    GEORGE MOORE Cl

the first Sattarday in July the chirch met and after prar
Redey for bisness and Joseph Von comfrd and prepared to
sell his land whare the meetin hous and grave yard Stanes
and his price was five dollars per eaker and the chirch agreed
to give it the chirch agread [to] leave it to a commetty how
much they should by 2 chose findely Reavis and beman to
know how much would do for that youce and they say that
one eaker and a half would do us Von throwed in a half
eaker and twenty rods 3 the chirch agreed that Bro Yokes &
wife have leters of dismison————Edward Revis and
Paul Beck and his wife.
                    this sined by order of the hole,
                                    GEORGE MOORE

the first Sattarday in August the chirch met and after worship Redey for bisness then came forad John Conner and
geave in his expearence and was received into the chirch 2

celecttion maid for money to pay for the land tha was pur-
chesed of mister Von Eight dolra was maid up six and half
dolars price of the land they [giving] the rest for the youce of
the chirch 3 asociation letter to be perpared aganst next
meting 4 and————when the communing shold be and
laid over————next meeting.

the first Sattarday in Setember the chirch met and after
prearr redey for bisness first the letter for the asosiation brot
fored and Red 2 agreaed upon to be filled up 3 Red and past
the hous so sined by order of the hole

GEORGE MOORE

the fryday before the last Saboth in sptember Church met
and after sarvis Redy for busness and all found in peace
Sined by order
GEORGE MOORE.

April first Saturday the Church met agreeable to appointment and after worship proceeded to business We agreed to
releace br George Moore from being Clerk and appointed
br James Tunnell in his stead

GEORGE MOORE Clk

May Friday before the first Saturday 1817 the Church met
agreable to appointment and after worship proceeded to
business were found in peace Saturday receivd br Herriford
as deacon Sunday Communion
Assigned by order
JAMES TUNNELL

June 1st Saturday 1817 the Church met agreeable to appointment and after worship proceded to business———— 1st

a request from Ogles Creek for Ministereal helps on the 3^d Saturday this Ins^t was granted

Assigned by order
JAMES TUNNELL

July 1,st Saturday 1817 the Church met agreable to appoint ment and after worship proceded to business the Church found in peace

assigned by order
JAMES TUNNELL

December 1st Saturday 1818 The Church met and after worship proceded to business the Church being found in peace

Assigned by order
JAS TUNNELL Clk

January 1st Saturday 1819 The Church met and after Worship proceded to business the Church being found in peace

March 1st Saturday 1819
The Church met agreable to appointment and after worship proceded to business
1st the Church found in peace
2,nd Nancy Young Received by letter

April 1st Saturday 1819 The Church met and after worship proceded to business————————
1st The Church found in peace
2nd Received Sister Suzanna Bedin by letter,

Assigned by order of the Church
JAMES TUNNELL

July 1ˢᵗ Saturday 1820 The Church met agreable to appointment and after Worship proceeded to business br Bagely
Moderator

1*st* agree to adjourn and meet at Br. Jones's this afternoon
to go into ordaination of Elders and Deacon

2*nd* the Church met at br Jones' agreable to adjournment
and after preayer proceded to business

first the prisbatry being formed to wit bretheren daved
badgly and william Jones Enered into the ordennation of the
ead-[Elder] and ordaind brother Jeames tunnel Elder in this
Church

2 Enterd into the ordenntion of a deaCon and ordained
brother abble more deaCon for this Church sind by order
of the Church

ALEXANDER CONLEE
Clark pro tem

on the friday before the first Saturday in October the Church
met and after prayr proceeded to business————————

1st none of the Brethren that was chosen last meeting to
labour with Bʳ John Moore being present but Br Beeman
therefore the matter is laid over till next meeting

2d The Church is not willing for any of her members to have
any thing to do with the bord of Western Missions

3ᵈ whereas Br Jones was appointe by the Board as a Missionary for one month the Church is willing he may receive the
wages appointed him for the same and then to be cautious
to receive no more from the Board for like service

Sep*t* 1ˢᵗ Saturday 1820 We a committee appointed to enquire into the conduct of br John Conner and Sister Molly
blak people and do find from examination from their own
confession that br Conner is guily of falshood in denying
that he had ever tried Sister Molly to sleep with her and
after confessing that he had tried her for the purpose of
proving whether she was a bad woman or not, and charge

sister Molly with agreeing to quit her husband and take
br Conner

assigned by order

JAMES TUNNELL Clk

The 1st Saturday in April 1822
The Church met according to Appointment and after prayr
proceeded to business
1st A letter from the Ogles Creek Church being read and
their request being granted—2nd Proceeded to nominate
members to attend at sd Church on the 3rd Saturday in
April to assist in setting distress in sd Church—Chose
Brethern Jones, Tunnel & Vickory & Ogle—
3rd Brother Russel & Wife granted letters of Dismission by
their requesting the Church for the same

July the 1 Satturday 1822 the Church met according to
apointment and after worship proceaded to Bisness 1 the
Church agree to prepare a letter against our next meeting
brthern william Jones James tunnel John vickry to bear
the letter to the next association.

CHAPTER XI

RECORDS OF THE FORKS OF ELKHORN BAPTIST
CHURCH, KENTUCKY, 1800–1820

[The Forks of Elkhorn Baptist Church was formed in 1788 as an
"arm" of the South Elkhorn Church. At its constitution, William
Hickman, one of the first baptist ministers in Kentucky, became
the pastor, where he remained many years. It is stated that
William Hickman baptized as many persons as any other minister
in the state. His style of preaching, as described by John Taylor,
was "plain and solemn, and the sound of it like thunder in the
distance; but when he became animated, it was like thunder at
home, and operated with prodigious force on the consciences of his
hearers." Under the supervision of William Hickman, the Forks
of Elkhorn Church was one of the best administered churches in
Kentucky, and its minutes, therefore are of great importance as
illustrating how a Baptist church on the early frontier was managed.]

1800   2nd Saturday in January The Church met at
        Mr Browns and after Worship proceeded to bus-
        ness 1st the Query from our last taken up and
        Debated & refer,d to our next meeting Feby
        [rest of date cut off when book was trimmed]
        1800 2nd Saturday March the Church met and
        after Worship proceeded to business
        1st the Query from our last referd

        2ndly, there was a Complaint lodged against
        David formerly the property of N Sanders &
        Bro R Wooldridge is appointed to Cite him to
        our next meeting

        3rdly agreed that the friday before the Second
        Saturday in May be appointed as a day of fasting

and prayer & that the Whole Church be Desired
to attend on Saturday to enquire into their Standing and that it be Communion the Lords day
following

2nd Saturday in Ap¹ 1800 The Church met and
after Divine worship proceeded to Business

Bro Hickman informed the Church that Several
Members of this Church living on the ohio wish
to Join a Constitution in that plan (Viz) at the
mouth of Kenty and this Church has agreed to
give them up to Said Constitution their names are
Mary Lindsay Elizabeth Bledso & John the
property of Jerʰ Craig

The Complaint against David is referd to our
next meetng & brothren Hayden & Hall is
appointed to Cite him to come at that time Also
bro R Wooldridge is appointed to Cite Sarah

Church Set the Lords day morning following and
recd by letter Bro Thos Wooldridge & wife

The Query from our last meeting respecting giving
the right hand of fellowship answer,d that it is
right to give the right hand of fellowship before
Baptism

2nd Saturday in June the Church met and after
Divine Worship proceeded to business
1st a letter from the Church at Portwilliam respecting the excommunication of Robt Scandland
taken up & after Debate it is Dismist

2nd the Charge against Bro Wm Ballard Brot By
Bro Cash for Drinking to an excess at his request,
is refer,d to our next meeting

3rdly Hannah the property of Benjamin Garnet is excluded from this Church for Whoredom

Yᵉ Church Set the Lords Morning following and recd by recommendation Billy Belonging to Geo Madison

2nd Saturday in July the Church met and after Divine Worship proceeded to Business

recd by Experience Condorces Belonging to Jas Saunders

Bro Ballard appeared before the Church made acknowledgements of his fauts and the Church acquitted him.   and the Church has agreed to give him a letter of Dismission Brethn Hickman Haydon and Scott is appointed as Messengers to our next association and they are also to prepare a letter against our next Church Meeting which is to be the 1st Saturday in August

Recd by recommendation Sister Frances Mastin. also by Experience Betsy Majors———

1800
1st Saturday in August the Church met and after Divine Worship proceeded to business

The letter to the Association read and approved of

recd by Experience Nancy Berryman———

open,d Church Lords Day morning & upon the request of Bro Fender & wife the Church agreed to give them letters of Dismission

2nd Saturday in Sept The Church met & after Divine Worship proceeded to business

Bro Hickman requested leave to baptize persons in the extreme parts of the Church and Desired that they should then be considered as Members of this Church, and the Church has agreed to Consider it till our next Meeting

it is agreed that it be considered till our next Meeting whether it is a Duty, the laying on of hands on Baptized persons or not

rec,d and Baptized John Rutherford Elizabeth Samuel & Aggness Ware

3rd Lords Day the Church Set & recd by letter Bro Saml Price

2nd Saturday in October the Church met & after Divine Worship proceeded to business

Rec^d by letter Sister Ruhama Thompson

at brother George Craigs request he is to have a letter of Dismission

Bro Hickmans request from our last Meeting taken up & withdrawn————————

the Query respecting the Duty of laying on of hands on newly Baptized persons referd to our next Meeting Rec^d by Exp^{er} & Baptism Nancy Fitzgerald & E Poe

2nd Saturday in Novr the Church met and after Divine Worship proceeded to Business

Rec^d by recommindation Sister Olimp Trabur

The following persons rec,^{d} by experience & Baptism Wm Wares Cate, Susanna Peek. Nancy Haydon & the Church Set the Lords day following & rec^d Haydon Edwards—also Elizabeth Gibbson

The Query from our last Meeting still continued

Quere what is the proper time of the day to administer the Lords Supper

Church Set the 5th Lords Day & rec^d by Experience Jane Scott. Sister Anderson Elijah Anderson Two Sister Peeks The following persons rec^d at Different times & places by Experience and Baptism

1 Jn.º Bartlet	31 Giles Samuel
2 Sally Bartlete	32 Wm Samuel
3 Keziah Colvert	33 Danl Peek
4 Nancy Rowlet	34 Tho.ˢ Martin
5 Dan! Rowlet	35 Jn.º Edwards
6 Br.º Goar,s, Will	36 Br.º Peek,s Thame
7 Do .. Lyddia	37 Jn.º Stevens
8 Alexander Andrews	38 Martha Stevens
9 —— Andrews	39 Patsy Majors
10 Susannah Edwards	40 Br.º Hubbles—Joan
11 Jn.º Browns Isabel	41 Jemimah Robison
12 Jesse Cole	42 Martin Nale
13 —— Bradly	43 Bird Hendricks
14 Jemimah Nancock	44 Benjamin Step
15 Sally Haydon	45 Susanah Price
16 Betsy Haydon	46 Patsy Gano
17 Ginny Hicklin	47 James West
18 Sarah Hall	48 Horatio Clift
19 Susannah Hencock	49 Lucy Samuel
20 Agness Ware	50 Br.º Maj,ʳˢ Robbin
21 Polly Hickman	51 Dupuys Mingo
22 Charity Rogers	52 Sister Cole
23 Elijah Rogers	53 —— Hendrick
24 Jesse Rogers	54 —— Nale
25 Wm Hubble	55 Nancy Samuel
26 Jn.º Price	56 Seth Ramsay
27 Nancy Smythers	57 John Green
28 James Peek	58 Elijah Martin
29 Cha.ˢ Palmer	59 James Majors
30 —— Sparks	61 Br.º J Price,s Phill & Anaky

62 Jn.º Browns Hannah   65 Mr Asa Bells Caty
63 Br.º G Samuel,s Pender   66 Conny Anderson
64 Br.º Stevens,s N Woman   67 Elijah anderson

2nd Saturday in Feb.ʸ the Church met and after
Divine Worship proceeded to Business

Col.º John Logans Ned offer,d his repentance for
his bad conduct he gave Satisfaction and the
Church agreed to Send to the Church at S Elkhorn
for a letter of Dismission

at the request of the following Member they are
Dismiss,d from this Church to Join in a Constitu-
tion Wᵐ & Obedience Hickman Gilbert and Lucy
Christian   Jn.º Major & Nancy Berryman

Mʳ Garnets Sue Excluded for lying Tattling and
ungarded conversation

Theoderick Bowler is excluded for immoral conduct & not hearing the church

The Church Set the Lords Day morning & recᵈ
Polly Smither by letter also a Negro Woman by
repentance Sally the property of Danⁱ Gano

recᵈ by letter Sister Agness Smith also Lucy
Ramsy by letter

Recᵈ by Dº & Bᵐ James Haydin Junⁿ Wᵐ Rowlet
Recᵈ also Sister Pemberton & Ryland Shackle-
ford
Recᵈ by letter Ned Belonging to Colº Logan

Recᵈ down on elkhorn the following persons
Gore Wᵐ Rowlet Br.º Gore,s Lewis
2nd Saturday in March the Church met and after
Divine Worship proceeded to business

at Sister Simonus,s request by bro Hickman the
Church has agreed to give her a letter of Dismission

Rec^d by letter Sister Price

Rec^d by recommendation Sister Elizabeth Rutherford

Rec^d by letter Br,o Benjamin Edrington & Wife

Rec^d by experience Betsy Hickman

Rec^d by recommendation Br° Joseph Baker & Wife

Rec^d by experience Pompey belonging to Br° Jn°
Major——

Rec^d by Experience Peter belonging to Br° Jn°
Price

The Church has agreed that Bro Wooldridge
& Br° Scott is at liberty to Exercise their Gift
when and where they may think proper

The following persons rec^d the Lords Day Morn-
ing by letter Sister Elizabeth Ship. also Jn° Alfred
Head by Repentance Br° Major's, James by
experience Susanna Major Nancy Gibson Lettuce
Ewing. Lewis Stevens & Hannah belonging to
Br° Major—also—Br° Henry Martin by letter

Rec^d at Different times
by letter Sally Mitchel & Betsy Smythers
by repentance Theodorick Bowler

Rec^d by Experience Ramsey Bowler
Mary Pemberton Ryland Shackleford Betsy

Baker Betsy Samuel, Nicholas Ware, Zachariah Pullam, Edward Roberts Dinal Rutherford & John Smythers

Rec^d at the Mouth of Elkhorn
Ja^s Hayden J^r Wm Rowlet Isaac Goar Sally Goar, Nancy Goar Barnet Clemens & Bro Goars Lewis—

2nd Friday in April the Church met agreeable to appointment and after Divine Worship proceeded to business————————

at the request of an arm of the Church at the Mouth of Elkhorn and Cedar by Br? John Bartlet for letters of Dismission in order to Constitute a Church in that place—The Church has agreed to their request Their Names are William Goar Polley Goar—Wm Rowlet Sister Rowlet Elijah Colvert Charity Colvert Sister Stevens Jn? Bartlet Sally Bartlett Keziah Colvert Dan! Rowlet Nancy Rowlet W^m, Rowlet J^r Isaac Goar Sister Goar Patsy Goar Bernard Clemens Ja^s Hayden Will, Lydia & Lewis, black people belonging to Br° Goar

Query is our present mode of receiving Members right or agreeable to the principles of the Gospel

Rec^d by repentance Sister Sarah Pullam

Rec^d by Experience Susannah Knap
Rec^d by Experience William Marshal also Benjamin Hickman James O Neal

2nd Saturday in April the Church met and after Divine Worship proceeded to Business

Opened a Door for the reception of Members & rec^d by Experience John Hickman, Peter Bain-

bridge, Cyrus Jackson, John Hickling, Betsy
Hickling, James Hickling, Polly Edrington, John
Ware—Susannah Hencock—Judith Bledso Polly
Smythy

Rec^d by repentance Richard Ship——

Rec^d also by experience Elizabeth Gale

The Church has agreed upon request ^Ye the follow-
ing Members be Dismiss,d for Constitution up the
N Fork of Elkhorn Thos Bradly Elijah Rogers
And^w Rogers Charity Rogers Conny Anderson &
Elijah Anderson

Opened a Door for the reception of Members on
Saturday evening at the Meeting house and rec^d
by experience Wm Montgomery & Madrid Jackson
—Lords Day Morning rec^d Hannah Hill Jesse
Browns Judah Mr Fitzgeralds Molly Patsy Hick-
man Bro Davis,s Fanny By letter W^m, & Nancy
Green————

Dismiss,d by letter Hannah Hill

2nd Saturday in May the Church met and Divine
worship proceeded to Business

Rec^d by Experience the following persons, Polly
Ware Elizabeth Marshal; Robert O Neal; John
Baker; James Robison; Hannah a black woman
belonging to old Sister Saml Eleoner Roberts;
Jenny, belonging to Br.^o Jno Samuels Benjamin
Stevens; Patsy Robison, Elizabeth Martin George
Brown, J^r.————

The Query respecting our present Mode of receiving Members Lost

The Church has agreed that Meetings be Appointed either Day or night in any part or Bounds of this Church to hear experience whereever Bro Hickman may think proper——

upon request the following Members are Dismiss,d from this Church for a Constitution up Glens Creek James Ford & Wife William Green & Wife Rich.d Ship & Wife Seth Ramsey & Wife Fanny Turpin

at a Meeting prior to this the following mode for receiving Members was adopted & is now agreed to be right Viz that the person Who offers his experience & is approved of is to have the right hand of fellowship & to be told that when Baptized he Shall have a right to all the privileges of the Church

Saturday Evening the Church met and after Divine Worship proceeded to Business
& rec.d by Experience Robert Hickling; John Brown Jr a Black woman belonging to Br.° W.m Brown Named Sarah Sam.l Gravat, James a Black man belonging to Geo, Madison; James Ware J.r; Benjamin Garnet; Frances Bartlet,

Church Set the Lords Day Morning following & Rec.d by Experience Polly Brown

at Meeting at Sister Bowlers the 12.th Day of May the following person were rec.d by experience Viz Patsy Bowler Iverson Ware & James ware

at a Meeting held W.m Ware,s the Church Set & rec.d by experience Patsy Samuel

at a Meeting at Br.° Hickmans the Church set & rec.d by Experience   Sanders at a Meeting at Br.º Giles Samuels the Church Set & recᵈ by Expᶜᵉ Wm Brown Jʳ Ja. Ware, Polly Brown Sally Brown Ross Rebekah Ware & Ben belonging to Wᵐ Ware Geo Browns Nick.......

at a Meeting at Baker Ewing,s 2nd Tuesday in June the Church Set & recᵈ by Experience Benjⁿ Martin

2nd Saturday in June the Church met and after Divine Worship proceeded to business

Open,d a Door for hear experience & recᵈ Col.º Logans N Woman Chainy, Milly Sparks Joseph Edrington Patsy Crutcher by expeᶜᵉ,

by repentance Sanders belonging to Sister Wooldrige

at the reqᵗ of Br.º O Dare he is Dissmᵈ also Br.º Garnet & Wife Dismissᵈ
The following persons recᵈ on Saturday evening of Lords day Morning—Morgan Bryant Elizabeth Edrington Sister Anderson Betsy Palmer. Sister Samˡˢ Jack Geo Madisons Sarah Head recᵈ by repentance Charles & Gilly
2nd Saturday in July the Church met and after Divine Worship proceeded to business..........

1ˢᵗ a Charge was brought by Br.º William Brown against Sarah his Negro Woman for theft and lying it was proved to the satisfaction of the Church and no Satisfaction recᵈ she is excluded ....

Opened a Door for to hear Experience and recᵈ Polly Reed Ambrose Jeffreys—also Sister Samˡˢ Jenny at Br.° Stouts request he and his wife is to have a letter Dismission—also Br.° Edmond Poe at his request is to have a letter of Dismission

Query; whether the Office of Elders is completely fill,d in this Church agreeable to scriptures

at a Meeting at M.ʳ Smeathers on thursday night the following persons were rec.ᵈ by experience Dorothy Stepp Joseph Hough & Br.° Wood Davis,s Negro Woman Hannah.........

A Charge was brought against Bro Ross by Br.° Haydon, from Information of Drinking to an excess Bre.ⁿ Edw.ᵈˢ & Hubble to Cite him to Next Meeting

Brethren Hickman Haydon and Scott is appointed Messengers to the Association & prepare our letter against Next Meeting
1.ˢᵗ Saturday in August the Church met and after Divine Worship proceeded to Business
Opened a Door for the reception of Members & rec.ᵈ by Experience Reuben Ware Nancy Ware..

The Query from our last is refer,d to our next Meeting

Br.° Ross came forward confess,d his faute & the Church agreed to bear with him

Query, is it right for the Members of this Church to commune with any other Church not of the Same faith and order The above Query Withdrawn—

The Church letter was read and approved of
2nd Saturday in Sep.ʳ the Church met and after Divine Worship proceeded to business

Charges brought against Br? Shackleford for various reports circulating respecting his Immoral conduct Gaming etc & Breth" J Price & Haydon is appointed to Cite him to Meeting to Morrow morning

A Charge Brought against Sister Wooldriges Sanders for putting away his wife & taking another Was taken up after conversing upon the Matter it was agreed to refer it to our next Meeting

at Bro Dan! Browns request he is to have a letter of Dismission

A request from M Connels run Church respecting helps is attended to & Brethren Ja⁵ Haydon Edrington, Finny & Hicklin is appointed

Brethren Wooldrige & Scott is appointed to attend the Conference at Howards Creek to Effect a Union with the Seperate Brethren——

The Query respecting Elder still refer^d to our Next Meeting
Tho⁵ Hickman came forward confess,d his fault & was restored

rec^d by Experience Bennet Pemberton————

at a Meeting at Br? Hickmans rec^d Polly Hickman also Dan! Brown

Church Set the Lords day Morning & Bre" Price & Haydon reported that they talked with Br? Shackleford & Desired him to come to Meeting he refused & the church excluded him

The Church set on Wednesday 23rd of Sep^r & rec^d by experience Mordecai Bashar & Jn? Roberts

2nd Saturday in October the Church met and after Divine Worship proceeded to Business

1ˢᵗ The Query respecting Elders refer,d to our next meeting 2ndly——upon Motion of Br° Hickman The Church agree,d to consider the gift of Br° Scott & Br° Wooldridge whether they were fit for ordination & the Church excepting one Member agree,d in the affirmative

3rdly The Church also took into consideration Br° Edwards,s Gift, and it is the advise of this Church that he make use of a Gift of Exhortation till further advise from them

4thly Sister Woolrige,s Saunders was brought again before the church for leaving of the wife that he had when he Join,d the Church & taking Rachel from another man and living in Adultery with her & the church was Divided The Church set Lord,s Day Morning and Excluded Saunders 2nd Saturday in Novʳ the Church met and after Divine Worship proceeded to Business—

Br° Clift came forward and confes,d his faute respecting his Drinking to an excess and the church agreed to bear with him—another Difficulty between he and a Member in the other church was represented to this church & Brethⁿ Edmᵈ Ware Carter Blanton & John Edrington together with three Brethren in the other church is appointed to attend enquire into the matter and try to Settle it——

The Query respecting Elders is refer,d to our next Meeting

The Matter respecting the Ordination of Bro Wooldlige & Br° Scott is refer,d to our next Meeting——

2nd Saturday in Dec.ʳ the Church met and after Divine Worship proceeded to business———

Open,d a Door for the reception of members and rec.ᵈ by experience Betsy Brown—

at the request of Bro Benjamin Stepp he and his wife is granted a letter of Dismission

Br.ᵒ Dan.ˡ Brown has returned his letter and Membership———

agreeable to appointed the Church met the on friday the 25ᵗʰ day of Dec.ʳ 1801 and after Divine Worship proceeded to Business—

The Query respecting Elders that has been refer,d for different Meetings back after Debate is withdrawn———

a Charge was brought against Br.ᵒ J Prices Peter for Drinking to an excess and fighting he came forward but did not Satisfy the church and the matter was laid over to our Jan.ʸ Meeting Query: have we any scripture authority for citing a publick transgressor before the church whether he repents or not———

2nd Saturday in January 1802 the Church met and after Divine Worship proceeded to business

a Charge was brought against Br.ᵒ Sam.ˡ Gravat for pilfering a pair of Gloves and for falsities when charged with it and the church has appointed Bre.ⁿ Nich.ˢ Ware, Robert Hicklin, and Geo Brown, to cite him to meet the church to Morrow Morning

> The church set lords day morning & Bre.ⁿ N. Ware—Rob.ᵗ Hicklin & Geo. Brown Reported that they talked with Br.ᵒ Gravit & desired him to meet the church in the Morning he refused & the church Excluded him

the above Query is refer,d to our next meeting after some Debate

the matter of charge brought against Br.° J Prices Peter is refer,d to our next meeting

2^d Saturday in February the Church met & after Divine Worship proceeded to Business

a 2^d Charge is brought against Bro J Price Peter For Drinking to Excess he came forward & was Excommunicated

the query Respecting publick transgresson was taken up & refered

the matter respecting the ordaination of Bro. Wooldrige & Brother Scott was taken up & the Church are of Opinion that Brother Wooldridge & Brother Scott Be ordaind ministers of the gospel—

JOHN PRICE

The Church set Lords day Morning and received by repentance Jn.° Browns Cate, Also receiv'd by Experience Jn.° Bacon's Bob

2nd Saturday in March 1802 the Church met & after Divine Worship proceeded to business
1st Bro. Horatio Clife was brought before the Church and charged with deceiving & defrauding Bro. Martin in the swaping of Horses. and Excluded for the same

2^{ndly} The Query respecting publick dealing taken up and refer'd to our next meeting

3rd At the request of Br.° Jn.° Roberts he and his Wife Elisabeth is to have a letter of dismission

THO^s SETTLE

The Church set Lords day morning
At Bro. Jn° Scotts request he & his Wife is to have
a letter of Dismission

T. S.

2nd Saturday in April 1802 the Church met and after
Divine Worship proceeded to business————

At the request of Sister Rachel Appelgate to have
a letter of dismission

At the request of Bro. John Rediford and wife and
Sister Dinner to have a letter of Dismission————

the Query respecting publick dealing taken up and
refered to our next meeting
Lords day Morning the Church met & after
Divine Worship proceeded to business Received
by letter a black Man belonging to Mary Allen
by the Name of William Also receiv'd by Experience Lewis Palmer
2nd. Saturday in May 1802 the Church met and
after Divine Worship proceeded to business

1st A Charge was brought by Br° Tho. Wooldridge
against Sarah a black free Woman for theft &
lying. it was proved to the Satisfaction of the
Church, and no Satisfaction received, She is
Excluded for the same

2nd. A Charge was brought against Robert a black man
belonging to Br° Jn° Majors for being equally
Guilty in the theft with his Wife Sarah and was
Excluded for the same.

3rd A Charge was brought against Br° Thomas Hickman for fighting, the Church has appointed
Brethn Carter Blanton & Jn° Bohanan to cite him
to appear before the Church next monthly meeting

4th A Charge was brought against Clary a black Woman of Br.º Edm.ᵈ Ware's for being too Intimate & Sleeping with Joe a Man of Capᵗ Taylors and is refered till next Monthly Meeting and that Br.º Edrington & Br.º Theodrick Boulware are requested to go & see a Woman of Capᵗ Taylor named Jany respecting the Matter and make report the next Meeting

5th The Query respecting publick dealing refer'd to our next meeting

6th Opened a door for the reception of members & recev'd by Experience Sarah a black Woman of Sister Samuels. Also Nicholas Coster

The Church Set Lords day morning & receiv'd by Experience Betsy Nolin

2nd Saturday in June 1802 the Church met and after divine Worship proceeded to business

1st Br.º Tho.ˢ Hickman came forward & made acknowledgment to the church for his faults & after a friendly Admonition the church agreed to bear with him

2nd Br.º Edrington & Br.º T Bowlware came forward & made report of the information they recᵈ from Janey & after the church heard the report they excluded Clary from them ————
3rd The Query respecting Dealing that has been refer,d heretofore was Drop,ᵈ by consent and the following Query adopted, Viz,
Query; is it right to take the 18th chapter of Mathew for our rule in dealing with all offenders ————& after a considerable time spent in Debate it recᵈ the following Answer

Viz Ans^w that not only the 18th of Mathew but all Scripture where it treats of Dealing with offenders is to be our rule

4th opened a Door for the reception of Members & rec^d by letter Vachel Lindsay and wife——also rec^d by experience Isabella Sparks
The Church set the Lords day Morning and rec^d by Experience Edmond belonging to Nathl Sanders Jun^n and Peggy Campbel

2nd Saturday in July 1802 The Church met and after divine worship proceeded to business.
1st receiv'd Br^o Harry Bartlett to fellowship again.
2nd Brethren, William Hickman Ja^s Hayden & Hayden Edwards is appointed as messengers to our next Association, Also to prepare our As^n Letter
3rd Received by letter Samuel Adair——
The Church set the Lords day Morning and rec^d by Experience Milley a negroe Woman belonging to Br^o Saml Price
1st Saturday in August 1802 The Church met and after divine worship proceeded to business.

1st Br^n Haden Edwards John Price William Samuel Giles Samuel Samuel Price directed to frame a rule upon the Scriptures for the guidance of the church in dealing with members committing offences against God, & one another & if approved of By the Church to be recorded as a standing rule——
2 Rec^d Br^o William Rowlet sen^r William Rowlet Junr & Sister Nancy Rowlet By letter
3^d Bro^r John Majors Robin and his wife Sarah restored to fellowship
4th Rec^d by experience George Garrett

5th Sister Bershaba Dun dismissed by Letter

6th Brother Giles Samuel appointed to cite Brother Andrews to mett this Church at her next church meeting to answer complaints.

7th Some difficulty arising in the mind of some of the Brethren respecting the Ordination of Brother Thomas Wooldridge It is agreed to be posponed and taken under consideration at our next church meeting

8th The Church Letter was read and approved of—
Wm HICKMAN Moderator

1802. 2nd Saturday in September The Church met and after Divine Worship proceeded to business.

1st At the request of Br.^o Hickman for Polley Reed—now Allen she is to have a letter of Dismission

2nd At the request of Bro. James Davis he and his Wife Frances and his Negroe Woman Fanny is to have a letter of Dismission

3rd At the request of Br.^o Hickman for James a black Member belonging to Mr Faulconer, he is to have a letter of Dismission.

4th Br.^o Andrews & Br.^o Marshal was brought before the Church for their misconduct to each other. Br.^o Marshal was acquited. Br.^o Andrews withdrew from the Church.

5th The matter respecting the Ordination of Br.^o Wooldridge is refer'd to our next Church Meeting.

2nd Saturday in October 1802 The Church met and after Divine Worship proceeded to business

1st The Order directing five Brethren to frame a rule upon the Scriptures for the guidance of the Church in dealing with Members committing Offences against God and one another taken up, debated upon and Ordered to be Erased out.

2nd The Ordination of Br^{o} Thomas Wooldridge which has been refer'd time after time, taken up and debated the Church was divided

3rd At the request of Br^{o} Stout he and his Wife is to have a letter of Dismission.

2^{d} Satturday in November 1802 the Church met and after Divine Worship proceeded to business

1^{t} Brother Ross Came forward & acknowledged & repubated his own miss Conduct in drinking too free & fiteing. The Church agreed to bear with him.

2nd Query Whether is it right to Exclude by a majority or Unanimity?

3rd At the request of Br^{o} Hickman, Br^{o} Joseph Baker and his Wife and Daughter is to have a letter of Dismission—Also Br^{o} Bird Hendrick his Wife and James his Slave is to have a letter of Dismission

4th Receiv'd by letter Jemima Rowlet.

2nd Saturday in December 1802 The Church met and after Divine Worship proceeded to business

1st Sister Betsy Hicklin withdrew from the Church in a disorderly way and is no more of us.

2nd Br? John Brown Junr withdrew from the Church in a disorderly way and is no more of us.

3rd Received by letter Larkin Bohanon.

4th The Query respecting the Excluding by a Majority or Unanimity taken up & the Church agreed to Exclude by a Majority of two thirds.

5th Br? Haden Edwards proposed to the Church that the present Moderator appoint a Moderator to act at our next Meeting The Church agreed to it.

6th Br? James Haydon appointed to act as Moderator at our next Church Meeting, in case of failure Br? Haden Edwards

1803   2nd Saturday in January The Church Met & after Divine Worship proceeded to business.

1st A Charge was brought against Br? Isaac Miles for saying that Br? John Bohanan did cover the truth with lies of Hypocrisy, and he was Excluded for the same.

2nd A Charge was brought against Br? John Hickman for Warranting one of the Brethren, and other Misconduct and he was Excluded.

3rd At the request of Br? Ja^s Hayden his Daughter Sally Forbush is to have a letter of Dismission. Als Br⁰ E. Jeter, Sister Elizabeth Martin & Sister Sally Sanders, Also Br⁰ Jaˢ Peak & his Wife and Elijah Martin

4ᵗʰ The Church appointed the following Breⁿ Danˡ Peak William Hubbell, Abraham Gregory, John Edrington and William Hall as a Committee to try & settle some grievances subsisting between Sister Stephens & Sister Hicklin

5ᵗʰ Br⁰ Danˡ Peak is appointed Moderator for our next Meeting

2ⁿᵈ Saturday in February 1803 the Church met and after Divine Worship proceeded to business—

1ˢᵗ The Committee appointed at our last Meeting to try & Settle some differences between Sister Stephens & Sister Hicklin was call'd on to make report. but some of the Committee being absent it is referred to our next Meeting & then to make report

2ⁿᵈ The Church appointed the following Brethren James Haydon Bennet Pemberton, John Edrington, Daniel Peak & Edmund Ware to Inspect & revise some rules drawn up by Brother Hickman for the guidance of Church

3ʳᵈ Brother Abraham Gregory appointed Moderator for our next Meeting in case of failure Br⁰ Carter Blanton

2ⁿᵈ Saturday in March 1803 the Church met and after Divine Worship proceeded to business————

1st. A Charge was brought against Br.º Ned & his Wife, black Members belonging to Col. Logan, Br.º Samuel Price is appointed to Cite them to our next Church Meeting———

2nd The Brethren appointed at our last Meeting to regulate some rules drawn up by Br.º Hickman for the guidance of this Church, laid before the Church some rules with their amendments, and after a considerable debate the Church Order'd that they shou'd be recorded

3rd Sister Hicklin & Sister Stephens profess'd to the Church their reconciliation to each other———

4th At the request of Br.º William Brown he & his Wife Elisabeth & his three Daughters, Polly, Betsy & Sally is to have letters of Dismission

5th Br.º William Hall is appointed Moderator for our next Church Meeting—
ABRAHAM GREGORY Moderator

Church Rules

1st Church Meetings to open and close by Singing and Praying

2nd That the Moderator is to Invite Members of Sister Churches to Seats with us and give their advice in any matter that comes before the Church but not to Vote on the decision of the Question

3rd The first business to come Orderly is the Moderator Inquire if their be any matter of

Complaint that has been treated agreeable to the Gospel.

4.th The admission of Members into the Church and Members into office shall be by Unanimity, and the Exclusion of Members & all other Questions shall be determined by a Majority

5.th But one person to speak at the same time and to address him or herself to the Moderator Standing

6.th All Motions made and seconded shall be attended to by the Church

7.th No person to be Interrupted while Speaking to the point

8.th No Member is allowed to Speak to the subject in hand more than twice, without leave of the Church

9.th The Moderator to have the same privilege of Speaking as any other Member provided he calls on some other person to fill his Seat

10.th At the close of the Meeting the Clerk be directed to read the business of the day and the Moderator sign his name or direct the Clerk so to do

1.st The Church set the lords day Morning and Excluded Vina for the Sin of Adultery

2. Br.^o Ned & his Wife came before the Church and Acknowledged their fault, the Church agreed to bear with them

2nd Saturday in April 1803 The Church Met &
after Divine Worship proceeded to business

1st Opened a Door for the reception of Members,
and receiv'd by letter, Sister Elizabeth Hiter

2nd At the request of Br? Haydon his Daughter
Jemima Hancock is granted a letter of Dismission

3rd At the request of Br? Hickman Sister Susannah Knap is granted a letter of Dismission

4th, The form in which letters of recommendation
is to be given to Members removing &c, was
ordered to be wrote as follows viz

The Baptist Church of Christ at the forks of
Elkhorn Holding Believers Baptism by Immersion only, Justification through the Obedience and righteousness of Jesus Christ's Effectual calling, final Perseverance of the Saints
in Grace &c. Whereas our beloved
have requested a letter of Dismission These
are to Certify that in good standing amongst
us, and when join'd any Baptist Church in
Union with us, is Dismiss'd from our care,
by order of the Church &c.

Br? Carter Blanton is appointed to Act as Moderator at our next meeting in case of failure Br?
Thos Wooldrige

WILLIAM HICKMAN Moderator

2nd, Saturday in May 1803 The Church met and
after Divine Worship proceeded to business—

1st A Motion was brought in and Debated on the
new system of Principles call'd Herrisy & at

length the following Question was taken, is the Son of God Equal & Eternal with the Father It was Answer'd by a great Majority in favour of the Son being equal with the Father, then the Minority was call'd upon to give their reason for Voting as they did, Several of them Answer'd they were not moved from their old faith

2nd, Br.° Hickman Chosen to Act as Moderator untill the Church thinks proper to appoint some other

3rd, Dismissed by letter Br.° James West Also Br.° Benjamin Garnet and Polly his Wife

4th, Receiv'd by letter Elizabeth Martin. By Experience Joe a black Man belonging to Geo. Carlisls—Also John Eidson
WILLIAM HICKMAN Moderator

2nd, Saturday in June 1803 The Church met and after Divine Worship proceeded to business

1st, At the request of Br.° John Edwards he is granted a letter of Dismission

2 Saturday in July 1803 The Church Met and after Divine Worship proceeded to business—

Tobie Excluded for aDultery the property of Bro^r FergerSon Bro. William Hickman and Bro. James Headen appinted as me ssiners to the next ASocation and to prepare the Church letter against the next Church meeting
WM HICKMAN

1st Saturday in August 1803 the Church met and after Divine Worship proceeded to business

1st Br.º William Hall requested of the Church that helps be call'd for to try and settle some grievances in the Church, the Church agreed that application should be made to M.ºConnels Run Church North fork Church & the Church at Coxes Mill for two Members from each Church & to meet on Friday the day before our next Church Meeting at this Meeting house

2^{ndly} Br.º William Hickman & Br.º James Haydon produc'd each one a letter which was read before the Church, and the Church thought proper to appoint Br.º Baker Ewing & Br.º Haden Edwards to take both letters & form a third one which is to be read before the Church tomorrow morning

WILLIAM HICKMAN Moderator

At a Meeting held on Friday the 9th of September 1803 Whereas this Church did at our last Church Meeting order her request to be Issued to three of our Sister Churches M.ºConnels Run Church, Northfork Church and Mount pleasant Church, praying them to send two Members from each Church in order to assist us in trying to relieve Br.º William Hall's grievances with Majority of this Church, and agreeable to this Churches request these Brethren came forward and took seats with us, Br.º William Hall laid before the Bre.ⁿ sent to our assistance his complaint against the Majority of this Church which was for continueing William Brown in Society after finding him guilty of falsehood without any recantation agreeable to the Word of God,—and after a discussion of the

business the Committee withdrew to form their
conclusion, which at their return we find was in
the following manner,—We the Subscribers being
call'd on as help to the Baptist Church of Jesus
Christ at the forks of Elkhorn are of Opinion that
Br? William Hall has a Just cause of Complaint
against the Majority of said Church for continueing W™ Brown in fellowship without a sufficient
Acknowledgement as in the case above mentioned,
Given under our hands the 9th day of Sept 1803

On a Question who can bear with Br? William Brown, answer'd we do agree to bear with him	Rodes Smith Jacob Martin Jesse Vawter
Question being put who can Accede to the Advice of the helps, Answer'd in the afirma- tive	Daniel James Benjamin Head John H. Ficklin

2nd Saturday in September 1803 The Church met
& after Divine Worship proceeded to business

A Charge was brought against Br? John Hicklin
by Br? W™ Onion for saying that he wou'd ag-
grivate John Brown Jun more than he ever had
done & if said Brown did lay the weight of his
hand on him, that he wou'd stick a knife in him,
and for saying that some of the Brethren had
advised him so to do & for not teeling who those
Bren Were—The Church Excluded him for the
Same Query, will this Church bare with a Member
who Justifies in Error, Answer by the Church no,

Then the matter respecting Br? William Brown's
Justifying himself in error was taken up and after
a considerable discussion on the business it was
put to Vote whether Br? W™ Brown had heard the
Church or not the Church thought he had not and
pronounc'd him Excluded

At Br.º Wᵐ Marshal's request his Wife is granted a letter of Dismission

At Br.º Larkin Behannon's request he is granted a letter of Dismission

WILLIAM HICKMAN Moderator

2ⁿᵈ Saturday in October 1803 the Church met & after Divine Worship proceeded to business
Br.º Samˡ Price Motion'd that Br.º Jn.º Gano be appointed to form rules for the Examination of the Church, The Church agreed to the Motion—Br.º Jaˢ Haydon Motion'd that our former rules of Acting by Majority be dispenc'd of at the admission of the above rules—After some arguments the motion was withdrawn.
A Charge brought against Br.º Annable for Quarreling, Fighting and Swearing, The Church was of Opinion he did not hear them and pronounc'd him Excluded

A motion made & seconded whether there shou'd be any thing raised by Subscription for the Support of Br.º Hickman or not answer'd there shou'd
Order'd that the Clerk draw a Subscription for the support of Brother William Hickman & bring it to our next Church Meeting

A complaint brough by Br.º Jaˢ Magors against himself for calling Br.º Rennex a liar, & fighting him the Church thought he gave Sufficient Satisfaction to them for his conduct

At the request of the following Brethren & Sisters they are granted letters of Dismission William Hall & Sarah his Wife Theodrick Boulware &

Patsy Boulware his Sister & Esther Boulware
James Haydon & Elizabeth his Wife,
Zacheriah Pullum & Caty his Wife.

CARTER BLANTON Moderator

2nd Saturday in November 1803 the Church met
and after Divine Worship proceeded to business—

1st The Church requested that the rules formed
by Br^{o} John Gano for the Examination of the
Church be read which was done—The Church
agreed that the following Bre^{n} James Haydon,
Baker Ewing & Jessey Vawter be appointed as a
Committee to Inspect and revise those rules
against our next Church Meeting

At the request of Br^{o} John Eidson he is granted a
letter of Dismission

WILLIAM HICKMAN Moderator

2nd Saturday in December 1803 the Church met
and after Divine Worship proceeded to
business.
Brother Edmond Ware laid in a complaint against
Brother Jack, Slave of Sister Samuel's it was
considered by the Church that he heard them and
suffered to continue his Membership

On motion by Br^{o} William Hickman & seconded—Brother Carter Blanton was appointed to
see Br^{o} Ross and Cite him to the Church to account for his conduct in drinking too much ardent
Spirits.

It being motioned and seconded that a Question
be put to this Church, whether they consider
themselves a Church of the Elkhorn Association

agreeable to the Confession of Faith as Established by that Association agreed to and as demonstration of our profession have agreed to record the following Articles Viz,

1st We believe the scriptures of the old and new Testament to be the Infallible word of God, and the only rule of faith and practice

2ndly We believe in one self Existing God, and that there is three persons in the divine Essence or nature phraised in the Bible, by, God the Father, God the Son, & God the holy Spirit, and yet these three are but one God, not admitting of a Priority or Seniority, in the Godhead or Essence

3rdly We believe in the doctrine of the fall of man, the depravity of human nature, the Inability of the Creature, to recover it's self to life

4thly, We believe in the doctrine of Sovereign Grace, Justification by the righteousness of Christ alone, final preseverance of the Saints, resurrection of the dead and a General Judgment

5thly, We believe the Joys of the righteous and punishment of the Wicked will be Eternal

6thly, We believe Baptism and the Lords Supper are ordinance of Jesus Christ and that Believers are the Subjects of these Ordinances and the true mode of Baptism is by Immersion

It is also agreed by the Church that any Member or Members not agreeing with the Confession as now Established may upon Application have letters of Dismission

WILLIAM HICKMAN Moderator

2nd. Saturday in January 1804 the Church met & after Divine worship proceeded to business.

Br.º Zacheriah Ross is Excluded from this Church for drinking too an Excess & for disobeying the call of the Church.

Bre.ⁿ Edmund Ware & Daniel Peak is appointed to cite Br.º Baker Ewing to our next Monthly Meeting to answer some complaints.

Br. Thomas Hickman is Excluded from this Church for drinking to an Excess & for fighting   WILLIAM HICKMAN M.

2nd Saturday in February 1804 the Church met & after Divine Worship proceeded to business—

1st A motion made & seconded that this Church fall upon some measure respecting Members of this Church who have mov'd out of the bounds of the Church without applying for letters of Dismission.—The Church thinks proper that Br.º W.ᵐ Hickman assist the Clerk in Writing to those Members and let them know that it is this Churches request that they make application for letters which will be granted them, provided they fetch a recommendation from the Church in whose bounds they live, or by sending such recommendation by a messenger.

2nd. Br. Baker Ewing is Excluded from this Church for Intoxication for misusing his Wife, & disobeying the call of the Church

3rd A motion made & seconded whether this Church thinks it is agreeable to the word of God for one Brother to Warrant another Brother the Church answer'd no, and if any have been guilty of the like that the Gospel steps of dealing shou'd be taken with them

WILLIAM HICKMAN Moderator

The 2nd Saturday in March 1804 the Church met and after Divine Worship proceeded to business.

Br.$^\circ$ John Gutthrie presented a letter from the Crossing Church and was rec^d as a Member to this Body—

Br.$^\circ$ Samuel Price & Sister Elizabeth Price made Application for a letter—Granted.

Br.$^\circ$ Joe Slave of Governor Garrard, granted a letter of Dismission upon the Application of Br.$^\circ$ Benjn Hickman—

WILLIAM HICKMAN, Moderator

The 2nd Saturday in April 1804 the Church met and after Divine Worship proceeded to business

Br.$^\circ$ Hickman motioned to the Church that he thought it necessary that the Meeting house & Grave Yard shou'd be post & railed in, the Church agreed that 2 Subscriptions be drawn, and put into the hands of Br.$^\circ$ Haden Edwards and Br.$^\circ$ Edmund Ware and that they make a trial & see if they can get a Sufficiency Subscribed to pay for it and to make report at our next Church Meeting—

Br.$^\circ$ Edmund Ware Motioned to the Church that some person be Nominated as a Deacon to fill the

Vacancy of Br? Hicklin Deceas'd—Br? Isaac Palmer Nominated—

The Church appointed Br? Haden Edwards & Br? Daniel Peak to see Br? Daniel Brown & Young Geo. Brown & Cite them to meet the Church tomorrow morning to answer some Complaints

WILLIAM HICKMAN Mod^r

Agreeable to order the above Mentioned Brethren Cited Br? Daniel & George Brown and they met the Church, the Church after Interogating them Admonish'd and acquited them

WILLIAM HICKMAN M.

The 2nd Saturday in May 1804 The Church met and after Divine Worship Proceeded to business

On Br? Hickman's motion to the Church in behalf of Sister Polly Peak now Baldwin & Susannah Peak now Lucus they are granted letters of Dismission

On a Motion made and seconded it is agreed that Breⁿ William Samuel Haden Edwards & Thomas Settle Superintend and let the Posting and Railing of the Meeting house and Yard by private contract.

On a Motion Br? Blanton & Br? Peak is appointed to Officiate tomorrow as Deacons for the term being

WILLIAM HICKMAN Moderator

The 2nd Saturday in June 1804 the Church met and after Divine Worship Proceeded to business

A Charge was brought against Br? James Oneal for Immoral conduct, by Br? Pemberton & Br? Fargeson—Br? Carter Blanton is appointed to cite him to our next Church Meeting—

Agreed to by this Church that the following Bre^n James Hayden Thomas Wooldridge Daniel Peak & Martin Nall is appointed to attend the South Benson Church on the 3rd Saturday in June and Inform that Church the reason why we did not receive Rachel belonging to Lewis Easterday, and to try and give them satisfaction—the said Bre^n is to be furnish'd with a Copy of the Charges against Sanders

Br? William Marshal & Elizabeth his Wife is to have letters of Dismission.

Receiv'd by letter Jeremiah Buckley & Frances his Wife also Isaac Wilson & Lucy his Wife

WILLIAM HICKMAN Mod^r

The Lords day Morning the Church met and after Divine Worship Proceeded to business—Received by Experience a black Woman belonging to John Stephens by the Name of Nancy

The 2nd Saturday in July 1804 the Church met and after Divine Worship Proceeded to business

A Charge was brought against Br? Pullum, by Br? Peak and others for abusing his Son John and for Swearing—Bre^n Joseph Edrington & Carter Blanton is appointed to Cite him to our next Church Meeting—

Br.° James Oneal is Excluded from this Church for Swearing and offering to bet on Horse Raceing & that on the Lords day—

The matter respecting Br.° Palmer's filling the place of a Deacon in this Church was taken up— and it was thought by the Church that some other be appointed and he Dismist.

Bre.ⁿ Daniel Peak, Abraham Gregory and John Price was recommended to the Church as being capable of filling the Office of a Deacon

Query is it not worthy of Dealing for a Member in time of Divine Worship to be found laughing and talking—Agree'd it is.

Bre.ⁿ William Hickman & Thomas Wooldridge is Appointed as Messengers to our next Asso.ⁿ and also to prepare the Church letter against our next Church Meeting

WILLIAM HICKMAN Mod.ʳ

The 1ˢᵗ Saturday in August 1804 the Church met and after Divine Worship Proceeded to business—

Agreeable to Citement Br.° Pullum came before the Church and Acknowledged his fault; the Church agree'd to bear with him

At Br.° Prices request by letter he is Dismist from being appointed to fill the Office of a Deacon. Br.° Gregory is appointed to fill the Office of a Deacon.

Br.° Peak is Dismist from being nominated to fill the Office of a Deacon.

Br.º Abraham Bledsoe is granted a letter of Dismission

Sister Esther Boulware return'd her letter and Membership

A motion made & secon'd that all those Members that has apply'd for letters of Dismission to Join some other Church & has not join'd be call'd on to Acc.ᵗ for such conduct—Also those that have grants for letters & do not draw them, nor relinquish their grant.

Br.º Haden Edwards, & Br.º Cole is Nominated to fill the Office of a Deacon.
Church letter read and receiv'd.

WILLIAM HICKMAN. Mod.ʳ

The 2.ⁿᵈ Saturday in September 1804 the Church met and after Divine Worship Proceeded to business.

A Charge was brought by Brother Onions against Bengamin & Lewis Stephens Members of this Church, the former for Improper conduct in time of worship playing of Ball and a pointed request to be excluded from the Church, the latter for the two last charges—They were accordingly Excluded.

Brother Jesse Cole's appointed to fill the Office of a Deacon.

Br.º Lewis Palmer upon request is granted a letter of Dismission.

Sister Elizabeth Haydon is granted a letter of Dismission upon request of her Father

Br.° Giles Samuel's Jack offered his Membership to the Church and was received for Baptism.

The request of the Church (that those Members who had formerly rec^d & applied for letters and had not Join'd other Churches or rec^d their letters) should be called on to account for such conduct, be postponed till the next Church Meeting.

WILLIAM HICKMAN

The 2nd Saturday in October 1804 The Church met and after Divine Worship proceeded to business

Brethren Edmund Ware & Benjamin Edrington is requested to Cite Br.° Zacheriah Pullum to our next Church meeting to answer some late charges, Also Sister Patsy Boulware to prove the charges against said Pullum.

Agree'd that the Ordination of the Deacons be at our next Church meeting and that Br.° Redding & Br.° Crutcher be requested to act in the business

November is the time to be prepared to defray the expenses of the table

A motion made & seconded that the Members of this Church do Annually come prepar'd at our Church Meetings in November to defray the expenses of the Table.

WILLIAM HICKMAN Mod.^r

The 2nd Friday in November 1804 the Church met and after Divine Worship proceeded to business

Brother Ware & Br.° Edrington reported to the Church that they Cited Br. Zachariah Pulliam to this Church meeting also that he acknowledged he was guilty of Swearing—he was Excluded for the same

Thomas Settle is requested to talk with Br.º Elijah Martin for not returning his letter and Membership——

Brother Daniel Peak is requested to talk with Br.º Morgan Bryan for not returning his letter and membership

Brother Gregory is requested to talk with Br.º Finney for not returning his letter—

At the request of the Church at Hopewell meeting House we do appoint our Brethren John Edrington & Edmund Ware to attend their Meeting the fourth Saturday in this Month

Receiv'd by letter Sister Polly Stout—

WILLIAM HICKMAN Mod.ᵗʳ

The 2.ⁿᵈ Saturday in November 1804 Br.º A. Gregory & Br.º J. Cole was Ordained Deacons— Sunday Evening after the Administration of the Lords Supper the Church set and Excluded Charles a Negroe Man belonging to Br.º Majors for a busing Winney a black member belonging to Sister Boulware

Also Excluded Molly a black member formerly belonging to M.ʳ Fitzgerald for telling lies

Excluded Hannah Davy's Wife for Swearing & keeping another Man beside her Husband

Condorus a black member belonging to Ja.ˢ Sanders was also Excluded for lying, & taking another Wife contrary to the Gospel

The 2.ⁿᵈ Saturday in December 1804 the Church met and after Divine Worship Proceeded to business

James Major was Excluded from this Church for Intoxication and Shooting for Liquor

Br? Red Major Came before the Church and was dealt with for Shooting for Liquor, and the Church directed the Moderator to give him a word of Admonition and was acquited

Robert Hicklin was Excluded from this Church for Horse Raceing

WILLIAM HICKMAN Mod.tr

The 2.nd Saturday in January 1805 the Church met and after Divine Worship proceeded to business Brother James Finney returned his letter of recommendation

Br? James Major restor'd to fellowship

A motion was made & seconded that the following Bre.n William Hickman Haden Edwards & Thomas Settle make some Alteration on the 3.rd Article respecting the manner of treating publick Offences—& report to the Church at our next Church Meeting

WILLIAM HICKMAN Mod.tr

The Church set on Sunday Morning
Br? Morgan Bryan return'd his letter of recommendation

Br? Major's Charles restor'd to fellowship

The 2.nd Saturday in February 1805 the Church met and after Divine Worship proceeded to business.

The Brethren Appointed at our last Meeting to make some Alteration on the 3rd Article made their report to the Church and after some debate was refer'd to our next Church Meeting.

WILLIAM HICKMAN Mod^{tr}

The 2nd Saturday in March 1805 the Church met and after Divine Worship proceeded to business

A Charge was brought against Sister Polly Edrington for frequently giving her Mother the lie, & calling her a fool and for Indeavouring by tattleing to set several of the Neighbours at strife with each other—She was Excluded for the same

Receiv'd by letter Sam a black Man belonging to Brother Edmund Ware

Br^{o} Nicholas Ware and Polly his Wife is granted a letter of Dismission

The alteration on the 3rd Article refer'd from our last meeting was debated on and was order'd to be refer'd to our next Meeting and that Br^{o} Wm Samuel and the Clerk make alteration on the same

Query what shall be done with our free Male Members that will not attend Church Meetings of Business

The above Query is refer'd to our next Meeting

WILLIAM HICKMAN Modt^{r}

The 2nd Saturday in April 1805 the Church met and after Divine Worship proceeded to business—

The alteration on the 3rd Article refer'd from our last meeting with its proposed alterations, was taken up and after some debate was Voted on

The Query refer'd from our last Meeting was taken up & Debated and it was concluded that it is the duty of every Member in this Church knowing any Member to live in neglect of attending Church Meetings or Preaching Meetings to Exort and persuade them to fill their seats at Meetings

Brother Elijah Martin return'd his letter of recommendation.

WILLIAM HICKMAN Mod.tr

The lords day Morning, the Church set and restor'd Annabel a Negroe Man belonging to Br.o Giles Samuel—

W.m HICKMAN Mod.tr

The 2nd Saturday in May 1805 The Church Met and after Divine Worship Proceeded to business

At the request of the Church at the Mouth of Elkhorn, we do appoint Brother Abraham Gregory & Br.o Carter Blanton to attend their Meeting the first Saturday in June in order to assist them in any Matter of Difficulty.

Received by letter Samuel Buckley.

WILLIAM HICKMAN Mod.tr

The 2nd Saturday in June 1805 the Church met and after Divine Worship Proceeded to business

Receiv'd by letter Elizabeth Buckley and David Partlow A Charge brought by Br.o Thomas Mastin against Br.o Martin Nall was refer'd until our next Church Meeting

The Church are of an Opinion that if any Member Conveys his property to defraud his Creditor's it is a Matter of Publick Dealing

WILLIAM HICKMAN Modt.

Sunday morning receiv'd Milley the property of M.ʳ Smith Hale by letter

W. HICKMAN Modt.

The 2nd Saturday in July 1805 the Church met and after Divine Worship proceeded to business

Brethren William Hickman Abraham Gregory & Thomas Wooldridge is appointed Messengers to our next Asso.ⁿ & to prepare the Church letter

Excluded John Baker for disobeying the Call of the Church and for profane Swearing &c.

Receiv'd by letter, Theodrick Boulware

At the request of Sister's Salley Sanders & Suckey Smith late Hancock by Br.º Hickman they are granted letters of Dismission

The Charge brought by Br.º Tho.ˢ Mastin against Br.º Martin Nall, refer'd from our last Meeting was Debated and ordered to be refer'd to our next Church Meeting

Br.º Martin Nall complains of Br.º Tho.ˢ Mastin for Chargeing him for mending one old piggin (at the price of 1/6) which he did not receive

WILLIAM HICKMAN

Sunday Morning Rec.ᵈ by letter Winney Kelly Also Lucy a black Woman the Property of Br.º Partlow

First Saturday in August 1805

The Church Met and after Divine Worship proceeded to business

1st The Charges that was brought by Br.° Tho.ˢ Mastin against Br.° Martin Nall which has been refer'd from time to time was taken up and Debated—

The Charges is as follows (viz.). for failing to come and see the ground and Settle as he agreed to do—then saying I agreed to take him for 4/6 which M.ʳ Thomas did Owe me I let him know there was no such thing, he said he would Sware it—and in Controversy between Thomas and myself for the 4/6 Thomas was due me Br.° Nall being first Sworn—he then said, I had taken the Debt on him and that I fell in Debt to him on p [rest of word has been cut off] Settlement— I Denied it and he said he could Prove it by his Motherinlaw—After a deliberate debate on the above Charges the Church Judged that Br.° Mastin faild to Substanciate the Charges Especially the one that went to prove Said Nall Forsworn but both being possess'd of a Momoss Spirit and Pointed Contradictions the Church thought best to Exclude them Both—

2 Br.° William Smither Complains against Br.° James Robertson for Horse Raceing and neglecting to hear the Church he is Excluded—

3 Bro Ambrose Complains against his fellow Serv.ᵗ Benjamin belonging to M.ʳ W.ᵐ Ware, for Stealing Fowls, he was Excluded.

4 Church letter read and approved—

5 Sister Patsey Boulwares letter returned—

6   Complaint brought against Bennet Pemberton for drinking to Excess Refer'd to Next Meeting—

7   The Church Profess'd to be Grieved with Grassy Spring Church—Drew up their Complaints and Sent them by the following Brethren James Haydon, Carter Blanton Abraham Gregory Daniel Peak and Theodrick Boulware to Enquire and make report at our next Meeting.

The 2ⁿᵈ Saturday in September 1805 the Church met and after Divine Worship proceeded to business—

Daniel Brown Excluded for Swearing and Gaming—

J. Haydons fellowship & letter.

A Question put to the Church, is Br.° Haydon in full fellowship in this Church, was answered in the affirmative and he is Requested to return his letter when convenient

Our Messengers made report to this Church that they were not receiv'd by the Church at Hopewell

Agreed by the Church that the Clerk do write to McConnels Run & the Great Crossing Churches Requesting them to send to our Assistance four Male Members from each Church to Aid us in trying to Settle some grievances that has arisen between this Church and the Church at Hopewell —and to meet at Hopewell on the 4ᵗʰ Saturday in September 1805.

Receiv'd by letter Anne McGraw

A letter is granted to Billey a black man the property of Mrs Allen

WILLIAM HICKMAN Modʳ

At a Call'd Meeting on Monday the 30th of Sep.t 1805 after Divine Worship proceeded to business

Our Members Sent to treat with the Church at Hopewell Informs us that they send four Members from the big Crossings, likewise four Members from McConnels Run at the request of our Church, met at Hopewell the 4th Saturday in Sept.—Our Brethren reported that the said Church would not receive the Charges, nor give any Satisfaction—
It is directed by this Church to send Information to the North Destrict Asson desiring a Committee to be sent to look into our Grievances

The Church has appointed Br.o Theodrick Boulware and Br.o Red Major to Carry the letter to the North District Asson from this Church
WILLIAM HICKMAN Modt

The 2nd Saturday in October 1805 the Church met and after Divine Worship proceeded to business

A Charge brought by Br.o Stephens against Br.o Edward Roberts for playing fives and Offering to bet one hundred dollars, Refer'd to our next Meeting

A Charge brought against Br.o Bennet Pemberton for drinking to Excess was taken up and he was Acquited

Br.o Theodrick Boulware reported that he bore the letter from this Church to the North District Asso. and they refus'd to send a Committe

This matter respecting Hopewell Church Refer'd till again taken up in future
WILLIAM HICKMAN Modt

The 2ⁿᵈ Saturday in November 1805 the Church met and after Divine Worship proceeded to business—

Br.º Blanton complains against Br.º Red Major for playing Carnal plays. The Church thinks proper that the Moderator reprove and Acquit him.
Br.º Edward Roberts is Excluded from this Church for playing fives and for offering to bet One hundred Dollars

Dismist by letter, Delpha a black Woman the property of Mᴿ N. Sanders

Dismist by letter, Charles, the property of Mᴿ Elijah Smith

Motioned and seconded that the Brother Deacons do Employ some person to put Glass in the Window against the pulpit and make a shutter to it

Agreed by the Church that Subscriptions be put into the hands of our Brethren William Samuel Carter Blanton & Tho. Settle to Raise Money to Repair the Schoolhouse which is in partnership between the Church and the Subscribers to the Schoolhouse The above mentioned Brethren is appointed as Trustee's to let and Receive the said Work

WILLIAM HICKMAN Modᵗʳ

Sunday recᵈ by Experience and Baptism Dorcas the property of Mʳˢ Nancy Hale

Br.º Majors Conkey is Excluded for profane Swearing, and refusing to come to the Church

M.ʳ Asa Bells Caty is Excluded for the Sin of a Dultery

WILLIAM HICKMAN Mod.ʳ

The 2.ⁿᵈ Saturday in December 1805 the Church met and after Divine Worship proceeded to business

Br.º Haydon Complains against Br.º James Major for threatening a Man's life and saying that his conduct had been so bad that he never wou'd tell it, The Church after a full Examination into the Charges agreed to bear with him.

At the request of Br.º James Haydon & Br.º Samuel Price The Church appointed the following Brethren William Hubbel Daniel Peak William Samuel Abraham Gregory and Carter Blanton to Settle some difficulties between them

Br.º John Price's Annaca is Excluded from this Church for Stealing

WILLIAM HICKMAN Mod.ᵗ.

The second Saturday in January 1806 the Church met and after Divine Worship proceeded to business

Br.º Palmer complains against Br.º Stephens and his Wife for not dealing with Nancy their Negroe Woman & bringing her before the Church and for puting her in Irons—Br.º Stephens was Acquited A second Charge against Sister Stephens for giving their Negroe Woman the lye—She was Acquited from both Charges

Charges brought against Br.º Ja.ˢ Major for saying that John Dupey slapt him in the face & he draw'd

himself up in the Chair and bore it, and that M.ʳ
Pulliam said he was the Patientest Man he ever see
in his life—

Charge the 2.ⁿᵈ for saying he gave Dupey no cause
to treat him in the Manner he did and for going
Repeatedly to where Dupey was and Quarreling
with him

The above Charges was substanciated—but when
taking a Vote who can bear with Br.° Major, the
Church agreed to bear with him

Br.° Ramsey Boulware said he cou'd not fellowship
Br.° Major and withdrew from the Church

Sister Polley Stout is granted a letter of Dismission

WM HICKMAN

The 2.ⁿᵈ Saturday in February 1806 the Church
met and after Divine Worship proceeded to
business—

Br.° Ramsey Boulware came before the Church
and Acknowledged his fault in leaving the Church
at our last meeting he is Continued

The Church appointed Br.° Daniel Peak, Br.°
Jesse Cole and Br.° Isaac Wilson to talk with Br.°
Ramsey Boulware and Br.° Red Major and try
to get a reconsiliation between them

At the request of Br.° John Samuel he & his Wife
Betsy is granted letter of Dismission—

At the request of Br.° Edmund Ware the Church
has agreed to send to the following Churches for
helps (to wit)

The Glens Creek, North fork & McConnels Run two Members from each Church to meet at this place the 2nd Saturday in March next to try and Settle some Grievances in the Church

WILLIAM HICKMAN M.

The 2nd. Saturday in March 1806 the Church met & after Divine Worship Proceeded to business

A Charge was brought against the Majority of this Church for bearing with Brother James Major after three Charges being Substanciated against the said Major without any Repentance

We the Subscribers being sent from the Baptist Churches at the North fork, Glens Creek and McConnels Run to Aid the Church at the forks of Elkhorn in Settleing a matter of Difficulty are Are of Openion that the Minority has some right of complaint because the Majority holds Majors without a Recantation, but we believe the Error of the Majority Aught not to make such a Split amongst professors of Christianity We therefore recommend to the Minority to Submit

Rodes Smith

The Church Acceeded to the
advice of the helps

Joseph Bonderant

John H. Ficklin

Richard D. Ship.

Tol.^r   Craig Junr

John Swon—

A letter of Dismission is Granted to Sister Betsy Buckley—

Brother Red Major came forward and Reprobated his past conduct of passion and unguarded
Expressions

Br.º Ramsy Boulware Offer'd his Repentance
which was Satisfactory and he return'd to the
Church

Br.º Thomas Gravet is Granted a letter of Dismission

WILLIAM HICKMAN Modt.ʳ

The 2ⁿᵈ Saturday in April 1806 the Church met
and after Divine Worship Proceeded to business—

Br.º Palmer brought a complaint against Br.º
Stephens and Wife for not leeting Nancy come to
see her Child—Referd to next meeting

Charge brought against Mʳ John Bacons Robben
by Br.º Peak for Lying and disobedience to his
Master—The Church took up the Matter & after
Investigation, Excluded him for the same Sister
Fitzgerald is to have a letter of Dismission

Appointed next Thursday a day of fasting and
Prayer.

Church took up a Complaint against Br.º Haden
Edwards for Gambling and Excluded him for the
same

Charge brought against Mʳ Coles Nancy by
Sister Stephens for saying Bro. Stephens said he
would give her a hundred stripes and every Six
Stripes dip the Cow hide in Salt and Water—And
saying while she was in Irons she Suffered every

day for Fire Victuals and Water—And for saying
when ever she and the Children fell Out they
would not hear her, but believe the Children &
whip her Refered to next Meeting——
WILLIAM HICKMAN Modtr.

The 2nd Saturday in May 1836 the Church met
and after Divine Worship Proceeded to business.

A Charge against Br.^{o} Majors James for drinking
to an Excess, refer'd to next meeting.

The Charge against Bro. Stephens & Wife refer'd
from last meeting, taken up, Bro. Stephens &
Wife is Acquited.

The Charges against Mr Coles Nancy, refer'd
from last meeting taken up & after Investigation
Excluded her for the same

Emancipating
Query rec'd
Query does this Church think that Baptist
Preachers are authorised from the word of God to
Preach Emancipation. Refer'd to next meeting.
WILLIAM HICKMAN Modtr,

The 2nd Saturday in June 1806 the Church met
and after Divine Worship proceeded to business—

The Charge against Bro. Major's James refer'd
from last meeting was taken up, he was Excluded
for drinking to an Excess and for refusing to hear
the Church—

A Charge against Mr Tho. Major's Hannah for
professing a desire to leave the Church and for
Refusing to give her reason Bro. John Major &

Bro. Benj.ⁿ Edrington is appointed to Cite her to our next Church meeting—

The Query refered from last meeting taken up and an amendment proposed & agreed to which reads as follows. Query does this Church think that Baptist Preachers are Authorised from the word of God to Preach Emancipation of Negroe Slaves, the above Query Voted out

A motion made & seconded whether does this Church Acceed to the advice in the minutes of the Association respecting Emancipation from Slavery —Unanimously agreed too—

GEORGE SMITH Modt.ʳ

The 2.ⁿᵈ Saturday in July 1806 the Church met and after Divine Worship proceeded to business

The Charge against Tho.ˢ Major's Hannah refer'd from last meeting taken up, she was Excluded for refusing to hear the Church

Sister Elizabeth Nall is Granted a letter of Dismission

The matter respecting Hopewell Church refer'd the 2ⁿᵈ Saturday in October 1805 till again taken up in future, was taken up the Church agreed to send her complaint to the Association

Motioned and seconded that the Church say what number of Messengers shall be sent to the Association, the Church agrees to send four, (to wit) Brethren, William Hickman, Theodrick Boulware, Carter Blanton and Abraham Gregory, The same is to prepare the Church letter

Bro. Jeremiah Buckley & Frances his Wife is granted a letter of Dismission

WILLIAM HICKMAN M.

The 1st Saturday in August 1806 after Divine Service proceeded to business

Church letter read and approved of.

Restored to fellowship Annaca the property of Bro. John Price

WILLIAM HICKMAN Mod.r

The 2nd Saturday in September 1806 after Divine Worship proceeded to business

Brother Thomas Wooldridge and Salley his Wife is granted a letter of Dismission, Also a black woman by the Name of Jane, formerly the property of Capt Hubbell

At the request of the Elkhorn Association this Church has agreed to send two of our Brethren Theodrick Boulware and Carter Blanton to the Town Fork Church the first Wednesday in October next to aid and assist that Church in a matter of difficulty

WILLIAM BUCKLEY Mod.tr

The 2nd Saturday in October 1806. after Divine Worship proceeded to business

Receiv'd by letter Priscilla Montgomery

Query What is best to be done with our Brethren that does absent themselves from Church Meet-

ings—And our Brethren that has mov'd a distance
& evil reports about them—Refer'd to next Meeting

At the request of the Church on Glens Creek we
have appointed four of our Brethren Wm Hickman, Daniel Peak, Abraham Gregory & James
Finney to meet at their meeting house the 3.rd
Saturday in this Month in Order to assist them in
their present difficulties

WILLIAM HICKMAN Modt.^r

The 2.nd Saturday in November 1806, after
Divine worship proceeded to business

1.st Receiv'd against Bro. Bennet Pemberton Complaints first for drinking to an excess, and getting
Intoxicated with Spirituous liquors at different
times in Frankfort—

Secondly for the like unchristian conduct at
different times at Thos Wingates—Thirdly for
treating the Church and cause of God with contempt by neglecting both meetings of business and
publick worship—Excluded him for the two first—
agreed that the third was Substanciated, but dispenced with it in as much as it had not been the
former rule of this Church—

2.nd Took up the Query refer'd from last meeting
—What is best to be done with our Brethren that
does absent themselves from Church Meetings—
Ans. It shall be the duty of all free Male Members
missing two Church Meetings, to come forward
the third meeting and give the Church their reasons
for so doing—and if they fail so to do—the Church
shall appoint Members who shall Cite them to the
next Meeting—

3rd Took up the other part of the Query refer'd from last Meeting—What shall be done with our Brethren that has moved at a distance & evil reports about them—Voted Out

4th The Church agreed to write to Peter Baimbridge, Joseph Hough, William Rowlet wife & Children that are Members here, to let them know that the Church is grieved with them for absenting themselves from us—

5th Agreed that Meetings of business and Meetings of Worship 2 be Stated Opened at 11 Oclock—

WILLIAM HICKMAN Moderator

The 2nd Saturday in December 1806 after Divine Worship proceeded to business

A Charge against Bengamin Martin for drinking to an excess, for Sewaring & neglecting Church Meetings—he is Excluded for the same

A Charge against Bro. William Hickman for inviting Carter Tarrant to preach at his house after being Excluded for disorder in the Hilsborough Church—the Church took the Question, is it right to Invite an Excommunicated Minister to preach? Answer'd by a majority of three fourths it is not— 2^{ndly} five said Bro. Hickman had Erred by so doing. Eight said he had not.

MORDECAI BOULWARE M.

The 2nd Saturday in January 1807 after divine Worship proceeded to business
Complaint brought against Sister Esther Boulwares Winney 1st for saying she once thought it

her duty to serve her Master & Mistress but
since the lord had converted her, she had never
believed that any Christian kept Negroes or
Slaves——

2nd For saying she believed there was Thousands
of white people Wallowing in Hell for their treatment to Negroes—and she did not care if there
was as many more—Refer'd to next Meeting

Took up the matter respecting our foreign Brethren—agreed by the Church that some of our
Brethren see Bro. William Rowlet and others who
have absented themselves from us for a considerable length of time and report to the Church at
our next meeting the cause why they do not attend
agreeable to the Churches request by letter

The Church appointed Bro. William Hubbell to
write to Brother John & James Ware who lives in
Shelby County respecting the Rules of this
Church

Bro. Theodrick Boulware is appointed to write to
Bro. Ja.^s Haydon respecting the Rules of this
Church

Motion'd, seconded & agreed to that the two Rules
made at our November meeting be entered in the
list of the Rules of this Church

Bro. Jeremiah Buckley & Frances his Wife declines
drawing their letter of recommendation
                                    WILLIAM HICKMAN Modt.^r

The 2nd Saturday in February 1807 after Divine
Worship proceeded to business

The Complaint refer'd last Meeting against Sister Boulwares Winney taken up She is Excluded for the same—

Bro. William Peak is appointed to Cite Bro. William Rowlet and as many of his family as are Members here to our next Church meeting to answer the complaint of the Church

The matter respecting Bro. John & James Ware refer'd to next meeting

Excluded Peter Baimbridge and Joseph Hough for disobeying the Call of the Church.

Took up the matter respecting Bro. James Haydon's failing to comply with the Churches request Agreed the same be refer'd to our next Church meeting and that if any of the Brethren can make it convenient to see Bro. Haydon they will request him to attend our next Church meeting to answer the complaint of the Church

Bro. Gregory is appointed to Cite the two young Bro. Palmers to our next Church meeting to answer the Churches complaint for non attendance

Bro. James Tate is appointed to Cite Bro Elijah Martin Vachel Lindsey & James Smither to our next Church Meeting to answer the Churches Complaint for non attendance.

Bro. Daniel Peak is appointed to Cite Bro. John Eidson to attend our next Church Meeting to answer the Churches Complaint for non Attendance

Bro. Ambrose Jeffries is appointed to Cite Bro. Daniel Brown and Bro. Bengamin Hickman to our next Church Meeting to Answer the Churches Complaint for non Attendance

Bro. Morgan Bryan is appointed to write to Bro George Brown at Louisville and inform him of the rules of this Church and request him to attend or write to our next Church meeting to answer for non attendance

Bro William Hickman is appointed to Cite Bro. David Partlow to our next Church Meeting to answer for non attendance.

Bro. Carter Blanton is appointed to write to Bro. Madrid Jackson and inform him of the late rule adopted in this Church and request him to attend our next Church meeting or write to the Church his reason for non attendance.

WILLIAM BUCKLEY Mod'r.

Sunday after Sermon the Church set and Excluded Joe the property of M.ʳ Geo. Carlisle and Charity the property of M.ʳ Francis Peart—who was Man & Wife, for frequently Quarreling and Parting

WILLIAM HICKMAN Mod

The 2ⁿᵈ Saturday in March 1807 After Divine worship proceeded to business

1.ˢᵗ Bro. O. Lindsey came forward & gave to the Church Satisfaction

2 Bro. E. Martin came forward & gave to the Church Satisfaction

3rd Took up the matter respecting Bro. James Haydon, and upon hearing he had Joined Another Church, he was Acquited

4th. The matter respecting the two Bro. Palmers refer'd to next Meeting

5th. The matter respecting Bro. James Smither refer'd to next Meeting

6th. The matter respecting Bro. John Eidson refer'd and Bro. D. Peak and Bro. E. Ware appointed to treat with him and make report to next meeting

7th The matter respecting Bro. Daniel Brown & Bro. Benj.n Hickman refer'd to next meeting.

8th The matter respecting Bro. George Brown refer'd to next Meeting

9th Bro. Partlow came forward and give the Church Satisfaction

10th The matter respecting Bro. Madrid Jackson refer'd to next Meeting

11th Bro W.m Hubbell appointed to write to Bro. George Garrard and request him to attend our next meeting and render his reason for non attendance

12th The matter respecting Bro. Rowlet & family —Also the two Bro. Wares refer'd to next Meeting

13th Took up the request of our Brethren A. Dudley &c respecting a Call'd Association— Refer'd till next Meeting

14th Bro. Nathaniel Thompson is granted a letter of Dismission

WILLIAM HICKMAN Moderator—

The 2nd Saturday in April 1807 After Divine Worship proceeded to business

1st The matter respecting the two Bro. Palmers refer'd from last meeting taken up and refer'd, and that Bro. Gregory & Bro. Palmer Cite them to next Meeting

2nd The matter respecting Bro. James Smither refer'd from last meeting taken up and refer'd to our next meeting

3rd The matter respecting Bro. John Eidson refer'd from last meeting taken up, Bro. Eidson Objects against the Rule of this Church which compells her members to attend Church meetings, or give their reason for non attendance—The Church agrees that Bro. Eidson consider the matter till next meeting

4th Took up the request of our Brethren A. Dudley & others respecting a call'd Association refer'd from last meeting and after some debate Voted it out

5th Bro. Benjamin Hickman came forward and give satisfaction to the Church for non attendance.

6th The matter respecting Bro. Daniel Brown refer'd from our last meeting taken up and refer'd to our next meeting and that Bro.

Benjamin Hickman is appointed to Cite him to our next meeting

7th. The matter respecting Bro. Geo. Brown refer'd from last meeting taken up and refer'd to next meeting.

8th The matter respecting Bro. Geo. Garrard refer'd to next meeting

9th. Dismist by letter William Rowlet & Jemima his Wife, William Rowlet Junr and Nancy Rowlet

10th. Dismist by letter a black woman by the name of Jane the property of Mr Richard Gano

11th. Motion & second that the 11 Article of our Church be dispensed off, agreed to by the Church and that all the references respecting the 11 Article be Entirely done away

WILLIAM HICKMAN Mod'r

The 2nd Saturday in May 1807 after Divine Service proceeded to business.

1st. Took up the following letter as a complaint against George Brown Junr and excluded him for the same the whole letter directed to be recorded

Jefferson County Kentucky
Dear Sir
I received your affectionate letter of the 14th of February; on the 29th of March informing me of a measure taken (in the forks of Elkhorn Church) to get the people

to come to Church meeting and that you were appointed
to write to me to attend Church Meeting in March,
Sixty miles is a prety good distance too to go to meeting
and as I got the letter too late to come or send word, I
expect to be fin'd about a dollar to be paid to the—I
cant say but I'll think, and I hope the Church will
cratch my name out as I shall consider myself as no
more of that Church not for the adoption of that rule
but as a duty you owe to me, for my conduct is not becoming of a professor of religion

GEORGE BROWN JUN.

March 29th. 1807—

MORGAN H. BRYAN

2 Query. does this Church believe it to be the
duty of her members to attend Meetings of
Church business—Answered in the affirmative,
they do.

3 Query. Is it not a matter worthy of Exclusion,
for parents to suffer their Children (that are
under their Jurisdiction) to attend Barbacues,
Balls &c. Refer'd to next Meeting

WILLIAM HICKMAN Modt.

The 2nd. Saturday in June 1807 after Divine
worship proceeded to business

1st. In answer to the query referred to this meeting
from the last Voted—The Church believe it a
duty of parents to prohibit their Children from
all licentious practices as far as possible, and
where there is any countenance given by parents
to their Children to frequent those places mentioned in the query. They ought to be disciplined, and if not reclaimed from such toleration, or countenance to be excluded.

2nd The propriety of raising monies for defraying the contingent expenses of the Church, being conversed upon, Voted that the mode of raising such money, be postponed to another meeting for the consideration of the Church

WILLIAM HICKMAN Modt.

The 2nd Saturday in July 1807 after Divine worship proceeded to business

Took into consideration the Query referred to this meeting from the last, respecting the mode in which money shall be raised to defray the contingent expenses of the Church. Agreed that the Clerk with the assistance of Bro. Blanton and Bro. Wm Samuel make out the proportion which each member has aright to pay of 25$ dollars according to their abilities, and report to the next Church Meeting

Bro. Edmund Ware is appointed to receive all such monies for the use of the Church. and to enter the same in a book to be kept for that purpose and likewise of the expendatures

Bro. Josiah Jackson withdrew from the Church indisorder and is no more of us—
Took up the request of Town fork Church agreed that the following Brethren William Hubbell, John Price, Josep Edrington & James Finney attend a meeting at Town fork Church on the 28th day of this month in order to assist them in business of Importance

The following Brethren appointed as Messengers to the Association William Hickman, Carter

Blanton, Theodrick Boulware & Edmund Ware. the same is to prepare the Church letter

Took into consideration the revisal of the Philadelphia confession of faith agreed that the old one be prefer'd—

Agreed by The Church that the sum of four Dollars be paid to any person that will keep the meeting house in good order, doors and windows shut &c for one Year.

JOHN PRICE Mod'r

The 1st Saturday in August 1807 After divine Worship proceeded to business

Excluded Jack—the property of Sister Samuel, for gambling and drinking to an excess

Complaint against Bro. Benjn Hickman for Joining the free Mason Society—Referred to next meeting and that Bro. Blanton is to cite him to the said Meeting—

From the request of the Church of Washington to give a statement of the cause of the Exclusion of Bro. John Samuel's Negro Man Ben, who wishes to Join them—if satisfaction be gained, we have no Objection

Church letter read and approved of—
The Brethren appointed to make a statement of the proportion which each member has aright to pay according to their several abilities, made report to the Church by a statement of the Members names with the sums annext thereto—The same agreed to by the Church

Bro. Maddra Jackson is granted a letter of Dismission

WILLIAM HICKMAN Mod.ʳ

The 2ⁿᵈ Saturday in September 1807 After divine Service proceeded to business—

1ˢᵗ Took up the Complaint against Bro. Benjamin Hickman and referred it to next meeting

2nd. Bro. William Hickman came forward and informed the Church that he was distressed on account of the practice of Slavery as being tolerated by the members of the Baptist Society, therefore declared himself no more in Union with us, or the Elkhorn Association—Therefore the Church considers him no more a member in fellowship

3ʳᵈ Bro. Plewright Sisk came forward and declared himself no more a member with us, for similar reasons with brother Hickman—Therefore the Church considers him no more a member in fellowship

ABRAHAM GREGORY Mod

The 2nd. Saturday in October 1807 After divine worship proceeded to business

1ˢᵗ Complaint against Bro. Daniel Brown for frolicking and dancing taken up and referred to next Meeting

2ⁿᵈ Complaint against Bro. Elijah Martin for treating the Church and cause of God with contempt by neglecting to attend, both Meetings of business and publick worship,—Taken up and referred to next Meeting—And that Bro. Tate Cite him to attend said Meeting

3rd Took up the complaint (referred time after time) against Bro. Benjamin Hickman for Joining the free Mason Society—and Excluded him for the same

4th Received by letter Thomas Buckley

5 Dismist by letter Sisters Mary McGee, Salley Mitchel Elizabeth Hiter and Milley Bledsoe
                    CARTER BLANTON Mod^r.

The 2nd. Saturday in November 1807 after Divine worship proceeded to business

1st Took up the complaint against Bro. Elijah Martin, referred to this meeting from the last, for treating the Church and cause of God with contempt by neglecting to attend both meetings of business and publick worship and he was Excluded for the same

2nd Took up the complaint against Bro. Daniel Brown (referred to this meeting from the last) for frolicking and dancing, and Excluded him for the same
                    JOHN SHACKLEFORD Mod^r.

The 2nd Saturday in December 1807 after Divine Worship proceeded to business

1st Complaint Bro. Wm Montgomery brought against himself for drinking to an excess, the Church agreed to bear with him.

2ⁿᵈ The Church appointed Bro. Edmund Ware to have wood furnised for the use of the house at the meeting house.

3ʳᵈ Question was taken does this Church want a Minister to preach to them, and administer the Ordinances, Voted they did, then agreed that next meeting be appointed to say what Minister they will get and by what means
JOHN SHACKLEFORD Modʳ

The 2ⁿᵈ Saturday in January 1808 after Divine Worship Proceeded to business

1ˢᵗ Brother John Shackleford made choise of as Minister to Preach to and Administer the Ordinances of this Church, and that he be requested to attend us one Year, on our Monthly Meeting days and as much oftener as he can make it convenient

2ⁿᵈ Agreed that Thoˢ Settle be appointed to receive what may be communicated for Bro. Shackleford Also keep a Memorandum of the Names of the Brethren from whom it is received and what sum from each—and report to the Church when call'd on
ABRAHAM GREGORY Modʳ

The 2ˑⁿᵈ Saturday in February 1808 after Divine service proceeded to business—

1.ˢᵗ Complaint brought against Bro. Iverson Ware for gambling—Referred to next Meeting—

2 Took up the subject concerning the Brethren who have mooved out of the bounds of the

Church without letters and fail to attend our
Meetings—Referred to next Meeting—

JOHN SHACKLEFORD Mod.

The 2ⁿᵈ Saturday in March 1808 after Divine
worship proceeded to business

1ˢᵗ Took up the complaint against Bro. Iverson
Ware for Gambling (referred from last meeting) He was Excluded for the same—

2ⁿᵈ Took up the subject (referred from last meeting) concerning the Brethren who have
moved out of the bounds of the Church
without letters and fail to attend our meetings—Agreed that the Clerk be directed to
make out a list of all the Members and present it to the next Meeting—

JOHN SHACKLEFORD Mod.

The 2nd. Saturday in April 1808 after Divine
worship proceeded to business

The matter respecting Bro. John Ware who has
moved out of the bounds of this Church and has
neglected to apply for a letter of dismission or
attend our meetings—Taken up and referred to
next meeting—

Excluded the following members who has moved
out of the bounds of the Church without letters
of dismission and neglect to attend our meetings
George Garrard—James Ware—William Rowlet
Sen. William Rowlet Jun. & Jemima Rowlet

The matter respecting our disorderly members
referred to next meeting

Motion made and seconded that the Clerk be
called on at our next meeting to make return of
the Money lodged with him for the benefit of
Bro. Shackleford

JOHN SHACKLEFORD Mod.ʳ

The 2ⁿᵈ Saturday in May 1808 after Divine
worship proceeded to business

1 The reference respecting Bro. John Ware is referred to next meeting

Bro. Theodrick Boulware & Bro. James Major is
appointed to talk to Bro. Nath! Thompson respecting his neglect of duty—and make report at
our next meeting

Bro. Finney and Bro. Gregory is appointed to see
Bro. Charles Palmer respecting his neglect of duty
and report to our next meeting

Bro. William Samuel and Bro. Stephens is appointed to talk to Bro. James Hicklin respecting
his neglect of duty and make report at our next
Meeting

Bro. Tate & Bro. Wilson is appointed to talk to
Bro. James Smither respecting his neglect of duty
and make report at our next Meeting

Agreeable to an order of the Church at our last
meeting the Clerk made return of the Money deposited with him for the benefit of Bro. Shackleford the sum is Twenty four dollars & twenty five
Cents, which sum he is hereby Authorised to pay
to Bro Shackleford—

Also the Clerk is requested to keep the subscription
paper and receive as before directed

Query. Does this Church think that her members has a rights to invite any Gospel Minister to preach in their houses—who is in in good standing in their own Church Taken up and agreed that they have aright

JOHN SHACKLEFORD Mod^r

2nd Saturday in June 1808 after Divine service proceeded to business

1st The reference respecting Bro. John Ware referred to next meeting

2nd Took up the reference respecting Bro. N. Thompson, and from the report of the Brethren the Church professed to be satisfied.

3rd The reference respecting Bro. Charles Palmer referred to next Meeting—

4th Took up the reference respecting Bro. J^{as} Hicklin and after conversing with him, the Church professed to be satisfied

5th The reference respecting Bro. James Smither referred to August meeting

6th Bro. Ware and Edrington, appointed to Cite Bro. G. Twiman to our next meeting, for neglecting to attend meetings of business

7th Bro. Bohannan & Bro. Blanton, appointed to Cite Bro. John Eidson to next meeting for neglecting meetings of business—

8th Bro. Gregory & Finney, appointed to Cite Bro. Lewis Palmer to next meeting for neglecting meetings of business

JOHN SHACKLEFORD Mod^r

The 2nd Saturday in July 1808 after Divine worship proceeded to business

The reference respecting Bro. John Ware taken up, Bro. Waller appear'd in his behalf and gave the Church satisfaction, Also applied for a letter of Dismission for Bro. Ware which is granted by the Church.

Took up the referrence respecting Bro. G. Twyman, and after conversing with him, the Church profess'd to be satisfied.

Bro John Eidson return'd his letter of recommendation, the Church after conversing with him profess'd to be satisfied

The matter respecting Bro. Lewis Palmer is referred to next Meeting

At the request of Bro. Isaac Palmer he is granted a letter of Dismission

Received by letter Bro. James Martin and Esther his Wife.

The following Brethren is appointed as Messengers to the Association Carter Blanton Edmund Ware and Theodrick Boulware the same is to prepare the Church letter

Bro. Gregory and Bro. Finney is appointed to Cite Bro. Benjamin Edrington to next meeting for neglecting to attend meetings of business—

Bro. Hubbell & Bro. Price is appointed to Cite Bro. Jesse Cole to next meeting for neglecting to attend meetings of business—

The referrence respecting Bro. Charles Palmer
referred to next meeting

Agreed by the Church that Bro. Edmund Ware
pay the Woman for sweeping the Meetinghouse
the year past—

Bro. William Samuel Bro. James Martin and Tho.
Settle be appointed to employ some person to keep
the Meeting house clean for one year—Also to
employ some person to repair the underpinning of
said house—Likewise some person to make some
repairs to the Roof of the same—The above
Expences for repairing and keeping the House
clean to be paid out of the Church funds—

Agreed by the Church that the Treasurer make
return at our next meeting of the Money Expended with an Acc^t of the Church—and also of
what is still remaining in the Treasury—

JOHN SHACKLEFORD Mod

First Saturday in August 1808 after Divine Service
proceeded to business

1   Took up the referrence respecting Bro. Lewis
     Palmer's neglecting meetings of business—
     and after receiving a letter from him, in which
     he charges the Church of acting partially—
     Also charges her of acting tyrannically in ex-
     pelling her former Pastor, which charges the
     Church declares to be false—Therefore the
     Church has Excluded him for the same

2nd Took up the referrence respecting Bro. Benjn
     Edrington's neglecting meetings of business—
     he came forward and gave the Church sat-
     isfaction

3rd The referrence respecting Bro. J. Cole referred—

4 The referrence respecting Bro. John Bohannon referred—

5 The referrence respecting Bro. Charles Palmer referred—

6 Treasurer reported that he has collected $19, 55, the Church Expenditures $5, 12, 5, So there remains in his hands collected $14. 42. 5

7 The referrence concerning Bro. James Smither, which was referred from June meeting to this, is referred to next meeting—

8 Took up the Answer of the Association of 1807 to a Query from the Northfork, respecting difficulties existing between two Sister Churches,—the church answered, they were satisfied with the said Answer.

9 Church letter read and approved of.
JOHN SHACKLEFORD Modt^r

The 2nd Saturday in September 1808 after Divine Service proceeded to business

1st Took up the referrence respecting Bro. Jesse Cole's neglecting meetings of business—he came forward and gave the Church satisfaction.

2nd Took up the referrence respecting Bro. John Bohannon and referred it to next meeting—

3.rd Took up and referred (the referrence concerning Bro. Charles Palmer) to next meeting

4.th Took up the referrence concerning Bro. James Smither. he came forward and gave the Church satisfaction

5.th Rec.^d by letter Sister Elizabeth Stephens

JOHN SHACKLEFORD Mod.^r

The second Saturday in October 1808 after Divine Worship proceeded to business

1.st Took up and referred the referrence respecting Bro. John Bohannon to next meeting

2.nd Took up the referrence concerning Bro. Charles Palmer, he came forward and gave the Church satisfaction

3.rd Agreed by the Church that Bro. Gregory & Bro. Price talk to Bro. John Shackleford and see whether he will attend this Church one year more on the same principles he has done the preceding year and report to the Church.

4.th The Bren. appointed to talk to Bro. Shackleford reported to the Church that he was willing to attend this Church the Ensuing year on the same principles as he did the preceeding year.

5.th Agreed by the Church that the Bro. Clerk make report to the Church at our next meeting of what Money is deposited with him for the benefit of Bro. Shackleford

CARTER BLANTON Mod.^r

Sunday after Preaching the Church set and received by letter Betty a black Woman the Property of Mrs Ewels and Peter the property of Mr Smith Hale

The 2nd Saturday in December 1880 after divine worship proceeded to business

1st Took up the referrence respecting Bro. John Bohannon's neglecting to attend Church meetings, he came forward and gave his reason for not attending—the Church Vote his reasons was not satisfactory, also Voted that his conduct and reasons before the church was worthy of Exclusion.

2nd Agreeable to the request of the Church at our last meeting the Clerk reported there is $11 .. 33 .. 3 Deposited with him for the benefit of Bro. John Shackleford, he is directed to pay the the same to Bro. Shackleford

3rd Rec^d and referr'd the following Query to next meeting Query Does this Church think it right to open her meeting house doors to Bro. Smith, Barrow & Tarrant and all those that we believe preaches the Gospel, that are in good standing in their own Churches, and try to be as friendly as in days past

4th Dismist by letter Sister's, Betsy Martin & Frances Hardin late Bartlet

JOHN SHACKLEFORD Mod

The 2nd. Saturday in Jan. 7. 1809 after divine Worship proceeded to business—

1ˢᵗ The Query referred to this meeting from our last, throw'd out.

2nd. The Brethren that Objected to Bro. Shackleford as not being their choise as a Minister, after some conversation concur'd with the Church in their choice

JOHN SHACKLEFORD Modʳ

The 2ⁿᵈ Saturday in February after Divine Worship proceeded to business—

1.ᵗ There being no business before the Church she adjourned—

JOHN SHACKLEFORD Modʳ

The 2ⁿᵈ Saturday in March 1809 after Divine Worship proceeded to business

1ˢᵗ Bro. Joseph Edrington is appointed to examine the Clerks Office in Woodford County to see if there is any Deed recorded there for the Meeting house lot—

JOHN SHACKLEFORD Modʳ

The 2ⁿᵈ Saturday in April 1809 after Divine Worship proceeded to business—

1ˢᵗ Brother J. Edrington reported that he examined the office at Woodford Court-house and finds that there is no record respecting the meeting house lot.

2. Appointed Brethren Blanton, Ware & T. Boulware to converse with Mʳ D. Brown

concerning the meeting house lot. also to know whether any more land can be obtained for the use of the Church, and upon what terms. To be reported next meeting—

3. Agreed to take up & refer for consideration untill next meeting that part of the fourth Rule which respects the exclusion of members.

JOHN SHACKLEFORD Mod.ʳ

The 2ⁿᵈ Saturday in May 1809 after Divine worship proceeded to business.

1ˢᵗ The Brethren that were appointed to converse with Mʳ Daniel Brown reported that he was willing to let the Church have as much land as she wants at ten dollars per. Acre Then agreed to continue the same three Brethren to act as trustees for her, to have the land Survey'd & obtain a Deed in their names for the use of the Baptist Church at the forks of Elkhorn—not to exceed One & a Quarter Acres. to be reported next meeting

2ⁿᵈ Took up the refference respecting that part of the fourth Rule which respects the Exclusion of members and agreed to alter it from two thirds to a majority

3 Agreed to raise twenty five dollars for the use of the Church and that Brethren Wᵐ Samuel —Blanton & Settle be appointed to proportion the same among the White mals Members and report nex meeting

JOHN SHACKLEFORD Mod.ʳ

The 2ⁿᵈ Saturday in June 1809 after Divine Worship proceeded to business

The Brethren appointed at our last meeting to act as trustees for this Church in Obtaining a Deed for the meeting house lot—Reported that they could not Obtain such a Deed as they thought would be satisfactory to the Church—
At the request of the Church M.ʳ Daniel Brown made his proposals in Writing which are as follows The proposals of M.ʳ Daniel Brown to the Church at the forks of Elkhorn

I am willing to relinquish my right and title to one Acre and a Quarter of Land to include the meeting house, School-house and grave yard without reward upon the following conditions Should the Church see cause to remove their place of worship or holding pub- lick meeting then and in that case the property or land to revert to me or my heirs, and should I not think proper to purchase the building on the aforesaid land the Church may have free liberty to remove what improvement they put on the same And also all per- sons having friends or connections buried on the same shall have free liberty to inclose the Graves in any manner they may think proper Upon my complying with these I am to receive all articles or Bond obliga- tory on me or my Deceast Father
Test

Jesse Cole	Daniel E. Brown
W. Hubbell	June 10.ᵗʰ 1809—

The Church agreed to the above proposals of M.ʳ Daniel Brown and appointed Brethren William Hubbell. Abraham Gregory & James Finney to act as trustees for her in obtaining a Deed in their names for the benefit of the Baptist Church at the forks of Elk-horn—Bro. Ware is to furnish Money to defray the expences of the same out of the Church funds—

The Brethren appointed at our last meeting to proportion the sum of twenty five dollars among the white male Brethren made their report which the Church acceded too.

Bro. Ware is requested to pay four dollars to the Woman for keeping the meeting house—Also to furnish the Clerk with one Quire of paper for the use of the Church

Bro Ware inform'd the Church that there is $5..37..5 uncollected of the first proportion list —beside 87½ Cents lost by members excluded & members moved away Also that there is Seven dollars now in his hands unexpended of

The Church appointed Bro. Wm Samuel to receive the ballance of the first proportion list which is uncollected if the Brethren please to pay it

Rec^d by letter Elizabeth Buckley

JOHN SHACKLEFORD

The 2nd Saturday in July 1809 after divine Worship proceeded to business

1st Agreed that Bro. Thos Settle be reappointed to receive what may be communicated for Bro. John Shackleford, and report as formerly when call'd on.

2nd Agreed that Bro. Thos Settle be call'd on to report next meeting what money he has receiv'd for the benefit of Bro. J. Shackleford.

3rd The Brethren appointed to obtain a Deed of Mr Danl E. Brown for the lot above mentioned for the use of the Church, reported and read the deed, which the Church says is satisfactory.

No person to
be buried on
the west end
of the Meeting house

4th Agreed that the Church suffer not any more burying on the west end of the meeting House lot—

5th Bro. Carter Blanton & Theodrick Boulware are appointed Messengers to the Association, who are to prepare the Church letter for inspection on next meeting—

6th Next meeting to be on the first Saturday in August.

First Saturday in August 1809 after Divine Worship proceeded to business

Agreed by the Church that Thos Settle give to Bro. Shackleford tomorrow afternoon, the money that has been deposited with him for that purpose, and make report of the same at our next meeting Church letter read and approved of. Bro. Edmund Ware appointed to go with our former Brethren to the Association

At the request of the Church at Northfork we have appointed the following Brethren William Samuel, Joseph Edrington and Theodrick Boulware to meet at Northfork Church on the Friday before the 3rd Saturday in August, to assist them in settleing some difficulties existing in that Church

Agreed that the proportion list be put into the hands of Bro. Edmund Ware, and he is hereby appointed to collect the same for the use of the Church

JOHN SHACKLEFORD Mod

The 2nd Saturday in September 1809 after Divine Worship proceeded to business—

Agreeable to direction at our last meeting, Thos Settle reported to the Church that he gave to Brother Shackleford the Money deposited with him for that purpose, which is Twenty Dollars, twenty five Cents—

JOHN SHACKLEFORD

The 2.nd Saturday in October 1809 after divine worship proceeded to business

At the request of Bro. Harry Bartlett he is granted a letter of dismission

Joe, the property of M. George Carlisle made application to be restor'd to the Church—Referred till next Church meeting—

JOHN SHACKLEFORD M

The 2.nd Saturday in November 1809 after divine worship proceeded to business

1.st Took up the referrence respecting Mr Geo. Carlisle's Joe and after Interrogating him he was restor'd to fellowship

2.nd Bro Wm Hickman came forward and offered his membership and after some conversation he was restord to membership and his former standing

3.rd At the request of Bro. William Smither he is granted letter of dismission for himself, his wife Esther and his two Daughters Polly Robertson & Nancy Shaw—

4.th Agreed that Tho. Settle be called on at our next meeting to make report to the Church of the Money deposited with him for the Benefit of Bro. Shackleford

JOHN SHACKLEFORD Mod

The 2nd. Saturday in December 1809 after divine worship proceeded to business.

1st Dismist by letter Sister Elizabeth Shadrick, Bro. David Partlow & his black Woman Lucy, Also Sister Susanna Easterday & Elizabeth Goldman.

2nd Agreeable to an order of the Church at our last meeting Thos Settle made report to the Church that there is Twenty two Dollars—deposited with him for the benefit of Bro. Shackleford, he is hereby directed to give up the same to Bro. Blanton, who is to convey it to Bro. Shackleford

WILLIAM HICKMAN Mod.

The 2nd Saturday in January 1810 after Divine Worship proceeded to business.

Receiv'd by letter Bro. William Forsee.

Dismis't by letter Sister Elizabeth Stephens.

WILLIAM HICKMAN. Mo

The 2nd Saturday in February 1810 After divine Worship proceeded to business.

1st On Motion of Bro. Carter Blanton 'Tis agreed that part of the 12 rule be altered to the following that preaching begin precisely at 11 Oclock and after a recess of a few Minutes the Church to form and proceed to business.

2nd On Motion of Bro. C. Blanton 'tis agreed that our next Church meeting be altered from the 2nd to the 1st Saturday in March on account of the Conference appointed to be held at this place on the Tuesday before our meeting in course—Agreed, that the letter signed by a number of our Baptist preachers respecting the conference, be Copied by Bro. Wm. Samuel.

WILLIAM HICKMAN Modr.

First Saturday in March 1810 After Preaching the Church proceeded to business

On motion of Bro. Joseph Edrington the letter Signed by a number of the Baptist Preachers directed to this Church for the purpose of dividing the Elk-horn Association by mutual consent was read, and received for discussion—After a considerable debate the Church appointed three Brethren (to wit) William Hickman Carter Blanton and Joseph Edrington, to meet the conference at this place on Tuesday next to act in behalf of the Church. On a motion the Church Instructed her members not to Aid in conference without there should appear three fourths of the Churches by their messengers on Tuesday next, and should three fourths appear then to act, but leave the choice of Assn. to a future day.

The Clerk is directed to furnish the above mentioned Brethren with a Certificate in behalf of the Church together with the Instructions

Dismist by letter Bro. William Onion.

Received by Experience Rebecca a black woman the property of Bro. John Major

WILLIAM HICKMAN Modr.

Second Saturday in April 1810 After preaching the Church proceeded to business.

Brother Morgan Bryan Dismissed by letter
WILLIAM HICKMAN Mod.

Second Saturday in May 1810 After preaching the Church proceeded to business.

Received by letter Jack Woodson a Man of Colour.

Receiv'd by letter Robin, the property of Bro. Forsee
W. HICKMAN Mod.

The 2nd Saturday in June 1810 after preaching and a recess of a few Minutes the Church proceeded to business—

Received a letter signed by a number of our Baptis Preachers, the same being twice read, is referred for consideration to our next Meeting.

Received by letter Ephraim, the property of Bro. Forsee

Bro. Ware is requested to pay four dollars to the Woman for keeping the Meeting House—
W. HICKMAN Mod.

The 2nd Saturday in July 1810 after preaching and a few minutes the Church proceeded to business

Received by letter Bro. Robert Goode Jun.

The letter signed by a number of our Baptist Preachers referred to this Meeting from our last for consideration, was talked upon and agreed to lay it aside.

Bro. Theodrick Boulware dismist by letter.

The Church Voted they would not send to the Ass.[n] this Year.

W.[m] HICKMAN Mod.[r]

The 2.nd Saturday in August 1810 Nothing Recorded.

The 2.nd Saturday September 1810 After preaching and a recess of a few Minutes, the Church proceeded to business

Took into consideration the 12.th Article of our Church rules and agreed to repeal it—

Took into consideration the necessity of appointing another Deacon. Bro. Carter Blanton chosen to fill the office of a Deacon but on account of absent members the final decision is referred to next meeting to know if there is any Objectors—

Dismis't by letter Sister Nancy Lowrey

WILLIAM HICKMAN Mod.[r]

The 2.nd Saturday in October 1810 after Divine worship proceeded to business—

The referrence to this Meeting from our last respecting Bro. C. Blantons filling the Office of a

Deacon, was taken up and he was Unanimousley chosen to fill the Office of a Deacon

Thomas Mastin restored to fellowship
WILLIAM HICKMAN Mod

The 2.nd Saturday in November 1810 after divine Worship proceeded to business

Philip Callender Received into the Church by Baptism

Ambrose Jeffries & Agnes his wife, has a letter of Dismission granted them by the Church

Brother Ware appointed to get glass to fill the Pulpit Window and defray the expence out of the Church fund

Bro. Joseph Edrington is appointed to have the Schoolhouse Chimney repaired & apply to Bro. Ware for Money to pay the expence
WILLIAM HICKMAN Mod.^r

The 2nd Saturday in December 1810 Nothing recorded
WILLIAM HICKMAN Mod

The 2nd, Saturday in January 1811 Nothing recorded
WILLIAM HICKMAN Mod

The 2nd. Saturday in February 1811 after divine worship proceeded to business.

Received by experience Sally Sanders and Rachel the property of Mᵣ Smith

WILLIAM HICKMAN Modʳ

Sunday after preaching the Church set and received by letter Gilbert the property of Mᵣ Samuel Lewis.

Wᵐ HICKMAN Modʳ

The 2nd. Saturday in March 1811 after divine worship proceeded to business

Sisters Elizabeth & Polly Smither, Nancy Abbet now Robertson, is granted letters of dismission Also Bro. James Finney is granted a letter of dismission

Wᵐ HICKMAN Modʳ

The 2nd. Saturday in April 1811 after divine worship proceeded to business

Received by experience William Graham & Peggy, his Wife and Jany his Slave—Als Anne Thomson a Woman of colour—

Benjamin Adair formerly a member of Flat Lick Church, requested admittance into this Church and was received, he also requested a letter of dismission which is granted him

WILLIAM HICKMAN Modʳ

The 2nd. Saturday in May 1811 after divine worship proceeded to business

Brother Vachel Lindsey & Anne his Wife, Sister Agnes Smith and Bro. John Smither is granted letters of dismission

Bro. Benjn Edrington is appointed to cite Bro. John Eidson to our next Church meeting to answer some complaints against him.

Received by experience Amy Reynolds & Sally Woodson Women of colour—Also Nancy Settle, and Liddy the property of Bro. Wm Forsee
WILLIAM HICKMAN Mod.^{r}

The Church set on Sunday morning and received by experience, Nelson the property of Mr Geo. Madison
Wm HICKMAN Mod.^{r}

The Second Saturday in June 1811 after divine Worship proceeded to business

Received by experience Sally Wilson

Bro. William Hubbell & Margaret his Wife is granted a letter of dismission
WILLIAM HICKMAN

The Church set on Sunday Morning & received by letter Sister Elizabeth Fitzgerald & her two daughters Peggy Fitzgerald & Betsy Fitzgerald— Also London the property of Mr James Fitzgerald
Wm HICKMAN Mod.^{r}

The second Saturday in July 1811 after divine Worship proceeded to business

Took up the reference respecting Bro. John Eidson. Bro. Benj.ⁿ Edrington who was appointed to cite him to the Church reported that he had cited him to the Church, and that Bro. John Eidson let him know that he should not attend— the Church excluded him for his hard censorious expressions against Bro. Peak and for disobeying the call of the Church.

Bro. Jesse Cole & Bro. Giles Samuel is appointed to cite Bro. Wm Montgomery to our next Church meeting to answer a complaint against him for Intoxication.

Tis agreed by the Church that we send messengers to our next Association

The following Brethren, William Hickman William Samuel and Jesse Cole is appointed as messengers to our next Association—the same is to prepare the Church letter

Rec.^d by letter sister Polly Grubbs

Rec.^d by Interogation Sister Sally Williams

Rec'd by Experience Olive Major.

WILLIAM HICKMAN Mod

Sunday morning, Rec.^d by Experience Isaac the property of Bro. Jno Major—Also William by Interogation the property of Bro. Mordecai Boulware—Rec'd by Experience Sally Shaddoa

Rec'd Jemima Harrison by interogation.

WILLIAM HICKMAN

July 21ˢᵗ Sunday afternoon Received Rebecca Vanmetre by Experience

Sepᵗ 1ˢᵗ 1811 Sunday Morning the Church set and Received by Experience Silas Noel & Maria his Wife, also Prudence Blackburn.

The 2ⁿᵈ Saturday in September 1811 after divine Worship proceeded to business

Took up the referrence respecting Bro. William Montgomery but at the request of Bro. Blanton it is referred to next meeting

Received by Experience Molley Long & Fanny Castleman

Received by Experience, Anaca the property of Bro. William Montgomery

Received by Experience, Frank, Jourdan & Sam the property of Mʳ Thoˢ Major.

Received by Experience, Betsy, Lucy, Rose & Paris the property of Sister   Major

Received by Experience Jane & Amos the property of Bro. John Major
                    WILLIAM HICKMAN Modʳ

September 15th. 1811. Sunday Morning the Church set and Rec'd by experience, Wat the property of Mʳˢ Patterson, and Mary the property of Mʳ Forsee also Charity the property of Bro. Thoˢ Martin

The second Saturday in October 1811 after divine worship proceeded to business.

The referrence respecting Bro. William Montgomery which has been referred to this meeting was taken up and referred to our next Church Meeting. on Acc^t of his being absent on some particular business.

Dismist by letter Sister Rebecca Vanmetre, Betsy Adair & Bro. Robert Goode.

Rec^d by letter, Dick the property of Bro. Edmond Ware

Rec^d by recantation Bennett Pemberton

Rec^d by Experience Rebecca the property of sister Boulware

WILLIAM HICKMAN

Sunday morning 13th October 1811.
Rec^d by Experience Walter Ayres & Agnes his Wife—Davy the property of Bro. Forsee. Jesse the property of Mr Isham Talbott, and Phillis the property of Bro. Julius Blackburn.

October 20th 1811
Rec^d by Experience Jonathan Blackburn Eli Clark a man of colour. Charles the property of Bro. Forsee, Lucy the property of Mr Early Scott

Dismist by letter Sister Salley Shaddoa.

The second Saturday in November 1811 after divine worship proceeded to business.

The referrence respecting Bro. William Montgomery that was referred to this meeting, was
taken up, and referred to our next Church meeting.
W^M HICKMAN Mod^r

Novr 10th. 1811. Sunday Morning
Rec^d by experience Rachel, the property of Bro.
Walter Ayres, and Jo. the property of brother
Julius Blackburn.

The 2nd. Saturday in December 1811 the Church
met, & after divine worship proceeded to business

On Motion the referrence relative to Bro Wm
Montgomery was taken up—& after due consideration of the Charge against him he was excused on his solemn assurance that the offence
wou'd not be repeated.
Received by experience Miss Sally Ware & Miss
Polly Blanton

Dismiss'd by letter Bro. Jeremiah Buckley &
Sister Frances Buckley his Wife
W^M HICKMAN—Mod^r

Sunday Morning Decr 15th. 1811
Rec^d by experience Sally the property of Bro.
Wm Forsee—Also Charlotte the property of M^r
George Madison—

At a Meeting at Bro. Wares on the—day of Dec^r
1811

Rec^d by experience Miss Betsy Bryan, Miss
Peggy Bryan & Mr James Triplett

Sunday. Jan.ʸ. 5th. 1812 after preaching Rec.ᵈ by experience Miss Betsy Eivel

The 2nd. Saturday in Jan.ʸ. 1812 after divine worship proceeded to business

Dismist by letter Sister Anne Palmer & her Daughter Betsy—Also Sister Jemima Gano & Sister Patsy Martin

A Charge was brought against Bro. Jonathan Blackburn for having been Intoxicated at a Meeting at Bro. Gregory's—After some conversation it was referred to our next Church Meeting

W.ᴹ HICKMAN Mod.ʳ

The 2nd. Saturday in Feb.ʸ. 1812 after divine Worship proceeded to business

The referrence taken up against Bro. Jonathan Blackburn for having been Intoxicated at a Meeting at Bro. Gregory's, and the Church agreed to bear with Bro. Blackburn.

A Charge brought against Wot a member of this Church, belonging to M.ʳˢ Patsey Patterson, for a Charge of Villany, and they Excluded him for the same

Rec.ᵈ by repentance a slave by the name of Tom the property of M.ʳ W.ᴹ Starling Jun.ʳ

Rec.ᵈ by experience M.ʳˢ Peggy Coleman

WILLIAM HICKMAN
Mod.ʳ

Sunday Morning Feb.ʸ 9.ᵗʰ 1812.
Dismist by letter, Sister Sally Shaddoa.

Recᵈ by experience Mʳˢ   Daniel

At a Night meeting at Bro. Giles Samuel the 21ˢᵗ
of Feb.ʸ 1812
Rec'd by experience Miss Fanny Samuel

The 2ⁿᵈ Saturday in March 1812 after divine
worship proceeded to business

Recᵈ by experience Mʳ Simon Beckham & Philadelphia his wife.
Miss Priscilla Ewel & Mʳˢ Mary Reed

Recᵈ by letter Sister Susanna Graham

Dismist by letter Bro. Samuel Buckley
                           Wᴹ Hɪᴄᴋᴍᴀɴ Modʳ

Sunday morning 15ᵗʰ of March 1812
Dismist by letter Sister Elizabeth Gale, and
Sammy a black man the property of Mʳ Geo.
Turpin

The 2nd. Saturday in April 1812 after divine
worship proceeded to business

A Charge brought against Sister Sally Brown a
member of this Church for improperly talking.
Continued untill our next meeting in course———

Charges brought by Brother Mᶜ Daniel against
Brother Jesse Cole

Charge 1st for making unrighteous landmarks on brother John Graves land————Not supported

Charge 2nd for accusing Brother Mc Daniels sons of destroying corner trees and trying to enforce a belief on the neighbours it was true————Not Supported.

Charge 3rd for making Illnatured expressions (that is to say) he had no more fellowship for me, than he had for the Devil————The 3rd Charge Acknowledged to by Brother Cole and the expressions reprobated the Church feel satisfied with brother Cole

On motion the Church took into consideration Bro. Silas Noels publick gift, and unanimously gave their approbation to his exercising it in the Church and neighbouring congregations, while acting with Christian propriety

Recd by experience Flora the property of Mr Benjamin Farmer

Recd by experience Mrs Elizabeth Buford
Wm Hickman Modr

Sunday morning April 12th. 1812
Recd by experience Isaac the property of Mr Francis Peart

A Charge brought against Mary the property of Mr Geo. Forsee for the Sin of lying & refusing to come before the Church to answer the complaint against her—She was excluded for the same

Sunday morning April 26th 1812
Recd by experience Mrs Susanna Farmer & Mr Reuben Ford.

The 2nd Saturday in May 1812 after divine Worship proceeded to business

Took up the referrence against Sister Sally Brown which was referred to this meeting—The Church directed the Moderator to admonish her

A Charge brought against Bro. Jonathan Blackburn for having been Intoxicated at Mr James Guthries Tavern on the 22nd Day of April 1812— The Church excluded him for the same

The Church have agreed to take up the Charges again that Bro. McDaniel brought against Bro. Jesse Cole at our last meeting, as she disapproves of her conduct at that meeting—and has appointed Bro. Price & Bro. Ayres to see whether Bro. Cole is willing to have them taken up at our next meeting.

WILLIAM HICKMAN Mod^r

The 2nd. Saturday in June 1812 after divine worship proceeded to business

Took up the referrence from our last meeting to this, respecting the Charges of Bro. McDaniel against Bro. Cole—Bro. McDaniel having obtained leave from the Church to explain his first charge against Bro. Cole—placed it in the following words—viz. 1st For runing an Incorrect line between himself and Bro. Graves without giving notice to Bro. Graves—Bro. Cole acknowledged the above charge,—But when Bro. Graves mentioned to Bro. Cole that he thought the line Incorrect. Bro. Cole stated he thought it was right or nearly so but proposed to get Bro. Price and run the line, which was consented to by Bro.

Graves, and Bro. Cole Immediately sent for Bro. Price, and Bro. Price came and run the line, and both parties agreed they were satisfied.

The 2nd. Charge was taken up, and it was agreed to let it stand as on the record.
The 3rd. Charge was taken up, and it was agreed to let it stand as on the record.

The Church agrees to send a letter & Messengers to the next Elk-horn Association—Bren. Hickman Samuel, Noel & Settle be appointed to write the Church letter against our next Church Meeting.

Bren. Blanton & Settle be appointed to assist Bro. Ware in making the Assessment amongst the Bren. of this Church, to raise money to defray the expences of this church

Bro. Carter Blanton is appointed to take the list when made out, and receive the Money for the use of the Church

WILLIAM HICKMAN Mod.

Sunday the 14th. of June 1812
Rec.d by letter Peter the property of Bro. Julius Blackburn

Rec.d Sister Peggy Sanders, by letter

Dismist by letter Sister Winny Kelly

Excluded Davy the property of Bro. Forsee for lying & other misconduct—

The 2nd Saturday in July 1812 After divine worship proceeded to business

Church letter read and approved of—

The following Bren. William Hickman, Silas Noel Carter Blanton & Edmond Ware is appointed messengers to our next Association

Bro. C. Blanton & Bro. Joseph Edrington is appointed to bear a friendly letter to the Licking Association

The following Bren. John Price Silas Noel, Carter Blanton William Samuel & Benjn Edrington is Appointed to View a convenient place to build a new meeting house on, and make report at our next Meeting—

Bro. Carter Blanton is hereby directed to pay four dollars to the Woman for keeping the Meeting house the year past, out of the money he has collected for the use of the Church

Rec^d by letter Bro. Joseph Eddins & Nancy his Wife

Dismist by letter Bro. Thomas Buckley and Sister Anne McGraw—

WILLIAM HICKMAN Mod^r

The 1st Saturday in August 1812 after divine worship proceeded to business—

The Committee appointed at our last meeting to View and make choice of a convenient place to built a new Meeting house on—

Reported, They cou'd not select a more convenient place, than the one, on which the Meeting house now stands—

On the motion of Bro. Wilson, The Church resolved that the friendly letter directed to the Licking Association should be read, and reconsidered After a considerable debate the Church agreed the letter should not be sent

Receiv'd by experience Matthew Reynolds a man of Colour

WILLIAM HICKMAN Mod.ʳ

Sunday Aug.ᵗ 2ⁿᵈ 1812.
Restored to the Church, Winney, the property of sister Esther Boulware

The 2nd. Saturday in September 1812 the Church met and after divine worship proceeded to business

Rec.ᵈ by Experience Susanna Parks.

WILLIAM HICKMAN Mod.ʳ

Sunday Morning 13th. September 1812.
Rec.ᵈ by letter Phill belonging to the Estate of Bro. James Martin Deceas'd—

W.ᴹ HICKMAN

Sunday Morning 20th. September 1812.
Rec.ᵈ by Experience Solomon Parks.

W.ᴹ HICKMAN Mod.ʳ

The 2.ⁿᵈ Saturday in October 1812 the Church met and after divine Worship proceeded to business—

The Church being satisfied that there is a call from the Minority at Bryans for an Association to meet at Bryans Station on the 4ᵗʰ Thursday in this Month, agreed to send four Messengers and appointed Brethren, Wᴹ Hickman Silas M. Noel, Wᴹ Samuel & Graham to meet at the time and place above mentioned.

The following Brethren Wᴹ Samuel Wᴹ Graham Carter Blanton Joseph Edrington & John Major are appointed as Trustees to superintend the Building of a new Meeting House near where the Steels Road intersects the Lexington Road, on Bro. Giles Samuels Land, and set on foot Subscription papers—

Dismist the following Members to Join in a Constitution at the Big Spring. Bro. Abraham Gregory & Millender his Wife—Bro. Jesse Cole & Nancy his Wife. Sister Prudence Blackburn, Sister Catherine Smith, Bro. Walter Ayres & Agnes his Wife

William Hickman Modʳ

The 2nd. Saturday in November 1812 after divine worship proceeded to business

Brother Carter Blanton is appointed to procure firewood for the use of this Church the ensuing Winter

The following Brethren, Carter Blanton, William Samuel and Isaac Wilson be appointed to superintend in the business of furnishing Bro. Hickman with the necessary supplies of provisions &c. he may stand in need of.

Dismist by letter Bro. Silas M. Noel and Maria his Wife

Recᵈ by Interogation Bro William Palmer

Wᴹ Hickman Modʳ

Sunday Nov.ʳ 15th. 1812.
After Preaching, On the motion of Bro. Hickman Sister Buthama Thompson is granted a letter of dismission

W. HICKMAN.

The second Saturday in December 1812 being very cold but a few of the members of the Church met, and after divine Worship, adjourn'd to our next meeting in course.

Wᵐ HICKMAN Modʳ

The 2ⁿᵈ Saturday in Jan.ʸ. 1813 the Church met and after divine Worship proceeded to business

The subject of the Minutes of the called Association was taken into consideration, disapproved of by the Church & a Committee appointed to draw a Remonstrance against them. William Graham Joseph Edrington William Hickman & William Samuel are appointed as a Committee

On a motion of Bro. Joseph Edrington the Church appointed Bren. Carter Blanton William Graham and Joseph Edrington to see Brother Giles Samuel respecting the piece of land to build the meeting house on. which we wish to be ½ Acres—and to get his Obligation to make a Sufficient right & title to the same when ever the Church may deem it necessary.

WILLIAM HICKMAN Modʳ

Sunday morning 9ᵗʰ Janʸ. 1813
Recᵈ by letter Sam & Sarah his wife the property of Mʳ Jesse Brown

The 2nd. Saturday in February 1813 the Church convened and after Worship proceeded to business.

The subject relative to the Minutes of the called Association was continued till next Meeting.

Agreed that Bro. Giles Samuel give his Obligation to make a Title to the land purchased by the Church of him to build a Meeting house upon to the following persons viz. William Hickman John Major, Carter Blanton William Graham, William Samuel. Edmund Ware. John Price Thomas Settle, Isaac Wilson & Joseph Edrington

William Hickman Mod^r

The 2nd Saturday in March 1813 the Church convened and after Worship proceeded to business.

The subject relative to the Minutes of the Called Assⁿ is again referred to next Meeting.

Ordered that Bro. Blanton funish the Clerk with a Quire of paper for the use of the Church.

W. Hickman Mod^r

Sunday morning 14th of March 1813
Dismist by letter Solomon Parks & Susanna his Wife

The 2nd Saturday in April 1813 the Church convened and after Worship proceeded to business

The subject relative to the minutes of the Called Assⁿ is again referred to our Meeting in course.
Sunday Morning Excluded
Philes, the property of } W. Hickman Mod^r
Bro. J. Blackburn

The 2nd Saturday in May 1813 the Church convened & after Worship proceeded to business—

The subject relative to the Minutes of the Called Assn is referred to our next Meeting in course.

W. HICKMAN, Modr

The 2nd Saturday in June 1813 the Church convened and after worship proceeded to business

The Committee appointed to draw a remonstrance against the proceedings of the called Assn Reported that they thought is unnecessary to draw a Remonstrance against them—And of course the subject was dropt.—

Received by experience Susanna Vaughan

Bro. Blanton is requested to pay the Woman for keeping the Meeting house the year past, the sum of four dollars out of the Church funds.

W. HICKMAN Modr

The 2nd Saturday in July 1813 the Church convened and after worship proceed to business

Dismist by letter Bro. James Triplett and Sister Betsy Buckley. now Hinton

Also Bro. Bennet Pemberton & Polly his Wife

Recd By letter Bro Charles Buck & Polly his Wife, and Sister Frances B. Harden

The following Bren. William Hickman Carter Blanton William Samuel Edmund Ware and

Charles Buck is appointed Messengers to our next Association. and to prepare the Church letter against our Church Meeting first Saturday in August next

W. Hickman Mod^r

The 1st Saturday in August 1813 the Church convened and after Worship proceeded to business—

The Church letter read and approved of—

W. Hickman Mod^r

The 2nd Saturday in September 1813. The Church convened and after Worship proceeded to business

On a motion of Bro. Blanton it is agreed that plates and glasses be procured for the use of the Church out of the Church funds, by one of the Deacons.— Agreed that Bren. William Samuel and Benjamin Edrington be appointed to procure the Charges and Evidences that Mr Jesse Cole has against Bro. Wilson and bring them forward at our Novr Meeting
Brethren—Carter Blanton & Joseph Edrington be appointed to employ some person to repair the Meeting house roof and under pinning

Dismist by letter Sister Susanna Samuel Sister Molly Martin & Bro. Harry Martin

W. Hickman Mod^r

Sunday Morning Sepr 12th 1813—Church convened and after worship, Excluded a black member by the name of Billy the property of Bro Mordecai Boulware—for lying and other misconduct.

Sister Lucy Nall returned her letter of recommendation.

W.ᴹ HICKMAN Mod

The 2ⁿᵈ Saturday in October 1813. The Church
convened and after worship proceeded to business

At the request of Bro. William Palmer he is
granted a letter of Dismission—

W. HICKMAN

The 2ⁿᵈ Saturday in Novʳ 1813. the Church convened and after worship proceeded to business.

The referrence respecting Mʳ Jesse Cole's Charges
against Bro. Wilson was taken up and after some
debate the Church agreed to dispence of it altogether as being out of order—

Brother Blanton is requested to pay for recording
the deed for the lot of ground the Meeting house
stands upon.

At the request of the Church at Hopewell we have
appointed our Brethren Charles Buck & Carter
Blanton to attend their meeting the fourth Saturday in this present Month Novʳ in order to assist
them in any matter of difficulty—

Brotheʳ Hickman absent & Bro. S. M. Noel acting
as Moderator. The Church agreed to contribute
the sum of $60 for the support of their Preacher
Bro. Hickman, to be proportioned upon the male
members by Brᵒ Wᵐ Samuel, Joseph Edrington &
C. Blanton & to be collected by the Deacons.

Brᵒ Carter Blanton is appointed to furnish fire
wood for the use of the Church the ensuing winter,

and to be paid out of the Church funds for the same

W. Hickman Mod^r

The 2nd Saturday in Decr 1813. the Church convened and after Worship proceeded to business—

The Church appointed Breⁿ Benj^a Edrington William Graham & John Stephens to make enquiry into Br^o Ramsey Boulwares conduct and make report at our next meeting—

W. Hickman Mod^r

The 2nd. Saturday in January 1814 the Church convened and after worship proceeded to business.

A Charge against Bro. Ramsey Boulware for cursing and swearing & wishing God might damn him if he did not kill his brother Richard (proven by two of the Brethren that were appointed at our last meeting to enquire into his conduct) and for his letter to the Church requesting to be excluded—The Church excluded him for the above conduct.

W. Hickman Mod^r

The 2nd. Saturday in February 1814 the Church convened and after worship proceeded to business

A Charge brought against Bro. William Montgomery for having been repeatedly Intoxicated with spirituous liquors.—Bro. Joseph Edrington and Bro. Carter Blanton is appointed to cite him to our next Monthly meeting to answer the complaint.

W. Hickman Mod^r

The 2.nd Saturday in March 1814 the Church convened and after Worship proceeded to Business.

The charge brought against Bro. William Montgomery at our last meeting and laid over to this is again referred to our next meeting. Brethren, Joseph Edrington & Carter Blanton is again appointed to Cite him to our next meeting.—

Agreed that we consider the following Querys What is the Scriptural mode of dealing with or proceeding against publick transgressors?

W.^{M} HICKMAN

The 3.rd Saturday in April 1814 the Church convened and after worship proceeded to business.—

The Charge against Bro. William Montgomery referred to this Meeting from our last was taken up—He came forward & reprobated his conduct for having been repeatedly Intoxicated. The Church Voted his continuance in society.—

The Query referred from our last meeting to this is referred to our next meeting

CARTER BLANTON Mod.^{r}

The 2.^{d} Saturday in May 1814 the Church convened and after worship proceeded to business.—

Dismist by letter Sister Mary Reed—Also Dick a black member late the property of Bro. Edmond Ware dec^{d}—

The following Brethren—John Major, William Graham Isaac Wilson, Joseph Edrington and John

Price were nominated for the consideration of the Church, out of which one is to be selected to fill the office of a Deacon.

Took up the Query referred to this Meeting from our last, respecting the mode of dealing with publick transgressors, and referred it to next meeting

Received by Experience Susanna Mastin & Barbary Dearing—

Rec.^d by letter Abner Fennell, and Nancy his Wife by Information

W. Hickman Mod.^r

The 2nd Saturday in June 1814 the Church convened and after worship proceeded to business.

Took up the Query referred to this meeting from our last respecting the mode of dealing with publick transgressors and after some debate agreed to insert the words (most proper) instead of the word Scriptural which will make it read as follows.

Query. What is the most proper mode of dealing with, or proceeding against publick transgressors?
The Church agreed to adopt the following answer We are not of opinion that the 18th of Matthew has any allusion to publick transgressions, but altogether to private offences. But if the law of God be publickly violated in the presence of two or more witnesses, that notice be given to the transgressor by one or more who saw it to appear before the Church, and if the Transgressor fail to attend, the Church proceed to excommunicate him as the Lord directs in his word.

Bro. William Graham chosen to fill the office of a Deacon.

Bro. Carter Blanton is requested to pay $4. to the woman for keeping the meeting house, out of the Church funds.

The following Brethren William Graham, William Samuel & Thomas Settle be appointed to make out a proportion list among the male members to raise the sum of twenty or twenty five dollars for the use of the Church.

Dismist by letter Sister Margaret Sanders

Rec^d by letter Bro. Charles Cullens.

W. Hickman Mod^r

The 2nd Saturday in July 1814 the Church convened and after worship proceeded to business.—

Sister Elizabeth Marshall returned her letter of dismission

The following Brethren is appointed as messengers to our next Association William Hickman Carter Blanton Charles Buck & William Graham—the same is to prepare the Church letter against our next Meeting.

At the request of the Church at Mount Pleasant we have appointed the following Brethren Charles Buck. William Samuel & Carter Blanton as a Committee to meet at Bro. Robert Church's the last Friday in this Month (July) and there to assist in settleing a matter of difficulty that exist between brother Robert Church and brother Alexander Macy.—

Brother Isaac Wilson is appointed to assist the Committee appointed at our last meeting in making out a proportion list amongst the mail members to raise the sum of twenty or twenty-five dollars for the use of the Church and make report at our next meeting—

Rec.^d by experience William Marshall

Elizabeth Hicklin restored to fellowship.

W. Hickman Mod.^r

Sunday Morning 10th of July 1814

John Behannon restored to fellowship

Excluded Joe, the property of Brother Julius Blackburn, for swearing and refusing to obey the call of the Church—

Wm Hickman Mod.^r

The first Saturday in August 1814 the Church convened and after worship proceeded to business.

The committee appointed at our last Church meeting to make out a proportion list amongst the male members, made their report which was received.

The Church letter was read and rec.^d

W. Hickman Mod.^r

The 2nd Saturday in September 1814 the Church convened and [after] worship proceeded to business.

Dismist by letter Sister Nelley Nall.

Bro. William Palmer returned his letter of recommendation.

W. HICKMAN Mod^r

The 2^d Saturday in October 1814 the Church convened and after worship proceeded to business.

At the request of the Church at Mountpleasant, we have appointed two of our Brethren (to wit) Joseph Edrington & William Graham to meet at Mountpleasant meeting house on the 3^d Wednesday in this present month of October to assist them in settleing some matters of difficulty.

JOSEPH EDRINGTON Mod^r

The second Saturday in November 1814 after worship proceeded to business—

Dismist by letter sister Susanna Farmer & her Negro woman Flora—Also sister Elizabeth Widner and Bro. William Marshall

Rec^d by letter sister Salley Neale

This Church has agreed to raise the sum of Sixty dollars for our Minister Bro. Hickman for the ensuing year and brother Carter Blanton and brother William Graham is appointed to call on the male members of this Church by Subscription to raise the amount and pay the same to them by our next monthly Meeting.

W. HICKMAN Mod^r

On Sunday morning received by experience Elizabeth Marshall for Baptism.

The second Saturday in Dec.ʳ 1814 the Church convened and after worship proceeded to business.

At the request of the Church at Hopewell we have appointed two of our Brethren, Carter Blanton & Joseph Edrington to meet at Hopewell meeting house on the fourth Saturday in this Month Dec.ʳ to assist them in settleing some matters of difficulty

Rec.ᵈ by letter Bro. Simeon Deering.

Dismist Elizabeth Marshall
W. HICKMAN Mod.ʳ

The 2ⁿᵈ Saturday in January 1815 the Church convened and after worship proceeded to business

At the request of the Church at Hopewell we have appointed two of our Brethren, Carter Blanton and Joseph Edrington to meet at Hopewell meeting house on the fourth Saturday in this Month Jany. To assist them in settleing some matters of difficulty.

WILLIAM HICKMAN Mod.ʳ

The second Saturday in Feb.ʸ. 1815 the Church convened and after worship proceeded to business

From information, the Church has agreed to send Bro. John Price & Bro. Cullens to Cite Bro. William Peak to appear at our next Church meeting—
W HICKMAN Mod.ʳ

Sunday morning Feb.ʸ. 12.ᵗʰ 1815. the Church convened and Received by experience Eliza Richmond

The second Saturday in March 1815 the Church convened and after worship proceeded to business

Bro. William Peak having attended according to the citation of the Brethren appointed at last meeting & the Brethren stating that they had informed him of information given to the Church that he had gone to Law with one of his Brethren, and he being called on stated that he had as an Administrator of an Estate brought Suit against a member, after long trials to collect without, therefore he was excused.—

Upon Motion, agreed that the answer to the Query of June last respecting publick transgressors shall read thus. It is the opinion of this Church that the18.ᵗʰ of Matthew has no allusion to publick transgressions, but altogether to private offences—Yet if the Law of God be publickly Violated notice shall be given to the transgressor by some Member of the Church that he shall appear before the Church to give the Church satisfaction & should he fail to attend, the Church proceed to excommunicate him as the Lord directs in his Word. and that this be our rule in future—

W. Hickman Modᵣ

Sunday morning 12.ᵗʰ of March 1815.
Recᵈ by letter Joe a black Member late the property of Sam! Moxley decᵈ—

The 2ᵈ Saturday in April 1815 the Church convened and after Worship proceeded to business—

The Clerk being absent. S. M. Noel appointed Clerk Pro-tem

Dismist by letter Sister Susanna Farmer Sister Elizabeth Fitzgerald and her two Daughters Peggy & Betsy & her Negro man London.

W. Hickman Mod^r

The 2^d Saturday in May 1815 The Church convened and after divine worship proceeded to business—

Whereas complaint was made at our last March meeting for business against Eli Clark a black member, by Brethren Robin & Jack—for parting with his Wife, getting drunk and dancing—he being then present acknowledged the charges—the same being now taken up & considered—he is by this Church excluded

Complaint brought in by Bro. Jack against Betty the property of Sister Major for unchristian like conduct parting with her Husband & drunkenness & swearing, and although by him desired to attend Church to answer therefor she refused to attend—She is therefore excluded

Complaint by same against Paris the property of Sister Major for swearing and failing to come to Church meeting according to promise—Bro. John Major to cite him to next meeting to answer to those charges—

Sister James Nancy Smither is granted a letter of Dismission

W Hickman Mod^r

The 2ᵈ Saturday in June 1815 the Church convened and after divine worship proceeded to business—

Took up the charge against Paris the property of Sister Major for swearing & failing to attend Church meeting and after receiving the necessary information he was excluded—

Bro. Wᵐ Hickman & Thoˢ Settle is appointed to prepare the Church letter against our August meeting.

Dismist by letter Sister Sally Williams

Dismist by letter Dick formerly the property of Bro. Ware, but now Bro. Jeffries

Bro. William Graham is requested to pay the Woman $4. for keeping the meeting house in order —out of the Church funds—

Dismist by letter Sister Elizabeth Buford

Recᵈ by letter Sister Betsy Hickman
                          W Hickman Modʳ

The 2ᵈ Saturday in July 1815 the Church convened and after worship proceeded to business—
                          W. Hickman Modʳ

The first Saturday in August 1815 the Church convened and after worship proceeded to business

Is this Church disposed to take the proper steps to assist in forming an Association in Franklin and to become a Member of it?—the above is referred to our next Meeting

The Church letter read and approved

Brethren appointed as messengers to our next Association William Hickman, Carter Blanton, Charles Buck and William Graham—

W Hickman Mod^r

The 2^d Saturday in Sept 1815 the Church convened and after Worship proceeded to business.

Took up the referrence referred from last meeting to this, respecting an Assⁿ and become a member of it—After some debate the Church voted in favour of the new Association and agreed to send four members (to wit) William Hickman William Graham Carter Blanton & Joseph Edrington to assist in that business.

Rec^d by recommendation Sister Love Fuller

Rec^d by experience Angeller the property of Larkin Samuel.

Dismist by letter Bro. Philip Calendar.

Dismist by letter Sister Polly Snell.

W Hickman Mod^r

The 2^d Saturday in October 1815 the Church convened and after worship proceeded to business.

Agreed to reconsider the matter respecting the referrence of our last meeting—that this Church send some of her members to assist in forming the Franklin Association and become of the same.
The above matter referred to our next meeting.
Bro. Noel took a seat and acted as Moderator.

Agreed to call for helps from three Churches to assist us at our next meeting concerning the above Referrence (to wit) Great Crossing Clear Creek

& South Elkhorn the number of members which they usually send to the Association.

Sundry charges made by Bro. Price against Anaky his servant for falsehood, & other improper conduct—were exhibited, & after hearing the case Voted that she was Censurable & is excluded—

Bro. Forsee laid in a charge against Bro. Montgomery for the sin of intoxication with liquor, and that he had taken the necessary steps, & Bro. Montgomery not appearing—& on Motion the same was continued till next meeting—

Brother Graham laid in a charge against Bͬ͘. James Ware for betting on Horse racing & gambling the accused not appearing, & the accuser stating that he had talked to Bͬ͘. Ware on the subject—who acknowledged he had been guilty of these things in a small degree and that they were improper, and believed he was not a fit member for society on Motion this case was likewise continued.

The clerk requested to write a letter to each of the Churches requested to assist us & that Bͬ͘ Wilson & Bͬ͘ Buck to convey them—

S. M. Noel Modͬ͘

The 2ᵈ Saturday in Novͬ͘ 1815 the Church convened and after worship proceeded to business.

At brother Hickmans request, Bro. S. M. Noel took a seat and acted as moderator.

The helps called for from three of our sister Churches (to wit) Great Crossing James & William Suggett Ben Taylor & James Johnson, from South Elkhorn Peter Higbee, John Kellar & James Marrs, from Clear Creek Lewis Sullivan,

Geo. Mac Daniel and John Graves came forward and took their seats.

Then took up the referrence referred to this meeting from our last, to reconsider the referrence referred to our September meeting, relative to this Church in assisting in forming the Franklin Association and become a member of the same—after some debate a Query was handed the Moderator as a basis of enquiry for the helps which reads as follows—

Is it consistant with good order and propriety for a majority of this Church to leave the Elkhorn Ass^n and join other Churches in forming a new one, against the declared Opposition of a respectable Minority and without dismission from the Elkhorn Ass^n—after some debate the Committee withdrew to form their conclusion, which at their return we find was in the following words—

We the helps approve of the course of the Church in consenting to reconsider the question of joining the Franklin Ass^n and advise the Church if she incline to join the Franklin Association to signify their wish to the Elkhorn Association at their next meeting.

Took up the case of Wm Montgomery and he not appearing although notified a second time to do so—upon Motion he was excluded—Same as to James Ware & same determination

S. M. Noel Mod^r

James Suggett
John Kellar
Lewis Sullivan
William Suggett
Peter Higbee
John Graves
Geo. Mac Daniel
James Johnson
Ben Taylor
James Marrs

The 2ᵈ Saturday in Decʳ 1815. the Church convened and after worship proceeded to business—

A Charge by Brᵒ Graham against Sam the property of Mʳ Thoˢ Major—for intoxication with Liquor and offering to fight—referred untill tomorrow and if not taken up then untill our next monthly Meeting.

Sunday after preaching received by experience
                                    W HICKMAN Mod

The 2ᵈ Saturday in Jan.ʸ. 1816 the Church convened and after worship proceeded to business

Query—Is it deemed a neglect of duty for free male members to omit tending Church meetings of business on every 2ᵈ Saturday in each Month without a reasonable excuse—Referred to next Meeting

Took up the referrence respecting Sam a black member the property of Thoˢ Major—for drinking to excess and offering to fight—excluded him for the same—
                                    W HICKMAN Modʳ

The 2ᵈ Saturday in Feb.ʸ. 1816 the Church convened and after worship proceeded to business.

Took up the Query referred to this Meeting from our last, amended it and agreed that the following answer shall be annexed to our code of rules

Any free male member who fails to attend each and every stated Church Meeting without a reasonable excuse, neglects his duty.

The following Members at their request is granted letters of dismission to join in the new constitution in the Town of Frankfort (to wit) Simon Beckham and Philadelphia his wife M.ʳˢ Polly Hickman Sally Cunningham, Patsey Ransdel, Betsy Loofborough, Sally Bacon, Benjᵃ Edrington and Lettuce his wife and Jane Daniel

The following Brethren, W.ᵐ Hickman, W.ᵐ Samuel Isaac Wilson, W.ᵐ Graham and John Major is appointed to assist in forming the new constitution in the Town of Frankfort—

S. M. Noel—Modʳ

The 2.ᵈ Saturday in March 1816 the Church Convened, and after Worship proceeded to business—

Sister Susan Graham is granted a letter of dismission to Join the new Church in Frankfort—

W.ᴹ Hickman Modʳ

The Next day the Church Set and granted a letter of dismission to Bro James Smithe and Bro George Twyman at their Request

W.ᴹ Hickman Mod.

The 2.ᵈ Saturday in April 1816 The Church Convened, and after Worship proceeded to business—

Bro William Palmer is granted a letter of Dismission————

W.ᴹ Hickman Modʳ

The 2.ᵈ Saturday in May 1816 the Church Convened and after worship proceeded to business.

Bro. Samuel Price has Returned his letter that he got from this Church on the 2^d Saturday in March 1804, and has Jind the same— — — — — —

Frank a black man belonging to Mr J. Marshall is Ex. from this Church for geting drunk Swearing & dancing

This Church has appointed William Samuel Cleark to the Said Church— — — — — — —

Brethren Blanton and Graham having been appointed to Make out a New apportionment for the present year to raise money for the use of the Church return,d the Same which was Read and approved of

W^M HICKMAN Mod^r

The 2nd Saturday in June 1816 the Church Conven,d and after worship proceeded to business

This Church has directed Bro William Graham to pay Caty a black woman four dollars of keeping the meeting house in order— — — — — — —

W^M HICKMAN Modr

The 2nd Saturday in July 1816 the Church Conven,d and after worship proceeded to business—

The following Brethren is appointed as messengers to our next Association William Hickman Charles Buck Carter Blanton and John Price and Brethren Hickman & Buck to prepare the Church letter against our next meeting

Motion by Bro. Hickman and Buck that we request a dismission from the Elkhorn Association to Join that of Franklin which was decided in the Negative— — — — — — — — — — —

Wm HICKMAN Mod^r

The 1st Saturday in August 1816 the Church Convened and after Worship proceeded to Business

The Church letter Read and approved. The Church has directed Bro Graham to Send one dollar and 25 Cents by our Messengers to pay the Expence of printing the minuts of the association—

Received by letter Sister Nancey Oliver and Morning Oliver— — — — — — — — —

Received by Experience Grace a black Woman belonging to Mr William Trigg

Wm HICKMAN Mod,

The 2nd Saturday in September 1816 the Church Convened and after Worship proceeded to Business— — — — — —

A motion Brought by Bro. Graham for bilding a new meeting house which was agreed to by the Church— — — — —
The above motion Refered to our next Church meating— — — — —
The Church have directed Bro. Graham to Imploy Some person to Repare the meeting house— — —

Received by letter Rose or Rosanna a woman of coller

The 2nd Saturday in October 1816 the Church Convened and after worShip proceeded to Business

Tuck up the motion Refered from our last meating ReSpecting Bilding a new meating house and the Church has Concluded to bild one on the present lot of ground whare the old one Stands, and the Said hous is to be fifty feet long and thoity foure feet wide and about Sixteen feet high the wales out of Brick— — — —

Brethren Blanton Graham and Stephens is apinted Commissioners to draw up a SubScription to Rase funds to bild Said house and make Report to our next February meating

W.ᴹ HICKMAN Modʳ

The 2.ⁿᵈ Saturday in November 1816 the Church Convened and after worship proceeded to Business and no Business dun—

W.ᴹ HICKMAN Modʳ

The 2.ⁿᵈ Saturday in December 1816 the Church Convened and after Worship proceeded to business

At The Request of The Church at Mackconnels Run this Church has appinted Three of Thare Members, Breⁿ Charles Buck ISaac Wilson and William Graham, to attend at the Said Church the 4ᵗʰ Saturday in December 1816 at a leven Oclock in the Morning to assist in Settleing Some dificulties in the Said Church

Said Leticia Erving is granted a Letter of Dismissien

Sister Nancey Oliver is granted a letter of Dismission—

This Church has agreed to appint, Breⁿ Carter Blanton ISaac Wilson and William Graham to

Rase by Subscription a Sufficient Sum for the Surport of Bro. Hickman Thare Preacher for the Ensueing year

Wm HICKMAN Mod.^r

The 2.nd Saturday in January 1817 the Church Convened and after worship Proceeded to Business

Sister Polley Grubbs is granted a letter of Dismission

Sister Jain Denney is granted a letter of Dismission

JOHN TAYLER Mod.^r

The 2.nd Saturday in February 1817 the Church Convened and after Worship Proceeded to Business

The, Brethren that was appointed at our last October meating to draw up a Supscription to Bild a new meating house has made Report to this meating, and the Church has directed, the Same Brethren, to Continue thare SupScription and make a Report to our next meating, and Brother Lewis R, Majors is directed to draw one and make a Report, at the Same time — — — — — —

Wm HICKMAN Mod.^r

The 2.nd Saturday in March 1817 the Church Convened and after Worship proceeded to Bisiness

Phil a Black man belonging to Brother Price was Exclued for Swaring and Telling the Church, that he which,d to be Exclued— — — —

The Church have agreed, to Call a meating on ThurSday next, to meat at the Meating house for the purpose of deciding weather theay will proceed to Bild the meating house

W.^r HICKMAN, Md^r

part of the Church meat on Thursday agreable to apointment of the Said Church and form^d Them Selves in a Body and it was Conclued it was Best to lay it over to our next meating in April

The 2nd Saturday in April 1817 the Church Convened and after Worship proceeded to Business—

This Church has agreed when ever two thousand dollars is ras^d by Supsouption to Bild a new Meating house the Said house is to be Let

W.^r HICKMAN Mod^r

Sunday the 13 of April the Church Received by Letter Rosanna a Woman of Caller

The 1st Saturday in May 1817 the Church Convened and after Worship proceeded to Business—

A Motion Brought by Bro.^r Blanton weather this Church will agree to Repare the meating house or not, and after some debate the Church agreed to lay it over to the next Church meating— — —

W.^r HICKMAN Mod

The 2nd Saturday in June 1817 the Church Convened and after Worship proceeded to Business

Charity a Black woman the property of Bro,
Thomas Martin was Excluded for living in
adultery and Desireing this Church to Exclude her

Bro. Charles Cullens is granted a letter of Dismission

Bro. Graham is directed to pay Cate a black
Woman four dollars for keeping the meating house
in order— — — —
The Church has tacken up the Reference Referd
from our last meating Respecting Repareing the
meating house, and agreed to Repare the Same in
the Best manner and to Bild a new addission on
the north Side to make it in the form of the Letter
tee it is a fram one about twenty four feet Square
and Surficient high for a good gallery above and
to be finished off in the Best manner and have
Apointed Brethren Blanton Graham and Stepens
and in Case of failure of Blanton Edringten is to
act in his place and the Said Bren is to Draw up
SupScription to Trye to Rase funds by the frends
Surficient for the Said Bilding, one half of the
money is to be paid when the work is let and the
other half at the time it is dun and to make ther
Report to our next Church meating— — — —

Wᴹ Hickman M

Sunday the 15 of June 1817 the Church Dismiss
Bren Simien Dearing and Wife by Letter — — —

Received by Experence Tener a Black Woman the
property of Mr Gill— — — —

The 2nd Saturday in July 1817 the Church Convened and after Worship proceeded to Business

The Church has appointed Br.ⁿ William Graham
and William Samuel as Commissioners to attend
the Franklin County Court to get a grant for a
Road from the Leestown Road by the meating
house to Intercect the Steels Ferey Road and the
Said Road is to be Thirty feet wide, and to make
Report to the Church — — — — — — —

The Following Brⁿ is Appointed as Messengers to
our next Association William Hickman Carter
Blanton John Price and William Samuel and the
Said Messengers is to prepare a Church letter
against the next Church meating and make a
Report

Wᵐ HICKMAN Modʳ

The 1ˢᵗ Saturday in August 1817 the Church Convened and after WorShip proceeded to Business

The Church Letter Read and Recive— — — —
Broʳ Joseph Edringten and wife granted a Letter
of Dismission— — — — —

Wᵐ HICKMAN Modʳ

The 2ⁿᵈ Sunday in Sepʳ 1817 the Church Convened and after WorShip proceeded to Business

Sister Salley Brown and Broʳ Nick The Property
of Mʳ George Brown granted a Letter of Dismissien— — — — —

The 2ⁿᵈ Saturday in Octoʳ 1817 the Church Convened and after WorShip proceeded to Business

Broʳ Charles Buck and wife is granted a Letter of
Dismission

The Church has appointed Br.ⁿ William Hickman and William Samuel as a Committey to Exemmen the Church Book and trye to Assetain the amount of the members in the Said Church, and the Members that has move out of the Bounds of the Church and make Report to the next Church meating..............

The Church Convened in the next day morning and granted Bro.ʳ John Major and wife Judith Letters of Dismission and two of his Slaves by the name of Amons and Rebecca..................

The 2ⁿᵈ Saturday in Nov. 1817 The Church Convened and after Worship proceeded to Bussiness

The Committey that was appointed at our last meating to Assetain the amount of the members Belonging to this Church and those that have moved out of her Bounds, has made thare Report and the Said Church agree.ᵈ to lay it over to our next Church Meating— — — — —

W.ᴹ Hickman Md.ʳ

The 2ⁿᵈ Saturday in December 1817 The Church Convened and after Worship proceeded to Business

The Church has agreed to Send a frendley letter to the following Bro.ˢ and Sisters James Hicklan Betsey Edsen Thomas Martain John Green Susannah Edwards and Jamina Harrison Infor'ming them that they must Come or Rite to the Said Church and let them know the Reason they have not taken Letters from the Said Church and Joined Some othe Church of the Same faith and order— — — — —

Joe the Property of Samuel Moxleys, Dec^dt is granted a letter of Dismission

Agreable to an order of Our Last Church meating the Committey have Exammened the Church Book and find the amount of members as following To Wit 25 White Males and 54 White fealmales and 47 Slaves and Persons of Culler the whole amounting to 126 members— — — — — —

Our Sisters Betsey Nowling and Salley Wilson having left the Bounds of this Church for a number of years and no member of this Church having any knowledge of Said Sisters it is thare fore agreed by this Church that the Said Sisters are considered no longer members of this Church untill they return and gaive Sattisfaction— — — — — — —

Wm Hickman Md^r

The 2nd Saturday in Jan. 1818 the Church Convend and after Worship proceeded to Business—

Bro^r John Price and wife Bro^r ISaac Wilson and wife Bro^r William Ferbee and wife Siste^s Francees Castleman Nancey Triplett Sarah Head Luccy Nawl and Love Fuller are granted Letters of Dismission to Join the new Contution in the Forks of Elkhorn in Franklin County— — — — — —

Wm Hickman Md^r

The 2nd Saturday in Feb^r 1818 the Church Convened and after Worship Proceeded to Business

A Charge Brought against Bro^r Reuben Ford for Gambling and geting Intoxicae^d in Licker by Bro^r John Gutherey and the Church has Received the

Said Charges, and appinted Bro̅ Gutherey, and he
is to Call on two more Members to Cite him
to the next Church Meating to Answer the Said
Charges— — — — —

W̅ HICKMAN Md̅

The Church Set the next day Morning and granted
Jack and his Wife Judey Letters of Dismission,
the Property of Sister Patseys Samuel

W̅ HICKMAN Md̅

The 2nd Saturday in March 1818 the Church
Convened and after Worship Proceeded to Business

Two of the members that was appointed at our
last meating have made thare Report against
Bro̅ Reuben Ford for Gambling & geting In-
toxicate^d in Licker and the Church have Excluded him for the Same— — — — —

Sister Salley Pullam is granted a Letter of Dismission— — — — —

W̅ HICKMAN Md̅

The 2nd Saturday in April 1818 The Church Convened and after Worship Proceeded to Bussiness

Bro̅ Samuel Price is granted a Letter of Dis-
mission
Rec^d by Experience Clovey the property of M̅
Richmonds

Anakey the property of Bro̅ John Price is Re-
store^d to fellowship in this Church— — — —

Sister Susannah Edwards is granted a Letter of Dismission— — — — —

Re^d by Experience Betsey ThompSon

Re^d by Experience Lucey Heart

W^M HICKMAN Mo^r

The Church Set the next days Morning

Lucey the Property of Mr Bell is granted a Letter of Dismission— — — — —

Peter the property of Bro^r Blackberns is granted a Letter of Dismission— — — — —

Hariot the property of Bro. Stephens Re^d by Experience— — — — —

Milly the property of R. Boulware, R.^{d} by Experience.

Happy the Property of Mr HenSleys, R^d by Experience— — — — — —

The 1st Saturday in May 1818 The Church Convened and after Worship proceede^d to Business

No Businness Came before the Church it adjorn^d

W^M GRAHAM Md^r

The 2nd Saturday in June 1818 the Church Convene^d and after WorShip proceeded to Bussiness

Sister Milley Sparks and her Daughter Milly Sparks is granted Letters of Dismission— — —

Sister PatSey Samuel is granted a Letter of Dismission

Bre.ⁿ Blanton and Graham are appointed by the Church to make out a new Assesment on the white male Members for the present year to Rase twenty dollars for the use of the Church and make a Report to the next Church Meating— — — —

Sister Sarah Andersen is granted a Letter of Dismission— — — —

Re.^d by Experence Rebecca Hicklan Peggy Hicklan and Polley Graham— — — — —

Phil a Black man belonging to Bro.^r John Price is Restor.^d to fellowship— — — — —

Sister Mary Peak is granted a Letter of Dismission— — — — — —

Wm HICKMAN Md.^r

The Church Convened on Tusday the 30.^h of June 1818 and Re.^d by Experence Lucey Finnel

The 2.nd Saturday in July 1818 the Church Convened and after Worship proceeded to Bussiness

A Charge Brought by Bro.^r Jack against a Black Woman Bettey belonging to Mrs Ewel for living in a Dultery and the Church Excluded her for the Same— — — — — —

Sister BetSey Edson is granted a Letter of Dismission

The Committey that was appointed at our last meating to make out Assesment on the white male Members have made thare Report and it amounts to Twenty four Dollars— — — —

Bre.ⁿ Hickman Blanton and Graham are appointed Messengers to Our next Association and are to prepare a Letter and make Report to our next Meating

Re.ᵈ by Experence Polley Webster Margret Guthery and ISabella Samuel

W.ᴹ Hickman Md.ʳ,

The 1.ˢᵗ Saturday in August 1818 the Church Convened and after Worship proceeded to bussiness

The Church Letter read and Receved— — — —

W.ᴹ Hickman, Md.ʳ

The 2.ⁿᵈ Saturday in September 1818 the Church Convened and After Worship proceeded to Bussiness

Peter the property of Bro. Blackburn was Excluded for living in adultery and fer lying— — —

Sisters Susannah Samuel and Nancey Samuel Hannah and Sam the property of Reuben Samuel and Sarah the property of Sister Samuel are granted Letters of Dismission

W.ᴹ Hickman Md.ʳ

The 2.ⁿᵈ Saturday in October 1818 The Church Convened and after WorShip proceeded to Bussiness

No Bussiness Came before the Church and It Adjurn.ᵈ

W.ᵐ Hickman Md.ʳ

The 2ⁿᵈ Saturday in November 1818 the Church Convened and after Worship proceeded to Bussiness

Brother Joseph Eddens and wife is granted Letters of Dismission— — — — — —

W.ᵐ Hickman Mod.ʳ

The 2ⁿᵈ Saturday in December 1818 The Church Convened and after Worship proceeded to Bussiness

and no Bussiness Came before the Church

W.ᵐ Hickman Md.ʳ

The 2ⁿᵈ Saturday in January 1819 The Church Convened and after WorShip proceeded to Bussiness

Brother William Peake and Wife are granted a Letter of Dismission— — — — —

Sister Salley Neal are granted a Letter of Dismission

Whare as Samuel Gravett was Excluded from this Church at thare January meating in the year 1802 and the Charge Standing on our Records fer pilfering a pare of Gloves and for faucities, and Some Testamoney Coming before this Church, that

prove's his Inecency, the Church has Restored
him in fellowShip— — — — —

Brother Samuel Gravett are granted a Letter of
Dismission
                                    W^m. HICKMAN Md^r

The 2nd Saturday in February 1819 the Church
Convene^d and after WorShip proceeded to Bussiness— — — — —

Brother Peter Bainbridge is granted a Letter of
Dismission— — — — —

The next days Morning the Church Convened and
Receved by Experence William Devinport
                                    W^m. HICKMAN Md^r

The 2nd Saturday in March 1819 The Church
Convened and after WorShip proceeded to Business

Sister Elizabeth Ewel and Sister Priscilla Ewel are
granted Letters of Dismission— — — — — —

Sister BetSey Major Re^d by Letter— — —

Brother John Green are granted a Letter of Dis
                                    W^m. HICKMAN, M

The 2nd Saturday in April 1819 the Church Convened and after WorShip proceeded to Bussiness

The Church hath agreed to give up the old Schoolhouse to the Manegers of the new Stone Choolhouse, all except the Stone Chemesery for the

benefit of Zachariah Pullam and Ezra Richmond on Condition that the Church Shall have liberty to have thare Church meating in the New Choolhouse

Sister Rosana a Woman of Coller are granted a Letter of Dismission— — — — — — —

The 2nd Saturday in May 1819 the Church Convened and after Worship proceeded to Business

This Church has agreed that Bro^r William Davenport Should Exercise a gift of praying Singing and Exertation in futer— — — — —

The Church Convened the next day morning and Re^d by Experence BetSey the property of Mr Samuel Lewis— — — — —

The 2nd Saturday in June 1819 the Church Convened and after WorShip proceeded to Bussiness

Bro^r Graham is directed to pay Catey a Woman of Couler five dollars for keeping the meating house the last year— — — — — —

Re^d by Experence Eliza Heart
Re^d by Experence James the property of Jarimah Randle— — — — —

The 2nd Saturday in July 1819 the Church Conven^d and after WorShip proceeded to Bussiness—

This Church has agreed to give up the meating house to Mr Bennet Settles the undertaker of the new meating house

The following Breⁿ William Hickman Carter Blanton William Samuel & William Graham are appointed Messengers to our next Association and is to Repare the Church Letter and make Report to this Church to Morrow Morning— — — —

Sister BetSey ThompSon are granted a Letter of Dismission— — — —
Bro^r William Davinport has liberty of this Church to Preach within the Bound of the Church— —

The Church Convened the next day morning and the Church letter was Read and Re^d— — — —
Wm HICKMAN Md^r

The 2nd Saturday in Septr 1819 the Church Conven^d and after WorShip proceeded to Bussiness

Bro^r Phillip, S. Fall Re^d by Letter— — — —

Sisters Elizabeth Hicklem Margret Hicklem and Rebecca Hicklam are granted Letters of Dismission— — — — —

Sister BetSey Sneed are granted a Letter of Dismission— — — — —
Wm HICKMAN Md,

The 2nd Saturday in October 1819 the Church Convened and after WorShip proceeded to Business— — — —

Bro^r Daniel Peake Came before the Church and Informed, the Church that he has been Informed, that thare is a Report that he and Wife has been in

the habit of Drinking to an Excess, and the
Church, has appointed Breⁿ Blanton and Ber-
hannon to Inquire in to the Report, and make
Report to the next Church meating— — — —

Quary will this Church point out what method one
Bro. Shall take with another Bro. Who failes to
pay him agreable to Contract

Answer the Bro. Shall deal with him a greable to
the 18.^h of Mathew, and if he fail to pay or Secore
the Debt he Shall be Excluded from this Church
Bro. William Davenport is granted a Letter of
Dismission— — — —

The 2nd Saturday in Nov. 1819 the Church Convened and after WorShip proceeded to Bussiness—

Bre. Blanton and Burhannan has made thare
Report, about Bro. Daniel Peak Drinking to an,
Excess, and the Church are Satisfied that he has
been, gilty and, the Church has agreed to Bare
with Bro. Peake, after directing the Mod^{tr} to
admonish him— — — — — —

The Church, has pointed Breⁿ Graham and
Samuel, Sisters, Gale and Bryant as a Commetty
to See Siste Peek about the Report of her Drinking
to an Excess and make Report to our next meating

Re^d by, Experence Henry Crutcher

The 2nd Saturday in December 1819 the Church
Convened and after WerShip proceeded to Business— — — — — —

The Same Commetty that was appointed at our last meeting to See Sister Peak failed to make thare Report, to this meeting, and thay are appointed to See her and make Report at the next Church meeting— — — —

This Church has Granted Bro. Phill N. Fall liberty to Preach the Gosple

W^r HICKMAN M^d

The 2nd Saturday in January 1820 the Church Convened and after WerShip proceeded to Bussiness

The Reference of Sister Peake taken up Referred to our next meeting and the Same two Brethren appointed to Wate on Sister Peake and Report to our next meeting— — — —

W^r HICKMAN Md^r

The 2nd Saturday in Feb. 1820 the Church Convened and after WorShip proceeded to Bussiness

The Reference ReSpecting Sister Peake was Taken up and Referd to our next meeting and Brethren L. R. Majer and James Majer is appointed to Site Sisters, Gale and Bryant to Come to the next Church meeting

W^M HICKMAN
Md^r

The 2 Saturday in March 1820 the Church Convened and after WorShip proceeded to Bussiness

The Charge against Sister Peake was Taken up and not So fulley proven to the Satisfacttion of

the Church, and the Church agreesse to Bare With
Sister Peake— — — — —

W^M. HICKMAN Md^r

The 2nd Saturday in April 1820 the Church Convened and after Worship proceeded to Bussiness

Received by Letter Brother Lewis Easterday and
wife, also Sister Elizabeth BledShoe

W^M. HICKMAN Md^r

The 2nd Saturday in may 1820 the Church Convened and after WerShip proceeded to Bussiness—

Sister Salley Stephens is granted a Letter of Dismission— — — —

Sam a Black man Belonging to W^M. Samuel is
granted a Letter of Dismission

W^M. HICKMAN M

The 2nd Saturday in June 1820 the Church Convened and after WerShip proceeded to Bussiness—
The Church has agreed to Send the following
Brethren, Hickman Fall Graham and Blanton as
helps to attend at the South BenSon Church on
the 3rd Saturday in June 1820 to attend to the
Ordanation of Bro. John Brown

W^M. HICKMAN Md^r.

The 2nd Saturday in July 1820 the Church Convened and after WerShip proceeded to Bussiness—

The Following Brethren is appointed Messengers
to Our Next Association W^M. Hickman Phillip S.

Fall and Carter Blanton and the Said Fall is to Repare the Church Letter against our next Church meating— — — — —

Re^d by Experence Edmond Vaughn J^r Q Cicey Vaughn his wife also Malinder a black Gale Belonging to Martha Majer also Lucey Gale and BetSey Western— — — — —

Sister Margret Cammel is granted a Letter of Dismission— — — —

The Church Sot the next day morning and R.^{d} Sister PatSey LivingSton— — — — —

The 5 Saturday in July 1820 the Church Convened and after WorShip proceeded to Buss^n

The Church Letter Read and Re^d

Re^d by Experence Polley Hughes— — — —
Wm HICKMAN, Md^r

The 2nd Saturday in September 1820 the Church Convened and after WorShip proceeded to Bussiness

Bro^n Blanton and Graham are appointed by the Church to make out assesment on the white male members belonging to the Church fer the present year the Sum of twenty dollars and make Report to our next meating— — — — — —
R^d by Experence Betsey Bacon and Nancy Bacon

This Church agree to Call helps to meat on the 3.rd Saturday in next month from the following

Churches, Church at Vear Sales Buck Run and North Fork, to Assist in the Ordination of Bro. Phillip, S. Fall and the Church has agreed to Set that day a part fer fasting and praying.

This Church has agreed to Change the Church meating from the 2.ᵈ Saturday to the 3ᵈ Saturday in Each month

W.ᴹ Hickman Md.ʳ

The 3.ʰᵈ Saturday in Octeʳ, 1820 the Church Convened and after WerShip proceeded to Bussiness

Reᵈ by Experence Permealey Daniel

Tuck up the Ordernation of Broⁿ Phillip S Fall, and helps from the Church at Vier Sales and from the Church at Buck Run Attended, a Prespetrey was formed Elder, William Hickman Elder John Scott, Elder Jacob Creatch, and the Said Fall was Ordain as a Minister to, Preach the Gosple of Jesus Christ

W.ᴹ Hickman Mdʳ

The 3.ʳᵈ Saturday in November 1820 the Church Convened and after WerShip proceeded to Bussiness

Breⁿ Blanton and Graham made thare Report assesing the white males of this Church fer the present year which amounted to 21 Dollars and 25 Cents— — — — —

Breⁿ Blanton and Graham is appointed by this Church Commissioners to Rase by SubScription a Surficient Sum fer our Preacher William Hick-

man fer the next year and make Report to this
Church— — — — —

Re^d by Experence Robert Snell
Bro^n Phillip. S. Fall is granted Letter of Dismission

The 3rd Saturday in December 1820 the Church
Convened and after WerShip proceeded to Buss^n

At the Request of the Church at Mount Present
we have Sent the following helps to Settle Some
deficalty in the Said Church Bre^n Lewis R.
Majer Henry Crutcher and William Graham, to
meat at the Said Church on 1st Saturday in
Jan^r next— — — — — —

Wm Hickman, Md^r

CHAPTER XII

MINUTES OF THE ELKHORN BAPTIST ASSOCIATION, KENTUCKY, 1785-1805

A Baptist conference held at South Elkhorn Saturday 25th of June 1785—members present who represented the diferent churches are as following

Churches	Deligates
South Elkhorn	Lewis Craig William Hickman & Benj Craig
Clear Creek—John Taylor John Dupey James Rucker & Richd Card	
Big Crossing—	John Tanner & William Jones
Gilberts Creek	George S Smith & John Price

Brother Lewis Craig chose moderator and brother Richard Young Clerk

Brethern Elijah Craig Augustine Eastin James Garrard and Henry Rock who were present were requested to take their seats in the conference

Agreed to be ruled in any matter that should come before them by a majority

Query—Whether the Philadelphia confession of faith adopted by the Baptists shall be strictly adhered to as the rule of our communion or whether a suspension thereof for the sake of Society be best? Answer—It is agreed that the said recited confession of faith be strictly adhered to.

Signed LEWIS CRAIG Moderator
RICH^D YOUNG Clerk.

Baptist Association held at Clear Creek friday the 30th September 1785 at 3 oclock.

Sermon by brother William Hickman from Exodus 23^d 30th 8. Brother Wood Chose Moderator Richard Young Clerk

Letters were read from six churches

Churches	*Deligates names*
Gilberts Creek	George S. Smith & John Price
Tates Creek	John Tanner William Jones & Willm Williams
South Elkhorn	Lewis Craig William Hickman & Benj Craig

Clear Creek—John Taylor James Rucker & John Dupey
Big Crossing William Cave Bartlett Collins & Robt Johnson
Limestone. William Wood & Edward Dobbins

Constitution

Being assembled together, and taking into our serious consideration, what might be most advantageous for the glory of God, the advancment of the kingdom of the dear Redeemer, and the mutual comfort and happiness of the churches of Christ, having unanimously agreed to unite in the strongest bonds of Christian love and fellowship, and in order to support and keep that union do hereby adopt the Baptist confession of faith first put forth in the name of the seven congregations met together in London in the year 1643 containing a system of the Evangelical doctrines agreeable to the Gospel of Christ, which we do heartily believe in and receive, but something in the third & fifth chapters in said book we accept if construed in that light that makes God the cause and author of sin, but we do acknowledge and believe God to be an Almighty Sovereign wisely to govern and direct all things so as to promote his own glory. Also in Chapter 31st. concerning laying on of hands on persons baptised as essential in their reception into the Church it is agreed on by us that the using or not using of that practice shall not effect our fellowship to each other; and as there are a number of Christian professions in this country under the Baptist name in order to distinguish ourselves from them we are of opinion that no appellation is more suitable to our profession than that of 'Regular Baptist' which name we profess.

The association adjourned till 2 oclock tomorrow Saturday 1st October 1785. The Association met according to adjournment and proceeded to business
William Cane chose Moderator
Resolved that all matters of controvery be determined by a majority of this association
A request from Gilbert Creek Church to the association for helps to enquire into the standing of said church, whether

they shall be dissolved or stand as a church; The request taken up & agreed that our brethren Lewis Craig, James Rucker, William Hickman & William Cane or any three of them are appointed to visit said church at Gilberts Creek and make report to the next association.

Query from Tates Creek Church—What may be thought best to be done with members that hold conditional salvation? Answer—We would give it as our opinion to the churches to use all tenderness to reclaim such persons from the error, but if they persist to deal with them as all other incorrigible offenders

A proposition to the association for their opinion on the following matter: Whether it is lawful for a Christian to bear office civil or military? Answer It is our opinion that it is lawful for any Christian to bear office either civil or military, except ministers of the Gospel—

Agreed that Quartely meetings be appointed as follows— At the Big Crossing the February before the first Sabbath in April next and that bro. James Rucker & bro. William Hickman attend the same.

At Tates Creek the Saturday before the first Sabbath in April next and that bro John Taylor and bro Richard Cane attend the same.

At Limestone the Saturday before the third Sabbath in July next and that bro Lewis Craig and bro John Tanner attend the same.

Association to be held at South Elkhorn the Saturday before the first Sabbath in August next and that bro William Wood be appointed to preach the introductory sermon or in his absence bro John Tanner.

Agreed that bro William Wood write the circular letter for the next association

Agreed that no Query be received into the association in future, but what is first debated in the church and inserted in the church letter.

Association adjourned till the first Saturday in August

Signed   WILLIAM CANE Mod.

RICH^d YOUNG Clerk

Baptist Association held at South Elkhorn Saturday 5th August 1786—

Brother John Taylor chose Moderator Rich Young Clk

1786

Churches	Messengers names
Tates Creek	John Tanner & William Williams
South Elkhorn	Lewis Craig George S Smith Benjamin Craig & William Hickman
Big Crossing	William Cane Bartlet Collins & Robt Johnson
Clear Creek	John Taylor John Dupey John Craig & Jas Hiler
Town fork	Edward Payne William Payne & Will Stone
Bryans Station	Ambrose Dudley & Augustine Eastin
Boones creek	George Shortage & Robert Fryer

Brother Elijah Craig requested to take a seat in the Association.

Letters were read from seven churches.

The three last mentioned churches were, after full satisfaction of their faith and order received amongst us at this annual meeting.

Association adjourned till Monday 8 oclock

JOHN TAYLOR Modorator

Monday 7th August 1786 the association met according to adjournment & proceeded to business

" A request from a number of baptists at or near the forks of Dicks river was read, and our brethren Ambrose Dudley, John Tanner Benjamin Craig & Bartlet Collins are appointed to attend a meeting at the aforesaid place the fourth Saturday in August next.

A form of marriage was produced & read and our brethren Elijah Craig, John Taylor, Lewis Craig, Augustine Eastin Ambrose Dudley and George S Smith are appointed a committee to inspect and correct said form and also to consider the expediency or inexpediency of a catechism and make report to the next association

A report made by our brethren Lewis Craig & William Cane who were appointed to attend at the church on Gilberts Creek and that the same was dissolved.

A motion was made, what power has this association with respect to the churches in union with it if any of them refuse its advice? Answer It has a right to reject them a seat in the association, provided the advice is not contrary to the terms of the general union

Query—Whether or not persons in a state of slavery may be said to be proper gospel members? Answer A slave may be considered a proper Gospel member.

Query Is it lawful for a slave being an orderly member and compelled to leave his wife and move with his master about five hundred miles, then to take another wife? As an opinion cant be had at this time agreed to refer the query to the next association and in the meantime advise the churches not to receive any more members under the above circumstance mentioned in said query.

Query—In regard to the duty of supporting a minister whether it be considered as a debt or liberal contribution —Debated drefered to the next association—

Supplies for the destitute Church at the Town fork. From South Elkhorn the second Saturday and Sunday in September. Clear Creek the second Saturday and Sunday in October Bryants the second Saturday and Sunday in November

Supplies for the destitute church at Boon Creek—From Clear Creek the first Saturday & Sunday in September. South Elkhorn the first Saturday & Sunday in October—Bryants the first Saturday & Sunday in November Tates Creek to assist in attend. The above meeting at Boons.

Agreed that the next association be held at Bryants the first Saturday in August next

Agreed that a yearly meeting be held at the town fork the second Saturday & Sunday in May next

Agreed that bro John Tanner be appointed to preach the introductory sermon at the next association on the subject of

sanctification or in the case of failure bro William Wood.
Association adjourned till the first Saturday in August
Signed JOHN TAYLOR Mod.
RICH^d YOUNG Clerk

Baptist Association held at Bryans Saturday August 4^h
1787 Brother Edward Payne chose Moderator   Richard
Young Clerk

1787

Churches	Messengers names
Tates Creek.	William Williams & William Turpin
South Elkhorn.	Lewis Craig Geo S. Smith Jno Staydent Jno Price
Big Crossing	Elijah Craig Jno Tanner Robt Johnson Jno Sayget

Clear Creek John Taylor James Rucker James Hite & Rich^d
Young
Town fork Edward Payne Willm Payne & Willm Stone
Bryants. Ambrose Dudley Henry Roach & E Waller
Boons Creek   George Shortage Orvin Winn & James
Whorley
Limestone Edward Dobbins Archibald Allen
Honying fork of Dicks river Wm Marshall & Mainard Thurley
Cowpers run   Augustine Eastin & James Garrard
Marble Creek   Robert Tryan & Samuel Bryant

The three last mentioned churches after giving full satisfaction of their faith & order were received at this annual
meeting
Association adjourned till Monday 9 oclock
Ew^D PAYNE Mod.

The association met according to adjournment & proceeded to business
Question—Whether the association shall receive churches
or determine any other matter touching fellowship by a
majority or unanimity? Answer By unanimity
Agreed that brethren William Marshall William Cane,
Lewis Craig James Rucker Robert Johnson and James

Garrard or any four of them be appointed to attend at William Shulls at Marble Creek the fourth friday in August if fair if not the next fair day to inquire into the grievance of a number of brethern in regard to the reception of said church into the union and make report to the next association & in the mean time said church is considered under supervision.

Agreed that bro John Tanner & bro James Garrard be appointed to write the circular letter

A report to be made to this association in regard to a form of marriage and a catechism was referred from the last association continued and agreed to be referred to the next association, and that the same brethern appointed formerly are to make the report.

Reference from last association. Query Whether it is lawful for a slave being an orderly member and compelled to leave his wife and move with his master about five hundred mile then to take another wife? Debated and withdrawn.

Query. In regard to the duty of supporting a minister, whether it be considered as a debt or a liberal contribution? Debated & cast out.

Query. Whether it is agreable to scripture for churches to suffer men to preach and have the care of them as their minister that are a trading and entangling themselves with the affairs of this life? Answer that it is not agreable to scripture but that it is the duty of the churches to give their minister a reasonable support and restrict them in these respects.

Query What rule are we to receive Baptist members by from the old country or elsewhere not of our association? Answer. All members coming from churches of our faith and order bringing an orderly letter of dismission from said orderly church, we advise to be admitted, and all baptists coming from churches of other order by experience

Query How are we to understand that part of the 13th chapter of Johns Gospel which relates to washing the saints feet? Referred to the next association and in the mean time it is requested that each church make up an opinion and make report to the next association.

Agreed that in the form of our Constitution after the word
regular that the word Baptist be added.

The Association adjourned till Teusday 9 oclock

Signed Edw^D Payne Moderator

The association met according to adjournment. A motion
whether this association has a right to concern with the internal affairs of a church when they stand & act on the principles of our constitution? Answer the association has no
right. In regard to the answer to the query of yesterday
which relates to the reception of baptist members into the
church? Agreed that the former answer be erased and answered as following, That the churches be careful to have
regard to the discipline received by the churches annexed to
the confession of faith in receiving all her members into
society.

Agreed that this association correspond by letter with the
Kitochton & Philadelphia associations and by delegates when
convenient and that brethren Augustine Eastin Edward
Payne Robert Johnson James Garrard John Tanner & Elijah
Craig are appointed a committee, any four of them to prepare
letters and empower a delegate if found convenient to send
one to each of the afore said Associations.

Agreed that the above mentioned brethren are appointed
to prepare a letter to the association at Coxes creek in Nelson
county and that brethren William Marshall John Tanner
Augustine Eastin and Maurice Hornsberry are appointed
delegates to attend the same

Agreed that there be two associations next year and that
the first be held at the big crossing the last Saturday in May
Brother Augustine Eastin is appointed to preach the introductory sermon

Brother William Payne is appointed to purchase a record
book & paper for the use of the association and that each
church is to pay a proportionable part of the expence.

Association adjourned till the last Saturday in May

Signed Edw^D Payne Modr
Rich^D Young Clk.

Baptist Association held at South Elkhorn Saturday 31st May 1788 at two oclock.

Sermon by bro. Augustine Eastin.

Brother William Cave chose moderator

Bro. Richd Young Clerk.—Proceeded to read letters from the Churches.

Churches	Ministers & Messengers	Baptized	Recd by letter	Disd by letter	excommunicated	Decd	total members
Tates Creek	Will Jones Will Turpin	1					16
South Elkhorn	Lewis Craig Geo S Smith John Conner Jno Hays	12			4	1	128
Big Crossing	Elijah Craig Jno Tanner Wm Cave Robt Johnson						48
Clear Creek	John Taylor Jas Rucker Jas. Hiter Richd Young	4	9				148
Bryants	Ambrose Dudley Wm A Waller John Mason	8	14			1	97
Townfork	William Payne William Stone						
Cowpers run	Jas Gerrard Augustine Eastin						
Boons creek	David Tompson Geo Shortage Owin Winn Jas Whaley	2	2		1		37
Limestone	Will Wood	3		2		1	30

Churches	Ministers & Messengers	Baptized	Recd by letter	Disd by letter	excommunicated	Decd	total members
Dicks river	Wm Marshall Maurice Hansberry Wm Gaines		1				20
Marble Creek	John Rice Robt Fryan Jas McMahan	8	9	6			35
		38	35	8	5	3	559

A report made by brethren Lewis Craig James Gerrard James Rucker & Robert Johnson who were appointed a committee to enquire into the greivance of a number of brethren in regard to the Constitution of the Marble Creek Church report, that the Church was legally and properly constituted, that the objections made was not a sufficient bar—Resolved that the Association agree in opinion with the Committee—

Brother John Tanner & bro Augustine Eastin are appointed to write the circular letter.

Association adjourned till Monday 9 oclk.

WM CAVE Modr

Monday 2d June 1788. the Association met according to adjournment.

Delegates attended from Salem Association on Coxes Creek with a letter, their delegates made some objections in regard to our Association tolerating the Churches in using or not using the laying on of hands on persons newly baptized and that brethren Lewis Craig Elijah Craig & Ambrose Dudley were appointed a committee to confer with said delegates & make report.

Brethren Lewis Craig Elijah Craig & Ambrose Dudley made a report that they confered with bro Wm Taylor &

bro Joshua Carman delegates from the Salem Association & that every obstacle was removed and their delegates received accordingly and a union declared.

Agreed that the Modorator give the right hand of fellowship to the delegates from Marble Creek, who took their seats bro. John Price Robt Fryan & James McHatton

Agreed that a plan be formed for receiving an accusation in the association against a Sister Church debated & agreed that a committee of three members be appointed to form a plan for this association to receive accusations against any of the churches in the union and the manner in which they shall be suspended or a disunion declared and that brethren William Wood John Tanner & Augustine Eastin were appointed accordingly and are to make report to the next association.

The query from the last Association in regard to that part of the 13th Chapter of Johns Gospel that relates to washing the Saints feet refered for further consideration

A motion from the last Association respecting a plan for a form of marriage, and also to consider the expediency or inexpediency of a Catechism continued, and agreed that brethren John Taylor Lewis Craig, Augustine Eastin, Ambrose Dudley & George S. Smith are appointed to form said plan & make report to the next association.

Query from the Church at Limestone Whether Churches belonging to the association that do not comply with that solemn duty of supporting their minister with a comfortable living so as to keep them from worldly incumbrance shall be held in the fellowship of this association? Debated, and referred for further consideration.

Agreable to a former order bro William Payne purchased a record book and paper for the use of the association.

Agreed that the next association be held at Clear Creek the last Saturday in October next and that bro Ambrose Dudley preach the introductory sermon & in case of failure bro William Wood.

Brother John Price and bro John Taylor are appointed to write the circular letter on the Subject of the Trinity.

Brethren William Wood John Taylor and John Tanner are appointed to attend the Salem Association in Nelson County the first Saturday in October next and that they are also requested to write a letter to said association in behalf of the Churches.

The association adjourned till the last Saturday in October next

Signed WILLIAM CAVE Mod
RICHD YOUNG Clk

The regular Baptist association held at Clear Creek Saturday the 25th October 1788 introductory sermon by bro Dudley.

From Tates Creek John Clarke & Absalom Crooke

S. Elkhorn Lewis Craig Geo S. Smith Jno Haydon & John Conner

Big Crossing Elijah Craig Robt Johnson Jno Suggett Wm Cave

Clear Creek Jno Taylor Richd Cave Jas Hiter & Richd Young

Bryants Ambrose Dudley Henry Roach & John Mason

Town fork Jno Gano Edwd Payne & Tho Lewis

Boones Creek Geo Shortage Geo & Owin Winn & Jas Whaley

Fork of Dick river Wm Marshall Mauris Hansberry Jno Steel & Wm Green

Marble Creek John Price Robt Fryan Arthur Fall & Jas McMahan.

Bro John Gano chose Moderator & bro Richd Young Clk
A church constituted at the forks of Elkhorn the 7th June 1788 and received into the association and their delegates took their seats accordingly William Hickman and Richard Thomas—

A church constituted at Buck run Octo 18t 1788 and received into the association and their delegate James Dupay received, & took his seat

A letter received from the Salem Association and their delegates Rhodensburgh Ashby and William King received accordingly.

Information was given to the association that there was a letter directed to be wrote from the Philadelphia association to this but that it never came to hand.

Voted that bro John Sutton take a seat in the association.

The association adjourned till Monday 9 oclock.

Signed   JOHN GANO Modr.
RICHD YOUNG Clerk

Monday 27h October 1788

The association met according to adjournment and proceeded to business.

Query from the Church at Limestone whether Churches belonging to the association that do not comply with that solemn duty of supporting their minister with a comfortable living so as to keep them from worldly incumbrance shall be held in the fellowship of this association? Debated and answered, That a Committee be appointed to visit the Church at Limestone in particular and all the other churches in general and to set in order any matters that may be wanting & make report to the next association.

Voted that the said committee consist of two ministers and two laymen, and that bro Gano & bro Dudley were chosen by ballot bro Lewis Craig is to attend their meeting with them at Bryants and the Town fork.

A letter received and read from the church at Coopers run and their delegates took their seats Augustine Eastin & James Brown.

A report made by bro Wood & bro Eastin who were appointed a committee to form a plan for receiving accusations against any of our Sister Churches which was referred for further consideration till the next association.

A form of marriage was presented to the association by committee for that purpose which was rejected, and the the motion struck out, and that it is advised that a catechism is necessary but not to be considered a term of communion.

The Query from the last association in regard to that part of the 13th Chap of John's gospel which relates to washing the saints feet which was referred for further consideration answered that the Churches which compose the association are not unanimous, but in the meantime the using or not using that practice shall not affect our fellowship each to other. She Still referred for consideration.

Query. What is to be done with members of a church who withdraw their membership? Answered. If they can't be reclaimed by Gospel steps they must be excommunicated

Query. In what light do the association view the conduct of a church in union with them admitting or receiving as a member or minister into their fellowship that stand excommunicated from a church of our denomination whether in or out of the association? Answer. It is disorderly for any of our Churches to receive an excommunicated member from any of the Churches of our denomination without first having a written information of the charge from the Church which they come from.

Agreed that brethren Gano, Dudley, Price, Taylor, Eastin, & William Cave are appointed a committee to enquire into the distress of South Elkhorn Association on friday next.

The circular letter read & approved Ordered that each church be furnished by the Clerk with a copy of the minutes of the Association & a copy of the circular letter

Ordered that Brethren Gano, Price & Young be appointed to write letters in behalf of the Association to the Salem, Ketockton & Philadelphia associations.

Agreed that Brethren Gano, Lewis Craig Price & Taylor be appointed to attend the Salem association the Saturday before the first Sabbath in October next.

Agreed that our next association be held at the Big Crossing the last Saturday in May next & that Bro Gano be appointed to preach the Introductory sermon—Bro Jno Price & Bro Aug Eastin appointed to write the Circular letter on the subject of God, decree.

The association adjourned till the last Saturday in May next.

RICHD YOUNG Clerk   JOHN GANO Modr

The minutes of the Baptist Association held at the Great Crossing the 30th day of May 1789. Bro John Gano preached by appointment II Cor. 11:28 Besides those things that are without, that which cometh on me daily the care of all the Churches. Letters from the Churches were read. Bro Gano chose modorator & Bro Price Clerk.

Churches	Messengers	Baptized	Recd by letter	Dis-missed	Excomd	Decd	No.
Tates Creek	Wm Jones John Clerk				3	1	15
S. Elkhorn	S 'Craig Tho Ammons Jno Hayden And Hampton	10	17	13			132
Crossings	E Craig Wm Cave Robt Johnson John Tanner	4	18				71
Clear Creek	John Taylor Rd Cave Jas Hiter, Saml Dedman	146	10	5	2	1	294
Bryants	Amb Dudley. Henry Roach John Mason Len Young	12	14	1	5	1	129
Town Fork	John Gano Wm Payne						18
Cooper run	A Eastin Joel Ellis Jas Gerrard	2	2				26
Boones Creek	David Tompson Geo Winn Alex Chambers		4				51
Limestone	Wm Wood Phil Drake Jno Wilson	10	15	1	3	2	54
Dicks river	Jno Sleet Morras Hansberry				1		27

Churches	Messengers	Baptized	Recd by letter	Dismissed	Excomd	Decd	No.
Marble Creek	Jno Price Robt Fries Jas Mc-Mahan	11	14				82
Forks Elkhorn	Wm Hickman Phil Thomas Richd Thomas	4	10	1	2		67
Buck run	Jas Dupey Jos Minter	10	9		1		34
	Total	209	113	21	17	5	1000

A letter from the general committee was read informing us of a union in old Virginia between the Regulars & Separate Baptists.

Brethren Gano, E Craig, Eastin & Price were appointed to write our answer to the same

Adjourned till Monday 8 oclock

Met pursuant to adjournment.

The letter to the General Committee and with amendment approved of.

The Committee appointed to visit the Churches reported that they attended the appointment & upon the whole the standing of the Churches appeared in a favorable light.

Advised that the Churches consider their services & make them such compensation as to the Churches may seem right.

The Circular letter was read & deferred for the present.

Agreed to drop the appellation regular in all letters going from this association.

A plan for receiving accusations against Sister Church— Referred Washing feet referred

The Committee appointed to visit S. Elkhorn reported they had visited said church accordingly.

Received the minutes of the United Baptists association of Kentucky with their messengers who were invited to set with us viz John Bailey, Jos Bledsoe, Wm Bledsoe & Andrew

Trible, desiring to treat with us respecting a union. Resolved that James Gerrard, Robt Johnson John Taylor & Augustine Eastin be a committee to act in conjunction with the asso. messengers for the purpose of appointing a time & place for the holding a general association & the number of delegates to be sent from each church between the United Baptist & the Elkhorn association.

The said committee came to the following resolution. That the second friday in August next at Harod, meeting house be the time and place for holding said meeting and that the association consist of one minister and two lay members from each church and where a Church has no minister they may avail themselves of one from a Sister Church or if they choose send three private members, which resolution was approved of Agreed that the Clerk furnish each church with a copy of the minutes & circular letter and that he receive three shillings from each Church for the same.

Query from Washington. Is it most agreable to Gospel rules to excommunicate disorderly persons in the Church only, or in public Congregations before the Church & world? The association is of opinion that the Church hath power to proceed either way but advise to excommunicate privately but in particular cases.

Query from Bryans whether the laying on of hands on new baptised persons be a gospel ordinance or not? Referred.

The first Thursday in August appointed a day of fasting in all the Churches.

Next association to be held at Boons Creek the last Friday in October. Bro Tanner to preach the association sermon.

Brethren Gano, Eastin, Garrard & E Craig are appointed to revise the rules of the Association & prepare a Circular Letter for the next association.

Jno Price Clk   Signed John Gano Mdr

The Baptist Association held at Boones Creek the 30th day of October 1789

Sermon at 2 oclock by Bro John Tanner My counsel shall stand & I will do all my pleasure—(Isai. 46:10.)

Proceeded to read letters from the churches.

Churches	Messengers	Baptz.	Red by letter	Disd	Excd	Dec^d	Total
Tates Creek	David Tompson Van Teage & Jas Dosher	4	4				27
South Elk	S Craig G Smith Jno Hayden & And Hampton	10	9	7			144
Big Crossing	Elijah Craig Jno Tanner W Cave			1		1	68
Clear Creek	Jno Taylor J Sutton J Martin & R Young	8	2	2	1		299
Bryans	A Dudley J Mason W Ellis & L Young	12	19		2		161
Town Fork	Jno Gano Edwd Payne & Tho Lewis	2					20
Cowpers run	Jas Gerrard Israel Ellis & Jas Stark	5	3				34
Boons Creek	Geo Winn Alex Chambers & R Sperr	4	9	2		1	61
Limestone	Thos Stoe & David Davis	17	5	1			72
Dicks river	Wm Marshall Theo Adams M Hansberry & Jno Sleet	5	12		1	1	44
Marble creek	Jno Price Rob Price Jas McMahan & Saml Reid	7	2				91
Fork Elk	Wm Hickman R & P Thomas	1	12				80
Buck run	John & James Dupey	4	5				42
		80	82	13	5	2	1143

A Letter was read from the Salem association and their delegates William Taylor Joshua Carman Josiah Dodge & Thomas Polk were received accordingly.

A Letter was read from the Ketockton association which gave a very favorable account of the progress of religion in that quarter. Also a letter was read from the Separate Baptist association South of Kentucky which was ordered to lie on the table.

Bro James Garrard chose moderator & Bro Richd Young Clerk.

The association adjourned till tomorrow 9 oclock Saturday Octo 31st 1789.

The association met according to adjournment after divine worship proceeded to business.

The Committee appointed to revise the rules of the association presented a number of articles which were read approved of and ordered to be recorded as following

1st. A Moderator shall be appointed by the association by ballot who shall preside during the association to preserve order & State questions & propositions that may be made agreable to the rules of this association

2d. No proposition or motion shall be debated unless made by one member & seconded by another.

3d. All motions & propositions shall be decided on as they are proposed nor shall any new motion be made or taken up while there is one undetermined before the association unless the first be postponed or referred.

4th. Any motion made & seconded may be withdrawn by the member making such motion before any decision had on it.

5th. Every motion shall be made in writing if required by the moderator or any other member and read by the clerk before any debate or decision had on it.

6th. Every member about to make a motion or proposition shall rise from his seat and respectfully address himself to the moderator.

7th. No member shall speak more than twice to any question without leave from the association nor more than once until every other member who chooses shall have spoken once.

8th. Every member in debate shall confine himself to the subject in hand & if he shall wander from the question shall be called to order by the moderator or any other member and every member called to order shall immediately sit down, unless permitted to proceed to explain himself.

9th. Every member shall keep his seat while the moderator puts any question, which he shall do standing.

10th. If any proposition should be made which to the association may appear improper to decide on the association may quash it by a previous Question which shall be in this form "Shall the main question be now put?"

A plan for receiving accusations against a Sister Church which stands referred, dismissed. Query referred respecting washing of feet.

Resolved that it is the opinion of the association that it is a Christian duty to be practiced at discretion.

Query which stands deferred respecting laying of hands on new baptized persons withdrawn.

Query whether the office of Elder distinct from that of a minister be a gospel institution or not referred to the next Association.

The Letter from the separate association South of Kentucky taken up & debated and a committee appointed to write an answer; Brethren Sutton, Tanner, Lewis, Craig & Price were appointed accordingly.

Resolved that Brethren John Taylor John Dupey & James Dupey be appointed a Committee to write the Circular letter.

Resolved that Brethren Dudley, Cave & Stoe be appointed a committee to write to the Ketockton association.

Resolved that brethren Geo Smith Edwd Payne & Richd Young be appointed a committee to write to the Salem association.

The association adjourned till Monday 9 oclock

Signed Jas Garrard Mdr Richd Young c

Monday 2ᵈ Novʳ 1789

The Association met according to adjournment. A Letter produced by the Committee appointed to write to the Separate Baptist Association South of Kentucky was read & approved of

A Letter produced by the Committee appointed to write to the Salem association was read & approved of.

A letter produced by the committee appointed to write to the Ketockton association was read & approved of.

Resolved that brethren Gano, Dudley Tanner, Edwd Payne & Lewis be appointed a committee to write to the Philadelphia association.

A circular letter prepared by the committee appointed for that purpose was read and referred to a Committee to be appointed to revise and report to the next association & that brethren Gano, Garrard, Tanner, Dudley & L Craig were appointed accordingly.

Query from Marble creek. Whether a woman slave that left a husband in the old Country and marry again here to a man that has a wife twenty miles from him who also refuses to keep said man as a husband ought her marrying in such circumstance to be a bar to her membership? Ans Debarred from Membership—

A request from Limestone to have an annual association which was agreed to and that also there be a yearly meeting for preaching and communion.

Resolved that the next association be held at Townfork the fourth friday in August next & that a yearly meeting be held at Marble Creek Beginning the first friday in June & to continue Saturday & Sunday.

Agreed that we adopt a circular letter from the Philadelphia association on the subject of Faith.

Resolved that brethren Elijah Craig S. Craig, Tanner, Dudley, Taylor & Eastin and Hickman are appointed to attend the next yearly meeting.

Resolved that bro Gano preach the Introductory sermon at the next association in case of failure bro Jno Price.

The association adjourned till the next association.

RICHD YOUNG Ck Signed JAMES GARRARD Mor

The Baptist association held at Lexington Aug 27th 1790 Introductory sermon preached by bro John Taylor Letters were read from eleven churches.

Churches	Messengers	Bap.d	Recd by letter	Disd	Exd	dec	total
Tates creek	David Tomson & David Wilcoxson	6	9	2		1	39
S. Elk	Lewis Craig Geo S. Smith Jno Hayden & And Hampton	17	16	5	4	1	167
Great Crossing	Jos Redding Elijh Craig Wm Cave	7					96
	& Robt Johnson	7	21				96
Clear Creek	Jno Taylor Richd Cave Jas Hiter & Richd Young	10	13	1	4	1	308
Bryans	Amb Dudley Heny Roach Wm Ellis & Jno Mason	20	24	2	2	1	200
Townfork	Edwd Payne Thos Lewis Wm Payne & Wm Stone	3	1	1	1	1	24
Cowpers run	Aug Eastin Jas Garrard Jerreel Lewis	25	10	1		2	66
Boons creek	Geo & Owen Winn Alex Chambers Jas Whaley	4	1	4			64
Hanging fork	Wm Marshall Feathergill Adams & Morris Hansberry	3	7				55
Marble creek	Tho Ammons Ro Fryan Sam'l Reid & Jas McMahan	28	3	2			119
Forks Elk	Wm Hickman & Anty Tomson	11	13	2	4	0	98
Buckrun	Jas Dupey Jo Minter	3	6	0	0	0	49
		137	124	20	13	7	1285
Indian Creek							8
Limestone	No Intelligence						72
							1365

Bro James Garrard chose moderator & Richd Young appointed Clerk

Agreed that in future the moderator do appoint the Clerk.

Query from Boones Creek. Is it agreable to Gospel for a member in Society who stands justly indebted and doth not pay according to contract to continue said member in society.

A letter was read from the general Committee in the City of Richmond & left for consideration.

The circular letter which was referred to a committee was reported by bro Dudley & Read.

Query from Cowpers run (which stands referred) whether the office of Elder distinct from that of a minister be a gospel institution or not?

Ans that it is the opinion of the association it is a gospel institution.

A letter was read from a church constituted on Indian Creek requesting to be received into the association & their delegates William Cromwell & Thomas Hubbard took their seats accordingly

The association adjourned till tomorrow morning nine oclock

August 28th 1790

The association met according to adjournment. After divine worship proceeded to business.

The Circular letter read amended & agreed to

Bro Jas Sutton being present his assistance was requested who took a seat.

Query from Boons creek withdrawn

And having debated on the letter from the general committee; Agreed that the association do answer it and that brethren Redding Johnson Eastin & Garrard were appointed for that purpose.

Agreed that Brethren Eastin Sutton Dudley & Reding be appointed to attend the Salem association.

A letter produced by the committee appointed to write to the general committee was read & approved of.

Agreed that all letters sent & also that àll letters received by this association from public bodies be committed to record

Resolved that a committee be appointed to write a circular letter to the Churches from the next association and that brethren Reding, Wm Cave, & Johnson were appointed accordingly.

Resolved that Querterly meeting be held at the following places & times to wit At Limestone the 2^d friday in November and that brethren Garrard Eastin John Taylor & Payne are appointed to attend the same.

At the Hanging fork of Dicks river the 4h friday in February and that brethren Lewis Craig, Reding, Hickman & Smith are appointed to attend the same.

And at the forks of Elkhorn the fourth friday in May and that Brethren Eastin, Marshall, Dudley, & Jas Sutton are appointed to attend the same.

Resolved that the next association be held at Cowpers run the fourth friday in August next & that Bro Gano is appointed to preach the Introductory sermon and in case of failure bro John Price.

Resolved that the Clerk be directed to furnish each church with a copy of the Circular letter and the minutes of the association

The association adjourned till the fourth friday in August next

Signed JAMES GARRARD Modr

The Baptist Association held at Coopers Run Meeting house friday August 26th 1791

Introductory sermon by John Gano from first Corrinthians 1 chap 10 verse "Now I beseech you brethren by the name of our Lord Jesus Christ that you all speak the same things and that there be no divisions among you but that ye be perfectly joined together in the same mind and in the same judgment. Letters were received from 13 Churches

Churches	& Messengers	Bapᵈ	letter Recᵈ	Restored	Disᵈ	Exᵈ	dead	Total
Tates Creek	David Thompson Wm Jones Jno Moore & Ralph McGee	28	11		9	4	1	60
South Elkhorn	Lewis Craig Geo Smith Jno. Haydon & Andrew Thompson	50	11	3	7	2	1	200
Clear Creek	Jno Taylor Jas Rucker Lewis Castleman Rh Young	10	1	2	36	4	4	277
Bryants	Ambrose Dudley Wm Wallar Jno Mason Alax Monroe	21	26		5	3	4	233
Townfork	Jno Gano Thos Lewis & Nathl Ashby	8	6		2		1	35
Coopers Run	A. Eastin J. Garrard J. Ellis & Jas. Stark	14	22			3	1	95
Boons Creek	Geo. Winn, Alexr Chambers Jno Hazlerig, Wm Hardage	20	5		3		2	74
Limestone	Wm Wood Phil. Drake Willis Conway	8	12		6	3		89
Dicks River	Wm Marshall Jno Steel & Jos. Helm	17	11		15	2		65
Marble Creek	Jno Price Rob Friar Arthur Fall	2	3		10	3	1	99

Churches	& Messengers	Bap^d	letter Rec^d	Restored	Dis^d	Ex^d	dead	Total
Forks Elkh.	Any. Thompson							
	Jno Brown &							
	Jno. Ethington	8	5		5			98
Buck Run	James Dupey &							
	Will Green	5	9					62
Indian	Will Cromwell							
Creek		1			2			7
		178	100	5	100	19	15	1299

Bro. Jno Gano chosen Moderator & Richard Young Clerk.
Two letters were read from the Church at the Great Xing &
seven delegates attended. but from an unhappy division be-
tween them the letters were ordered to lie on the table and
all the delegates to stand nuter till the matter of dispute
shall be settled by this association.
A letter was read from the Church constituted at Mays
Creek and their delegates David Morris Cornelius Drake &
John Shotwell were recd into the Association.   25 [1]
A letter was read from the Church constituted at the Cove
Spring & their delegate Maurice Hhonberry recd into the
association   19
A letter was read from the Church constituted on Green
Creek & their deligates George Shortage Elijah Postem and
James Williamson was recd into the Association   10
A letter was read from the Church constituted in Tenessee
County Cumberland Settlement and their delegates Richard
Thomas and William Wilcox was recd in the association 21
A letter was read from the Church Constituted at Strouds
fork and the deligates Reubin Smith & Joel Havens were
recd into the association   9
A letter was read from the Church Constituted at Taylors

[1] The numbers indicate the members in these newly constituted churches.

Fork & their deligates Thomas Jones & Clop Thompson
were recd into the association   19
Brethren Jno Sutton & Able Griffey being present at the
Association was requested who took their seats accordingly
A letter was recd and read from the Salem Association and
their deligates William Taylor and Joshua Carman took
their seats. A letter and the minutes of the Ketockton
association was recd and read
Resolved that a committee of eight members be appointed to
write to the same association to the, Ketockton association and a circular letter to the churches, and that Brethren
Price, Smith Carmen Griffey Woods Ashby Dudley and
Dupuy were appointed accordingly—
A motion was made to appoint a committee to enquire into
the distress of the Church at the Great Crossings debated
and referd till tomorrow
The association adjourned till Tomorrow 9 oclock
                                            Jno Ganoe Moderator

    Saturday the 27th Augus 1791
The association met according to adjournment and after
divine worship proceed to business. Agreeable to the reffer-
ence of yesterday the association agreed to take up the
matter respecting the distress of the Church at the Great
Crossing.
Resolved that a committee of 15 members of this body be
appointed to meet both parties of the Baptists people of the
Crossings at their former meeting house on the 7th day of
September next at 10 OClock and that Brethren Taylor,
Smith, Price, Ganoe, Dudley, Garrard, Dupuy, Young
Eastin, Shortage, David Thompson Haydon & Anthony,
Thompson were appointed accordingly and are to make re-
port to the present association
On a motion resolved that when the association adjourn
that it meet at the Crossing meeting house the 7th day
of Sept next at 10 OClock On a motion resolved that a com-
mittee of five members be appointed to take under their
consideration the Baptist confession of Faith and the dis-

ciplin so far as to them may appear necessary and report their proceedings to our next association, and that Brethren Eastin Garrard Wood, Gano & Smith were appointed accordingly. and that in case of death or any other disability of any of the members that the remaining part provided it be a majority have full power to keep up the number of five.

Resolved that our sister association of Salem be requested to assist us in the revision of the Confession of Faith and treaties of discipline agreeable to a resolution of this association. Resolved that a committee of three men be appointed to draw up a memorial to the Convention to be held at Danville the—day of Aple next requesting them to take up the subject of religious liberty and perpetual slavery in the formation of the constitution of this district and that they make report to this association at the Great Crossing the 8th of next month and that Brethren Eastin Gerrard & Dudley were appointed accordingly.

Resolved that Brethren Wood Gerrard and Payne are appointed deligates to attend the next Salem association

At an association continued by adjournment and held at the Big Crossings meeting Sept 8th 1791—

A Report made by the Committee appointed to enquire into the distress of the church at the Great Crossings was read and approved of and directed to be recorded as follows

A circular letter as prepared by the committee for that purpose was read and approved

A letter was prepared by the committee appointed to write to the Ketocton association was read and approved—

A letter was prepared by the committee appointed to write to the Salem association was read, and approved.

A memorial was prepared by the committee appointed to the ensueing Convention on the subject of Religious liberty and perpetual slavery was read and approved.

Resolved that the next association to be held at Tates Creek the last Friday in Agust next and that Bro Garrard is appointed to preach the introductory sermon & in case of failing Brother Dudley On a motion agreed to take up the matter respecting the distress of the Baptist people of the Crossing.

The association advise the Brethren at the Crossing not to consider the members recd by either, party since the division, members of the Church untill they give satisfaction to the whole body in case of a union between them.

Resolved that the association advise the Churches to provide a fund and send their bounty by their delegates to the next Association, and to be under their direction.

Resolved. That this Association recommend to the church at the Crossing that they so far take our advice as to meet us in our next Association with the twenty nine withdrawn Members united to them

The Committee agreeable to the appointment of the Association met at the Great Crossing Meeting House Sept the 7th 1791

Brother James Garrard chosen Chairman and Richard Young Clerk—

Present John Taylor, Geo Smith John Price, John Gano, Ambrose Dudley, James Dupuy, Augustin Eastin, George Shortage David Thomson, James Rucker, Jno. Haydon John Mason and Anthony Thomson—

1st Difficulties proposed by Robert Johnson There was a Committee against Mr Craig which some wished him cited to appear before the Church without taking any Gospel steps.

The Committee are of opinion that the Brother who was offended with Mr. Craig ought to have taken the steps of Gospel as mentioned in the 18th of Matthew, and that the Church ought not to have received the complaint as not being in Gospel order

2nd The Church failed to recd Mr Craig when he wished to offer his repentance for two meetings the Committee are of opinion that the Church was to blame for not hearing him.

3rd No member Voted that he could not bear with the Church and a majority voted, that they could bear with the conduct of the Church fifteen members who were nuters were supposed to have no priviledge in the church without any trial

The Committee wase of opinion that the afforesaid fifteen members ought not to be deprived of Church liberties.

4th Twenty nine members withdrawed contrary to good order.

It is the opinion of the committee that the said members withdrew themselves in disorderly manner.

A farther difficulty in regard to the adoption of the Treaties of discipline at a time when a member was on trial. Answered that the church had a right to receive it at any time but that they had no right to apply it to the person then on trial. Difficulties propose by Joseph Reding whether the Church did right in the exclution of Mr. Craig the first saturday in Jan last

The committee are of opinion that from what appears on the records Mr Craig was justly excluded for his misconduct, but we think the Church was wrong in receiveing the accusation Contrary to the 18th of Mathew

Jas Garrard Chairm
Rich^D Young Clerk

The association adjournd till the last friday in August next.

Jno Gano Modear
Richard, Young. Clerk

At an occational meeting of the Elkhorn Association met at Bryans Decr 26th 1791

Letters from 13 Churches were read and the messengers names enroled as follows.

Tates Creek—David Thompson, John More & William James
South, Elkhorn—Lewis Craig Geo S Smith Jno Haydon & A
    Hampton
Clear, Creek—J Taylor Jas Rucker Lewis Castleman, R. Young
Washington—Wm Wood Phil Drake Miles, W. Conway.
Cooper, Run—Augustin Eastin James Garrard James L. Smith
Bryans—Ambrose Dudley Alex Monroe William Waller & Jno
    Mayson
Forks Elkhorn—Wm. Hickman, Rd Thomas Anthony Thompson
Strods Fork—John Strode
Town Fork—John Gano Edward Payne Thos Lewis North Ashby
    Wm Payne
Cove Spring—Morias Hansberry

Mays Lick—Mathew Grey
Buck Run—Jas Dupuy Wm Green
Marble Creek—John Price Arthur Tall Tobt Fryar Sam Reed

Brother James Garrard chosen Moderator & Bro John Price Clerk

The Church at Clear Creek by their letter request to be received into this assn and their messengers John Verdeman & Wm Maneffee took their seats accordingly

The same request from a Church at Columbia on the N. W. side of Ohio John Smith & John L Gano the messengers who presented their letter, took their seats accordingly

The situation of the Church at the Crossings came under our consideration and it was agreed that they had complied with the advice of the last Association their messengers Elijah, Craig Wm Cave Robert Johnson and John Payne were permitted to take their seats

Quere from the Church at Bryans, Is Baptism valed when administered by a Pedo Baptist Minister upon proffession of Faith—refered till the next Association

Resolved that this association disapprove of the memorial which the last Association agreed to send to the convention on the subject of Religious liberty and the abolition of slavery.

A letter from the general committee of the united Baptists Churches of Virginia (with the minutes of their proceeding) was received and read in which they requested a correspondence to be opened with this Assn It was agreed to commence a correspondence with them and our Brethren Augustin Eastin & James Garrard are requested to write the first letter to them in behalf of this Association.

Brethren William & Philip Drake are appointed to write a circular letter against the meeting of the next Association

Signed by order of the Association

JAMES GARRARD Modr.

JOHN PRICE Clk.

At an association held at Tates Creek Madison County August 31st 1792

Brother James Garrard delivered the introductory from

Ephe. 5. 1. "Be ye therefore followers of God as dear Children."

After worship proceeded to business

Bro. Jno. Gano chosen Moderator & Augustine Eastin Clerk Letters from 23 Churches were read viz.

Churches	Messengers	Baptised	Recd by letter	Dismissed let.	Excommunic'd	Dead	Total No. each churches
Tates Creek	John Moore Wm Jones & Ralph Magee		8	7	2		63
South Elk.	A Lewis Craig Geo S. Smith Jno Price & J Keller	2	1	14	12	1	170
Great Xing	Elijah Craig Robt Johnson Will Cave John Payne	9	14				85
Clear Creek	John Taylor Donald Holmes L Castleman A. Dale	1	2	14	6	2	260
Bryans	Ambrose Dudley. Wm Waller Alex Monroe & J Mason	35	6	8	4	2	254
Townfork	John Gano Will Payne Thomas Lewis	5	9	1			49
Coopers Run	Augustin Eastin Jas Garrard Jazreel Ellis, & Wm Hutcheson	24	11	8	1	1	120
Boons Creek	Geo Winn Owen Winn Jas Moony J. Whaley	7	2	2		1	79
Washington	Wm Wood Ro. Taylor Jno Taylor Jr.	6	8	3			100

Churches	Messengers	Baptised	Recd by letter	Dis- missed let.	Excom- munic'd	Dead	Total No. each churches
Hanging fork	Jno Mason. Wm. Marshall & Jno Steel	2	1	2	1		53
Marble Ck.	Jno Price. S. Denny. Danl. Bryan	2	1		1	1	97
Fork, Elkhorn.	Wm Hickman A. Thompson	2	9	1	3	2	93
Buck Run.	Jno & Jas. Dupuy. & Wm Green	4	1		1		67
Indian Run.	J. Withers & T. Hubbard				1		5
Mays lick.	Nathl. Hixon T. Mills,	14	12		1		47
Green Creek.	G. & Jno. Shortridge & E Poston		2				12
Cave Spring.	M. Hansberry & Will Davis	1	5		1		23
Taylors fork	Jas Lee. Ch. Waterman						
Columbia.	W. Ter. Jno Smith Tho Wade	6	3			1	37
Strodes Creek.	Joel Heavens				2		8
Indian Creek.	S. L. Ish. Munson. Frs. Mann						17
Sugar Creek.	F Adams. Wm. Walden. Luke Adams	2					12
Cedar Creek.	Jno James., Jno Verdeman	1					19
Tennesse	no inteligenge						
Cumberland.							21

Two Churches viz Indian Creek (South Licking) & Sugar Creek made for reception in this union & were received.

Our sister Association of Salem, sent her letter an minutes which were read and her Messengers, William Taylor & Joshua Morris took their seats.

A letter was received and read from the congregation of Baptist on Cave Run Woodford County setting fourth that the association advised the Brethren at the Great Crossings not to consider the persons received by either party since the division, members of the Church untill they give satisfaction to the whole body in case of an union betwen them which advise they say they have complied with.

On motion ordered that the same lie on the table.

Adjourned till 9 OClock tomorrow morning

Saturday Sept 1st met pursual to adjournment After divine service business follows

A request from the Church at Clear Creek to reconsider the advise given by the association adjourned from Coopers Run to the Great Crossing in Sept last which advise is refered to in the Cave Run letter and stands in minute No 6 agreed to take up sd request after much deliberation thereon. Resolved that it is the opinion of the association that the advise given to the Church at the great Crossing by the Association convened at that place in Sept last, requesting the Church to put away her members in case of an union betwen them and, the party that left thim in a disorderly manner was not agreeable to the principals upoñ which this Association is united.

Ordered that our Brethren James Garrard Robert Johnson and James Price be a Committee to write to the Salem Association, and John, Taylor, John Price and George S Smith are our messengers to the same.

The letter from the Cave Run Congregation of Baptists ordered to be read and their case taken up.

Agreed that our Brethren, John, Gano, Wm, Hickman, John, Taylor, Ambrose, Dudley, George, S, Smith & Lewis, Craig. be a committee to attend them at house to hear and try to accommodate the unhapy difference betwen them and the Great Crossing Church, and report to the nex association.

The Committee appointed by the last association to revise the confession of Faith Continued

The Circular letter by Brethren Wood and Drake read and received

Our Brethren Eastin and Garrard are appointed a committee to continue our correspondence with the general committee of the united Baptists of virginia and send them our minutes and Circular letter.

Our Brethren John Gano and John Taylor will (by divine permission) attend the Church at Columbia to answer their request relative to ordination

Our motion agreed to defer the Queres in the different letters untill next Association.

On motion agreed to permit the minutes and circular letter and the Churches pay the expense of the same to Ambrose Dudley and George S Smith, who are to superintend sa Business and foreward them to the Churches and different corresponding associations and as we receive the minutes and letter of the Middle District Association South of James River Virginia met at Ceder Creek 1st Saturday 1791 agreed to send them a copy of ours as a token of our love and good will to them.

Next association to be held at Bryans Station their Saturday in may next Brother William Wood to preach the Introductory Sermon and in case of failure Brother John Smith.

Signed by order of the Asso.
John Gano Modro
A Eastin Clerk

At an association Began and held at Bryans May 18th Continued by adjournment untill the 21st 1793

At 12 OClock Brother William Wood delivered the introductory Sermon from Isa 27–13 And it shall come to pass in that day the great Trumpet shall be blown and they shall come which are ready to perish.

Letters from 25 Churches were read

The Churches are in general peace but appear to be in a

languishing state few additions haveing been made this year.

Brother James, Garrard, was moderator and Augustin, Eastin, Clerk.

Churches	Messengers	Baptised	Rec'd by letter	Dis- missed	Excluded	Dead	No'
Tates Creek	D. Thompson W. Jones and D. Wilkinson				1		62
South Elk.	H. Lewis Craig Jno Shackleford J. Keller J. Haydon	1	10	20	2		265
Clear Creek	Jno. Taylor John Sutton J. Hitter J. Whitaker	1	4	9	2		265
Great Xing	Elijah Craig R. Johnson Will Cave Jno. Payne	0 7	9	1			100
Bryans	Ambrose Dudley W. Waller Alex Monroe. Leond. Young	6	9	35	4	1	228
Townfork	Ed. Payne. Steph Barton William Stone	6	9	1		1	60
Coopers Run	A Eastin. Jas. Garrard Jaz Ellis, Jas. Starke	1	2	7	1		114
Boons Creek.	George Winn Owin Winn and J. Hazlerig J. Bradly		1	7	1	1	66
Washinton	Will Wood J. Turner and J. Downing	8		3			105
Hanging fork.	Jno. Mason, J. Steel, J. Helms			5	3		46
Marble Creek.	Jno. Price, Robert Fryer S. Denny		1		1		97

Churches	Messengers	Baptised	Rec^d by letter	Dis-missed	Excluded	Dead	Nor
Fork, Elk. H.	William Hickman J. Brown Anthony Thompson		4		2		103
Buck Run.	James Duper & William Green	3	4	3		1	70
Indian Run.	Wm. Marshall J. Wethereford		1				6
Mays Lick	letter	2	5	2	1		51
Green Creek	George & J. Shortridge	1	5				17
Cove Spring.	Morias Hansberry J. Barber						23
Taylors fork	J. Lee & J. Jones						20
Indian Cr.	S. L. Chs Webb Isaac Munson	2	6				25
Columbia	no intelegence						
West Ter.							37
Strodes Fork	J. Oliver	1			2		7
Tennessee Cum.	No public intelegence						21
Grapy Lick	Wm Payne Saml. Deadman	1	6				32
Flat Lick	James Sutton Thos. Starks	1	4				13
		41	80	96	17	4	1847

The Churches at Grapy Lick and Flat Lick at their request were received into this Association and their messengers names enrolled.

Agreed that our Brethren James, Gawarard, and, William Wood and Augustin Eastin be a Committee to arrange the business of this Association and make report on monday morning. Adjourn monday morning 9OClock

Monday May 20th

Met pursuant to adjournment The Committee of Business made report viz

1st Quere from Bryans Is Baptism valid when administered by a Pedobaptist Minister on profession of Faith—

Agreed to advise the Churches to act with discretion in all cases of this nature that have happened prior to this date and that they act with care and caution in similar cases in future.

2 Quere from Town Fork. What is the origin and divine authority of an Association the use and extent of its power the principals on which admission into or rejection from it are justifiable (differed)

3 Quere from the Forks of Elkhorn What is the work of an Elder when considered distinct from a minister or Deacon (defered)

Nothing is more earnestly to be desired among the people of God. than union and fellowship; Agreed therefore, that an attempt be made for a union with the Baptist Association south of Kentucky and that our brethren Ambrose Dudley James Garrard John Taylor John Price & Augustin Eastin, are hereby appointed a committee to attend their next association with full power to confer freely on terms of union and if hopeful appearances of effecting the same they may with them (Brethren) apoint a time and place for the Churches in both unions to convene by their Deligates to carry said union in effect.

Brethren John Price & Ambrose Dudley are requested to write the circular letter to the Churches—William Wood to the Philadelphia Association of Baptists—John Mason and Joseph Helms to that of Salem, and Elijah Craig to that of Ketocton all to return tomorrow morning.

Agreed to mak an attempt to open a corispondence with the Redstone Association of Baptists and that Brother James Sutton be requested to write a letter for that purpose and present it tomorrow morning.

The Committee apointed by the Association at Coopers Run and continued from our last to revise the Confession of

Faith reported that some phrases in the 3rd and fifth Chaps
would be better if put in words easier understood by weak
minds and in Chapter 24th instead of the words "a lawful
Oath is a part of Religious Worship" offer the following
amendment "An oath should be taken in Religious Fear etc."
is all in their opinions that wants any amendment the treatist
of deciplin they think wants amending and enlarging they
are requested to fill up their appointment and report to the
next association.

A letter proposing the printing a Register of the Baptist in
North America by John Asplund was read

The Committee appointed by the last Association to visits
the cove Run Congregation of Baptist made report from the
hopeful appearance of a reconciliation between them and the
Great Crossing Church agreed to defer that Business untill
next Association.

A private letter from our sister Church at Tennessee (Cumberland Settlement) was read by which they appear to be in
great distress for the want of ministral helps and earnestly
request assistance.

Adjourn till 9 OClock tomorrow morning

Tuesday May 21st

Met pursuant to adjournment The Circular letter of the
Churches and letters to the different Associations being
presented and read were approved.

Brethren James Garrard and Ambrose Dudley were
appointed Messengers to the association of Ketocton
and Philadelphia and Brother Jas Sutton to that of
Salem

The Church at Washington requests ministerial helps to
attend their Meeting on the 3rd Saturday in August next
Brethren Elijah Craig Augustin Eastin and John Shackelford
will (by Divine permission) attend their request

Supplies for the Hanging Fork Taylors fork and the Cove
spring Brother James Sutton 3d Saturday in June begining
at the Cove Spring—Brethren Wm Hickman and George S
Smith 3rd Saturday in august begining at Taylors fork and

Brother John Shackleford first Saturday in September begining at the Hanging fork.

Agreed that Brother John Price receive the money for printing the Minutes and circular Letter and superintend the same and after takeing out one copy for each of the coresponding Associations and general Committee of the united Baptists of Virginia that he send to the Churches the number of copies of said Minutes and Letter in proportion to money that each of them may put into his hands.

On motion agreed that the moderator appoint a Treasurer to receive the money sent by the Churches in aid of a Fund about to be raised by this association who appointed Brother Edward Payne.

On Setting the last years accounts there appears to be 31/ in hand of Brother Ambrose Dudley he is directed to pay it to the Treasurer.

On motion agreed to take up the case of the Church at Tennessee and try to engage some of our ministering Brethren to assist them—Brethren James Sutton and John Mason agree to pay a visit the 1st of july and continue with them 6 weeks and at their return John Sutton and F, Adams will also visit them and continue with them a like term. a subscriptition was proposed in the association to defray the Expences of the above Brethren on their journey and the sum of £ 10–6–8 was raised by the members. Agreed that said money should be put into the hands of the Treasurer and that £ 3–6–o out of the fund be added to the above sum and that he pay the same to said Brethren by the moderators orders

Ordered that the Treasurer pay our Clerk for paper and services 14/

Brethren James Dupuy and and William Green are requested to write a circular Letter for the next asson.

Agreed that our next association be at South Elkhorn the 2nd Saturday in October next and that Brother Augustine Eastin preach the introductory sermon and in case of failure Brother. Elijah Craig

JAMES GARRARD Mor
ATTEST A EASTIN Clerk

At an Association began and held at South Elkhorn October 12th 1793 and continued by adjournment until 15th of same month

At 12 OClock Brother Augustin Eastin delivere the introductory sermon from Mathew 3, 16 "There they that feared the Lord etc"

Letters from 25 Churches were read

The Churches are in peace but appear to be in a languishing state few additions haveing been made this year

Brother John Gano was chosen Moderator and Augustin Eastin Clerk

Churches	Messengers	Baptised	Rec^d by letter	Dis-missed	Excl^d	Dead	No.
Tates Creek	No intelegence						62
South Elk. H.	Jno Shackleford Geo. S. Smith Jno Haydon Jno Keller		10	4			152
Clear Creek	James Rucker Donald Holmes James Hiter Richd Young		1	2	2		264
Great Xing.	Elijah Craig. Joseph Redding Robert Johnson Will Cave	8	8		1	1	165
Bryans	William Waller Alex Monroe Leonard Young Jno. Mason	1	5	6	3	1	223
Town fork	Jno Gano Ed. Payne Will Stone			4			64
Coopers Run,	Wm, Hutchinson, Jno, Kirkpatrick	2	3	2	3	1	114
Boons, Creek	Jas, Whaley James, Money			1			66
Washington	Wm, Wood Miles, W, Conway	2	5	14			99

Churches	Messengers	Baptised	Rec.ᵈ by letter	Dis-missed	Excl.ᵈ	Dead	Noʳ.
Hangfork	John, Steel Joseph, Helm			1			43
Marble Creek	John Price Robert Frier Saul, Denny, Saml Reeds			7		1	90
Forks Elkhorn	Wm Hickman John Brown Thomas Hickman	1	5	0	2		105
Buck, run	John Dupuy James Dupuy		2				70
Indian, run	Wm, Marshal John Weathers	1	3				10
Mays, lick	H, M, Curry, Cornelius Drake		9	1			58
Cove spring,	Morias Hansberry Wm Gains John Barbee						22
Taylors fork	James Lee		2				22
Green Creek	William Langore John Shotridge	2	4				36
Indian Creek, S. L.	Isaac Mouson & Jno Jones	2	2				31
Cumberland	W,(est) T,(ennessee) Francis Dunlavy		10		1	1	
Sugar Creek	Feathergail, Adams, Wm, Walden		2				12
Strodes fork	James Ball Levi Ashbrook		6				13
Grapy lick	Wm Payne Thos Hansford	17	9				58
Ceder, Creek	John Vardiman		2	2			19
Flat lick	Jesse Bowles Thos Starke	1	1	1			14
Tennessee, Cumb,	No Inteligence						
Springfield	Jno. Summers Jr, Wm Smith						
		37	80	51	16	5	1695

The last mentioned Church Viz Spring field petitioned for admitance into this union & was received and her messengers names ordered to be enrolled.

Letters and minutes were received from our Sister Association of Salem and letter read and brother William Taylor her Messenger took his seat.

Agreed that Brother John Price Wm Payne and Robert Johnson Assist the Clerk to arrange the business of the Association and report on monday morning

Adjourn till 9 oClock on monday morning

Monday October 14th

The Committee appointed to arrange the Business of the Association reported Viz

1 A reference from the Great Crossings The Brethren from the Great Crossings inform us; they are happly reconciled with the Cove run Congregation of Baptists and now from one Church. The Association agree in and rejoice at sd reconciliation

2 The proceedings of the Committee Appointed by our last Association to visit the Baptist Asson. South of Kentucky and of the general convention who met in consequence of an appointment of sd Committee A large majority of this Asson. approve of sd proceedings: in consequence of which it is agreed that our Brethren John, Price Augustin, Eastin Robert Johnson Edward Payne and John Mason are here by appointed a committee to meet those Brethren who lately broke of from the South Kentucky Assocn and confer with them on further terms of union and report to us. Who reported they had agreed to form, a, union with sd Brethren, and, Churches they represent on the following terms Viz We do agree to receive the regular Baptist Confession of Faith but to prevent its usurping a tiranical power over the Consciences of any, we do not mean that every person is to be bound to the strict observance of every thing therein Contained, Yet that it holds forth the essential truths of the Gospel, and that the Doctrins of Salvation by Christ and free and unmerited grace alone ought to be believed by every

Christian, and mantained by every minister of the Gospel and that we do believe in those Doctrins relative to the Trinity the Divinity of Christ, the sacred authority of the Scriptures the universal depravity of human nature; the total inability of men to help themselves withot the aid of divine grace; the necesity of repentance towards, God, and faith in the Lord Jesus Christ, the justification of our persons entirely by the righteousness of Christ imputed; Believers Baptism by immersion only and self-denial. And that the supreme Judge by which all controversies of religion are to be determined, and, all decrees of Councils opinions of ancient writers doctrins of men and private spirits are to be examioned and in whose sentance we are to rest, can be no other than the Holy Scriptures, delivered by the Spirit, into which scripture so delivered our faith is finially resolved

Agreed that the sense of this Asson. be taken on terms; a large majority express their satisfaction with the same, and agree to form an union thereupon—upon which those Brethren of the South Kentucky Asso. refered to above were Called in and the right hand of fellowship (the token of union) given to them by the Moderator.

3 A refference from the Town fork letter of 1792 what is the origin and devine Authority of an Association the use and extent of its power the principals on which admission into and rejection from are justifiable.

Agreed that our Brethren John Gano Joseph Reding and Francis Dunlavy are hereby appointed a committee to prepare an answer to sd quere for the inspection of our next Association.

The circular Letter by Brethren James Dupuy and William Green was read and ordered to ly on the Table.

From a request of the church at Columbia agreed to set apart wednesday 23 Just as a day of fasting and humiliation before God for the preservation and success of our Army against the Enemy and for the suppression of vice in our land we also recommend our Brethren to send a copy of this order to the different denominations of Christians among whom we reside hopeing they will join us in our petitions.

Agreed that our Ministering Brethren be requested to consider the situation of our Sister Churches South of Kentucky and visit them as often as possible,

Adjourn till 10 oClock tomorrow morning

Tuesday Morning

A number of members being absent agreed that a post-script be added to our circular letter signifying our grief for the absence of so many members from their seats

The circular Letter being read a second time Brethren Francis Dunlavy and John Price are requested to retire with Brother James Dupuy and make some amendments.

A Letter was read from an Association of Baptists on the Holston river requesting a Corispondence with us, Agreed that Breth Augustin Eastin James Garrard & Edmond Mountjoy are here by appinted a committee of Corespondents to keep up a corispondence with the general committee of the united Baptists of Virginia the Middle District Asso. South of James River and the sd Association of Holston and send them copies of our minutes and letter.

Agreed that Brethren George S Smith John Price John Shackleford & John Taylor are our Messengers to a Conference to be held at Jessamine Meeting-house by our United Brethren the 4th Saturday in Nov next.

Agreed that our Brethren, Augustin Eastin, James, Garrard Edmund, Mountjoy & Francis, Dunlavy, are here by appointed a Committee to prepare a plan and point out the uses of the association Fund for the Consideration of our next meeting.

Agreed that at our next Asson the Moderator Close the service by Preaching a Sermon.

Whereas some disadvantages have arisen from the unsetled meetings of this association agreed therefore that in future there be but one anuel meeting and that the time of the same be on the 2nd Saturday in August—Brother George S Smith is appointed to Preach the Introductory

Sermon at our next; and in case of failure Brother John Shackleford and the place of the meeting at Marble Creek

Agreed that quarterly Meetings be at Indian Creek (S Licking) first Friday in December next and continue three days Brethern George, S, Smith James Dupuy & Donald Holms be requested to attend the same. At Mays Lick last friday in March to continue three days and that Brethren Augustin Eastin James Garrard John Smith & Robert Clark be requested to attend the same and at Cove Spring the first friday in June to continue thre days and that Brethren Joseph Reding William Hickman Ambros Dudley & John Taylor be requested to attend the same.

Agreed that Brother John Price is requested to receive the money for printing the Minutes and Circular letter and superintend the same and after takeing out one copy for each of the Corisponding Associations and general Committee of the United Baptists of Virginia and that he send to the Churches the No of Copies of sd Minutes and letter in proportion to the money that each of them may put into his hands.

Ordered that the Treasurer pay the Clerk 14/ for paper, and, service

The following Churches contributed to the Fund Viz Columbia 2 Dollars, Indian Run half a dollar

JOHN GANO Modr

A EASTIN Clerk

The State of the Fund is as follows Viz Was in the hands of Brother after Printing the Minutes

1792	£	/.	//.	o
Coopers, run paid in May 1793		I	o	o
Great Crossings paid at the same time		o	12	o
Forks of Elkhorn paid a dito		o	3	o
Columbia paid in October 1793		o	12	o
Indian Run paid at same time		o	3	
		4	I	o

1792	£	/.	//.	o
Expenditures				
Clerk received in May 1793 for paper and services		o	14	o
Ditto received in October for same		o	14	o
		1	8	o
Bal		2	13	o

ATTEST, A EASTIN CLK

At an Association began and held at Marble Creek August 7th 1794 and continued by adjournment untill the 9th At 12 oClock Brother George Smith delivered the introductory sermon Rom 12th 5th so we being many are one body in Christ and every one members one of another,

2 Letters from 24 Churches were read

3 Brother Ambrose Dudley Chosen Modr and John Price C

Churches	Messengers	Baptised	Rec^d by letter	Dis^d by Do	Excluded	Dead	No^s
Tates, Creek	Dod, Thompson, Raph, Mcgee, Wm, Jones						62
S. Elkhorn	Jno, Shackleford, G, S Smith Jno Keller	1	1	4	1		149
Clear Creek	Jno, Taylor, Jas, Rucker, Jas Hitter		1	4	5		256
G, Crossings	E, Craig, Wm Cave, Robert Johnson B H Collins						167
Bryans A,	Dudley, Wm, Waller, Jno, Mason Lend Young	6	2	1		5	219
Town Fork	Wm, Stone, Henry, Payne, Thos Lewis	4	2	2	1		55

Churches	Messengers	Baptised	Rec'd by letter	Dis'd by Do	Excluded	Dead	Nos
Coopers run	Jas, Garrard, Jerrel Ellis Edmund Mountjoy	3	4	3	2		115
Boons Creek							66
Washington	Robt Taylor A Houghton		16	1	1	2	107
Hang, Fork	John Steel	3	4	5		1	44
Marble, Creek	John Price Robt Fryer			6			84
Forks, of, Elkhorn	William Hickman Thos Hicklin	6	4	3	2	1	114
Buck, run	John Dupuy James Dupuy		1	3	1	2	63
Indian, run							10
Mays, Lick	J Losson	1	4				63
Cove, Spring	Jno Mason Morias Hansberry	1	3				27
Taylor Fork	Jesse Lee Charles Westerman		2				22
Green Creek							26
Indian Creek	Ise Mason George Eaton		6	2			35
Columbia	John Smith Francis Dunlavy	6	3	1		1	55
Sugar Creek							12
Strodes, Fork	Reubin Smith John Oliver						
Grapy Lick	Wm Payne Saml Dedman	5	15	2			78
Cedar Creek							19
Flatt Lick	James Sutton Caleb Hall	9	6				28
Spring, Field,	Jas White John Smith	1	2		1		19
Total		36	76	38	16	13	1904

Brother James Garrard & William Payne appointed to write the Circular letter Brother John Smith John Taylor & John Price are appointed to arrange the business of the Association.

Adjournd till Monday Morning 8 OClock.

Monday Morning August 9th

Met according to adjournment and after divine service proceeded to Consider the union formed last Association and agreed to the following decliration. This Association taking into Consideration the unhappiness in some of the Churches as appears from their letters expressing their apprehensions of the Associations departing from their constitutional principals in forming an union with five Churches (late of the Association South of Kentucky) at our last Association. In order to remove all uneasiness from the minds of our brethren we do declare that we never had any design or desire to depart from the Constitutional principals of the Elkhorn Association; believeing them to contain the essential truths of the Gospel upon which Christian union and fellowship can only be suported and in which we hope through grace to remain

Agreed to dissolve said union on account of several Churches being desatisfied therewith, and, that Brethren John Price and Robert Frier write to the said Brethren informing them thereof.

Agreed that Quarterly meeting be held at South Licking the third Friday Saturday & Sunday in November & that Brethren David Thompson Elijah Craig Wm Payne and James, Rucker attend; the Second saturday and sunday in March at Washington and that Brethren Augustin, Eastin, John, Price, and James Sutton attend; Grapy Lick the friday before the second sunday in June and that Brethren John Shacleford Ambrose Dudley John Taylor and James Garrard attend.

Agreed that Brethren John Taylor & James Sutton write to the Salem Association and be our messengers there.

Agreed that Brethren John Smith and Francis Dunlavy prepare, an answer to the Quere from Town fork.

Agreed that the same Brethren who were appointed to prepare a plan for an association Fund and point out its use. be continued and make report to the next Association.

Agreed that the next Association be at Coopers run on the second saturday in August and that Brother Elijah Craig preach the Introductory sermon and in case of failure Brother John Mason. Brother Wm Payne appointed to write the Circular letter for the next Asson

AMBROSE DUDLEY Modr

JOHN PRICE Clerk

At an Association began and held at Coopers run August 8th 1795 and continued by adjournment untill the 10th 1st At 12 oClock Brother Elijah Craig delivered the introductory sermon from John 31st 16.

2nd Letters from 23 Churches were read

3rd Brother James Gerrerd was Chosen Moderator, and, John Price Clerk.

Churches	Messengers	Baptised	Rec^d Do	Dis^d by letter	Excluded	Dead	Total
Tates Creek.	John Wilson & Danl Williams			6		3	46
South Elk. H.	Jno Shackleford. A. Williams J Keller J Price	2	11	10	3		149
Clear Creek.	J Sutton. R. Cave J Hicks, R Young		3	6	4	1	248
Great Xing.	E. Craig Will. Cave Robt Johnson		10	14	5		147
Bryans.	Wm Waller Jno Mason Leonard Young	1	17	32	2	2	200
Townfork	Jno Gano. Wm Stone Nat Ashby		3	2	1		52

Churches	Messengers	Baptised	Rec⁴ Do	Dis⁴ by letter	Excluded	Dead	Total
Coopers Run.	A Eastin, J Garrard, J. Ellis, E Montjoy	I	8	3	3		119
Washington	William Wood		15				122
Hanging fork	Joseph Helms		4	I			47
Marble Creek	Jno Price, A Frier Saml. Reed		I	4	4	2	75
Fork Elk. H.	Wm Hickman Tho Hickling J Murphy	2	6	6	3	I	109
Boons Creek	No intelegence						66
Buck Run	Joseph Minter		6	3	2		63
Mays lick	Lawrence Cabill Jno Johnson	2	7	2	5		65
Cove Spring	Wm Gaines Lipson Norvill	I	10	I		I	35
Green Creek	Geo Shortridge Manl Tabbut	I	5				29
Indian Creek	Isaac Munson Geo Eaton	I	5				41
Sugar Creek	Fethugil Adams Jno Martin						11
Columbia	No intelegence						55
Grapy Creek	Wm Payne & Moses Frazier	2	9	5	2	I	80
Cedar Creek.	Robert Smith Wm Manifee		3				21
Flatlick	Richd Thomas Tho Stark Wm Thompson	3	5	4			32
Springfield,	Donald Holmes Will Smith	2	3		I		20
Indian Run	Wm Marshall James Dean				2		9
Strodes fork.	John Oliver			3	I		9
Bracken	Lewis Craig Thomas Killis						45

Churches	Messengers	*Baptised*	*Rec^d Do*	*Dis^d by letter*	*Excluded*	*Dead*	*Total*
Licking	Wm Decorsy Benj Archer						12
Forks Licking	Alexr. Monroe George Monroe						18
Great bend of Ohio	John Taylor						23
		18	131	102	38	11	1948

Brethren Donald Holmes and John Shackleford appointed to
write the Circular letter.

Brethren Will Wood E. Craig, & John Price appointed to
arrange the business of the association.

Several strang Ministers being present are invited to take
seats with us.

Adjourned until Monday nine Oclock.

Monday morning Aug. 10. Met according to adjournment
and after divine Service proceeded to business.

Four Churches lately Constituted desired admission into
the association which was accordingly agreed to.

Brethren Augustin Eastin and John Sutton appointed to
write to the Salem association, and our brethren John Gano
and William Hickman are appointed our Messengers to sd
Association

Agreed to consider the quere from Town fork What is the
origin and divine authority of an association the use and
extent of its power—The principals on which permission into
or rejection from it are justifiable.

Answer; That the divine authority of an association are
the commands in God's word for Christians to assemble together in his name for worship and counsel and union to
Christ and one another and that its use is for mutual edification and assistance to cultivate unniformity of sentiments in

principals and practice and that its power is to regulate and governe itself as a body and give such advice to the Churches as may be for their peace. And that any Church who agrees to the principals on which we ourselves are united ought to be admitted and any Church who openly opposes those principals ought to be rejected.

Received a report respecting an association fund & voted it out of the Association

Request from tates Creek to reconsider the union of the united Baptists.

Quere from Marble Creek: Was not the Association of 1794 guilty of covenant breaking in disolving the union of the united Baptists upon the principals the did? Referred.

Agreed to appoint a committee of five Brethren to confer with the five Churches formally in union with us respecting a full union and report to the next association, the following Brethren were appointed, John, Gano, James, Garrard, Augustin, Eastin, Ambrose, Dudley and John Price.

Quere from Ceder Creek respecting reordaining a Deacon. Answered no necesity for it.

The Circular letter read and approved of. The letter to the salem Association read and approved of.

Agreed to recommend to the Churches to set apart the 2nd Saturday in september as a day of fasting and prayer to implore the divine blessing upon our state and upon the Churches that the Lord would bless his own institution of a preached Gospel that he would check rapid of impiety & infidelity

Quarterly meetings to be held at Green Creek the 2nd friday Saturday and sunday in November and that Brother Wm Payne and Brother Ambrose Dudley attend the same

At Hanging on the 2nd Friday Saturday & Sunday in March and that Brethren John Gano and William Hickman do attend the same At Mays Lick the 2nd Friday Saturday and Sunday in June and that the Brethren Augustin Eastin James Garrard Lewis Craig and Wm Wood do attend the same

Agreed that the next Association be held at Town Fork

the 2nd Saturday in August next and that Brother Gano
preach the introductory sermon and in case of failure brother
William Wood. And Brother Gano will write the Circular
letter for the year 1796.

JAMES, GARRARD, Modr
JOHN, PRICE, Clerk

At an Association began and held at Town fork August
13th 1796 Saturday 13th At 12 oClock Brother Gano delivered the introductory sermon from Psalms 133.1 verse.
Letters from 28 Churches were read Brother Ambrose
Dudley Chosen Moderar and Brother John Price Clerk

Churches	Messengers	Baptised	Rec^d by letter	Dis^d by letter	Ex-cluded	Dead	Total
Tates Creek	Jno Moore Danl. Williams		2	4			40
S. Elk. H.	J.Shackleford, J White, J Keller J Haydon		10	7	6		146
Clear Creek.	R. Cave, J Hiter R. Young. A Dale	3	5	25	5		225
G. Crossing	J Redding, R. Johnson J Wilson	2	13	50	6	3	102
Bryans	A Dudley W. Waller, J. Mason, B Collins		19	20	3	4	194
Coopers Run.	A Eastin, J Garrard J Ellis		11	9	3	2	114
Townfork	J. Gano. F Barret, E. Payne, J. Beatty	1	5	4	2	1	51
Washington	Wm Wood, Meredith Helms			36	1	1	91
Hangingfork	John Steel R. Smith	1	3	7	2	1	42
Marble Creek	J. Price, R Frier, D. Bryan		3	2	1	2	68
F Elkhorn	Wm Hickman T. Hickling J. Haydon		17	1	1	5	123

Churches	Messengers	Baptised	Rec^d by letter	Dis^d by letter	Ex-cluded	Dead	Total
Boons Creek,	G. Winn, O. Winn, J. Hazlerig			7	9	1	43
Buck Run	J. Minter, Wm. Green		6	1	7	1	60
Mays lick	J Porter, C Drake Wm Allen	3	10	3			75
Stoney Point	J Mason, L. Norrill		1	2			34
Green Creek	R. Ashby, Wm. Williams		4	2	1	1	28
Indian Creek.	T. Veach, G Forrest			1			40
Columbia	Jno Smith, Peter Smith,	1	11	6	2		72
Grap lick	M Frazier S Dedman	5	16	4	2		96
Flat lick.	J Jamison J Felps	1	2	1			34
Springfield.	Wm Payne. D. Holmes	1	10	4		1	27
Indian Run.	Wm Marshall Wm Lerenby		8	1	1		15
Tennessee	No intelegence						21
Strodes fork	do						9
Bracken	L Craig R Smith J Blassingham P. Drake	24	29				92
Ceder Creek	no intelegence						21
Mouth of Licking,	Thomas Landsey						12
Forks of Licking,	Alex Moroe Jno Saunders	1	1	1			18
Bulets Burg,	Jno Taylor, Wm Cave						
M Connels Run	E Craig J Payne						75
Stone Lick	J Singleton R Park						20
		43	193	204	43	24	1934

Two Churches lately constituted desired admission into the Association which was accordingly agreed to

Received a letter and Messenger from the United Baptists Association and appointed our Brethren Joseph Redding, Lewis Craig and Ambrose Dudley to confer with them respecting an union.

Received a Letter and Messengers from the Salem Association.

Brethren Augustin Eastin, & John Price are appointed to arrange the business of the Association.

Brother John Gano and Elijah Craig write to the Salem Association. Peter Smith and Wm Payne to the Cotocktin Association. Brother Toler being present was invited to take a seat with us. Adjourn till Monday 9 OClock

Monday Morning August 15th

Met according to adjournment and after divine service proceeded to business. Complaints being made by some members of the Association against Boons Creek Church. Do advise said Church to call for Counsel from the Sister Churches and endeavour to settle those differances between themselves and said Members

Agreed that in regard to an union with our united Baptist Brethren it is the wish of this Association that every possible and friendly effort be made in Christian love to cultivate untimasy and harmony in converseing praying and preaching together which will give an oportunity to know how near we agree in Gospel Principles and Discipline And that a Committee be appointed to confer with any Committee they may appoint and whatever plan they may agree to be made known to the differant Churches for their consideration.

Brethren John Gano Augustin Eastin Joseph Redding and Ambrose Dudley accordingly are appointed.

Quere from Marble Creek withdrawn by their Messenger.

Quere from McConnels run. Is the ancient and general custom of preaching funeral Sermons founded on the Scriptures or not.

Refered. Brethren William Payne & William Hickman appointed our messengers to the Salem Association.

Quere from Licking Whether the Church is Justifiable in shuting the door against a member of a Sister Church (that offers his membership) for the cause of retailing of Liquors agreeable to Law; Answered No.

The Circular letter read and approved of:

The Letters of the Catocktin and Salem Associations read and approved of:—

Quarterly meetings to be held at Cedar creek the second Saturday and sunday in November. and that Brethren Robt Smith John Shackleford and Joel Noel and John Mason do attend the same.

At the Forks of Licking the second Saturday and sunday in March and that Brother, John, Taylor, and, Brother, Augustin, Eastin do attend the same

At Tates Creek the second Saturday and Sunday in June and that Brother Joseph, Redding, Brother Donald, Holms, and Brother John Price do attend the same

Next Association to be held at Clear creek the second saturday in August and that Brother John Shackleford preach the introductory sermon and in case of failure Brother Augustin Eastin, and Brother Joseph Redding will write the circular Letter for the year 1797

AMBROSE DUDLEY Modr
J PRICE, Clerk

At an Association began and held at Clear creek August the 12th 1797.

At 12 OClock Brother John Shackleford preached the introductory Sermon Ephesians 3 Chapt 8 Verse

Letters from 30 Churches were read.

Brother Ambrose Dudley Chosen Moderator and Brother John Price Clerk.

Churches	Messengers	Baptised	Rec'd by letter	Dis'd by letter	Excluded	Dead	Total
Tates Creek	Jno Moore Ralph Magee						37
S. Elk. H.	J Shackleford, G Smith J Haydon J Keller	18	7	21	2	1	147
Clear Creek	J. Sutton, R. Cave, R, Young, J Hiller		4	16		1	212
G Crossing	J. Redding, R, Johnson, J Willson	6	5	4	2	1	106
Bryans A,	Dudley, Wm, Waller, J, Mason, B, Collins	10	7	16	3	2	185
Townfork	J Gano J Beatty Wm Stone	1	4	1		1	54
Coopers Run	Augustin Eastin J Ellis Edmund Montjoy	1	2	3	5	2	107
Washington	John Taylor	77	25	4			200
Hanging fork	J, Smith. Reuben, Smith			2			39
Boons Creek	L, Bradly, J, Haselrig, S Talbot		3	1	2		48
Marble, Creek,	J Price Robt Fryer	1		5	3	2	58
F of Elkhorn,	Wm, Hickman, T, Hickling J, Edrington J Haydon		12	3		3	127
Buck run	J Minter Wm Green			15			43
Mays Lick,	D, Holms C, Drake, T, Longly	43	18	3			137
Stony, point,	J Mason Lipscomb Norrel			5			29
Indian, Creek	Isc Muson, G, Forrest			4			34
Bracken	L Craig W Holton S Hieat J Blassingame	126	17	33	6	4	157

Churches	Messengers	Baptised	Rec^d by letter	Dis^d by letter	Excluded	Dead	Total
Licking	W Decoursy James Jones	1	10				23
Ceder, Creek	T Hansford J Rinfow		2			1	31
Forks, of Licking	G, Hume J, Thobald		1				20
Bullets Burg	J Taylor G Eave W Cave		20			1	57
M Connels run	E. Craig J Payne R Smith	4	4			1	81
Stone Lick	H M Curry J Singleton	42	9	3			76
Goshen	William Payne Green	1	12				28
Green Creek	R Athley L Simpson	2	2	5	1		26
Lick Creek	Tros Heckly J Barbee						13
Beaver Creek	W Hiller John Cooper						16
		340	190	172	26	20	2335

Three Churches lately constituted desired admission into the Association which was accordingly agreed to.

Received a Letter and Messenger from the Salem Association

Also a letter and Messenger from the United Baptist Asson respecting an union.

Brethren Joseph Redding John Price and Robert Johnson are appointed to arrange the business of the Association.

Brother, Donald, Holms, appointed to write to the Salem Association Adjourned till monday morning 9 oClock

Monday morning August 14th

Met according to adjournment and after prayer proceeded to business. Brother——Jones and Brother Sanders Walker being present were invited to take a seat with us.

Quere from M Connels run, Is the ancient and general practice of preaching funeral sermons founded on the scripture or not?

Answered That funeral procession attended with singing, conforms to much to the anti-Christian customs and ought to be omitted in the Churches of Christ; but there can be no impropriety in a servant of Christ preaching at that time and place for he is to be instant in season or out of season Christian prudence ought to decide on the subject but to suppose a sermon necessary to the decent burial of the Dead we wish discountenanced. Received a report from the Committee appointed to visit the united Baptist respecting an union They reported that they confered with a committee appointed by the united Baptist association on the following principals

1st Respecting man and his utter inability to recover him-Self on which they were agreed, 2dly How and by what means he is recovered (there they agreed) 3dly on regeneration. (in this they agreed) 4thly. On Justification. (on this they agreed) 5thly. On the perseveance of the Saints (here they agreed) 6th. on Church disciplin. (here they agreed) 7th Whether any of our members holding the doctrine of general provision would be a bar of union? This was not answered. The Association approved of the conduct of this Committee and the following proposition was made. Shall we unite with said united Baptists agreeably to the report of the Committee, and acceeded to by them which was agreed to and the right hand of fellowship interchangeably given by the moderator and messengers of said united Baptists association.—

Quere from McConnels run are the Churches bound by scripture to contribute to the support of pastoral ministers? Answered that God hath ordained that they who preach the Gospal should live of the Gospel

Agreed that the Columbia and agjacent Churches be dismissed to form an association; and when formed are dismissed from us.

Agreed to appoint a committee of five Brethren to meet

the Churches of Mason County at Washington to consult with them relative to forming an association John, Gano, Ambrose, Dudley, Augustin, Eastin, John Taylor & George Eve are appointed to attend the first saturday in November. The Letter to the Salem Association was read and approved of and that Brethren William Waller John Taylor and William Payne are appointed our messengers to said Asson.

Brethren Ambrose Dudley Elijah Craig and John Price are appointed our messengers to the united Baptist Association.

The Churches are cautioned to be ware of Robt Smith formerly a member of the Baptist Church at Bracken haveing been excluded from said Church and now preaching in different parts of the state.   Brethren John Gano William Wood Ambrose Dudley Augustin Eastin and John Mason are appointed a committee to guard against any irregularities in the ministry.   The Circular letter was read and approve of

The complaints brought against Boons creek Church last association are accomodated

Next association be held at the Forks of Elkhorn the second saturday in August and that Brother John Sutton preach the introductory sermon and in case of failure Brother John Gano Brother Sutton to write the circular letter

A Dudley Modr
J Price—Clk

At an Association began and held at the forks of Elkhorn August 11th 1798 Saturday at noon the Association was opened with Divine worship Sermon from Peter 2nd Epistle 1 Chap 15 verse Moreover I will endeavour that ye may be able after my decease to have these things always in rememberance.—By Brother John Gano. Brother Ambrose Dudley Moderator Brother John Price Clerk.

Churches	Messengers	Baptised	Rec'd by letter	Dis'd by letter	Ex-cluded	Dead	Total
Tates, creek	John Moor, Thomas, Watts						35
S, Elkhorn	J, Shackleford, J, Keller, J, Lucas.	2		16	1	2	132
Clear, Creek	Carter, Tarrant, R, Cave, A, Dale, J, Theber,		13	1		3	321
G, Crossings	Jos, Redding, D, Neil, J, Willson		6	3	1		108
Bryans,	A, Dudley, B, Collins, J, C, Richardson, J Mason	8	14	13	2	4	188
Townfork	J, Gano, Absalem, Bainbridge	1	1	1		2	53
Coopers run	E, Montjoy, Charles, Smith			10		1	97
Washington	No Intellegence						200
Hanging fork	Joel, Andrew, Ginblin		1	3			37
Boons Creek,	Saml, Habbirt, G, Nallingham						40
Marble creek,	J, Price R, Frier, Daniel Bryan	1	2	3			58
Forks of Elkhorn,	Wm, Hickman, F Hickling		6	8	2	1	121
Buck run,	Saml, Berry, Wm, Green						43
Mays Lick,	D, Holms. F, Young, N Hixon	16	5	5	5	4	144
Stony Point	Jno, Mason, Lipscomb Norrel		2	2			29
Indian creek,	I, Munson Francis, Mann,		3	2			35
Grapy Lick,	Lewis, Corban, William Jeems		10	11	1	1	92
Flatt Lick	John, Jameson, Caleb, Hall	2	5	2		1	43

Churches	Messengers	Baptised	Rec'd by letter	Dis'd by letter	Ex-cluded	Dead	Total
Mount Sterling, Indian run,	D, Barrow J Payne J Coons Wm Marshall Wm	2	7	2			39
	Patterson						19
Braken	Lewis Craig Stephen Hiat	11	3	32		6	166
Ceder Creek	J James Jas Renfroe	1	2	5			28
Licking	John Decourcy	15	9				27
F. of Licking	Saml Bryan Jas Theblis	1	1			2	27
Bulletsburg	John Taylor		5	3			95
McConnels run	J Payne R Smith F Herndon				1	1	84
Stone Lick	Elijah Anderson John Crow	2		7			72
Green Creek	Saml Shortrige					1	25
Goshen	No intelegence						28
Lick Creek	Jas Dupuy John Barbee		3				16
Raven creek	Wm Herndon		7				23
Flower Creek	John Taylor						15
Louis Creek	Wm Cherrith	1	1			1	16
	Total	63,	105,	129,	14,	29,	2376

Two Churches applied for admission and and received a letter and Messenger from the Salem association. Also a Letter and Messenger from the united Baptist Association.

The Circular Letter prepared by brother John Sutton read and rejected. Brother Donald Holms appointed to prepare a Letter to the Churches, Brother Jos. Redding and John Price are appointed to arrange the business of the Association. Brother Johnson and William Cave to write to the Catockton association. Brother John, Taylor and Robert Friyer to write to the United Baptist Association. Brother

John Gano and Wm Payne appointed to write to the Salem Assoc.

Adjourn till Monday 9 oClock

Monday 13th

The association met according to adjournment and after worship proceeded to business The Church at Columbia is dismissed from this Association

Agreed to consider the Quere from Marble Creek, Whether it is consistent with our duty to God and our Children to have them taught while at School to read Books of human institution until they are well acquainted with read the scriptures and whether the reading such books has not a tendency to lead their tender minds into a disestum of the Bible. Answered That the design of sending our Children to School is to have them taught to read and such Books. Tho' of human institution if moral in their nature as will answer that end are the best and after our Children are tought to read we ought to give them every encouragement to read the scriptures.

Agreed to caution the churches of certain John Duncan who has sustained the Character of a Baptist preacher but is not in union with us or any of our sister Churches as we know of and that he is not a man of a fair and religious Character also there is a certain Peter Bainberge in the same situation.

The Letters to the several associations and Circular Letter to the Churches were read and approved of

The next Association to be held at Great Crossings on the second saturday in August next and that Brother David Barrow preach the association sermon and in case of failure Brother Donale Holms, Brother John Price write the Circular Letter and that it be on the Subject of Family Worship.

Agreed to recommend to the Churches to consider the propriety of publickly Catechising their Children.

J PRICE Clk.   AMBROSE DUDLEY Modr

At an Association began and held at the Great Crossings August 10th, 11th, 12th 1799 Divine Worship was opened and a Sermon delivered by Brother Dvd Barrow from John 11th 56 What think ye that he will not come to the feast.

Letters from 28 Churches was read a general complaint of supiness with some additions yet we bless God peace seems to pervade the whole

Brother Ambrose Dudley Chosen Moderator Augustin Eastin Clk

Churches	Messengers	Baptised	Rec'd by letter	Dis-missed	dead	Ex-cluded	Total
Tates Creek	John More Thomas Watts						30
So, Elkhorn	J, Shackleford G Smith J, Kitter S, Ayres	7	5	1		4	146
C, Creek	C Tarrant R Cave A, Dale, R Young						218
Bryans	A Dudley B Collins S Young J Mason	4	1	10		2	173
G, Crossings	J, Redding J, Wilson D, Neal R Johnson		3	6		2	101
Town, Fork	A, Bainbridge J Baily E, Payne W, Stone	1			1	2	45
Coopers, Run	A, Eastin E, Mounjoy, W, Carbin		5	2	1	1	97
Hanging Fork	Letter		1	2		1	35
Boons Creek	G & O Winn Denice Bradley	1	8				39
Marble, Creek,	J, Price W Carr S Wood		8	4	1	3	60
Fks, Elkhorn	Wm Hickman J Haydon	2	2	11	1	2	110
Stony Point	John Mason		3	1		1	30
Indian, Creek	Isace Mason Moses Indicut	2	5	1			41

Churches	Messengers	Baptised	Rec^d by letter	Dismissed	dead	Excluded	Total
Grapy Lick	Lewis, Carbin William, Jones		10				82
Mount Sterling	D Barrow W Smith Jacb Counts	3	6	4		1	214
Flat Lick	Thos, Starke Caleb, Hall	1	1	2			43
Indian run	W, Marshall W Lozenby F, W Carty	2		1			20
Cedar Creek	James Renfrow Wm Bevards						26
M of Licking	W, Decourcy W, Robb F Lindsey	6	2	6		1	46
Forks Licking	A Monroe J Theobald	1	2				27
Bulletsburg	John Taylor George Eve		6	1		1	63
MConnels run	E Craig J Martin R Smith J Payne	2	2				86
Green, Creek	J Crow D Filbert Eli Thomas	2		4			23
Goshen	William Payne	0	3	5	1	1	27
Lick Creek	James Dupuy	2	7		1		24
Raven, Creek	W Williams Andrew Hampton		1	1	1		22
Flower, Creek	F, Griffin John, Ashbrook						19
Hariken, Creek	Even and Saml Jones						11
Elk Lick	Theodore Jaco						6
Russells Creek	John White						15
Drennons Lick	Morgan Bryan						10
							(—)

The last four churches were newly constituted and made aplication for admittance into association and was recd and their messengers took their seats.

Received a Letter and Messengers, (Thomas Ammon and Andrew Tibble) from the united Baptist Assn Also a Letter and Messengers (Wm Taylor and John Penny) from the Salem Association Also a Letter and Messengers (Davie Thompson and Lewis Craig) from the Association called Brackens which was formed by a member of our Sister Churches on the eastwardly side of Licking Also a friendly corisponding Letter from the Ketockton Association Verginia.

Agreed that Brother Daved Barrow write a Letter to the United Baptists Association and Brothers G Smith and John Shackleford to write a Letter to the Salem Association Absalem Baimbrige and John Payne to write to the Braken Association and John Taylor and George Eve write a Letter to the Ketockton Assn. and present the same on monday morning for inspection. Circular Letter by John Price read and ordered to ly on the table.

Brother Daved Thompson Ambrose Dudley and John Taylor to preach to the audiance that may attend to-morrow
Adjourned till Monday 9 OClock

After worship—The Letters wrote by the different persons appointed for that purpose were read and approved of, and the following persons were appointed to attend the different coresponding Associations in this state Viz John, Price, and, Absalom, Baimbridge the United Asson A Dudley J Redding and W. Hickman that of Salem and Augustin Eastin John Taylor and Alexander Monroe that of Bracken.

We find the Churches composeing our Body divided respecting a catechism and the act of catechiseing their Children agreed to let the matter rest at present

The following Churches Viz Hanging fork, Stony point, and cedar Creek, at their request, have leave to join the United Asson

Lick Creek at her request has been to join the Salem Association,

The Church at the Hanging fork asks counsel on the following question

May those who formerly embraced the System of unaversalists, now join us without an utter renunciation of those sentiments We advise they may not— — —

We advise the Churches of our union to be aware of encourageing any stranger to preach among them without proper Credentals and a fair character— — —Circular Letters read a second time and are recd— — —Brother Barrow to write the circular Letter for the next year on the subject of charity, Next Association to be held at Bryans 2nd saturday in August, Brother A Eastin preach the introductory sermon and in case of failure Brother E Craig

   A, Eastin Clk   A Dudley Mod

At an Association began and held at Bryans in Fayette County August the 9th 1800 Brother Augustin Eastin agreeable to appointment preached the introductory sermon from Psalms 73, 24 Thou shalt guide me.

After Sermon Business was opened with Prayer when Brother Ambrose Dudley was Chosen Modr and Brother John Price Clerk.

Letters from 26 Churches were read and messengers names enrolled as follows

Churches	Messengers	Baptised	Rec^d by Letter	Dismis	Dead	Excluded	Total
Tates Creek	John Moore Thomas Watts						29
S Elkhorn	J Shackleford G Smith J Keller	1					127
Clear, Creek	R, Cave J, Tanner R, Young A Dale	7	12	3	1	2	230
Bryans	A, Dudley B, Collins, L Young J, Mason	1	5	12		2	170
G Crossings	J Redding G Eve D Neal J Willson	5	11	18		2	107

Churches	Messengers	Baptised	Rec'd by letter	Dismis	Dead	Excluded	Total
Townfork	J Gano A Baimbridge W Stone N Ashly		3	1			46
Coopers run	A Eastin E Mountjoy W Corbin		1	5		1	93
Boons Creek	Thad Dolin Leonard Bradly		2	2			39
Marble Creek	D Thompson J Price R Frier	2	3	6			59
F Elkhorn	Wm Hickman J Taylor J Scott	6	10	12	2		109
Indian Creek	Isaac Mason Moses Endicott	2	2			1	112
Grapy Lick	L Corbin W Jeems S dedman	3	2	6	1		80
Flat, Lick	Caleb Hall	3	2	2	1	1	40
Mount Sterling	D Barrow J Payne	4	8			1	55
Indian run	J Dean Wm Patterson			4	1		15
M of Licking	J Griffith F Barbee	13	1	24	3	1	38
Forks Licking	Alexander Monroe	1	1	1			24
Bullits Burg	J Taylor Wm, Craig, J, Kertley	22	9	12	1		82
McConnels Run	E Craig J Payne R Smith	4	3	3	—	—	90
Green Creek,	R Athey. E R Thomas	2	2	—	—	—	27
Goshen,	Wm Payne and J. Barker	3	2	—	—	—	32
Raven Creek,	Wm Williamson Wm Ninnord	1	—	—	2	—	21
Flower Creek,	J Ellis. J Ashbrook	1	4	—	—	—	25
Hariken Creek,	J M. Wharten J Barker	1	3	—	1	—	14
Elk Lick.	J Mulberry Abraham Field	—	3	—	—	—	9

Churches	Messengers	Baptised	Recᵈ by letter	Dismis	Dead	Excluded	Total
Drennens Creek,	Morgan Bryan	—	7	—	—..	—	18
Dry Run	J Leatherer L Chrislar	—	—	—	—	—	21
		82	96	101	13	12	1642

The Church at Dry Run being lately constituted made application for admittance into this union and was Received.—

Letters from several correspondent Associations were read from the Ketockton Salem and the united. Brother Redding & the Clerk appointed to arrang the business of the Association. Messengers appointed them Brother Taylor & Hickman Salem Baimbridge & Smith Dudley the United Baimbridge, Payne, Redding & Eve the Bracken, Brother Eastin to write to the Salem Association,

Brother Payne to the Ketockton Asson Brother Barrow to the united Association Brother Baimbridge to the Bracken Asson Adjourn till 9 OClock Monday morning

Met pursuant to adjournment.

The circular letter read revised and aproved of The Letters from the coresponding Association red and approved of

Brethren Eastin, Dudley and Price appointed a Committee of corespondence to write to the Philadelphia Association. Harikin Church dismissed to Join the united Association. The Church at Buck run desolved by mutual consent.

Next association to be held at South Elkhorn the second saturday in August next Brother Dudley to preach the Introductory sermon and in case of failure Brother Eve. Brother Eastin to write the Circular Letter for 1801.

JOHN PRICE Clerk.   AMBROSE DUDLEY Modr.

At an Association began and held at South Elkhorn Fayette County. August the 8th 1801 The Association was opened with divin worship sermon from Gallations 6 & 14

But God forbid that I should glory save in the Cross of Christ.

Letters from 26 Churches were read Brother David Barrow Moderator Brother J Price Clk

Churches	Messengers	Baptised	Rec^d by letter	Dis^d by letter	Dead	Excluded	Total
Tates Creek	Daniel Williams Thos Hall	35	1	5		1	60
S. Elk. H.	J. Shackleford, G. Smith, J. Keller, J. Young	309	39	25	2	10	438
Clear Creek	R. Cave, J. Rucker, S. Gill, R. Young	326	22	24		1	558
Bryans,	A Dudley. J. Mason, R. Robertson J. Robn	367	39	18		4	561
Great, Cross- ings	J, Redding J. Sug- gett R, Johnson J, Johnson	376	19	76	3	1	423
Town, fork	J Gano A Bain- bridge W Stone B Stout	71	7	6			118
Coopers, run	A Eastin E Mount- joy H Corbin	30	1	28		1	100
Boons Creek	T Dolin D Bradly G Mure	44		11		1	82
Marble Creek	J Price A Bouers H Carr R Frier	133	9	9	1	3	188
Forks Elkhorn	W Hickman J Scott J Haydon	216	17	47	2	3	267
Indian Creek	M Endicott G For- rest	22	5	1	—	1	67
Grapy Lick	L Corbin R Mc- Donald W Jeans	107	11	3		2	195
Flat Lick	Ths Stark R Thomas	43	5	2		4	86
Mount Ster- ling	D Barrow J Payne E Smith	6	6	1			66

Churches	Messengers	Baptised	Rec^d by letter	Dis^d by letter	Dead	Excluded	Total
Indian run	B Withers W Larenby W Williams	37	4	2			55
Mouth of Licking	C Thompson J Thellar			3	1	3	30
Forks of Licking	A Monroe J Turner	12	2	4			34
Bullets Burg	J Taylor W Cave J Craig J Kertly	104	7	5	2		186
McConnels, run	E Craig J Payne R Smith	156	3	21		5	220
Green Creek	J Harebrig J Hedges R Athey	51	5	6			77
Goshen	Wm Payne C Tracy J Barker	50	11	1		1	92
Beaver Creek	NC Williams A Hampton W Campbell	106	2	2	1		127
Town, Fork	T Griffin J Ellis	10	3	1			39
Elk Lick	J Mulbury A Fields	29	3	1			40
Drennens Creek	Morgan Bryan	12	2	11			21
Dry Creek	M Vicors L Crisler	6	7				34
Mouth of Elkhorn	W Rowlet E Calvert	19	4	—	—	—	45
Eagle Creek	A Robertson J Gail	—	—	—	—	—	20
Cylas	C Smith W E Boswell W Kendrick	90	22				132
Gline Creek	J Ford H Green	22	20				52
N Elkhorn	G Eve J Willson J Thompson	170	25	5		5	206
Twins	J Arnold M Barker	0	0	0	0	0	33
S Benson	T Berryman	8	4			1	17
Dry run	T Foster J Withers	16	13				60
Port William	B Craig Wm C Neal	20					97
N Fork	J Nouter	10					29
		3011	318	318	42	47	4853

Ten Churches applied for admission and were recd Received Letters and Messengers from the Salem Bracken & Tates Creek Associations

Brother Joseph Redding A Dudley & J Price are appointed to arrange the Business of the Asson

Adjourn till Monday 8 oClock

Monday 10th of August met according to adjournment after prayer proceeded to Business

Circular read, and, approved Letters to the corisponding Associations read and approved.

Request from South Elkhorn missionaries to the Indian nations. Agreed to appoint a Committee of five members to hear and determine on the Call of any of our ministers & if satisfied therewith to give them credentials for that purpose: To set subscriptions on foot to receive collections for the use of said mission and it is recommended to the Churches to encourage subscriptions for said, purpose and have the money Lodged with the Deacons to be applied for that purpose wheneve Called for by the Committee the following Brethren are appointed David Barrow Ambrose Dudley John Price Augustin Eastin G Smith or any three of them

Agreed that a Committee be appointed to attend the separate Association and write them a friendly letter and use such means as may appear right to them to bring about a union and if it should appear necessary that they call a convention of the Churches to carry the union into effect the following Brethren are appointed David Barrow Ambrose Dudley J Price Wm Payne & J Redding.

Agreed to appoint a committee to draw a plan to restore excluded members emigrating to this Country and present it to the next Association Brother Dudley Eastin and Price are appointed. Brother Wm Payne to write the Circular Letter for 1802 Agreed that the Churches who are in union with us that reside in the North part of our Bounds are at Liberty to use their own discretion in forming an Association and that Brother Eve and Baimbridge do advise them.

Messengers appointed to attend the corisponding Associations to be held at Coopers run the Second Saturday in August next Introductory Sermon Brother Gano and in case of failure Brother Redding.

Agreed that Brother Walter Cave Richard Young Charles Smith J Payne James Haydon John Mason be appointed a committee to receive the bounty of the Churches for the benefit of our aged Brethren John Gano David Thompson & J Sutton as an indication of our Love and care of them in their old age and it is recommended to the Churches to make frequent Contributions & send them to the committee who are to distribute the same as to them may appear right and render an account to the Association what they have received and from whom and how they have distributed the same.

DAVID BARROW Modr
J PRICE Clk

At an Association began and held at Coopers run Bourbon County State of Kentucky Augus 14th 15th 16th 1802

The Association was opened with divine worship Brother Redding preached the Association Sermon from first John 4th 19th we love him because he first loved us. Brother Augustin Eastin Chosen Moderator and John Price Clerk

Letters from 26 Churches were read

Churches	Messengers	Baptised	Rec'd by letter	Dismisse by Let	Excluded	Dead	Total
Tates Creek	John More John Watts	32	5	2	3	1	91
S Elkhorn	J Shackleford J Keller S Ayres	15	3	147	15	3	294
Clear Creek	R Cave J Rucker D Mitchum R Young	10	3	138	5	1	378
Bryans	A Dudley J Mason Le Young B Collins	44	12	308	6	2	292

Churches	Messengers	Baptised	Rec.d by letter	Dismisse by Let	Excluded	Dead	Total
Great Crossings	J Redding R G Johnson J Johnson Jo Suggett	29	11	20	15		421
Town Fork	J Gano A Baimbridge H Payne T Cox	6	5	3	3	4	120
Coopers run	A Eastin E Montjoy W Corbin	17	3	4	4	1	98
Boons Creek	T Dolin D Bradley J Baly	5	1	9	5		73
East Hickman	A Brown D Barker M Whitam		1	40	3		146
Forks Elkhorn	W Hickman J Haydon H Edward	20	7	11	6	—	305
Indian Creek	John Mason G Forest L Neach	33	3	7	1	1	95
Grapy Lick	L Corbin W Jeans R McDonnald H Stanford	25	3	32	2		193
Flat Lick	T Stark A Parker	20	5	20	1	1	8
Mount Sterling	D Barrow J Payne E Smith	2	3	3	1		62
Mount Moriah	W Patterson L Waters P Withers	3	2	14	1		46
Mouth Licking	M Gray J Johnson	1	7	3			35
Forks Licking	A Monroe J Theobald	13	12	6			54
Bullets Burg	W Cave J Kirtley	20	6	15	1	2	197
McConnels run	E Craig J Payne J Hawkins T Henderson	24	2	2	6	1	216
Green Creek	J A Wilkinson R Any N Talbot	40	11	12	6		120
Goshen	J Thompson L Ashbrook	4	3	7	5		84
Raven Creek	A Hampton E Chinn	5	2	58	4		72

Churches	Messengers	Baptised	Rec'd by letter	Dismisse by Let	Excluded	Dead	Total
Flower Creek	B Grovens T Rush	1	1	4	3		31
Elk, Lick	A Field J Mulbury	5		3	2		40
Drennons Creek	Joel Jackson	4	2		2	2	23
Dry Creek	M Viker L Chrisler	5	2				41
Mouth Elkhorn	Holloman J Bartlete	6	1	6	1	1	45
Eagle Creek	J Reese S Cobb		1	1			20
Silas	C Smith W Hendrick F Craig B Rendrik	16	4	7		3	140
N Elkhorn	G Eve J Willson J Martin	21	6	1	9	3	220
Glens Creek	J Bonderant Wm Garnett	3		5	2		43
Twins	J Scott S Brockman	3	5		3		38
S Benson	W Hickman	11	3			1	30
Dry run	F Foster Withers W Rhodes N Long	4	19	2		1	80
Port William	W Parker D Applegate	1	3	4	7		83
N, Fork	J Newton J Undewood	15	12			1	55
Twelve Mile	B Riggs S Betreal	15	7	2		1	23
Rock Bridge	R Thomas H Willson J Neale		5				41
Clover Bottom	A Buckhannon W Lisonley						23
Brushfork	T Ammon J Barnet J Ralkett						92
Bank Lick	T Griffin G Hume	7	10			1	22
Hills Borrough	C Tarrent A Dale G M Daniel	29	3	38			172
Davids, fork	B Robertson J Robertson R Mitchel J Welch	5	12	4	13		297
Mill Creek	J Conner W Vanard	3	4	3	6		38

Churches	Messengers	Baptised	Rec^d by letter	Dismisse by Let	Excluded	Dead	Total
Mount Pleasant	W Hugh A Williams S Craig						120
Mount Gillond	R Frier G Riley						39
Union	R King W Hall						13
Ridge of drennons Creek	J Melon A Mcguire						54
		488	275	994	143	29	5310

The twelve last Churches upon their request were received into the Association Letters from the following Coresponding Churches were received from Salem by their Messengers Brother William Keller; from Tates Creek by Brother Andrew Tibble. from Green River Brother Robert Stocton, from Bracken Brother Philip Drake. Appointed the following Brethren to write to the different association Redding to Tates Creek Tarrent to Green River. Baimbridge to Bracken. Barrow to Salem. Adjourn tell Monday 9 oClock.

Met pursuant to adjournment Th following Brethren are appointed messengers to the Associations. To the Green River Tarrant and Price. to the Tates Creek Redding and Corbin. To the Bracken Barrow and Baimbridg to the Salem Suggett and Reisse.

The Letters read and approve of. The Circular Letter read an approved. A request from the Crossing Church not to admit McConnels run Church a seat in the association. Rejected. Also a memorial from the minority of said Church. Rejected. Agreed to appoint a committee of eleven members to attend the McConnels run Church the Wednesday before the fourth Sunday in October Namely Barrow Eve Enoch & Wm Smith Jelson Payne Thomas Stark Edmund Mountjoy Alexander Monroe Richard Young Lewis Corbin John Scott, seven of them may act in giving all the friendly aid they can. Quere from south Elkhorn What constitutes Baptism valid

Answer the administrator ought to have been Baptised himself by immersion legally colled to preached the gospel ordained as the scriptures dictates & that the candidate for Baptism make a profession of his faith in Jesus Christ and that he be Baptised in the name of the father of the Son & of the Holy Ghost by dipping the whole body in water.

The Committee appointed to form a plan for the use of Churches in our union to direct them in the reception of excluded persons who have moved to this state do advise that the Church which the person wishes to join write to the church from which said person was excluded and get a statement of the offence committeed & the acknowledgement of which they are to judge but in case the Church is dissolved they are to act at discretion.

Whereas the Church at Townfork is not satisfied respecting our union with the Baptists who were denominated separate we recommend it our Brethren James Gerrard Ambrose Dudley Robert Johnson and David Barrow to visit said Church and give them all the friendly aid they can

The following Brethren are appointed to attend the united association. Barrow and Jelson Payne North of Kentucky Richard Cave south of Kentucky

Next association to be held at Town fork on the Second Saturday in August.

Brother Eve appointed to preach the Introductory sermon and in case of Failure Brother Lewis Corbin. Brother Price appointed to write the Circular Letter for next association Agreed to continue the same Committee respecting the Indian Missionary

J Price Clk　　　　　A Eastin Modr

An occasional Association held at the Great Crossings on the 3rd Saturday in April 1803

Letters from 33 Churches also a letter and messengers from 8 Churches on Green River Brothe Robert Stockton & Brother John Murphy Also a Letter from the Church at Pitman.

Tates Creek Thomas Wats
South Elkhorn J Shackleford, J Keller J Parker S Ayres
Bryans A Dudley L Young A Thompson J Mason
Great Crossings J Redding R Johnson J. Suggett J, Johnson
Townfork E Payne W Stone. H. Payne. L. Turner
Cooper, run Edmund Montjoy
Boon Creek A Bainbridge J Beaty
East Hickman John Price A Bower
Indian Creek J Munson G Eaton G Foster
Grapy Lick L Corbin S Dedman H Sanford
Mount Sterling D Barrow W Smith
Mount Moriah P, Withers. S, Cromwell
McConnels run J Martin J Cook R Smith J Payne
Elk Lick. T Gillam. J Fields
Goshen. H Morris C Tracy
Ridge Dren. Creek. J Mellon A Mcguire
Mountain Island J Gill
N Elkhorn G Eve R Davis W Buckly J Thompson
Silas W Bosel H Hendricks D Carkston
Glens Creek J Bandran Will Green
Twins J Scott S Brokman
Dryrun T Foster J Withers W Rhodes
N Fork J Voters J Ficklin
Raven Creek C Chinn W Stowers
Hills Borough C Tarrant A Dale S Gill
Davids fork B Robertson J Robertson J Witch R Mitchel
Rock Bridge. Robert Thomas J Neal
Mill Creek J Coner W Williams
Mount Pleasant G Smith W Hughs
Mount Gillard R Frier G Riley
Brush fork J Barnet Vincent Pelfs
Clear Creek. J Rucker R Cave R Young D Mitchum
Mouth of Elkhorn. J Bart B Lambert
David Barrow Moderator & J Price Clerk

Agreed that a committee of five Brethren be appointed to
visit the Coopers run Church and endeavour to convince
them of their heresy respecting the trinity and make report
to the Association in August next and that Flat Lick Indian
Creek and Union be considered in the same situation. The
following Brethren D Barrow J Price A Dudley, Joseph

Redding. Carter Tarrant or any three of them are appointed
to visit Coopers run the Saturday before the 2nd Sunday in
June and Flat Lick the Friday before and Indian Creek the
Monday after and Union the tuesday following and that those
Churches be informed thereof.
An Enquiry. Does this Body beleive the doctrin of the
Trinity as contained in the Confession of Faith. Answered
unanimous They do.

At an Association began and held at Townfork on Saturday
the 13th of August 1803
  Brother Eve preached the introductory sermon from Rev.
11th Chap 1 verse Letters from the Churches were read.
Ambrose Dudley Chosen Moderator—J Price Clerk.

Churches	Messengers	Bapised	Rec^d by Let.	Di^d by Let.	Excluded	Dead	Total
Tates Creek	Thos Watts Jesse Johnson			5	7	2	76
S. Elk. H.	Jno Shackleford Jno. Keller J Parker S Ayres	3	3	8	6	3	283
Clear Creek	Richd Cave Jas Rucker, D. Mitchum, R. Young			27	5	3	343
Bryans.	A. Dudley, B. Collins, L. Young, J. Mason.	10	13	7	6	4	293
Great Xing.	J Redding. R. Johnson Jas Suggett Jas Johnson	2	4	4	13	5	405
Town fork	John Gano E Payne H Payne Wm How	3	12	12	3		110
Boons Creek	Absalom Baimbridg C Grimes D Bradley		2	2	4		72
East Hickman	J Price A Bourn Walter Cave	2	2	5	2	4	141

Churches	Messengers	Baptised	Rec'd by Let.	Dis'd by Let.	Excluded	Dead	Total
Forks of Elkhorn	Wm Hickman J Haydon	3	6	32	6	2	276
Indian creek	Isaac Munson Gresham Forrest		5	4	12		66
Grapy Lick	L Corbin S Dedman R M Daniel Wm Jeans	1	4	11	5		183
Mt Sterling	D Bannon J Coons Wm Smith E Smith	1	1	2		1	61
Mt Moriah	Levi Waters Peter Weathers			3	3		39
McConnels, run	R Smith J Payne J Cook J Martin	2	5	9	3	2	210
Goshen	W Morris Charles Tracy	1	4	3	4	1	78
Elk Lick	Joel Mulbury Abraham Field	1	1	5	2		37
Raven Creek	Crischester Chinn Wm Campbell	5		9	3		60
Drennens Creek	Morgan Bryan Richard Rice	1	2	1	2		23
Mouth of Elkhorn	Bery Lambert Wm Hollyman		3	2	4	2	41
Mountain Island	John Rice John Gull		2		2		21
Silas	E Craig W E Boswell W Rendrach D Clarkston		8	8	2	2	141
North Elkhorn	G Eve J Willson Wm Buckly J Tomson	2	5	6	10	2	204
Glens Creek	John Bonderant J Garnett		1		1	1	47
Twins	John Scott Thomas Harris	1	2		1		40
S Benson	William Hickman	9	3		1	1	50

Churches	Messengers	Baptised	Rec'd by Let.	Dis'd by Let.	Excluded	Dead	Total
Dry run	Thomas Foster James Wethers Pitts Young		2	3		2	77
Port William	George Craig John Bernard		1	1	1	2	81
North fork	Jesse Vauter John Ficklin		6	3	1	1	58
Rock Bridge	R Thomas Jacob Neal Henry Willson	1	11	1			50
Clover Bottom	A Buckhannon Wm Lisonby R H Thomas	5	3	2			29
Brush fork	V Self Thomas Ammon J Barnett						
Hills Borough	Carter Tarrent Spencer Gill A Dale		18	8	4	2	191
Davids fork	B Robertson J Welsh R Mitchel	1	1	17	7	2	270
Mill Creek	J Conner W Vernard		4	5			33
Mt Pleasant	G Smith A Williams, W Huehs, S Craig		10	11	3		119
Mt Gillard	Robert Frier Garrard Riley	7	1	3			44
	William Hall Richard King						10
Ridge of drennon creek	Isaac Mattin J Baker		5	21	1	1	33
Flat Lick							16
Republican	John Todd						8
		64	194	215	138	47	2442

Appointed the following Bretren to arrange the Business of the Association Barrow Collins and Price. Brethren Gregg Creath and Taylor to preach tomorrow. Adjourn till Monday 9 oClock

Letters from the corisponding associations were received. from Salem by their Messenger John Taylor. From Tates Creek Peter Woods Joel Noel From Green River Elijah Summers From Bracken Wm Payne and Lewis Craig. North District Moses Bledsoe and Daniel Willson South, District Jesse Frier North Bend Thos Griffin and Wm Cave Appointed the following Brethren Messengers to the Associations. To the Salem Hickman and Brown and to write the Letter. South District Dudley Redding an Price. Green River Tarrant and Price. Coopers run Church dropt from the union of this Association for denying the doctrin of the Trinity and holding that Jesus Christ is not truly God. Agreed that that part of Flat Lick Church that holds to their Constitution and to the divinity of Christ be considered the Church Appointed our brethren Barrow Morris Eve Redding and Dupuy to visit the Brethren at Green Creek.

At the request of the Townfork Church the Association voted unanimously that the union with the Baptist South of Kentucky does not in the least remove them from their Constitutional principals. The Corisponding Letter read and approved. Brother Baimbridg appointed to write the Circular Letter for the next year brother Corbin to preach the Introductory Sermon and in case of failure Brother Tarrant. The association to be held at south Elkhorn the second in August 1804.

J Price Clerk........Ambrose Dudley Modr.

At an Association held at North Elkhorn the 2nd Saturday in August 1804

Brother Lewis Corbin preached the introductory sermon from Psalms 84 – 11 For the Lord God is a sun and a shiel the Lord will give grace and glory no good thing will he withhold from them that walk uprightly.

Letters from the Churches were read Brother Ambrose Dudley Chosen Moderator and John Price Clk

Churches	Messengers	Baptised	Rd by Letter	Dd by Letter	Excluded	Dead	Total
Tates Creek	Thomas Watts Jesse Johnson	3	8	7	1		80
S Elkhorn	J Shackleford J Keller A Parker S Ayres		1	6	8	3	360
Clear, Creek	R Cave J Rucker D Mitchum R Young	1	1	10	9	1	325
Bryans	A Dudley B Collins L Young J Mason		8	10	16	5	274
Great Xings	J Redding R Johnson J Suggett J Johnson		12	10	18		333
Townfork	J Creath H Payne W Stone	3	1	1	3		113
Boons Creek	A Bainbridge D Bradly J Beaty	3	5		3		77
East Hickman	J Price A Bourn W Cave			2	4	3	130
Forks of Elkhorn	W Hickman T Woldridge	1	7	17	8	3	260
Indian Creek	G Eaton M Endicott		5	6	12		55
Grapy Lick	L Corbin R McDonnel W Jeans	8	11	4	2		168
Mt Sterling	D Barrow J Coons Dis	1	4	6	2		60
Mt Moriah	T McCarty Peter Weathers			8	1	1	27
McConnels run	J Payne R Smith		9	13	6	4	199
Goshen	D Thomson C Tracy Dis	1	5	10	8		71
Elk Lick	A Fields J Mulbury				1	1	33
Raven Creek	C Chinn W Campbell		3		3	1	63
Drennons Lick	Morgan Bryan Dis	1	3	0	1		26

Churches	Messengers	Baptised	R^d by Letter	D^d by Letter	Excluded	Dead	Total
Mouth of Elk-horn	W Grave J Bartlett				3		37
Mountain Island	J Reace J Hawkins	I	I		I		26
Silas	E Craig H Hendrick D Clarkson						
N Elkhorn	G Eve J Willson W Rackly		16	8	I	5	206
Glens Creek	W Green J Ronder-ant		4		I		42
Twins	T Jones W Blarton Dis			2	I		37
S Benson	W Hickson Jr T W Quiddy B Robinson	I	3		2	I	50
Dry run	T Foster J Weathers		5	3		I	78
North fork	Jesse Vauter John Fickling		I	5	4		50
Rock Burg	R Thomas Thomas Parsly		4	3		I	50
Clover Bottom	Ab Buckhannon W Lisenby		2			I	30
Brush Fork	J Barnett V Self	4	I	3	5		86
Hills boro-rough	C Tarrent A Dale S Gill	I	5	6	4		188
Davids fork	B Robinson J Welsh J Greavs A Will-son		I	24	10		243
Mill Creek	J Connel W Wil-liams		3		4		34
Mount pleas-ant	G Smith W Hughs S Craig		6	I	I		120
Mount Gillard	R Frier G Riley	I					44
Union	W Hall R King		6		2		14
Drennons ridge	Isaac Martin John Bakers Dis	3	3	I	5	I	39

Churches	Messengers	Baptised	R by Letter	Dᵈ by Letter	Excluded	Dead	Total
Republican	J Todd T Marshall	5					13
Flat Lick	Thomas Neal W						
	Manse	8		2			23
Stony Point	G Shortridge J Williamson J Hedges						62
	Total	22	163	180	165	34	4220

Received Letters and messengers from the Corisponding
Associations from Long run by their Messengers Elder John
Taylor and Elder Wm Reller. from North Bend Elder Wm
Craig & Christopher Willson. From Salem Elder Warren
Cash North District Elder Isaac Crutch and Brother Jelson
Payne. Green River Elder John Murphy From the South
District Elder John Rice and Elder Jeremiah Vardaman the
following Brethren were appointed to write letters to the
corisponding Associations brother Joseph Redding to the
Long run Brother Robert Johnson to the North Bend
Brother Craig to Salem Brother Baimbridge to Green River
Brother John Payne to Tates Creek Brother Richard Young
to Bracken Brother Elijah Craig to north District. Elder
Jeremiah Vardaman Elder Jacob Creath and Elder David
Barrow appointed to preach on Sunday. brothers David
Barrow brother Ambrose Dudley and brother John Price
were appointed to examine the letters and arrange the busi-
ness of the association.
   Adjourned till Monday 9 oclock

   August 13th 1804 Monday 9 oclock met pursuant to
adjournment after prayer proceed to business Queres from
several churches Nearly the same
   Viz Is it not a cause of distress for the churches to be
constituted so near each other as they frequently are with
us and is it not the duty of the association to endeavour

to remedy this evil. is it not necessary for the Association to form some plan for the constitution of Churches and ordination of Ministers Debated and ordered to ly on the Table. Quere from Mount Gillard. Is it the Constitutional right of a member that is in good standing in the Church to which he belongs and living nearer a Sister church of the same faith and order to have a letter of Dismission an an application. Rejected. Request from the Crossings.

To appoit a day of fasting and of Prayer and that our Brethren of other denominations be invited to join us agreed that the last Wednesday in september be appointed for that purpose. Agreed that Mount Sterling Goshen and Grap Lick Churches have leave to act at their discresion in joining the North District Association. Drenens Lick and Drennens Ridge twin Churches are dismissed to join the Long run Association. The Circular Letter read and approved. The Letters to the corisponding Asson read and approved and the following Brethren appointed Messengers. To the Long run Association Brethren Joseph Redding W Hickman J Vauter. To the Green River Association Jas Suggett and Absalam Baimbridge. To the Backen Association Ambrose Dudley and John Price to the North District Association. Jacob Creath A Dudley Lewis Corbin and George Eve To the Tates Creek association Wm Buckly & J Price. To the Salem Association Jas Suggett and Jon Rease To the North Bend Association George Eve and Lewis Corbin To the South District Association Joseph Redding and John Shackleford and Absalem Baimbridg and said brethren to write a Letter of Corispondence to said Associations.

Agreed that our next Association be held at Bryons the second Saturday in August next and that brother Carter Tarrent preach the introductory sermon and in case of failure Brother Ambrose Dudley Brother James Johnson appointe to write the Circular Letter for 1805

Received a request from some black Brethren who dessented from Coopers run Church on the account of the arian heresy agreed that brother Todd Corbin and Craig be appointed to visit said brethren and advise them to join some of the adjacent Churches. Agreed to insert in our minutes the death of our aged and beloved Brother John Gano who departed this life August 9th 1804 aged nearly 80 years he lived and died an ornament to Religion

A DUDLEY Moderator
J PRICE Clerk

At an Association began, and, held at Bryans August 10th 1805 brother Carter Tarrent preached the introductory Sermon from Mark 16, 15 and he said write unto them go ye into all the wourld and preach my gospal unto every creasure."

Letters from 35 Churches were read.

Brother Ambrose Dudley Chosen Moderator and Brother John Price Clk

Churches	Messengers	Baptised	Red by Letter	Disd by Letter	Excluded	Dead	Total
Tates Creek	A Bower Thos Watts			2	4	16	64
S Elkhorn	J Shackleford J Keller S Ayres P Higber	1	13	6	16	2	259
Clear Creek	R Cave R Young		2	9	10	2	206
Bryans	A Dudley B Collins L Young J Mason		10	5	12	1	267
Great Xings	J Redding R Johnson J Suggett J Johnson			19	8		370
Town Fork	J Creath Wm Stone Benjamin Stout		6	7	2		109
Boons Creek	A Baimbridge T Dairter D Bradley		4	6	1		74
Et Hickman	J Price W Carr		4	3	4	3	124
Fks of Elkhorn	Wm Hickman E Gregory T Wooldridge	2	12	4	10	1	237

Churches	Messengers	Baptised	Rd by Letter	Disd by Letter	Excluded	Dead	Total
Indian Creek	Isaac Munson Moses Endicott		2		5		52
Mt Moriah	J Rucker P Withers		3				32
McConnels run	S Brown John Payne Rhodes Smith	2	6	7	42	2	195
Elk Lick	J Mulberry						33
Raven Creek	J Powers M Pigg	1	1	4	21	1	55
Mouth of Elk-horn	William Goare	1		5			33
Mth Island	J Rease S Simpson		4	5			20
Sylas	C Craig J Clarkson		8	2	1	3	131
Nth Elkhorn	Wm Henrick J Chinn G Eve J Willson J Thomas	2	7	16	9	2	185
Glens Creek	William Buckly William Green		1		2		39
Benson	Wm Hickman Jnr, Wm Brown	2		2	1	0	50
Dry Run	Thos Foster James Withers		3	5			76
Nth fork	Jesse Vauter John Ficklin	1	4	2	1		53
Rock Bridge	Richard Thomas David Thomas		4	1			52
Clover Bottom	Jas Chambers Wm Lisonby R M Thomas		5	6			29
Brushfork	T Ammon J Barnet Vincent Self	2		4	3		81
Hills Borough	C Tarrent A Dale Spencer Gill	1	8	5	6	1	185
Davids fork	B Robinson J Wealch A Willson J Greavs		4	16	12	2	191
Mill Creek	J Cannon W Williams		9	2	3		39

Churches	Messengers	Baptised	Rec'd by Letter	Dis'd by Letter	Excluded	Dead	Total
Mt Pleasant	G S Smith G Smith Wm Hughs S Craig		2		4		180
Mᵗ Gillard	Robert Frier G Riley	1		1			45
Union	William Hall Richard King	5	5		1		23
Republican	J Todd H Sidwell		3		1		14
Flat Lick	W Maurice T Neal	1	3	3			23
Stony Point	L Corbin J Wilkinson R Ather		9	1			67
Long Lick	John Vauter John Lucas	2	3				19
	Total	23	147	150	137	21	3550

The Church at Long Lick Lately Constituted applied for admission into the association and was received The Circular Letter read and referred to the Committee of Arrangements.

Received Letters and Messengers from the several Corisponding Association. Viz from the Salem Association by their Messenger Elder Walter Slattard From the Tates Creek Association by their Messengers elder Andrew Tibble & Elder Squire Boon From the Bracken Association Elders W Payne and Singleton From the North Bend Association by their Messengers Elder Isaac Rentfre & brother Christopher Willson. from the South District Association by their Messenger Elder John Rice from the North District Association by their Messengers Elder David Barrow & Robt Elkin from the Long Run Association by their messengers Elders John Penny and Philip Webber. from the Green River Association by their Messenger Elder Robert Stockton From Rupel's Creek Association by their Messenger Elder Elijah Summers.

Brother Elijah Craig appointed to write to the Salem

Association. Brother George Eve appointed to write to the Bracken Association. Brother Joseph Redding appointed to write to the Tates Creek Association Brother Absolom Baimbridge appointed to write to the North Bend Association Brother John Payne appointed to write to the South District association and Brother Jacob Creath appointed to write to the North District Association brother Robert Johnson appointed to write to the Long Run Association Brother James Suggett appointed to write to the Rupels Creek Association. Brothers C Tarrent G Eve L Corbin & John Price are appointed to arrange the business of the Association. Brothers Jeremiah Vardeman David Barrow & Joseph Redding chosen to preach on the Lords day. Adjourn till Monday 9 oclock

Sunday brother Joseph Redding preached 2 Cor. 5th 17th Therefore if any man be in Christ he is a new Creature old things are past away behold all things are become new. Brother Jeremiah Vardeman from 1. Cor 16. 22 If any man love not the Lord Jesus Christ let him be Anathema Marentha. Brother David Barrow preached from 2 Cor 5. 10 For we must all appear before the Judgment seat of Christ." To a very large assembly.

Monday met pursuant to adjournment. After Prayer proceeded to business The Circular Letter read and thought not proper to send to the Churches. Brother Robert Johnson G S Smith with Absalom Baimbridge were appointed to prepare one. Quere from South Elkhorn. Who is the Church of Christ to be governed by agreeably to the Scriptures Refered. Quere from Boons Creek What is a member to do who is in good standing and applies for a letter of dismission and is denied? Withdrawn—Request from the Church at the Crossings Clear Creek and Hillsborough to revise the Confession of Faith and Church disciplin agreed to appoint a Committee of seven members to consist of four ministers & three private brethren accordingly Elders A Dudley J Redding J Price C Tarrent Brethren R Johnson B Collins &

John Payne were appointed who are to revise the Confession of Faith and Church Discipline to meet as often as deem it necessary to prepare such amendments as they may Judge proper and report the same to the next Association and if approved to be recommended to the Churches & our brethren in union for their inspection.

Quere from Glens Creek Is it right for Baptists to join in & assemble at barbacues on the 4th of July? Answered No. Letter of Corispondence to the Salem Association read and approved Brother Jas Suggett and Jno Reace appointed to attend the same A Letter to the Tates Creek Association read and approved Brothers Carter Tarrent and Wm Buckly appointed to attend the same. A Letter to the Bracken Association read and approved Brothers A Dudley & George Eve Lewis Corbin & John Price appointed to attend the said Association. A Letter to the North Bend Association read and approved Brothers Jas Redding appointed to attend A Letter to the South District Association read and approved. Brethren John Shackleford & Jacob Creath appointed Messengers thereto.

A Letter to the North District Association read and approved Brethren Ambrose Bourn & Richard Cave & Jacob Creath appointed to attend—

A Letter to the Long run Association read and approved & Brethren Joseph Redding and Jacob Creath to attend

A Letter to the Green River Association read and approved Brethren Jacob Creath Wm Hickman and C. Tarrent to attend.

A Letter to the Rupells Creek Association read and approved Brother Absalom Baimbridge to attend.

This Association Judges it improper for ministers Churches or Associations to meddle with emacipation from Slavery or any other political Subject and as such we advise ministers & Churches to have nothing to do therewith in their religious Capcities.

Next association to be held at the Crossings on the 2nd Saturday in August next Brother Absalom Baimbridge to preach the introductory sermon and in case of failure

Brother Jacob Creath Brother George Eve write the Circular Letter to the Churches.

AMBROSE DUDLEY Modr.

J PRICE Clerk

PS The names of the messengers being called at the close of the meeting a number haveing disorderly gone off before we were regularly dismissed it was agreed that they should be publickly reproved by name, in the minutes. A Motion was afterward made that their names should not be inserted in the Minutes & no further reproff given untill the next Association.

CHAPTER XIII

MINUTES OF THE ILLINOIS ASSOCIATION
OF BAPTISTS, 1807–1820

Part of the Several Baptist Churches in the Illinois met at Anthony Badgleys on friday the 9th of January 1807 & having there agreed to Strive to gain a fellowship with each other Apointed two members out of each Church to bring the dsign into effect, we the Committee met at brother David Badgleys & Proceeded to business, brother Wm Jones Moderator, we the Committee agree to unite on the following Principles—

1 that there is one only true God, the Father Son & the Holy Ghost—

2 we beleive the old & new Testaments to be the word of God & the only rule of Faith & Practice—

3 we beleive that by nature we are fallen & depraved creatures

4 that Salvation regeneration Sanctification & justification is by the life death resurrection & assention of Jesus Christ

5 that Saints will finally Persevere through grace to glory—

6 that beleivers Baptism by immertion is necessary to the receiving of the Lords Supper

7 that the Salvation of the righteous & punishment of the wicked are Eternal—

8 we beleive that no minister have a right to administer the Ordinances until they legally come under the imposition of hands

9 that it is our duty to be tender & affectionate to each other & Stoody the happiness of the Children of God in general & to be engaged Singularly to promote the honour & glory of God—

10 we beleive in Election by grace

11 we beleive that it is our duty to Commune with other Baptists

12 that each Church may keep up their own government as to them may Seem best

13 the Several diferent Churches have agreed to unite on the foregoing Principles

January the 10th 1807 A Committee was chosen by the Several Churches consisting of nine members three out of each Church namely Mississippi bottom David Badgley Isaac Hill George Valentine—
New design Church Isaac Enochs Joseph Chance & Wm Whiteside Richland James Downan Robt Brazle & Joseph Cook Strange brethren Wm Jones & John Finley to Settle the distresses that remain among the Churches
bror Wm Whiteside Moderater & proceeded to business

1 we the Committe beleive that it would be rong in a Church government to grant a letter of dismission & call the member back to the Church & on refusal Excommunicate without any immorallity in the member so dismissed—

2 we believe it would be rong in any Church to receive Excluded members from a Sister Church until a reconciliation takes place between the Church & member So excluded.

3 we believe from the records of the bottom Church that Henry Clark was justly excluded from the Church & that he the P— Clark by deception got into the Silver Creek arm of the new design Church & this committee lays it upon the Arm to write a letter Countermanding the letter the Arm gave him & Send it after him

4 We the committee do agree that if any Church Shall disfellowship a Sister Church without takeing Gospel Steps, it Shall be deemed a matter of dealing with them, the Same rule to extend to the Members—

5 The committee took up the distress between the Bottom Church & Richland Church concerning Mr Bradsby & believe that Bradsby was a member of the richland Church & that he was justly dealt with & lawfully excluded & that he imposed himself on the bottom Church—

6 It is hereby understood that any difficulty that is now Subsisting among any members of any of the Churches they

have a right to deal with them in Gospel order in the Church where they are a member & helps to be called in matters of difficulty—

7 This committe agree to delegate members from each church to meet as an advisery Counsil to keep up a Union & fellowship & to consult rules of decorum which may be apointed as often as thought necessary, this Advisary Counsil to meet on the third friday Saterday & Sunday in June next at brother Downans—we agree that all Church Splits that have been heretofore be finally done away.

Signd by order of the Committee
Isaac Enochs Clk

Minutes of the Illenois Ass^n of Baptist held at the Richland Church at James Dowans on the 3^d friday in june 1807 & continued by a-journment until Sabath day following being the 23rd at 12 oclock Elder Wm Jones delivered the introductory Sermon from Proverbs 18 & 24 a man that hath friends must Shew himself frendly & there is a friend that Sticketh closer than a brother after Sermon business was opened with prayer David Badgley was chosen Moderater & Wm Whiteside Clerk. letters from five Churches was read their Messengers names enrolld & a list of their numbers taken as follows

New design church James Lemen & Isaac Enochs	16
Mis bottom D Badgley James Henderson & James Gilham	11
Richland Jas Downan Rot Brazle V& Brazle	11
Wood river Wm Jones Isaac Hill Joseph Cook	12
Silvercreek J Chance Peter Mitchel Edw Radcliff	12

Total—62

A celect Committee was chosen to make rules of Decorrim for the Ass^n & make report tomorrow at 9 oclock The names of the Committee Viz David Badgley Wm Jones Ja^s Downan Isaac Enochs & Ja^s Gilham The committee met on Saterday the 21 acording to a journment & agreed on the following rules

1 that an introductory Sermon be preached at every Ass^n
2 the delegates names to be calld & Moderater & Clerk chosen

3 a letter from each church taken & read & their deligates names enrolld

4 the deligates names to be called over when thought Proper by the Association

5 a Treasurer to be apointed to keep the Ass^{ns} fund

6 The Ass^n Shall apoint one or more Persons to examine the fund & make report annually

7 a cellect committee to be chosen to arange the business of Association & make report—

8 The Ass^n being conveined & any person offering to Speak Shall arise & adress the Moderater & then make his Speech—

9 in the time of a publick Speech a profound Silence Shall be observed & neither talking nor whispering Shall be admited—

10 Any motion made & not Seconed Shall fall—

11 no motion Shall be taken up & debated without the concent of a majority—

12 all Motions Shall be determined by a majority except in cases which may be thought proper otherwise than by a majority

13 none may Speak more than 3 times to one Subject without the consent of the association.

14 we think it proper for the members to bear the appelation of brother or friend

15 no person Shall absent himself in the time of business without the consent of the Ass^n

16 the Moderater Shall not leave his place without another to fill his Seat as moderater—

17 it Shall be the duty of the Clerk to furnish each Church with a coppy of the minutes of the Ass^n—

18 it Shall be the duty of the ass^n to allow a reasonable compensa- tion to the clerk out of the fund for his Services—

19 any Person who Shall break through any of these rules or go counter to any of them Shall be dealt with as the ass^n Shall think proper

20 the Lords day Shall be Spent in Preaching by any who the association may appoint at each ass^n—

21. This ass^n Shall apoint when & where the next ass^n Shall be holden & allso appoint Some one to Preach the introductory Sermon or in case of falier Some other to be apoined at the Same time to fill the vacancy—

22 question asked does this Communion extend throughout the Union answered the Communion shall extend throughout the

Union The Committee made their report which was taken up in order & aproved—

Wm Whiteside was apoint Clerk the next Ass^n to be holden at Isaac Enoches on the Second friday Saterday & Sunday in october
David Badgley apointed to Preach the introductory Sermon & in case of falier Elder Jo^s Chance Signd by order of the association

DAVID BADGLEY Moderater
& WM WHITESIDE Clk

Minutes of the Illenoi Ass^n of Baptist holden at Isaac Enochs in the richland Creek Church St Clare County on fiday the 9th of October 1807 & continued by ajournment until Sunday the 11th

1 The Introductory Sermon was delivered by Elder David Badgley from John 3–16 for God so loved the world that he gave his only begotton Son that whosoever beleiveth on him Should not Perish but have everlasting life
2 after Sermon business was opened by Prayer & Elder Wm Jones Chosen Moderater. letters from 7 Churches was read & their Messengers (names) enrolld & list of their numbers taken as follows

Churches	Messengers names	Recd by Experience	Recd by letter	Number
Newdisgn	Wm Whiteside S Terry G Demint	9	1	20
Miss bottom	D Badgley G Valentine D Waddle	1		14
Silver Creek	J Chance Ed Radcliff Am Riter	5	2	22
Richland	Jas Downan V Brazle R Brazle	7	1	19
Wood River	Wm Jones I Hill Jos Cook		2	14
Kain Spring	Jno Hendrickson Wm Null			7
R L Creek	Jas Lemon Wm L Whiteside I Enochs			17
	Total	22	6	113

D Badgley Jos Chance Jno Hendrickson Isaac Hill Jas
Downan with the Moderater & Clerk was chosen a celect
Committe to arange the business of the Assn & make report
ajournd until 3 oclock
met at 3 oclock; the Committee made their report
1 The matter of Henry Walker which was laid over from last
Assn to be done Something with
2 The request of the richland Church to be taken up
3 Some to be apointed to Examine the fund & make report
4 a querry by the Committee to know how excommunicates
from foreign Countries is to be received
5 that Some more rules of decorum be Enacted
6 that Some be apointed to Preach the introductory Sermon
7 a time & place to be apointed for the next Ass^n
8 that the clerk be alowed out of the fund for his Servises
Ajournd

The Ass^n met acording to ajournment, the Committee
made their report which was receiv^d & taken up in order—
1. The matte of the friend Walker taken up & thown out
2 the request of the Richland Church taken up & laid on the
Preachers to apoint the times to Preach
3 Isaac Enochs & Stephen Terry apointed to examine the
fund. they report that they find in the treasury $—6.62$\frac{1}{2}$—
4 it is answered that the excommunicates Shall give Satisfaction to the church from whence they were excluded &
if that cannot be come at consistantly the Church to whom
application is made Shall write to the Church who excluded
Such applicant Requesting the charge to be exhibited with
a request to have the Previledge of acting in the matter
for them but if the Church Shall be desolved, then the
Church to whom application is made by the excluded
member Shall be clear in takeing it up & acting as to them
may Seem best—
5 an amendment to the 16th article of decorum that the
moderator Shall not give his judgment until the voice of
the Ass^n is taken & the moderater Shall have no vote
excep the Ass^n is equally devided—

6 any Person Speaking in disorder & neglecting or refusing
to hear the Moderater Shall be taken under dealings

7 ordered that the clerk Shall have 25 cents for each coppy
of the minutes of the association

9 our next ass⁰ to be holden at Jas Lemons on Second friday
in june 1808—association

10 agreed that the name of our ass⁰ be Calld Illenois

11. Wm Whitesde apointed Treasurer—
Signed by order of the Association

WM JONES Moderater
WM WHITESIDE Clk.

Minutes of the Illenois Ass⁰ of Baptist holden at J Lemons
in the New design on friday the 10 of june 1808 & continued
by ajournment untill Saterday 11 on friday 12 oclock Elder
Jos Chance Preached the introductory Sermond from Jno
21 & 15 Simon Son of Jona lovest thou me more than these—
after Sermod business was opened by prayer Jos Chance
Moderator letters from 7 Churches was read their Messengers names enrolld & a list of their no taken as follows

Churches	Messengers Names	Recd by Experience	Recd by letter	Excluded	Numbers
Newdesign	Jno Griffin S Terry GDemint	10	—	—	29
Silvercreek	J Chance. Jas Garrison Eᵈ Radcliff	6	3	—	29
Miss bottom	D Waddle G Valentine A Badgley	4		4	14
Rich L Creek	Jno Steel B Ogle I Enochs	4	4		25
Richland	R Brazle Wm Brazle Jos Downan	2	5		24
Wood river	Jos White Jno Finley Wm Jones				15
Kainspring	Jno Nicols T Cumstock Jno Hendrickson	1			8
	Total				144

a celect committee was chosen to arang the busness of the
assn Viz Jno Griffin I Enochs Edwd Radcliff Val Brazle Jas
Downan Jno Hendrickson Wm Jones with the Moderater &
clerk ajournd until 8 oclock tomorrow
The committee met at 3 oclock a request from the wood
River Church to have our next assn to be holden at the
meetinghouse in woodriver Church—
application by the delegates of the Ricland Church to the
assn to ordain John Baugh apreacher of the Gospel. a querry
by the Deligates of the KainSpring Church is it right to'
exclude a Preach member & restore him to his membership
& also to his gift wihout helps from the Sister Churches. A
Querry from the deligates of the woodriver Church to know
what is to be done with a member who transgresses before
the world & comes forward & confess part & not (what the
wold Says) is the whole. Qerry from the commitee Is there
any Society of People Professing Christianity that we
(Baptist) can receive to Church fellowship & they never
have Submited themselves to the ordinance of Baptism in
that, that we believe to be right, & if there is who are they—
The committe ajourned until Saterday 7 oclock Met acording
to ajournment after divine worship an inquiry to know what
is to be done with David Badgley concerning his credentials
a request to take into consideration Some plan to Supply
every Place with Preaching that no lack be in any Place—
a Proposition that the Assn make Some rules for the Organ-
nization of our Assn a Proposition by the Wood river Church
concerning a letter from S Carolina concerning Thos Musick
that some be apointed to examine the fund & make report—
an introductory Sermon to be Preached at the next Assn
The Committee ajournd—
The Assn met acording to ajournment after Divine worship
Proceded to business
1 a motion made to lay over apointing aplace for our next
   association to be holden—carried
2 Elders Joseph Chance John Hendrickson & Wm Jones
   apointed a Presbetery for to ordain brother John Baugh—
3 the Querry from Kain Spring. it is advised by the assn

that his membership may be restored by the Church but as the advice of this counsil. they had better call helps to restore him to his publick gift—

4 the Querry from the delegates of the woodriver Church taken up & left to each church to act concerning testamony as to them seem best—

5 A querry by the arm of of the Richland Church to know what Shall be done with members having letters of dismission from the United Baptist churches & living in disorder—thrown out—

6 the motion concerning D Badgleys Credentials agreed that he keep them until the next meeting of the church where he was a member—

7 a Proposition to Supply the diferent Churches taken up & agreed to Send two together, to wit, Jos Chance & James Lemon/ Jno Hendrickson & Benm Ogle/ Wm Jones & Jos Lemon/ Jno Baugh & Robet Brazle/

8 it is agreed that the ordained Ministers that atends the Assn Shall pintout one when met at the place to Preach the introductory Sermond

9 agreed that the man that Preaches the Introductory Sermon Shall Stand as Moderater until the letters is received & read & then a Moderater Shall be chosen by private ballat—

10 The letter from S Carolina taken up & read

11 It is the opinion of this Advisary counsil that it is disorder to invite or Suffer any Disorderly Baptist to preach in our houses or to countenance them in it—

12 Wm Jones & Isaac Enochs apointed to examine the fund. they report that they find in the fund $1.87½

13 our next assn holden at the Wood river meeting house & to commence on the friday before the 1st Saterday in October 1808—

14 Querry is there any Society of People Professing Christianity that we (Baptist) can receive into Church fellowship & they never Submited themselves to the ordinance of Baptism in that way which we believe to be right & if there is who are they—

Answered we know of none. Signed by order of the association

JOSEPH CHANCE Moderator
WM WHITESIDE Clk

Minutes of The Illenoi Association of Baptist holden at Wood River Meeting house on friday the 30th of of September 1808 & continued by ajournment until Sunday the 2nd of October.—friday Elder John Hendrickson Preached the Introductory Sermond from 2nd Corenthians 5 & 26 after divine worship letters was received from the differant Churches. their Messengers names enrolled & a list of their numbers taken as follows—

Churches	Messengers Names	baptised	Dismist	Nombers
N dsign	G Denint Jos Lemon S Terry	2		30
Silvercreek	Jos Chance Jas Garitson P Mitchel	1		30
Miss bottom	D Waddle A Badgley G Valentine		5	7
R L creek	Jos Lemon I Enochs Ben Ogle			29
W River	Wm Jones Jos White Jno Finly			16
K Spring	John Hendrickson			8
Feifees creek	Abraham Musick James Richardson			11
	Total			131

The letter from the Richland Church faild but two of their Messengers being present took their Seats. to wit Jno Baugh & R Brazle

A celect committee was chosen to arange the business of the assn Viz Wm Jones Jos Chance Jno Baugh with the Moderater & Clerk. ajournd until tomorrow 7 oclock—Saterday October the first the Assn met Persuant to ajournment after divine worship the committee made their report which was receivd & taken up in order—

1 A remonstrance from woodriver Church against sending ministers into the Sirqiut. Discontinued

2 Querry is it consistant with the Gospel for a brother baptist to go to law with a brother in the union before taking gospel Steps & if it is in what case. laid over to next assn

3 agreed that no Querry be received by this Assn except it be by the Authority of a church or where the committee is Queried—

4 the examination of the fund past over

5 the next Assn to be holden at Silver Creek meeting house on the 3rd Saterday in june next & Sunday monday follow

6 Fefrees creek desires this Assn to consider them with ministerial helps. agreed that the church Shall be Supplyed monthly until our next Assn by one Preacher

7 The matter of Thos Musick taken up & it is the opinion of this Assn that he ought to be taken into fellowship of this body of Baptist & that if infuture any further testimony Shall be forwarded to convince us that he was guilty of fornication they are to give him up to be as he was before, for we beleive the testimony of Margaret Bridges was not Sufficient to exclude him

8 upon the matter of David Badgley taken up & he is restored into fellowship on his acknowledgment. Signd by order of the Association

JNO HENDRICKSON Moderator
WM WHITESIDE Clk

Minutes of the Illenoi Assn of Baptist holden at Silver Creek Meeting house on Saterday the 17 of june 1809 when Elder Jno Baugh Preached the introductory Sermond from Rev 12–4 after divine worship Jno Baugh Moderator letters from 8 churches was read their messengers names enrolld & a list of their numbers taken—

Churches	Messengers Names	by experience	Rec'd by letter	Dismissed	excluded	Dead	Numbers
N design	S Terry G Demint Jas Lemon	1		2			29
Silvercreek	J Chance Jas Garitson U Short	5	1	1		2	33
Richland	Wm Little Jas Downan Jno Baugh	1	4		3		14
Miss bottom	G Valentine Jas Hendrickson David Waddle	2			4		10
W River	Jas Gilham J Finly Wm Jones						19
R L Creek	L Rutherford I Enochs B Ogle	8	3		1		39
Fifees Creek	T. R Musick L Martin A Clark		3	1			18
Kainspring	John Hendrickson	1					8
L G Paririe	R Brazle V Brazle Wm Brazle						9
Cold Water	John Alin Jacob Eastwood						9
	Total	18	11	8	4	2	188

NB the two last mentioned Churches was lately costituted & prayed admittance into the Assn & receivd and their Messengers took their Seats as a bove—
A celect committee was chosen to arange the business of the Assn ajourned until monday 8 oclock. when the Assn met & after divine worship the report of the committe was receivd & taken up in order

1 the querry laid over from last assn concerning brother going to law with brother. thrown out—
2 a querry from Silvercreek. thrown out—
3 a querry from Kainspring taken up & Ans^d in the afirmative
4 a querry from Richland creek taken up. 1st we beleive an association is an Advisary Counsil 2nd we beleive the

apostles mode of Seting ministers forward to the Ministry
was to find the gift in the man & then if thought fit by the
Presbytery to be Set at liberty by the laying on of hands
5 a request from Cold water church for Ministerial helps
answered we will Strive to help them
6 in ansr to the Church in the Mississippi Bottom we will
Strive to help them—
7 Jas Downan & Stephen Terry apointed to examine the
fund & make report. they report they find the fund in
arears to the clerk 87½ cents
8 the assn alows the clerk one month to write the copies &
each church to Send for their coppy
9 Our next assn to be holden in the Mississippi Bottom
begining on friday before the first Saterday in October
next at the Schoolhouse near James Garitsons. Signed by
order &c &c

JNO BAUGH Moderator
WM WHITESIDE Clk

The 1st Friday in October in the Year of our Lord 1809
The Association met at the Schoolhouse near Br Garretsons
in the Mississippi Bottom where the Introductiory Sermon
was delivered by Elder Robert Brazel from 2d Chron, 4th
Chap & part of the 3d, 4th and part of verse 5th and after
Divine Service Br Brazel Moderator proceeded to business
the Association divided assunder and the party desiring to
support the General Union of United Baptists at large being
Assembled Chose Br Wm Jones Clerk & proceeded to business letters from five Churches were read their Messengers
names enrold and a list of their numbrs taken

Churches	Messengers		
Missippi Bot-tom	George Valentine D Badgley		11
Wood River	Jno Rissel abs William Jones		28
		Exc m	
Cold Water	Jno Allen Wm Patterson	2	11

Churches	Messengers			
Looking Glass Prairie	William Brazel, Val Brazel, Robt Brazel			9
Feifees Creek	Richard Sullen, Jas Wallen			
		Ex	let	
	abs, Alex. Clark abs.	7	1	37
				78

A Celect Committee Chosen to arrang the business of the
Association by Name Br David Badgly with the Moderator
and Clerk The Committee made their report and it was
received and the Committee Discharged—

1st an amendment to the Union in the 12th article we thnk
that no Church have any right to make any rule to cross the
Union of the United Baptists at large—

2. Query from the Bottom Church is it right for a Church to
gave letters of dismission if so on what ground—Answer we
believe it right to gave letters in case of the person moving
out of the bounds or wanting to join another Church nearer
to them of the same faith and order—

3d The request of Wood River concerning Br Musick laid
over till the next Association—

4th We bilieve it right not to commune with those that have
left the General Union at large.

5th Agreed that our next Association be held at Wood River
meeting House on the friday before the first Saturday in
December next signed by order

ROBERT BRAZEL Mod.
WILLIAM JONES Clk.

Minutes of the Illenoi Assn of Baptist holden at Woodriver
meeting house St Clare County the first friday in December
1809 Elder D Badgley delivered the introductory Sermon
from Rom 8 9

1 Elder D. Badgley chosen Moderater & Eld Wm Jones Clk
2 letters from 6 churches read & their Messengers names
enroled—

Churches	*Messengers Names*
L glass	Wm Brazle Valentine Brazle
woodriver	Jos White Jno Russel Wm Jones
Cold water	Wm Patterson Jacob Eastwood
M Bottom	D Badgley G Valentine D Waddle
Silvecreek	Dan Stooky Jos Carr Moses Short
Fifeescreek	Thos R Musick Ely Musick Eleck Clark

3 a committee chosen to arange the business of the Assn by name Wm Brazle Jacob Eastwood Dan¹ Stooky Thos R Musick with the moderater & Clerk—

4 ajourd until tomorrow 9 oclock

5 Met Persuant to ajournment & after worship the committee made their report & it was received.

6 The referance from last Assn thrown out

7 Cold water requests for visits to be paid them it is left to the Preachers

8 Thos R Musick Robt Brazle D Bagley D Waddl Moses Short Wm Brazle Wm Jones Jno Finley is apointed to meet with the defferent churches to help them in their Present distresses to establish those who wish to live with the United Baptists & (if need be) to costitute churches to meet first at Daniel Stars, Bottom Church on the 12 of February next 13th at Newdesign 15 at Jos Carrs Silvercreek 16 at Lashing Rutherfords R L Creek, 17 at Jno Philipses Richland—18 at Robt Brazles L G Perarie 19 woodriver

9 we advise each Church to Send paper to the next Assn to write their own Minutes on—

10 next Assn is apointed at Fefees Creek on friday before the Second Saterday in october next

11 appointed Eldr Wm Jones to preach the introductory Sermond & in case of falier Eld D Badgley

12 ajournd to the time & Place above mentioned
    Signed by order &c

DAVID BADGLEY Mod͆
WM JONES Clerk

Minutes of the Illenoi assn of Baptist conveined at Fiefees creek Louisany Territory on friday before the Second Saterday in October 1810 elder Wm Jones delivered the introductory Sermond from 1 Peter 2 V 9.

1 Elder Wm Jones chosen Moderater & Moses Short Clerk
2 letters from 6 Churches was red & their messengers names enroled & a list of their numbers taken, as followeth

Churches	Messengers Names	by experience	Recd by letter	dismist	excluded	Dead	Total
Coldwater	Jno Allen Thos Ellace	1	1	3	8	1	10
Lookingglass	Wm Brazle R Brazle B Chapman				1	1	9
Woodriver	Jno Finley Jas Beman Wm Jones						29
Miss Bottom	D Waddle G Valentine Jas Henderson						
Fifees creek	Lewis Martin A Musick T R Musick	5	5		1	1	48
Ogles creek	D Badgley Jno Philips	1	6				13
Turkey hill	Nathan Arnet Moses Short						14
Shole creek	Simon Lindley						
	Total						123

3 Shole creek Church is a new constitution which made apliation & was receivd & Ogles Creek is the Church formerly called Richland & Turkey hill is the Church formerly called Silvercreek
4 a committee chose to arage the business of the Assn to wit
5 ajourd until tomorrow 9 oclock
6 Met Persuant to ajournment & after worship prceeds to business
7 Elder Jno B Brook & br jno Wren being Present was invited to take a Seat with us—

8 the arangement read & receivd & the committee discharged

9 we Approbate the proceedings of the committee chosen at last Assn to visit the Churches

10 Querry from the Ogles creek church is the conduct of the Emacepats (Emancipationists) justifiable or not answered, that it is not

11 querry from L G Perara Church is it right to invite those people who went from us & declared an Unfellowship with the Union to Preach in our Stands Ansr. no

12 Sholecrek church being destitute of a minister the following brethren agree to visit them. 1st D Badgley & Wm Brazle 2 Wm Jones & M Short 3 N Arnet & B Chapman

13 the bottom Church being destitute of a minister the following brethren agree to atend them, in their turns 1 Wm Jones 2 N Arnett 3 D Badgley 4 R Brazle

14 the following brethren apointed to Preach tomorrow to wit Jones Badgley B Brook & Arnet. The next Assn is apointed at the L G Perara to convainee the friday before the 4th Sunday in September next. elder T. T. Musick is apointd to Preach the Introductory Sermmon & in case of falier N Arnet.

15 it is agreed that the assn receive no querry until it hath been first debated in the church where it arose & cannot be determined

16 it is agreed that when the moderater See cause that can fill his Place with whom he Pleases then dismist a bove Signd by order of the Association Wm Jones Moderater

MOSES SHORT Clk

Minutes of the Illenois Assn holden at the Looking G Perarie the Saterday before the 4th Sunday in September 1811

1 the Introductory Sermon delivered by Elder Jas Rentfro from 1 Peter 4th–12–13 verces

2 letters from 3 churches read & their messengrs names enrold

Churctes	Messengers Names	Rec-by L.	Dis.t	Ded	To.t
Ogles Crk	D Badgley D Samples Jas Rentfro	11	2	1	20
Shole creek	Wm Jones John Finley	8			11
Woodriver	James Beman				26

The L G Perarie letter faild but two of their Mess^s being Present took their Seats (to wit) R Brazle & B Chapman

3 El. Wm Jones chosen Moderater & El R Brazle Clerk

4 a committee of the whole apointed to arang the business of the Assn

5 the report of the committee receivd & atended to acordingly

6 a request from woodriver church (being destitute of a Minister) for Ministerial helps. Elr Jas Rentfro agrees to atend them the first 5 months. El D Badgley the 3 next Elr R Brazle the 2 next & Elr Wm Jones the 2 next months.

7 a request from Oglescreek to Soften the matter concerning the Emacepating Preachers . . . referd —

8 brethren Jas Rentfr & Jas Beman apointed to notify the absent churches when & where our next Assn is to be

9 we apoint our next Assn to holden at Elr D Badgleys the friday before the 4th Saterday in November next & that Elr Thos R Musick Preach the introductory Sermon & in case of falier Elder Nathan Arnet—

10 we recommend it to the churches to make known their libirality by Sending Some money to the next assn to defray the expences of the same—

11 ajourd to the time & Place above mentioned. Signed by order of the Association Wm Jones Moderater

ROBERT BRAZLE Clk

1810

The advice given in Febry, 1809 by the Committee to the Churches / To reclaim all the Baptist members who live nearer to them than any other Church wishing to support the United Baptists at large and all that will not be reclaimed to Exlude them and to be cautious not to receive any member or members that live near in the bounds of any other sister Church lest contempt should be thrown on the Church to the wounding of their Bretheren and to gave up all their members that live nearer to any other sister Church to join with them unles the Church should be broken up in so doing — when such members who separate themselves from the Churches are excluded write they went out from us and therefore they are no more of us —

Minutes of the Illenoi Assn Holden at Elder David Badgleys in St Clare County Illenoy Teritory on the 22 23 & 24 of November 1811 The Introductory Sermon was delivered by Elder Thos R Musick from Isai 61.7 Letters from 6 Churches was read & their Messengers names enrolld & a list of their numbers taken

Churches	Messengers names	dismist	Rec^d Experience	Rec^d by letter	exclu^d	Dead	Total
Fephees Creek	T R Musick Chr^n T Nelterbrand Jno Mcdonald Seth Emmons	12	58		1	1	82
Cold water	David Burk		3				9
Wood River	Jas Beman George Moore						24
M Bottom	G Valentine David Waddle				1		6
Lookinglass	Robt Brazle Wm Brazle	2			1		6
Ogles creek	David Badgley Jas Rentfro		1	3			23
							150

The Turkey hill & Shole Creek letters failed but brethren Nathan Arnett & Wm Jones being presents took Seats with

us brother Thos R Musick was chosen Moderater & br Jas
Rentfro clerk

1 the following brethren was apointed to arange the business
of the assn Wm Jones R Brazle D Badgley S Emmon G
Moore N Arnett G vallentine D Burk with the Moderater
& clerk

2 ajoured until tomorrow 9 oclock — 23 Met Persuant to
ajournment & after worship Proceeded to business—

3 the arangement read & receivd & the Committee discharged

4 in answer to the referance from last Assn to releive the
minds of any that maynot understand us, we say we did
not nor do not mean the rule concerning the Emancepating
Preachers to extend to any that have not departed from
the General Union or given hurts by disorderly conduct

5 a request from Fephees creek for ministerial helps to
ordain a minister,—bren D Badgley N Arnet & Jas Rentfro is apointed to that business

6 the Bottom Church being destitute of a minister the
following brethren agrees to atend them Jas Rentfro in
Decmͬ february March July & August R Brazle in
january & April Thos R Musick in May & June—

7 Money Sent from the Churches (to wit) from Fephees
creek $1.37½ Ogles creek 50 Woodriver 75 bottom 50
Coldwater 5.08

Jas Rentfro apointed treeasurer & also to Procure a book
& record all the business done by this Assn therein & bring
it to the next assn

9 bror Wm Jones apointed to write a circular letter &c

10 bretheren Musick Arnet & Rentfro apointed to Preach
tomorow

11 The next assn to commence on the 3rd friday in September next at bro Elick Clerks Lucianina Territory & that
broͬ S. Arnett Preach the Introductory Sermon & in case
of falier J Rentfro

Dismist in love

THOS R MUSICK Moderater
JAS RENTFRO Clerk

Minuts of the Elanoy asoscation Holed at Brother Alec Clarks Misouri Teritory on the 18th 19th 20th of september 1812 first the Introductory Sermon Delivred by Elder Jas Rentfro from 2 Timothy 2 Chap and 15th Verce—
2 letters from Nine Churches read and Recd and their Mesengers Names Enrold

[Churches]	[Messengers]	Exp	leter	Dismist	Exclood	dead	Total
Feefees Creak	T. R Musick S Emmon Abrm Musick mon Abrm Musick	12	2	10	6	0	86
Cold water	Jno. Allen Thos Ellace William Paterson	3			1		13
Wood River	Jas Beman						27
Ogles Creek	Jas Rentfro B. Miller						55
Shole Creak	William Jones						9
Turkey hill	Wm Thomson Jas Balls	11	4				33
Nigro fork	S. Graham A Helterbran						11
Beauf	John Sullins						17
							269

These last two Churches is New Constitutions since the last asoscation and prays admitance into this asoseation and it is granted

3d Brother Rentfro Chosen Moderater and Brother Thos R Musick Clark—

4th The Circular letter Cald for and Read and Referd To the Committee for Consideration—

5th a Committee Chosen to a Range the busyness of the asoscation and make Report to morow at Nine oclock

Br Jones Br Allan Br Beman With the Moderator and Clark—

6th Saturday the 19th The asoscation met and after divine worship proceeds as follows

7th The committee chosen to arange the busyness of the asoscation Makes their Report and it is Received and the Committee discharged—

8th The Matter Concerning the Book for the asoscation Taken up The asoscation Consider that Brot Rentfro Receive for his services and the Book a Compensation of Six dollars and fifty cents—

9th The Asoscation think it Nesesary to Chose a standing Clark for the asoscation Thos R Musick is Elected Clarke

10th The Circular letter Calld for Read and Received—

11 The Request of the arm from Turkey Hill Church Taken up—The asoscation advise the arm Make application to the body to which they belong and if they Concur with them then they have a Right to apply to any Sister Church of the Union or Churches for Sutable helps for that purpose—

12th To know the liberality of the Churches from ogles Creak 1 dollar 62½ cents Wood River 50 cents Shole Creak 50 Cents Nigro fork 1 dollar feefees Creak 1:25 Beauf 50 and Cold water 50—

13th Brother paterson apointed to Examin the fund and make a Report he Reports that their is found Remaining in the Treasury three dollars

14th It is the Mind of the Asoseation that the Clark furnishes Each Church with a Copy of the Minuts and Receive 25 Cents for Each—

15th When and where the Next asoscation is to be holden It is apointed at wood River and to begin the fourth Friday in August Next—

16th Who to preach the Introductory Sermon Brother Arnet and in Case of falure Brother Emmons—

17th Who to write the Circuler letter answer Brother Rentfro

JAS RENTFRO Modetor
THOS R MUSICK Clarke

To the Churches whom we Represent
Very dear Brethren whereas Religion is held in great dispute
in the world we have thought proper to address you on the
Subject. We believe Religion to be a sistom or sumery of
principals through which we discover something of th divine
being and our duty towards him and Man our fellow Creature
We believe in the Father the Son and the Holy ghost one
only true and liveing God and that he made man Upright
but they have Sought out many inventions Eclis–7–29 and
became a became a falen and depraved Creature Conceived
in Sin and brought forth in Inequity pet 5–5 Children of
wrath by nature Eph. 2–3 haveing no power of their own to
make Satisfaction for sin or Change the Coruptions of their
Hearts but God being Unchangeable and the only fountain
of love first John 4–16 therefore laid help on his son and sent
him to our Relief first John 4–9–10 Who Rendred Satisfaction to his law and became the propesion for our Sins Romans
3–25 and the End of the law for Righteousness to Every one
that believe Romans 10–4 therefore he hath Sent the Holy
Ghost the Spirit of Truth into the hearts of his people John
14–17 and it became the day of his poro [power] to them
psalms 110–3 they wer Made a willing people and being con-
vincd of their lost and helpless setuation ware inabled by faith
in the son of God to lay hold on Eternel life haveing the Spirit
of God to bare with their spirits that they ware born of God
that his Church is a garden Enclosd. a spring Shut up a
fountain Sealed Songs 4–10 have bean made to Cry out how
amiable are thy Tabernicle o Lord of host one day in thy
Corts is better then a thousand Elcewhere pslms 84–10–12
and haveing Respects to all his Commands have given our
Selvs to the Lord and one another by the will of God Col
2–12 Romans 6–4 henceforth that you should not live to your
selves but Unto God therefore Earnestly Contend for the
faith once delivred to the saints Jude 3 and Stand as faith
dorekeepers in the house of God—
Watching against sin and try to shun all apearance of Evil
keep up your Respective Church Meeteings let Brotherly
love Continue hab 1–31 let Each one Esteam his Brother

better than him Self and be kind to all men Makeing mention of them in your prayers for this is good and Axceptable in the sight of God our saviour Who will have all men to be saved and to Come to the knowledg of the Truth first Timothy 2–24 second peter 3–9 tho much to be lemented that the greater part seems to Come short of it let us try to keep up our Asocations to Relieve the distresed minds amonst us if any and head the groath of Userpation if thair should be any phil, 3–2–7–8 first Timothy 1–7 acts 15–5–6
May the Lord build you up in your most Holy faith in Christ Jesus our Lord amen

Jas Rentfro Modtr
Thos R Musick Clke.

Minuts of the Elenoys Assoscation Holden at Wood River Meeteing house Elenoys Teritory Maderson County on the 27th–28th–29th of August 1813 The Introductory Sermon delivred by Br Arnet from psalms the 126–and 6 verce— Letters from Seven Churches was Red and the names of their Deligates Enrold—

Churches	Deligates	by Ep-earance	Re^d by letter	Dis-missd	Excluded	Dead	Total
Nigro fork	Abraham Heller br Seth Emmons	1	1	1	1	0	12
Feifees	C J Houders. R sul-lins T. R. Musick	0	0	10	8	2	59
Lo glass prary	Robt Brazel	1	0	0	1	1	6
Turkey hill	N Arnet J Kerr W Thompson	0	0	0	1	1	31
ogles Creak	R stockton Benet Millen	1	10	6	2	0	66
Wood River	Jas Beman J Rusel Jos White	0	0	0	0	0	24
Shole Creak	William Jones	0	0	0	0	0	8

Committee Chosen to arange the busyness of the Asocation and Make Report to Morow at Nine oclock—

B Jones Br Emmons Br Brazel together with the Moderator and Clarke—

4 The Asoscation Met accordeing to Ajournment and the Committe Made their Report and it is Received and the Committee Discharged—

5 Brother Robt stockton Chosen Treasurer protem—

6 the Liberality of the Churches to pay the Expences of the Assocation........$5 37½

7 John Houdershall to Examin the fund pay Charges and Return the overplus—

8 Who to fill the stand tomorow N Arnet W Jones T. R Musick—

9 When the Next asoscation and where it is to be Holden at T. R Musicks in st Louis County in Missouri Teritory and to begin the friday before the forth Lords day in September 18th—

10 Who is to preach the Introductory sermon Br Emmon

11 Who to Write the Circular letter Br Arnett—

Signd NATHEN ARNETT Modr
THOS R MUSICK Clark

The Circular Letter

Mesengers Composeing the Elenoys Asoscation Holden at Wood River Meeteing House the 27th 28th and 29th of Augt 1813 To the Churches whom we Represent Sendeth Christian Salutation, Dearly Beloved Brethren It appears from the accounts of the letters to the Asoscation that a Very small Addition has bean since our last asoscation it appears to be a time of general declintion in Religion a time when Enequity abounds and the Love of many Waxes Cold Ought not this to be a matter of lamentation and yet we fear theirs but few that does sincearly lament it, it is said in scripture that much Increase is by the strength of the ox, O brethren what is the Matter do you use your oxen well to make them strong do you pray for them do you Endeavour to strengthen them by a due attendance on their appointments when in your power and Endeavour to practise what they teach you Wo to them that are at Ease in sion, it is aufull for a profisor to groe so much Gallio like as to Cear so much for none of these things Brethren we would wish to Rouse your fealings for their is need and when you view the aufull gloomy situation we are in, dont let Dispare overwhelm your minds so as to discourage you, Remember King Jesus Reigns yea and his love is as great as when he sweated in in Jethsemine or blead in Calvery O Breathren shall he love us somuch so Undeservedly and we love him none or so little O let us try to search after his beauty his glory and Excellency and Endeavour to love him because he first loved us and then when we have him his yoke will be easy and his Commands delightfull Especially the New Command to love one another yea surely if we love jesus we shall love those that bares his Image wher ever we find it this is Charity that one Apostle sais Covers a Multitude of sins and a nother sais without it I am Nothing this would leade us to all Reasonable allowances for human frailties or depraved nature to take Admonation kindly from Each others and to pray for one another that the grace of God might abound which may God grant for Christs sake—Amen

NATHEN ARNET Mod
THOS R MUSICK Clke

Minutes of the Illinois Association holden at Thos R Musicks in the Missouri Territory St Lousis County the 23d 24th 25th of September 1814—

1st The introductory Sermon delivered by Elder David Badgley from John the 10th Chap and 14th verse—

2d Br David Badgley Chosen Moderator—

3d Letters from Eight Churches was read and the names of their Delegates enroled—

		No
Feefees Creek	T. R. Musick Wm Walten Cha Hubbard Richard Sullin	52
Wood River	George Moore	20
Ogles Creek	David Badgley David Samples	53
Nigro Fork	Abrm Holterbrand	11
Cold Water	Chs Collard Jno Mcdonnold Thos Ellace	14
Prairie Delong	William Thompson	10
Femosage	David Desk Thos Smith	12
Beauf	Lewis Williams Jno Sullen Wm Henson	17

4th The Committee chosen to arrange the business of the Association and to make report tomorrow at 10 Oclock Br Charles Hubbard, Br George Moore, Br David Samples

Br Abraham Helterbrand Br Thos. Ellace Br. Thos Smith Br Jno Sullin together with the Moderator and the Clerk—

5th The liberallity of the Churches received four Dollars and 75 Cents—

6th Thomas R. Musick Chosen Treasurer for the Association protem—

7th Adjournd till tomorrow ten Oclock—

8th Saturday the Delegates met According to Adjounment an proceed as follows—

9th the Committee called on They make report it is received and the Committee discharged

10th The petitions from Prariri delong taken up the Church begs Admittance into This Association and is Received. Also begs Ministers to visit them Br John McDonnold is to visit them at their November Meeting which is the 2d Saturday in each month

11th The Femosage Church begs atmittance in to this Association they are received—

12th Who to write The Circular letter for next Association Ans. Br Thos R Musick—

13th Br Jno McDonnold appointed to examine the fund and make report after Examination he frays the expences of the Association reports that there is one Dollar and 75 Cents—

14th When and where the next Association is to be holden Ans at Br David Badgleys in the Illinois Territory St Clair County and to begin the friday before the third Lords day in September 1815—

15th Who to preach the Introductory Sermon at the next Association Ans Br Lewis Williams in case of falure Br Jno McDonnold

16th Br John McDonnold appointed to Search the General fund and make report to the next Association—

17th The Minutes cald for Read and Received them dismised in love

Signd by order of the Association

DAVID BADGLEY Moderator
THOMAS R. MUSICK Clark

Minutes of the Illinois Association of United Baptists holden
at Br Davids Badgleys begun the 15th day of September
1815
1st Br Lewis Williams preached the Introductory Sermon
from John 10th Chap & 2d 3d and 4th verses—
2d Letters from Nine Churches read and the names of their
delegates enrolled—

		No
Feefees Creek	Jno Howdershell Wm Martin Thomas R Musick	54
Wood River	Jas Beeman Jno Finley Wm Jones	26
Beauf	Josh Massey Phil Miller Mosias Manpin	32
Prairie delong	Wm Thompson Preston Bricky	12
Femeoshage	Thomas Smith Daniel Colgan	13
Negro Fork	Lewis Williams	11
Cold Water	John McDonnold	10
Looking Glass Prairie	Wm Brazel Wm Roberts R Brazel	12
Ogles Creek	David Badgley	46

3d Br Jones Chosen Moderator Thos R. Musick Clark Br
Massey Assistant Clark—
4th The Committee chosen to arrange the business of the
Association and make report tomorrow nine Oclock—
5th the names of the Committee John Howdershell John
Finley Phillip Miller Wm Thompson Daniel Colgan Lewis
Williams John McDonnold Robert Brazel David Badgley
together with the Moderator and Clark—
6th Money thrown in to fray the expences of the Association
Femosage $1 00 Feefees Creek $1–00 Cold Water 0–50
Negro Fork 0–50 Prairie delong 0.25 Beaf 2.00 Wood River
1–00 then adjound till tomorrow nine Oclock—
Saturday September 16th 1815
Members met pursuant to Adjournment an proceeded as
follows—
The Association call for the report of the committe dis-
charged.

The business of the association to be taken up as it stands on the minutes—

From last Association Br John McDonnald to examine the general fund and make report to this association—and reports there was found in the hands of Br Renfrow 3 Dolars and in the hands of Brother Stockton $3.12½ cents and in the hands of Br Musick 1.75 cents Br Musick appointed Treasurer and that he call for the money in the past Treasurers hands—

Br John McDannald to examine the fund—

The prayrs of the Prairiedelong churce Ministerial helps given at the fourth Saturday and sunday in each month first Br Jno. McDonnald in July Robert Brazel October and May Wm Jones Novemeber and August Thos R Musick June Wm Brazel April—

The Querry of the Prairie delong church taken up to wit, is it right for any body of people praying for a Constitution and being absent at the time of the Constitution and their names not being enroled in the Constitution afterwards to deny the Church privilege, to deal with them for immorral conduct on that account Answer no, we thik them belonging to the Constitution—

Why the seats of the Turkey hill Church is emty in this Association these two Years—

We believe it right to appoint a committee to go to Turkey hill Church and enquire into the order of that Church and make report to the next association—We authorise the Committee to set in Church order with the Turkey hill Church as it respects any thing that may be before them Resolved that the Committee shall consist of ten members from the different Churches, to wit, Wood River Church Bretheren Jones, Beeman Finley Ogles Creek Bretheren Badgely, Samples, Halkum, Looking Glass Prairie Bretheren Robert Brazel Wm Brazel, Roberts Prairie delong Brother William Thompson—

The circular letter read and approved Shall the minutes of this Association be printed Answer it is left to Br T. R. Musick to superintend that business and if he can get them

printed on reasonabl terms to get them printed and distribute them to each Church according to the number of members when Printed—
who is to fill the Stand tomorrow—
Answer who feels the impression—
Who to write the Circular letter for next Association—Ans Br Jones—When and where the next association to be held Answer the first friday in October 1816 at the Baptist Meeting House in the settlement of St, John that Br Wm Jones Preach the Introductory Sermon in case of failure Br David Badgley
Signed by order of the Association,

WILLIAM JONES Mod

THOS R. MUSICK Clk.

Circular Letter
To the Churches whome we represent
Dearly beloved Bretheren—
We learn from your letters, that Religion seems at a low ebb at this time among us which ought to be lamented much by all true believers and as there is a cause for these things it appears necessary that each one should by searching after the cause in order that it may be done away from among us although religion is a matter of the greatest importance of all things, yet it seems the least set by among mankind and many who have professed to have had religion now says there is no reallity in it and says it is only a fancy of the brain, Dear Bretheren permit us to address you on that important subject Some says they think christianity to be a grand imposition and yet they cannot think that Thousands of the learned Romans and wise Greeks who agreed to despise the Jews above all other men took for their Saviour that very Jesus of whome his own countrymen had been ashamed and whom they had Crucificd as an imposture is not this as absurd as to believe that thousands of wise men and men of learning too, could be induced to believe from the tale of two or three Hottentots to worship a certain Hottentot, whom that nation had condemed to be hanged asserting he was more guilty of Death then the bloody ringleaders of a Seditious mob, If you believe with some infidels that the history of Christ is a mere fable and that there never was such an extraordinary person

you must think that the Heathen the Jews and the Mehomitians have agreed with the Christians there sworn enemies to carry on a most amazing imposture which they all agree in—If the Gospel is a delusion you must believe saint Paul who was a man of sense education and interpidity was seduced by no body to Preach near thirty years with astonishing Zeal and great hardships an imposture against the abattors of which he just before breathed nothing but threatening and Slaughter—If the Gospel is forged you must believe that the Apostles handed down to posterity as a sacred treasure, Epistles where he mentions his amasing conversion from gross immoralities and congratulate them about the spiritual or miraculous gifts in which they abounded, and gaves them particular directions how to use the gift of tongues to edification when yet they were totally unacquainted with any such thing If you conclude that the Apostles were cheats and liars you must believe that they took a great deal of pains to bring pain and misery want and distress upon themselves for nought but to bring themselves to an untimely death—But we are informed that in the latter days many will depart from the faith giving head to seducing Spirits and doctrines of devils—Dear Bretheren let us look to the word and make it the man of our Council and look to him who is able to guide us in the paths of peace and holiness without which no one can see the Lord Dear Bretheren have your lamps trimmed and your lights burning and you yourselves like men waiting for the coming of your Lord and master and may the God of all love guide and direct all his people is our prayers

WILLIAM JONES Mod

THOS. R. MUSICK, Clerk.

Minutes of the Illinois Association of the United Baptists holden at the new meeting House in the Settlement of St. Johns, began friday the fourth of October 1816 and continued by Adjournment the two following days—

1st Elder William Jones preached the Introductory sermon from 2d Cor, 11 Chap 29 verse—

2d Letters from Nine Churches was read and the names of their Delegates enrolled—

		No
Looking glass Prairie	Robt Brazel Wm Brazel	14
Ogles Creek	David Badgley Jeremiah Hand	63

		No
Wood R(i)ver	Wm Jones and John Finley	22
Prairie Delong's	Letter received and read but no delegate	11
Beauf	K. Caldwell Josh Massy, Chas. Collard	30
Feefees Creek	Richd Sullin lewis Martin Chas. Hubbard T. R. Musick	58
Femme Osage	Flanders Calleway	12
Cold Water	Letter received and read no delegate	13
Mount Pleasant	Boons Lick Green B. League	28

3d Wm Jones Chosen Moderator T. R. Musick Clk.

4th A committee Chosen to arrange the busines of the Assoication and make report tomorrow nine Oclock—

Th. Caldwell Robert Brazel David Badgley Flanders Calleway Lewis Martin John Finley Green. B. League together with the Moderator and Clarke—

The Association met according to adjounment and after divine worship Proceeded—

1st the Committe came and made report of their proceedings The report received and the committee discharged—

2d the committee appointed last Association to visit Turkey Hill Church came to this Association and brought their proceedings that they had given letters of dismission to some and excluded some and the Church was dissolved— The Association received their report with thanks and the Committee discharged—

3d the Circular letter called for read and receaved

4th Query from Feefees Creek Church concerning the 7th chapter of the first Corinthians and 36th verse, it throw'd out—

5th Prairie delong prays for ministerial helps to be sent to them by the association motioned for the Ministers to volunteer. Br Robert Brazel agrees to attend them two months, March and August, Br Collard and Br League two months February and September Br Wm Brazel one month May T. R. Musick June the fourth Saturday and Sunday in each month is the time of their Church Meetings—

6th the case of Wm Hensley taken up whome the Church on Beauf had excluded for Preaching unsound doctrine and for leaving the Church in a disorderly way and joining himself to a disorderly Body the association cautions each Church of the United Baptists against him and not to countinance him in Preaching among them

7th Question shall we correspond with any other Association—Ans. we shall—

8th With what Association and how—ans with the Wabash district association by letter and delegate, it is thought necessary that two be nominated and in case they should fail two more—first Br Wm Jones and David Badgley in case of failure Br Robert Brazel and Wm Brazel Question who to write the Corresponding letter—Ans Br David Badgley and Br Jones with a Committee and to sign it in behalf of the association and that Br. R. Brazel write a letter to the Association that we correspond with the nature of the split that took place in the Illinois Association and that he call someone to assist him—

9th The fund to be examined and a report made to the Association Br Coldwell and Br Finley they report that there is Twenty one Dollars the Bretheren that corresponds to have a reasonable compensation allowed them—

10th Who to superintend the printing the minutes Ans T. R. Musick and to distribute them when printed who to write the circular letter for next Year Br League who to fill the stand tomorrow Wm Brazel Robt Brazel Wm Jones David Badgly T. R. Musick

11th When and where the next association is to be holden Ans at Wood River and to begin the fourth friday in September 1817

12th Who to Preach the Introductory sermon Ans Br Collard and in case of failure T. R. Musick Then the Association adjourned till time and place appointed

WILLIAM JONES Mod
THOS. R. MUSICK Clk,

The circular letter lost or mislaid so that it cannot be printed Money thrown in to defray the expenses of the Association—

Femeosage	$3 00
Mount Pleasant	4 00
Wood River	2 00
Looking Glass Prairie	1 00
Prairie delong	0 75
Ogles Creek	2 50
Beauf	2 75
Cold Water	0 75
Feefees Creek	2 50
Total	$19 25

The Circular above mentioned is wrote on the first leaf in this book from the Original by the Authors own hand—

(In the Year 1816 ought to have been 1817.)

We wish to address you this year on the subject of A Union A Union we conceive consists in a proper acquaintance and oneness with each other which alone proceedeth from the Triune God which from a beam of his divine light poor sinners are brought to a sence of their lost and helpless situation and to a dependance on God for eternal Salvation through our Lord Jesus Christ and being Born again they have Union with God and one another for he that loveth God loveth him that is born of God and to maintain a union and as an earnest of his Love God has given his Holy Spirit to seal his Children and his word for the man of Their Counsel and when they walk according to the Holy commandments they prove they have a Union with God and one another for the keeping of the commandments is the only proof of their Love to God and one another Therefore dear Bretheren try to be fervent in the Spirit obeying the word of God from the heart it will prove as the only means in the hands of God to drive away baroness of mind and leanness of soul and to be separate from sinners and to be careful not to have Union or Communion with those that obey not the Gospel of our Lord Jesus Christ then would each of us be careful for the wellfare of union and for those that stand upon her walls to blow the Gospel Trumpet then would union travel and bring forth and be comforted and God Glorified Amen

(Copy of the original lost in the year 1816)

(NOTE.—The above circular Letter for 1816 was copied on the inside of the front cover of the Minute Book.)

Minutes of the Illinois Association of the United Baptists holden at Wood River Meeting House began the fourth friday in September 1817 and continued by adjournments from time to time till Sunday evening following—

1st Br Charles Collard Preached the Introductory sermon from John 1st Epistle 2d Chap. and 28th verse

2d Letters from Nine Churches read and the names of their Delegates enrolled—

		No
Ogles Creek	Bennet Millen Wm Johnson David Badgley	29
Prairie delong	William Thompson	13
Cold Water	John Allen	17
Femosage	Flanders Caleway Daniel Colgan	14
Negroe fork	Samuel Grayham Lewis Williams	16
Beauff	Charles Collard James Greenstreet James Brown	
Looking Glass Prairie	Robert Brazel Wm Brazel	15
Feefees Creek	Thos R. Musick Jno Howdershell Richard Sullen	52
Wood River	James Beeman Jno Finley Wm Jones	

3d Three Churches by letters and delegates begs admission into this association—and is received—

Canteen Creek	Alexander Conlee Jacob Gunterman Alexander Stire	39
Upper Quiver	Charles Hubbard John Null	
Shole Creek	William Roberts	14

4th Br Collard Chosen Moderator

Liberality of the Churches taken	$; Cts
Prairie delong	1.62½
Cold Water	1.25

Liberality of the Churches taken $; Cts.

Femosage	3.00
Lookingglass Prairie	1.00
Beauff	1.00
Feefees Creek	2.50
Negroe Fork	1.25
Wood River	1.00
Ogles Creek	3.00
Upper Quiver	2.00
Canteen Creek	1.62½
Shole Creek	1.00

5th a Committe chosen to arrang the business of the association and make report to morrow Nine Oclock Br Jones Br Brazel Br Williams with the Moderator and Clark— the Association met acording to adjournment and proceeds as follows—

1st the proceedings of the Committee cal'd for received and the Committee discharged—

2d The man appointed to write the Circular letter last Year failed and Br Collard appointed to write it and bring it forward

3d The rules of Decorum requested to be read and it was done—

4th Shall we continue as the last Association appointed to Correspond with the Wabash association—We shall—

5th The letter that Br Robert Brazel was to to write last Association cal'd for read and Received

6th The Corresponding letter cal'd for read and received

7th It is thought necessary that a Copy of letter that Br Robert Brazel wrote to be kept Br Jones and Br Robert Brazel to write it—

8th It is thought right that our Delegates be compensated and that they have Ten Dollars Each—

9th Men appointed to examine the fund and make report— report $25.00—

10th Mount Pleasant begs a dismission from this Association. the Clark is appointed to write them a letter of dismission—

11th The request of Wood River Church taken up Requesting to divide this Association into two Associations that the other or West side of the Mississippi be a sepperate Association and that it bear the name of the Missouri Association—it is carried—

12th And appoints the first Association the friday before the seond Lords day in November next, at Thomas R Musicks Old Place—

13th Wm Brazel and Robert Brazel to write a Corresponding letter to the Missouri Association and the same Bretheren to attend—

14th the request of Cold Water Prairie delong and Upper Quiver requesting preachers to be sent to them it is left to the discression of the Preachers—

15th The Association appoints that the Clark furnish this Association with one copy of the Minutes and the other side of the River with one

16th Br Williams appointed to preach the Introductory sermon for the Missouri Association and in case of failure Thos. R. Musick—

17th When and where the next Association is to be holden it is to be holden the friday before the second Lords day in October 1818 at Job Badgleys St Clair County Illinois Territory and Wm Brazel to Preach the Introductory sermon and in case of failure Br Robert Brazel and Br Jones to write the Circular letter for next association—

18th The Association Relaeses our Treasurer from collecting the Money from the past Treasurers—

The proceedings of the Association Read received and signed by order and adjourn'd—

CHARLES COLLARD Moderator
THOMAS R. MUSICK Clark

To the Baptist Churches of the Illinois Association greeting dear Bretheren we would wish to adres you on the alimportant subject of Christian duty and that is to take the word of God for the man of your council Oh Bretheren hearing from the different parts of Zion we find that she is languishing Bretheren put on the whole armour of God having on for an helmet the hope of Salvation and the Breastplate of Righteousness havin your Loins girt about with Truth and your feet shod with the preparation of the Gospel of peace but above all take with you the Shield of Faith whereby you may wield all the fiery darts of the Wicked one praying always with all prayrs. Seeing that the blessed Jesus our head and husband pray'd to his father when in the days of his humiliation but has ascended to your father on high and sends such blessings into the souls of his Children as is not equally to be told know Dear Bretheren consider that prayr is the institution which the Lord of Life and Glory has appointed for us, ask and ye shall receive do you not feel that you are needy, where should you go but to Jesus seeing he has Grace to help in time of need Bretheren of God heard the Crys of his Children in days of Old and that he did his word will show, so a Paul and Silas when in Chains and god heard them so the Lord delivered them and feard the hurt of the keeper of the jail so as to bring him to the acknowledging of saving Grace, so a peter bound in Chains when the Church pray'd—ah behold the Angels of God decending for his deliverance and a Cornelius a devout man met with the Angel of God these things bretheren we find on record and many more may behold by searching the Scriptures O Bretheren keep a close walk with God deny yourselves of all ungodly and worldly lusts live to the honour of that blessed Jesus who suffered that you and we might live see him in the garden and on the Bloody Tree behold and hear him cry before he died it is finished keep your selves unspotted from the world let your lights so shine that others beholding your good works may Glorify your Father which is in Heaven the Grace of our Lord Jesus Christ be with you all Amen—

CHARLES COLLARD Mod.

THOS. R. MUSICK Clk,

Minutes of the Illinois Association of United Baptists held at the house of Job Badgleys, St. Clair County Territory of Illinois October 9th 10th & 11th 1818

Friday October 9th 1818

1st the Association having convened Elder William Brazel preached the Introductory sermon from John 6th 39th and this is the Fathers will which hath sent me that of all which he hath given me I should lose nothing but should raise it up again at the last day

2d Rev. David Badgley chosen Moderator & Rev William Jones Clerk—

3d Letters from the following Churches were received read and the names of their ministers and messengers enrolled

Ministers names [1] in Italicks

Churches	Delegates	Baptised	Rec'd by letter	Dis'd by letter	Excluded	Died	Whole No.	Monies Paid $	Cts
Cantine Creek	Andrew Turner								
	Samuel Wood								
	Alexandrer Conlee		1				40	2	56¹/₄
Shoal Creak	James Street								
	William Roberts	3	5				20	1	25
Wood River	William Jones								
	John Vickery								
	John Finly	1	3	1			30	4	50
Ogles Creek	David Badgley								
	Risdon Moor junr								
	Abraham Badley	4				1	33	2	75
Prairie delong	Robert Stockton		3				16	0	75
Looking Glass	William Brazel								
	Robert Brazel								
Prairie	William Paydon		1				15	1	75
Bethel	George Shipman	1	10	3			15		
	Total	9.	23.	4		1	169	13	56¹/₄

Whole number last Year 12 Churches 385 members Dismissed last Year to constitute the Missouri Association 6 Churches 142 members aggragate increase this Year 1 Church (Bethel received this Session) and 32 members—

4th The delegates to the Wabash Association report, that the Wabash Association readily agreed to open a Correspondance—

5th A letter from the Missouri Association by their delegate Th. R. Musick was received requesting a Correspondance,

[1] The original manuscript fails to indicate the names of ministers.

which upon being found established upon the Principles of the United Baptists in General Union were cordially received as a Correspondant and their Delegate invited to a seat—
—6th Elders Robert Brazel, James Street, and Brother John Finley. Chosen a committee of arrangement, together with the Moderator and Clerk—
7th Rev. William Jones appointed Treasurer
8th A letter was received from the New design Church of Emancipating Baptists which was read and referred till tomorrow—
Adjourned till 9 oclock tomorrow morning—

Saturday October 10th
The Association met and proceeded to business
9th the Committee of arrangement reported and were discharged—
10th The Rules of decorum read—
11th The letter from New design Church called for and Robert Brazel, William Brazel and John Finley appointed to write an answer which read and Accepted—
12th The circular letter by Br Jones read and accepted
13th Brethren Street and conlee chosen to audit the Treasurers account, report $13.56½ cents in the funds
14th Bro. J. M. Peck a Missionary from the Baptist board of of foreign Missions arrived and invited a seat with us
15th Brother William Jones appointed to write the corresponding letter to the Misouri Association and himself with Bro. David Badgley chosen Delegates—
16th Br. Risdon Moore Jun. to write the Corresponding letter to Wabash Association and Brethren Robert Brazel and Wm Brazel chosen delegates—
17. Resolved to propose a Correspondence with the Bethel Association Brethren David Badgley and Wm Jones to write a letter & be our Delegates for that purpose to said Association which sits the Saturday before the 4th Sabbath in Sept, 1819 in the Baptist Church in Belleview settlement, Washington County, M. T.
18. By the request of Looking Glass Prairie Church this

Association recommend to the Churches to meet on the first Monday in each Month to pray for a revival of Religion and the blessing of God on Missionary exertions in the spread of the Gospel—

19 Br Peck presented a circular from the Baptist board of foreign Missions which was read whereuppon Bro. Peck gave a relation of the great exertions making to spread the Gospel and Translate the Scriptures into heathen Languages and the astonishing success which follows the labours of the Missionaries in heathan lands together with a brief statement of the great revivals of Religion in manny parts of our Country and the world—all of which was highly interesting—therefore Resolved that Rev. David Badgley of Ogles Creek St. Clair County be our Secretary to correspond with the board of Missions—

20 Bro. Peck presented a plan of a society to employ Missionaries and promote common Schools amongst the Whites and the Indians which we desire to see carried into effect and which we recommend to the Churches—

21. Appointed Br Badgley to write an outline of the rise and progress of the Baptists in the Illinois to be preserved with the documents of the Association

22. Donation to the funds $1— total $14.56½ Cents—

23. Appointed Bretheren Jones and Peck, to print the Minutes for which $9 were appropriated—

24. Ordered that the remains of the funds be applyed to defray the expences of the delegates to the Missouri Association

25. Appointed Brethren Musick, Peck, and Jones to Preach tomorrow—

26. Our next Association appointed in the Looking Glass Prairie meeting House the Friday before the second Lords day in October 1819—

Br. Street to Preach the Introductory Sermon—

Bro. Wm Roundtree in case of failure—

27. Br. Robert Brazil to write the next circular letter—

28. agreed to hold Quarterly Meetings in this Association as follows first at Shoal Creek at their Meeting in November,

Second at Wood river do. May. Third, Prairie delong do.
July, Fourth do. Bethel (on Shoal Creek) do, September,
Adjourned prayr by Bro. Peck—

Lords Day Oct. 11th

A respectable concoures of people having met Br. Peck
Preached a Missionary Sermon from Exod. 33, 15. If thy
presence go not with me, carry us not up thence. A collection
for the Indian Fund of the Western Baptist Mission society
of $11.25 was received by Bro Peck—
Bro. Jones preached from Hebrews 4th 3d Br Musick from
Isa 53. 1,
Bro. Peck closed by giving some interesiting accounts of
Religious revivals in the Northern States and elsewhere

Circular

The Illinois Association to the Churches we represent—
Dear Bretheren—
The visible Church of which we are members is the kingdom of
Christ on the earth, in which the word of God is the only rule to
direct both in doctrine and practice. It is by the holy Spirit of God
that men are awakened to see the necessity of Salvation; being
Born again they are led by his Spirit and as dear Children cleave
unto their Heavenly Father, his word becomes precious unto them
and his Commandments delightful the precious words of the Redeemer are to be observed by all his professed children, for he says
if ye love me keep my Commandments, and again if a man love me
he will keep my words, and my Father will Love him and we will
come unto him, and make our abode with him, and John says
(1.Epis.4,21) he that loveth God loveth his Brother also, and again
we know that we have passed from Death unto Life because we love
the brethren. In Tertullians time 196 years after Christ such was
the loving behaviour of Christians to each other that the heathen
would point at them as they passed along and say "see how they
love one another!" O that it were so now.—Let us brethren take
the Prophets, Apostles and Ancient Saints for examples in our
conduct, the Psalmist cries, come and hear all ye that fear God and
I will declare what he hath done for my soul. Was the courts of the
Lord the delight of the sweet singer in Israel? They ought to be
our delight Brethren let us say with pious Dr. Watts

My soul how lovely is the place,
To which my God resorts,
'Tis heaven to see his smiling face,
Though in his earthly courts.

To the solemn pledge of our Redeemer gone forth where two or three are geathered together in my name, there am I in the midst of them And does not the Appostle exhort his Brethren—Not forsaking the assembling ourselve together as the manner of some is, Then surely Brethren strict dicipling ought to be maintained and every measure taken to preserve harmony and prevent divisions. Ministers ought to have great care over the Churches taking the oversight thereof being particular to Preach the Gospel in its purity to warn the Churches against error, for the enemy is busy, and if the Husbandmen sleep he will sow tares. The members of the Churches Should love pray for and, hold up the hands of their Ministers, keep a close walk with God and pay strict attention to Church meetings, it is very discouraging for a minister to wride eight of ten Miles to meeting and then find his Brethren neglectful. Good order should be paid to all our business, let us pay early attention to attend our Associations and be a little more liberal to meet its expences, and keep up a correspondence with our sister Associations for this is one means to spread the Gospel. finally abound in every good work and may the grace of our Lord Jesus Christ be with you all,—Amen.

Signed　　　　　　　　　　　　DAVID BADGLEY Mod.
WILLIAM JONES Clerk

Minutes of the Illinois Baptist Association held at the Looking Glass Prairie Meeting House St. Clair County Illinois State October 8th 9th and 10th 1819

1st According to appointment the Association met Br J. M. Peck preached the Introductory sermon from Romans 5th 8th

2d Br Badgley Chosen Moderator and William Jones Clark

3d letters from the following Churches received read and the names of the delegates with the Ministers enrolled, to wit,

Counties Churches	Delegates	Bap	let.	dis	Ex	Rec	ded	total	$
Madison Canteen Creek	Thomas Ray Alexander Conlee Samuel Wood	o	o	1	1	o	3	44	3.00
Bond Shole Creek	James Street no intelegence	o	o	o	o	o	o	20	000
Madison Wood River	William Jones James Beaman John Vickery	o	3	o	o	o	o	35	2.00
St. Clair Ogles Creek	David Badgley Risdon Moore junr Daniel Wilbanks	o	7	10	1	o	o	28	4.00
do. Prairie delong	Israel Straight	o	o	o	1	1	o	11	.50
do. Looking Glass Prairie	Robert Brazel William Brazel	2	o	o	o	o	o	18	2.50
do. Bethel	William Roundtree	o	o	o	o	o	o	15	0.00
Monroe Union	Daniel Star	1	2	3	o	o	o	6	.50
Washington Elkhorn	William Thompson James Fisher	1	6	o	o	o	o	13	1.50
St. Clair Richland Creek	William Kinney J. J. Whiteside Wm L. Whiteside	o	o	o	o	o	o	24	1.00
	Total	4	18	14	3	1	3	194	15.00

4th the three last Churches received this session

Letters from the following Associations received and their delegates invited to a seat The Wabash association neither letter nor Delegate

Missouri—J. M. Peck J. E. Welch Lewis Williams letter Minutes

Bethel no delegate Rec^d a Letter

Mount Pleasant William Thorp Letter

The last association proposed a Correspondance which was readily embraced and the right hand of fellowship given to their delegate—

5th Bretheren Robert Brazel, Conlee, Starr, with the Moderator and Clark appointed a Committee of arrangement—

6th. R. Brazel appointed to write a Corresponding letter to the Wabash association. I [t] was received and ordered to be sent to Br Isaac McCoy,

Brother S. Wood to write to the Missouri asso, which was accepted and bretheren William Jones, David Badgley, Risdon Moore and Daniel Wilbanks to bear it as our Delegates Brother William Brazel to write to the Bethel Association and Bretheren Badgley, Jones, and R. Brazel to bear it as our Delegates Brother Alexander Conlee to write to the Mount Pleasant Association and Bretheren William Kinney, Wilbanks and Samuel Wood to bear it as our delegates

7th—Circular letter called for and delivered to the Committee of arrangement for inspection

8th A letter from the Elk horn Baptist Church received requesting to unite with us Upon examination they were found in good standing and received—

Adjourned till tomorrow morning 9, o'clock.

Brother Badgley Prayed

Saturday October 9th

The association met agreeable to adjournment

Brother Peck prayed

9th The Committee of arrangement made their report and were discharged

10th The circular letter written by Brother Robert Brazel read and adopted—

11th Corresponding letters to sister Associations read and delegates appointed—

12th. Heard a corresponding letter from the Baptist Board of Foreign Missions containing interesting intelegence of the prosperity of the redeemers Kingdom

13th The Quires from Wood River considered 1st is it right to correspond With the Baptist Board of foren Missions— answer yes. 2nd Is there any use of the United Society for the Spread of the Gospel and if so, wherein does it usefulness consist—Answer yes, and its use is to supply destitute places with Preaching

14th Application was made from the Richland Creek Church by their delegates bretheren William Kinney J. J. Whiteside, William L. Whiteside paying for admission as a member of our Union which was accepted and the delegates invited to a Seat—

15th The Querie from Ogles Creek Church considered Is the imposition of hands in the Ordination of a Deacon indispensibly necessary—

Ans. Yes, See Acts 6th 5th 6th Titus 1st 5th

16th A Querie from the Committee of arrangement What advice will the Association offer to a Church of her Body who has a member among them who preaches the doctrine of falling from Grace—refered to a committee of Bretheren R. Brazel, Welch and L. Williams—

17th Appointed Brother Ray to write the next circular on the subject, Why the Baptists do not Commune with other religious societies—

18th Brother Badgley reported that he had made some progress in composing an outline of the history of this Association and requested some person to aid him therefore Brother Jones was appointed—

19th The committee appointed on the last Querie report as follows:—

We affectionately give our advice that such member if a licentiate, be solemnly admonished by the church and iformed that such Preaching is subversive of the Gospel of Christ and if he continue the Church should inform him that they do not concieve his gift profitable and request him to return his licence: and if he refuse, after the first and second admonition to proceed to the highest church censure Titus 3rd 10th— The report was received unamously—

20th Quarterly meetings appointed as follows

1st Shoal Creek 4th Saturday in November, Brother Jones to Preach the first Sermon—

2nd Wood River 1st Saturday in May Brother Badgley to Preach—

3rd Prairie Delong 4th Saturday in July Brother Kinney to preach—

4th Bethel on Sugar Creek 1st in September Brother Robert Brazel to Preach—

21st Brother Jones to receive the money from the Churches and superintend printing the minutes—

22d Appointed the next association at the Meeting House of Canteen Creek Church Madison County the Saturday before the second Lords day in October 1820—

23d Brother Kinney to Preach the introductory Serm in case of failure brother street

24th Resolved that a public collection be taken on tomorrow one half appropriated to the expence of pinting the minutes and the other half to the travelling expenses of the delegates sent abroad—

25th Appointed brethren Welch, Peck, and Williams to Preach tomorrow—

26th The minutes to be distributed according to the number of members in each church

Adjourned

Brother Peck prayed

Lords day October 10th

The following ministers a solemn and attentive assembly—

Elder Lewis Williams from Isa. 26th 1st

—— James E Welch from Isa. 9th 6th

—— J. M. Peck from Isa. 9th 7th

Collection $4.75

The closing scene was quite solemn and affecting and we trust will be long remembered by some present—

Circular Letter

The Illinois association of United Baptists to the churches they represent Sendeth Greeting

Dear Bretheren

What we have done will appear from our minutes, but we wish to caution you against the prevailing errors of the times, the prophecies of Christ and the Apostles are now fulfilling. wolves are appearing in sheeps clothing and false Prophets crying Lo here, and lo there, but our Lord tells us not to believe them for they shall deceive many and if it were posible the very Elect. Some maintain that mankind are born into this world pure but believe them not for David says Behold I was shapen in iniquity and in sin did my Mother conceive me Ps 51st 5th adam was a sinner when he begat a son in his own likeness. Job asks, who can bring a clean thing out of an unclean, not one Job 14th 4th some declare that it will not do to trust in the righteousness of Christ for pardon, but Paul says, Christ is the end of the law for righteousness, Rom. 10th 4th And Jeremiah cals him the Lord our righteousness Jer, 23d 6th and Christ Jesus is made unto us wisdom righteousness &c—

Some will deny the personal divinity of Christ and the doctrine of the attonement, or the vicarious sufferings of Jesus Christ our Lord, the Scripture says whosoever denys the son the same hath not the Father,"—

some tell us that the Lord has done his part and left it for us to dour part, thus placing the whole of our salvation in our hands, forgeting that all we have, has been received from the Lord, and that he worketh in us to will and to do of his own good pleasure, David describes the blessedness of the man to whome the Lord imputeth righteousness without works, others will maintain that after a person becomes righteous and declared to be Justified he may finally fall away and be lost, but the Lord says, my sheep hear my voice and I know them and they follow me, and I gave unto them Eternal life, and they shall never perish neither shall any pluck them out of my hand John 10th 27th 28th—

Dear Bretheren let us not be surprised because men will not receive the words of divine truth without repetition but in the mouth of two or three witnesses every word shall be established. The doctrine that the world receive are not the truth for the natural man discerneth not the things of God for they are foolishness to him neither can he know them for they are spiritually discerned and the carnal mind is enmity against God not subject to his law. The narrow limits of a circular letter will not contain all we might say, but dear brethren suffer a word of Exortation: read the word of God with prayrful attention, and notice these things: and may the God of Grace keep you from all evil and error, and preserve you to his second comeing, Farewell.

Signed by order of the association
DAVID BADGLEY Moderator
WILLIAM JONES Clerk

Minutes of the Illinois Baptist Association held at the Canteen Creek Meeting house Madison County Illinois State October 14, 15 and 16th 1820.

1st According to appointment the association met, Brother William Kinney preached the introductory Sermon from Isa. 28, 16—

2d Brother D Badgley chosen Moderator and William Jones Clerk.—

3d Letters from the following Churches received read, and the names of the Delegates enrolled

Counties	Churches	Delegates	Baptized	Received by Letter	Dismissed by Let	Excluded	Restored	Died	Present No.	Moneys paid
Madison	Canteen Creek	Thomas Ray Jacob Gonterman Alexander Conlee	7	8	1			1	52	3.00
Bond	Shoal Creek	Edmond Booz	5	17	8	1	1		23	0.75
Madison	Wood River	William Jones James Tunnel John Vickery	1	9	11				34	2.62½
St Clair	Ogles Creek	Daniel Wilbanks Risdon Moore David Badgley	2	2					26	3.00

Counties	Churches	Delegates	Baptized	Received by Letter	Dismissed by Let	Excluded	Restored	Died	Present No.	Moneys paid
Do	Prairie	William Peach								
	DeLong	Robert Stockston		7	5			1	14	1.00
Do	Looking	William Padon								
	Glass	William Bridges								
	Prairie	Robert Brazel			3	1			14	3.00
Washinton	Bethel	John Creel	3	5	3				23	1.00
Monroe	Union	Robert Haskins								
		Daniel Starr	1	2	3	3		1	6	0.50
Washington	Elkhorn	Wm Thompson sr								
		Wm Thompson Jr		8	4	1	1	1	16	0.75
St Clair	Richland	John J. Whiteside								
	Creek	Wm L. Whiteside								
		William Kinney							28	4.00
Bond	Hurricane	James Street								
	Fork	Henry Pratt							25	1.50
Madison	Providence	John Finley							20	1.50
	on Macoupin									
St Clair	Twelve M. P.	Samuel Smith								
		Timothy Higgins							5	0.50
Madison	Sangamo	Simon Lindley								
		William Crow							27	1.00
St Clair	New Design	Joseph Chance							19	1.00
		Total	19	58	38	6	1	5	332	25.12½

The five last Churches Received this association—
4th Corresponding letters Called for Wabash no intiligence, Missouri no letter Br J M. Peck Zadock Darson their Delegates being present took their seats. Mount Pleasant a letter but no Delegates Bethel no Intiligence—
5th Br Finley, Kinney and Ray with the Moderator and Clerk appointed a Committee of arrangement—
Brother Risdon Moore to write to the Wabash Br Robert Brazel to Missouri Br Peck to Bethel. Br Kinney to write to Mount Pleasant—

6th Circular letter called for delivered to a special Committee for inspection

7th Street, Peck and Jones to Preach tomorrow and that Preaching begin at 10 Oclock—

8 Adjourned until Monday 9 Oclock

Lords Day, October 15, 1820.

The Bretheren preached to a numerous and attentive congregation Br Street from Rev. 10,1. Br Peck from Cor 4, 5. and Br Jones from Rev. 14, 3.

October 16th

Met according to appointment and proceeded to business—

1 The report of the Committee read and Approved of and the Committee discharged—

2 Br Badgley reported to the Association the Outline of the Baptists in the Illinois

3. It was refered to a Committee until the next Association and Appointed Br Badgley, Jones, Kinney, Risdon, Moore and Joseph Chance—

4. A letter to the Wabash Association read and received Wm Kinney, Joseph Chance, and risdon Moore to bear it

5, a letter to the Missouri Association read and received Badgley, Jones and Wilbanks to Bear it—

6. A letter to the Bethel Association read and received Br. Brazel and Street to Bear it—

7. A letter to the Mount Pleasant Association read and received and say Wm Crow and Alexander Conlee to bear it

8. The circular letter called for read and approved—

9. Br. Jones appointed Treasurer—

10. Br Moore and Wilbanks to Examine the fund and report $25—,12 ½ at this time

11. The next association to be holden on the fourth Saturday in August, 1821 at the Meeting House at Richland Creek Church

12. It is agreed that the Association with all the Churches belonging to her Commence their Meetings on the 1st, 2d, 3d, and 4th Saturday in the month—

13. Brother Street to Preach the introductory sermon at the next Association in case of falure, Br. Jones—

14. Br Wilbanks to write the Circular letter on the subject of Church Dicipline—

15. The Clerk to superintend the printing of the minutes and number and distirbution to be left to his judgement and the balance of the money if any left to go toward his services —

16. The Query from the Canteen Creek Church is the principle and practice of the Baptist Board of foreign Missions in its present Operations justifiable agreeable to Gospel order— answered as folls, Whereas our information respecting the mangement of the Board of foreign missions has as yet been but small we therefore feel willing to drop the Query respecting them, and also to drop any further Correspondance with them

Adjourned.

Circular Letter

The ministers and members composing the Illinois Association to the Churches whom we represent Send Christian love.

Dear Bretheren

From the earliest period of ou correspondence we have studiously selected for the subject of our Annual addresses those doctrines and duties which appeared the most calculated to confirm you in the faith of Christ and increase that light and perfection, which would honour and commend the cause of the Redeemer but while you have endeavoured to keep yourselves unspotted from the world as a chast virgin to Christ you have excited unpleasant feelings and drawn forth censures among the religious denominations around you because you have refused to admit them to your Communion table therefore we propose as the subject of this letter to adduce some reasons why our denomination have pursued this course—

1st It is inviolably maintained by us that the Ordinance of Baptism is an important prerequisite to communion. the following order was observed on the day of penticost—

The three Thousand Converts were first pricked in their hearts then gladly received the word, then were Baptised after were added to them that is the Church in Jerusalm which was composed of the appostles and others to the number of about one Hundred and twenty Indeed most sectaries who pretended to consistancy have heretofore refused communion to those converts who in their view were unbaptised and since the clearest light of scripture fully convinces us that nothing short of complete immersion in water, and only to professed believers and by a proper administrator is Gospel Baptism—that neither pouring or sprinkling either Infants or Adults is in any respect admissible but introduced into the Church by misguided men, we think it improper to introduce such persons as we view unbaptised to our communion

2nd Different sects have different views relative to the use of the Lords supper. as well as about the requisite quallifications for admmission Some suppose and Praach that it is a means of Grace for the unconverted to use for their Salvation and consequently admit all enquirers after truth while others suppose a mere morial Character is all the prerequisite qualification, while we believe it is only an emblem of Christs Death and a means of growth in Grace to believers who are incorporated in Church relation If we should throw open our doors indiscriminately to all proffessers we should be compelled to eat and drink with those who did not pretend to be real Christians. Should we adopt only a partial communion and with those whom we esteemed real Christians we should still give umbrage to the rest, and still be charged with want of Charity; but communion at the Lord,s table is not to be celebrated by us as individuals but in an incorporated or church capacity hence the propriety of limiting it to those only who are regular members and in fellowship in the Church.

3d. There ought to be corresponding sentiments required of those who come to the communion table together We are admonished to speak the same things, and are asked if two can Walk together except they be agreed. Even if we are agreed on the subject of Baptism while it is our unhappiness to be divided on the most essential doctrines of Salvation we are forbid uniting in the Ordinance of the supper. For what kind of communion could there be between two denominations while the ministers of the one declare publickly that the coctrines of the other originated in Hell. Does the doctrines of Heaven and the Docktrine of hell hold communion or is there fellowship with light and darkness. It is a lamentable fact which comes under your own knowledg, that men who profess to be illuminated by truth will in publick and in the heat of their zeal declare that the doctrines which some other denominations hold as sacred Truths come from Hell and perhaps Close with a prayr that it may return thither again and yet in the face of all this will invite the same to their communion table. This is called Charity, but beloved brethren we expect that you know that, Charity rejoiceth in the truth and we beseach that while you hold fast the form of you profession and earnestly contend for the faith once delivered to the saints be ready to Unite with those from whom you may Differ as far as the principles of eternal truth will justify and while you firmly oppose that shadow of Unions so often urged be instant in prayr and exert yourselves to bring about that Union which is in sentiment, affection, and practice, which may the Lord hasten in due time. Amen

Signed,   DAVID BADGLEY Moderator
                                           WILLIAM JONES Clerk.

CHAPTER XIV

DOCUMENTS RELATING TO THE FRIENDS TO HUMANITY OR THE ANTI-SLAVERY BAPTISTS IN KENTUCKY AND ILLINOIS

MINUTES

of the

BAPTIZED LICKING–LOCUST ASSOCIATION, FRIENDS OF HUMANITY,

Held at Ebinezer, Mason County, Kentucky, September 26th, 27th and 28th, 1807.

AT 11 o'clock Elder CARTER TARRANT preached, who was also succeeded by Elder DAVID BARROW

Letters from the Churches were received, and CARTER TARRANT chosen moderator, and John Winn, Clerk.

N.B. Ministers names in small capitals.

State of the Churches.

Churches	Messengers	Baptised.	Rec. by reco.	Dis. by let.	Excluded.	Dead.	Total.
1 Licking-Locust,	DONALD HOLMES, MAHALAEEL SHACKLE, JAMES DUNLAP, John Winn.	1			1	1	40
2 Bracken,	JAMES THOMSON, Job Stout, Wil-						

Churches	Messengers	Baptized.	Rec. by reco.	Dis. by let.	Excluded.	Dead.	Total.
	liam Carter and Abel Morgan.				1		38
3 Foxes creek,	James Wright & Samuel Powel.						11
4 West creek,	Henry Jackson.		1	4			6
5 Ebinezer,	Thomas Longley, George Forquir, John Davis and Nathaniel Hickman.			2			27
6 Bethel,	Sears Crains & Jeremiah Beck.	1			4		18
7 New-hope,	CARTER TARRANT and William Lisinby.		12	2	2		31
8 Laurence's creek,	HAMPTON PANGBURN, Thomas Longley, junr. William Maston.						10
9 Etham,	JOHN STEPHENS, Jonah Reynold, Samuel Belvel & John Bever.		3				9
	N.B. The last two churches received at this meeting.	2	16	9	7	1	190

1. Invited Elders BARROW, GRIGG and MORRIS to set with us; who accordingly took their seats.

2. The Circular was read and referred to the committee of arrangements.

3. Brethren SHACKLE, HOLMES, BARROW, GRIGG, TARRANT & WINN, appointed to arrange the business of the association.

4. Brethren BARROW, GRIGG and TARRANT, to preach to-morrow. Adjourned till Monday morning 9 o'clock.

The Brethren aforesaid, preached to a numerous audience on Sunday.

Monday morning 9 o'clock, we met according to adjournment.

1. *Resolved*, That as an association it is not our duty to interfere in the queries or difficulties of any of the churches.

2. Circular letter read and approved.

3. Elder BARROW's piece on Slavery read, unanimously approved of, and recommended to be printed.

4. Query? What is the most scriptural manner of carrying on correspondence among the Churches? A. Referred to the Churches.

5. Query? Is the office of moderator a scriptural office? A. No.

6. What is the best declaration of faith? A. The scriptures of the *old* and *new Testaments*.

7. The following brethren are to visit the Churches in the following months, viz. PANGBURN, in November; SHACKLE, in May; GRIGG and STEPHENS, in June; THOMSON and LONGLEY, in July; HOLMES and DUNLAP, in August; TARRANT and ELROD, in September.

8. Our next Association is to be held at New-Hope, in Woodford county, and to commence the last Saturday in September, 1808; Elder DAVID BARROW to preach the introductory sermon, and in case of failure, Elder JACOB GRIGG.

9. Elder TARRANT to prepare and superintend the printing of these minutes. Then adjourned to the time and place aforesaid.

CARTER TARRANT, Moderator.

John Winn, clk.

To the Churches in union with us—grace and peace be multiplied!!

DEARLY BELOVED,

WE are now distinguished from our former brethren, by reason of our professed abhorrence to unmerited, hereditary, perpetual, absolute unconditional Slavery—a system of oppression, by whch one part of mankind assumes a right of domineering over another part, as if the latter had been designed by their common creator, to support the crimes of the former; by whom they are bought and sold, denied the rights of humanity and the comforts of life—tormented, afflicted and abused at the discretion of wicked men—without the means of information, concerning God and themselves, and so rendered unfit for civil or religious society, or to perform the duties incumbent on rational beings, as parents, children, husbands, wives, &c—and their children, and their childrens children for ever, are doomed to the same unhappy fate. So that no crime can possibly be committed by man, which can deserve of man a punishment equal in degree and duration to the sufferings of these people, and which they are forced to endure, without the shadow of a crime laid to their charge, and without any cause that we know of, but that this system was introduced by wicked men, and sanctioned by wicked laws. We can easily conceive of servitude of various kinds, as hired servants, bond (or indented) servants, servants on account of debt, misdemeanor or crimes, all which are perfectly consistent with scripture and reason; but this nefarious system is an outrage against both. As a political evil every enlightened wise citizen abhors it; but as it is a sin against God, every citizen is in duty bound to testify against it.

One would think that no human being could look at this system but with abhorrence, and that to frame arguments against it, would be an insult upon the common sense of mankind: But (strange as it may appear in other nations, and to future generations,) there are professors of christianity in Kentucky, who plead for it as an institution of the God of mercy; and it is truly disgusting to see what pains they take to drag the holy scriptures of truth, into the service of this heaven daring iniquity. Sometimes they appeal to Noah's curse, as if that prophecy had been designed by the Almighty, as a foundation of the African slave trade—again they will talk of Abraham's servants, as if the degraded sons of Africa and Abraham's warlike bands, were very much alike. Some will plead the permission given to Israel, to buy of the devoted Canaanites; as if that merciful dispensation could bear any resemblance to this cruel system. Some have urged Onesimus the servant of Philemon, as if they did not know that he was also a brother beloved, both in the flesh and in the Lord. Now they exchange the word slave for servant, and then plead the scripture duties of servants, as an argument in favour of this system; although they have never produced one instance of such a servant as this system holds to view.—Sometimes the word *yoke* is harped upon, as if every servant was not under the yoke, according to the nature of his servitude. Some will plead the slaves (or bodies) and souls of men, traded upon by the wicked Babylonians, as if they would rather be thought such, than lose the gains of oppression. Some will plead the practice of anciant heathens, and the custom of the Negroes enslaving each other in their own country, as if they would rather imitate Pagans and Negroes, than let the oppressed go free. Some will plead their purchase, as if riches would justify wickedness. Some their right by heritage, as if the iniquity of the fathers could justify the crimes of their children. Some will plead the piety of many slave-holders, as if invincible ignorance in one man, could justify sin in another, or as if men comparing themselves with themselves, and measuring themselves by themselves, were wise, which the apostle denies: 2. Cor. x. 12. Some will plead our civil government, as if the church was beholden to the world for assistance in matters of religion, and had no king nor constitution of her own, and as if the laws of Kentucky constrained men to commit wickedness in the land, a stigma on our constitution, which no friend to the state will relish. And some will even challenge us to bring one text against it, as if they did not know that pride, covetousness and cruelty, are contrary to scripture: Nor have they concealed their attachment to this wickedness: They have published it as on housetops, in their councils, their annual associations of Bracken, Elkhorn and North District, for several years past, in their cruel censures.

against the Friends of Humanity, Blinded by covetousness and intoxication with the cup of Babylon, they call evil good and good evil. Rev. xvii. 4, & xviii, 3 – Isai, v. 20. In perverting the scriptures to favour oppression, they cause divisions and offences, contrary to the doctrines which the saints have learned of God, and ought to be marked and avoided: Rom. xvi, 17, 18–1. Thes. iv, 9. But God has made their wrath to terminate in our existence, as a. distinct society—separated (we hope) for ever from the friends of oppression. Blessed be God, for his gracious interposition in our behalf, and the unexpected success he has granted to our feeble efforts in his own cause. How zealous ought we to be, in our opposition to every appearance of evil.

As to the question, What shall be done with these people? We answer, That when we as a people are willing to do our duty, we shall obtain a suitable answer to this question, and not before.

If this system in its nature and tendency is contrary to any one text in the Bible, or to any fair inference drawn from it, then it is a sin against God, to be hated as such by his children. We wish it to be tried by the following passages, as a small specimen of what might be added:–Lev. xix, 18, 33, 34–Isa. i. 16, 17, 18–Isa. xxxiii. 15–Isa. lviii. 6–Jer. v. 28, 29 and xxi. 12, also xxii, 13–Joel iii. 3–Amos viii. 4–Matt. xix. 19, & xxi. 39–Mark xii. 31–James v. 1, 6–Eccl. iv. 1. Ministers may try the propriety of their silence on this subject by such scriptures as followeth: Isa. lviii. 1, and lxii. 6–Ezek. iii. 17, 18–Matt. x. 26, 27, 28–Mark iv. 21, 22–Luke xii. 1, to the 9th–John xviii. 20–2 Cor. iv. 2. Persons who are convinced of the iniquity of this system, and yet continue in fellowship with its friends, are requested to compare their conduct with the following passages: Matt. vii. 30–2 Cor. vi. 17–2 Thess. iii. 6, 7, 8–1 Tim. vi. 4, 5–Rev. xviii. 4, 5.

But we would not lose sight of our duty to God and Man in other respects although the above system is the subject of our letter:—let us study to manifest by our conduct that we have respect to all the commands of Jehovah. May

we grow in Grace and in the Knowledge of our Redeemer!
Amen.

CARTER TARRANT, Mod.

John Winn, Clk.

Printed by W. Hunter, Frankfort, (K.)

THE BAPTIZED CHURCH OF CHRIST FRIENDS TO HUMANITY AT TURKEY HILL, ILLINOIS

State of Illinois, St. Clair County, September 27th, 1822

1st We whose names are here enrolled do agree to unite our membership as a church for Christ to watch over each other in Christian love, having fellowship one for another.

2nd We agree to be constituted on the scriptures of the old and new testaments, believing them to contain sufficient rules for our faith and practice.

3rd We agree to be known by the name of the Baptized Church of Christ, friends of humanity, on Turkey Hill.

Rev'd James Pulliam, Judath Pulliam, his wife, Delilah Woods, Dolly Pulliam, Nancy Wilderman, and Polly Rettenhouse.

Turkey Hill Church was constituted agreeable to the order of the churches by Elders Joseph Lemen, James Pulliam, and James Lemen jr.

Church Rules

This Church agrees to adopt rules concerning slavery, which was made on the 29th of August, 1807, by an association held in Woodord County, Kentucky, and on the day and year above written, which rules are as follows (viz)

Quest. Can any person be admitted a member of this Church whose practice appears friendly to perpetual Slavery.

Ansr. We think not.

Quest. Is there any cases in which persons holding Slaves may be admitted to membership into a Baptized Church of Christ?

Ansr. No except in the following ways.

1st. In case of persons holding young slaves and recording a deed of their emancipation at such an age as the church to which they offer their membership may agree to.

2nd. In the case of persons who have purchased in their ignorance and are willing that the church shall say when the slave or slaves shall be free.

3rd In the case of women, whose husbands opposed to emancipation.

4th In the case of widows who has it not in their power to liberate them.

5th In the case of idiots, old age, debility of bondage that prevents such slaves from procuring a sufficient support, and some other cases which we would wish the church to be at their liberty to judge of agreeable to the principles of humanity.

Quest. What shall be required of those who shall withdraw from other churches on account of perpetual slavery and apply for admission among us.

Ans. If there are no charges against them their acknowledgement of the Doctrine of the gospel is sufficient.

Quest. Shall members in union with us be at liberty in any case to purchase slaves?

Ansr. No, except it be with a view to ransom them from perpetual slavery, in such a way as the church may approve of. Signed by order of the Church.

Rules of Decorum

1st. The Church meeting shall be opened and closed by prayer.

2nd. No person shall be a member of this Church, holding the principles of perpetual involuntary hereditary slavery.

3rd. All matters of debate before the Church shall be decided by a majority except in receiving and exempting of members.

4th. No matter of distress shall be received into the Church but such as come in gospel order.

5th. Only one person shall speak at a time who shall rise

from his seat, and address the Church, in a scriptural manner when he is about to make a speech.

6th. The person thus speaking shall not be interrupted unless he break the rules of this decorum.

7th. The person thus speaking shall strictly adhere to the subject in hand and in no wise reflect on the person who spake before so as to make remarks on his steps failings or imperfections.

8th. No person shall speak more than three times on one subject without liberty obtained from the Church.

9th. No person shall abruptly break off or absent himself from the Church during the setting of the same without liberty obtained from it.

10th. No member shall have the liberty of laughing or whispering in a time of a publick speech.

11th. Any member who shall willing and knowingly break of these rules shall be reproved as the Church may think proper.

The Baptized Church of Christ Friends to Humanity at Turkey Hill met according to appointment on the 26th of October 1822 at Mr. George Wilderman's and after divine worship proceded to business, fellowship being called for, this Church being found in peace. Signed by order of the Church.   DAVID R. CHANCE, Clerk.

The Baptized Church of Christ Friends of Humanity met at James Pulliam's on the 23rd of August, according to appointment. The church found in peace.

1st. A sermon was delivered by Brother James Pulliam from the 2nd Epistle of Peter, first chapter, 5, 6, 7 and 8 verses the Church then proceeded to business, the Church nominated Brother James Pulliam and Charles Messenger to write a letter to the Annual Meeting held at Newdesign Monroe County in October next and also appointed them as deligates from this Church, to sit in Conference at the sd meeting—the Church also appointed Brother Charles Messenger their Clerk and in the evening of said day Sisters

Barbara Million and Elizabeth Pritchet joined by experience and to be baptized as soon as practicable the Church in peace—Signed by order of the Church.

CHARLES H. MESSINGER.

The Baptized Church of Christ, Friends of Humanity, at Turkey Hill, met according to appointment at Mr. John Pulliam's, on the 27th of December, 1823. Fellowship being called for, the church was found in peace.

Brother James Pulliam lodged a report, against Sister Nancy Million, of hard sayings against some of the members, and sister Sus. Shook, and sister Sally Whiteside, was appointed to site her to the next church meeting, and also to give a report of her answer. Signed by order of the Church,

CHARLES H. MESSINGER.

(NOTE.—The Church seems to have met every four weeks. In most cases the minutes are all the same. Unless some special business is recorded such routine minutes are omitted here.)

The Baptized Church of Christ, Friends of Humanity, at Turkey Hill, met according to appointment at Mr. George Willderman's on the 24th of January, 1824, and after divine worship proceded to business. The case of sister Million was lade over to next meeting. Signed by order of the Church.

CHARLES H. MESSINGER.

The Baptized Church of Christ, Friends of Humanity, at Turkey Hill, meet according to appointment, at Brother James Pulliam's, on the 28th of Feb. 1824. And after divine worship proced to business. The case of Sister nancy Million, taken up, discussed, and she expeled. And sister Dicy Smith withdrew her membership, and is no more of us and we are not accountable for her walk. Signed by order of the Church.   CHARLES HOLT MESSENGER, clk.

The Baptized Church of Christ, Friends of humanity, at Turkeyhill, met according to appointment, at Mr J. Wilderman's, on the 25th of Sept. 1824: and after divine worship proceeded to business. Fellowship being called for, the church was found in peace. On motion of Bro. Pulliam the Church concurs with the different churches of the union, in returning thanks to God by prayer and thanksgiving, for the deliverance which we have had in this great struggle, to defend the cause of emancipation in our State government. Signed by order of the Church.

CHARLES H. MESSIGNER, Clk.

The Baptised Church of Christ Friends of Humanity met at Brother James Pulliam's 25 June fellowship being called for the Church being in Distress for Brother John Blagdon he being charged with profanity and intoxication but confessing his error and asking forgiveness the Church forgave him the Church continues in peace. Signed by order of the Church EPHRAIM HARRIS Clerk.

The Baptised Church of Christ friends to Humanity met at Brother James Pulliam's August 27th, 1826 and after divine service fellowship being called for Distress being caused by the improper conduct of Brother James Rutherford the Church appointed Brothers Green B. Batison and Ephraim Harris to cite the said brother to appear at Brother James Pulliams staurday in September 12 Ocl a door being opened for the admission of members Robbert Chesney joined by Experience. The Church appointed Brothers William Holt and Abner Carr and Benjamin Chesney as Delligates to the annual or yearly meeting.

Brother Ephraim Harris was appointed to wright the Church letter.

Signed by order of the Church

EPHRAIM HARRIS Clerk.

The Baptized Church of Christ friends to Humanity met at Brother James Pulliams Oct 24th and after Divine service fellowship being called for the Church is found in peace. Signed by order of the Church.

The case of Brother James Rutherford being brought up

and he being found guilty of disorderly condut the Church saw fit to expell him. Signed by order of the Church.

EPHRAIM HARRIS Clerk.

The Baptized Church of Christ Friends to Humanity of Turkey Hill met at Brother James Pulliams January 26th (1828) and after divine service fellowship being called for the Church is found in peace. This Church has licensed Brother Nathan Arnot to exercise his gifts in public.

Signed by order of the Church. EPHRAIM HARRIS Clerk.

Jan the 23—1830

The Baptised Church of Christ friends to Humanity at Turkey Hill. Met according to appointment at Brother Conrad Carrs House on Richland Creek, and after divine worship fellowship was called for the church proceded to business. The ordination of B. Nathan Arnott was taken into consideration and the Church proceded to appoint five of our Ministers as a Prispitery to take Brother Arnot through an examination and report the same to the Church, to wit Brother James Lemen James Pulliam Joseph Chance Benjamin Ogle and Brother Daniel Hilton. After examination of Brother Arnott the Brethren reported that Brother Arnott being examined they find him redy for ordination whereon the 24th day Sunday he was ordained. Sunday night a door being open to receave members Rebecka Arnott joined by recomendation. This Church is in peace.

Signed by order of the Church, EPHRAIM HARRIS Clk.

1831   Feb 26th on Saturday   1831

The Turkey Hill baptized Church of Christ Friends to Humanity met at Brother George Wilderman's and after divine service the Church proceded to examin charges laid against Brother Solaman Stevens of immoral conduct and of absence from every Church meeting since he joined theirfore we think it improper to count him as one among us and we are not accountable for his conduct hereafter. Brother Willial(m) Holcom was appointed to call Brother William G. Gofourth to attend the next Church meeting to answer to charges laid against him.

The Church continues in peace.   EPHRAIM HARRIS Clerk.

March 26th 1831

The Turkey Hill Baptised Church of Christ Friends to Humanity met at Brother James Pulliams and after divine service proceded to consider the business of selecting a place most suitable for holding the next yearly meeting postponed the selecting of a place till June the Church restored Brother William G. Gofourth, to fellowship on his acknowledgment.

The Church continues in peace. EPHRAIM HARRIS Clerk.

June 25th 1831

The Turkey Hill Baptized church of Christ friends to humanity met agreeably to appointment at brother Clement Bostwick's after divine service the church sat together to put things in order that might be found wanting the reference from last meeting was taken up brother Gofourth came before the church according to citation and gave satisfaction. On motion sister Tempy Cotton was excluded for the charge of pregnancy. There appearing no further business the meeting then closed in order.

N.B. On motion Brother William Holcomb was chose as standing clerk.

Signed WILLIAM HOLCOMB.

MINUTES
OF THE ANNUAL MEETING OF THE FRIENDS OF HUMANITY, HELD AT NEW DESIGN, MONROE COUNTY, ILLINOIS, SEPTEMBER 7, 1821.

ACCORDING to appointment the Friends of Humanity met, and brother Daniel Hilton delivered the Introductory Sermon, from Paul's first epistle to Timothy, 4th chapter and 8th verse: "For bodily exercise profiteth little, but godliness is profitable unto all things, having promise of the life that now is, and of that which is to come."

1. The letters from the churches were read, and the names of their ministers and delegates enrolled.

Churches	Ministers & Delegates
Cantine Creek.	*Benjamin Ogle,* *James Lemen, jr.* *Joseph Lemen,* *John Clark,* Stephen Terry Levi Day
Fountain Creek.	*James Lemen, sen.* *Daniel Hilton,* *Josiah Lemen,* *Moses Lemen,*
Silver Creek.	*James Pulliam,* David R. Chance, William King, George Mitchell,
Providence.	No intelligence.

Ministers' names in *Italics*.

2. Agreed that James Lemen, jr. write a Circular Letter.

3. Agreed that our next annual meeting be held at Silver Creek, near Captain Griffin's, on the Friday before the first Saturday in June, 1822, and continue the two succeeding days, and that brother James Lemen, sr. preach the Introductory Sermon, and in case of failure, brother Benjamin Ogle.

4. Appointed brothers James Pulliam and Robert Lemen to superintend the printing of our Minutes and Circular Letter.

By order of the Annual Meeting,

RT. LEMEN *Clerk.*

A CIRCULAR ADDRESS,

FROM THE MINISTERS AND DELEGATES COMPOSING THE ANNUAL MEETING OF THE BAPTIZED CHURCHES OF CHRIST, FRIENDS OF HUMANITY, TO THE CHURCHES THEY REPRESENT.

WRITTEN BY JAMES LEMEN, JR.

Beloved Brethren:

ALTHOUGH our present condition of life is such, that we are permitted to meet but occasionally, yet the Author of our existence has provided means whereby we may converse with each other, though absent in body, which is by way of letter. Therefore, we most gladly avail ourselves of this method of communication, and through the medium of a circular, transmit to you a tender of our sincere affection and christian fellowship. Be pleased to receive this as such.

We can inform you, that according to appointment, we, your delegates, met at the time and place specified in our minutes; and, to our comfort, and satisfaction, found suitable preparations for the comfortable accommodation of all who attended our annual meeting. The first day was spent in attending to divine worship; on the second, the letters from the different churches were called for. Providence and Cold Water Churches presented none; but we have since received a letter from Providence Church, which informed us that their number was thirty-seven, and also requested a visit from some of our preachers. For further information relative to the manner in which our meeting was conducted, we will refer you to our minutes, an examination of which will furnish you with information relative to our present number, with the exception of the two churches above mentioned.

Dear Brethren, when by a retrospective glance we retrace the roll of but a few seasons, and realize the commencement of our labors on the waters of Cantine and Silver creeks, contrasting those times with the present, ought not the response of our hearts to be, the Lord hath done great things for us, whereof we are glad. In 1810, a small handful, seven in number, withdrew, their membership from the general union, on the account of involuntary slavery, believing it to be an iniquity which ought not to be tolerated by christian churches. Formidable indeed, were the powers which we then had to combat, and alarming were the oppositions which we had to encounter. But none of these things moved us, being sensible, that unmerited, involuntary, perpetual, absolute, hereditary slavery, is contrary to, and a violation of the principles of nature, reason, justice, policy, and scripture. In 1811, the Lord was pleased graciously to move on the minds of a few faithful members on Silver creek, (also seven in number) who called for a constitution, and in February of the following year were constituted, three of whom have departed this life in the triumphs of faith. Several years were spent, in faithful labor, ere there was a discovery of any fruits thereof. At length Almighty God smiled propitiously on our efforts and almost instantaneously swelled our number to its present, and still making daily additions. Beloved brethren, while we behold that arm which quietly props the universe, thus gloriously displaying its power, in our defence, do we not fell conscious that our cause is just. It is the cause of oppressed humanity. We have seen the sable sons of Africa torn from their native land by the hand of a ruthless enemy, and condemned to perpetual bondage, to be driven at pleasure, like hogs and sheep to market, there to be disposed of for silver or gold; where husband and wife, parent and child, are torn from the fond embraces of each other; where the groans of the distressed father, or of the more deeply affected mother; the tear of the weeping child, are seen and heard only to be disregarded, let humanity drop a tear, and blot from the catalogue of human offences the enormity of such crimes, that it may not be told in "Gath nor publised in the streets of Ashkelon, lest the daughters of the Philistines rejoice, lest the daughters of the uncircumcised triumph." Alas! this evil has not only found its way into our nation, and spread its poison there, but, restless to obtain still greater victories, has approached the portals of the sanctuary of the Most High; and, lamentable to relate, has found admittance there, and defiled even the temples of the living God; causing the children of light (who have been redeemed from cruel bondage, and restored to the enjoyment of perfect liberty) to grow forgetful of the change, and to impose involuntary servitude on their brethren in the gospel, and thus becoming masters, can say to one brother, come, and he cometh, and to another, go, and he goeth; new maxims which the gospel knows nothing of. And will a God of equal justice rest quietly in his pavilion, when "justice has fallen asleep, and judgement gone away backwards;" while the poor are bought for silver, and the needy for a pair of shoes, (Amos viii. 6.) has he not already declared that his people of late have risen up against him as an enemy, plucking off the robe with the garment from them that would pass by securely as men averse from war, (Micah ii. 8.) He has also declared what the consequences shall be: Woe unto him that buildeth his house by unrighteousness, and his chambers by wrong; that useth his neighbor's service without wages, and giveth him not for his work, (Jer. xxii. 13.) Behold the hire of the laborers who have reaped down your fields, which is of you kept back by fraud, crieth: and the cries of them which have reaped are entered into the ears of the Lord of Sabaoth, (James v. 4.) Seeing God hath taken cognizance of these things in the archieves of heaven, and is now looking through the windows of his habitation to see whether any will appear on the side of the oppressed, shall we refuse to come up to the help of the Lord against the mighty; will we not, like the men of Gideon, come forth in haste, unappalled, before a host of oppositions, and exclaim in the consciousness of our rectitude, we struggle for liberty! Our cause is just! It is the cause which induced our forefathers to quit their peaceful homes, and go forth in martial array to meet the enemy in the tented field, (with victory or death written on their forehead) regardless of either their blood or treasure. And although some unfortunately found an untimely grave in the desolate wilderness, and went down to the chambers of silence without either a change of apparel, a sheet or a coffin, while the bones of others were left to bleak upon the mountains without a burial, yet their cause being righteous it still prospered in the hands of their survivors, who at length obtained a glorious conquest; a conquest which the pages of future history will be found to relate. Thus the enemy being driven like a flock of frighted goats before an impetuous storm, back to their native shore, to own the eclipse of their glory, the war-worn veterans of America could return in peace to their former habitations, bearing laurels of victory in their hands, at whose return the daughters of America could join in song with the daughters of Israel, and sing, Britain hath slain her thousands, but America hath slain her tens of thousands. Thus having obtained their freedom, could form a government of their own, the principles of which all nations are, or will be, proud to imitate; and we trust that under the influence of a just providence, we shall be able to boldly and nobly defend our cause, and to build up a society the government of which will be a pattern for societies yet unborn to follow. The holy scriptures are on our side, which will be seen from the passages to which you have been cited. Moreover, the constitution of the United States, and of this state, are both in our favor. The former declares that all men are born equally free and independent, while the latter states that there shall be neither slavery nor involuntary servitude introduced into this state, otherwise than for the punishment of crimes, whereof the party shall have been duly convicted. Thus the scene is changed, and now instead of being charged with flying in the face of authority, we can exhort our congregations to be subject to the higher powers. But lest our address should appear more like a volume than a circular, we shall now conclude with a short exhortation. Recollect, brethren, that we are constituted on the scriptures of the Old and New Testaments and have also taken them for our form of government. Must it not be said of them as was said of Goliah's sword, "there is none better." Therefore, endeavor to become conversant with those holy pages. Read them prayerfully, that you may have a correct understanding of what you read for the doctrines we hold. The manner of our building up and governing churches is all drawn therefrom. Being thus taught, thus constituted, thus governed, possessing an established heart, you can confidently answer the messengers of the nation, the Lord hath founded Zion, and the poor of his people shall trust in it, (Isa. xiv. 32) and also bid them to turn in this way, and to walk about Zion, and go round about her; tell the towers thereof; mark you well her bulwarks; consider her palaces; that ye may tell it to the generations following, (Ps. xlviii., 2, 13.)

MINUTES
OF THE ANNUAL MEETING OF THE FRIENDS OF HUMANITY, HELD AT NEW DESIGN, MONROE COUNTY, OCT. 10, 1823.

According to appointment the Friends of Humanity met, and the Rev. John Clark delivered the Introductory Sermon, from Psalm 48th, 12th and 13th verses: Walk about Zion and go round about her; tell the towers thereof; mark ye well her bulwarks; consider her palaces that ye may tell it to the generations following.

Saturday the 11th, the letters from the Churches were read, and the names of their Ministers and Delegates enrolled.

1. A Circular, written by the Rev. Benjamin Ogle, was read and received.

2. Agreed that the Minutes and Circular be printed, and brothers James Pulliam and Robert Lemen superintend the printing of two hundred copies.

3. Agreed that brother Joseph Lemen preach the next introductory sermon, and in case of failure brother James Lemen.

4. Agreed that brother Robert Lemen write the next circular.

5. Agreed that our next annual meeting be held at Silver Creek, Salem Meeting House, on the Friday preceding the third Saturday in August, 1824.

THOMAS M. HAMILTON, *Clerk.*

Churches	Ministers and Delegates	
Cantine	Benjamin Ogle	
	Joseph Lemen	
	James Lemen	Ministers
	Obadiah Osborn	
	Austin Symmes	
	James Downing	
	Stephen Terry	
	Samuel Beedle	Delegates
	Levi Day	
	Robert Lemen	
Silver Creek	William King	
	Ransom Caudle	
	Isaac Griffin	Delegates
	Peter Mitchell	
	Samuel M'Guire	
Fountain Creek	Daniel Hilton	
	Josiah Lemen	
	Levi Daines	Ministers
	Herman Dase	
	Moses Lemen	
	T. M. Hamilton	
	Jacob Eastwood	
	Andey Kinney	
	Daniel Barker	Delegates
	Theron Brownfield	
	Henry Hull	
Turkey Hill	James Pulliam, Minister	
	Charles Messinger, Delegate	
Merremack and Cold Water	John Clark, Minister	
	Jeremiah Hamilton	Delegates
	Nicholas Darter	
Grand Blaze	William Smurl	Delegates
	William Boly	
Crooked Creek	David R. Chance, Minister	
	Henry Lee	
	Samuel Shook	Delegates
	Malachi Ware	

CIRCULAR.

Dear Brethren,

The time having rolled on, which has favored us with another opportunity of offering to your serious consideration, things, which we conceive, to be most conducive to our own happiness, and the increase of the kingdom of our Redeemer; we, therefore, would call your attention to the duties which we owe to God, our rightful Sovereign, and also the duties we owe one to another. Our blessed Savior tells us that to love the Lord our God with all our heart, and with all our soul, and with all our mind, in the first and great commandment; and that the second is like unto it, viz: Thou shalt love thy neighbor as thyself. We trust, brethren, that we have not nor ever will forget this golden rule; which, if observed by all, would unite all in one:

"How blest would every nation prove.
Thus ruled by equity and love:
All would be friends without a foe,
And form a paradise below."

Are we not, brethren, under the strongest obligation to serve our God, when [illegible] for a moment, his great [illegible] towards us, without going back [illegible] the when we espoused, as we believe, the best of causes. Ought not our hearts to glow with love and gratitude unto him, when we call to mind our infantile state; when we were but very few in number, and our opposition very great: when we had to go through deep waters, and even through the fire; yet has he brought us through all unhurt, according to his promise, "When thou passest through the water I will be with thee," &c. The Lord has been, and still is, carrying on his work among us; adding to our number, we trust, such as shall be saved. Have we not often times been astonished at his goodness towards us, notwithstanding our many failures, when we have assembled together to worship our God. And often times in the presence of our foes, while discharging our duty, trusting in the Lord, has he not poured us out such a blessing as there was scarcely room enough to contain it; even to the astonishment of our opponents. Might we not then, in confidence, say with the psalmist David, "Thou preparest a table before me in the presence of mine enemies: thou anointest my head with oil; my cup runneth over. Surely goodness and mercy," &c. But we must still remember, that we remain in a state of trial, and that it is not the least of our trials to have lost several eminent characters, who were pillars in the house of God; but our loss is their infinite gain: They were honorably discharged, and are now reaping the fruit of their labor; while we are left to combat with the world, the flesh, and the devil, without their aid. Yet let us remember, that we are fighting under the same general (for whose sake saith the Apostle Paul, we are killed all the day long, we are accounted as sheep for the slaughter,) who will, ere long, bring us off more than conquerors.

Among the worthies whom we have lost for a season, and who died in the full triumph of faith, and brother in the gospel, James Lemen, senior, of blessed memory: though called by many rigid and austere,[1] because, like the prophet Michaiah, he never would prophecy good concerning them, but evil; for the most of them, Ahab-like, were not willing to quit their sins.

As an evangelical preacher, nothing could deter him from travelling by day or by night, through heat and cold, wet or dry, to bear the glad tidings of salvation, to a world of dying men and women; crying aloud and sparing not; lifting up his voice like trumpet; going on in the discharge of his duty; doing the work of the Lord faithfully, notwithstanding the many persecutions and oppositions he had to encounter; yet none of these things seemed to move him; so that he might finish his course with joy. And so it seemed that he did.

Brethren, though we are left awhile to mourn the loss of one, whose help is much needed at this present time; yet let us not murmur at the providence of God; nor ask for a moment, why it is, that such useful men, both in church and state, are taken away; while so many who seem to be of little

---

[1] This was chiefly in consequence of his opposition to slavery.

use, are spared. But let us endeavor to justify, the ways of
God to man, and ere long, we shall be called to join our
brethren; where we, with them, shall be able to comprehend
the mysteries of his providence. For the Apostle Paul saith,
"Now we see through a glass darkly: but then face to face:
now I know in part; but then shall I know, even as also I
am known."

In our former circulars, we briefly touched on the enormous crimes, prevailing apace in the land of light and vision—
the land of professed liberty and equality; trusting that our
state possess a sufficient number of true, real republicans,
lovers of their country, who would forever guard our constitution and soil from being, in the least degree, polluted
by the heaven-daring crime of oppression. But to our utter
astonishment, we have such men (not to say reptiles, in our
bosom or in the bowel of our state) who have exerted every
nerve to introduce the barbarous God-provoking practice of
unmerited slavery into our happy, peaceable, and highly
favored state, under the borrowed (not to say stolen) cloak
of humanity. Many of them have the assurance to tell us,
that they are as much opposed to the spirit and practice of
slavery as any one. What a contradiction is this! Let the most
distressed character, if he be a person of [color] apply for redress! Will they hear his complaints? Are they not deaf to the
cries of the most broken in heart? O where is judgment! Is
not their backs turned towards it? Is not justice far from
them? Is not truth disregarded, and trampled, as it were,
under their feet, while equity is barred out from amongst
them?   What shall we say, or what character shall we
attribute to such people? Let the Lord by the mouth of the
prophet Isaiah speak concerning such characters. "A people
who delighted in transgressing, and lying against the Lord,
and departing away from our God. Speaking oppression and
revolt. Conceiving and uttering from the heart, words of
falsehood; and judgment is turned away backward, and justice standeth afar off, for truth is fallen in the street, and
equity cannot enter."

When we take these things into consideration, should we

not be up and a doing; standing continually on our watch tower; particularly those who are called of God to be watchmen, placed, as it were, on the walls, looking out for the enemy? When they see the evil coming; should they not warn the people, and that faithfully? Is not the door threatened to be open for the introduction of an evil into our state, which is the most afflicting that ever was introduced into any state or nation; for it is a source that has brought forth all other abominations, and will bring down ere long, if not prevented by repentance, the most severe judgments; even the devouring sword which is threatened against the disobedient; "If ye refuse, and rebel ye shall be devoured by the sword, for the mouth of the Lord hath spoken it." Some tell us, that it is a political evil, and does not belong to our mission; therefore, we ought to be silent on the subject. But we would ask; Is it not a moral evil? Is it not a transgression of the moral law of God? It must be answered in the affirmative. If so, then we may conclude, that it is not only our privilege, but our indispensable duty to cry against, not only one, but every abomination. The truth is, they dread the preachers, for they are men of considerable influence, at least some of them; and, had, they it in their power, they would soon place them where they would no more dread them; even, where they would be no more troubled with their reproofs. What would not the spirit of oppression do? What lengths will it not go? But let us be thankful to God for the good laws of the land, and, particularly, for those of our own free state; that secure to all men their just rights; that declare all men to be born equally free. But notwithstanding all the advantages and encouragements we have let us not forget that mighty weapon prayer, but be instant in supplication at the throne of grace; calling daily upon God; who is able to turn the counsels of the wicked into foolishness, and bring off his chosen victorious. Let us not forget, brethren, while we feel compassion for the oppressed, to exercise pity for the poor oppressors, and pray. not as some have done, for fire to come down from Heaven to consume them; but that God would have compassion on them; and cause them to see their folly, that they may put away every evil, and seek that repentance, that needeth not to be repented of; that their souls may be saved with an everlasting salvation.   Remembering, brethren, that the Lord hath saith in his word, "That he came not to destroy men's lives but to save them." And, again, "I will have mercy and not sacrifice."

MINUTES

OF THE

ANNUAL MEETING

OF THE

BAPTIZED CHURCHES,

FRIENDS OF HUMANITY,

held at

MACOUPIN,

GREENE COUNTY, ILLINOIS,

SEPTEMBER THE TWENTY-NINTH, ANNO DOMINI ONE THOUSAND EIGHT HUNDRED AND TWENTY-SIX, AND THE TWO SUCCEEDING DAYS.

———

EDWARDSVILLE:

PRINTED BY JEREMIAH ABBOTT

1826.

M I N U T E S, &C.

According to appointment, the Friends of Humanity met, and the Rev. John Clark delivered the Introductory Sermon, from Isaiah, 27th Chapter, and 6th verse:—"He shall cause them that come of Jacob to take root: Israel shall blossom and bud, and fill the face of the world with fruit."

First. Chose brother James Lemen Moderator.

2. Chose brother Elijah Dodson Clerk.

3. The Circular, written by the Rev. John Clark, was read and received.

4. Agreed that the Minutes with the Circular be printed, and that there be three hundred copies.

5. The Corresponding Letters were read, and the names of the Ministers and Delegates enrolled.
From Providence Church no intelligence. Adjourned until tomorrow, 10 o'clock.

Saturday, September 30.
Conference opened by the Rev. John Clark.

6. Agreed that brother Moses Lemen preach the next Introductory Sermon, and, in case of failure, brother James Pulliam.

Churches	Ministers and Delegates	
Cantine Creek, St. Clair co. Ill.	Benjamin Ogle Joseph Lemen James Lemen Austin Symmes Samuel Wood	*Ministers*
	Samuel Bedle Gideon Scantling Isaac Bacye John Turner Robert Lemen	*Delegates*

Churches	Ministers and Delegates
Silver Creek, St. Clair co. Ill.	Peter Mitchell, Isaac Griffin, ~~Ministers~~ / Moses Land, William Mason, Perick Huggans } Delegates
Fountain Creek, Monroe co. Ill.	Daniel Hilton, Levi Daines, Josiah Lemen, Moses Lemen } Ministers
	Andey Kinney, Zara Briggs, James Taylor } Delegates
Turkey Hill, St. Clair co. Ill.	James Pulliam, Minister
	William Halcomb, Abner Carr, Benjamin Chesney } Delegates
Macoupin, Greene co. Ill.	John Clark, Minister
	Major Dodson, John G. Lotton, Elijah Dodson } Delegates
Crooked Creek, Madison co. Ill.	David R. Chance, Minister
	Samuel Shook, Delegate
Cahokin Creek, Madison co. Ill.	James Mayberry, Samuel Lair, John Love, Levi Day } Delegates
Lebanon, Monroe co. Ill.	Theron Brownfield, Richard Christal } Delegates
Cold Water, St. Louis co. Mo.	John Clark, Jeremiah Hamilton } Ministers
	William Patterson, Archibald Loller } Delegates
Grand Glaze, Jefferson co. Mo.	Hermon Dace, Minister
	William Smurl, James Foster } Delegates
Sugar Creek, Jefferson co. Mo.	John M. Meens, Minister
	John Kile, James Kile } Delegates

7. Agreed that our next annual meeting be held at New Design, Monroe County; commencing the last Friday in September, 1827, and to continue the two succeeding days.

8. Agreed that brother Theron Brownfield contract with a printer, and superintend the printing of the Minutes and Circular letter.

9. Agreed that brother John G. Lolton write the next Circular Letter, for the 1827.

10. Agreed that our next annual meeting be a camp-meeting.

Signed by order of the Conference.

ELIJAH DODSON, *Clerk.*

CIRCULAR.

Very Dear Brethren,

The Apostle Jude, in his general epistle, exhorts the faithful to contend for the faith once delivered to the saints; which faith means the doctrines of the Gospel. The same exhortation has been, and will be necessary still, until the great promise be fulfilled, that the watchmen should see eye to eye, and the knowledge of God cover the earth as the waters to the great deep. Till that happy period come, even the children of God are liable to err, both in doctrine and practice: Especially those who possess strong minds, and depend too much on their own understanding, and who have not considered the wonderful simplicity of the gospel; (adapted to the weak as well as to the strong;) but vainly imagine that they can fathom the immense depth of the mystery of godliness, by the inadequate line of human reason; (a task too profound for angelic minds;) not considering that the gospel is calculated to hide pride from self wise, self-potent man, and to secure the primary glory of salvation, to God alone. To this cause, though not to this only, we may attribute the introduction of the Unitarian doctrine, which, of late, has been infused into the minds of thousands, who, notwithstanding, truly fear God and work righteousness. But the main cause, is our ignorance of the various dispensations of the Gospel; such as the heathen, patriarchal, Mosaical, John Baptist's, or the beginning, of the Gospel, and the luminous dispensation of the Spirit that commenced on the day of Pentecost. Each of these dispensations has its proper [function] plainly described in the Old or New Testament; and strange as it may appear, even people in this enlightened age, are converted under one or another of these dispensations. Few, very few, of late years, have received, at their conversion, the luminous faith of the day of Pentecost; they seem, like Apollos, to know only the beginning of the Gospel; i.e. the baptism of John.

Another grand cause of all the mischievous errors that even disturb the peace of the church in almost every age, was, and is, this false maxim, "That we are not to believe what we cannot comprehend." But according to this trite rule, we can neither be Christians, Deists, nor Atheists: We cannot be Christians, for we must believe in miracles, the immortality of the soul, the resurrection of the body, and in one God existing in three distinct persons, though we cannot comprehend the manner. Neither can we be Deists on that plan; for a Deist must believe in the eternity, omniscience, omnipresence and omnipotence, of God. Nor can we be Atheists on that principle, if Atheism consist in believing that all things existed from all eternity, and governed by blind chance.

Another article of the faith which we must closely adhere to, and contend for, is, salvation by faith alone. For though Antinomianism has been made to hide her deformed face for years; yet Pharisaism stalks abroad without a veil. The gospel doctrines of justification, new birth, and sanctification by faith alone, or its tantamount, the rightrousness of Christ imputed to, and implanted in the penitent believer, is laid as the only foundation of our hope. The name of Jesus, which St. Paul mentions ten times in one paragraph, is seldom mentioned in preaching or praying; as if such teachers were determined to exclude him out of the church which he has founded, and out of the world which he has created and redeemed.

But there is one thing more to be particularly treated on, and that is the injustice and unmerited cruelty exercised on the poor, sable posterity of Ham; and that in a land in which equal rights, liberty, and philanthropy are much boasted of. But such boasting is preposterous, while more than fifteen hundred thousand souls, or perhaps one-fifth of our population, are kept in abject bondage, and treated, in many respects, as beasts of burden! But the mercy of God appears to be interposing in the behalf of these outcasts of men. Colonization and manumission societies are forming, and auxiliaries increasing and extending from Boston even to St. Louis, for the qualifying, if needful, and transplanting them to their ancestors native land; wherein they may enjoy their unalienable rights, and prove an everlasting advantage to the natives of that benighted quarter of our globe. But what may we expect will eventually follow, if the slave-holding states will not avail themselves of this momentous opportunity that now offers, not only to avert the just and tremendous judgments of Jehovah, but to extricate the nation from a most dangerous part of its population, increasing rapidly in number, and exasperated to the highest pitch of revenge, by the most unmerited, unjust, barbarous, and degrading treatment, which has been, and still is exercised on them, without any means or hope of redress, till their number and prowess will awfully effect it! We say, what may we expect to follow, but an awful storm, perhaps now [already] pending over a guilty! land! And may we not look for the heaviest p[unishment] to fall on the professors of the most benign religion that even existed who keep in continual countenance this shocking system, by their unprecedented example: for how shall the avaricious, unawakened sinner be ever convinced of the enormity of this horrid practice, or of the reality of the christian religion, while gospel churches, so called, receive in to their communion, and hold in high esteem, those who buy and sell, whip, drive and pinch, without remorse, those whom they profess to believe are the offspring of Jehovah, and the purchase of his blood! But it is said that some professors use them well; they feed and clothe them well and work them moderately, and neither buy nor sell. But will this plea answer before the flaming bar of Jehovah? Will not the just Judge of all the earth inquire: "Have you diligently used every necessary means to qualify those heirs of endless duration, for the enjoyment of all the blessings, in time and eternity, which I have purchased for them; and which, ye knew, were their unalienable right? Or have you fasted sumptuously, day by day, on the fruit of their involuntayr labor, and bequeathed them, at your death, to drudge for your graceless children or friends, that they might live in luxury, and soar in pomp and splendor, as if you were resolved that they should live the life and die the death, not of the righteous, but of the rich glutton."

O brethren, was there ever a time that called louder for a reformation than this time? And the reasons are evident; for never were people more enlightened, more favored, and sinned more egregiously! Let us never forget the appelation by which we are distinguished, that we bear not that significant title in vain; but that we evidence our detestation, by every prudential means, to a practice, the turpitude of which, baffles human language to describe. Let our prayers be frequent and fervent, that the Fountain of Mercy and Grace, may grant such repentance, as shall, through the intercession of the Friend of Sinners, avert his righteous judgments, and raise his church on the ruins of all antichristian doctrines and practices,—pure, without spot or wrinkle,—"fair as the moon, clear as the sun, and terrible as an army with banners."

MINUTES

OF THE

ANNUAL MEETING

OF THE

SOUTH DISTRICT BAPTIST ASSOCIATION,

FRIENDS OF HUMANITY,

Held with Upper Silver Creek Church, Madison County, Illinois,

Commencing October 4, 1839.

———

Chester, Ill.

Smith & Abbott, Printers.

1839.

MINUTES.

Friday, October 4, 1839.

The ministers and brethren composing the South District Baptist Association, met according to appointment at eleven o'clock.

Elder James Lemen preached the introductory sermon from Math. ix. 37, 38—"The harvest truly is plenteous but the laborers are few. Pray ye therefore the Lord of the harvest, that he will send forth laborers into his vineyard."

The letters from the churches were called for by the former Moderator, and the names of the ministers and messengers enrolled.

The following brethren from other associations and churches, being present and entitled to a seat as corresponding brethren by our rules, their names were enrolled as follows: Elders Moses Lemen and W. F. Boyakin, and brethren A. H. Richardson and R. Trabue.

Eld. James Lemen was chosen moderator, Daniel Converse, clerk, and James H. Lemen, ass't clerk.

Elders Joseph Lemen, N. Arnett, James Pulliam, John Padon, and Wm. Holcombe, with the moderator and clerk, were chosen a committee to arrange and digest the business of the association.

Brethren John Linley, Wm. Skinner, J. S. Brown, Asa Parker, and Valentine Vanhooser, were chosen a committee to arrange the exercises of the meeting.

Adjourned until 9 o'clock to-morrow morning; prayer by Elder James Lemen.

Saturday Morning, Oct. 5.

The association met pursuant to adjournment—prayer by Eld. Newman.

Correspondence from sister Associations:—North District association: M. Lemen, M. Bailey, Ashur Chase, Wm. Roberts. Saline association: W. F. Boyakin, R. Nichols, Charles Wade. Edwardsville association: Elders Z. B. Newman and Z. Darrow. Colored association: A. H. Richardson and R. Trabue.

The committee appointed to prepare a letter of correspondence to the Edwardsville association, setting forth our principles and doctrine, particularly relative to slavery, and ask of them a letter declaring their principles and doctrine, in relation to the same subject, and whether slavery exists in any of the churches of that body, presented their correspondence, which was read and received, and the messengers invited to seats.

The committee appointed to procure ministerial labors for that part of the State south and east of the Kaskaskia river, made their report, which was received, and from which it appears they have collected the sum of $97.56; they have paid to Elders N. Arnett and W. F. Boyakin $25 each, for services rendered last year; and Elder James Lemen $30, and Eld. Joseph Lemen $10, for services rendered the present year, leaving in their hands the sum of $7.56; and recommend the passage of the following resolution:

Resolved, that Eld. James Lemen be appointed to attend every church in this association, in the course of the ensuing year, and report at the next annual association their state and condition; and that a public collection be made to pay said minister for his labors, which was laid on the table for further consideration.

Resolved, that we recommend to each church in this association to make choice of some preacher to act as their pastor, and to contribute to his temporal necessities as God may give them ability.

Resolved, that we cheerfully co-operate with the Illinois Baptist Convention, in endeavoring to supply the destitute in our State with the preached gospel; and that we appoint Eld. W. F. Boyakin to attend and represent is at the annual meeting of said Convention, commencing at Bloomington on Thursday the 10th inst.

Resolved, that we recommend to the churches of this association, to encourage the religious and moral instruction of children and youth, through the medium of Sabbath schools.

Resolved, that this association consider it the duty of

all heads of families, who profess the religion of Christ, to worship God by prayer in their families.

Resolved, that this association deeply deplore the neglect of the Lord's day, by too many members of our churches, and for this reason do earnestly urge a more strict observance of the same.

On motion of Eld. N. Arnett.

Resolved, that a contribution be taken up at some convenient time, to defray the expense of delegates to the Convention and other associations, for the past and present year.

Resolved, that the next association be held with Silver creek church, at Salem meeting-house, on the Friday before the third Sabbath in September next.

Resolved, that the Theological Seminary at Upper Alton, is regarded as an indepensable appendage to the College, with a view to the training of our young brethren for greater usefulness, in the ministry; and that the churches be urged to look out such gifts as God seems to designate for the ministry, and provide means for their theological education.

Resolved, that we again urge the principle of Temperance, in abstinence from all intoxicating drinks; and recommend to our churches and brethren vigorous and persevering action; and we would especially call their attention to the act of the Legislature, by which a majority of the voters in each Justice's district, by petitioning the county commissioner's court, can prevent any more licences being granted to sell intoxicating liquors.

Resolved, that Eld. James Lemen be appointed to attend every church in his association in the course of the ensuing year, and report at the next annual association their state and condition; that a public collection be made to pay him for his labors; and that brethren J. Begole, J. D. Hughes, Merlin Jones, Robert Lemen and D. Converse, be appointed a committee to receive and pay over all monies collected by public or private contribution to the use of said brother Lemen. In case of death or inability to act on the part of brother Lemen, said committee shall select some other suitable minister to perform the said service, to be remunerated as provided in the case of brother Lemen.

Resolved, that the churches of this association be requested to hold a protracted meeting in conformity with bro. James Lemen's arrangements in visiting the different churches; and said churches are requested to furnish funds to help compensate brother Lemen for his labors in visiting them.

Resolved, that the public collection recognized by a previous resolution, be made to-morrow.

Whereas, the Springfield Association, at its last session, passed a resolution desiring to open a correspondence with the South District Association, by a corresponding circular published in the minutes;—therefore

Resolved, that we reciprocate the correspondence; and that our corresponding secretary transmit a suitable number of minutes to the Springfield association.

Elds. Joseph Lemen and James Pulliam appointed delegates to the Edwardsville association.

Elds. Nathan Arnett and J. Padon, delegates to the North District Association.

Elds. Josiah Lemen and Abner Barker, delegates to the Missouri association.

Elds. Wm. Steele and Joel Terry, delegates to the Saline association.

Eld. Moses Lemen to the Colored association.

Resolved, that 1000 copies of the Minutes of this association be printed, and that brethren Josiah Lemen, Richard Green, and Edward Rodgers, be appointed to superintend the printing thereof, and when printed to be forwarded to brother J. D. Hughes, Belleville, for distribution among the several churches and corresponding associations; and that said committee prepare the corresponding letter to be published with the minutes.

CORRESPONDING LETTER.

The South District Baptist Association to the Associations with which we correspond.

Dear Brethren:—We have especial reasons for gratitude to the great Head of the Church, for the displays of his grace among our churches the past year. We have, in common with other associations in this State, enjoyed times of refreshing from the presence of the Lord.

Our associational meeting has bee harmonious, and we trust it will redound to the glory of God, and the promotion of his cause. Our churches generally are in favor of the various forms of Christian benevolence, and many of them are engaged in promoting the circulation of the Scriptures, Foreign and Domestic Missions, &c.

For further information of our proceedings we refer you to our Minutes. We shall endeavor by our Minutes and Messengers, to keep you advised of our condition and prospects, and to co-operate with you in every good work.

And, relying on the blessing and promises of God, let our field of labor be the world, and the object of our prayers and efforts the subjection of our fallen race to the dominion of the prince of Peace. May the grace of our Lord Jesus Christ be with you all.—Amen.

JAMES LEMEN, Moderator.

DANIEL CONVERSE, Clerk.
JAS. H. LEMEN, Ass't Clerk.

TABLE OF THE CHURCHES.

N. B. Ordained Ministers' names in small capitals; those of Licentiates in Italics.

Churches	Ministers & Messengers
Canteen-creek	JOSEPH CHANCE, JOSEPH LEMEN, JOEL TERRY, Merlin Jones, Wm. Hart, Elisha Freeman, Samuel Beedle, L. Lancaster.

Churches	Ministers & Messengers
Silver-creek	HENRY ROSS, NATHAN ARNETT, SILAS GASKILL, David Howell, Isaac Griffin, Solomon Teter, James Jackson, Joel Jackson
Fountain-creek	JOSIAH LEMEN, DANIEL HILTON, *Wm. Lemen, L. Bostwick, C. BOstwick, A Barker, A. B. Harris,* J. Wiswell, J. Hilton, J. Tolin, J. Kinney.
Clinton Hill	WM. STEELE, Wm. Petree, Joseph Huey.
Upper Silver-creek	JOHN PADON, SAML. WOOD, *A. Parker, Wm. Vanhooser, J. S. Brown, T. Craig,* V. Vanhooser, Wm. Skinner, John Linley, A. B. Vanhooser.
Waterloo	J. B. OLCOTT, PETER RODGERS, Wm. Ditch, R. Wyatt, D. Converse, J. Taylor, Jackson Johnston.
New-Salem	*B. J. Henderson, S. Wilton,* John H. Powers, Peter B. Carnes, D. Powers, J. Simpkins, Wm. Henderson.
Belleville	JAMES PULLIAM, Geo. Wilderman, Reuben Berry, John D. Hughes.
2d Shoal-creek	WM. BURGE, *R. Clyne,* Geo. Varner, Wm. Clyne, M. Smith, Wm. Smith, J. A. Wall.
Georgetown	Richard Green, Geo. Thompson, Enoch Eaton, W. Lyon, J. McDonough, Henry Gordon.
Elk Horn	Benjamin Chesney, A. Jackson.
Beaver-creek	Joseph Myers, S. H. Stevens.
High Prairie	SAML. RODGERS, *Wm. Holcombe,* H. Marler, J. Robinson, G. W. Carr,
Ebenezer	Simeon Ferrel, R. Goodwin, J. Smith, Wm. Stallings,
Asher-creek	CHARLES RADCLIFF, J. McKinney, Wm. Frieds, S. Radcliff, J. Taulbee.

The Edwardsville Association to the South District Baptist Association, Friends to Humanity, send Christian love—

Dear Brethren:—

We have received your letter and delegates with much Christian pleasure, and respond to your inquiries in the same spirit of frankness with which they are made.

Our views as an association on the subject of slavery were expressed fully in our minutes of last year which we here transcribe

"Whereas we regard the spirit and practice of involuntary and hereditary slavery as a violation of the principles of liberty, of human rights, and of the gospel of Christ, which requires us to "do unto others as we would have them do unto us:—"

Therefore Resolved, That in our individual and associate capacity we bear decided testimony against this evil, pray for those who are in bonds, and for those brethren who hold slaves that they may be directed in the way of their duty according to the will of God and the principles of humanity and especially pray that God will devise appropriate means and direct in their application for the removal of slavery and all kinds of oppression from our country and the world.

Resolved, That by the foregoing resolution we are not to be understood as committing ourselves to any society or organization for moral and political action whatever, otherwise than the faithful discharge of our religious duties in subjection to the churches to which we respectively belong"

The foregoing preamble and resolutions were preceded by another which disclaims every species of authority over the churches, and which we regard as a fundamental principle in Baptist church government. It is as follows:

"Resolved, That while we hold as a sacred and New Testament principle that each church, organized according to the laws of Zion's King, is strictly and substantially independent of all other bodies and persons, in government and discipline, and can alone judge of the qualifications for membership, yet as an association, we feel it to be our privilege to express our opinions and bear our testimony against any and every species of evil that may exist"

Had the sentiments of this association on slavery been generally known to those brethren that objected against consumating the correspondence at your last meeting, it would probably have precluded the necessity of your inquiries

It will be recollected by a number of your ministers and

brethren who attended the union meeting held in Edwardsville October 16 and days following of 1830, and who cordially united with other brethren in recommending the formation of the Edwardsville association, that the views of the
Friends to Humanity were fully explained, a statement made
of their origin and progress, and the ground originally
occupied in the old Illinois Union,—that a response was
made by leading brethren who were formed into the Edwardsville association, satisfactory to all on the subject of slavery—
that it was recommended unanimously that the new association should assume the same ground the old Illinois Union
occupied before any attempt was made to open a correspondence in slave holding states. Hence it was agreed at the time
this association would confine its correspondence to such
associations as exist in free states and who manifest their
disapprobation of the system of African slavery in such a
mode or form as may appear best calculated to promote the
principles of Humanity

With respect to your inquery whether any members of
churches in our body hold slaves, we would reply in all Christian frankness. And first we would state that on well known
Baptist principles existing from the apostolical age and in
which we are persuaded you will heartily agree that no association or body of people on earth has any power to call
churches or members to account in the way of discipline:—
that each church has its own keys of government, is alone
authorized to judge the qualifications of its own members and
deal with them as delinquent. The right of an association to
Inquire into the order and discipline of the church and the
standing of individuals, supposes power to prosecute, discipline to its end, if evil is found to exist, which if carried out
in some other denominations would be entirely subversive
of the right and independence of churches and the whole
system of New Testament discipline. We therefore think that
every object may be gained and all evils avoided by churches
acting as churches in such matters and associations acting
as associations and if the churches make no complaint, it may
be taken for granted they tacitly approve of the act.

We have heard no complaint but rather general approbation of our brethren relative to the expression made by our last association on the subject of slavery. Hence we conclude the churches agree to the principles above.

But we would say to you in the same frankness with which your letter and inquiry is dictated, that we learned there are two or three instances in our churches of members who are the legal holders of slaves, one of whom is a member of the committee appointed to draft this letter. But we have no doubt in his case and believe also in the other cases they come with in the limits of "Tarrant's Rules" and are entirely consistent with the principles of humanity. These brethren profess decided opposition to slavery in principle and profess to be desirous to emancipate their servants fully, soon as their comfort happiness and prosperity can be secured in the best possible way, consistent with the principles of humanity.

We hope these explanations will be fully satisfactory and that a perfect understanding shall exist hereafter between us on this subject.

We have appointed our brethren B. F. Edwards, Zadock Darrow, . . . Leverett, G. B. Newman, Joseph Taylor, and E. J. Palmer to attend your next Association as our messengers and solicit an interest in your prayers

By order of the Association

E. ROGERS, Moderator
J. M. PECK Clerk

Rock Spring Ill
May 25, 1839

CHAPTER XV

THE GREAT WESTERN REVIVAL AND BAPTIST INDIAN MISSIONS

I. Letters describing the Great Western Revival with particular emphasis upon the part played by the Baptists in that movement.

1. Extracts of a letter from a Gentelman to his Friend at the City of Washington, dated Lexington, Kentucky, March 8, 1800 (Ripon, Baptist Annual Register, 1801–1802, pp 805–806.)
2. From the same to the same, March 9, 1801.
   (Ripon, Baptist Annual Register, 1801–1802, pp 806.)
3. Extracts of a Letter from a Gentleman to his Sister in Philadelphia, dated Lexington, Kentucky, August 10, 1801.
   (Baptist Annual Register, 1801–1802, pp 806–807)
4. Extracts of a Letter from the Rev. Dr. Rogers, dated Philadelphia, November 2, 1801.
   (Baptist Annual Register, 1801–1802, pp 807–808.)
5. Letter to Rev. Dr. Rippon, Editor of the Baptist Annual Register, London, from Bourbon County, Kentucky, January 7, 1802.
   (Baptist Annual Register, 1801–1802, pp 1007–1010.)

II. Minutes of the Salem Association, Kentucky, 1802, showing the great increase in members due to the revival.

III. Extracts from the Journal of Maj. S. H. Long, describing the Indian Mission under Isaac McCoy, June 2 and 3, 1823.

I.

A BRIEF ACCOUNT

of the

REVIVAL OF RELIGION IN KENTUCKY

and several other parts of the United States

Extract of a Letter from a Gentleman to his Friend at the city of Washington, dated Lexington, Kentucky, March 8, 1801.

Dear Brother,

I am glad to inform you, there is a great revival of religion near this place; 51 have been added to our church since you left us; 62 to Bryant's station since the 8th of February, exclusive of to-day, at which place 46 were received yesterday, and a number more expected to join. I suppose upwards of 220 have been added to that church.—53 were baptized at Clear Creek in one day. There is also a great reformation at Boone's Creek, Marble Creek, Shawne Run, etc. In short, all the churches near this, that I have heard from, who adhere to primitive Christianity, are in a prosperous state. In some it appears like a fire that has been long confined—bursting all its barriers, and spreading with a rapidity that is indescribable—attended only with a still small voice. This, my brother, is a harvest indeed; and we may, on this occasion, use the language of sacred inspiration, —"The flowers appear on the earth; the time of the singing of birds is come, and the voice of the turtle is heard in our land." It may be truly said, the Lord is doing great things for us, and I will add, whereof I am glad—Oh, that the great Husbandman would still carry on his work, and separate the precious grain from the tares!

From the same to the same, March 9, 1801.

I am sorry to hear of your destitute situation, in not hearing the gospel preached—but I will tell you one thing, not because you are ignorant of it; the Lord can communicate spiritual health, strength, growth, and vigour, without it, when he sees cause to place any of his dear children in such a situation as you are.—It is with pleasure I inform you, 58 were baptized at Bryant's yesterday—from 8th February to 8th March, 120 have been added to that church, among whom were a number of our acquaintance, and several poor black people, some of whose experiences have astonished me—This is the work of the Lord, and it is marvellous in our eyes—But alas, poor L[exingto]n, yet in measure stands out, though I trust even in this Sodom there are a few brought to a saving knowledge of Christ. I was told yesterday, that the wicked son of E . . . . D . . . . has been brought into the gospel fold.

Your friend and brother
in the gospel of Christ.

Extract of a Letter from a Gentleman to his Sister in Philadelphia, dated Lexington, Kentucky, August 10, 1801.

Dear Sister:

I hasten to give you an account of the revival of religion, and some of the remarkable circumstances thereof. The nicest pencil could not pourtray to your imagination, the full idea of the meeting that took place at Kainridge, in Bourbon county. I shall confine myself only to a few particulars:—

This meeting was published about one month generally, throughout the Presbyterian connexion, as one of their annual sacraments: thither assembled the religious of every denomination, some from one hundred miles distant, but more particularly the Presbyterians and Methodists, who are in full communion with each other;—lastly the Baptists, who preach with each other, but do not commune. To this general assembly I set off last Friday, and arrived there on Saturday about 10 o'clock; I then began to note some of the most extraordinary particulars. I first proceeded to count the waggons containing families, with their provisions, camp equipage, etc. to the number of 147; at 11 o'clock the quantity of ground occupied by horses, waggons, etc was about the same size as the square between Market, Chesnut, Second and Third streets, of Philadelphia—There was at this place a stage erected in the woods, about 100 yards from the meeting-house, where were a number of Presbyterian and Methodist ministers; one of the former preaching to as many as could get near enough to hear.— In the house also, was another of the same denomination, preaching to a crowded audience—at the same time another large concourse of people collected about 100 yards in an east direction from the meeting-house, hearing a Methodist speaker—and about 150 yards in a south course from the house was an assembly of black people, hearing the exhortations of the blacks. The number of communicants who received tokens were 750, nor was there a sufficiency of them— those tokens are small pieces of lead, the size of a five-penny bit, with the letter A or B impressed thereon, and distributed by the ministers to the members of the several churches, not excluding any Baptist that applies for them.[1]

Last Sunday the association was held at Higby's, 6 miles from here, where it is said there were from 8 to 10 thousand persons; and on the same day, in the two counties adjoining, there were, at two congregations, from 18,000 to 25,000 souls.

Extract of a Letter from the Rev. Dr. Rogers, dated Philadelphia, November 2, 1801.

The printed minutes of Elkhorn Baptist association, held in Kentucky, August 8th, 1801, were put into my hands for perusal, last Friday; by which it appears that the said association consists of 36 churches, 10 of which had applied at the above time for admission, and were accepted. The addition to this association had been, in one year only, by

---

[1] Oh, that these People had introduced among them PRESIDENT EDWARDS'S Narrative of the work of God in Northampton, N. E. and his After-thoughts on the Revival. The former of these may be had of Messrs. Burton, Paternoster Row, London.—EDITOR.

baptism, 3011. Four of the churches had received, by baptism, 1378 members: between 300 and 400 severally, viz.

Great Crossings Church	376
Bryant's ditto	367
Clear Creek ditto	326
South Elkhorn ditto	309

Some had received, the same year, between 200 and 300, others between 100 and 200; in some, under 100, down to 50, 20, 10, 8, or 6 persons.

Besides the Elkhorn, there are several other Baptist associations in that state, viz. Salem, Bracken, Tate's Creek, etc. I am most credibly informed, that upwards of 10,000 at the lowest calculation, had been baptized in one year only, preceding the above period. Surely this must be the work of God, and it is truly marvellous in our eyes.

The following is an account of the prosperity of Zion, in the Shaftsbury, Warren, and Stonington Baptist Associations.

	Members added in one year
Warren	620 year, 1800
Shaftsbury (Vermont)	395 ditto, 1801
Stonington (Con.)	114 ditto, 1801
Total	1129

Extract of a Letter from the Rev. Mr. Moore, to the Rev. Mr. Richards, in Baltimore, dated Moores-field, November 9th, 1801.

I am informed by private letters, that God is still calling sinners out of darkness, into his marvellous light, in the Elkhorn Association. In a letter I saw yesterday, from a gentleman in Kentucky, to his friend in Montgomery county, there is a paragraph to the following effect: "The work of the Lord, amongst us, is extraordinary; there were, on the Last Lord's Day, 30 persons baptized, and 70 others waiting to receive that ordinance; among other instances of almighty grace, my father (80 years of age) has professed to know Jesus of Nazareth, and was baptized in his name.

A PECULIAR WORK IN AMERICA

To the Rev. Dr. Rippon

Bourbon County, Kentucky, January 7, 1802

Sir,

In June last I wrote the following letter to send to you, but several things prevented my sending it; if it will afford you any new information, or be of any service, you may use it as you please.

Men of much diffidence will scarce ever introduce themselves in the company of strangers; but I wish that all the friends of real piety should partake with us in the pleasure arising from the prospects of religion at present in this country. I do not remember for about 27 years past, ever to have heard such complaints of deadness and supineness in religion as were contained in our church letters, at the Elkhorn Association, in August 1799. It appeared as if every harp was untuned and hung upon the willows. Though peace and tranquillity were prevalent, and the Churches appeared sound in the Faith, their general state seemed to strike all the friends of vital piety. It was likewise observed to be the case with every other denomination of Christians, in this country. At our Association in August 1800, the face of the churches' letters was generally altered, and hopes expressed, in very strong terms, of a divine visitation, with some small encrease in many of them; in one Church only, the encrease had been large. The meeting of the Association was lively and refreshing, and great seriousness appeared in the very numerous audience which attended of I think not less than 2000 persons. When I set out on my return home, at the house where I had lodged, I left about a dozen persons bathed in tears. About this time, in one of the Churches called *Great-crossing*, the Lord appeared working powerfully upon the hearts of several persons. The work increased abundantly, so that in a few months there were baptised, at that place, from thirty to forty at each of their meetings, which meetings were monthly, and they continue to baptise until now; they have baptised about 353, though this has been the most unhappy Church in our union. This work immediately spread, and has more or less pervaded the whole of the baptised Churches except one, on the North side of the Kentucky River. The greatest increase I have heard of, in any one Church, is that of *Bryan's-station*, which is 358, and the smallest is a little Church called *Indian Creek*, which is 8, though now the deepest solemnity and concern appear in that place, and it is expected a number will be baptised there next Lord's day, which is their stated meeting. Cooper's run, one of the old Churches in this country, has had a small visitation, which was truly refreshing, but has added, by baptism, about 30. From the best information I can get, about 2464 have been baptised in the different Churches since August last, among whom are a great many children of professors, and this work is increasing every day, and spreading into new places. I assisted at the Constitution of a Church yesterday, which has risen up in an intire (sic) new place, detached from every other Church in the union, and after the Constitution baptised seven persons, which will make their number 17. In this one place the people are greatly agitated: they go—to Meeting, and will continue all night, exhorting, praying, and singing; sometimes the professors of religion appear in raptures, as if they were ready to take their flight to Glory, and distressed souls, lying on the floor, crying out for mercy, in such distress, as if they saw the yawning pit of destruction ready to receive them; some get speedy relief, and give very satisfactory accounts of their views, and a sense which they have of the corruption of human nature, and of their own hearts; of man's inability to help himself; of the exceeding sinfulness of sin; and of the way of salvation through our Lord Jesus Christ, and the feeling sense they have of the comforting and powerful influence of quickening Grace.—Others continue in this distressed state for several weeks, without any comfort. These people are a mixed multitude, made up of Presbyterians, Methodists, and Baptists, engaged in worship together. In one other of the Baptist Churches, those extraordinary bodily agitations are prevalent; in the rest, as far as my acquaintance extends, there is great solemnity and seriousness, and the new converts give very satisfactory accounts of a work of grace on their hearts.

On the *South side* of the *Kentucky River*, I understand, there have been large additions to the Baptist Churches; but I shall pass them over, and give you some account of the Presbyterians in conjunction with the Methodists. An union in part has taken place between them, so that they commune together, and they are trying much to bring about a general communion of all Christian professors. Great accounts have been received of a wonderful work of God among the above people in the State of Tennessee, for these last eighteen months; but nothing of it appeared here until a few weeks past, in a meeting at a place called Concord, distant from me, about twenty miles; the people met from different parts—some whole families in waggons, and prepared to stay on the place of meeting; it was what they call a sacramental occasion:—they began on Friday, and did not wholly break up until Tuesday following. Here something strange appeared; 30 or 40 persons would be lying on the ground at one time, crying out for mercy, some saying, they had been professors of religion from early life, but were strangers to its life and power till now; old men, of regular conduct and good standing in the Churches, were among them; and two of this description with whom I have conversed, who are elders, and men of good natural abilities, tell me, they have been possessors of vital religion many years, one of them says twenty five, lay almost motionless for some hours, overwhelmed with a sense of their former ingratitude, and wonderful views of the way of salvation through Christ. Two of the Presbyterian Ministers were quite overcome with a sense of the divine goodness, and lay for some time on the ground in a helpless condition.—Persons who went among them with the vilest intentions, were struck to the earth, and confessed all their follies. Some Deistical characters have been made to bow even to the ground; and many other persons of all descriptions. The same week a whole family that had attended, through this meeting, without any visible agitation, were struck down at home, and several as they were returning home were so taken. I have attended one of their meetings in my own neighbourhood, where there was a great deal of this work. It is different from anything I have seen, though I have seen great bodily agitations before this. Persons of all ages are wrought upon in this way, from ten or twelve years to grey hairs; some, as I said are soon relieved, others continue under great distress of mind: yet in some instances it is worn off, and the persons say they were only scared, and now seem very indifferent about future things. I leave you to make your own remarks,[2] only I add, whatever may be the case with some persons, (for there are several things I do not approve of) I hope the great power of God is in this work. The two *noisy* Baptist Churches mentioned above, are among this people, and the tumult is spreading through different parts of this state, and perhaps will pervade the whole of the Presbyterean and Methodist Congregations.

I am, Sir,

With esteem and affection, sincerely yours,

(The minutes of the Salem Association for 1802 illustrate the effect of the Great Western Revival upon the Baptist churches in Kentucky. During this year 495 were baptized, and 189 were received into the churches by letter in this association. The *Circular Letter* is also a good example of the advice and warning issued to the churches in the time of the revival.)

[2] It would be a more easy than it is a welcome task to make remarks on what has been so generally called *the great work of God in America;* suffice it at present to say, That if, amidst the disorder and enthusiasm which have remarkably, of late, disgraced many of the Assemblies in Kentucky, the *Lord* has been really sowing the *good seed,* nothing is more to be feared than that it will too soon appear to the sorrow of the Church of God, that Satan has been very diligently sowing *tares.* O that the less informed among the Americans were in possession of President Edwards's excellent volume on the *Affections,* and would most seriously read it.—EDITOR

II.

MINUTES

OF THE

SALEM ASSOCIATION,

HELD AT COX'S CREEK MEETING HOUSE, NELSON COUNTY,

OCTOBER THE FIRST AND SECOND, 1802.

The introductory Sermon was preached by Brother John Taylor, from the 5th verse of the 8th chapter of *Paul's Second Epistle to the Corinthians*, "*And this they did, not as we hoped, but first gave their own selves to the Lord, and unto us by the will of God.*"

Brother William Taylor, chosen Moderator; and Brother William May, Clerk.

Letters from the different Churches in the Union were read, and the Messengers' names enrolled.

Churches.	Messengers.	Restored.	Baptized.	Received by Letter.	Rec'd by Relation.	Dismissed by Letter.	Excluded.	Dead.	Total.
Cedar Creek	Joshua Morris, Anthony Foster Atkinson Hill	3	51	2	1	8	2	2	111
Beargrass	George Hicks, James Fontain	1	7	4			1	2	69
Cox's Creek	William Taylor, William May, Joseph Lewis		29	6	1	15	4	2	163

Churches	Messengers	Restored.	Baptized.	Received by Letter.	Rec'd by Relation.	Dismissed by Letter.	Excluded.	Dead.	Total.
Brashear's Creek	James McQuaid, David Standiford, Isaac Ellis, Daniel Colgan		11		2	12	7		131
Hardin's Creek	James Rutter, Thomas Philips		25		1	5			
Simpson's Creek	Warrin Cash, Walter Stallard, Benjamin Cooper		68	7	1	7	2		182
Chinoweth's Run	William Taylor, Bartlet Asher, Edward Taylor		2			15	1		41
Fox Run	Moses Boon, William Ford								29
Buck & Elk Creek	Reuben Smith, Eliab Cooper, Thomas Spencer	1	9	4		8	3	1	143
Mill Creek	John Daesley, Thomas Hubbard								
Beech Creek	Moses Scott, Samuel Tinsley, John Howe		2	7		10	3	1	146
Harrod's Creek	William Kellar, John Netherton, Samuel Faris, Thomas White		6	6		5	10	3	145
Long Run	Joseph Collins, Benjamin Hughes, Benjamin Bridges		2	3		81	8	1	117

Churches.	Messengers.	Restored.	Baptized.	Received by Letter.	Rec'd by Relation.	Dismissed by Letter.	Excluded.	Dead.	Total.
Salt River	John Renny, Edmund Waller, Martin Utterback, Hardy Holeman	1	24	8	1	8	6	1	137
Ridge	Josiah Herbert, Isaac Edwards								12
Tick Creek	Philip Webber, Edmund Hensley		4	4		6	5		99
Fourteen Mile Ck.	Elisha Carr, James McCoy		17	5	5	4	1		42
Plumb Creek	William McCoy, George Waller	2	3	3		7	4		58
Six Mile creek	William Tool, Seth Cook		3	6		6	5	1	107
Eighteen Mile ck.	John Coons.		1	16		1	6		73
Corn Creek	John Taylor, Presley Gray, William King		18	12	1				60
Rock Lick	William Jones, Robert Loudon, Ralph Cotton		5	15	1				40
Burk's Branch	James Mullican, William Mullican		2	4	2		1		23
Floyd's Fork	Jonathan Stark	1	10	4			1		42
Cane and Back Run	James Anderson, Jesse Drake, Jesse Jones, George Markwell		9	21	1	5	1		61
Little Mount	Stephen Ashby, Daniel Wise		4	4	2		2		59

Churches.	Messengers.	Restored.	Baptized.	Received by Letter.	Rec'd by Relation.	Dismissed by Letter.	Excluded.	Dead.	Total.
Sulphur Fork	William Langore, William Fore			1		1			16
Lick Creek	William Kindall, Joseph Brown	2	17	8	3	2			31
Wilson's Creek	Edmund Polk, William Chinoweth		13	11	1	5			36
Salem	Daniel White, Robert Middleton, Hinson Hebbs			17					45
Hite's Run	Thomas Piety, Peter Cummins		1	3					13
Rock Creek	Morris Brady		24	1					32
Lick Branch	Hadley Head, George Bohannon			5	1			1	28
Rolling Fork	Samuel Miller, William Coy		71			5		2	77
Cedar Creek Salt River	William Overall, Samuel Simmonds	1	1						16
		12	495	189	24	216	73	17	2470

The following churches, viz. Wilson's creek, Salem, Hite's run, Rock creek, Lick branch, and Rolling fork, were received into this Union.

Received the minutes and circular letter from the Green river Association; and her messenger took his seat.

Brethren Joshua Morris, William Ford, and William May, appointed a committee to arrange the business of the ensuing day. And then the Association adjourned till to-morrow 9 o'clock.

SATURDAY

Met according to adjournment;—when the corresponding letter from the Elk-horn Association, together with her minutes and circular letter, were received; and her messenger, Brother Reese, invited to a seat with us.

Attended to the Query, referred by the last Association to the present; "Is it consistent with good order for a Minister within the bounds of a Church, to hear Experiences and baptize Persons, without the consent of such Church?" Answered in the negative.

The circular letter was read and approved.

Query from Cedar creek Church, "Are Members of Sister Churches invited to a seat in time of Church Business, intitled to a vote?" Answered in the negative.

Query from Hardin's creek Church, "Is it advisable to receive the evidence of a credible person in the world, against a Member who might publicly transgress, and yet deny it?" All things considered, we think it not advisable.

Agreed to unite with the South District, and Tate's creek Associations, on the terms they united with the Elk-horn Association; whereupon Brethren John Rice and Jeremiah Vardiman, Messengers from the South District, and Brother Reading from Tate's creek, were invited to their seats.

Agreed to receive the Church at Cedar creek (waters of Salt river) into this union.

Agreed that the Churches on the North side of Salt river, have liberty to form themselves into an Association, to be held at Long Run Meeting House, on the third Friday in September next; to bear the name of "Long Run Association:" Brother William Taylor to preach the introductory sermon; in case of failure, Brother John Taylor to be prepared.

Brethren Joshua Morris, Walter Stallard, and William May, appointed to write to the different Associations;

Brother Penny and Brother John Taylor to be our Messengers to the Elkhorn; Brother Cash, the Tate's creek; Brother Penny, the South District; Brethren Morris and Stallard, the Green river; and Brother William Taylor, the Long Run Association.

Brethren Joshua Morris and Joseph Lewis, to prepare the circular letter for the ensuing year.

The next Association to be held at Cedar creek, on the first Friday in October next. Brother Morris to preach the introductory sermon; in case of failure, Brother Cash to be prepared.

Quarterly meetings to be held the ensuing year, the first at Mill creek on the fourth Saturday in November; to be attended by Brethren Stallard and Pierson—the second at Lick creek, on the fourth Saturday in April; to be attended by Brethren William Taylor and Joshua Morris—the third at Cedar creek (Salt river), to be attended by Brethren Morris and Cash, on the fourth Saturday in July.

Agreed to appoint Quarterly Meetings on the North side of Salt river; the first at Sulpher fork, to be attended by Brethren Keller and M'Quaid, on the fourth Saturday in November the second at Bear-grass, on the fourth Saturday in April; to be attended by Brethren John Taylor and Reuben Smith—the third at Clear creek, on the fourth Saturday in July; to be attended by Brethren Webber and Kellar.

Brethren Lewis and May to superintend the printing our minutes and circular letter, and distribute them among the Churches.

Query from Floyd's fork, "What is the use and authority of an Association?" Answer—An Association is only an Advisory Council.

WILLIAM TAYLOR, *Moderator.*

William May, *Clerk.*

CIRCULAR LETTER.

. . . .

. . . .

TO THE CHURCHES WITH WHOM WE ARE IN UNION.

Dear Brethren,

THROUGH the Goodness of God, we have been favoured with another Meeting; and in token of our love to you, shall recommend to your serious consideration, a few Hints on the important Subject of Watchfulness.

In the first place, watch against a spirit of dogmatical Arrogance and Bigotry; remember you are far from infallibility or perfection in Knowledge; and others have an equal right of private Judgment with yourselves. Watch against a spirit of Curiosity, and a fond love of Novelty; remember you are warned not to affect to be Wise above what is written, or to intrude into Things that are unseen; but at the same time, watch against lazy Indifference to a progressive acquaintance with the Things of God; and remember that the Bible contains an inexhausted Mine of religions Knowledge, which you have not fully explored. Watch against all Notions which flatter human Pride and that encourage the Idea of Merit in a Sinner; and ever remember that the Design of God in the Gospel, is to abase all the Haughtiness of Man, that his free Grace may be exalted as the only Source of a Sinner's Salvation; and watch equally against Sentiments which tend to encourage Licentiousness or Sloth; remember it is Christ's Design to bring apostate Creatures back to God. Watch against all Sentiments that oppose God's moral Government, and make void his Law, either as representing the unregenerate, as fallen below all Obligations to any Thing spiritually Good, or the regenerate, as raised above every Idea of Duty; remember that the Law of God is too Holy, Just, and Good, to admit of any Abrogation or

Abatement. While we warn you against every Thought that would impeach the Equity of the Divine Government; we would equally caution you to reject every Idea that militates against the sovereign Freeness of Grace. Watch against degrading Ideas of the person of Christ; remember he is the only foundation of a Sinner's Hope; and the efficacy of his atoning Sacrifice, depends on the Dignity of his Person as God over all blessed forever. Watch against the Denial of the Personality, Divinity, and effectual Operations of the Holy Spirit; remember that the foundation which God hath laid, is adapted to sustain an Holy Temple, & no other kind of Building will accord therewith. In fine, watch against all Sentiments that would lessen your Abhorrence of Sin; prevent Holy Joy in God, or make you Careless of your moral Conduct; remember he who hath delivered us from the Curse of the Law, hath not lessened our Obligations to Obedience; let each one watch his own Heart, remembering the Charge given by the wisest of Men, "Keep thy Heart with all Diligence; for out of it are the issues of Life." Watch against Hypocrisy and self Deception; remember that God cannot be deceived, and will not be mocked. Watch against Formality and self Righteousness; remember, as an Antidote against the former, that God demands the Heart,—and as a Preventative from the latter, that by the Deeds of the Law there shall no Flesh be justified. Watch, lest any one should be found to have only the Semblance of Conversion, and not really be Born of God; remember that counterfeit Grace will soon be detected.—Watch against those corrupt Mixtures which sometimes attend the Experience of real Christians; many sinful Exercises of the Heart may attend, even the Exercise of Grace in the Seasons of our sweetest Enjoyments; remember it is not your being assuredly right in one Thing, that will prove you right in another. Watch against Backsliding from God; remember one Neglect leads to another, and God has said, the Backslider in Heart shall be filled with his own Ways. Be watchful over the whole Tenor of your Lives; remember the Grace of God teacheth us to live soberly, righteously and godly, in this present World.

Watch over your Tempers, Appetites, affections & Passions; & against the beginning of Temptations. Whatever you make an Idol of, will be a cross to you, if you belong to God; and a Curse to you, if you do not. Study relative Duties; show that you love universal Holiness; remember he that faith he abideth in him, ought himself also to walk even as he walked, Watch particularly over your Disposition and Behaviour towards each other; remember Christ hath said, *By this shall all Men know that ye are my Disciples, if ye have Love one for another.* Finally, watch against all earthly mindedness, and a worldly Spirit.

Farewell.

WILLIAM TAYLOR, Moderator.

William May, *Clerk.*

Frankfort, (k.)
Printed by William Hunter,
Printer to the Commonwealth.
1802.

III.

EXTRACTS

FROM THE

TOPOGRAPHICAL JOURNAL [1] OF MAJ. S. H. LONG

The Commander of an expedition authorized by the War Department for exploring a portion of the U. S. Territory situated westwardly and northwestwardly of Lake Superior.

First entry dated April 30, 1823. The visit to the McCoy Mission occurred June 2 and 3, 1823.

Having a desire to visit the school and missionary establishment, under the care of the Rev. Mr. M'Coy, we pro-

---

[1] The Manuscript Journal consists of three volumes and is in the collections of the Minnesota Historical Society, St. Paul, Minn.

ceeded down the river by a circuitous route of six miles, and arrived at the place of our intended visit. There we were gratified with meeting with an institution, embracing every preliminary appropriate in an establishment for reclaiming and civilizing the savages. Seven months only have elapsed since the site occupied by the establishment was clad in a forest.

Mr. M'Coy the principal was unfortunately absent on a visit to Grand River of Lake Michigan, at the time of our visit, but the result of his labours, zeal and industry, spoke loudly in his praise.—A large and comfortable dwelling house, a school house, a Blacksmith's shop, and other out houses—a large garden,—a pasture ground, enclosed with a good fence, together with a large field of plowed ground, planted with corn, etc., etc., are among the fruits of his industry and perserverance.—But a still stronger proof of his worth, was exhibited in the improvement of his Indian pupils. He has now under his charge, no less than about 40 pupils, about half of them the children of Indian parents, and the other half of mixed blood, Indian and French.—Of this number 14 were girls, who are taught reading, writing, arithmetic, plain and ornamental needle work,—nitting and spinning, together with the various business of the kitchen. —The residu are boys who are taught in the same branches of education, and during their leisure from study, and the requisite amusements are gradually instructed in the art of agriculture.—Particular attention is paid to their morals and deportment, and the pupils appear uniformly to conduct themselves, with as much decorum and propriety as are usually to be met with, in schools of white children of the same age. They appear to be of all ages, from six or seven to about seventeen. Their course of instruction is altogether in the English language, and many of them appear to make very rapid proficiency.—

Mrs. McCoy, is a lady of about thirty-five years of age, and appears admirably fitted to matronize an establishment of this kind.—Her disposition is remarkably mild, her deportment winning and sedulous.—She seems to entertain a mother's affection for them all, while they appear to treat her invariably with the respect and love of children.

There are two young men who officiate as subordinate teachers,—as also a young lady, who instructs the girls needlework, etc.

The school is made up of children from the Potawotomes, Miamis, and Otaways.—The number is expected to be enlarged as soon as more building can be erected for their accommodation. Timber is already prepared for the construction of as many more as are now built.—While every effort is made immediately connected with the establishment, to advance its interests and utility.—Among the difficulties they have to encounter one of the most formidable was that of procuring the requisite supply of provisions, which they have hitherto been under the necessity of transporting by land, over bad roads, from Kentucky and Ohio.—So precarious was this dependence that, sometimes owing to the impracticubility of transportation, and at others, to the loss of provisions accidently incurred on their passage, they have occasionally been reduced to the last extremities.—In order to guard against further embarrassment of this kind, arrangements are making to procure ample supplies from agriculture, at the establishment itself.—A field of about 50 acres, is to be planted with corn and sheep are now at the disposal of the institution. The wool of these is to be spun and woven by the girls, and is supposed sufficient to clothe the children of the establishment.

For the support of this establishment, government has appropriated $1,000 per annum, to be expended in support of a teacher and blacksmith.—Additional support to a very considerable amount is afforded by the Baptist Missionary, and other charitable institutions and annual donations.

It is denominated the Carey Mission station,—and is exclusively under the management of the Baptist Missionary Society of Washington City.—A similar establishment, under the auspices of the Main (?) Society, is contemplated at the Fork of Grand River of Lake Michigan.

Distance 25 miles.

Tuesday 3

It is contemplated to adopt the Lancastrian mode of education at this establishment as soon as they can render their organization more complete. This mode has been practiced by Mr. McCoy at Fort Wayne (where he first commended the duties of his mission) with much success, and was found particularly well adapted to the disposition and character of Indian youths.—At this place we got the shoes of some of our horses refitted,—by the assistance of the smith of the institution.

The site of the institution had been formerly occupied by a populous village of the Potewatomies, no traces of which now remain, except the corn-hills upon the ground then under cultivation. Their appearances are both numerous and extensive,—covering not less than 1,000 acres of ground, now clad in deep growth of timber and furze. Arrow points, knives, etc. are found distributed over the whole in considerable plenty.—According to the statements of the Indians, the village after having dwindled for many years must have been finally abandoned, between fifty and one hundred years since. Aged squaws recalling to mind the scenes of their youth which they enjoy here, speak of them with tears and sighs.—They point out the particular spots on which the cabins of their parents stood,—and recount the scenes of their younger days till utterance is suppress(ed) by the most heart-rending sobs.

We took our leave of this interesting establishment, at half past 7 A.M.—leaving the good people to whom its management was entrusted, with hearts as heavy at the separation as they were glad at our arrival.

Secluded from civilized society, they are exceedingly happy to receive visits from those with whom they are able to associate and converse.

BIBLIOGRAPHY

MANUSCRIPTS

Church Records:

Record-Church Minute Book, Severn's Valley (Kentucky), 1787–1884.
Minutes Boone's Creek Baptist Church Fayette Co. Virginia (now *Kentucky*), 1785–1830. 2 vols.
Minute Book—Mountain Island Church (Kentucky), 1801–1836.
Minutes of the Glen's Creek Baptist Church, Vol. I (Kentucky), 1801–1824; Vol. II, 1825–1851.
Minutes of the Long Run Baptist Church (Kentucky), 1803–1817.
Minutes of the Forks of Elkhorn Baptist Church (Kentucky), June 7, 1788 to June 30, 1903.
Minutes of the Brashear's Creek Church (Kentucky), 1807–1818.
Minutes of Bogg's Fork Baptist Church (Kentucky), 1829–1886.
Minutes Plum Creek Baptist Church (Kentucky), 1812–1899.
Minutes White's Run Baptist Church (Kentucky), 1810–1847.
Minutes of the Hill Grove United Baptist Church (Kentucky), 1822–1870.
A Record Book for the United Baptist Church of Christ at Valley Creek (Kentucky), 1803–1844.
Minutes of Claylick (Baptist) Church (Kentucky), 1822–1834.
A Record of the Proceedings of an Arm of the West Fork Church constituted at the Salubrious Spring M.H. on the Saturday before the 4th. Lord's Day in Jany. 1814 to 1827; later known as Bethel Church.
An Historical Sketch of the Rise and Progress of Bethel Church (Kentucky). Prepared by Jno. Pendleton Clk. at the request of the Church in 1817.
Record of the Proceedings of Bethel Church Christian Co. Kentucky, Vol. II, 1828–1870.
Historical Sketch of Elk Creek Baptist Church (Kentucky), 1794–1894 by W. W. Gardner.
Records of Wood River Church (Illinois), 1812–1822.
Records of Turkey Hill Church (Friends of Humanity), (Illinois), 1822–1850.
Records of Fountain Creek Church (Friends of Humanity), (Illinois), 1821–1868.
Records of the Blue River Association (Indiana), 1816–1819.
Records of the Silver Creek Association (Indiana), 1813, 1819.
Records of the Laughery Association (Indiana), 1819.

The Holman Correspondence, 1818–1842. Private letters relating to Baptist matters in Indiana, written to Jesse L. Holman of Aurora, Indiana, a United States judge and prominent in political and Baptist circles. (About 140 items.)

Minutes of the Coffee Creek Association (Indiana), 1826–1906.

A Record of the Articles of Faith, Rules of Decorum and Constitution and Also the Proceedings of the Little Pigeon Association of United Baptists of America Commenced October 1821 (1821–1854).

Proceedings of the Indianapolis Association of Baptists for the First Thirty Years of its History (Vol. I, 1826–1856).

The Record Book of Vernal Church (Indiana), 1817–1873. (Typewritten copy.)

History of Vernal Church.

Records and Minutes of the Fourteen Mile Regular Baptist Church (Indiana), 1798–1873. (Transcribed from the original.)

Record Book of Bethel Church (Owen Co., Indiana), 1822–1885. (Typewritten copy.)

General Association of Baptists of Indiana, 1833–1835. (Photostat.)

Record of Door Valley Church (near La Porte, Indiana), 1840–1891. (Copy.)

Record of Silver Creek Baptist Church (Indiana), 1807–1836. (Copy.)

Church Record Blue River Church (Indiana), 1847–1929.

Minute Book Bear Creek Church (Indiana), 1828–1929. (Copy.)

Records of Sharon (Baptist) Church (Indiana), 1810–1830. (Copy.)

Smith, Ulmer E.—*History of Bethel Baptist Church* (Owen Co., Indiana).

Other Manuscript Materials:

Journal and Notes of Rev. David Barrow of a Tour From Virginia to Kentucky, 1795–1797 (Draper MSS., Shane Collection in Wisconsin Historical Society).

Autobiography of Jacob Bower (Shurtleff College Collection).

Edwards, Morgan—*Materials Towards a History of the Baptists in Virginia to 1772* (American Baptist Hist. Society Collections, Chester, Pennsylvania).

Diary and Memoirs of Rev. W. M. Pratt, 1838–1872.

Journal of Maj. S. H. Long (3 MS. vols.). (Minnesota Historical Society, St. Paul, Minnesota.)

Church Letters Transferring Church Membership, covering the years 1805–1829. (Shurtleff College Collection; photostats in the University of Chicago Library.)

Letters and Reports of Isaac McCoy (Department of the Interior, Office of the Indiana Affairs, Washington, District of Columbia).

The Draper Collection (Shane Manuscripts, Vols. 11, 12, 14 and 15). (State Historical Society of Wisconsin.)

Letters of John M. Peck. (Photostats in the University of Chicago Library; originals in Shurtleff College Collection.)

BIBLIOGRAPHY 631

PRINTED SOURCE MATERIALS

Association Records, Partly in Manuscript, but for the Most Part Printed:

Minutes of the Elkhorn Baptist Association (Kentucky), Vol. I, 1785–1835; Vol. II, 1836–1845; Vol. III, 1846–1876; Vol. IV, 1877–1890.

Minutes of the North Bend Association (Kentucky), 1803–1865.

The Book of the Records of Long Run Association (Kentucky). Held at Long Run Meeting House the first time, September 16th and 17th, 1803 and continued by adjournment from time to time within the Bounds of the Association, 1803–1852.

Minutes of the Salem Association (Kentucky), 1802–1822.

Minutes of the Kentucky Baptist Association, 1826–1840.

Minutes of the Sulphur Fork Association (Kentucky), 1826–1838.

Minutes of the Goshen Association (Kentucky), 1818–1827.

Minutes of the South District Association (Kentucky), 1807–1824.

Minutes of the Franklin Association (Kentucky), 1824–1839.

Minutes of the Green River Baptist Association (Kentucky), 1822–1833.

Minutes Russell's Creek Association (Kentucky), 1813, 1816, 1831–'32, 1836.

Minutes of the Baptized-Licking-Locust Association, Friends of Humanity (Kentucky), 1807.

Minutes Tate's Creek Association of United Baptists (organized, 1793), 1824.

Minutes of the Licking Association of Particular Baptists (Kentucky), 1823–1828.

Minutes North District Association of Baptists (Kentucky), 1802–1840.

Minutes of the South Concord Association of United Baptists (Wayne County, Kentucky), Vol. I, 1825–1870; Vol. II, 1871–1892.

Minutes Boone's Creek Association (Kentucky), 1823–1840.

Minute Book of the Illinois Baptist Association, 1807–1849.

Minute Book of the South District Association (Illinois), 1830–1864.

Minute Book of the North District Association (Illinois), 1825–1840.

History of the North District Association, by H. L. Derr, 1825–1840.

Minutes of the Wabash District Association (Illinois), 1830.

Minutes Georgia Baptist State Convention (1822–1830).

Minutes of the Philadelphia Baptist Association from A.D. 1707 to A.D. 1807. Being the First 100 years of its existence—Edited by A. D. Gillette, Philadelphia, 1851. Also the minutes, 1788–1819 bound but not edited.

Minutes of the Huntington Baptist Association (Indiana), 1813–1819.

Minutes of the Silver Creek Association (Indiana), 1821–1929.

Minutes of the Indiana Baptist State Convention, 1833–1866.

Minutes of the Flat Fork Association (Indiana), 1823–1899.

Printed Sources Other than Association Records:

The Baptist Annual Register (London), Edited by John Rippon; Vol. I, 1790–1793; Vol. II, 1794–1797; Vol. III, 1798–1801.

Asplund, John—*The Universal Register of the Baptist Denomination in North America.* No. I, Southampton, Virginia, 1790.

"*Massachusetts Historical Society Collections,*" Vol. VI.

Rhode Island Colonial Records, Vol. I.

Barrow, David—*Involuntary, Absolute, Hereditary Slavery Examined on the Principles of Nature, Reason, Justice, and Scripture.* Pam., 1808.

Cartwright, Peter—*Autobiography, The Backwoods Preacher* (Cincinnati, 1856).

Finley, J. B.—*Autobiography* (Cincinnati, 1856).

Fishback, James—*A Defence of the Elkhorn Association* (Lexington, Kentucky, 1822).

Leland, John—*The Rights of Conscience Inalienable* (Richmond, 1793).

Leland, John—*Writings,* edited by Miss L. F. Green (New York, 1845).

Parker, Daniel—*A Public Address to the Baptist Society* (Pam., 1820).

Pendleton, J. M.—*Church Manual* (Philadelphia, 1867).

Proceedings of the Baptist Convention for Missionary Purposes held in Philadelphia, in May, 1814 (Philadelphia, 1814).

Publications of the Narragansett Club—(Providence, Rhode Island, 1866–1874).

Taylor, John—*Thoughts on Missions* (Pam., 1819).

Taylor, John—*Clear Creek Church and Campbellism Exposed* (Frankfort, Kentucky, 1830).

Madison, James—*Letters and other Writings,* 4 vols. (Philadelphia, 1865).

Works Containing Source Materials

Babcock, R.—*Memoir of John Mason Peck* (Philadelphia, 1864).

Backus, Isaac—*A History of New England with Particular Reference to the Denomination of Christians called Baptists,* 2 vols.—Second edition with notes by D. Weston (Newton, Massachusetts, 1871).

Benedict, David—*A General History of the Baptist Denomination in America,* 2 vols. (Boston, 1813).

Bishop, Robert H.—*Outline History of the Church in the State of Kentucky*—Containing the Memoirs of Rev. David Rice (Lexington, 1824).

Burkitt, L. and Read, J.—*A Concise History of the Kehukee Baptist Association* (Halifax, North Carolina, 1803). Revised (Philadelphia, 1850).

Campbell, Alexander—*The Christian Baptist,* 1822–1830 (Cincinnati, 1885).

Carden, Allen D.—*The Missouri Harmony,* etc. (Cincinnati, 1833, first edition 1831) (R. G. McCutchan Collection, Greencastle, Ind.).

Cox, F. A. and Hoby R. J.—*The Baptists in America—A Narrative of the Deputation from the Baptist Union in England to the U. S. and Canada* (New York, 1836).

Davidson, Robert—*History of the Presbyterian Church in the State of Kentucky* (New York, 1847).

Elton, R.—*The Reverend Jonathan Maxcy,—Literary Remains* (New York, 1844).

Fristoe, F.—*History of the Ketocton Baptist Association* (Staunton, Virginia, 1808).

James, Charles F.—*Documentary History of the Struggle for Religious Liberty in Virginia* (Lynchburg, 1900).

Keith, Benj. F.—*History of the Maria Creek Church* (Vincennes, Indiana, 1889).

McNaul, W. C.—*The Jefferson-Lemen Compact* (Chicago, 1915).

Mead, Stith—*A General Selection of the Newest and Most Admired HYMNS and Spiritual Songs,* etc. (Richmond, 1807) (R. G. McCutchan Collection).

Purefoy, G. A.—*A History of the Sandy Creek Association* (New York, 1859).

Ricker, Joseph—*Personal Recollections, a Contribution to Baptist History and Biography* (Augusta, 1894).

Rothert, Otto A.—*A History of Unity Baptist Church, Muhlenberg County Kentucky* (Louisville, 1914).

Scall, Stephen P.—*A Selection of Christian HYMNS* (Bloomington, Ind., 1827) (R. G. McCutchan Collection).

Semple, Robert B.—*A History of the Rise and Progress of the Baptists in Virginia* (Richmond, 1810). Revised and extended by Rev. G. W. Beale (Richmond, 1894).

Smith, Joseph—*Old Redstone, or Historical Sketches of Western Presbyterianism* (Philadelphia, 1854).

Sprague, W. B.—*Annals of the American Pulpit* (New York, 1858–1869), Vol. VI, *Baptists.*

Stott, W. T.—*Indiana Baptist History, 1798–1908* (Franklin, Indiana, 1908).

Sweet, W. W.—*Circuit Rider Days Along the Ohio* (New York, 1923).

Sweet, W. W.—*Rise of Methodism in the West* (Cincinnati, 1920).

Taylor, James B.—*Memoir of Rev. Luther Rice* (Baltimore, 1840).

Taylor, John—*History of Ten Baptist Churches* (Frankfort, Kentucky, 1823).

Wayland, F. and H. L.—*Memoir of the Life and Labors of Francis Wayland,* 2 vols. (New York, 1868).

Wood, Furman—*A History of the Charleston Association of Baptist Churches in the State of South Carolina* (Charleston, 1811).

Wright, Stephen—*History of the Shaftsbury Baptist Association from 1781 to 1853* (Troy, New York, 1853).

Denominational Periodicals:

The American Baptist Magazine and Missionary Intelligencer (Boston), *1817–1821.*

The Baptist Magazine, Vols. 1 to 46 (London, England), 1809–1854.

The Latter Day Luminary (Philadelphia, 1818–1821; Washington, 1822–1824).

New York Baptist Register (Utica, New York), Vol. 1, 1824 to Vol. 8, 1831.

Columbian Star and Monthly Index (Philadelphia), Vol. I, 1829 to Vol. 5, 1833.

The Baptist Advocate (Philadelphia), Vol. I, 1840 to Vol. IV, 1843.

Religious Narrator and Philadelphia Journal of Christian Effort (Philadelphia), Vol. I, 1833.

The World As It Is and As It Should Be (Philadelphia), Vol. 1–2, 1832, 1833.

American Revivalist and Rochester Observer (Rochester), Vol. 1, 1828.

Baptist Banner (Shelbyville, Kentucky), Vol. I, 1834 to Vol. 3, 1836.

General Tract Society (Philadelphia), Vols. 1–4, 1836–1839.

The Christian Watchman (Boston), Vol. 1, 1819 to Vol. 20, 1839.

The Baptist Advocate (New York), Vol. 1, 1839; Vol. 2, 1840.

The Journal and Messenger (Cincinnati), Vol. 1, 1831 to date.

The Baptist Preacher (Boston), Vol. 1, 1826–1827 to Vol. 3, 1829–1830.

The Massachusetts Baptist Missionary Magazine (Boston), 1803–1816.

The Baptist (Nashville), Vol. 1, 1834.

The Western Baptist Review (Frankfort, Kentucky), Vol. 1, 1845–1846.

Baptist Repository and Home Mission Record (New York), Vols. 1–5, 1828–1833.

The Regular Baptist (Cincinnati), Vol. 1, 1839.

Baptist Memorial and Monthly Chronicle (New York), 1842–1854.

New York Missionary Magazine and Repository of Religious Intelligence for the year 1800 (New York), Vol. I.

GENERAL WORKS

Adams, A. D.—*Neglected Period of Anti-slavery in America* (Boston, 1908).

Baptist Encyclopedia, 2 vols. (Philadelphia, 1883), W. Cathcart, editor.

Benedict, David—*Fifty Years Among the Baptists* (New York, 1860).

Beveridge, A. J.—*Abraham Lincoln*, 2 vols. (Boston, 1928).

Birney, W.—*J. G. Birney and His Times* (New York, 1890).

Brand, E. P.—*Illinois Baptists, a History* (Bloomington, Illinois, 1930).

Broadus—*The American Baptist Ministry One Hundred Years Ago* (Baptist Quarterly, Vol. IX, 1875), pp. 1–20.

Brown, J. M.—*Political Beginnings in Kentucky* (Louisville, 1889).

Buck, S. J.—*Illinois in 1818* (Springfield, 1917).

Carroll, B. H.—*Genesis of American Anti-Missionism* (Louisville, 1902).

Christian, J. T.—*A History of the Baptists, 1740–1790* (Nashville, 1926).

Cleveland, C. C.—*The Great Revival in the West* (Chicago, 1916).

Coburn, Mrs. Henry and others—*Souvenir, Seventy-fifth Anniversary of First Baptist Church Indianapolis, 1822–1897* (Indianapolis, 1897).

Collins, L.—*Historical Sketches of Kentucky* (Cincinnati, 1847).

Curry, J. L. M.—*Struggles and Triumphs of Virginia Baptists* (Philadelphia, 1873).

Curtis, T. F.—*Progress of Baptist Principles in the Last One Hundred Years* (Boston, 1860).

Duncan, R. S.—*A History of the Baptists in Missouri* (St. Louis, 1882).

Dunlevy, A. H.—*History of the Miami Baptist Association.* (n.d.)

Edwards, Morgan—*History of the Baptists in Virginia* (MSS.).

Esarey, L.—*History of Indiana*, 2 vols. (Indianapolis, 1915).

Fisher, M. M.—*History of Negro Baptists* (MSS.).

Gammell, William—*History of American Baptist Missions in Asia, Africa, Europe and North America* (Boston, 1850).

Gates, E.—*Early Relations and Separation of Baptists and Disciples* (Chicago, 1904).

Gates, E.—*The Disciples of Christ* (New York, 1905).

Gewehr, W. M.—*The Great Awakening in Virginia, 1740–1790* (Durham, N. C., 1930).

Goodsell, Charles T.—*The Baptist Anti-Mission Movement in America* (Master's Thesis, University of Chicago, 1924).

Guild, R. A.—*Life and Times of James Manning and the Early History of Brown University* (Boston, 1864).

Harris, N. D.—*History of Negro Servitude in Illinois* (Chicago, 1904).

Hart, A. B.—*Slavery and Abolition* (New York, 1906) (American Nation Series, Vol. 16).

Hawks, F. L.—*Contributions to the Ecclesiastical History of the United States of America* (New York, 1839).

History of the Baptist Denomination in Georgia compiled for the Christian Index (Atlanta, 1881).

Holcombe, Hosea—*A History of the Rise and Progress of the Baptists in Alabama* (Philadelphia, 1840).

Houck, L.—*A History of Missouri*, 3 vols. (1908).

Howe, J. Edwin—*History of the Perry County Indiana Baptist Association, 1821–1891* (Cannelton, Indiana, 1922).

Howell, Robert B. C.—*The Early Baptists of Virginia* (Philadelphia, 1857).

Humphrey, E. F.—*Nationalism and Religion in America* (Boston, 1924).

Knight, R.—*History of the General or Six Principle Baptists* (Providence, 1827).

Jarratt, Devereux—*An Argument between an Anabaptist and a Methodist on the Subject and Mode of Baptism* (Fredericksburg, Virginia, 1814). (Reprint).

Jones, S.—*Early Baptists of Philadelphia* (Philadelphia, 1877).

Jubilee of the General Association of Baptists in Kentucky (Louisville, 1887).

Leavell, Z. T., and Bailey, T. J.—*A Complete History of Mississippi Baptists*, 2 vols. (Jackson, 1904).

Leonard, D. L.—*One Hundred Years of Missions* (1913).

Locke, M. F.—*Anti-Slavery in America* (Boston, 1901).

McCoy, Isaac—*History of Baptist Indian Missions* (Washington, 1840).

Manly, B.—*Kentucky Baptist Pioneers* (Louisville, 1876).

Martin, A. S.—*The Anti-slavery Movement in Kentucky Prior to 1850* (Louisville, 1918), Filson Club Publication No. 29.

Mercer, Jesse—*History of the Georgia Baptist Association* (Washington, Georgia, 1838).

Milburn, W. H.—*The Lance, Cross and Canoe, Flatboat, Rifle and Plow in the Valley of the Mississippi* (New York, 1892).

Minutes of the One Hundredth Anniversary of the Miami Association of Regular Baptists, including Historical Sketch of the Miami Association by George E. Stevens, pp. 37–63.

Newman, A. H.—*A History of the Baptist Churches in the United States* (New York, 1894), American Church History Series, Vol. 2.

North Carolina Baptist Historical Papers, eleven numbers, Vols. 1–3, 1897–1900.

Nowlin, W. D.—*Kentucky Baptist History*, 1770–1922 (Baptist Book Concern, Louisville?, 1922).

Paxson, F. L.—*History of the American Frontier* (Boston, 1924).

Peck, J. M.—*"Father Clark" or the Pioneer Preacher* (New York, 1855).

Peck, J. and Lawton, J.—*An Historical Sketch of the Baptist Missionary Convention of the State of New York* (Utica, 1837).

Ranck, George W.—*The Travelling Church* (Louisville, 1891).

Ray, D. B., and Lucas, J. R.—*Church Discussion: Baptist and Disciples* (Cincinnati, 1873).

Riegel, R. E.—*America Moves West* (New York, 1930).

Riley, B. F.—*A History of the Baptists in the Southern States East of the Mississippi* (Philadelphia, 1898).

Riley, B. F.—*History of Alabama Baptists.*

Roosevelt, Theodore—*The Winning of the West*, 4 vols. (New York, 1890).

Rusk, R. L.—*The Literature of the Middle Western Frontier*, 2 vols. (New York, 1925).

Smith, J. A.—*A History of the Baptists in the Western States East of the Mississippi* (Philadelphia, 1896).

Smith, Z. F.—*History of Kentucky* (Louisville, 1901).

Spencer, J. H.—*A History of Kentucky Baptists*, 2 vols. (Cincinnati, 1885).

Starbird, George M.—*The Adaptation of the Baptist Associational Movement in America to its Environment* (Master's thesis in MSS.—University of Chicago, 1924).

Taylor, G. B.—*The Life and Times of J. B. Taylor* (Philadelphia, 1872).

Taylor, James B.—*Virginia Baptist Ministers*, 2 vols. (Philadelphia, 1859).

Thom, W. T.—*The Struggle for Religious Freedom in Virginia* (Baltimore, 1900). Johns Hopkins Uni. Studies, Series XVIII.

Thompson, L. N.—*Lewis Craig, The Pioneer Baptist Preacher* (Louisville, 1910).

Tibbetts, J. C.—*History of Coffee Creek Association* (Indiana), *An Account of Present Churches and Biographical Sketches of Its Ministers* (Cincinnati, 1883).

Tong, H. F.—*Historical Sketches of Baptists of Southeast Missouri* (St. Louis, 1888).

Trowbridge, M. E. D.—*History of Baptists in Michigan* (Philadelphia?, 1909).

Vedder, H. C.—*A History of the Baptists in the Middle States* (Philadelphia, 1898).

Vedder, H. C.—*A Short History of the Baptists* (Philadelphia, 1892).

Waggener, H. F.—*Baptist Beginnings in Illinois* (Master's Thesis in MSS.—University of Chicago, 1928).

Waller, John L.—*Historical Sketch of the Baptist Church in Kentucky* (pamphlet, Durrett Collection).

Weeks, S. B.—*Southern Quakers and Slavery* (Johns Hopkins Uni. Studies, Extra Vol. XV, Ch. 9).

Williams, C. B.—*History of Baptists in North Carolina* (Raleigh, 1901).

Williams, John A.—*Life of Elder John Smith* (Cincinnati, 1870).

INDEX

"Abolition Intelligencer," edited by David Barrow, 85

Abolition society, formed in Virginia, 80; membership of Quakers and Methodists, 80

Aged brethren, bounty of the churches for, 490

Alabama, anti-mission Baptists (1846), 66; colliding elements in Baptist ranks, 66

Allegheny Mountains, 22, 121, 130; Baptist migration over, 17; settlements across, 18

Alton, Illinois, 208

American Anti-slavery Society, 101

American Bible Society, 97

American Board of Commissioners for Foreign Missions, admission of Presbyterian and Dutch Reformed representatives, 58; Congregational in origin, 58; first missionaries Hall, Judson, Newell, Rice, 58; organized in 1810, 58

American churches, new western problem, 18

American Colonization Society, founded in Washington in 1816, 98

Anglicans, among frontier settlers, 19

Anti-mission agitation, 32

Anti-mission Baptists, 58–76; Primitive, 67; theology of, 74–75; Two-Seed-in-the-Spirit, 67; ultra-Calvinistic, 67

Anti-mission feeling in Baptist churches in Tennessee, 63

Anti-mission movement, harmful effect of in West, 76

Anti-mission neighborhood, Brown County, 215

Anti-missionism, in Illinois, 207, 208; peculiar frontier Baptist phenomenon, 67; responsibility for rise of, 67

Anti-slavery Baptists, 77–101; circular address (1821), 577–581; circular letter of 1823, 583–587; circular letter of 1826, 593–596; circular letter of 1839, 603–607; in Kentucky and Illinois, 563–607

Anti-slavery cause, in 1818–1824, 96

Apple Creek Anti-mission Association, Illinois, 64

Arminian views, compromise with Calvinistic, 23

Arminianism, of Cumberland Presbyterians, 75; of Methodists, 75; of New Lights, 75

Asplund, John, register of the Baptists in North America, 455

Association, divine authority of, 468; first Baptist (1707), 4; formation of in Franklin, 388, 389, 391; letter, 318; messengers to, 325, 406; origin and divine authority of, 454

Association officials, moderator and clerk, 56

Associations, circular letters of, 54, 57

Atheism, in former pastors of South Creek Church, 124

Backus, Isaac, 16, 17; New England Baptist leader, 5

Badgley, David, founder of New Design Church, 31; preacher in Illinois, 129

Badgleys, Anthony, 510

Balls, 335

Baptism, 198, 199, 273, 612; by immersion, 303; members received by, 276; ordinance of, 517, 518; validity of, 493; validity of when administered by Pedobaptist minister, 454

Baptist anti-missionism, 58–76; causes of, 72; opposition to centralization of authority, 72; opposition to paid and educated ministry, 72–73

Baptist beginnings in Illinois, 88

Baptist Board of Foreign Missions, 63; beginning of, 62; opposition by Parker, 69; questions regarding, 554

Baptist church, first in Illinois, "New Design Baptist Church," 89

Baptist church government, 21, 69

Baptist churches, business meetings, 48; frontier, formation of, 46; frontier, located on streams, 45; in Connecticut, 6; in Maine, 6; in Massachusetts, 6; in New England, 6; in New Hampshire, 6; in Rhode Island, 6; in Vermont, 6; messengers from, 55; receiving of members in, 52 f.; *Separate*, 119

Baptist families, from North Carolina, 27; from Virginia, 27

Baptist missionaries, 34, 58

Baptist missionary, first, for the West, 59

Baptist preachers, 21, 24, 357; arrest of, 13; division of Elkhorn Association, 356; first in Kentucky (Marshall, Barnett, Whitaker, Skaggs, Lynn, Gerrard), 19; licensed, 40; Luke Williams, Missouri, 42, 43; on frontier, two types of, 40

Baptist principles, 43, 54; contrary to missionary enterprise, 68

Baptists, 610, 611; agitation for religious liberty, 15; anti-slavery, 32; anti-slavery controversy among, 80; anti-slavery movements, 77–101; Arminian, 4, 7, 43, 44; as political factor, 12; associational organization, 55; at close of Revolution, 3; attitude of, toward paying pastors, 37 f.; attitude toward slavery, 78; barbecues, 508; Calvinistic, 7, 43, 44, 120; churches in Kentucky, 25; doctrinal position of, 44; effect of anti-mission movement on, 76; emancipation movement, 89; emancipation work among, 81; English, 3, 4; first church in America, 3; first churches on frontier, 53; Free Will, 43; from New Jersey, 28; from New York, 28; from North Carolina, 20; from Pittsburg, 28; from Virginia, 20; frontier churches, 45; frontier groups, 43; General, 43; German, 29; Great Awakening, 3; in Cincinnati, 28; in Illinois, 30; in Indiana, 30; in Ken-

tucky, 25, 81; in Louisiana, 35; in Maryland, 7; in Massachusetts, 3; in middle colonies, 4, 6; in Mississippi, 35; in New England, 7, 16, 17, 29; in North Carolina, 7, 9, 12; in Providence Plantation, 3; in South Kentucky, 152; in Tennessee, 26, 27; in United States at close of Revolution, 17; in Virginia, 7, 12, 14, 36; in Virginia, manumission of slaves, 79; Irish, 4; justification of slaveholding, 87; members in Kentucky, 25; of Kentucky, attempts to unite Regular and Separate, 23; of New England, 16; of Rhode Island, 7; on frontier, 18, 24; Particular, 43; Primitive or "Hardshell," 43, 44; propaganda of Rice for missions, 61; protest against slave trade, 77; raising up of preacher, 410; Regular, 7, 43, 120, 132; rise of anti-mission, 58; Roger Williams, 3; second church, 3; *Separate*, 43, 132; taxation, in Illinois and Missouri, 64; typical frontier preacher, 36; United, 43; Virginia General Committee, attitude toward slavery, 79; Welsh, 4; work among slaves, 78

Baptized Church of Christ, Friends to Humanity, Turkey Hill, meeting of September 27, 1822, 569; meeting of December, 1823, 572; meeting of February 28, 1824, 572

Baptizing in South River, 119

Barbecues, 335, 508

Barrow, David, 563, 564; emancipation champion among Kentucky Baptists, 81; expulsion from North District Association, 83; on slavery, 565; pamphlet of, 82; president of Kentucky Abolition Society, 85

Beargrass settlement, 123

Beaver Association, near Pittsburg, 29

Beaver Creek Church, Kentucky, constitution and rules of, 258–261; records for 1803, 258 ff.

Bible Society, 206

Black Hawk, 206

Board of Home Mission Society, 226

Boon County, 161

Boone, Daniel, 18, 20

Boone, Squire, Baptist preacher, 18
Boone's Creek Church, Kentucky, records of, 253–258
Boon's Creek Church, Tennessee, 27
Bower, Jacob, 37, 40 f.; activities of in—1834, 218; 1835, 218; 1836, 219; 1837, 219; 1838, 219; 1839, 220; 1840, 220; 1841, 221; 1842, 222; 1843, 222; 1844, 224; 1845, 224; 1846, 225; 1847, 225; 1848, 225; 1849, 227; 1850, 227; 1851, 228; 1852, 228; 1853, 228; 1854, 228; 1855, 229; 1856, 229; 1857, 229;— anti-mission opposition to, 209–216; appointed a missionary, 209; autobiography of, 185–230; Baptist missionary in Illinois, 64; missionary in Missouri, 64; begins to preach, 202; conversion of, 193–195; frontier Baptist preacher, 185–230; in Illinois, 204; in St. Louis, 228; joins Baptists, 199; lack of education, 203; left Kentucky, 204; license to solemnize rite of matrimony, 204; move to Scott County, Illinois, 205; ordination of, 204; religious struggle of, 191; tour in Kentucky, 222; united with Sandy Creek Church, Illinois, 205; work in Missouri, 223–225; youth of, 187
Bracken Association, attitude toward emancipation, 82
British West Indies, ports of, 19
Brush Run Church, Pennsylvania, 70
Bryant's Church, Kentucky, 152; membership, 612
Buck Run Church, Kentucky, 177–184; constitution of, 177–180; rules of decorum, 180–182
Burial ground of church, 353
Burma, first Baptist mission, 59
Business, of church, 48–49; 352

Cain Ridge meeting, 24; of 1801, 610
Call to preach, 235–238
Calvinism, effect of on Baptist progress in West, 76
Calvinistic views, compromise with Arminian, 23
Campbell, Alexander, 26; anti-missionism of, 67, 70; attacks on missionary societies, 74; attacks on non-scriptural denominational practices, 70; Baptist from 1813 to 1830, 70; Brush Run Church, Pennsylvania, 70; changed views on missions, 71 f.; educational work in western Virginia, 70; head of "Reformers," 66; organization of church of *Disciples*, 71
Campbellism, 57
Campbellite, preacher, 205
Campbellites, 213, teaching of, 212
Cantine Creek, Baptist church, antislavery basis of, 91; members of, 92
Carey Mission Station, 627
Carey, William, English Baptist pioneer missionary, 58
Cartwright, Peter, on use of liquor, 52
Catechism, 483
Catholic religion, in upper Louisiana, 32
Catholic settlement, 183
Cave, Richard, 148, 151, 164
Charges, against the church, 345
Choosing a pastor, Marshall and Ireland, 120
Christian Baptist, The, 26; founded in 1823 by Campbell, 70
Christian experience, 53
Church, burial ground of, 353; formation of new, 279, 281; fund for, 350, 382, 383; grievances in, 322; land for, 350; Record book, 401, 402; request to be received into Association, 439; trustees, 351
Church business, 48–49, 352
Church constitution, Buck Run, 45; Mount Tabor, 45
Church covenant, 177
Church discipline. *See Discipline*
Church finances, 345, 346, 394, 405, 414
Church grieved with Grassy Spring Church, 317
Church letter of dismission, 297
Church letters, 239–247, 341, 401; Ogle Creek Church, Illinois, 239; Twelve Mile Prairie Church, Illinois, 239; Wood River Church, Illinois, 239
Church members, 612
Church rules, 295–296
Churches, desiring admission to Association, 468; supply of, 518

Cincinnati, Ohio, 28; Baptist churches in vicinity of, 29

Circuit, remonstrance against, 519

Circular address, anti-slavery Baptists, 1821, 577–581

Circular letter, 439, 440, 469; rejected, 479; of 1823, anti-slavery Baptists, 583–587; of 1826, 593–596; of 1839, 603–607; Illinois Association, of 1812, 532; of 1813, 534; of 1815, 539; of 1817, 546; of 1818, 550; of 1819, 556; of 1820, 560 f.; Friends to Humanity, of 1807, 566–569; Salem Association, of 1802, 623

Circular letters, Associations, 57

Clark, George Rogers, of Kentucky, 20

Clear Creek, 149

Clear Creek Church, Kentucky, 48, 124, 151–165; formation of, 46; membership of, 152, 612; meeting house, 155

Clerk, of association, 56; standing for Illinois Association, 531

Coles, Edward, Baptist from Virginia, 95

Coles, Governor, Baptist, 97

Complaints, against Boone's Creek Church, 472

Concord Association, Tennessee, 28

Confession of Faith, 22, 303, 459, 496; revision of, 444

Congregationalists, active against slavery, 78; Calvinistic, 4; of Rhode Island, 7

Connecticut, Baptist churches in, 4; Baptists from, 28; churches of, in Philadelphia Association, 6; *Separates* and *New-Lights* from, 8

Constitution of United States, against slavery, 97

Constitutions, of frontier associations, 55

Converts, baptized at Clear Creek, 152

Cook, D. P., anti-slavery representative in Congress (1819), 96

Corn Creek Church, Kentucky, 165–177; growth of, 168

Cox's Creek, Kentucky, 23

Crab Orchard, Virginia, 142

Craig, Elijah, 119

Craig, John, founding of Elkhorn Association, 22

Craig, Lewis, 21, 87, 148, 150, 151, 152, 153, 154, 157, 417; leadership of, 55; moderator, 47; sketch of life, 151

Craig's Station, 22, 123, 147, 149

Cumberland Association, Tennessee, 28

Cumberland country, Tennessee, 27, 28; Mero Association, 55

Cumberland Presbyterians, Arminianism of, 75

Day of fasting and humiliation, 460

Day of fasting and prayer, appointment of, 503

Deacon, appointment of, 358; office of, 308, 309, 359, 378, 381; ordination of, 310, 311, 554; work of, 454

Decorum, rules of, 570–571; Illinois Association, 512, 513, 515

Deed, lot for church, 352

Deism, in South River Church, 124

Delaware, Baptist churches in, 3

Disciples Church, withdrawal of Kentucky Baptists to form, 26

Discipline (church), 49, 50, 51, 252–253, 291, 292, 294, 300; adultery, 285, 296, 298, 320; betting, 308, 319; business dealing, 316; calling another member a liar, 301; deceiving and defrauding, 287; destroying corner trees, 368; disobeying the call of the church, 304, 330; false accusation of lying, 320; fighting, 257, 261, 286, 292, 301; frolicking and dancing, 338, 339; gambling, 323, 337, 340, 341, 402, 403; immoral conduct, 251, 274, 277, 284, 307; improper conduct in time of worship, 309; intoxication, 51, 159, 257, 260, 273, 283, 285, 286, 287, 292, 304, 312, 317, 318, 324, 327, 328, 337, 339, 362, 366, 369, 379, 380, 402, 403, 411, 573; "lies of hypocrisy," 293; lying, tale-bearing, 313, 368, 370, 377; making unrighteous landmarks, 368; misusing his wife, 304; non-attendance (at church), 327, 330, 331, 332, 333, 338, 339, 342, 343, 344, 346, 348; playing carnal plays, 319; quarreling, 301, 321; rules of, 259; running

an incorrect line, 369; selling an unsound mare, 263; stealing, 282, 286,
320; swearing, 301, 307, 308, 310, 315,
319, 379, 383, 573; refusing to hear
the church, 325; refusing to obey the
call of the church, 383; shooting for
liquor, 312; swapping of horses, 287;
talking improperly, 367; threatening
a slave, 323; treating the church with
contempt, 327; use of "hard, censorious expressions," 362, 368; vil-
lainy, 366; withdrawing from church
in a disorderly way, 293

Discipline (family), 250

Discipline (of slave members), 272, 295,
298, 302, 330, 331; adultery, 399, 405;
betting, 390; dancing, 394; gambling,
390; intoxication, 390, 392, 394; lying
and disobedience, 323, 390; offering
to fight, 392; swearing, 394, 397; telling the church he wished to be excluded, 397

Dispute, about doctrines, 121

Distresses, among the churches, 511

Doctrine, of falling from grace, 554;
minister excluded for preaching unsound, 541; particular and eternal
election, 239

Doctrines, Baptist, 460, 476

Dorris, Joseph, 22; pastor Sulphur
Creek Church, 28

Edwards, Governor Ninian, slaveholding Baptist, 90

Edwards, Jonathan, President, 611

Edwards, Morgan, 7

Edwardsville Association, 98

Edwardville, missionary church in, 213

Elder, office of, 439; work of, 454

Elkhorn Association of Kentucky, 25,
36, 55, 56, 612; annual meeting ar-
ranged for, 461;—1787, 422; 1788,
425; 1789, 431; 1790, 437; 1791, 440;
1792, 447; 1793, 451, 457; August 7,
1794, 463; August 8, 1795, 466;
1796, 470; August 2, 1797, 473;
August 11, 1798, 477; August 10, 11,
12, 1799, 480; August 9, 1800, 484;
August 8, 1801, 486; August 14, 15,
16, 1802, 490; April, 1803, 494;

August, 1803, 496; August, 1804, 499;
August 10, 1805, 504;—attitude toward slavery, 81; churches, 420;
churches in 1715, 45; constitution,
418; division of, 356; first west of
Alleghenies, 22, 23; messengers of,
422; messengers to, 370; minutes of
1785, 417–509; minutes of August 8,
1801, 611; occasional meeting, 446;
rebuke to friends of emancipation, 82;
union with South Kentucky Association, 23

Emancipation, 164, 570; first church,
organized by Carmen and Dodge, 81;
of negro slaves, 325; query concerning, 324; societies, 82; weakening of
interest in, 99

Emancipationists, 526, 527

English Baptists, General, 43; Particular, 43

English government of Illinois, 89

English prisoners, join South River
Church, 122; stationed through country, 122

Episcopalians, of Rhode Island, 7

Established Church, in Virginia, 78

Excluded members, Illinois Association,
517; rules regarding, 511

Excluded persons, reception of, 494

Excommunication, of church members,
273

Experience, members received by, 274,
275, 276, 280, 281, 283, 288

Experiences, 621

Fairfax's Manor, 128

Fallen Timbers, Battle of, 30

Families, size of on frontier, 140

Fighting, church discipline, 261

Finley, James B., first Methodist missionary, 67; on use of liquor, 52

Finley, Robert, founder of American
Colonization Society, 98

Foot washing, 423, 427, 429

Foreign Missions, J. M. Peck, 549

Forks of Elkhorn Church, Kentucky,
25, 182; formation of, 46; members
of, 46; records of, 272–417

France, trade policies of, 19

Freemasons, morality of, 171, 172; op-

posed by Baptists, 170; opposed by
Methodists, 170
French inhabitants, Illinois, 89
Friends to Humanity Association, 32,
83, 84, 88; annual meeting at Mac-
oupin, Illinois, 1826, 588; annual
meeting at New Design, Illinois,
September 7, 1821, 575; annual meeting at New Design, October 10, 1823,
581; annual meeting, at Silver Creek
Church, Illinois, October 4, 1839, 597;
at Turkey Hill, Illinois, 1822–1831,
569; Baptized Licking Locust Association, 1807, 563; detailed account
of, *History of Jefferson-Lemen Compact*, 95; discontinued in 1835, 94;
division into three districts, 93; expansion, 93; formation of Illinois Association in 1820, 93; growth stimulated by pro-slavery forces, 96; in
Illinois, 88, 98, 99, 101; important
factors in disintegration of Illinois Association, 99 ff.; in Kentucky and
Illinois, 563–607; in Kentucky, death
of, 86; Missouri Territory, 92; movement in Illinois, 93; not strong in
Kentucky, 85; progress response to
political and social forces, 94; regarded as schismatic in Illinois, 91
Frontier Baptist Church, formation of,
46
Frontier Baptist churches, records of,
248–271
Frontier Baptists, doctrinal position of,
45
Frontier meeting houses, 53
Funeral processions, 476
Funeral sermons, 476

Gano, General John, of New York, 29
Gano, John, 9; rules of, 302
Gano, Reverend Stephen, of Rhode Is-
land, 29
Garrison, William Lloyd, 101
General Baptists, Arminian, 9
General Committee, united Baptist
churches of Virginia, 447, 456, 461,
462
General missionary convention of Bap-
tists, 59

Georgia, anti-mission Baptists, 1846,
66; Baptists from, 34
Gilbert's Creek, 123, 147
Gilbert's Creek Church, Kentucky, 87,
147–150
Great Awakening, Baptist, 3, 4; in New
England, 8, 44
Great Crossings Church, Kentucky, 152,
182; controversy, 450; distress of, 443,
444, 445; membership, 612
Great Miami, 161
Great Revival, in New England, 4, 6, 8
Great Western Revival, 24; letters de-
scribing, 608
Greenbrier settlement, 130
Grievances, arbitrated, 299

Hall, missionary sent to India by Amer-
ican Board, 58
Happy Creek Church, Virginia, 125
Hard times, at close of Revolution, 19
Harmer's defeat, 125
Harris, Samuel, 9, 11, 119
Harrison, Governor, of Indiana Terri-
tory, 89
Hawks, F. L., historian of Protestant
Episcopalians in Virginia, 16
"Helps," 321, 326, 327, 336, 353, 378,
384, 385, 396, 415, 416; asked to
settle grievances, 317; from neigh-
boring churches, 47, 49; letter re-
questing, 389, 390, 391; ministerial,
541; on ordaining a minister, 529;
request for, 299, 455
Henry, Patrick, friend of religious free-
dom, 14
Heresy, 495
Hickman, William, 86, 184, 272, 273,
328, 417; leadership of, 55; patriarch
of Kentucky Baptists, 83
Holston Association in Tennessee, 27, 55
Home Mission Society, 208
Hyper-Calvinists, 75

Illinois, anti-mission Baptists, 1846, 66;
as part of Indiana Territory, 89; attitude toward paying pastors, 37;
Baptist Convention organized October 9, 1834, 217; Bower united with
Sandy Creek Church, 205; emancipa-

tion movements among Baptists, 81; first Baptist church in, 31, 42, 89; first religious service in, 31; forces contending for slavery, 97; French inhabitants, 89; Friends to Humanity Association, 88, 98, 99, 101, 563; New Design church, 31; New Design settlement, 31; Ogle Creek Church, 239; oldest association anti-mission in 1824, 65; records of Wood River Baptist Church, 261–271; Richland Creek Church, division on slavery question, 90; St. Clair County, 246; home of J. M. Peck, 60; Scott County, 205; separated from Indiana Territory in 1809, 90; Wood River Church, 239

Illinois Anti-slavery League, existence doubted by Solon J. Buck, 95

Illinois Baptist Association, 33, 55, 91, 262, 510–562; attitude toward slavery, 86; circular letter—of 1812, 532; of 1813, 534; of 1815, 539; of 1817, 546; of 1818, 550; of 1819, 556; of 1820, 560 f.;—finances of, 543, 544; formed in 1807, 31; meetings of—October 9, 1807, 514; June 10, 1808, 516; September 3, 1808, 519; October, 1809, 522; December, 1809, 523; October, 1810, 525; September, 1811, 526; November 22, 23, 24, 1811, 528; September 18, 19, 20, 1812, 530; August 27, 28, 29, 1813, 533, 534; September 23, 24, 25, 1814, 535; September 15, 1815, 537; October 4, 1816, 540; September, 1817, 543; October 9, 10, 11, 1818, 546; October 8, 9, 10, 1819, 551; October 14, 15, 16, 1820, 557;—members dismissed to form Missouri Association, 547; minutes of 1809, 91, 520; principles, 510; reception of Peck, 61; Wood River Church, 62, 245

Illinois Baptists, 30; emancipation sentiment of by 1830, 98; taxation, 64

Illinois Constitution, against slavery, 97; slave holders dissatisfied with, 97

Illinois Intelligencer, The, 94

Illinois Territory, indentured service law, 90

Immigration, to Kentucky and Tennessee, 20, 21

India Fund, of Western Baptist Mission Society, 550

India, missionaries to, 58

Indian nations, missionaries to, 489

Indian towns, 149

Indian wars, 29

Indiana, anti-mission Baptists (1846), 66; Baptist churches in southeastern, 30; Baptist churches in southwestern, 30; Baptists in, 30; Fourteen Mile Creek Church, 30; Harrison County, 244; Pigeon Creek Church, 54; settlement of, 29; Silver Creek Church, 30, 53, 54; Territorial Law of 1807, 90; Wabash Association, 30, 55

Indiana Baptist Association, attitude toward slavery, 86

Indiana Territory, Posey County, 242

Indians, 131, 157, 165

Intoxication, discipline for, 50

"Involuntary, Absolute, Hereditary Slavery Examined on Principles of Nature, Reason, Justice and Scripture," David Barrow, 82

Ireland, James, 114, 117, 119; choosing of as pastor, 120; departure from South River Church, 121

Isaac McCoy Mission, 625–628

Janitor, for church, 337

Janitor service, 388, 394, 409

Jealousy of frontier missionaries, 73

Jefferson, Thomas, 91; assists anti-slavery movement, 77; bill for establishment of religious freedom, 15, 16; friend of religious freedom, 14; patron of James Lemen, 88

Jenkins, Jonathan, anti-slavery representative in Congress, 90

Judson, baptized in Baptist church in Calcutta, 58; converted to Baptist principles, 58; first missionary to Burma from America, 59, 211; missionary to India of American Board of Commissioners for Foreign Missions, 58

Kaskaskia, Illinois, 30, 88, 89

Kentucky, 123, 125, 134, 148, 156; anti-mission Baptists (1846), 66; Boone's

Creek Baptist Church, 253; Boone's Creek Church, records of, 253–258; brief account of religious revival in, 609–612; Bullittsburg Church, 39; center of anti-slavery agitation, 80; churches in central, 23; Clear Creek Church, 46, 124, 152; clergy with emancipators, 80; compensation to preachers, 211; constitution and rules of Beaver Creek Church, 258–261; Cox's Creek, 23; discipline in Mount Tabor church, 49; Dunkards in, 197; Elkhorn Association, 36, 55; emancipation movements among Baptists, 81; first Baptist preacher in, 19; first Baptist revival in, 42; Friends to Humanity Association, 88, 99, 563; Gilbert's Creek Church, 21; Great Crossing Church, 25; Harrodsburg, 19; immigration to, 20, 21; leaving of Jacob Bower, 204; Methodists in, 197; migration into, 18; minutes of Elkhorn Baptist Association (1785), 417–509; Mount Pleasant Church, 149; move of Marshall to, 121; Muhlenberg County, 189; population of, 24; Pulaski County, 243; records of Forks of Elkhorn Baptist Church, 272–417; records of Severn's Valley Church, 248–253; revival movement in, 25, 164; Salem Association, 23, 55; Salt River, 163; Scott County, 182; Separates and Regulars in, 44; settlers, 22; settlers from, 30, 34; Shelby County, 188; six associations in 1800, 24; slavery question, 32; South Elkhorn Church, 50, 150; South Kentucky Association, 23; Taylor's influence in, 106; traveling church in, 151

Kentucky Abolition Society, 84 f.
Kentucky Baptists, 27, 33, 116, 182, 197; failure of emancipation schism, 85; justification of slave holding, 87; membership in 1820, 26; William Hickman, 83
Kentucky Constitutional Convention, address of David Rice, 80
Kentucky River, 147, 149
Ketocton Association, 12, 424, 437, 443

Land, for meeting house, 374, 375
Land sale, 267
Lane, Dutton, 9
Laying on of hands, 119, 275, 436
Leland, John, 12; slavery resolution of, 79
Lemen, James, 89, 90; advocacy of non-fellowship with individual slaveholding Baptists, 90; attitude toward slavery, 88, 97; delegate to Constitutional Convention, 96; example of farmer-preacher, 42; exclusion by Richland Creek Church, 92; founder first Baptist church in Illinois, 30, 31, 42; opposition to, 91; protégé of Thomas Jefferson, 88
Lemen family, only members of Cantine Creek Church, 92
Letter, from member withdrawing, 335; to Association, 406
Letters, of dismission, 523
Lexington, Kentucky, letter dated 1801, 609
Liberator, 101
Liberia, 98
License, form of ministerial, 40
Licking Association, friendly letter to, 371
Limestone Church, Kentucky, 152
Lincoln, Abraham, father of, 54
Lincoln, Thomas, father of Abraham, 54
Lindsey, Vachel, 361
Liquor, use of on frontier, 52. See also Discipline
Little Miami, Baptist settlement on, 28
London Confession of Faith, 45
Long, Major S. H., extracts from journal of, 625–628
Long Run Association, 621
Louisiana, Baptists in, 35; first church in, at Bayou Chicot, 35; population of, in 1803, 33; territory of, 34
Louisville, 123
Lunies Creek, branch of Potomac River, 128
Lunies Creek Church, Virginia, 128–146; members, 129
Luther, Martin, 73
Lutherans, among frontier settlers, 19; in Virginia, 14

Mad River Association, Ohio, 29
Madison, James, friend of religious freedom, 14
Manning, James, 7
Maria Creek Church, Indiana, loyalty to missions, 62; pamphlet of Daniel Parker, 69
Marriage, form of, 420, 429
Marshall, 128, 129
Marshall, Daniel, 8, 120
Marshall, John, 9, 11
Marshall, William, 107, 117; ministry of, 119
Maryland, churches of, in Philadelphia Association, 6
Mason, George, friend of religious freedom, 14
Masons, church member excluded for joining, 339; objection to, 337
Massachusetts, Baptist churches in, 4; stronghold of Congregationalism, 16
Massachusetts Baptist Missionary Magazine, 58
McCoy family: Isaac, Baptist missionary to Indians; William, Kentucky minister, 30
McCoy, Isaac, 553; appointment as missionary to Indians of Indiana and Illinois, 60; establishment of mission called Carey, near Niles, Michigan, 61; Indian work at Fort Wayne, 60
Meeting house, building of, 371, 395, 396, 397, 398; deed for, 351; janitor service, 371, 376; land for, 349, 374, 375, 378; procuring firewood for, 371; repair of, 305, 345, 377, 399; sweeping, 345
Members (church), 401; disciplined for offenses (*See Discipline*); expulsion of, 159-160; moving away without letters of dismission, 304; moving out of bounds of church, 341; negro, 282, 288, 289; non-resident, 329; of Forks of Elkhorn Church, 46; received, 278; received by experience, 288; received by repentance, 279, 280; restored to fellowship, 326, 407; rule admitting slave, 421; rule for receiving Baptist, 423; transfer of, 337
Mero Association, Tennessee, 27, 55;

dissolution of, 28; Head of Sulphur Creek Church, 28
Messengers, 245; to the Association, 344, 382, 406
Method of dealing with offenders, 289
Methodist Conference of 1780, attitude toward slavery, 78
Methodist preachers, 24
Methodists, 610, 611; Arminianism of, 75; attitude toward missions, 212; Indian mission established at Upper Sandusky, Ohio, 67; conflict with Daniel Parker, in Kentucky, 69; missionary society organized in 1819, 67; on frontier, 24
Miami Association, of Ohio, 29, 55; organization of, 82
Miami Indians, 627
Migration, Baptist, 21
Millennial Harbinger, 1829, founded by Campbell, 70
Minister, appointment of, 340, 342; how chosen on frontier, 47; support of, 384, 421, 423, 427
Ministerial education, opposition to, 73
Ministerial "helps," 47, 49
Ministry, irregularities in, 477
Minutes and Circular letter, expense of, 451
Minutes, printing of, 395, 456
Missionaries, Baptist, 58; home, 549; to Indian nations, 489
Missionary, definition of, 212
Missionary periodicals, 58
Missionism, 210, 214
Missions, Baptist associations, 58; contrary to scriptures, 74
Mission Society, supported by Presbyterians, Baptist and Dutch Reformed churches, 58
Mississippi, anti-mission Baptists(1846), 66; Baptists in, 35; territory of, 34
Mississippi River, 18
Missouri, anti-mission Baptists (1846), 66; attitude toward slavery, 96; Baptist settlers in, 32; Bethel Baptist Association, 33; ceded to United States, 33; churches in Cape Girardeau County, 33; delegates from, 553; entry into Union in 1821, 96; first

Baptist church in, 33; French settlers in, 33; religious freedom in, 33; gambling and lawlessness in, 33; settlers in, 34; Tywappity Baptist Church, 33

Missouri Association, 33, 547, 548

Missouri Baptists, taxation, 64

Missouri Compromise, 96

Moderator, of association, 56

Mohawk Indians, 8

Money, for printing minutes and circular letter, 462; raising of, 336

Monongahela River, 134; five branches of, 130

Morgan Association, Illinois, 206, 207; denunciation of missions, 214

Muskingum Association, Ohio, 29

Negro members, 50, 320; discipline of, (See Discipline); Forks of Elkhorn Church, 46

Negroes, 190, 329; free, 96

Newell, missionary to India of American Board, 58

New England, Congregational churches in, 4; Great Awakening in, 8; Great Revival in, 4; origin of "separate," 119; southern churches of Philadelphia Association in, 6; struggle for religious freedom in, 16

New Jersey, Baptist churches in, 3; Baptists from, 28; churches of Philadelphia Association in, 6

New York, Baptists in, 4; Baptists from, 28; Churches of Philadelphia Association in, 6; migration westward through, 18

New-Lights, 5, 8; Arminianism of, 75; conflict with Daniel Parker in Kentucky, 69

Newport, 4; Baptists in, 3

North Carolina, 11, 22; anti-mission Baptists of 1846, 66; Baptist ministers from, 26; Baptists from, 32; Baptists in, 9, 12; Kehukee Creek, 9; Sandy Creek Church, 27; Separates and Regulars in, 44; settlers from, 34; Stearns and Marshall in, 8

North District Association, attitude toward emancipation, 82; expulsion of David Barrow, 83

North Fork Church, 182

Northwest Ordinance, 90

Northwest Territory, 89; first Baptist church in, 29; slavery question in, 77

Ogle's Creek Church, request for "helps," 269

Ohio River, 18, 28, 30, 55, 56, 80, 123, 161, 162

Ordinance of 1787, prohibiting slavery in Northwest Territory, 78, 89

Ordination, 285, 287, 291, 413; certificate of, 40; design of, 138; how legally performed, 138; of deacons, 270, 310, 311; of Jacob Bower, 204; of Taylor, 137 ff.

Opekon Creek, Virginia, 8

Otaway Indians, 627

Otis, James, anti-slavery movement of, 77

Pack horses, 123

Parker, Daniel, anti-missionism of, 67, 72, 74; arch enemy to frontier missions, 68; in Tennessee, 68; opposition to Baptist Board of Foreign Missions, 69; pamphlet of 1820, 69; publication of Church Advocate, 69; removal to southeastern Illinois, 69; three pamphlets of, 69; Two-Seed-in-the-Spirit doctrine of, 75, 207

Pastor, compensation of, 155

Peck, John M., 98, 207, 208; account of activities of Friends to Humanity prior to 1818, 95; agent American Bible Society, 97; Baptist mission work in Missouri Territory, 60; delegate from Missouri, 553, 555; early life of, 59 f.; first Baptist missionary for west, 59; founder of United Society for spread of Gospel, 60; Gazetteer of Illinois, 60; Guide for Emigrants, 60; how inducted into ministry, 39; in St. Clair County, Illinois, 60; missionary from Baptist Board of Foreign Missions, 548, 549; missionary in Missouri, 34; missionary sermon, 550; part in slavery controversy, Illinois, 60; reception into Illinois Association, 61; travels in Missouri and

Illinois, 60; voluminous writer, 60; with settlers of Mississippi Valley, 60

Pennsylvania, Baptist churches in, 3; Baptists, 4; churches of Philadelphia Association in, 6; migration westward through, 18

Pequot Indians, 77

"Period of the Great Persecution" (1768–1774), 12

Philadelphia, letter from Dr. Rogers (1801), 611

Philadelphia Association, 7, 9, 424, 437, 454; attitude toward slavery, 79; churches of, 6

Philadelphia Confession of Faith, 22, 120; adopted in eastern Tennessee, 27

Piggot's Fort, Illinois, 30

Pittsburg, Baptist from, 28

Plates and glasses for use of church, 377

Potawatomy Indians, 627

Preachers, 24; employment of, 347; licensed, 40; ordination of, 40, 285; raising up of, 39, 368, 410; support of, 38, 348, 353; typical frontier Baptist, 36, 40

Presbyterian preachers, 24

Presbyterians, 134, 610, 611; Abram Clark, 129; attitude toward missions, 67, 212; in New England, 119; in Virginia, 14, 15; on frontier, 19, 24

Price, first missionary to Burma from America, 211

Primitive Baptists, 44, 67

Principles of Illinois Association, 510

Pro-slavery forces, stimulated growth of Friends to Humanity in Illinois, 96

Providence Plantation, 3, 77

Providence, Rhode Island, first Baptist church in America, 29

Public offences, manner of treating, 312, 380, 381

Quaker colonies, 3

Quakers, abolition of slavery, 78; of Rhode Island, 7

Quarterly meetings, Elkhorn Association, 419

Reading, Isaac, 114, 116, 120

Reading, Joseph, 19, 116, 117, 120, 121, 128, 129, 134, 135, 136, 137, 139

Record Books, of early churches, 49

Redstone, 123

Redstone Baptist Association, Ohio and Pennsylvania, 29, 70

Redstone County, 139

Redstone, Virginia, 131

Reformer, groups in Baptist churches, 71; in associations, 71

Reformers, disciples of Alexander Campbell, 66, 71

Regular, 44

Regular Baptists, 22

Reid, James, 9

Religious liberty, 444, 447; agitation for, 15

Religious experience, of candidate for ordination, 231–238

Repentance, for bad conduct, 277

Revival, at Buck Run Church, 183; at Clear Creek Church, 157

Revival movement in Kentucky, 25; brief account of, 609–612

Revivalistic methods, on frontier, 24

Revolution, 13, 121; agitation for religious liberty during, 15; Baptist position at close of, 17; basis of movement for emancipation, 77; in Virginia, 20

Rhode Island, Baptist churches in, 3, 4, 16

Rhode Island College, 7

Rice, David, Kentucky Presbyterian preacher, 80

Rice, Luther, 59, 61; baptized in Baptist church in Calcutta, 58; considered by Taylor modern "Tetzel," 73; converted to Baptist principles, 58; first missionary to Burma from America, 58, 59, 211; propaganda for missions among American Baptists, 61

Richland Creek Church, Illinois, division on slavery question, 90; opposition to Lemen, 91

Road, building of, 400

Robertson, typical figure in Kentucky, 20

Rolling Fork Church, withdrawal from Salem Association, 81

Roman Catholic church, in Louisiana, 35

Roosevelt, Theodore, 20, 21
Rule, for guidance of church in dealing with members committing offenses, 290–292; for proceeding against public transgressions, 386; for receiving accusations against a sister church, 432, 436; for receiving Baptist members, 423; regarding payment of debt, 439; respecting the exclusion of members, 350
Rules, of John Gano for Examination of the Church, 302
Rules (church), on slaveholding, 569–570
Rules, of the Association, 435

Sabbath Schools, 206
St. Clair Anti-convention Society, 97
St. Clair County, Illinois, 89
St. Louis, African Baptist church founded in 1818, 34; colored churches, 228; first Baptist church in, 34
Salary, preachers, 353, 354, 355
Salem Kentucky Association, 23, 25, 55, 426, 443; attitude toward slavery, 79; circular letter of 1802, 623; minutes of October 1–2, 1802, 617; withdrawal of Mill Creek and Rolling Fork churches, 81
Salt River, Kentucky, 163
Sandy Creek Church, North Carolina, 8, 9, 11
Scioto Valley, second Ohio Association, 29
Schoolhouse, repair of, 319, 359
Schools, common, 549; for Indians, 549; for Whites, 549
Semple, Robert B., early Baptist historian, 4, 9, 10, 11, 13
Severns Valley Church, Kentucky, 19, records of, 248–253
Separate Baptist Association South, of Kentucky, 436
Separate Baptists, 9, 10, 11, 12, 22; attitude toward negroes, 78
Separate congregations, 5
Separates, 6, 8, 44
Sevier, typical figure in Kentucky, 20
Shackleford, John, minister of South Elkhorn Church, 37
"Shakers," 200

Shenandoah Church, 135, 138, 139
Shenandoah River, 119
Shurtliff College, Alton, Illinois, 229, 231
Silver Creek Indiana, church, 53; antimission agitation, 62
Slave marriage, 437
Slave members, discipline of. See Discipline (slave)
Slave members, 258, 272, 274, 278, 290, 292, 298, 307, 314, 315, 320, 329, 362, 363, 364, 423
Slaveholders, dissatisfied with Illinois Constitution, 97
Slavery, 421, 565, 566, 569, 600; abolition of, 444, 447; excitement over, 96; introduction into Illinois, 89; letters on, 94; members withdrawn on account of, 338; Ordinance of 1787, 89; regulation of, 77
Slavery controversy, Illinois, 60
Slavery question, 328
Smith, George S., doctrinal preacher, 149
Smith, John, one of first ministers in Ohio, 29; U. S. Senator from Ohio, 29
South Carolina, 239, 243, 518; Baptists from, 32, 34
South Elkhorn, Baptist meeting at, 22
South Elkhorn, Kentucky Church, 148, 150, 151; membership, 612
South Kentucky Association, 23
South River Church, Virginia, 118–128; choosing a pastor, 120; great baptizing at, 120; members of, 121, 122; rapid growth of, 120
Spain, trade policies of, 19
Spanish authorities, in Mississippi, 34
Spanish official, in upper Louisiana, 32
Spottsylvania County, persecutions in, 12
Stearns, Shubal, 8, 9, 11, 119
Sugar Creek Association, Indiana, antimission feeling, 65
Supplies, for destitute church, 421
Support, of preachers, 340, 342, 378, 384, 421, 423, 427
Sutton, John, founder of New Hope Church, Kentucky, 81

Tarrant, Carter, 164, 328, 563, 564; emancipationist, 82; founder of New

Hope Church, Kentucky, 81; moderator, 568, 569; Rules, 89

"Tarrant's Rules," 83 f.

Taylor, John, 19, 28, 45, 46, 47, 48, 417; anti-missionism of, 67, 72, 73; as preacher, 105; baptized by James Ireland, 115; beginning of ministry, 116; born Fauquier County, Virginia, 105; chosen pastor Clear Creek Church, 154; conversion and call to ministry, 106–118; hardships of, 141–144; influence among Baptists, in Kentucky, 106; leadership of, 55; move from Clear Creek, 161; move to Kentucky, 105, 116, 122; ordained as itinerant preacher, 116, 137 ff.; pamphlet on missions, 68; raising up of preacher, 39; slave holder, 87, 166, 175; "Ten Churches," 41, 42

Temperance, 206

Tennessee, anti-mission Baptists, 66; Baptists in, 26; church in, 456; Clinch River, 26; Concord Association, 28; Daniel Parker in, 68; eastern, churches in, 27; French Broad River, 26; Head of Sulphur Fork Church, 22; Holston Association, 55; Holston River, 26; immigration to, 20; McMinn County, 245; Mero Association, 27; migration into, 18; settlers from, 34; Wautauga River, 26; White County, 244

Tennessee Association, 27

Tennessee River, 26

Territorial Law of 1807, regarding slavery, 90

Theology, of anti-mission Baptists, 75

Thoughts on Missions, pamphlet of John Taylor, 68

Tigers Valley, 134, 135

Timber clearing, 166

Tinsley, Thomas, first Baptist preacher in Kentucky, 19

Trinity, doctrine of, 496

Turkey Hill Church, dissolved, 541

Two-Seed-in-the-Spirit, anti-mission Baptists, 67; doctrine of Parker, 69, 75

Tywappity, first Baptist church in Missouri, 33

Union and fellowship, 454

Union Church, 254, 255

United Baptists, 44

United Baptists Association of Kentucky, 432

United Society for Spread of Gospel, 60, 61

Universalism, 188

Universalists, 224, 484

Upper Alton, 229; missionary church in, 213

Virginia, 156; Abingdon, 21; Act establishing Religious Freedom, 17; antimission Baptists (1846), 66; antislavery activities in, 82; Baptist ministers from, 26; Baptist preachers, 21; Baptists in, 11, 12, 13, 36; Berkeley County, 9; birthplace of John Taylor, 107; General Assembly of, 15; Happy Creek Church, 125; home of Edward Coles, 95; James Lemen, 31; Lunies Creek Church, 128; old records from, 148; Opekon Creek, 8; pastors from, 47, 152; Philadelphia Association, 6; Richmond, 14; settlers from, 34; *Separates* and *Regulars* in, 44; Shenandoah Valley, 29; South River Church, 118–128; struggle for religious freedom in, 16; Upper Spottsylvania Church, 21; Whitefield (George M.), 8; Yorktown, 21

Virginia Baptists, manumission of slaves, 79

Virginia Convention, 14

Wabash Association, Indiana, 55; antimission agitation, 62

War for Independence. *See Revolution*

Washing feet, 56

Washington, city of, 609

Washington, George, attitude toward bill for religious freedom, 15

Waller, John, 119

Wayne, General Anthony, 30

Warren Baptist Association, 16

Welch, James E., Baptist mission work in Missouri Territory, 60; delegate from Missouri, 553, 555; missionary in Missouri, 34

Western Baptist Mission Society, Indian fund, 550

Wheeling, 123

Whiskey, 141

Whitefield, George, 8, 134

Whitewater Valley, settlements in, 30

Williams, Luke, Missouri Baptist preacher, 42

Williams, Roger, 3; pronouncement against the slave trade, 77

Wood River Baptist Church, Illinois, 245, 246; Illinois Association, 62; records of, 261–271

Woodford County, 149, 161

Worship, time of, 355

Wyandotte Indians, Methodist Mission, 67

DATE DUE

MAY 26 '65			
FEB 25 '66			
JAN 26 '67			
MAY 10 '67			
DEC 12 '73			
JAN 6 '76			
JAN 2			
APR 7 '76			
APR 19 '76			
GAYLORD			PRINTED IN U.S.A.